THE ANATOMY OF RUSSIAN DEFENSE CONVERSION

THE ANATOMY OF RUSSIAN **DEFENSE CONVERSION**

Vlad E. Genin, General Editor

Foreword by William J. Perry

INSTITUTE FOR INTERNATIONAL STUDIES,
STANFORD UNIVERSITY
Stanford, California

MORRISON INSTITUTE FOR POPULATION AND RESOURCE STUDIES,
STANFORD UNIVERSITY
Stanford, California

VEGA PRESS
Walnut Creek, California

First Published, 2001.

The paper used in this publication meets the minimum requirements of American National Standards for Information Sciences – Permanence of Paper for Printed Library Materials, ANSI Z39.48-1984.

Library of Congress Catalog Card Number: 00-105562

ISBN: 0-9702587-0-4 (alk. paper)

Printed in the United States of America by
BERTELSMANN, Valencia, California

DISCLAIMER

This book represents the personal work of the authors and is written for academic expression only. The opinions, interpretations, and conclusions expressed here are those of the authors and do not represent policies or positions of the Department of Defense, the Department of State, the Department of Energy or any other agency of the United States Government. This book does not represent the policies or positions of the Russian Government or any of its agencies or organizations. Neither does this book represent the policies or positions of any foreign government.

The goal of this book is to introduce the visions and viewpoints of different authors from different countries on Russian defense conversion. In certain cases their visions and viewpoints may differ from, or even oppose, each other. The information and data presented by them may not correspond.

The publisher is not responsible for the content or data presented in this book.

*Dedicated to our mothers,
who made us responsible
for the peoples' future*

CONTENTS

ABBREVIATIONS

ABM	Anti-Ballistic Missile
ACA	Arms Control Association
AO	Joint Stock Company
BRAC	Base Realignment and Closure Act
BTWC	Biological and Toxin Weapons Convention
BW	Biological Warfare
CBM	Confidence Building Measures
CC	Central Committee (of the Communist Party of the U.S.S.R.)
CDE	Conference on Disarmament in Europe (The Stockholm Conference)
CEO	Chief Executive Officer
CFE	Conventional Forces in Europe Treaty
CIA	Central Intelligence Agency
CIS	Commonwealth of Independent States (Countries of the former Soviet Union, excluding Baltic States)
CPSU	Communist Party of the Soviet Union (U.S.S.R.)
CSBM	Confidence and Security Building Measures
CSCE	Conference on Security and Cooperation in Europe
CTO	Chief Technical Officer
CTR	Cooperative Threat Reduction
DARPA	Defense Advanced Research Projects Agency
DEF	Defense Enterprise Fund
DGA	General Delegation for Armaments
DOD	Department of Defense
DOE	Department of Energy
EBRD	European Bank for Reconstruction and Development
ECA	Economic Cooperation Administration

FBI	Federal Bureau of Investigations
FEI	Fuel-Energy Industry
GATT	General Agreement on Trade and Tariffs
GDP	Gross Domestic Product
GGNRA	Golden Gate National Recreational Area
GKO	Russian State Bonds
GMP	Good Manufacturing Practice
GMPA	General Management Plan Amendment
IMF	International Monetary Fund
INF	Intermediate Range Missiles Forces Treaty
IPP	Initiatives for Proliferation Prevention Program
IPR	Intellectual Property Rights
ISBM	Intercontinental Ballistic Missiles
ISO	International Standards Organization
ISTC	International Science and Technology Center
JV	International Joint Venture (*Mezhdunarodnoe Sovmestnoe Predpriatie)*
KB	Design Bureau
KGB	Soviet Agency for the State Security *(Komitet Gosudarstvennoi Bezopasnosti)*
MDC	Multinational Development Corporation
MFA	Ministry of Foreign Affairs *(MID)*
MIA	Ministry of Internal Affairs *(MVD)*
MIC	Military Industrial Complex (*VPK - Voenno-Promyshlennyi Kompleks)*
MOD or DM	Ministry of Defense *(MO – Ministerstvo Oborony)*
MTC	Military Technical Cooperation
MTCR	Missile Technology Control Regime
NASA	National Aeronautics and Space Administration
NATO	North Atlantic Treaty Organization
NDS	Sales Tax *(Nalog na Dobavlennuyu Stoimost)*
NII	Research/Scientific Institute/Lab *(Naucho-Issledovatelskii Institut)*
NIS	Newly Independent States (Countries of the former Soviet Union)
NMD	National Missile Defense
NPT	Treaty on Non-Proliferation of Nuclear Weapons
OECD	Organization for Economic Co-Operation and Development
OPIC	Overseas Private Investment Corporation
OSCE	Organization on Security and Cooperation in Europe
Ph.D.	Doctor of Philosophy (U.S. highest scientific degree)

first sets the historical context of the Soviet command economy, and the extent and way in which the military was emphasized.

It is not surprising that there is considerable disagreement among the authors about the processes and accomplishments of conversion, because the problem is not a simple one to analyze. The list of contributors to the book includes Russian and Western authors, both academics and practitioners from government and industry. The editors are to be congratulated for assembling such a diverse group of authors.

It is important to continue both the analyses of conversion and the efforts to improve on the past record if Russia is to capitalize to any significant degree on the huge investment the Soviet Union made in the military industrial complex. The reemergence of Russia as a major economic power will take many years -- much longer than expected in the optimistic days following the collapse of the Soviet Union -- but it is hard to conceive that a country endowed with such a talented population and such vast resources will not achieve this in time. Defense conversion is but one element of economic reform, but it can be an important one.

LIFE IS ABOVE ANY IDEOLOGY

Evgeniy I. Shaposhnikov

I can recall various military exercises involving the simulated exchange of hundreds of nuclear strikes. Afterwards, the probable losses were estimated, and the fighting forces and management system regrouped to deliver one or more additional strikes. All of this was "rehearsed" in a prescribed regimen. There were countless rationales, concepts, doctrines, articles, and even literary works, to demonstrate the superiority or inferiority of various approaches. The best brains of all mankind were attracted to this work. For decades the Russian people were told in many different ways that the whole capitalist world was made up of enemies who dreamt of swallowing up the free socialist system. People in capitalist countries were told twenty-four hours a day that the USSR was an "evil empire". Such behavior does not reflect well on mankind, because the true interests of human beings are incompatible with plans for annihilation.

At the same time, historical experience shows that when faced with the real threat of fascist enslavement, countries and peoples with opposing ideological principles joined forces to fight this threat. In other words, they acted like human beings. Life is above any ideology.

However, the leaders and politicians of the countries that defeated fascism lost their historical chance after WW II to strengthen the relationship between their countries, and offer the world new forms and ways of existence. During the postwar decades, the world was on the brink of thermonuclear war more than once, and sometimes only a miracle, or fear, or the remnants of common sense were able to avert this threat.

The Russian Army – like the country itself, it has a rich history. The army developed cyclically, each cycle lasting for a certain period of time.

The first cycle began with Peter the Great and ended with the 1917 October Revolution; from the "romantic youth" of the state and army to their decrepitude and collapse; from the military reforms of Peter the Great, through the war against Napoleon of 1812 and later the uprising of Decembrists, to the military reforms of General-Field Marshal Milyutin (1860-1870) and the October Revolution.

The second cycle lasted from 1917 to 1992. The first, "heroic youth," period of this cycle began with the creation of the Red Army in 1918 and ended in 1961 with the first major postwar reduction in the army by Nikita Khrushchev—a reduction of 1.2 million troops. During this time, a new empire was created through the new Army. The State again used the formula "State-Army-People", which was implemented by the state through its own system of terror. The ideology of "camp under siege" and "state fear", powerful brainwashing, and the forced introduction of Communist ideology successfully mobilized the population's consciousness. In that system, a man was just a cog in the machine, and could at any moment become "gulag dust". Before and during WWII, the Army was not only an object of pride to the state and the people, but an instrument for "gathering land." Its prestige in society increased with victory in war.

The second cycle's second period (1961-1979, from the postwar reduction of the Army to the beginning of the war in Afghanistan) was the period of "powerful maturity". The Army had been modernized, the powerful Warsaw Pact was working, and successful "military-political cooperation" with the Third World was taking place. The Soviet military presence in the Eastern Europe also implemented the concept of "advanced boundaries" as a counterweight to worldwide capitalism. "Successful" demonstrations of force were conducted in Hungary (1956) and Czechoslovakia (1968). The prestige and status of the Army were supported by the state and by society.

The third period, the decrepitude and destruction of the Soviet system and the Soviet Army, lasted from 1979 to 1992. The total militarization of the USSR led to economic and political crisis. The main events of the third period include disintegration of the Warsaw Pact, withdrawal of the Soviet Army from Europe, severe reductions in Soviet military presence abroad, and the growth of social problems in the Army and society.

The war in Afghanistan led not only to the loss of direction for the Army, but to the destruction of the dominant Communist ideology. For the first time in its history, the Army began to ask who it was and why. For the first time, the full scale of the issue of military-civilian relations was realized. The problems of civilian-military relations and the Army's internal democracy became acute. As part of the state machine and as an instrument of Communist policy, the Army was severely criticized by society and the mass media. The Army's prestige declined. Social problems among servicemen worsened. The failure of the 1991 putsch signaled the end of the great Army of the great Empire.

The third cycle—Democratic Russia—began in 1992 with the formation of the Russian Army on May 7. It began its new history as a huge "splinter" of the great Soviet Army, which survived as the main state institution.

In order to reform the Army, vast sums of money were needed, which Russia did not have. The state began to drastically reduce its arms purchases (almost to zero) and expenditures on scientific developments. As a result, the MIC—the backbone of the entire Soviet economy—found itself on the brink of collapse.

Withdrawal of Russian troops from the countries of Eastern Europe and the states of the CIS, difficulties in deploying them to new locations, and the participation of the Russian Army in peace-making actions in hot spots, etc., brought the Army to a critical point in its existence. In the deep systemic crisis in the state and the Army, the issue of military reform became of paramount importance for the survival of the young Russian democracy and for the Russian Army itself.

A nineteenth-century Russian commander once likened the Army to a strong and healthy forest, planted in the soil of the state, feeding from this soil and protecting it from storms and inclement weather. Society and the state should remember that if we do not want to feed our army, we will feed somebody else's, and a good army is not cheap.

Once we have provided reliable defense for the country, stabilized the domestic political-economic situation, and strengthened law and order, we can move on to the next phase, namely radical military reforms and reductions of several aspects of the armed forces to a necessary and sufficient level. Firstly, we should work on matters that do not require tremendous expenditures, and will allow us to save significant sums of money, such as drastically reducing the types and variations of weaponry, military equipment, support and control systems, ammunition, fuel, lubricants, and spare parts. Supporting such a chaotic assortment in a budget deficit situation is not only impermissible it is immoral. This would facilitate the conversion process and the restructuring of defense industry, particularly:

1. Maintaining production of arms at the minimum quantities necessary to outfit the armed forces, sell arms abroad under military-technical cooperation agreements, and to outfit reserve forces;
2. Continuing conversion of the remaining MIC enterprises that are not involved in arms production;
3. Eliminating, privatizing, or selling particularly burdensome parts of the MIC.

This would lead to radical restructuring, reductions, and mergers of defense plants and scientific research organizations, as the existence of major and subsidiary factories and research institutes in each branch of the Armed Forces, and virtually all branches of the defense industry, is absolutely unnecessary. An independent audit could easily establish that dozens of such organizations are spending large amounts of money duplicating each other's efforts without any concrete results. Therefore it is necessary to stop financing the services of such parasitic structures, and invest in factories and scientific organizations that can produce successful results.

Restructuring and conversion of the Russian MIC, as a part of the solution to the global problem of disarmament and preventing the outbreak of world wars, received wide support from the world community. At that time, in the early 1990s, the civilized world understood the scale of the military, political, social, economic, and financial problems associated with conversion. However, with the passage of time, interest in Russian conversion waned, then became indifference, and was recently replaced with disregard.

Conversion of the Russian MIC, like the future of democratic Russia, greatly depends on the participation of civilized international society. It is still not too late to work together to create the necessary conditions and mechanisms for intensifying the process for irreversibly converting and restructuring the MIC.

I am convinced that mankind does not want world leaders to create new military blocs, new tensions in international relations, or new cataclysms. Mankind does not want decisions that arise from hidden or overt dictates, new confrontations, or a new cold war. Therefore, the most rational and authoritative world leaders must not miss their historical chance to ensure stability in Russia, thereby guaranteeing global stability.

PROLOGUE

Vlad E. Genin

"No people had suffered and sacrificed like the Russians. No state, no nation had ever gone through trials on such a scale and retained its coherent structure. The vast machine creaked and groaned. But it still worked. One more effort and victory would come..."[1]

Winston S. Churchill, *The World Crisis* (1916-1918)

This book addresses a vital issue for the entire civilized world: the importance of successful conversion of Russian defense enterprises. Had this book had been written when the 1980s were becoming the 1990s, and everything seemed so promising in Russia, there would have been little to say about the many tragic failures in Russian reforms, and the subsequent chaotic socioeconomic conditions. But in fact, this book is being published, at the start of a new century, at a time when the future of Russia is still highly unpredictable. The Russian strategic arsenal includes 1,397 launchers with 6,546 warheads[2]. Among them there are 756 intercontinental ballistic missiles

1 Winston S. Churchill, The World Crisis (New York: Charles Scribner's Sons, 1931), p. 376.

2 Editor's Note: START 1 Aggregate Numbers of Strategic Offensive Arms,

with 3,590 warheads. But missiles are only delivery vehicles. They are able to deliver different warheads, including nuclear, chemical and biological ones, which are capable of destroying whole countries.

During the past few years, conditions have been so unstable that no one can tell whether there will be a recovery or ongoing social and economic catastrophes, a return to military confrontations, or the limitation of individual rights and freedoms. This book is intended to give the reader insight into why defense conversion is so important, not only to the future of Russia, but to the rest of the world as well.

* * *

The concept of peace on our long-suffering planet is based upon several major issues, one of the most important of which is disarmament. In the recent past, the Soviet Union's military aspirations shocked the world. In the mid 1980s, the country made a choice: to move toward a civilized society, a free market economy, and global peace.

Disarmament entails defense conversion. This process, for which the new Russia, the West, Eastern Europe, and others had high hopes, was supposed to convert Russia's huge, militarized economy into a civilian economy.

As planned, conversion of the Russian defense industry – Military Industrial Complex (MIC) could have been one of the greatest victories of the Russian people. It was meant to help reduce the threat of a new, devastating war; to ensure peace on Earth; and to help the Russian people to achieve western living standards.

Bureau of Arms Control, U.S. Department of State, Fact Sheet, October 1, 1999. Adjustments based on Federation of American Scientists Nuclear Force Guide. Status of Nuclear Powers and Their Nuclear capabilities as of January 1, 1999.

However, Russian defense conversion, as a full-scale process, did not take place, which contributed to Russia's deepest social and economic crisis, and the threat of worldwide proliferation of the most dangerous nuclear, chemical, and biological weapons. The fate of this noble process was a tragedy, primarily for those previously involved in the defense sector. What happened instead was "headlong conversion", the results of which can be felt across Russia, from the Baltic Sea to the Pacific Ocean. Its devastating consequences can be seen when we look at empty, frozen, gradually deteriorating former defense plants, once the flagships of the Russian industry, and when we visit poverty-stricken cities where we see the misfortune of millions of former engineers and workers.

Ask any sensible honest Russian today whether it was worth it to work hard your entire life, sacrificing everything for the sake of communist dogma, and remaining poor, bringing your children and grandchildren into the world with no hope for a better future, all in the name of "proletarian hegemony"[3] over all countries and people? Tragically, "No," is the answer from any Russian, any citizen of the great country that gave birth to such outstanding people as the founder of the Russian Academy of Science Lomonosov and the chemist Mendeleev, the inventor of the radio Popov and the pianist Gilels, the mathematician Lobachevsky and the first rocket and Sputnik designer Korolev, the poet Pushkin and the artist Repin, the composer Tchaikovsky and the cellist Rastropovich, the helicopter designer Sikorsky and the outstanding nuclear scientist and great human rights activist, Nobel Laureate Sakharov.

---

3 Editor's Note: Soviet Communist Party slogan.

Ask any ordinary Russian mother what she dreams about at the beginning of the new century and the new millennium. Unfortunately, first of all, she hopes not to curse herself for bringing her children into this world. She hopes not to turn gray over humiliating problems such as a house with no heat, a shortage of food and clothes, a lack of medicines and linens in hospitals. She dreams about just being a woman and a mother, to give all the warmth of her heart to her children. The warmth that lights our lives even today brings back memories about the dearest mom in the world. Ask mothers who became “stalkers” in the former secret "closed cities" of the defense industry. Or ask those who live in the horrifying “radioactive zone” and who have to relive the nuclear tragedies of the Urals, Siberia, and Chernobyl over and over again along with their children. Ask them what they need: nuclear missiles or “clean" food, guns or butter?

Since the dawn of time, it has been inherent in human nature to build. Hopes and expectations motivate people to build homes, create the family hearth, cultivate gardens, and produce food, clothes, computers, cars, and children's toys--everything that is most welcome in every house. Now people are mastering the new, boundless world of cyberspace--a planet called Internet with its new global markets and unlimited opportunities.

Nevertheless, humankind continues to fight. Some have fought to plunder and enslave other nations, like Napoleon and Hitler. Some have fought their own people, like Stalin, who was the architect of the ideals of *the Gulag*--the network of Northern concentration camps where millions of Russians were shot or worked like slaves and died from the cold and diseases. Others have fought to liberate their motherland from fascism, like the Soviet soldiers during WWII. Some have fought to export the dictatorship of a dying communist dogma, as deceived and maimed Russian youth did in Afghanistan. Others have fought to protect the ideals of common humanitarian values, humanity, and human rights. Even today NATO, Russia, and Ukraine use armed forces to protect a fragile peace in the Balkans, in the heart of what seemed to be "Europe Undivided"[4], as the only recourse to halt the legacy of dictatorship: new, metastasizing, inhuman national conflicts that challenge humankind. They took up arms against the shameful crime of genocide, which we promised in Nuremberg, after the end of WWII, would never happen again, but which unfortunately repeated itself in the last year of 20th century, even as everyone believed that the century had, at last, become civilized.

Every civilized country should have as many weapons as is necessary for its defense. Russia is no exception. The central issue is whether the purpose of the weapons is to protect everything that was built over the centuries—people's values, rights, and homes--or to destroy them.

Russia has one of richest military arsenals in the world. Today Russian intercontinental ballistic missiles are more powerful than before, while Americans lead the pack in home theaters and Internet electronic commerce systems. Unfortunately, history is repeating itself. Forty-one years ago American leaders discussed a similar problem with Russian leaders: "Isn't it better to talk about the relative merits of washing machines than the relative strengths of rockets? Vice President Richard Nixon asked during the "kitchen debate" in Moscow in 1959. Both

---

4 James E. Goodby, Europe Undivided: The New Logic of Peace in U.S. – Russian Relations (Washington, D.C.: United States Institute of Peace Press, 1998).

Nixon and Khrushchev knew that Soviet rockets were more powerful, while the Americans had a clear lead in washing machines". [5] Nikita Khrushchev, First Secretary of the Central Committee of Communist Party of the USSR was accompanied by his successor-to-be, Leonid Brezhnev, who before and during his 18-year leadership orchestrated an unprecedented arms race, and who finally, in his last years, began to put forward peaceful initiatives to the West.

Russia is not only a well-armed country, but also one of the world's major manufacturers and exporters of weapons. The Soviet defense industries worked not so much for the idea of national defense as for the notorious idea of "world domination by the proletariat dictatorship"[6], a myth that, over the decades, was thoroughly propagated by all Russian textbooks and by word of mouth. This myth was created by generations of communist leaders to satisfy their geopolitical ambitions. In the bottom of their hearts, many of these leaders and their comrades in arms did not believe in this myth, but they were too cowardly to admit it.

Russia no longer needs as many weapons as its defense industries are capable of producing. The Russian government has been experiencing financial difficulties in buying its army even a minimal quantity of necessary arms. The industry's conversion to civilian applications did not happen. The only way the defense industry envisions the full utilization of its unconverted industrial potential is through exporting its military output. But to whom? This is the most critical question. The historical records of Russian weapons exports include terrorist and undemocratic regimes as buyers. One hopes that selling

---

5 Thomas Hine, Populuxe (New York: MJF Books, 1999), p. 131.

6 Editor's Note: Soviet Communist Party slogan.

weapons to terrorists is not a political aspiration of the new leaders of the new Russia. Nevertheless, the defense industry can no longer afford to remain in its present uncertain, degrading situation; meanwhile, influential voices are calling for Russia to fill a fruitful niche in the overseas weapons markets. They say that creating a mechanism for filling this niche will help feed hungry Russia.

The political agenda of the founders of Soviet communism (and Stalinism in particular) and their successors included the task of the country's defense, along with several other major issues extremely important to their ideological ambitions for international domination. They started the unprecedented arms race and the idea of expanding the Soviet Union's international influence by creating and supporting the "camp" of procommunist regimes. Besides the 15 republics of the Soviet Union, this camp included the countries of Eastern Europe and Cuba. Among the camp's allies were numerous countries in Asia, Africa, South America, and the Middle East, as well as terrorist groups in different parts of the world.

The economic foundations of socialism were not based on humankind's natural aspirations to be free, to create a better life, or even become wealthy. The wealthy life promised by communist ideologists after the "victorious procession of communism" [7] was merely a utopian dream. This is why, in order to maintain the ideals of communism, ideologists imposed on the Soviet republics and the members of the socialist camp a myth about the Soviet way of life, the main principle of which was "Lenin's modesty".[8] The camp was surrounded by a solid iron curtain, which prevented the people from seeing how much better

---

7 Editor's Note: Soviet Communist Party slogan.

8 Editor's Note: Soviet Communist Party slogan.

life was in the civilized world. They were not allowed to compare the two standards of living, to recognize their poverty.

Looking at photos of ordinary Russian people taken between the 50s and 60s, one sees warm-hearted people, more than modestly dressed, who seriously believed in a better and brighter future. These well-educated people were selflessly building a communistic society. They lived their lives not only without cars, but also often without TVs, refrigerators, or stylish Western clothes. Many families lived in multi-family apartments with a communal kitchen and bathroom. At the time, such poverty was called "a modest life without the "Western grimace"[9]. The command propaganda for the "modest" way of life was an absolute necessity, and was forced upon the populace.

In order to implement a dictatorial political order; frighten political enemies; strengthen communist ideology; and support socialist countries, "third world" nations, and terrorist organizations, many weapons and, accordingly, a huge and a very expensive defense industry were needed. The ineffective socialist economy was not able to provide the necessary funds. The only way was to seize people's resources and pay only pennies for their labor.

During the years of the USSR existence, the country was proud of the skyrocketing development of its "industrial defense potential" in the North and Siberia. However, nobody knew then the real price – the hundreds of thousands of human lives the dictatorship sacrificed for the construction of the *Belomor Canal*, the *Gulag* factories/concentration camps, and the new defense plants in remote areas that were built on the bones of political prisoners, mostly innocent people arrested during the years of Stalinism. Even later, in the 1970s, one could see in documents

---

9 Editor's Note: Soviet Communist Party slogan.

for defense plant construction projects, particularly the passages on human resources, the ominous words: "This part of the industrial facilities will be built by a *spetskontingent* [special contingent, i.e., prisoners]."

During the "victorious" decades of Soviet existence, the Soviet people sincerely admired its flourishing achievements in science, culture, and art, and its unique achievements in space exploration. The country was proud of the unprecedented mass construction of five-story apartment buildings, started by Khrushchev, which provided millions of people with small yet private, and nearly free apartments.

One can see the change in the Russian people themselves, in what they want for their lives. During the last decade, Russian society has become dramatically stratified. Some people, such as the so-called "New Russians", have become enormously wealthy, while most of the population has lost its middle-class status and some have become extremely poor. But when Russian young people are asked whether they miss the "modest" life of their parents in 1950s and 1960s, the answer is "no". Moreover, the same points of view are kept by top modern communist ideologists. Is the military jacket of "the proletarian father," Stalin, still in fashion among them? No. After tasting the Western lifestyle, didn't these modern ideologists of communism, ultra-nationalism, and reactionary anti-capitalism reject "Lenin's modesty", which they had formerly promoted for a long time? Are they full of contempt for American computers, Italian furniture, Spanish interior accessories, or late-model German Mercedes and Audis, to which they prefer the "modest" domestic full-size *Volga* cars or *ZIL* limos? No, they are normal people with normal human desires. The expression "social being determines consciousness," uttered sarcastically by the USSR propaganda, became revered among legislators in the Russian Duma, the Ukrainian Verkhovna Rada, and government offices in Minsk, Chisinau and other capitals of former Soviet republics. The Western lifestyle, which is one of the main achievements of the 20th century, is no longer fantastic or unattainable. It has become a life goal for all Russian people, including politicians of all temperaments and ideologies.

This is a result of half a century of life with no devastating world wars, the opening of the iron curtain to make contact with the West - values which must be protected. The anathematization of these ideals would be the most serious crime against humanity, the end of civilization.

Russia was the cornerstone of the huge Union of the Soviet Socialist Republics. However, this "brotherhood of socialist countries" was built on the sands of myth. For seven decades, propaganda glorified "the unified family of the Soviet people". In the 1960s, the "Moral Code of the Soviet Builder of Communism" was written, according to which "one person to another is friend, comrade, and brother," while in actuality, nationalism was Soviet state policy.

The fifteen Soviet republics were proclaimed "sisters". A unique sculptural fountain created by a talented artist was erected in Moscow, in the center of the *VDNKh,* Russia's main exhibition park in honor of all the republics of the Union. Fifteen female figures danced in a circle, symbolizing the eternal friendship of the fifteen sister republics of the USSR. The "eldest sister" Russia danced along with her sisters Latvia, Moldavia, Belorussia, Kyrgyzstan, Tajikistan, Lithuania, Estonia, Ukraine, and others… The Russian people could not have imagined that all these "sisters" hated the Union ferociously. They did not know then that many of the republics had been forced to join the Union against their will. The Baltic States, the Western regions of Ukraine, Belorussia, and Moldavia were occupied by the Soviet Union before the beginning of World War II as the result of an ominous deal between Stalin and Hitler. It turned out that during all these years the republics had not wanted to live under the same roof with their eldest sister Russia in the household called the USSR. They wanted to live independently, although on pain of death these republics, particularly their leaders, swore an eternal allegiance to the Union, to the "unified family". But secretly they waited for the day when they would be able to run away from home.

That day finally came. The final accord was played in 1991 in the quiet coolness of the Belorussian *Belovezhskaya Puscha* - a virgin forest, where the leaders of Russia, Ukraine and Belorussia signed the death sentence for the USSR as a unified state. Its family disintegrated completely. The Soviet family was formally replaced only by the name Commonwealth of Independent States (CIS) and subsequently, Newly Independent States (NIS).

If the political leaders of the former republics did not want to join the Soviet Union, this raises the question of whether the effort and the resources spent on the unprecedented development of the world's largest defense industry, on the production of huge amounts of weapons, on the creation of the gigantic Soviet Army in order to fulfill the country's "international duty", and on the latest, most devastating war in Afghanistan, were justified? The answer is "no."

Since the Soviet Union did not bring any benefits to the former republics, they feel no gratitude towards it. It was a very painful and hard lesson for the USSR and its successor, Russia. But it is a fact.

Do the former republics of the USSR recall today the years of their existence in the "unified family" as years of happiness? No. Do they want to become "sisters" again? In most cases, no, despite the fact that independence has not made peoples' lives better.

Are the former members of the "socialist camp"--Hungary, the Czech Republic, Poland, Romania, Bulgaria, and others—grateful to the USSR for the use of tanks to "protect" the communist ideals in these countries in 1956 (the occupation of Hungary) and in 1968 (the occupation of Czechoslovakia)?

Did these civilized European States really need the USSR and the "senior comrades" from the Soviet *Politburo*? No. Not yesterday, not today. Ask former "comrades" from Vietnam, Chile, China, and other Asian, African, and South American countries: do they feel nostalgia for the USSR? Their response will also be "no".

So why then, if nobody wanted it, did the USSR have to spend the lion's share of the gross national product to process so much more iron ore than it actually needed, to smelt so much metal, to build so many defense plants, to produce so many missiles, cannons, tanks, ships, aircraft, and guns? Why was it necessary to spend billions on military science, to form countless top-secret research institutions, laboratories, experimental plants, and "special defense departments" of the USSR Academy of Science and its branches in all the republics? It is hard to believe this was all created for a "dowry" for each formally independent sister-republic, which was to leave the family nest sooner or later. Thus, the construction of this huge military machine—the defense industry, the army, and their infrastructure—was in vain.

After the spring of 1985, the people of the new Russia learned a great deal about their tragic and contradictory history. Undoubtedly, today is not the Stalinist or post-Stalin era. Since Gorbachev's glasnost, the people of Russia have learned to understand how the civilized world does everything. First of all, they have learned to hate war.

In today's world without informational borders, it is almost impossible to delude people with simplistic images of external enemies. The people are quite capable of evaluating everything themselves. Russians, being a wise nation, have learned during the last decade how to walk the thin line between protecting their values and infringement on somebody else's. They understand perfectly well how much weaponry is necessary to maintain peace and how much is needed for bloody military conquests. They learned at last how the countries of Western Europe, thanks to the Marshall Plan, rose from the ashes of World War II and built a new life for their people.

A decade and a half has passed since Mikhail Gorbachev, the first President of the USSR, began perestroika, when progressive Russian people could see on the horizon the dawn of a much better life. This was the start of a new and very promising stage of cooperation between West and East. In this torrent of bright changes and big hopes, conversion of the Soviet military-industrial complex looked like a natural, logical part of the bigger reform process.

In 1988, conversion, after Gorbachev's famous announcement about its beginning, sounded like a new spring, full of life and hope. People hoped that all these political changes would bring them prosperity, and were confident that their children would have a much better life. People hoped that the last stretch of the path to a better life and happiness would soon be finished.

They did not know that the legacy of the Soviet Union—a planned economy, with its heavy burden of military expenses—was terminally ill, and the end was near. Nobody told the people what the upper echelons already clearly understood: that the country could not go on this way any longer. Very few knew that the defense industry was the heart of the country's militarized economy. The weak, sickly militarized economy urgently needed to be treated with simultaneous economic reforms and defense conversion.

The unprecedented deep political and economic reforms and defense conversion started by Boris Yeltsin, the first President of post-USSR Russia, merged to form a unit. Russia has been striving to make the transition to a free market economy that would introduce the democratic attitudes that it has yet to fully experience. However, the shift from a predominately military-industrial complex to a civilian industry-based economy was attempted too early, before many needed economic and political factors were in place.

Russia's top defense industry executives did not have a clear vision of the future of the industry in conjunction with market-based economic reforms. Neither was it clear who needed Russia's grossly hypertrophied "defense potential", the pride of some officials even today. Its enterprises were founded within the context of a planned economy, and built on the principles of gigantism. Its huge plants are almost impossible to transform into new, flexible manufacturing divisions, with small business units. Nobody in Russia suggested either an effective, realistic method for defense conversion, or a feasible plan with practical workable solutions and steps. Officials produced radically different diagnoses of the situation in the defense industry. Accordingly, different treatments were prescribed. It is well known that when a patient is misdiagnosed with two entirely different ailments and receives two completely different treatments, the results can be terrifying. The prescribed type of conversion, which had no concrete plan, no basis in analysis of international experiences, and incomplete financial and technological support, resulted in another “headlong” conversion marathon.

Today the frozen defense industry is suffering horrible pains. Common sense suggests that without a correct diagnosis and a new effective treatment, the illness will become incurable. The “headlong" conversion that contributed to the defense industry's problems could lead to total and irreparable deformities, which will be devastating for Russia, and will compromise stability in the rest of the world.

"Headlong" conversion brought tremendous social problems. Many citizens who formerly worked in the Russian defense industry, including the once-prosperous "closed cities”, are now practically unemployed. No jobs, no incomes. Racketeering, banditry, robbery, theft, and contract killings of politicians, businessmen and bankers are flourishing. The list of new professions in Russia now includes “bodyguard” and “killer”, i.e., hit man. Just recently, such societal and medical problems as drug addiction, prostitution, and diseases, including long forgotten tuberculosis, were added to wide -spread alcoholism.

The hardships people are suffering constitute a tragic paradox of the new Russia. The essence of this paradox is that while progressive, fundamental reforms of the country’s political and economic systems were taking place, the population was becoming more and more impoverished. While considerable arms reductions have become a reality, thanks to new political thinking in the country and the international peace process, decreased government military orders and the huge financial deficit have forced many defense enterprises to virtually halt both military and civilian production.

History shows that similar crisis situations provide the most fertile soil for the rise of dictatorships, as in Germany of the 1930s. Its motto was a flourishing economy and the victory of the Third Reich. Its means to that end was aggression and violence. Russian Communists and ultra-nationalists, as successors of the Soviet regime, sometimes call for similar means. To overlook the danger of a repetition of that combination of motto and means is to ignore history's lessons. Passivity and inertia would be the best lubricants for guaranteeing such a repetition. As history demonstrates, the price of stopping such movements once they are well begun can be extremely high. And that price will be reckoned not only in hard currency, commodities, and lost opportunities, but also quite probably in human lives.

Many years have passed since the conversion process began, and everybody in Russia is tired of hearing the word "conversion". It has been consigned to oblivion, and the new term *restrukturizatsiya* (restructuring) has come into use in Russia. But is it indicative of a new, systematic approach to the problems facing the MIC, or is it just a deceptive word that marks the abandonment of the idea of conversion? In Russia today, there are numerous objections to defense conversion. They have been increasing as the economic crisis and its negative consequences deepen. After many failed, mismanaged attempts at "command conversion", quite a few directors of unconverted, "forbidden" defense enterprises, who oppose reforms, are lobbying for the renewal of military procurement orders. They have no other choice than to "restart" their plants and move toward profitability, offering paying jobs to their employees. It is unfortunate that for many of them it no longer matters whether they produce pharmaceuticals or biological weapons, precision machine tools or millions of new guns. Weapons would actually be the best choice for them, since they can produce weapons perfectly, with no need to meet urgent technological and business challenges.

Again and again, communists and ultra-nationalists remind the world of their existence. Their goal is to revive dogmas rejected by the world, without making any constructive efforts to help Russia to overcome the present crisis. They claim they can feed the people of the country and eliminate unemployment through the export of Russia's most advanced weapons. To whom are they going to sell them? It does not matter. Any band of terrorists will do, as long as they can "add fuel to the fire", leading the world to the brink of a new devastating world war, which will write off the bills accumulated by their own unfortunate people.

As in the Cold War era, communists and ultra-nationalists are again blaming the notorious West for all the economic and social disasters in Russia, the country that departed from the shore of “poor” socialism, but which has not yet moored at the “rich” shore of capitalism, as promised by the reformers. It is still easy for ordinary, impoverished Russians to direct their hatred towards the West.

And again, as at the beginning of perestroika in 1985, the world is waiting for the word from the new leaders of Russia, particularly its new President Vladimir Putin, whose historical mission is to make a final choice regarding the future of the country’s defense industry. A lot will depend on what the defense industry looks like in the first few years after 2000 and beyond: what will the new Russian politicians and the world community make out of it, and will this industry produce weapons or civilian products in the future?

The first alternative is a new, intensive round of logically organized conversion, which will dramatically decrease military production and transform Russia from an arms supplier to a real Motherland for its own people. One of the main issues of conversion is how to restructure the industry, eliminate all excessive production facilities, and re-tool the remainder for civilian use. And of course, Russia will not be able to cope with this task without the help of Western countries.

The second alternative is to switch back to the production of huge amounts of weapons, and to sell them to dangerous terrorist regimes. But then it will be extremely difficult to stop the dangerous consequences of this course of action. If weapons are sold to terrorists today, tomorrow they may be used against their producers. The latest examples of this are the deadly terrorist acts with hundreds of casualties in several Moscow residential areas and other regions of Russia in 1999.

Russian history shows that it is possible for a country to provide weapons to half of the world, yet not be able to feed its people. Will the country be able to feed its increasingly hungry population in the future by selling weapons? This is a big question.

* * *

We trust that this book will contribute to a better understanding of the history of Russian defense conversion and its future prospects. It will help to shed light on specific issues, implications, and tragic political, economic, and social consequences of mismanaged defense conversion processes, which are causing Russia and her people to suffer. We hope that the new Russian leadership and the world community understands the need to resolve the present problems and ordeals in Russia, the severity of which could lead to global instability, military confrontations, terrorism, and threats to international security.

We hope that Western society will gain a better understanding of the importance of increasing support for these Russian defense conversion ideals, on behalf of both Russia and the entire world. Russia's problems have already crossed the country's borders, "contaminating" other regions. When everything is collapsing in a country with a full arsenal of deadly weapons, it is no time to be a silent witness. It is an issue of vital importance to the whole world.

PART ONE

The USSR Defense Industry: From Militarization to Conversion (1917-1985)

INTRODUCTION

Vlad E. Genin

The Russian defense industry has had a unique developmental history. Destructive wars, tragic chapters in the country's history, social and political upheaval, cataclysms, the negative role of dictatorial leaders, and, recently, the poor results of headlong conversion have made the defense industry what it is today.

The formation process of the USSR/Russia Defense Industry, and the beginning of its conversion, is one of the most complicated phenomena of the 20th century. It is so multifaceted and so multifarious, that without studying all of its aspects, it is impossible to see the whole picture of today's Russian MIC and the range of its problems. Its ups and downs may seem mysterious, sometimes even incomprehensible. This phenomenon is a complex system consisting of a variety of elements: historical, political, international, military, economic, technical, environmental, and social. The world still cannot fully understand the true scale of this phenomenon, and how it affects the different spheres of Russia's life, and the life of the international community.

As the disarmament process began, the fate of the Russian defense industry changed dramatically. It had to face a very difficult task – conversion: the task of adjusting itself to the new political and socio economic environment and circumstances. It was the beginning of deep systemic changes, unprecedented in the world experience.

Why did the Russian defense industry react so painfully during the course of conversion? Why did the panacea that worked for all other countries regardless of their histories turn out to be completely unacceptable for Russia?

A thorough review of the defense industry, of the circumstances in which it developed, and of its historical heritage, will help us to understand this phenomenon. An objective historical analysis of the Russian MIC will give us the tools to predict the probable course of its conversion efforts.

1.1. NATIONAL SECURITY DOCTRINES

Introductory Remarks

Vlad E. Genin

Any State must know how to defend itself. But throughout history, global political leadership objectives and territorial ambitions have been regularly included under the rubric of defense. Although history shows that the desire for aggression and occupation was often disguised as a philosophy of defense against an external enemy, the doctrine of defense was becoming the doctrine of war.

The blood of the young Soviet Republic was drained by World War I, Civil War, starvation, and poverty. The country was still very far from creating the modern generation of weapons. Nevertheless, at the end of the 1920s, the grandiose, almost unimaginable, plans to build the most menacing army in the world were developed in the corridors of power.

How the Soviet Army survived Stalin's 1937 pre-war repressions remains a mystery. Stalin eliminated all outstanding commanders: Tukhachevskii, Yakir, Guy, Gamarnik and many other so-called "saboteurs", thereby virtually decapitating the Army. Many prominent weapons designers, including Tupolev and Koroliov, were subjected to "cleansing" and repression.

During World War II, the army suffered a great deal of casualties, as well as the loss of military equipment and weapons. But it completed the war very well equipped and stronger than ever before.

After Stalin's death in 1953 the country started to recover from the horrors of his dictatorship. Khrushchev's "thaw" was coming, and it seemed that all old dogmas of "the proletarians are the grave-diggers for the bourgeoisie"[1] and previous military doctrines should have sunk into oblivion. The country and the whole world were expecting great positive changes. But as we all remember, "the spring thaw" quickly became the "winter frost" of the intensifying Cold War, which peaked in the last years of Brezhnev's eighteen-year long leadership.

What was the foundation for creating the first national security doctrines in Russia? What was their influence on the principles of the Army's formation?

David Holloway

War and the preparation for war exerted a profound influence on the Soviet state and the Soviet economy. The Soviet Union was born in war and revolution. After twenty years of social and political upheaval, it faced in 1941 the test of a terrible war with Germany. Soon after the end of World War II, the Soviet Union was caught up in an arms race with the United States and the other Western powers. For all the years of its existence the Soviet Union gave high priority to the creation of military power. It created a vast defense industry, which enabled it to play a major role in the defeat of Nazi Germany, and to achieve strategic parity with the economically more advanced Western powers during the Cold War.

The priority given to military power was determined not just by specific threats that faced the Soviet Union, or by specific political

1 Editor's Note: Soviet Communist Party slogan.

ambitions. It was rooted in the official ideology of the Soviet state, in its view of the twentieth century as a period of transition from capitalism to socialism, in which the capitalist powers would resist the inevitable progress of revolution. The Bolsheviks hoped that their seizure of power in Russia would spark off revolution in Europe. By the early 1920s, however, it began to become clear to them that revolution in Europe was not about to happen soon. The Soviet Union would have to survive as the only proletarian state in a capitalist world. The idea of "building socialism in one country" began to gain ground in the Party in the mid-1920s. Trotsky attacked this notion as a betrayal of the revolution and surrender to the peasantry, but its ultimate significance was very different.[2]

In the bitter industrialization debate of the 1920s, military considerations played an important role. The Bolshevik leaders realized that the economic basis of Soviet military power was weak. As the idea of "socialism in one country" gained acceptance, the lack of modern armaments grew more worrying, for the Soviet state might have to fight alone against the capitalist powers. In January 1925, Mikhail Frunze, Trotsky's successor as People's Commissar of War, warned that a future war would not be like the Russian Civil War:

"Of course it will have the character of a class civil war in the sense that the White Guards will be on the enemy's side, while we, on the other hand, shall have allies in the camp of our enemies. But in equipment, in the methods of waging it, it will not be a war like our civil war. We shall have to deal with a splendid army, armed with all the latest technological advances, and if we do not have these advances then

2 E.H. Carr, *Socialism in One Country, 1924-1926* (London: Macmillan, 1959), vol. 2, p. 50.

the prospects for us may prove very unfavorable. This should be taken into account when we decide the question of the general preparation of the country for defense."[3]

The needs of the Red Army figured prominently in the first Five Year Plans. In December 1927, Voroshilov, the Commissar for Army and Navy Affairs, told the 15th Party Congress that the chief military purpose of the First Five Year Plan was to raise the "technical strength of the Red Army to the level of first class contemporary armies."[4]

1929 was a turning point in military policy, just as it was in industrial and agricultural policy. In that year Stalin launched the policy of forced collectivization, and pushed for higher targets for industrial production. In July, the Politburo issued a decree on "The State of Defense of the USSR," calling for the Red Army to have no fewer troops than its probable enemies in the main theatre of war, and to attain superiority in the decisive types of armament – aircraft, artillery, and tanks.[5] In the same year, the Red Army adopted new Field Service Regulations. The Regulations Commission noted that "we have every reason to expect that [our] technological might will increase from year to year. We must not only refuse to accept a technological lag, but on the contrary we must surpass our bourgeois neighbors in arms and equipment."[6]

---

3 Quoted in *50 let Vooruzhennykh Sil SSSR* (Moscow: Voenizdat: 1968), p. 198.
4 Quoted in E.H. Carr, *Foundations of a Planned Economy 1926-1929*, vol. 2, London: Macmillan, 1971, p. 314. For a discussion of the military factor in the first Five-Year Plan see R.W. Davies, "Soviet Military Expenditure and the Armament Industry," in *Europe-Asia Studies*, 1993, no. 4.
5 *KPSS o Vooruzhennykh Silakh Sovetskogo Soiuza* (Moscow: Voenizdat, 1969), pp. 264-266.
6 S. Kozlov, *Razrabotka i Razvitie Sovetskoi Voennoi Doktriny* (Moscow: Voennaia Mysl), 1966, no. 7.

The Bolsheviks believed that in a future war they were likely to face a coalition of powerful capitalist states, and that was why they needed a strong army. They believed too that military power rested upon industrial power, and consequently gave high priority to the creation of a modern armaments industry. Tsarist Russia had had an extensive arms industry, to which the First World War had given new impetus. But this was badly damaged in the Civil War, and neglected in the first years of Bolshevik rule. By the late 1920s, the Soviet Union had virtually no tank industry, little or no warship production, and low artillery and ammunition production; the aircraft industry was the brightest spot in an otherwise gloomy picture. Production of arms and equipment rose rapidly during the 1930s. In the early 1930s, foreign weapons were acquired and used as the basis for Soviet designs. By 1940, the Soviet Union had a strong defense-industrial base.[7]

The Soviet leaders rejected the concept, which was popular with Western military theorists in the 1920s and 1930s, of small highly mechanized forces. They sought instead to marry the mass army to modern military technology. During the 1930s, the Red Army's leaders devoted great attention to determining how the new weapons would be employed in war. Tukhachevskii and a group of officers close to him developed the concept of the "operation in depth" as a way of using modern arms in mobile offensive warfare. The main idea was that modern armaments made it possible to strike the enemy not only in his front line, but also simultaneously in the whole depth of his order of battle. The enemy could thus be prevented from bringing up his reserves and stopping the breakthrough. This concept, which was based on the

---

7 Nikolai Simonov, *Voenno-Promyshlennyi Kompleks SSSR v 1920-1950-e gody* (Moscow: ROSSPEN, 1996), pp. 81-137.

mass use of artillery, tanks, and aircraft, reflected – and in turn reinforced – the belief that military power rested on industrial might.[8]

The picture was not one of unalloyed progress, however. Stalin's purge of 1936-38 destroyed the High Command that had been trying to mold the Red Army, with its new arms and its new doctrine, into an effective fighting force. Most of the military innovators, including Tukhachevskii, were arrested, to be replaced by men with less experience. The resulting loss of direction was reflected in the general disarray of the Red Army in 1938-41, and contributed to its poor showing in the war with Finland in the winter of 1939-40.

On June 22, 1941, the war that had been so long expected took Stalin by surprise when Germany attacked the Soviet Union. By the end of November 1941, several million Soviet troops had been killed or taken prisoner, and the German armies had reached the outskirts of Moscow. The Soviet authorities had lost control of more than 40 per cent of the population, 40 per cent of the grain production, and 60 per cent of the coal, iron, steel, and aluminum output of the country.[9] In December 1941, the Red Army launched a counter-offensive outside Moscow and halted the German advance. But the Soviet Union could take the offensive in an effective manner only when industry began to produce armaments in large numbers. Losses of equipment were enormous in the opening stage of the war, and military production was disrupted by the German advance. By the end of 1941, however, large numbers of plants had been evacuated to the east of the country, and in 1942, arms production started to rise sharply. Once it was supplied with weapons,

---

8 M.N. Tukhachevskii, "O Novom Polevom Ustave RKKA," in his *Izbrannye Proizvedeniia*, vol. 2 (Moscow: Voenizdat, 1964), pp. 255-256.

9 G.S. Kravchenko, *Ekonomika SSSR v Gody Velikoi Otechestvennoi Voiny* (Moscow: Ekonomika, 1970), pp. 123-124.

the Red Army could search for the right combination of arms, men, and doctrine to put into practice the principles of maneuver and offensive that had been espoused in pre-war military thought.

On February 9, 1946, Stalin declared that the "Soviet social order has shown itself more stable and capable of enduring than a non-Soviet social order, that the Soviet social order is a form of organization, a society superior to any non-Soviet social order."[10] In the same speech, he claimed that the policies of collectivization and industrialization had made victory possible, and he announced that the Soviet Union would return to the task of building up heavy industry. It would take at least three more Five Year Plans before the Soviet Union would be ready for "all contingencies."

World War II left a powerful imprint on postwar defense policy. The memory of the German surprise attack remained strong. Victory, moreover, was claimed by Stalin – and understood by many – as confirmation that prewar policies had been correct. At the end of the war, Stalin decided to invest heavily in the new military technologies: the atomic bomb, jet and rocket propulsion, radar.[11] For Stalin, the postwar period was also a prewar period. He argued, on the basis of Lenin's theory of imperialism, that another world war was inevitable; and by analogy with the period between World War I and World War II he expected it to take place in 15-25 years.[12] Stalin gave top priority to the development of nuclear weapons. But in the years before the Soviet

---

10 "Rech' Na Predvybornom Sobranii Izbiratelei Stalinskogo Izbiratel'nogo Okruga Goroda Moskvy," in Robert H. McNeal (ed.), I.V. Stalin, *Works*, vol. 3, 1946-1953 (Stanford: Hoover Institution Press, 1967), p. 2.

11 See David Holloway, Stalin and the Bomb: the Soviet Union and Atomic Energy, 1939-1956 (New Haven: Yale University Press, 1994), pp. 134-149.

12 Ibid., pp. 150-153.

Union acquired a stockpile of nuclear weapons, the main counterweight to American atomic air power was air defense, which received heavy investment, and the Ground Forces, which were trained and equipped to carry out the kind of large-scale offensive strategic operations that the Red Army had conducted in 1943-45.

Stalin's death led to a reassessment of the role of nuclear weapons in foreign and military policy. Georgii Malenkov declared in early 1954 that such a war would mean the end of "world civilization," and argued that peaceful coexistence with the capitalist world was therefore imperative. Malenkov's colleagues in the Party leadership rejected his position.[13] They were aware of the terrible destruction that nuclear weapons could cause, but they were not willing to accept that a world war would put an end to the historical progress of humanity toward communism. At the XXth Party Congress, in 1956, Khrushchev modified the Stalinist position by declaring that, "thanks to the growing might of the Soviet Union, war was not fatally inevitable". But a new world war was not impossible, and if it did take place, it would end in the victory of socialism. Thus, Soviet policy was to have a dual character: it was to be directed toward the prevention of war with the West, even as the two sides engaged in a historic political rivalry. At the same time, the Soviet Union had to prepare for a world war, which, though not inevitable, might nevertheless take place. The Soviet Union, moreover, had to prepare to win that war.

This formulation, which underpinned Soviet military doctrine until the 1980s, was fateful in its consequences. In stressing the importance of avoiding a new world war, it took account of the terrible destructive power of nuclear weapons. But in pointing to the victory of

13 Ibid., pp. 335-340.

socialism in the event of war, it laid the basis for an extremely expensive, open-ended defense effort. Soviet military doctrine provided the rationale for very large forces by arguing that the Soviet Union had to be able to win a global nuclear war. The doctrine did not set any limits on what systems the Soviet Union should build and deploy. Khrushchev tried to deal with the burden of defense spending by reducing the production of conventional systems such as aircraft and surface ships, and by cutting the armed forces. He made significant reductions in the mid-1950s. But he met with stiff resistance from the military and the defense industry.[14] Besides, the missile and submarine programs Khrushchev launched were very expensive, and the cost of defense production rose sharply in the late 1950s and early 1960s.[15]

Brezhnev was much more friendly than Khrushchev to military demands. The late 1960s and early 1970s saw a build-up not only of nuclear forces but also of conventional forces in Europe and along the border with China. By the early 1970s, the Soviet Union had clearly reached parity with the United States in strategic arms, and there were signs that the Party leadership (and the military leadership too) no longer believed that it made sense to think of victory in a nuclear war. In 1985, Marshal N.V. Ogarkov, former Chief of the General Staff, wrote that the rapid growth in the number of nuclear weapons in the 1970s and 1980s had led "to a radical review of the role of these weapons, to a break with previous views of their place and significance in war, of the methods of conducting battles or operations, and even of the possibility of waging

---

14 I.V. Bystrova, "Razvitie Voenno-Promyshlennogo Kompleksa," in V.S. Lel'chuk and E.I. Pivovar, eds., *SSSR i Kholodnaia Voina* (Moscow: Mosgorarkhiv, 1995), pp. 160-203.
15 Simonov, op.cit., p. 299.

war at all with the use of nuclear weapons."[16] There were some signs too of a growing realization that the military effort constituted a heavy economic burden.

But it was only under Gorbachev that the basic political underpinnings of Soviet military doctrine were altered in such a way as to make it possible to think of reducing Soviet military forces significantly and transferring resources to civilian purposes. The "new thinking", which Gorbachev and Foreign Minister Eduard Shevardnadze elaborated in the late 1980s, provided a new conceptual framework for defense policy: human interests take precedence over the interests of any particular class; the world is becoming increasingly interdependent; security must be mutual, especially in the context of U.S.-Soviet relations, since if one side is insecure it will only make the other side insecure too; there can be no victors in a nuclear war; security has to be based increasingly on political rather than military instruments. The "new thinking" rejected many of the basic assumptions of earlier Soviet doctrine, and provided a rationale for reducing defense outlays and converting the defense sector – or at least parts of it – to the production of civilian goods.

Gorbachev did not move at once to cut the defense effort. In the first years of his rule defense expenditures appear to have risen.[17] In December 1988, however, in a speech at the United Nations, he announced a unilateral cut of 500,000 men in the armed forces, and in January 1989 he revealed that "the defense budget will be reduced by 14.2 percent, the production of armaments and military hardware by 19.5

---

16 N.V. Ogarkov, *Istoriia Uchit Bditel'nosti* (Moscow: Voenizdat, 1985), p. 47.
17 Joint Economic Committee, U.S. Congress, *Allocation of Resources in the Soviet Union and China -1987* (Washington D.C.: U.S. GPO, 1989), p. 23.

percent."[18] In May, Gorbachev told the Congress of People's Deputies that the Soviet defense budget in 1989 amounted to 77.3 billion rubles or about 9 percent of the Soviet national income. He said it would be reduced by ten billion rubles (about 13 percent) in 1990-91.[19] In June 1989, Premier Nikolai Ryzhkov stated that 40 percent of the output of the defense sector was for civilian use, and that that proportion would grow to 46 percent in 1990, and to over 60 percent in 1995.[20]

---

18 Bill Keller, "Gorbachev Tells of Military Cuts," *New York Times*, January 19, 1989. These figures were later embodied in a law of March 1989 on the reduction of Soviet armed forces.

19 "Ob Osnovnykh Napravleniiakh Vnutrennei i Vneshnei Politiki SSSR," *Pravda*, May 31, 1989, p. 2.

20 N.I. Ryzhkov, "Sluzhit' Interesam Naroda," *Pravda*, June 8, 1989, p. 3.

1.2. THE HISTORY AND STRUCTURE OF DEFENSE INDUSTRY

Introductory Remarks

Vlad E. Genin

It is impossible to create a militarized State without the support of a very well developed industrial foundation. During the 1920s and 1930s, the USSR did not yet have such a foundation. Nevertheless, the country, which was behind the rest of the industrial world at that time, was able to create a considerable defense potential in record time.

At that time, the number of defense plants was not great enough to meet the fast-growing demands of the military for the newest weapons, military devices, equipment, heavy machinery, and supplies. However, very few people knew about the existence of the secret program of "assimilation" of civilian enterprises – a unique practice for the industrial world of those years.[21]

The Soviet MIC seemed then to embody the best achievements of socialism. It was a symbol of scientific and technological progress. Its name was somehow connected with all technical innovations: airplanes, ships, automobiles, radio devices, jet propulsion, and emerging missile technology. It was the country's best example of executing production plans.

---

21 Assimilation meant immediate conversion of civilian enterprises to military production within a few days. Assimilation programs served as the foundation for the militarized Soviet economy.

Everything related to it was beyond any criticism. This MIC was successful and flawless.

The real size of the MIC is still unknown. It has always been a sort of "State within a State." Even now, with the top-secret enterprises declassified, there are many varying evaluations of the power of the Soviet defense industry, its financial strength, and its material resources. These evaluations differ from each other dramatically; some are even contradictory. Even today we do not know what the gigantic MIC cost the people of the Soviet Union. It was a mystery "hidden behind seven sealed doors". However, just a few decades later, life would prove that behind this grandiose façade a gigantic, bulky and clumsy mechanism was hidden, preventing the country from moving forward economically.

David Holloway

The Stalinist leadership created the command-administrative system precisely in order to enable it to direct resources toward its own high priority goals. Since the central goal of Stalin's industrialization drive was to turn the Soviet Union into a powerful military-industrial state, investment in the defense industry received high priority. But the defense industry could not be the sole object of investment, for, as was clearly recognized, it could flourish only if supported by a strong industrial base, and in particular by the development of metallurgical, fuel, machine-tool, electrical supply, and chemical industries. Moreover, the defense industry placed quite special demands on these industries, for example for high-quality metals and high-grade fuels. The defense industry in the 1930s had to operate under severe constraints, which the

Party leaders tried to minimize by giving it preferential treatment in the supply of manpower and materials. The priority system was designed to reduce the constraints under which the defense sector developed, and to shield it from shortages and bottlenecks elsewhere in the economy.

There existed a conflict between immediate investment in military production and the building up of a strong civilian industry, which would eventually provide the basis for military power. In order to minimize this conflict the Party leadership tried to ensure that civilian plants could be shifted rapidly to military production if the need arose. New civilian plants were designed with military production in view. Special shops were set up in many plants to smooth the way for defense production. Mobilization plans were drawn up for industry as a whole to make possible a rapid increase in military production in the event of war. The early stages of the war with Germany showed, however, that these plans were not always easy to implement.[22]

The basic organizational form of the Soviet defense industry was established in the 1930s, as an integral part of the new command-administrative economy. The production of arms and materiel was carried out in enterprises subordinate to branch ministries (people's commissariats), and was subject to plans drawn up by central planning agencies. At first, arms production came under the People's Commissariat of Heavy Industry. In 1936, a People's Commissariat of the Defense Industry was established, and, in 1939, this in turn was divided into four separate people's commissariats – for ammunition, armaments, ships, and aircraft. In 1940, there were about 300 enterprises in the defense industry, employing around one million workers. In that

---

22 *Istoriia Velikoi Otechestvennoi Voiny Sovetskogo Soiuza*, vol. 2 (Moscow: Nauka, 1961), p. 161.

year defense production accounted for 18.7 percent of total industrial production.[23]

After the initial setbacks, Soviet defense production grew rapidly during World War II, as civilian industry was mobilized to produce arms and materiel. In 1942, military production constituted 63.9 percent of industrial output; in 1943 – 58.3 percent; by 1945, it had fallen to 40.1 percent.[24] These results were made possible only by massive sacrifices on the part of the people of the Soviet Union. Nevertheless, the capacity of industry to produce enormous quantities of tanks, artillery, aircraft, and ammunition made a major contribution to the Soviet victory. World War II confirmed in the minds of the Party leadership three important requirements of military-economic policy: to maintain a high level of arms production; to provide the basis for economic mobilization in time of war; to ensure the viability of the economy in wartime.[25] How much sense these principles make in the nuclear age is open to question, but they exerted a strong influence on Soviet policy after World War II.

World War II also saw the birth of new technologies: the atomic bomb, jet and rocket propulsion, and radar. In the immediate postwar period Stalin decided to invest heavily in the development of these technologies, which in turn gave rise to new science-based branches of industry, alongside the more traditional branches. By the 1970s, there were nine industrial ministries in the defense industries group: the Ministry of the Aviation Industry; the Ministry of General Machine Building (strategic missiles); the Ministry of the Defense Industry (conventional arms); the Ministry of Machine Building (munitions); the

---

23 Simonov, op.cit., p. 326.
24 Kravchenko, op.cit., p. 351.
25 Kravchenko, op.cit., p. 333.

Ministry of Shipbuilding; the Ministry of Medium Machine Building (nuclear weapons); and three ministries devoted to the development and production of electronics – the Ministries of the Electronics Industry, the Radio Industry, and of the Means of Communication). Not all of the output of these ministries was devoted to military purposes; a significant portion was civilian (e.g., passenger aircraft and merchant ships). And military goods were produced in the enterprises of other ministries.

The defense sector was both an integral part of the Soviet economy, sharing many of its general characteristics, and the highest priority sector of the Soviet economy, with special features of its own. Like other industrial ministries, the ministries in the defense sector had their own research institutes, design bureaus, and production plants, and their output was planned and coordinated by higher economic agencies. Special bodies were created at different times to direct the work of the defense industrial ministries. In the 1970s and 1980s, the Military-Industrial Commission (*Voenno-promyshlennaia kommissiia*), an agency under the Council of Ministers, coordinated the activities of the defense sector.

As a result of its high priority, the defense industry had some distinguishing characteristics. It tended to receive the best machinery and equipment. Its workers were better paid than those in civilian industry, and it offered more benefits – for example, in housing and health care; the quality of its labor force may therefore have been higher. Labor discipline was stricter than in civilian plants, and this contributed to higher quality output. High priority was an important advantage in an economy where supply problems were chronic. Economic planning agencies dealt more quickly with requests and orders from the defense industry – an advantage in a system where bureaucratic delays could be considerable.

The high priority given to defense was reinforced by the power of the Ministry of Defense as a customer. Not only did the Ministry enjoy the support of the Party leadership; it also had institutional mechanisms through which it could monitor defense production and exercise quality control over the output of defense plants. The Ministry had a network of military representatives (*voenpredy*) in the design bureaus and production plants. These representatives had three main functions: to prevent production bottlenecks by speeding up the supply of materials and parts; to supervise the pricing of military products; and to ensure that military production met quality standards. These arrangements did not ensure that the Ministry always got what it wanted. Tension could arise between the military and the defense industry – for example, over quality (the defense plant might not be able to get the components it needed) or over innovation (the enterprise might delay shifting to production of a new model). But the Ministry of Defense did nonetheless enjoy a degree of consumer power unusual in the Soviet Union.

The priority system was established to shield the defense industry from shortcomings in the rest of the economy. One consequence of this attempt was, ironically, to encourage a tendency found elsewhere in the economy: the pursuit of autarky by ministries, through the creation of supply industries under their own control. This tendency appears to have been strong in the defense sector. In the 1970s, for example, the Ministry of the Electronics Industry produced hundreds of materials and components it needed because it could not rely on outside suppliers (i.e., on other ministries) to meet its quality requirements.[26] This pattern shows that the defense industry had high priority, since it had been given its own supply industries. But it also shows that the priority system was not wholly effective in ensuring that other branches would supply the defense industry with what it needed – otherwise it would not have needed its own supply industries. In spite of the high priority it enjoyed, the defense sector was not wholly isolated from the rest of the economy and its shortcomings.

One of the most striking features of the defense industry was the secrecy that surrounded it. That secrecy was officially justified by the need to prevent hostile powers from gaining information about the Soviet military effort. No doubt it did contribute to this goal. But it was not only the desire to keep foreign governments in ignorance that lay at the basis of Soviet secrecy, since a good deal of information about the Soviet military effort, which was available abroad, could not be published inside the Soviet Union. The General Staff was anxious to protect its claim to professional expertise by discouraging civilian institutions from learning details of current policy; in this way informed criticism could be kept to a minimum, and the General Staff's monopoly of expertise preserved. The secrecy surrounding the defense industry helped to buttress its priority by preventing criticism of the efficiency of the defense industry. Khrushchev complained in 1963 that "because the production of defense industry enterprises is secret, shortcomings in the work of such enterprises is closed to criticism."[27] Secrecy helped the defense industry to lay a claim to scarce materials and products, without having to provide a detailed justification. Secrecy was not an accidental feature of the

---

26 P.M. Stukolov, ed., *Ekonomika Elektronnoi Promyshlennosti* (Moscow, 1976), pp. 14-15.
27 *Pravda*, April 26, 1963.

Soviet defense economy, but an essential element in its mode of operation.

The compartmentalization of knowledge and information in the defense sector reinforced the centralized system of policy-making, because only those at the top had a full picture of what was going on, and hence the power of control and initiative. But not everyone at the top had full access to information. In his memoirs Mikhail Gorbachev writes of the late 1970s and early 1980s that "all the figures relating to the MIC [military-industrial complex] were held in the strictest secrecy even from members of the Politburo. You only had to mention that some defense enterprise was working unsatisfactorily for Ustinov to pounce on the "immature faultfinder," and no one in the Politburo was brave enough to stand up to him."[28] And if Ustinov (who was then Minister of Defense and a member of the Politburo, and had been a leading figure in the defense industry since World War II) was ready to do that to Politburo members, he was even readier to do it to those of lesser status.

One consequence of the secrecy surrounding the Soviet defense industry is that it was impossible for foreign analysts to know what the size of the Soviet defense effort was, and what burden it placed on the economy as a whole. Western governments and research institutes expended a great deal of effort in trying to assess how much the Soviet Union spent on defense, and what the level of defense expenditure said about Soviet intentions. Even with the declassification of Russian archives, it is still difficult to assess how much the Soviet Union was spending on defense. According to Nikolai Simonov, author of the most detailed economic analysis of the Soviet military-industrial complex, the

---

28 Mikhail Gorbachev, *Zhizn' i Reformy*, kniga 1 (Moscow: Novosti, 1995), p. 207.

government kept the price of defense products lower than their cost of production. "By pricing raw materials, semi-fabricated goods used for the production of armaments, munitions and military equipment at lower than their real cost, the state achieved an increase in their [i.e., arms etc.] production in accordance with the demands of the military establishment."[29] But the government had to make good the difference by providing subsidies to the defense industry. Simonov calculates that according to official figures, military expenditures amounted to 14.2 percent of the national income in 1950, but that that figure rises to 20 percent if subsidies to the defense industry are taken into account, and to 21.2 percent if the special accounts for the nuclear and missile programs are included.[30] By 1955 that proportion fell to 14.1 percent, as a result of post-Stalin cutbacks.[31] Unfortunately, data of this kind do not exist for the later period. But the way in which prices were set for materials and components used in defense production indicates that Gorbachev's 1989 statement that military expenditures constituted 9 percent of the national income is likely to have been a significant understatement.

It is clear that the Soviet military-industrial complex enjoyed high priority, but also that the mechanisms for regulating defense spending and balancing it against other priorities were very weak. Soviet military doctrine provided for an open-ended commitment of resources to defense, within the context of the Cold War. Furthermore, the pricing system and the secrecy that surrounded defense deprived the Party leadership of the basis for informed decisions about the priorities of

---

29 Simonov, op.cit., p. 312.
30 Ibid., p. 329.
31 Ibid., p. 330.

national policy. These conditions provided the environment in which a massive military-industrial complex could develop.

1.3. THE PERFORMANCE OF THE DEFENSE SECTOR: CAPACITY AND OUTPUT

Introductory Remarks

Vlad E. Genin

In the 1970s, the Cold War was in full swing. The Socialist system challenged capitalism. It did not at all appear as though the U.S. and U.S.S.R. planned to peacefully coexist, although such plans were frequently announced at summit conferences.

A new round of the arms race was started. The mountains of weapons continued to grow. East and West were spending large sums of money on the development and production of the most advanced weapon systems. But while the national economies of the United States and countries of Western Europe could afford to pay these bills without taking the essentials away from their people, the arms race in the USSR "ate" almost everything that people earned with their hard work. The industries that produced food, clothing, medicine, various consumer goods, and the construction of residential houses, were ugly stepsisters in comparison with the beautiful older sister – the defense industry. There were still attempts to convince people that the country needed massive protection against the encroachment of imperialism. The question arises: was there really any constant danger of the conquest of the USSR by "imperialistic" powers? Did the arms race ever have any achievable goal, or did it simply chase after ghosts, or even worse, its own shadow?

David Holloway

During the Cold war the Soviet Union succeeded in creating a formidable military machine that – fortunately – was never tested in the global war for which it trained and planned. For that reason it is difficult to make a final judgment on just how formidable it really was. It is true that the Soviet Army lost the war against the Mujahadeen in Afghanistan, but that was not the kind of war, which it had been created to fight. The Soviet Union certainly had enough nuclear weapons to destroy its potential enemies many times over, and it had the capacity to deliver those weapons to at least some targets even if attacked first. The Soviet Armed Forces were successful in removing from the minds of Western political leaders any thought of attacking the Soviet Union, and they also underpinned the Soviet position in Eastern Europe. It was generally accepted by the late 1960s that the Soviet Union had attained strategic parity with the United States, and in Europe it enjoyed a preponderance of military power.

To support this military machine the Soviet defense industry continued to grow in the 1970s and 1980s. By the late 1980s, the defense sector (defined as the nine defense-industrial ministries) had approximately 2000 enterprises, about 100 of which were giant plants employing an average of 18,000-20,000 people.[32] Forty percent or so of the output of the defense sector was civilian in 1989. According to one source, about 400 enterprises were engaged in purely civilian production;

---

32 The figure of 2000 is given by several sources. See John S. Earle and Ivan Komarov, "Measuring Defense Conversion in Russian Industry" (Stanford University: CISAC, September 1996), p. 7. The figure on the 100 large plants is taken from Clifford G. Gaddy, *The Price of the Past: Russia's Struggle with the Legacy of a Militarized Economy* (Washington D.C.: Brookings Institution Press), p. 199.

about 1,000-1,100 were purely military; and the other 500-600 companies had mixed production.[33] By the late 1980s, the defense complex employed as many as 7-9 million people, not all of whom were engaged in defense production.[34]

The Soviet Union had to match the military might of the Western powers on the basis of a much weaker economy. Even the most generous estimates placed the Soviet GNP at no more than 60 percent of the U.S. GNP. And the Soviet Union's allies in the Warsaw Pact were economically less advanced than the United States' allies in NATO. In order to match its more advanced rivals in military production, the Soviet Union had to mobilize a much larger proportion of its economy. Even now it remains difficult to say what that proportion was. By the mid-1980s, the CIA estimated, the Soviet Union was spending 15-17 percent of its GNP on defense, an estimate that in retrospect does not seem too high, and may well be too low.[35] The Soviet defense industry turned out arms and equipment in large numbers to satisfy the requirements of the Soviet Armed Forces, the troops of the KGB and the MVD, and the export market. The numbers produced by the Soviet industry were generally much higher than those produced by Western defense firms.

---

33 Julian Cooper, cited ibid., p. 7.

34 See the range of estimates discussed by Earle and Komarov, op.cit., p. 6.

35 Joint Economic Committee, U.S. Congress, *Allocation of Resources in the Soviet Union and China – 1986* (Washington D.C.: U.S. GPO, 1988), p. 15. The estimation of Soviet defense expenditure was a highly controversial issue. Some economists argued that the CIA understated the military burden because it excluded activities such as civil defense and military aid. If this broader definition were used, they argued, the military burden rose from 20 percent of GNP in 1970 to about 25 percent in the mid-1980s. Still others argued that even this estimate was too low – that the proportion was about 30-35 percent – not because the CIA underestimated the size or cost of the defense effort, but because it overestimated the size of the Soviet GNP.

The Soviet Union was able to compete successfully in terms of quantity; it produced far more weapons than NATO.

Quality was a more difficult area for the Soviet defense sector. The technological level of Soviet industry was lower than that of Western industry, and the Soviet Union did not show any signs of closing the technology gap during the Cold War. A careful and comprehensive study of Soviet industry, which looked at a range of technologies from the early 1950s to the early 1970s, found that "in most of the technologies ... studied there is no evidence of a substantial diminution of the technological gap between the USSR and the West in the past 15-20 years, either at the prototype/commercial application stages or in the diffusion of advanced technologies."[36] According to this study, the Soviet Union tended to perform better in traditional areas such as electric power transmission, and in the iron and steel and machine tool industries. Soviet performance was less good in the more advanced, science-based branches such as computers, chemicals, and industrial process control instruments. These branches, it hardly needs to be said, acquired greater and greater significance for military power during the Cold War.

A similar picture of Soviet technology emerges from assessments done by the U.S. Department of Defense in the 1980s. The Department concluded in a 1980 study that the United States led the Soviet Union in fifteen of "the twenty most important basic technology areas," and was equal in the other five. In 1982, the United States was estimated to lead in fourteen of these areas, to tie in four, and to lag in two. The methodology behind these assessments is not clear, but the

---

36 R. Amann, J. Cooper, R.W. Davies, eds., *The Technological Level of Soviet Industry* (New Haven: Yale University Press, 1977), p. 66.

general picture to emerge is the same as that in the academic study referred to in the last paragraph: that the Soviet Union technological base was weaker than that of the United States, and of the West in general.[37]

This of course was no secret to the Soviet leadership. Ever since Stalin's death, the Soviet authorities had taken steps to try to improve the level of science and technology, and in particular to stimulate the transfer of scientific knowledge into industrial production. They also made strenuous efforts to acquire Western technology and to incorporate that into Soviet products, both civilian and military, thus demonstrating an awareness of Soviet backwardness. In the military field, designers did show ingenuity in creating effective weapons systems on the basis of a lower technology base. Two case studies of Soviet tanks and ICBMs offer some support for the view that in the Soviet Union military technology was at a higher level than civilian technology. Soviet designers were able, working from a lower technology base – especially in the science-based branches of industry, to create powerful and effective weapons. This suggests that the processes of turning science and technology into finished products was more effective in the defense sector than in civilian industry, but it does not support the view that the defense sector turned out technology of a qualitatively different level.[38]

In 1976, the CIA told Congress that "although some Soviet weapons systems have capabilities that exceed those of U.S. systems in such things as range, these are the result of design choices and do not reflect a higher state of technology."[39] In the following year the

---

37 See David Holloway, *The Soviet Union and the Arms Race* (New Haven: Yale University Press, 1983), pp. 134-140.

38 See R. Amann and J. Cooper, eds., *Industrial Innovation in the Soviet Union* (New Haven: Yale University Press, 1982), pp. 276-279.

39 Joint Economic Committee, U.S. Congress, *Allocation of Resources in the*

Director of the CIA testified that "while virtually all of the Soviet inventory weapons fall within U.S. production technology, the Soviets simply do not have the technology required to produce many of the U.S. weapons nor could they produce close substitutes."[40] A similar picture emerges from U.S. Department of Defense assessments in the 1980s. The United States was shown to enjoy a general lead in deployed military systems, though the lead was not as great as that in the comparison of basic technology areas. This points to the success of the Soviet defense sector in creating effective weapons on the basis of a generally lower technological level.

By the mid-1980s, the Soviet defense sector embraced the most advanced parts of Soviet industry. Within the enormous sector were gathered huge numbers of able scientists, engineers, managers, and workers, who had succeeded in designing, developing, and producing large numbers of advanced weapons and military equipment. In the mid-1980s, the new Party leader, Mikhail Gorbachev, decided that the military-industrial complex would have to be cut back so that resources could be channeled to other purposes. For all the successes that the complex had achieved, it had become a brake on the development of the Soviet Union. Gorbachev believed that the only way in which the military-industrial complex could be brought under control was by bringing the Cold War to an end. He achieved that latter goal successfully. But converting the resources of the military-industrial complex to civilian purposes has proved more difficult to achieve.

Soviet Union and China – 1977, Part 3 (Washington D.C.: U.S. GPO, 1977), p. 40

40 Ibid.

1.4. MIC: THE VIEW FROM INSIDE

Introductory Remarks

Vlad E. Genin

The Soviet MIC was comprised of the following nine ministries (Defense Industry, General Mechanical Engineering, Mechanical Engineering, Medium Mechanical Engineering, Electronics Industry, Telecommunications Industry, Radio Industry, Aviation Industry, and Shipbuilding Industry), as well as all the institutes, design bureaus, and factories that developed and produced weapons and military technology.

The specialists in the extremely security-conscious MIC were not permitted to tell others where they worked, let alone what they worked on. They had to take written oaths of secrecy—called "giving one's signature"—and they remain silent to this day. These people are taking the wealth of interesting knowledge they accumulated to the grave. A rich, unique chapter of history, not just Russia's but the world's, is being lost forever. The most comprehensive data and information about MIC's real capacity and output, plans and results achieved were on the desks of senior executives of the *Oboronnii Otdel TsK KPSS* (Department of Defense Industries of the Central Committee of the Communist Party of the USSR). They were studied and analyzed intently and comprehensively by those responsible for the future of the apparently flourishing MIC.

Until recently, no open, accurate

information on the Soviet MIC was available, which led, as is often the case, to polarized points of view on Soviet military expenditures. Adherents of one viewpoint portray the MIC as an enormous Soviet military industrial monster, a sort of "state within a state". According to the other point of view, the MIC was not a monster at all: it was like a bull in a china shop.

Vitaliy L. Katayev

The MIC was a highly classified "empire".[41] The image of the powerful Soviet MIC was created and maintained (willingly or unwillingly) by the combined efforts of the political institutions and special services of the Soviet Union and those of its foreign opponents.

Western experts, when analyzing and preparing information for their leaders on the military capabilities of the Soviet Union, always inflated the numbers. The military-political leadership of the Soviet Union found this image useful. This helped them keep quiet about the discrepancy between the real capabilities of the MIC and its artificially created image. This image, strange as it may seem, was actively reinforced by well-known Soviet scientists and academics, who criticized the government for its alleged "enormous expenditures, nearly 70% of total spending, to support the MIC". But people in the Soviet Union were accustomed to believing high-ranking scientists. Many foreign analysts also believed their statements.

As a result, many outright lies appeared in the press, often appearing there to forward the personal interests of their authors. But the motives weren't always personal; these myths were often advantageous

41 Editor's Note: Kataev was the Deputy Chair of the Department of the Defense Industry of the Central Committee of the CPSU.

to both sides during the Cold War. They were used to increase the military budgets in Western countries. The Soviet Union also needed to catch up to the levels its experts quoted, which were based on inflated data regarding the military capabilities of the enemy. Thus, the unprecedentedly costly secrecy of the MIC was advantageous not for the Soviet Union, but for the military industry of the United States and of the Soviet Union's other enemies.

The Soviet leadership regarded the power of the MIC as a suitable balance to the threat from overseas, as a guarantee of state security. Most importantly, however, the government found it convenient to use the enormous defense expenditures as an excuse for the country's economic difficulties. Both the Soviet Union and other countries used the same tactics: when the leader is in trouble, he should divert public scrutiny away from himself by, for example, carrying out a military strike or beginning a war under a specious pretext. The war did not necessarily have to be a shooting war: a Cold War, a war of expenditures, would suffice.

The MIC was a sort of Soviet Texas—everything existed on a grand scale. But not everything in the MIC was well organized. It was a conservative and brittle system, and did not allow for drastic organizational changes. It was something like a bull in a china shop, despite being strictly managed and controlled by party organizations that had defense departments in the Central Committee and Oblast committees of the Communist Party.

The highest link in the chain of command for both military-technical and military-economic issues in the MIC was the Department of the Defense Industry of the Central Committee of the Communist Party (subsequently the Defense Department of the Central Committee, and later the Department for Defense and State Security under the President of the Soviet Union). All new technologies were introduced by the Voenno-Promyshlennaia Komissiia (the Military Industrial Commission) of the Soviet Council of Ministers. Gosplan determined the volume of weapons production according to the conclusions of the state commission for testing these weapons, and the recommendations of the Military-Industrial Commission.

For a long time, the Soviet Union had no official military doctrine, just a range of ad hoc measures. The Army had no institutional character, so each defense minister molded it according to his own vision. Keldysh, president of the Soviet Academy of Sciences, first called Brezhnev's attention to this deficiency in the 1960s. He worked with Ustinov, the Minister of Defense, to propose the concept for a doctrine to be included in the text of a resolution of the Soviet Defense Council, which was drawn up in Yalta in 1969.

Nobody tried to figure out how much weaponry and military equipment the army required. Therefore, there was no understanding of what volume of production was necessary or sufficient for the defense industry. The Ministry of Defense always demanded as much weaponry as possible. Gosplan determined plans for arms production based on the economic capability of the country, although it gave first priority to defense orders. Gosplan reached the final figures for weapons and military technology production by arranging a compromise between the defense executives' requests and country's production capacity.

A large number of military design bureaus and factories in the Soviet Union had "doubles". Theoretically, this was to facilitate mobilization of production capacity in the event of war, as well as to ensure healthy competition. But within a command system, competition was virtually nonexistent. The decision to produce a given weapon was made, as a rule, not on the basis of military needs or technical merit (although these were taken into account) but rather on the basis of authority of its sponsors, and the personal relationships between the Chief Designers, the General Secretary of the Central Committee, and the Ministry of Defense.

The MIC industries were obliged to increase their production volume by at least 2-3% every year. Therefore, production of many types of weapons was not stopped even after the army was saturated with them.

The "production-use" chain did not work efficiently for weapons. The Defense Department of the Central Committee exercised strict, exacting control over the production of each and every type of weapon, but after it was produced and delivered to the army, the Central Committee had no more control over it. The slightest attempt by the Defense Department to organize such control of the army was suppressed, and the initiators were considered to be dissidents, which negatively affected their careers. In theory, the army had its own control agency— *Glavnoe Politicheskoe Upravlenie Sovetskoi Armii* (the Main Political Directorate of the Soviet Army), equal to a department of the Central Committee. But that was only theory: weapons were the least important issue for this directorate.

The army did not have a well-developed system of weapons accounting, even for such weapons as intermediate- and short-range missiles. When the Soviet Union counted these missiles in order to declare the number in the text of the Memorandum for the Intermediate Nuclear Forces Treaty, the number was re-declared several times. The military was unable to count these missiles properly the first time, even though a nuclear missile is considerably easier to find than a needle in a haystack.

All decisions about arms production were spontaneous and subjective, but nobody realized it. Even today, such a statement is controversial. However, except for some isolated cases, the fact of the matter is that long-term planning, even within the framework of five-year plans, did not work.

In the mid 1980s, the Soviet Military Doctrine was formulated, and it entered into force in 1987. The foundation of the Doctrine was military sufficiency. This document was the first in the history of the country to attempt to establish the fundamental character of the armed forces and of the production of weapons for them, thus forming a basis for rational planning. This was also an attempt to understand what kind of defense industry potential the government needed under this Doctrine.

The adoption of the Doctrine in the Soviet Union overcame a psychological barrier. The mere accumulation of weapons and the sustaining of continuous production were no longer ends in themselves. MIC factories began to make the transition to the increased production of civilian goods. Civilian goods, which were manufactured in the 1970s as an afterthought, began to be a subject of increasing attention. Defense plants were directed to produce civilian goods in quantities worth as much as or more than the total value of the enterprise's payroll. Seven of the nine industries (the exceptions were the shipbuilding and the atomic industries) reached this level after two to three years. This was an important milestone, since civilian production was previously determined by the resources left over from defense orders.

The first step was to increase the profitability of the factories. Plans for domestic and export deliveries of weapons and military technology were reviewed. The quantity of free exports was sharply reduced.

The military-industrial system was unique in that it was made up only of "pure" defense factories. The MIC did not include the armed forces' production facilities, nor did it include civilian factories, or plants at which part of the capacity was used for the MIC or Ministry of Defense orders.

Approximately 8-9% of the Soviet Union's management, scientific, technical, and industrial potential worked in the MIC. Perhaps this number will disappoint some people, but it is accurate, and naturally, not taken from the newspapers. These numbers were used by the Central Committee, the President of the Soviet Union, and the President of Russia. Today, these data are history.

The following illustrates the state of the MIC in the mid-1980s. The Soviet economy employed 135 million individuals—approximately half of the population. The defense industry was concentrated in 1,770 enterprises, with a total of 10.45 million employees. Within the MIC, the production of military equipment accounted for only 55% of the personnel in the defense industry, with the remaining employees involved in civilian production or work in the social sphere.

The high qualifications of the workers, and the constant strict control produced results: 8.4% of the working population in the MIC produced approximately 20% of the GDP.

Of the total number of defense industry workers, 33.7% worked in the aerospace industry; 20.3% worked in radio technology, electronics, and communications; and 9.1% worked in shipbuilding.

Management accounted for 7.1%, engineering and research workers accounted for 14.1%, the labor force accounted for 77.4%, and service personnel made up 1.4% of MIC employees.

Apart from the MIC, 546,000 workers in the civilian sector of the Soviet economy also produced military equipment (but not weapons). In addition, 388,000 individuals in the Ministry of Defense were involved in the maintenance of military equipment.

The country had a total of 5,100 design bureaus and technical institutes, both civilian and military, and 3,200 scientific institutes, including 32 research complexes of the Soviet Academy of Sciences. Within the MIC, there were 450 scientific research and 250 design organizations. Eighty percent of these were located on Russian territory.

In the other former Soviet republics, the military and research potential of the Soviet Union was manifested in world-famous scientific and R&D institutes and factories. Ukraine had large scientific schools—the Paton Institute of Electrical Welding and the Glushkov Cybernetics Institute—and the largest enterprises within the MIC for missile and rocket, aviation, tank, and radio-electronic technology. Latvia had the Institute for Organic Synthesis (bio-organic chemistry, genetic engineering), and in Belarus, there was the heavy military truck industry.

The largest non-Russian defense enterprises were in Ukraine and Belarus only—the republics that were believed least likely to secede from the union. For example, NPO Yuzhnoe, located in Dnepropetrovsk and Pavlograd (Ukraine), employed over 55,000 individuals. Yuzhnoe provided over 70% of the Soviet Union's ICBMs.

A small part of the defense industry was scattered across the Warsaw Pact countries. Transactions between the USSR and these facilities were generally barter-based.

In the 1970s, the MIC consumed the following share of the materials produced in the USSR for military production purposes: rolled ferrous metals—6%; steel pipes—1.7%; rolled aluminum—25%; and wood—5.5%.

The MIC's assets accounted for 5.9% of the total Soviet economy. In the final years of the Soviet Union, capital investment in the defense industry made up 11-12% of investments in the whole country. This was not enough to support state-of-the-art defense production. Obtaining the necessary funding from the ministries involved in the defense sector was a difficult, sometimes impossible, task for factory directors. Only the Chief Designers of leading design bureaus that were popular with the Central Committee could obtain investments, which they did by bypassing the ministry.

The physical plant and equipment of MIC enterprises was seriously worn out: by the end of the 1980s, 28% of the production equipment had operated for 6–10 years; 21%–for 11-15 years; and 16%–over 15 years. Many unique machines worked only in the hands of certain expert workers. If such a worker quit, nobody could replace him, and the machine would sit idle.

Soviet equipment did not permit high-quality production (that is, production having the necessary cleanliness, precision, reliability, and environmental safety). For this reason, for example, the weight indicators of Soviet aircraft were much worse than their foreign counterparts.

Underdeveloped technology at all stages of production, beginning at ore processing, constantly hampered efforts to create the newest high-quality military equipment that the design bureaus regularly proposed. Therefore, in the blueprints of many projects, markedly inferior specifications, and accordingly, parameters were accepted. This distortion was prevalent throughout the Soviet MIC.

Nor were the high-tech production facilities of the defense complex always used for military purposes. In 1988, MIC enterprises produced 40-50% of the total USSR civilian goods output; in 1990—58%, in 1991—60%, including almost all the advanced, science-based products of Soviet industry:

- Televisions, tape recorders, movie and still cameras, sewing machines—100%
- Refrigerators, freezers—97% (refrigerators from the Krasnoyarsk missile plant were exported to over 30 countries)
- Vacuum cleaners, washing machines—70%
- Motorcycles—50%
- Civilian aircraft, tractors, automobiles, trams, railroad cars, ships, drilling and medical equipment, diesel engines—22%.

To increase the quality of civilian production, the MIC dedicated 25-28% of its work to R&D in 1988. In that same year, the MIC ministries were given control over 240 mechanical engineering enterprises for light industry and food processing. The goal of this action was to improve processing equipment. The country's food processing industry had production losses of 30%. However, MIC enterprises were not ready for this type of reorientation. An enormous amount of effort and money was wasted in an attempt to create machinery for meat-processing production lines at missile plants. Ten years were spent on developing a portable television camera, but a commercial product was never made.

The workers in the main high-tech branches of the MIC received 20-30% increases in wages and benefits in the 1960s, due to the efforts of Brezhnev and Ustinov. MIC enterprises were better than their civilian counterparts at resolving social issues. This was important, considering that there were over 50 "closed cities" in the Soviet Union that were completely dependent on the MIC. The high wages and good benefits at that time were an incentive for high-quality specialists to join the MIC, but they lasted only 10-15 years. In the 1980s, they leveled off, and then MIC wages fell behind those of other industries. At that time, when reduced international tensions caused a drop in defense procurement orders, a deadly stagnation of military technology set in, accompanied by a large outflow of qualified personnel into more stable and higher-paying industries. There was also a psychological factor involved: not all MIC personnel could bear the burden of secrecy or the strict technological discipline, with duplicate (sometimes triplicate) quality control. They were forbidden to go abroad. Cities with extensive MIC infrastructure were closed to foreigners. All these factors led to a noticeable decline in the number of qualified workers.

The first year after the collapse of the Soviet Union, Russian budget allocations for weapons and military equipment purchases were reduced by a factor of 7.5, and R&D was reduced by a factor of 11, which led to irreplaceable losses in the scientific and industrial potential of the MIC, not to mention personnel. In addition, Russia lost the 20% of MIC enterprises that are located in other republics.

A large part of the intellectual potential concentrated in the MIC continued to fall apart even up to the end of the 1990s. This intellectual potential could serve not only Russia, but the whole world. Its loss could be compared to the loss of Russian ballet or Russian sports. For the world community, it would be highly advantageous to offer multifaceted aid for irreversibly converting the Russian MIC in order to retain and use the potential for peaceful purposes, including business.

1.5. THE SOVIET SYSTEM OF MOBILIZATION PREPAREDNESS

Introductory Remarks

Vlad E. Genin

Mobilization preparedness and its spirit accompanied all generations of Soviet people. And it worked. During the very first days of World War II, the country started converting all of its civilian industries to military production. At the same time, the colossal task of transferring all enterprises, primarily defense plants, from the European part of Russia to Ural and Siberia, was performed. No other country in the world had ever recovered so quickly from the stunning impact of an attack by another nation, nor had any performed the nearly impossible task that the USSR undertook: not just to increase arms output, but to create new types of weapons—e.g., rocket artillery (the "Katyusha").

People expended heroic efforts, working 16-20 hours a day in facilities that were still under construction. Some of the new plants in the Urals and Siberia were still under construction and did not yet have roofs or heaters. Twelve-year-old children worked selflessly along with adults. They had to stand on little stools to operate machine tools designed for adult workers.

Probably none of this would have been possible if the country had not lived its life under the terms of the mobilization preparedness system.

Soviet propaganda promoted the idea of a better life for people as being secondary to finishing the process of mobilization preparedness. However, this process was in perpetual motion.

Vitaliy V. Shlykov

Many years ago, I came to the conclusion that it is futile, and a waste of time, to try to find an exact or even relative share of the Soviet defense burden in terms of GNP, national budget, etc. I even attempted to express my views on the subject.

In June 1993, I gave an interview (using the pseudonym Colonel Petrov, a former Russian intelligence officer) to the defense analyst and journalist, Pavel Felgengauer, entitled "Infamous Inventions of the KGB"[42]

Here is an excerpt from that interview, expressing my attitude toward the problem of militarization: "The essence of militarization of the Soviet economy was the result of the economy's structure, which can't be expressed as a percentage of budgetary, or even non-budgetary, expenditures and subsidies to the MIC. Birman and his colleague, William Lee from U.S. military intelligence, intuitively felt the monstrous degree of militarization of the Russian economy. But, in turn, without understanding the core of the problem, they underestimated the degree of militarization of which they accuse others. From my point of view, the Soviet economy was militarized by 100 percent. But it can't be proven by budgetary calculations."

---

42 *Segodnya*, June 18, 1993. The interview dealt with accusations by the U.S. economist and Soviet émigré Igor Birman, that U.S. Sovietologists, and especially the CIA, had grossly underestimated the Soviet Union's defense expenditures.

On another occasion, in October 1993, in hearings before the Senate Intelligence Committee of the U.S. Congress, I stated that "there has been no demilitarization of the Russian economy" and that "this is the historic crime of the democratic leadership of Russia."[43]

Of course, I had in mind the structural militarization of the Soviet economy, rather than the size of the USSR's armed forces or the defense industry's share of the GNP or national budget. To understand how this structural militarization came about, one has to go to the origins of Soviet militarism.

From its very first days, Soviet Russia was a country determined to have military security at all costs. Possessed by a unique sense of its own destiny, and hoping to establish a new world order "free of capitalistic exploitation," the communist leadership of the country saw a military confrontation with the rest of the world as inevitable. To be prepared for that confrontation, the Soviet State had to be turned into a permanent military camp. As with military preparation for war, economic war preparation had to begin, and continue in peacetime.

Mikhail Frunze, the most famous Soviet military theoretician, and the driving force behind Soviet military reform in 1924-1925, which laid the groundwork for transforming the Red Army into a modern well-equipped fighting force, demanded that the country's economy should be prepared for war to the same degree as the armed forces. He wrote: "The work [in the economic sphere – V.S.] should be organized in the same fashion as is being done by the general staffs of the armed forces with respect to the pure military aspects of war. We should have the same operating plan for mobilization of the economy that we developed for the

43 Congressional Record, Vol. 139, No. 140, 18 October 1993, p. S13580.

armed forces. Such a plan should take precise accounting of both our requirements and our resources." [44]

According to Frunze, all State employees at every level of the state hierarchy – economic, financial, cultural or any other – should ask themselves when making any official decision "to what extent does this decision contribute to the defense of the country?"[45]

The III All-Union Congress of Soviets, the highest legislative and executive body at the time, decreed that the government should take all necessary measures to "increase the defense capability of the country through expanding the defense industry and organizing all other state-run industries of the Union in such a way that even in peacetime, all wartime needs are met."[46]

In all major theoretical works by the founders of the Soviet military system, the line dividing the civilian from the military part of the economy seemed to evaporate. Industrial policy was supposed to promote a geographical distribution of industry, which lowered the vulnerability of major industrial centers after outbreak of hostilities. Practically all the leading figures in the Soviet leadership were convinced that victory in a future war between Socialism and Capitalism should go to the side best able to harness the latest technology. The Soviet State, they argued, was in an exceptionally favorable position to use civilian technology for military purposes, because a socialist system was more capable of exploiting the advantages of the emerging new technologies by closely linking the military and civilian economies.

---

44 M.V. Frunze, *Sobraniye Sochinenii* (Moscow-Leningrad: Gosizdat, 1929), vol. 2, p. 102.

45 Ibid, p. 103.

46 *S'ezdy Sovetov Vserossiiskiye i Soyuza SSR v Postanovleniyakh i Rezolyutsiyakh*, (Moscow, 1935), p. 351.

It was decided that the equipment of the Red Army had to be based on dual-use technologies, i.e., those applicable to both military and civilian needs. The civilian aviation and automobile and tractor industries were expected to provide the basis for mass production of military aircraft and tanks, and they were explicitly organized and equipped to do so. For instance, tractor plants had to be able to produce any type of tank equipment, and new types of automobiles were allowed to go into production only if they could meet the standards of tank production. This was supposed to make the mobilization of civilian industry in wartime relatively easy.

The Soviet system of economic planning lends itself perfectly to this integration of civilian and military economies. The experience of managing the economic life of the Soviet Union in peacetime was the best school for the planners of industrial mobilization. To make sure that mobilization would not cause any organizational disruption, all the government's main peacetime economic agencies had special mobilization departments.

Their development over time (1922-1985) is shown in Table 1.5.1.

Branches of this high-level mobilization apparatus, the departments (sectors, sections, etc.) of which were labeled "special," "mobilization" or "first" departments, were established and continued to function over the entire period of the USSR's existence, in each republic and province, in the executive committees of local Soviets, and in practically all factories and plants.

The central feature of this system of mobilization preparedness was the plans drawn up in individual enterprises for the conversion of the economy to wartime needs; e.g., for the manufacture of tanks instead of

TABLE 1.5.1.

Development of the Soviet Industrial Mobilization System

Years	Principal Directorates and Decisions
1922	Establishment of the Committee for Demobilization and Mobilization in the Supreme Council for the People's Economy under the Council of People's Commissars.
1926-27	Council for Labor and Defense Supreme Council for People's Economy Department for Mobilization Planning Mobilization Planning Directorate established with branches at republican, regional (*oblast*) and district (*rayon*) levels. Military production systematized by type (industry). Decision is made to use civilian enterprises for defense production.

1936

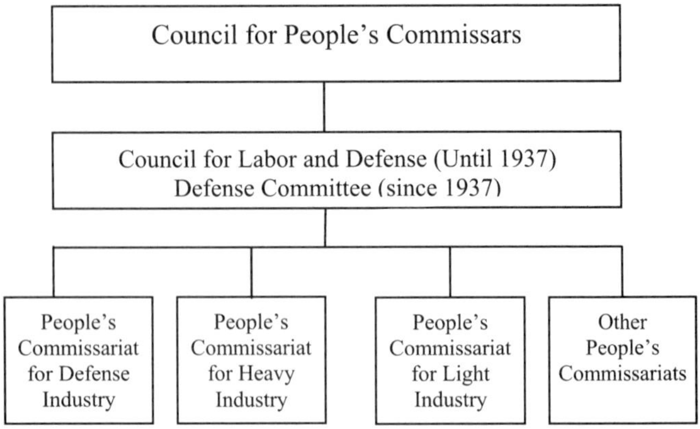

The new People's Commissariat for Defense Industry is charged with mobilization preparedness. (The Council for Labor and Defense functioned from 1920 to 1937, when it was dissolved and its responsibilities for mobilization preparedness were inherited by the Defense Committee).

Continued on the next page

<table>
<tr><td>1938</td><td>The Military-Industrial Commission (VPK) under the Defense Committee is established by decision of the All-Russian Communist Party (January 31,1938).</td></tr>
<tr><td>1939</td><td>
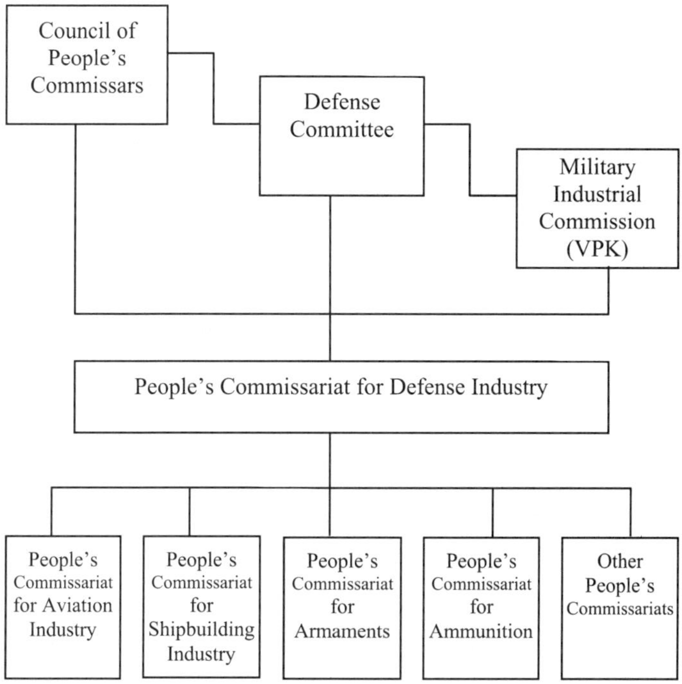

Military mobilization departments established in all defense commissariats.</td></tr>
<tr><td>1941</td><td>All military mobilization departments dissolved on August 14, due to war.</td></tr>
</table>

Continued on the next page

<table>
<tr><td>1946</td><td>

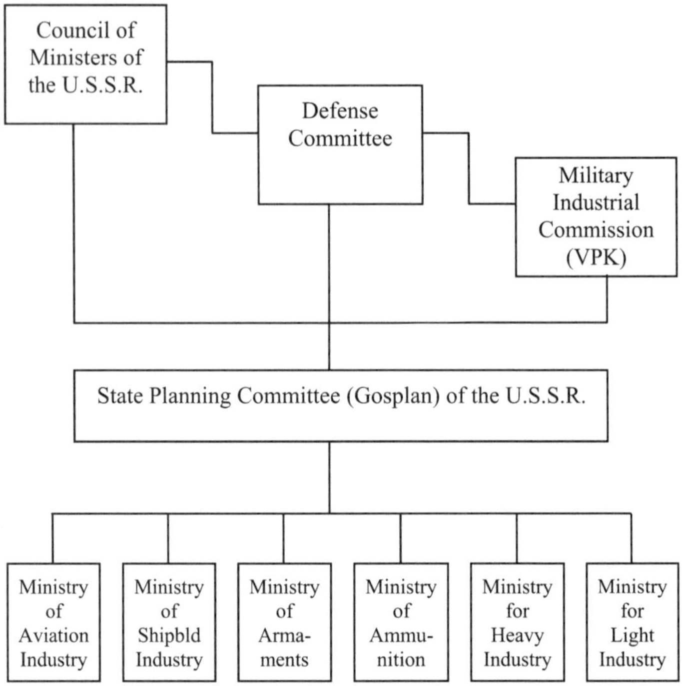

Decree of the Council of Ministers adopts statute on the military mobilization departments in all industrial ministries, determines list of enterprises obligated to possess "special departments" and "special sectors" for mobilization planning.</td></tr>
<tr><td>1954</td><td>A so-called "First" (mobilization) department established in Gosplan.</td></tr>
<tr><td>1958</td><td>Decree of Council of Ministers establishes on January 8, 1958 a Gosplan directorate for defense industries, consisting of industry departments and the "first" (mobilization) department.</td></tr>
<tr><td>1961</td><td>The Central Committee and the Council of Ministers issue a decree on September 11, 1961, which approves The Main Statutes on Mobilization Preparedness of the People's Economy of the U.S.S.R..</td></tr>
</table>

Continued on the next page

1966	By Decree of the Central Committee and the Council of Ministers, mobilization preparedness of the economy is to be concentrated in Gosplan, Councils of Ministers of Union republics, and ministries (executive agencies). Structure of mobilization agencies is confirmed and list of enterprises where mobilization agencies are created is refined.
1968	An overall summary department for the defense industries is established within Gosplan and the tasks of the "first" (mobilization)department are refined.
1969	By decree of the Central Committee and the Council of Ministers a new version of *The Main Statutes on Mobilization Preparedness of the People's Economy of the U.S.S.R.* is issued.
1985	A department of the defense industries and administrative agencies is established in the Council of Ministers, with the responsibility, among other things, for the mobilization preparedness of the country.

tractors or automobiles. Such plans encompassed not only production targets but also technological and educational needs. At the same time, increasing emphasis was put on building up emergency stockpiles of raw materials, energy resources, components, production equipment, clothing, and foodstuffs.

Essentially, everything concerning economic mobilization is still considered taboo even in present-day Russia.[47]

The only time in Soviet history when mobilization issues were discussed in the open was in the 1920s. For instance, in his book *Obshchie osnovy mobilizatsii promyshlennosti dlia nuzhd voiny* (General Principles for Mobilization of Industry for War Needs)[48], Karatygin strongly emphasized the necessity of bringing civilian industry as close as possible to the military production sector, as well as the need to develop those branches of industry which could serve both wartime and peacetime needs. He thought it necessary to introduce a detailed registry of enterprises, materials, production equipment, raw materials, and labor for the entire country, with the purpose of obtaining a continuous, all-encompassing picture of the military value of all economic assets of the country.

The first (and the last) official statement about the establishment and existence of special State structures for economic mobilization took place at the XV Congress of the Communist Party in December 1927, when Defense Minister Voroshilov reported that Mobilization Departments had been established in all people's commissariats and that

---

47 Niels Eric Rosenfeldt, *Stalin's Special Departments* (Copenhagen, 1989). Harriet F. Scott and William F. Scott, *The Armed Forces of the USSR* (Boulder, Colo.: Westview Press. 1979), pp. 229-230.

48 P. Karatygin, *Obshchiye Osnovy Mobilizatsii Promyshlennosti Dlya Nouzhd Voiny*, p. 1925.

the Supreme Council for People's Economy had been provided with a special body, the task of which was centered on the mobilization of industry.

Mobilization preparedness was not confined to industry. In fact, it had an all-embracing character. One of the main purposes of the collectivization of agriculture was to precisely establish and increase mobilization stockpiles of foodstuffs. The activities of a special governmental Committee for Reserves, created in 1932, contributed in no small degree to the horrible famine that affected parts of the USSR in 1932-1933.

The whole structure of the Soviet industry was built in such a way as to give priority to the defense sector. Beginning with the first Five Year Plan in 1928, industries were divided into "A" ("heavy", i.e., defense-oriented) and "B" ("light", or civilian) groups, with the "A" branches having first choice for all resources. Huge investments in science and education were made almost exclusively with an eye to future military needs.

Mikhail Frunze wrote that the "outcome of future wars depends now to a greater degree on the people of pure science than on the military command. Any important invention or discovery applicable to military purposes can immediately give great advantages to military opponents."[49] That is why, he pointed out, there should be established "a most close relationship with the people of science so that this relationship could be a preparatory force in peacetime which could be used in wartime to the fullest possible extent."[50] Such an approach was

---

49 M.V. Frunze. Op. cit. Vol. 1. P. 254.
50 M.V. Frunze, *Izbranniye Proizvedeniya* (Moscow: Voenizdat, 1957), vol. 2, p.50.

the true reason for the huge growth of the Soviet scientific establishment and its achievements.

In 1913, Russia had little more than 10,000 scientists. In 1941, the USSR already had 98,000 scientists. In 1985, their number exceeded 1.5 million, while the scientific sector, as a whole, employed 4,546,000 people.[51] According to Mikhail Maley, four out of five scientists in the country worked for the MIC.[52]

With a view to future war needs, the educational system had to supply as many specialists for the defense industry as possible, far exceeding the current needs of the peacetime economy. For example, in the 1970s-1980s, the USSR was educating three times more engineers each year than the United States. This also explains the heavy emphasis in secondary and high schools on physics, chemistry, mathematics, etc., at the expense of the humanities.

Likewise, strict controls upon the movement of labor and the obligatory registration of all citizens (by means of the *propiska*, or "residence permit," which had to be carried by everyone) [53] were not only the result of a natural desire by the totalitarian state to control its citizenry, but also an effective instrument for the mobilization of labor in case of need.

World War II strengthened the Soviet leadership's conviction that the mobilization preparedness of a country was more important than the overall size of its economy.

---

51 *Narodnoye Khozyaistvo SSSR Za 70 Let* (Moscow: 1987), pp. 62, 412.

52 *Moskovskiye Novosti*, February 21, 1993.

53 Editor's Note: Propiska is roughly analogous to the US Green Card. The difference is that a Green Card gives its holder the right to live and work anywhere in the US, while the "propiska" gives its holder only the right to live and work in a specified city, town or village.

The part of Russian territory that was occupied by the German army by November 1941, had before the war produced 63 percent of Russia's coal, 68 percent of its pig iron, 58 percent of its steel, 60 percent of its aluminum, 38 percent of its grain, 84 percent of its sugar, and 38 percent of its livestock. Three hundred and three ammunition plants on that territory were either completely lost, or had to be evacuated to the Urals or Siberia. From June to December 1941, the production of steel products dropped by 70 %; the production of non-ferrous metals – by more than 98%. In the same period, Russia also lost 41 percent of its railroad lines.[54] In 1943, The Soviet Union produced only 8.5 million tons of steel (compared to 18.3 million in 1940, and 8.1 million in 1942), while German industry (including iron and steel plants captured in Europe) produced 34.6 million tons.

And yet, despite the huge economic losses dealt by Operation Barbarossa, Soviet industry substantially outproduced Germany in all major armaments (tanks, aircraft, artillery, and ammunition). For example, in 1941, the Soviet Union produced 4,000 more aircraft than Germany, and in 1942, 10,000 more. In 1941, it produced 6,590 tanks to Germany's 3,256; and in 1942, 24,688 tanks were produced, versus 4,098 by Germany.[55] This Soviet war-production "miracle" was possible only because the mobilization preparedness of the Soviet economy was much better than Germany's.

The first day after the German invasion, June 23, 1941, the Politburo implemented an already-approved mobilization plan for

---

54 N.Voznesenskii, *Voyennaya Ekonomika SSSR v Velikoi Otechestvennoi Voine* (Moscow, 1948), pp. 2, 43.

55 Paul Kennedy, *The Rise and Fall of the Great Powers* (New York: Random House, 1987), p. 352. Vitaly Shlykov. "Our Tanks are Fast." *International Affairs*, no. 9, 1988.

ammunition production. On June 30, a mobilization plan for the entire Soviet economy, for the third quarter of 1941, replaced the regular peacetime plan for that quarter, which had been approved by the Politburo and Gosplan shortly before the war, on June 14, 1941.[56]

Because the USSR had outproduced Nazi Germany in war materials despite the initial loss of so much of its economic base, Soviet political and military leaders emerged from World War II with a deep conviction that the Soviet planned economy was the most effective system for harnessing a country's resources for war effort.

A textbook for Russian officers, written by the staff of the Lenin Military Political Academy of the Soviet Army, put it this way: "The economic laws of socialism...allow in case of war a most efficient mobilization of all the resources of the people and the socialist republics for the defeat of an enemy. On the contrary, the laws of the capitalist economy with its anarchy seriously hamper the effective mobilization of material resources for war."[57] A special theory was developed, which was designed to prove that the military economic potential of a country could radically differ from the size of its economy. According to the same textbook, "countries with approximately equal economic capabilities can possess different military economic potentials. This difference was determined, first of all, by the economic system, social and political conditions in the country, and level of material and technical development."[58] From this theory came the conclusion that the

---

56 Klaus Segbers, *Die Sowietunion im Zweiten Weltkrieg. Die Mobilizierung von Verwaltung, Wirtschaft und Gesellschaft im "Großen Vaterländischen Krieg."* (R. Oldenburg Verlag, Munchen, 1987), p. 42.

57 *Marksizm-Leninizm o Voine i Armii* (Moscow: Voenizdat, 1968), p. 260.

58 Op. cit., p. 259.

production of armaments in a socialist country is much less expensive than in the West.

"It should be noted that the high cost of modern weapons in the United States, and other capitalist countries, is due not only to the complexity of these weapons but also to the existence of industrial corporations, which use their monopoly position to artificially raise prices for the produced military goods."[59] This point of view was completely taken over by Russian generals, industrialists, and politicians after the collapse of the USSR.

To prove their point, they often quote the difference in the price of armaments for export and internal consumption. According to Mikhail Maley, a Kalashnikov submachine gun cost 6,000 rubles (less than 10 dollars in 1992) for the Russian Army, and 150 dollars for an export customer. A S-300 SAM launch system was being offered for export at 150 million dollars, while at the same time it was being delivered to the Russian armed forces for 1.5 million rubles. A MIG-29 fighter plane in 1992 had a 24 million dollar price tag for export, and a 7 million rubles[60] price tag for the Russian Air Force. Also, a T-72 main battle tank was offered for export for 1 million dollars, and 200,000 rubles for the Russian Army, respectively. Western observers also thought that Soviet weapons were cheaper than those in the United States (about 50 percent less for tanks and more than 61 percent less for jet engines).[61]

---

59 Op. cit., p. 255.

60 Editor's Note: Equivalent to $350,000 in 1992.

61 Arthur J. Alexander, *Decision-Making in Soviet Procurement*, Adelphi Paper No. 147/8 (London: IISS) Winter 1978/79, p. 63.

After World War II, there was a brief period of "re-conversion" to civilian production. But the economy was not demilitarized. Some of the military enterprises indeed returned to the production of civilian goods they had been producing before the war, but kept or even increased their mobilization preparedness, and all that goes with it (stockpiles of production equipment, materials, components, etc.).

The economic resources were simply channeled into broadening the industrial base for future war needs, far in excess of those during the last war, because now the Soviet leadership was getting ready to take on the whole Western world.

In his famous speech on February 9, 1946, Joseph Stalin declared that the USSR should aim to produce yearly 50 million tons of pig iron, 60 million tons of steel, 60 million tons of oil and 500 million tons of coal. In his words, "only in this case would our Motherland be guaranteed against any contingency."[62] This goal, set before the country by Stalin, was clearly based on the experience of the Soviet Union in WWII when steel was practically an equivalent to tanks, artillery, ammunition, etc., and oil was used for one purpose only – to fuel tanks, aircraft, military trucks and ships. Stalin was probably sure that if the USSR could outproduce Germany (with its access to the industrial potential of continental Europe) in armaments production with only 8 million tons of steel a year, then, he could easily repeat this performance, even if confronted by the rest of the world, with 60 million tons of steel.

But these simple calculations were thoroughly undermined by developments in military technology after WWII. It became necessary

---

62 I.V. Stalin, *Rechi na Predvybornykh Sobraniyakh Stalinskogo Izbiratel'nogo Okruga g. Moskvy 11 Dekabrya 1937 g. i 9 Fevralya 1946 g.* (Moscow: Gospolitizdat, 1953), pp. 22, 23.

for the USSR to rapidly develop and produce nuclear weapons, missiles, jet aircraft, radar systems, etc. Unlike the traditional armaments of WWII, these weapon systems demanded for their production a degree of specialization unknown before.

This specialization of arms production took place in all industrialized countries. In the United States, during WWI, 80 percent of war goods came from standard civilian production lines. By 1941 the standard proportion had dropped to 50 percent; by 1963, it was only about 10 percent.[63] But nowhere was the borderline between civilian and defense production so strictly drawn as by the development and production of high-tech weaponry in the USSR.

In the Soviet Union the new trend to compartmentalization of defense production took on often grotesque forms, epitomized by the so-called "closed cities," the number of which grew to more than 80.

This not only meant that more mobilization planning was needed, it also drastically changed its character. The archipelago of closed communities demanded for its mobilization preparedness not just steel or aluminum, but new highly sophisticated materials, instruments, and equipment, but, above all, a reserve of highly competent specialists in often exotic fields of knowledge.

This made mobilization planning much more complicated, and less transparent. The Gosplan used input-output analysis (so-called *balans narodnogo khozyaistva*) for its mobilization planning. Yearly and five-year data were collected and analyzed. But the input-output coefficients were highly inflexible and very slowly took account of technological changes in the economy. Usually the coefficients in use

---

63 "The Economics of Industrial Preparedness and Raw Materials Stockpiling". Doctoral dissertation by William Scott Stambaugh, 1982.

were ten to fifteen years old, which makes calculating mobilization needs extremely difficult for the latest high-tech military equipment.

However, that never bothered the Soviet General Staff, which traditionally was responsible for formulating the mobilization requirements for the economy. The reason for its indifference was that its views on mobilization planning were almost an exact replica of those it held in the 1930s.

The Soviet generals were always prone to exaggerate the mobilization capabilities of their opponents. For instance, several years before WWII, they based their planning for war on the assumption that in case of mobilization, Great Britain and France (considered natural enemies in those days) could produce 30,000 and 18,000 tanks a year, respectively[64]. To see the magnitude of the error committed by the Soviet defense intelligence one has to remember that in 1936 Great Britain produced 42 tanks; in 1937 – 32; in 1938 – 419; in 1939 – 969; in 1940 – 1,399; in 1941 – 4,844; in 1942 – 8,611; in 1943 – 7,476; and in 1944 – 2,476 tanks. In the Cold War years, this propensity of the Soviet General Staff to overestimate the enemy's strength reached new heights, which may look incredible to a Western observer.

In the 1960s-1980s, the Soviet General Staff claimed that the U.S. defense industry could produce 50,000 to 70,000 tanks a year. That meant an overstatement by a dozen times[65]. Even in the early 1990s, at the height of Gorbachev's *glasnost*, the Soviet military command believed that in the span of six months, after the beginning of

---

64 G.K. Zhukov, *Vospominaniya i Razmyshleniya* (Moscow: Izdatelstvo Agentstva Pechati Novosti, 1970), p. 103; *Vooruzhenniye Sily Britanskoi Imperii* (Moscow: Gosvoenizdat, 1938), p. 29.

65 V. Shlykov, "Fatal Mistakes of the U.S. and Soviet Intelligence," *International Affairs*, no. 10, 11-12, 1996.

mobilization, the United States would reach a production rate of 50,000 tanks[66].

The mobilization capability of the West to outproduce the Soviet Union in other types of weapons (aircraft, artillery, ships, armored personnel carriers, ammunition, etc.) was exaggerated in a similar grotesque fashion. According to the Soviet defense planners, the U.S. ammunition industry consisted in 1990 of 98 state-owned ammunition plants (38 of them kept in reserve but ready to resume production at a month's notice), and 540 privately owned ammunition factories.

These ammunition plants, as reported by the same Soviet planners, could, in case of mobilization, out-produce the Soviet ammunition industry in terms of aircraft bombs by 13 times; in unguided missiles by 17 times; and in tank and field artillery rounds by 5.3 times.[67] It must be obvious that the General Staff used these and similar figures to spur the Soviet defense industry to correspondingly increase its own mobilization capabilities.

A bizarre situation developed. The Soviet economy had long over-filled Stalin's dreams of 1946 as to the amounts of steel, coal and oil to be produced to protect the USSR "against any contingencies." And yet it was deficient in all these materials, and tried to produce more and more. At the same time the *kolkhoz*[68] fields all across the country were strewn with many millions of tons of scrap metal from broken-down tractors, while the factories were churning out new ones at an ever-increasing pace. Industrial equipment and machinery grew heavier from

---

66 Statement by Col. Gen. Vyacheslav Gordienko, *Krasnaya Zvezda*, 18 April, 1991.

67 V. Shlykov, "Economic Re-Adjustment Within the Russian Defense Industrial Complex." *Security Dialogue*, vol. 26. no. 1, March 1995, p. 29.

68 Editor's Note: Soviet collective farms.

year to year. Truck drivers were pouring millions of tons of gasoline into the gutters to get rid of it, and thus prove that they had driven enough mileage to earn a couple of extra rubles (their salary depended on the covered mileage and the mileage was measured by the fuel spent). All along the railroads, there were heaps of fertilizers decaying in the rain, while the agricultural output was getting smaller and smaller. The explanation for this paradox was simple: the fertilizer factories were built, and kept up in operation, as reserve facilities for the ammunition industry.

In their desperation, many economists came to the conclusion that this waste was an inherent feature of any centralized economic planning, and the only way to get rid of the waste was to liberalize prices and let market forces put an end to this insanity. They overlooked the fact that in WWII, Soviet industry had functioned quite efficiently, and probably less wastefully, than, say, Germany.

It is much easier to understand what caused the incredible wastefulness of the Soviet economy if one takes into account the mobilization system of the USSR. Though the exact size of the Soviet mobilization effort is still a highly guarded secret, it can be safely assumed that the Soviet mobilization requirements for a future world war were approaching those of the United States, with which the USSR tried to reach parity in every field of military effort. Taking the estimates of U.S. mobilization capabilities as a basis for calculation by the Soviet General Staff, one can easily approximate with the help of input-output tables, the quantities of metals, oil, rubber, and other materials necessary to produce the required amount of armaments in the timeframe envisioned by the General Staff planners.

The figures one gets are staggering. They shed a lot of light on what went on in the Soviet economy.

First, the defense industry had to continue producing a lot of armaments in peacetime just to keep the production base "warm."

Second, this explains the true reason behind the steady growth of civilian production inside the defense industry. The satisfaction of consumer needs was never uppermost in the minds of those who had created, and fostered, the civilian sector of the defense industry. It had to serve two main purposes: on the one hand, to act as an immediately available pool of additional labor, machinery, and floor space to speed up mobilization efforts in case of war; and on the other hand, to subsidize out of its profits weapons production and thus keep the price of produced military equipment artificially low. This was one of the reasons for the ostensible cheapness of Soviet arms.

In the old Soviet economy of deficits, nobody worried much about the low quality and shoddy looks of civilian goods produced by the defense factories. The customer had to take them, because there was nothing else. The MIC jealously kept its monopoly for the production of consumer durables (goods such as TV sets, radios, refrigerators, washing machines, etc.), justifying this monopoly by mobilization needs.

Third, to satisfy mobilization demands many enterprises had to keep uninterrupted production in volumes greatly exceeding the peacetime needs of the economy, for technological reasons (aluminum plants, coke ovens, etc.).

A case in point is aluminum. Recently, Russia produced 3 million tons of aluminum a year, while the internal demand didn't exceed 200,000 to 300,000 tons. The rest went for export. The USSR produced 4 million tons of aluminum, while exports were insignificant. A certain amount of the metal was consumed by the defense industry for arms production, but the greater part of the aluminum output was used for producing low quality goods, or simply turned into scrap. The main reason for this waste was to keep the aluminum industry in a state of permanent readiness to satisfy a huge jump in defense requirements for aluminum in case of mobilization. The same explanation goes for the excessive production in the USSR of steel, titanium, and many other metals, materials, and industrial and transportation equipment.

For many years, the cargo truck was the main mode of transportation on Russian roads, because the army needed big trucks, not cars. But it was too expensive for the army to maintain all of the trucks it needed in case of mobilization on army bases. So, in effect, many trucks produced for the army were sent to different sectors of the economy, though each truck had a special mobilization registration in the local military administration, so as to be available to the military should a war break out. As a result, there are many transportation organizations with surplus military trucks to be mobilized in an emergency. Because of the mobilization requirements, most of these organizations are still state enterprises with large administrative staffs. And now the large, empty trucks one sees in big cities are delivering letters, or doing private errands for these organizations.

The automobile plants, in their turn, had to entertain huge surplus capacities. For example, the ZIL automobile plant in Moscow is saddled with a subsidiary foundry in Yartsevo (Smolensk Oblast), with a production capacity of half a million tons of cast metal which is currently being used at one percent of that capacity.

It is doubtful that in the last decades, the Soviet leadership was aware of what was going on in the economy, and of the real cost of maintaining the high level of mobilization preparedness. It was obvious that the lack of a developed consumer sector, due to chronic shortages of resources for civilian needs, had undesirable consequences for the population, and retarded the development of the economy. So from time to time, ambitious projects for satisfying civilian needs were developed (in agriculture, housing, consumer goods production, etc.) for which huge financial expenditures were allocated (in 1989, agricultural subsidies amounted to 90 billion rubles, far in excess of the official defense budget).

Actually, the proclaimed changes of key development targets from "group A"[69] to "group B"[70] (in Gosplan parlance) to ensure expanded production of consumer goods and services boiled down to a redistribution of inflated investment rubles, and not of material and manpower resources. Or, to put it in other words, these seemingly large financial resources were backed by relatively low quality material resources.

These new goals were set in addition to the earlier goals (maintaining mobilization capacities; development of new high-tech weaponry; and mass production of new, ever more sophisticated armaments); they did not abolish the accepted practices in the distribution of resources, or destroy the existing system of priorities. As a result, the entire system of economic management was oriented, as before, to those priorities.

In fact, these inept attempts to improve the living standards of the population contributed to the worsening of the general situation in the

---

69 Editor's Note: Group "A" was considered to be the main industrial sector, which included defense industries, metallurgy, machine building industries, etc.

70 Editor's Note: Group "B" included light industries (textile, shoes, sewing, etc) and food processing industries.

country, because they meant additional expenditures of materials and labor. They also led to a huge increase in the number of uncompleted construction projects, numbering in the several hundred thousands during the last years of the USSR's existence. So from year to year, deficits, and with them hidden inflation, increased. Such a structurally distorted economy could not last forever.

There were economists in Gosplan and the Academy of Sciences, especially those dealing with input-output tables, who felt the approaching catastrophe. According to Ivan Materov, who worked in 1981-1991 in Gosplan, input-output calculations already showed in 1982 that if the existing structure of the Soviet economy was kept intact, the economy would ultimately collapse by 1997.[71]

To prevent the impending collapse, a simple redirection of the defense industry to civilian production was not sufficient. What was needed was a conversion in a broader sense, meaning a complete restructuring of the economy. In this, both the Gorbachev and Yeltsin governments failed miserably.

---

71 The Weekly Konversiya, Information Agency RICA, January 27, 1992, p. 3.

1.6. THE STRUCTURAL MILITARIZATION OF THE SOVIET ECONOMY: THE UNKNOWN PHENOMENON

Introductory Remarks

Vlad E. Genin

It is common knowledge that Russia inherited a militarized economy from the USSR. The industry of any country consists of civilian and defense sectors. At first glance, the more military enterprises a country has, the higher the degree of militarization. And conversely, a predominance of civilian industry enterprises over military ones seems to indicate the opposite— the peaceful nature of the economy.

The controversy over the degree of militarization of the Russian economy has been going on for more than ten years. For many reasons, the positions of the two sides, within both Russia and the Western countries, remain diametrically opposed. It does not appear that these opinions will converge any time soon. Even the militarization of the economy itself is being considered from different points of view: one side studies its scale and scope, i.e., quantitative characteristics of this phenomenon; the other – the depth of its penetration into the Russian economy, and the degree of its organic effect— i.e., the "system" approach.

There were clear signs of structural militarization of the national economy. Labor was always paid unbelievably badly in all industries of the Soviet militarized economy, in particular in civilian industries. Designers, metallurgists, tool developers, and industry workers received extremely low wages, though they all contributed considerably to the wealth of the country with their work. Under the terms of the State controlled economy, the defense industry was buying all of its supplies at a very low price, sometimes lower then the actual production cost.

This practice very painfully impacted all the other non-defense enterprises. Many of them became unprofitable. However, the worst effect it had was on people who received scanty salaries, but who had to pay for every day consumer goods at very high prices. An average employee paid the same amount of money for several pounds of sausage as the military paid for one AK-47 assault rifle. The army still buys the latest models of this gun for $10 - $15 apiece. It is hard to believe that such an unprecedented low price actually covers the production cost, especially the labor cost.

Many Russians remember very well that each factory, even those that had nothing to do with the defense industry, had a notorious "First Department" overseen by KGB. "Special orders" of the defense ministry were run through these departments.

They also remember *"assimiliatsia"* (assimilation): in case of war a civilian enterprise – for instance a cotton textile factory – must be converted to gunpowder manufacturing in seventy-two hours. Almost no one, sometimes not even the management of these plants, knew for sure what was happening there, who the customers were, and what the specific purpose of "special orders" or "assimilation", was. Nobody at that time could see the whole picture of the militarization of the economy. The people were just cogs in the gigantic military machine created when Stalin was in power. Neither did anyone at that time realize the size and scale of this secret militarized web, which entangled the whole country with its invisible threads.

Vitaliy V. Shlykov

In the early 1990s, many politicians, economists, and the mass media of Russia were blaming all the economic problems of the country on the inordinate burden of a militarized economy. Many reformers believed that if we could get rid of this burden, we could build a new and healthy economy. Thus, the concept of conversion was born. According to the opinion of the former acting Prime Minister Egor Gaidar, "If the heavy load of the defense industry on the economy, expressed as a portion of combined military expenses in gross national product, is much higher than the corresponding indicator in Japan, it is senseless to include in their plans the repetition of the Japanese miracle." He believed that if conversion succeeded, the State could reduce its expenses and increase its income, and the market would be flooded with a new generation of consumer goods. Defense conversion was called "the catalyst of the structural reconstruction of the economy". This idea was not simply to reduce the rate of growth of military expenses, but to greatly reduce their absolute magnitude.

And, actually, when Gaidar came to power, the first thing he did was to drastically lower military expenditures. In 1992, the volume of arms purchases had already been reduced by 67 percent. In the following years, the reduction in military purchases continued. According to former Russian Minister of Defense Igor Rodionov, between 1991 and 1996, allocations for outfitting Russia's armed forces were reduced by a factor of fifteen. Rodionov stated that soon after accepting his office, the serial production of complex weapons systems was practically nonexistent.

So, on the surface, Russia had, for the most part, demilitarized its economy according to widely accepted criteria (absolute volume of defense spending and procurement, its share of GNP, etc.). But there was no improvement in the standard of living for the major portion of the population, as openly acknowledged by independent experts and the Russian government itself. Moreover, the so-called civilian sector, especially in industry and agriculture, fell into an extremely steep decline.

It is considered nearly axiomatic that lower military expenditures have a beneficial effect on the economy. Most economists concur that the economic success of Japan or Germany is explained first and foremost by low levels of military expenditures. In Russia's case, the military budget's share of the GNP fell to the level of Germany's (less than 3.5 percent in 1997), but the "Russian economic miracle" is still not evident.

So, what are the reasons for this anomalous reaction by the Russian economy to the reduction of military expenditures? There are two diametrically opposed explanations for this phenomenon, which have been expressed by politicians and economists for almost ten years, without any compromise between their points of view.

One group of observers is convinced that the immense size and complexity of the defense establishment inherited by Russia from the USSR makes impossible any improvement in the Russian economy without huge new investments for defense conversion.

Lev Makarevich, a prominent expert from the Association of Russian Banks, wrote the following: "For seven decades, trillions of dollars were spent on the military industrial complex. It accounted for 25-30 percent of the GNP (compared to 5-6 percent in the United States). Only the military ruble was fully supported 100 percent by material resources. The support of the civilian ruble was less than a kopeck.[72] If the best, most productive, and most effective was always given to the defense sector, then the civilian sector, from agriculture to food and light industry, was only given crumbs. As a result, the country received an unprofitable, environmentally dangerous, non-marketable production sector, which wouldn't be able to exist without multiple billions in subsidies.[73]

In 1992, Mikhail Maley, at the time President Yeltsin's counselor on Defense Conversion, stated that defense conversion in Russia would take fifteen years, and cost 150 billion dollars. Since then, these figures have been quoted in almost every discussion concerning the problems of Russian defense conversion, requiring no proof or justification. The opponents of this point of view are convinced that the scale of militarization of the Soviet economy and the influence of the military industrial complex on the civilian economy are grossly overestimated.

The former Chairman of the Military Industrial Commission (*Voenno-Promyshlennaia Kommissia* – VPK) and of the State Planning Committee (Gosplan), Yuri Masliukov, asserted in August 1996, in an interview with the newspaper *Zavtra*, that "The MIC, contrary to accepted opinion, did not consume 70 percent of the country's resources.

---

72 Editor's Note: There are 100 kopecks per ruble.

73 *Finansoviye Izvestia*, June 25, 1996.

I tell you, it consumed exactly 7 percent, while producing in the machine building sector alone approximately 55 percent of all consumer goods for the internal market."[74] In Masliukov's opinion, all of Russia's national economic problems arose from the fact that the military industrial complex was destroyed. "The military industrial complex," Masliukov states, "is first and foremost the realization of the dream of having a comprehensive defense of the homeland from outside encroachments. If the government had not used all of its might to smother the military industrial complex instead of gradually turning this powerful intellectual potential into a guiding force for civilian development, then there would be no problem now in existence which the military industrial complex could not solve."

So, who is right in this protracted argument? Was the USSR on the eve of a breakthrough into the economic leadership of the 21st century, due to the accomplishments of the military industrial complex in the field of advanced technologies, as Masliukov believes, or was its economy crushed under the burden of excessive military expenditures?

Precise determination of the level of the USSR's militarization is an essential prerequisite to answering these questions. A critical examination of the evidence presented by both sides of the controversy is necessary.

The largest estimate for the absolute size of the defense burden on the Soviet economy is given by Lev Makarevich. "For well-known historical reasons," he writes, "the Soviet economy was created, and functioned, as an exclusively military economy. It was served by four-fifths of the industrial capacity, which was mostly located in Russia; three-fourths of the country's labor and scientific resources; and nine-

74 *Zavtra*, no. 31, August 1996.

tenths of the country's research and development sector. More than half of all raw materials, materials in general, and energy were spent on it. They were simply mobilized for the needs of the military industrial complex, bypassing the market, i.e., buying and selling, and equivalent exchange."[75] Unfortunately, Makarevich did not bother to produce any evidence to support his allegations.

An attempt to quantify the defense burden of the Russian economy was made by Professor Viktor Belkin in his article entitled "53 Years After the Outburst of War, Our Economy Still Suffers From the Defense Burden"[76]. According to Belkin, in 1994, Russia was spending from 20 to 25 percent of its GNP on defense. This figure sharply contradicted the official defense budget, which comprised about 6 percent of the GNP in 1994. Belkin justified his estimates in the following way.

The number of military personnel in Russia, including the Ministry of Defense, border guard troops, interior troops, various security forces, railroad troops, etc., according to Belkin, was approximately 3.5 million in 1994 [In 1997 the figure, according to official sources, is closer to 4 million. – V.S.]. Another 3 million people were occupied in the defense industry. Basing his estimates on U.S. experience, Belkin concludes that in the United States, for every employee in the defense industry, there are 2.5 employees in other industrial branches, supplying weapons producers with electricity, metals, components, etc. Belkin asserted that the aggregate number of people employed in Russia in the production of arms was 10.5 million. To this figure he added another 3.5 million people, who supplied the

---

75 *Finansoviye Izvestia*, June 25, 1996.
76 Izvestia, June 22, 1994.

personnel in the armed forces and the defense industry with food, clothing, housing, medical and educational services, etc. As a result, Belkin calculated that a total of 14 million people were employed in sustaining the armed forces, a fifth of Russia's labor force. He equated one-fifth of the Russian working population, which were employed directly, or indirectly, in the defense sector with 20 percent of the country's GNP.

Belkin deduced that an extra five percent of the GNP was a defense burden, reflecting the fact that 3.5 million healthy young people in the military were withdrawn from the production of civilian goods and services. According to Belkin, spending from one-fifth to one-fourth of a country's GNP on defense in peacetime is absolutely unacceptable, because after 10 percent of the GNP is spent on defense, normal economic development becomes impossible. This, writes Belkin, is what has been happening to the Russian economy since the early 1970s until now. His conclusion is that without drastically reducing this excessive defense burden, Russia's economic crisis cannot be overcome.

The main argument of the opponents of this point of view is that the Soviet defense sector consumed a comparatively modest share of the country's economic resources. According to official data, at the peak of its output in the late 1980s, the Soviet defense industry employed only 9.5 million people out of the USSR's total labor force of 130 million. It consumed 20 percent of steel plate, 9.3 percent of rolled steel, 23.6 percent of aluminum, and less than 3 percent of all timber utilized by Soviet industry. All capital investments in the defense industry in 1990 were valued at 111 billion rubles, or 12.6 percent of all capital investments in Soviet industry. These are impressive figures to be sure, but scarcely sufficient to warrant the talk of a total militarization of the economy.

Even smaller was the defense industry's share of the Soviet economy as a whole – 6.4 percent of capital stock and 5.6 percent of steel plate. The portion of imported, that is the most modern, industrial equipment in the defense industry, was 17.9 percent as compared to 22.2 percent in the civilian industrial sector.

All of the above figures were produced by Igor Belousov, Deputy Prime Minister of the USSR and Chairman of the VPK, at a session of the Presidential Council on September 27, 1990, at which I was present. On that day, the Presidential Council, under the chairmanship of President Mikhail Gorbachev, discussed all day long the draft program for converting the Soviet defense industry.

According to another speaker at that session, Oleg Baklanov, who was at that time the Secretary of the Central Committee of the CPSU responsible for the defense industry, the value of all military goods produced in the Soviet Union in 1990 was equal to 30 billion rubles. In 1991, according to Baklanov, the value of military goods was planned to be reduced to 26 billion. The next speaker, Yuri Semionov, Director of the Koroliov Missile and Space Enterprise, supported Baklanov's statement, and said that while everybody was going around shouting that the Soviet Union had been pouring trillions of rubles into the space exploration, the entire Soviet space program, from the day of its inception, cost no more than 80 billion rubles. According to Semionov, the Soviet space achievements were mainly the result of "dedication and enthusiasm" of the people involved in the program.

The United States also spent a lot of resources during the years of the Cold War to determine the scale of Soviet militarization, without coming to any statistically conclusive results[77]. U.S. experts seem to be almost as divided in their estimates as their Soviet counterparts.

As for Russia, the dispute goes on with unabated heat. There are many people who still see the Soviet defense industry as a sort of militaristic leviathan, unaccountable to anyone, and a voracious devourer of the country's resources, absolutely incompatible with the market and democracy.

Most of the data, for example, in the claim by Lev Makarevich mentioned above (four-fifths of the industrial strength, three-quarters of the country's labor, etc., used for defense purposes), don't stand up to even perfunctory examination. Already known figures of Soviet defense production, from the Cold War years, allow one to conclude that the defense industry couldn't possibly have been consuming half of the 120 million tons of steel, 3 million tons of aluminum, 500 million tons of oil, 600 million tons of coal or 600 cubic meters of natural gas annually produced in the USSR.

Professor Belkin's estimates are also highly questionable. Referring to the experience of the U.S. defense industry, and multiplying the number of the employees in the Russian MIC by 2.5 times, is a highly questionable procedure. A typical Soviet defense plant undertakes most of its activities in-house, while in the United States, a much larger part of the workload is delegated by the main weapons producers to external, specialized subcontractors.

Belkin's estimate of 3 million people employed by the Russian defense industry also needs qualification. Even at the peak of the arms race in the 1980s, from 40 to 50 percent of defense industrial output

77 V. Shlykov, "Fatal Mistakes of the U.S. and Soviet Intelligence," *International Affairs*, no. 9, 10, 11-12, 1996, and no. 4, 1997.

consisted of civilian goods. Enterprises of the MIC produced a wide range of industrial and transport equipment, tractors and agricultural machinery, 100 percent of the TV sets produced in the USSR, 70 to 80 percent of all refrigerators, washing machines, and most household appliances.

Unfortunately, exaggerated claims about the size of the Soviet defense sector were made not only by experts without any access to reliable information about the defense industry, but also by high-ranking politicians and officials. So, in April 1990, Mikhail Gorbachev announced that Soviet defense expenditures amounted to 20 percent of the national income. Then, at the end of 1991, the Chief of the General Staff of the Soviet Armed Forces, General of the Army Vladimir Lobov, declared that the military expenditures of the USSR made up one-third or even more of the GNP.[78]

These crudest estimates quickly became common currency the both inside and outside of the Soviet Union. Not only did they cause wide antagonism toward the military industrial complex, but also they prevented any sensible discussion in a society permeated by secrecy about anything connected with defense. Needless to say, neither Gorbachev nor Lobov ever produced any kind of evidence in support of their claims.

When questioned by Oleg Baklanov at the Presidential Council on September 27, 1990, as to where he got his "favorite estimate" of 20 percent of GNP spent on defense, whereas Baklanov could come up with only 3 percent, Gorbachev fidgeted a bit, and said that he got his figure "from scientists." In Gorbachev's words: if Baklanov wanted a more

---

78 *Voenno-Istoricheskii Zhurnal*, no. 11, 1991, p. 3.

precise estimate, he should give more classified information to the scientists to help them prove their point.

Those who claimed that the extremely high efficiency of the Soviet defense industry allowed it to keep quantitative and qualitative military parity with the United States at a fraction of the latter's expenses, sounded less convincing. Nobody in the world, and especially inside the USSR, believed that the Soviet Union was spending about 2 percent of its GNP (20 billion rubles a year), as official figures indicated, on its defense in 1968 to 1988. Everybody knew that under the Soviet non-market economic system, the defense sector enjoyed priority access to all kinds of resources: skilled labor, the best scientists, the newest technology, and guaranteed supplies of other inputs at subsidized prices.

Research conducted at the end of the 1980s by the Institute for Economic Forecasting of the Soviet Academy of Sciences, showed that if the output of the USSR machine-building industry were to be rated at world market prices, the share of military equipment would account for more than 60 percent of the output, and consumer goods not more than 5 percent[79]. These figures indicate that the degree of militarization of the Soviet machine-building industry was phenomenal.

Sad to say, these conclusions of the Institute for Economic Forecasting were either ignored by most officials and economists, or used uncritically as proof that the machine-building industry was using 60 percent of physical resources (that is metals, energy, labor, machinery, etc.) for defense production. Nobody seems to have noticed that the results of the research of the Institute could be used to put an end

79 *Studies on Soviet Economic Development*, Pleiades Publishing, vol. 2, no. 1. January-February 1991, p. 48.

to the unproductive polarization of positions about the scope of the USSR's militarization, if properly developed.

It was obvious that the high degree of militarization of the machine-building industry was due to extremely low productivity in the civilian sector of industry. The reason for this was that for more than half a century, all of the best technologies, material, and human resources of the country, had been channeled into defense and related industries, while civilian industry and infrastructure were doomed to partial or complete inefficiency. The backwardness of the civilian sector was proportional to the funds diverted from it into military production. This kind of economy can exchange its products only on a compulsory or non-commercial basis, through direct distribution of resources at artificially fixed prices. In other words, an economy like this can function only if it defies the laws governing market systems. If such an economy were to switch abruptly to prices corresponding to world prices, the system of ties between them would eventually and inevitably collapse. And this is exactly what has been happening in Russia over the last five years.

An economy that does not respond to such measures as cutting defense purchases, and does not allow the transfer of financial resources from the defense sector into the civilian economy, is one that is structurally militarized, as opposed to the familiar temporary militarization, which can be measured by the share of defense spending and defense production in national budgets, GNP, etc. In a structurally militarized economy, all defense procurement can be stopped, but this drastic measure will not automatically, or by the "invisible hand of the market," result in a corresponding increase in efficiency in the civilian sector, or produce other noticeable changes for the better in the economy.

In fact, these measures can cause the economic situation in the country to deteriorate further.

The explanation for this paradox lies in the fact that in a structurally militarized economy, the major waste of resources goes on not in the defense sector (Igor Belousov probably was correct in his estimates of the quantity of material resources that are consumed by the defense sector), but in the civilian economy. Due to its extreme backwardness, the simple maintenance—not renewal—of the civilian sector calls for masses of primary resources: raw materials, energy, and construction facilities. To maintain its pitiful agriculture, the Soviet Union had to produce six to seven times more tractors, and several times the quantity of fertilizers, than the United States. According to Mikhail Maley, the metallurgical complex alone consumes more resources than the defense ministry with its six million employees.[80] First Deputy Prime Minister Boris Nemtsov insisted in 1997 that the productivity of Russia's housing and utility sector was only one tenth or one fifteenth of Sweden's, a country with similar climatic conditions.[81]

A large part of the equipment for the civilian sector had been supplied by the defense industry. In Russia's particular situation, production of this equipment fell over the last few years at an even greater rate than arms production. Thus, the civilian sector (except, perhaps, for the oil and gas industry), deprived of needed modernization, became even more wasteful than before.

Such an economy is completely unknown in the West, where defense cuts sooner or later lead to a flow of resources from the defense to the civilian sector. There, countries undergoing defense conversion

---

80 *Komsomolskaya Pravda*, September 17, 1993.

81 *Moskovskiy Komsomolets*, June 19, 1997.

are at an advantage, because they can rely upon functioning capital markets, and on an existing system of prices, which are cleared by the market. They also have numerous specialists, people able to provide various intermediary services, etc. People move to new jobs, new specialties, or new locations. Factory buildings are sold, machinery is auctioned in a very active market, and land is sold to new owners. Defense conversion in the West is thus a vague activity. Demand falls in one sector, and rises somewhere else.

Very little of this has happened in Russia so far, despite huge cuts in defense purchases, nor is it likely to happen in the foreseeable future, even if defense cuts continue. The failure to comprehend these fundamental differences between the economic systems of Russia and the rest of the industrial world explains the excessive optimism of the Western public and politicians about the prospects of market reform and defense conversion in Russia. Unfortunately, the difficulties of dismantling a structurally militarized economy have been ignored by Russian reformers themselves.

Their most obvious mistake was a firm belief that money can play a decisive role in changing the ways of the Russian economy, and that it can be managed with the help of a budgetary and credit policy. It is certainly tempting to use financial indicators in summing up the results of economic development and formulating its goals, instead of getting bogged down in the intricacies and problems of technological and structural imbalances between the civilian and military sectors of the economy. Moreover, this practice of using financial indicators as a guide in economic policy is accepted all over the world, and is intellectually and administratively not very demanding, having ready-made, previously-tested recipes galore.

But the biggest mistake of the reformers was the failure to understand and remove the main stumbling block on the way to eliminating structural imbalances in the Russian economy – the Soviet system of mobilization preparedness, which the new Russia inherited from the USSR.

1.7. THE SPECIFICS OF SOVIET DEFENSE ENTERPRISES

Introductory Remarks

Vlad E. Genin

It is generally understood that Soviet defense enterprises were different from Western defense and civilian commercial enterprises. Their structure, their subordination to strategic and political imperatives, and their functioning under the planning system are the elements that are generally quoted to explain these differences. Some analysts also consider that Soviet enterprises should not be called 'enterprises,' as this implies a specific mode of operation and a culture that Soviet enterprises obviously lacked. Indeed, profit-seeking, economic efficiency, quality production, flexibility, and innovation are some of the characteristics that Soviet enterprises did not share with their counterparts in market economies. In fact, they presented the opposite characteristics: waste of resources, little attention paid to quality, no profit drive, rigidity, etc.

Both arguments seem to lead to the same questions. Was the framework in which Soviet enterprises evolved the source of their culture and mode of operation? And is it possible to reform these modes of operation and culture by reforming the framework, i.e., by destroying the Soviet system and creating a market economy instead?

Sonia Ben Ouagrham

Soviet defense enterprises evolved in a world where all enterprises – civilian and military – were both production units and political entities. They operated in the same economic framework – the command economy – and mainly served the objectives of the State. The incentives and constraints created by such an environment generated specific types of flexibility, innovation, and profit, which were very different from those prevailing in the market, but very well adapted to the Soviet environment. In addition to being production units and political entities, Soviet defense enterprises also were political actors. Their representation in the highest bodies of the State and of the Party allowed them to exert a direct political influence, and to a certain extent to control their economic environment. Thus, the Soviet system created a world deprived of commercial links, and with no clear border between economic and political actors. In such conditions a change in the enterprises' culture and mode of operation cannot happen unless the economy is re-commercialized, and economic agents are separated from political actors.

1. Mode of Operation of Soviet Enterprises

1.1. Soviet Enterprises as Production Units

Defense enterprises, like all other Soviet enterprises, were economic actors, with a specific mode of operation. All of them were State enterprises, subordinate to the central plan. They enjoyed a soft budget constraint. Their production had guaranteed outlets; they did not directly interact with their foreign and domestic partners and clients. Prices were centrally fixed; the monetary and distribution circuits were segmented, which reinforced the automatic validation of their production; and production was resource-constrained.[82]

These characteristics translated into a specific mode of operation. As production was defined by the central authorities (or central plan), and as its distribution and financing were guaranteed, enterprises did not have to organize distribution networks. They also did not have to improve the quality of their production to meet their clients' needs or to face competition.

Although competition existed in the Soviet system, it did not take place at the end of the production cycle – when production was distributed – but at the beginning of the production cycle, where the allocation of resources was concerned.

The system of price setting and the malfunctioning of the central planning system did not encourage enterprises to control their costs. The main requirement imposed on industry was to produce, and therefore to obtain the means required for production.

As demand was always higher than supply, Soviet enterprises had to substitute some goods for others in order to use those that were less affected by shortages. This could lead to a decrease in the quality of products, but it also generated a specific kind of innovation, which did not consist in new production processes, but in using existing goods in a different way. For instance, it could translate into new construction methods allowing the use of inputs of various quality levels. Or it could

---

82 For a complete description of the Socialist systems, see Janos Kornai, *The Socialist System. The Political Economy of Communism* (Princeton University Press, 1992).

take the form of new ways to assemble old components in order to obtain higher performance, without changing the production process.[83]

The irregular production cycle did not allow enterprises to modernize their equipment. Indeed, the use of modern production technologies implies a continuous flow in the supply system. As this was not guaranteed in the Soviet system, enterprises preferred using manual labor. Therefore, the creation of "labor stocks" allowed enterprises to adapt to the irregular flow of the supply system. And even though this did not allow them to make productivity gains, it allowed them to develop a certain flexibility that was adapted to their environment. Similarly, Soviet enterprises hoarded resources and tried to achieve self-sufficiency, in order to adapt to the irregular supply system and to unexpected changes in their production plans. These practices lead to the waste of resources, but they were also elements of flexibility and efficiency in the Soviet environment.

The specific flexibility, efficiency, and innovation developed by enterprises in the Soviet system lead to high production costs and a low-quality production. Their specific mode of operation also implied a short temporal horizon. Finally, all this leads to a definition of profit which is very different from that prevailing in a market environment: profit is not defined as an accumulation of money, but it is defined in terms of power. And this is closely related to the fact that Soviet enterprises were also political actors.

---

83 Sonia Ben Ouagrham, "La Convesrion des Enterprises de Defense en Russie: Une Analyse Regionale," Doctoral Dissertation, Highest School of Social Sciences, Paris (France), January 1999.

1.2. Soviet Enterprises as Political Entities

Indeed, like any other enterprises, defense enterprises were also political entities, in which directors, trade unions, and Party delegates were representatives of the State. Directors were nominated by central authorities on the basis of their technical competence (big research institutes were named after their directors, who were famous scientists or researchers) or according to their loyalty vis-à-vis the Party. Therefore, directors were neither entrepreneurs nor managers (this is not to say that none of them had these qualities). They had to execute the plan, but they were accountable for their actions only before higher authorities. They also belonged to a dominant group of the Soviet bureaucracy.

Trade unions also depended on political authorities. Their mission was to promote productivity and competition and to ensure discipline. Trade unions were not supposed to protect workers' rights against abusive rules, or to help them obtain better work conditions; rather, they were supposed to serve as "drive-belts" between the management and the employees, reinforcing the execution of orders received from above.

Another feature of the Soviet system lies in the pervasiveness of the Party. All organizations and administrations had a dual management: their own and that of the Party. Decisions by the Party were supreme; political and ideological imperatives were superior to economic issues. And membership in the Party was an essential element of social promotion.

As a result, the Soviet system mixed political and economic actors, and the decisions of the Party defined the political and economic orientations of the Soviet Union. Through their horizontal and vertical organization, both the Party and the trade Unions[84] formed a system that shaped economic, political and social relationships.

1.3. The Place of Defense Enterprises in This System

In this system, defense enterprises were dominant actors. They received priority in the supply system and their representation in the Party allowed them to influence central decisions, and consequently to soften the constraints of the Plan.

Defense enterprises were represented at the highest level of the Party hierarchy. One of the secretaries of the Party Central Committee was in charge of supervising the military complex. Defense departments also existed within the Republics' Central Committees, as well as in the regions and cities where defense enterprises were concentrated. At each level, these departments were in connection with Party cells in ministries, enterprises, and research institutes.

Such a high degree of representation of defense enterprises in the Party, and more particularly in the higher bodies of the Party, was very beneficial to them. They could, for instance, negotiate less constraining plans, and they could also determine their production and prices. And they had more influence to obtain the means to achieve self-sufficiency, and to avoid big fluctuations in the orders of Central authorities. In a nutshell, defense enterprises exerted a certain control over the rules that presided in their environment, and they had the ability to soften their constraints.

It appears that Soviet enterprises differed from Western enterprises not because they had no flexibility, were inefficient, or were

---

84 Trade Unions were organized by branch (vertical) and by region (horizontal), and the Party had a pyramid structure, with offices in all regions, and cities.

unable to innovate. They did in fact possess all these qualities, but in a form adapted to the environment. Soviet enterprises' legitimacy was political: their existence depended on bureaucratic decisions. Their development as well as their survival depended on their negotiating power. The plan was not a means of economic management, but an instrument of power[85], both used by central authorities to impose their will on lower bureaucratic levels, and by the lower levels in order to increase their negotiating power. Enterprises had quantity objectives, and they were only marginally interested in costs and quality of production. In this system they were dominant economic and political actors.

In a market economy, economic and political actors are largely separated, even though enterprises' decisions can have a political impact and vice-versa. Enterprises are mainly motivated by profit. They must respect a certain financial discipline (reducing costs, saving resources, credits and investments justified by the expected sales), increase their market share, and pay attention to the quality of their production. Enterprises have an economic legitimacy: their existence, development, and survival depend on the existence of true economic demand, and their ability to meet that demand. Directors are accountable for their actions before their employees and the sanctions for bad management come from the market.

2. Conditions for Successfully Changing the System

In the light of the discussion above, a reform of the system should have two objectives. The first requires that economic actors and

---

85 For a discussion of this concept see Eugene Zaleski, "La planification stalinienne, croissance et fluctuation economiques," Arie Zacks, "Diversification et reconversion de l'Industrie de D'armamement," *Les Dossiers du GRIP*, n165, January 1992, p.212.

political actors be separated. The second entails the creation of an environment allowing enterprises to operate according to market rules.

The first objective requires the abolition of the Party's domination over economic decisions, and the restriction of enterprises' activities to the economic sphere. The second objective requires the abolition of the planning system, and the creation of a market, with all of its attendant institutions.

However, these objectives generate two difficulties. The first lies in the definition of the market. If the aim is to switch from a planning system to a market economy, it is extremely important to determine the type of market that is aimed at. Although they have common features, Western market economies stem from very different cultures and histories, which generated various societies. They were also formed over a long period of time, and all the elements composing them generated specific behaviors, which provide them with their own coherence. Therefore, the idea of transforming the Soviet system instantly is impracticable, as is that of trying to recreate in Russia the replica of an existing Western market economy. However, all market economies have common features, and the transformation in Russia could be based on these features.

The second difficulty lies in the fact that the destruction of the Party and of the planning system deprives the State of its control over economic agents. Without such instruments no economic policy can be applied. Therefore, the authority of the State has to be re-established prior to the destruction of its control instruments.

2.1. First Objective: Separating Economic Agents From Political Actors

In the former Soviet republics, and especially in Russia, separating political actors from economic agents is quite a challenge, owing to the pervasiveness of the Party at all the levels of the State and the economy, and because of the characteristics of the planning system.

As mentioned above, all administrations and organizations in the Soviet Union had dual management. The Five-Year Plan was endorsed by the highest bodies of the government, and economic priorities were dependent on political objectives. Changes in the political sphere could lead to changes in economic priorities, and directors had to develop the means to adapt quickly to such changes. The predominance of political imperatives over economic considerations, in addition to the incentives and constraints associated with the implementation of the plan, generated behaviors that further aggravated the confusion between political and economic actors.

The implementation of the plan was compulsory. The enterprises that managed to completely implement and even exceed the plan were rewarded with a bonus, which could take the form of the allocation of more resources for the next plan, or greater political influence. On the other hand, the enterprises that failed to implement the plan were sanctioned by a decrease in the resources allocated to them, which eventually led to even greater difficulty in implementing the following plan. In such circumstances, directors, political leaders, and all those who were involved in the implementation of the plan and who could suffer from a failure, had great incentive to manipulate information in order to post positive results.

Such manipulations were permitted by the organization of the planning system. Although the planning system imposed a centralized decision-making process, it also resulted in a highly decentralized system of decision implementation. This is mainly due to the fact that, contrary to the Party's wishes, the planning system imposed no direct subordination among its various services. Plan services depended on the organizations or administrative bodies with which they were associated (Republics, regions, cities etc.), and had to form their own economic staff. As both political and economic actors shared the same interest of implementing and exceeding the plan, they commonly distorted information, both while the plan was being defined (by minimizing their production capacities in order to obtain lower production loads) and at the end of the plan period, when announcing results that may have been higher than actually achieved. In other words, the characteristics of the system generated a common interest in misrepresentation among political and economic actors, which contributed to the confusion of the economic and political spheres.

The separation of economic agents from political actors must therefore take place both at the economic and political levels.

At the political level, the abolition of the Party as the paramount source of power and decision-making is essential. It is also crucial to clearly define the respective powers of the Federal State and those of the regions, as well as the respective prerogatives of the executive and legislative branches of power at the federal and regional level. This implies creating a set of explicit rules guaranteeing that the representatives of the State do not deal with topics that are beyond their competency, and that the authority of the State and its representatives is not challenged, except in specific conditions and in a framework specified by the law.

At the economic level, the separation of political and economic actors requires giving enterprises the ability to control their production (definition, supply, distribution etc.) and to define clearly the framework in which exchanges have to take place.

No market economy operates without a set of laws and rules that regulate exchanges and determine where agents' responsibilities lie. Commercial laws, rules protecting consumers and intellectual property, and defining the rights and responsibilities of share-holders, prudential regulations related to the banking system, a network of insurance companies, etc., are all necessary for a competitive market to operate. Furthermore, such rules and laws must apply to all equally (any exceptions must be explicitly justified).

It goes without saying that the priority system and the bargaining culture which prevailed in the Soviet system are obstacles to competition, and do not allow the emergence of a set of rules common to all. Their abolition is a prerequisite for a successful system change.

However, although it is quite easy to put an end to the priority system, it is much more difficult to change behaviors. If reform is to be effective, the existence and orderly working of a legal system, with an effective law-enforcement system (police, prisons, fine collection agencies, etc.) is essential. It is worth noting, however, that the implementation of the law must not be too rigid, for in transition periods unexpected events may hamper the implementation of the law or make the laws irrelevant. The State must therefore be able to intervene in order to change laws or the framework for their implementation.

2.2. Commercialization of the Economy

A common characteristic of modern market economies is a system of commercial exchange. Producers and buyers interact directly, and exchanges are performed on the basis of a negotiation between agents. The commercialization of the economy therefore implies removing the obstacles to direct relationships between producers and buyers. To achieve this, the abolition of the planning system and of controls on foreign economic relations, and the liberalization of prices to follow the market, are essential elements.

However, in Russia's case, the commercialization of the economy implies not only softening State controls on the economy. It also implies allowing free exchanges to take place, and therefore the creation of a unified economic environment.

The unification of the economic environment must take place at different levels. At the geographic level, it requires the existence of a developed communication and transportation system – roads, railroads, telephone lines – allowing goods to be exchanged and agents to interact without too many obstacles. Considering the poor state of the Russian communication system, Russia will have to invest heavily in the development and modernization of its industrial infrastructure.

At the commercial level, the unification of the economy requires the creation of a distribution network with wholesale markets and a system of retail outlets, allowing producers to expand their markets and reach a wide variety of clients directly. As distribution networks were formerly segmented and organized by the State, this is a very important aspect of the economic unification process.

At the financial level, the unification of the economy implies the creation of a banking and financial system as well as a unified currency.

One of the characteristics of the Soviet economy was that the monetary system was segmented: different "currencies" were used by different agents for different transactions. For instance, individuals could use only fiduciary money to buy goods; checks and credit cards did not exist. Enterprise-to-enterprise exchanges as well as the payment of salaries were made by wire transfers; foreign exchanges were performed using either "transferable ruble"[86] or foreign currencies, depending on the recipient. All money transfers were performed by the State bank[87], and were subject to the planning system. The State bank was the unique loan provider, the only body issuing money, the only compensation and clearing center, and the only financial auditor. As it controlled money flows and the issuing of credits, the Central Bank did not have to develop a set of prudential rules to regulate financial operations.

The segmentation of the monetary system also contributed to the segmentation of the distribution system, as some goods could be acquired with a specific currency only. For instance, goods in special "Beriozka" shops were available mostly to foreigners and diplomats and could be bought only with foreign currencies or "diplomatic" rubles. Although distribution and monetary circuits were not hermetically sealed, they were rigid enough to maintain a separation between agents.

The commercialization of the economy also requires that enterprises change their mode of operation. In order to encourage them to produce higher quality goods, to pay attention to costs and to be competitive, competition must shift from the beginning of the production

---

86 The Transferable Ruble was mainly used for transactions with satellite countries.

87 The Soviet banking system was composed of the Central Bank and of several specialized banks (Investment bank, bank of foreign trade, a savings bank), which in fact were agencies of the Central bank, which played the role of both a central and commercial bank.

process (competition for the allocation of scarce resources) to the end of the production process (when goods are sold). In order to do so, the restrictions on enterprises' resource supplies must be lifted. The development and modernization of distribution and communication networks will contribute to this. The creation of a financial and banking system – composed of a central bank and commercial banks – is also a vital element for shifting competition from the beginning to the end of the production process. Enterprises will have several sources of financing at their disposal, providing them with the means required for their daily operation (working capital, liquid assets) as well as for long-term investments. By ensuring the liquidity of agents, the financial and banking system will also allow the lengthening of enterprises' time horizons. By offering enterprises alternative sources of financing, it also allows them to get more independent of the State budget, and get accustomed to the market mode of coordination.

Re-establishing private property is certainly a key element of the commercialization of the economy. It should encourage a more efficient use of resources, the practice of competition, and flexibility on the supply side. However, private property has no virtue if it not accompanied by accountability. Clear rules as to what private property means must therefore be implemented. Otherwise, privatization will not generate a favorable change in behavior, and may even lead to a greater waste of resources.

Commercial information is another characteristic of market economies. True enterprises can get information about the profile of their competitors, and detect expansion opportunities through different channels: chambers of commerce, business directories, published firms' financial statements, etc.

Such information is all the more important in Russia, because the mobilization of the economy, and the predominance of political and ideological imperatives over economic considerations, have resulted in the creation of a highly integrated production system, which was spread all over the territory of the USSR. However, the system was not balanced. While some enterprises had redundant production, others could not satisfy the demands for civilian goods. Information about the market – about consumer demand, competitive activities, and the status of other enterprises – is extremely important in restructuring the production system.

Owing to the scale of the Russian territory and to the Soviet habit of distorting information, commercial information must be collected, checked and guaranteed by Federal agencies.

Conclusion

The mode of operation and culture of Soviet defense enterprises are direct responses to their environment. In theory, reforming the environment should provoke a change in the enterprises' culture and mode of operation. However, a reform of the framework – commercialization of the economy, and separation between economic and political actors – may lead to results just the opposite of what is wanted unless the measures that need to be implemented are carefully prioritized.

Furthermore, in the transition period, the State has an important role to play. Decreasing State control over the economy does not imply total disengagement. The State must be a stabilizing institution, and allow exchanges to take place by providing enterprises with clear information, by creating a set of rules regulating exchanges, by creating a judicial system able to implement the law, and by creating communication networks open to all, among other things. In other words, the State must create a unified economic and legal environment, and reduce the uncertainty generated by the system change. To accomplish this, it is essential that State's functions should be clear and known to all.

PART TWO

New Political Thinking and Disarmament: Precursors to Conversion

INTRODUCTION

Vlad E. Genin

The early 80s were a critical period for the U.S.S.R. Within three years, three successive leaders of the country passed away, one after another: General Secretaries of the Communist Party of the Soviet Union Leonid Brezhnev, Yuri Andropov, and Konstantin Chernenko. These years saw the passing of leaders from the immediate post-Stalin generation.

They were replaced by men whose political views had been formed in the 60s and 70s. These new men recognized the danger of the imminent crash of the system in all its aspects: domestic politics, the economy, and international relations. Recognizing these dangers, they clearly saw the necessity of radical changes in the country. And in 1985, one of them, Mikhail Gorbachev, became the leader of the state.

There is no doubt that he will be remembered as a courageous person, and a progressive political and international public figure. He will go down in the history of the 20th century as one of those outstanding people who struggled to help mankind to escape the Armageddon of nuclear war.

It was Gorbachev who dared to challenge the Communist political system and command economy of the U.S.S.R., which, like quicksand, was sucking the country down to destruction. Gorbachev took upon himself the most crucial and dangerous mission of actually making things happen, instead of treading water with the Party bonzes in the safety of the Kremlin. It is obvious that he might have been deposed by the Politburo's hardliners, had they only known the full depth of the new leader's commitment to bringing glasnost, democracy, and a market economy to the U.S.S.R.

Balancing on the edge of the abyss, the U.S.S.R. desperately needed to break free from the chains of false doctrines and a thoroughly rotten system. The Party elite understood better than anyone the scope of the problems that Russia was facing, 65 years after the Tsar's dethronement. They were unable to make a difference in their own country. But later, the same people were too ready to unconditionally blame Gorbachev for all the problems in post-Communist Russia and the new independent states.

The year 1985 marked the beginning of the new, Gorbachev way of thinking. The Cold War, after having dragged on for four decades, was effectively over. The Gorbachev era became a time of hope for the Russian people. It offered the country a chance to evolve into a civilized state. It was the time of perestroika and glasnost, when Russia got its first and perhaps only chance in the 20th century to enter the global community as an equal partner, instead of being an international bogeyman...

2.1. FROM THE FORMER U.S.S.R. TO THE NEW RUSSIA

Introductory Remarks

Vlad E. Genin

In the late 70s and early 80s, the threat of a nuclear war was the most acute world problem. This threat evolved mostly out of the unheard-of escalation of weapons production, and the nuclear marathon in Europe and other regions; the main players being the U.S.S.R. and the countries of the Warsaw Pact on one side, and the United States and NATO on the other.

Several major, epoch-making changes in Soviet policy, which were thought up by Mikhail Gorbachev, became precursors of the defense conversion process in the U.S.S.R. and later on in Russia. First, a sharp turn toward global peace, and a transition from confrontation with the United States and other Western countries to the strengthening of political, economical, and military cooperation with them. Second, major participation in the global disarmament process, which was unprecedented in human history, and, consequently, the beginning of limitations on arms production. Third, revolutionary socio-economic changes inside the country, which moved it toward a new political system and economic reforms. Fourth, a rapid reduction in governmental military procurement orders. Fifth, both the movement toward free market economy and conversion of the country's defense sector.

These dramatic changes were caused by new international political thinking introduced by Gorbachev, as well as the impossibility for the U.S.S.R. of continuing to participate in the crippling arms race. Under the unbearable burden of weapon production expenses, the U.S.S.R. was slowly sinking like an old ship left to rust away. The country also paid a heavy price to learn the hard lesson of the Afghanistan war. The huge expense incurred in supporting the armies of socialist countries and many so-called "friendly regimes" was draining the economy of the country. Enormous amounts of money and free military equipment left the country for Cuba, Vietnam, Iraq and other Soviet-supported states.

In the United States, a new administration headed by President Ronald Reagan brought with it a tough, no-nonsense attitude towards issues of global security and the nuclear opposition of the two political systems. Development of an unprecedented comprehensive anti-missile defense was launched. The international situation grew tense, and reached a critical point.

Mikhail I. Gerasev

A multitude of military-political problems showed that the international political situation was truly critical. A completely new stage of the arms race development had just begun. Specialists called it the "Technological Stage." It involved all kinds of arms, systems, and other various aspects of military preparedness.

The abrupt worsening of the international political situation and the Soviet-American relationship was caused by the strategic military parity between the East and the West. The stability of the strategic military balance obviously decreased, especially after the deployment of intermediate-range missiles in Europe. As a result, the missiles' flight time to the vitally important centers of both parties in Europe was reduced to 4 to 5 minutes, which in turn reduced the critical minimum time for a thorough evaluation and verification of the information, and for decision-making after the receipt of a signal of a nuclear missile attack. The possibility of an unauthorized nuclear attack, and the reliability of automatic control of the nuclear forces, was widely discussed by the Eastern and Western public sectors. In other words, the ability of politicians to control the mechanism that could eliminate life on Earth came into question.

The changes in the strategic military balance also caused the modernization of strategic arms. From the end of the 1960s to the beginning of the 1980s, nuclear arms, considered to be exclusively offensive weapons, technically and operationally, created a balance of forces in which the defense prevailed against the offense. The unprecedented changes in the political and military situation caused by the development of nuclear arms led inevitably to a new strategic balance.

Gradually, both parties increased the amount of smart weapons – arms intended for highly accurate strikes on strategic targets on the other side, which would potentially weaken their power to retaliate. During 1970s, large-scale anti-missile defense programs were developed, which, if successful, would lead to a further weakening of the defensive power of the opposite side.

Anti-missile defense programs gave unlimited freedom to the supporters of all kinds of technical military programs. In the 1970s, the U.S. and the Soviet governments were able to contain military-technical preparation, and the increasing appetites of the military establishment, with the help of mutual agreements, but by the mid 1980s, this approach had become questionable.

By 1985, the country started to feel tired, because of the endless military-technological competition, and the "fortress under siege" syndrome. In 1985, the new Soviet government, under Gorbachev's leadership, introduced a very important new concept: that of considering international military security a political problem, which could be solved only by political means. This idea contradicted the technological military way, which made the solution of the international safety problem dependent upon the quantity and quality of the weapons.

By evaluating the statements by Gorbachev and the other members of Soviet leadership, and the documents issued after the very important Soviet forums of the perestroika era, such as the 27th Congress of the Communist Party of the Soviet Union (CPSU), and the 19th Conference of the CPSU in 1986-1987, the following three very important conclusions can be reached:

First, the characteristics of modern weapons meant that all of the traditional forms of defense, despite the gigantic human and material resources they consumed, could not guarantee safety.

Second, in terms of the further development of the arms race, and its expansion into space, the peak of nuclear weapons perfection could eliminate East-West military parity as a restraining factor.

Third, the military-political situation in the mid-1980s came very close to escaping the control of the political authorities.

When Gorbachev came to power in the U.S.S.R., the United States started realistic weapons reduction and disarmament programs. Only one month after Gorbachev was elected General Secretary of the

CPSU, on April 7, 1985, the Soviet Union stopped further deployment of its intermediate-range missiles. By October 1985, the U.S.S.R. had considerably reduced the number of these missiles. On July 29, 1985, the U.S.S.R. announced introduction of a moratorium on all nuclear testing, beginning on August 6, 1995, and ending on January 1, 1996, and called upon the United States to follow its example.

The most important result of cooperation between the two countries was the U.S.S.R.-U.S. Agreement, signed on December 8, 1987, which concerned the liquidation of intermediate-range and short-range missiles. It was symbolically important, despite the fact that the terms of this Agreement meant the destruction of only 4% of the nuclear weapons in the world. It was also very important economically.

According to Soviet estimates, the ratification of the Agreement could result in a savings in the State budget of about 300 million rubles.[1]

This particular Agreement was intended not merely to reduce but to liquidate an entire class of weapons, and was the first Agreement to acknowledge the necessity of converting certain defense enterprises. The following Soviet enterprises were affected: the Votkinsk Machine-Building Plant, the Barrikada Plant in Volgograd, the Lenin Heavy Machine-Building Plant in Petropavlovsk, and the Kalinin Experimental Plant.

When the Agreement had been signed, the problem of non-nuclear weapons limitation and reduction became very critical, especially in Europe.

---

1 Editor's Note: In the 1980s, the official exchange rate was 0.6 dollars per ruble. However, it was an artificial ratio and did not reflect the real value of the ruble. In the reality, this amount of money was equal to the cost of constructing approximately 30,000 new residential apartments.

After long negotiations, the new Agreement regarding regular military forces was signed at the end of 1990. According to the terms of this Agreement, the considerable military arsenal of the U.S.S.R. had to be reduced in these terms:

Tanks – from 41,400 to 13,100;

Armored cars – from 48,900 to 20,000;

Artillery systems – from 42,400 to 13,100.[2]

This new Agreement dealt not only with the withdrawal from Europe of considerable quantities of military machinery and equipment, but also with their partial destruction and a corresponding reduction in defense industry production, to be effected in the near future.

When Gorbachev was in power, a very important role in the process of disarmament was played by the Strategic Arms Limitation Treaty (SALT I), which reduced strategic offensive weapons. For the first time in history, both countries were committed to reducing strategic nuclear weapons by approximately 30%. Each party was obliged to reduce the number of strategic delivery vehicles to 1,600, and nuclear warheads to 6,000.

Unfortunately, during the perestroika era, the problem of limitation and liquidation of tactical nuclear weapons was not solved, mostly because of the collapse of the U.S.S.R. In the second half of the 1980s, both the West and the East proposed a number of disarmament initiatives. Although very few of them were implemented, apart from those just mentioned, these agreements affected the most important, and the most expensive, components of military arsenals, excluding naval weapons. It was very important that the aforementioned Soviet/U.S. commitments to disarmament influenced the reconstruction of the

---

2 *Pravda*, July 12, 1990.

defense industries, led to the revision of military activity plans, caused widespread realization of the necessity for conversion programs and the diversification of production to civilian output.

To evaluate the effect of disarmament activity on the Soviet defense industry, it is necessary to emphasize a very important concept of the so-called "New Political Thinking," as suggested by the Soviet leadership during the Gorbachev era. One of the most important concepts was the following: in terms of confrontation, it is impossible to provide any guarantees of peaceful coexistence; it is impossible to eliminate the threat of nuclear disaster. Even if we assume that in terms of confrontation, we could achieve a considerable limitation of the arms race and the reduction of military arsenals, it would not exclude the resumption of the arms race should there be any aggravation of the international political situation. Hence this first step toward peaceful coexistence and disarmament was not sufficient; for complete relief from the nuclear threat, it was also necessary to make this course irreversible, and to stabilize international relations on the basis of peace and trust.

From the new point of view of political thinking, implementation of these ideas suggested an entirely new type of relationship between the countries, which operated under different political and economic systems. The idea concerned not just the absence of war between the countries, but also mutual understanding, broad cooperation, absence of confrontation, and the elimination of ideological influence on international relations.

In the second half of the 1980s, much progress was achieved in disarmament. The international situation was considerably improved. The U.S.S.R.'s relations with the West were stabilized, and the preconditions for the further inevitable improvement of relationships were created. Thus, not only disarmament agreements, but also the new political situation and the new prospect for cooperation with the West strengthened the forces of the supporters for the gradual reduction of the Soviet defense industry.

The State policy of glasnost (openness) was a very important step in helping Soviet citizens realize the necessity for deep fundamental changes. The mass media started to broadcast and publish more truthful information about the economic burden of the arms race, about the gigantic Soviet military arsenal, and also about the practically endless and uncontrolled financial demands of the military forces and the defense industry.

Before 1991, the operations of the defense industry were controlled by resolutions of the Central Committee of the CPSU, the Soviet Council of Ministers, the Military Industrial Commission *(Voenno-Promyshlennaia Kommissia)* and also by joint decisions of the different divisions of the Defense Industry Ministries, which were coordinated by the Military Industrial Commission.

The legal foundation for the functioning of the Defense Industry were the five laws, nineteen resolutions of the Central Committee of the CPSU and Council of Ministers, and seven decisions of Military Industrial Commission, as stated in the 1993 draft of the "Concept of the Industrial Policy in the Russian Defense Industry". This shows how the financing of the defense industry lacked any control by the public, or even by legislative bodies.

The largest part of the military budget was spent on the purchase of weapons from the defense industry and NIOKR [3]. This spending

3 Editor's Note: This term stands for Scientific Research and Special Design Projects.

represented about 62% of the country's total military budget. In 1991, this number was reduced to 53% due to the dramatic reduction of the NIOKR budgets.[4]

Naturally, many Soviet and foreign experts believed that the official data about the Soviet military budgets were lower than the real numbers. If the Soviet military budget were to be calculated in terms of world prices, the annual expenses would not be 70-90 billion rubles, but rather 300-350 billion dollars, as was estimated by some Soviet specialists.[5]

At the same time, some details about the military power of the U.S.S.R. were published: on January 1, 1989, the number of Soviet military troops was 4,258,000, and one year later, after the beginning of troop reduction, the number was 3,993,000, approximately twice the number of U.S. regular military troops.[6]

In 1989, when the agreement concerning the reduction of the Conventional Forces in Europe Treaty in Europe was signed, the U.S.S.R. had 63,000 tanks, 69,000 artillery pieces, 8,200 military aircraft, more than 76,000 armored personnel carriers, 260 strategic submarines, including 113 nuclear submarines, and 157 surface warships.[7]

The existence of such a powerful military force was justified by the necessity of maintaining military parity with NATO. But the economic resources of the two blocs were very different. In 1985, the economic power ratio of the Warsaw Pact and NATO was 1 to 2.5; with the national revenue ratio accordingly at 1,901.7 billion dollars to

---

4 *Pravda*, December 16,1989.

5 *Nezavisimaya Gazeta*, 10.9.1991.

6 *Krasnaya Zvezda*, April 8, 1989; Pravda, December 16,1989.

7 *Krasnaya Zvezda*, April 7, 1989; Foreign Affairs Ministry Bulletin, No.2, 1990.

4,350.7 billion dollars, and the population ratio at 1 to1.6, to the advantage of the NATO countries.[8]

Another important factor that made the arms race an even heavier economic burden, was the practice of military-technical cooperation with Soviet allies. These allies, as a rule, were poor developing countries. At the end of the 1980s, Soviet exports to the world market were less than 5%, but Soviet weapons exports, as estimated by Western specialists, accounted for 28 % of the world's weapons exports (32% of the total military supply to developing countries). A quarter of all the weapons produced in the U.S.S.R. were exported.[9] But most of the debts incurred by the allies of the U.S.S.R. were written off, or the payments were postponed indefinitely. Thus, the citizens of the U.S.S.R. had to pay for their country's relationships with its allies. Moreover, if clients did eventually pay for the weaponry, they would usually do so with their low quality goods instead of the hard currency that the U.S.S.R. needed badly—also for the further development of the defense industry. Among the major clients, only Iraq and Lebanon paid with hard currency, but when they later fell under an international economic blockade, even they were unable to pay their debts that way.

The main problem, however, was that since the country's industrialization began under Stalin, the defense industry was the core of the Soviet national economy, a core that was growing very fast. The main resources of the country were pumped into it, diverted originally from the agricultural sector, then from the oil and gas industry. Giving priority to the defense industry, the Soviet leadership overlooked the

8 *Pravda*, March 2, 1989.

9 *Moscow News*, December 3,1989.

"Technical Revolution" that started in the Western countries. From 1975 to1985, Western countries began a massive reorganization of their industries using new technologies, while the Soviet civilian (commercial) industries were in a state of stagnation. The defense industry reached an unbelievable size, and it formed the major part of the national economy.

Military-political opposition to the West, paradoxically, made the U.S.S.R. even more economically dependent on it. By the middle of the 1970s, the Soviet national economy found itself on a much lower technological level than other developed countries. It became a supplier of natural resources and raw materials to the economically developed sector of the world. The Soviet economy was falling further and further behind. The export operations of the U.S.S.R. had a very definite colonial character. The highly technologically developed defense industry of the U.S.S.R. survived, supported by "oil dollars." It was not based on a solid post-industrial economy, but on a backward, failing one.

The situation worsened with the emerging economical crisis, in particular, the crisis in the energy supply industries in the early 1980s. This had a significant impact on the reduction of military expenditures.

Perestroika was to create a new economic basis for the defense industry (through the so called *"uskoreniye"* policy– the policy of accelerating economical development), which was one of the main new directions under Gorbachev's leadership, along with perestroika and glasnost. Unfortunately, the policy of acceleration brought unexpected results. After 1988, the national economy became more and more difficult to control, and the policy of acceleration was gradually abandoned.

It became obvious that in implementing the reforms, the country's leadership concentrated all of its efforts on ideological, political, and organizational problems, neglecting economic problems. According to the Kremlin's new thinking, perestroika was considered a way to change the political and public systems. The Soviet leadership still relied upon the economic structures formed during the last several decades, hoping to correct all political and economic mistakes and improve old structures by using Western economic practices. As a result, the implementation of economic reforms slowed down, especially in the defense industry, and economic difficulties prevented the military complex from reorganizing, and by 1985 the crisis worsened.

One of the major problems that Gorbachev inherited, and which he was not able to solve, was the prevalence of large-scale monopolies in the economy. For example, in 1991, 87% of heavy machinery was produced by a single manufacturer. Approximately 30%-40% of industrial products were manufactured by monopolies.[10]

At that time, small business enterprises virtually did not exist. Even the enterprises supplying the big manufacturers with spare parts were monopolies in the U.S.S.R. In 1988, the new law *O Kooperatsii*[11] was approved. It was supposed to encourage the development of small businesses, but this process was very slow. It could not meet the needs of the national economy. Thus, the reforms proclaimed in the U.S.S.R. were different from the economic reforms in China, for example. China had three major sources for economic reforms: direct defense industry conversion, the export of weapons to finance the import of regular consumer goods, and foreign aid. Among these sources, China mostly relied upon defense conversion with some foreign help.

10 IMF, A Study of the Soviet Economy, Vol. 2, Paris, 1991.
11 Editor's Note: On Cooperatives.

Although the proclaimed goals of the two countries were similar, the measures they took were different. Gorbachev preferred the comparatively easier option: foreign aid and the export of weapons. As a result, the country's foreign debt had increased considerably by the end of his presidency, and the credits received were consumed, but not used for economic reforms.

The Soviet leadership was hoping to continue exporting weapons in large quantities to support its defense industry and the other internal needs of the country. But, as was noted before, two major hard currency clients, Lebanon and Iraq, were under an international economic embargo, so the hopes were never realized.

But by the end of the 1980s, at least, two processes in the economy created the prerequisites for the inevitable and relatively fast demilitarization of the economy:

First, the unsuccessful reforms and a deepening economic crisis. Second, a process of increasing integration with the world's economy. As a result of very cautious reforms, the U.S.S.R. was connected to the world market system. The prospect of accelerated integration into the world market made it necessary to review price-determining mechanisms. This prospect also made the process of demilitarization inevitable. The process of matching internal prices with the prices on the world market would force the U.S.S.R. to reduce the production of weapons by 75% - 80%.[12] Thus, as a result of rising prices and salaries, the internal market and the world market together suppressed the defense industry. Disarmament and defense conversion were the only solutions for the crisis.

---

12 *Nezavisimaya Gazeta*, October 9, 1991.

2.2. ECONOMIC CONCEPTION OF CONVERSION

Introductory Remarks

Vlad E. Genin

Even now, the opinions of specialists in both Russia and other countries about the true fundamental reasons for defense conversion are quite different. In Russia, the variety of the opinions is much wider than overseas.

According to one school of thought, the U.S.S.R. and its successor Russia reached the critical point in their political and socio-economic developments, after which there were only two alternatives: the abyss or a new way of thinking followed by a turn toward civilized development – peace and free market economy.

Another school of thought explains that it was the result of the Soviet Union's defeat in both the arms race and the Cold War.

Some opinions represent extremist, reactionary points of view. For instance, Communists are accusing modern leaders of betraying Russia to the West. According to the opinions held by Western specialists, there were other, deeper reasons.

Sonia Ben Ouagrham

Conversion was launched under the Gorbachev administration as the result of an evolution of the Soviet nuclear strategy.

The Soviet nuclear doctrine developed by Marshal Sokolovski was based on the following principle: should a war break out, nuclear weapons would be used from the very beginning. The U.S.S.R. would avoid a surprise assault by initiating a massive nuclear strike[13] supported by conventional military means.

Such a military doctrine represented a threat to NATO members, and damaged the credibility of the "Flexible Response," which was based on a progressive transition from conventional to tactical and, finally, strategic weapons. NATO responded to that unfavorable strategic situation by designing the "Air Land - Battle" (1982) and "Follow-on-Forces Attack" (1983) concepts. By relying on new technologies, they aimed at attacking the second echelon of Soviet forces in order to deprive the first echelon, the most powerful, of its support and reinforcements.

The Soviet Union realized how much these NATO concepts threatened its traditional doctrine, which was based on two echelons and massive military formations: any concentration of forces could be forced to commit military action by NATO forces. Furthermore, the offensive approach and the element of surprise, which were the pillars of the Soviet strategy, were challenged by Western technological progress in the fields of reconnaissance and information collection.

Aware that a nuclear war was unlikely, Soviet officers started defining future wars as conventional wars based on smaller, mobile, and independent formations, equipped with sophisticated conventional arms able to wage single-echelon combat.[14]

---

13 Although the doctrine did not state it explicitly, this offensive strategy involved a preemptive strike.

14 Sonia Ben Ouagrham, Le Disarmament et La Conversion de l'Industrie Militaire en Russie, op.cit.

But in order to wage conventional wars, the Soviet Union needed not only modern armaments, but also an economic system strong enough to meet war needs and support the survival of the system. Unfortunately, the planned economy had generated a number of malfunctioning enterprises, and the military-industrial complex, which still enjoyed high priority in the allocation of resources, was unable to meet the requirements of modern technology. Reinforcing the economic system and restructuring industry became vital elements for the survival of the Soviet system. Hence, the new policy of glasnost, perestroika, and the accelerated rhythm of disarmament agreements. They mainly aimed at alleviating the burden of the arms race, and allowing time for the U.S.S.R. to restructure and defeat its enemy.

Thus, conversion in the Soviet time was initiated and organized by the State, and for mainly hidden strategic ends.

2.3. THE REAGAN REVOLUTION IN ARMS CONTROL

Introductory Remarks

Vlad E. Genin

The UN complex in New York City is symbolized by the sculpture "Let Us Beat Swords into Plowshares". This work by the talented sculptor Yevgenii Vuchetich, which is seamlessly inserted into the architecture of this international organization, reflects one of the noblest aspirations of mankind: disarmament in the name of constructive work.

The long and thorny path to disarmament was, perhaps, the most difficult test of political will and maturity in the civilized world. For centuries, disarming a defeated foe on the field of battle was a relatively simple task. Mutual worldwide disarmament of nuclear superpowers after decades of confrontation in the Cold War was the main dilemma set before the world at the end of the 20th century. A dilemma properly resolved by world leaders.

At first glance, it seemed to many that the road to disarmament was the prerogative of the military and politicians. Unlike a highway, however, it did not run through flat valleys or rolling hills. On this road, there were unavoidable gorges, rivers, and swamps that could not be crossed without building bridges, which are highly complex structures.

At the most difficult, sometimes impassable sections of the road to disarmament, the diplomats went to work.

They were able to build bridges, to find compromises for most difficult issues. Their ability answered the question "to be or not to be" for disarmament in the 1980s, and decided the fate of the world.

Many aspects of conversion are closely tied to the arms reductions negotiations process; indeed, it was the precursor to conversion. The negotiators in Vienna, Geneva, and Stockholm decided the type and number of weapons that were to be eliminated, thereby predetermining the future of the Russian defense complex.

The "Goodby-Grinevsky Compromise" is a phrase well-known to those familiar with the history of diplomacy and international relations; it has become an historical term. Two legendary figures—U.S. Ambassador James Goodby and Soviet Ambassador Oleg Grinevsky—earned their place in history while conducting the START (Strategic Arms Reduction Treaty) and CSBMs (Confidence and Security Building Measures) negotiations.

Due largely to their talent, courage, and capacity for endurance, these diplomats built a bridge of mutual agreement between two countries. The responsibility for finding a mutually acceptable solution to disarmament, the difficult and sometimes contradictory task assigned by the White House and the Kremlin, lay largely on their shoulders.

James E. Goodby

Ronald Reagan's foreign policy has been held up by some conservatives as a model for future presidents. Its reliance on military supremacy and its aggressive defense of American interests are seen as perfectly in tune with a unilateralist foreign policy aimed at achieving a benign global hegemony. Left out of the picture is one of Ronald Reagan's most important legacies: the revolution he wrought in our thinking about nuclear weapons and about relations with Moscow. Reagan was what we would call today an abolitionist. He wanted to rid the world of nuclear weapons, and he set the course for dramatic reductions in these weapons. He was ready for a very different relationship with Moscow even before the advent of Gorbachev. Together with Gorbachev, Reagan transformed the geopolitical landscape. A neo-Reaganite foreign policy, to be true to the original, should seek to continue on the course that Reagan pioneered.

I witnessed this Reagan revolution from the vantage point of Vice Chair of the U.S. START I delegation, 1982-83, and head of the U.S. delegation to the Conference on Disarmament in Europe (the Stockholm Conference), 1984-85. In the latter capacity I met with Reagan in the Oval Office several times. Although these were essentially "photo ops," there was also an opportunity for some conversation between the two of us.

I had seen during my work on START I that Reagan was ready for radical ideas in nuclear arms control. George Kennan at that time had been publicly urging 50% cuts in nuclear weapons. As a result of good cooperation between the Joint Chiefs of Staff and my office in the State Department, we were able to present Reagan with a proposal that came close to what Kennan was suggesting. It was already clear that Reagan liked to see such proposals in the form of speech inserts, so I drafted some language for a speech that the President later, in the Spring of 1982, made at his alma mater, Eureka College.

Still, I had not realized the depth of Reagan's feelings on the subject of nuclear weapons until something I said later, partly in jest, at one of our Oval Office meetings triggered a strong response from the president. Usually relaxed and easy-going in demeanor, on this occasion Reagan turned to me with a steely glint in his eyes and said in emphatic tones: "you tell people that I'm willing to go as far as anyone else in getting rid of nuclear weapons." This remark was made in early 1984, and it told me once and for all that Ronald Reagan, unlike all of his predecessors, meant what he said when he spoke of his abhorrence of nuclear weapons. It explained everything about the remarkable Reykjavik meeting with Mikhail Gorbachev in October 1986, when the two leaders spoke seriously about eliminating nuclear weapons.

Another experience with Reagan was revelatory about the man's interest in doing business with Moscow. Although this episode did not directly involve nuclear weapons, I saw it as part and parcel of Reagan's desire for a new relationship with the Soviet Union. His thinking on this point, as I understood it, antedated Gorbachev's later policy of seeking to liquidate Cold War ideological differences between the United States and the Soviet Union.

The president had named me to head up the U.S. delegation to the Conference on Disarmament in Europe, a part of the Conference on Security and Cooperation in Europe (CSCE), now the Organization for Security and Cooperation in Europe (OSCE). My Soviet counterpart was Ambassador Oleg Grinevsky, a talented and independent-minded diplomat who had solid credentials as a nuclear arms control negotiator dating back to the 1960s. He had been the equivalent of Assistant Secretary of State for the Middle East in the years preceding his appointment to head up the Soviet delegation to the Stockholm Conference.

On my way to Helsinki for the preparatory conference of the CDE I had stopped off in Bonn, and there met with Ambassador Murad Hoffmann at the Foreign Ministry. Hoffman strongly urged me to establish a close relationship with Grinevsky if I could, and on the strength of that advice I invited Grinevsky to an introductory lunch in a private room at the Klaus Kinkel restaurant in downtown Helsinki. Grinevsky left no doubt in my mind that he was ready to do business and that he was a pragmatic, no-nonsense negotiator.

Secretary of State George Shultz also instructed me to work closely with Ambassador Grinevsky. The opening shots in the Stockholm Conference between Shultz and Soviet Foreign Minister Gromyko had been tough, no-holds-barred speeches. Nonetheless, as I said good-bye to the Secretary at Stockholm airport, George Shultz made clear to me that he wanted something to come of this negotiation and that he expected me to work as closely as I could with Oleg Grinevsky to make that happen.

It is possible that I read too much into Grinevsky's remarks on the several occasions that we met together in early 1984, but it seemed to me that he saw an outcome for the conference along the same lines that had been passing through my own mind. I will admit that it was a fairly obvious outcome, since there were only two areas where NATO and Warsaw Pact positions overlapped: a renunciation of the threat or use of force, along the lines of the U.N. Charter obligations, and a series of modest confidence-building measures to improve upon those already in place since 1975 in the Helsinki Final Act of the CSCE.

On one occasion, after an excellent lunch at Erik's, courtesy of the Greek ambassador, Grinevsky and I walked up and down the wharf to which the boat-restaurant was tied up. His vision of the final outcome was a non-use of force pledge as the central core, around which would be wrapped several confidence-building measures that we both could agree on. This coincided with my own opinion and I cheerfully reported to Washington the gist of what I understood Ambassador Grinevsky was suggesting. To get the attention of Washington policymakers, I described the conversation as "the walk on the wharf." I intended the description to be perceived as the "poor man's" version of Paul Nitze's legendary "walk in the woods." And so it was, touching a vein of humor that really and truly does exist deep underground in Washington.

Because of this report, I was asked through a back channel from the State Department to provide some language for a speech that Reagan would give during his upcoming June visit to Europe. I was happy to oblige, and sent by back-channel a paragraph tying non-use of force to practical confidence-building measures. The president used this material just as he had used the material I had drafted on nuclear reductions.

It took more than two years of negotiations after Reagan's speech to produce the Stockholm accords but, essentially, that was the deal that emerged.

The lesson in this for me about Reagan's foreign policy is that he was willing to be non-traditional in dealing with Moscow, even before the advent of Gorbachev. The usual U.S. way of negotiating with the Soviet Union was to hold back concessions until the 11th hour and then some, in order to extract a few hard-won concessions from Moscow. This, in fact, is what most of the allies thought would happen with non-use of force, which was seen as a concession to the Soviets. Reagan played his hand differently. By announcing at an early stage in the Stockholm Conference what his bottom line amounted to, he established a focus for the conference, fortified his own credibility, and won the support of the neutrals, a crucial step in consolidating a consensus behind the U.S. and NATO position. There was no bargaining leverage lost in the maneuver, so far as I could see. Reagan, to the contrary, offered quite openly the deal that everyone privately wanted, and gained strength in the process.

Reagan's secretary of state, George Shultz, deserves a great deal of credit for making Reagan's wishes come true. In effect, he forced the pace of the Stockholm talks in the fall of 1985 when he convinced Soviet ambassador to the United States Anatoly Dobrynin that the negotiators should begin drafting their final report. He then authorized me to speak with President Reagan's national security adviser, Bud McFarlane, to explain what I wanted to do procedurally to make that happen. With the approval of Secretary Shultz and Bud McFarlane, I traveled to Moscow by way of London, where I met with the "Quad," the British, French, and Germans. My subsequent talks in Moscow with Ambassador Grinevsky were promising, I thought, and the top levels of the State Department agreed. Secretary Weinberger disapproved of the whole exercise, and told McFarlane that he thought I had exceeded my instructions. Nonetheless the procedural framework I set in motion in response to Secretary Shultz's initiative, which became known as the "Goodby-Grinevsky compromise," permitted the Stockholm talks to enter the final stage of drafting an agreement.

There were other episodes during Reagan's presidency in which I was not directly involved, but which I studied closely both during my participation in his administration as an ambassadorial appointee and later, after I became a university professor during Reagan's second term. These included the Strategic Defense Initiative and the Reykjavik meeting. Each of these episodes revealed a president who was dead serious about escaping from the nuclear trap, and willing to exercise personal leadership to do so.

To underscore just how dramatic a change this was from the policies of his Democratic predecessor, President Jimmy Carter, I will describe briefly where nuclear weapons policy was as the Carter administration drew to a close. By the end of President Carter's time in office, he had endorsed every major strategic program of his predecessors in the Oval Office, except for the B-1 bomber. He had approved the MX missile, assigned highest priority to production of cruise missiles, improved Minutemen III warheads to the point where they could effectively attack hardened targets, authorized advanced development of a similar capability for the new missiles for Trident submarines, authorized research and development on a new multi-role bomber, and had supported development of command and control systems which could survive a prolonged nuclear war. Following his signing of the SALT II Treaty, he also launched a major program of defense spending to improve all elements of the U.S. armed forces. After the Soviet invasion of Afghanistan, he added still more funds to the defense budget.

Carter's actions completed a revolution in the American concept of strategic nuclear war, which had started with Nixon's NSDM-242 (the "Schlesinger doctrine") and had been carried forward in the guidance on nuclear weapons employment policy developed during the Ford Administration. The strategic revolution completed by Carter was essentially a shift from the concept that strategic nuclear war would consist of massive attacks, which would be enormously destructive but brief, to the concept that a strategic nuclear war might be protracted, could take place incrementally, and might initially involve primarily military targets.

The contrast between Carter and Reagan in their attitudes towards nuclear weapons and the way they interacted with their advisers could not have been more striking. Late in his term, Carter had become weakened politically and seemingly hemmed in by his advisers. He made decisions that he was apparently not comfortable with, probably against his better judgment. Reagan did not change Carter's nuclear doctrine, but he reversed twenty years of merely "capping" the nuclear arms race, and pushed through a new policy that amounted to a return to nuclear disarmament rather than nuclear arms control. He told his advisers what he wanted, sometimes giving them little time to react. Reagan's policies could be seen just as an exercise in public opinion. The question is whether it was more than that, whether Reagan's ultimate goals went beyond the obvious and legitimate short-term political objective of creating conditions in which his nuclear weapons programs could be realized.

I had my own opinion, but on April 12, 1999 I talked with Paul Nitze about his views of Ronald Reagan. He thought that Ronald Reagan and Harry Truman were kindred spirits. In particular, in Nitze's view, what Reagan said, he deeply believed. Furthermore, Ambassador Nitze mentioned that he had advised Reagan even before he became president that Mutual Assured Destruction was a poor idea. He could envisage no circumstances, Nitze had told Ronald Reagan, in which it would be wise to use nuclear weapons, even—and especially—in retaliation. In such a case, Nitze said, nuclear weapons would be used against centers of industry and population. As regards the phrase "a nuclear war cannot be won and must never be fought," a phrase used by

Reagan and Gorbachev, Ambassador Nitze remarked that he had said something similar himself, perhaps even in conversations much earlier with General George C. Marshall, and he thought Reagan had absorbed that idea. Ambassador Nitze's recollections fit perfectly with a passage in Don Oberdorfer's book, *The Turn,* in which former Senator Howard Baker says that Reagan wanted "to make the world safer from nuclear weapons or to abolish nuclear weapons."

Reagan was not the first president who spoke of escaping from the straitjacket of nuclear deterrence. Nor was he the first to suggest changing the ground rules of the nuclear age. Reagan's contribution was to suggest that a defense against attacking nuclear-armed missiles would enable the nuclear powers safely to disarm—eliminate nuclear weapons altogether. The President of the United States announced to the world on March 23, 1983 his vision of the future:

"It is that we embark on a program to counter the awesome Soviet missile threat with measures that are defensive...to give us the means of rendering these nuclear weapons impotent and obsolete."

How the president chose to describe the objective of strategic defenses came to be critical to Reagan's subsequent management of the project, particularly with respect to the decision to deploy defensive systems. The president insisted that his goal was protecting people, not missiles. Even when his own experts argued that the goal should be changed to "strengthen nuclear deterrence through defending U.S. strategic forces," Reagan held firm. He knew that a terminal defense for missile sites could be constructed more rapidly and with greater chance of success than a defense of populations, but he refused to condone a deployment limited to missile sites. Speaking at a briefing on the Strategic Defense Initiative on August 6, 1986, for example, he reiterated that "our research is aimed at finding a way of protecting people, not missiles. And that's my highest priority and will remain so...to deploy systems of limited effectiveness now would divert limited funds and delay our main research." As reported in a *Washington Times* article by Gregory Fossedal on February 6, 1987, after the Reykjavik meeting, Reagan came close to a decision to plan for deployment of kinetic kill vehicles, but on the understanding that this would be an area defense and an integral part of a comprehensive system.

A president who overrules his experts does so at the risk not only of being wrong, but also of being perceived as naïve and irresponsible. Reagan's decisions in the case of the Strategic Defense Initiative show him firmly in charge of policy, and accepting this double risk. Had he consulted his experts thoroughly before the March 23 speech, and followed their advice, there probably would not have been a Reagan proposal on strategic defense. Had he listened to his technical advisers after the decision, he probably would have shifted the objectives of research to defense of missiles instead of defense of people. This would have led to deployment decisions, and to serious consequences for the stability of U.S.-Soviet nuclear relationships.

There was a consistency in Reagan's basic policy statements, even if they flew in the face of conventional wisdom and the laws of physics. He publicly cast doubt on the long-term stability of mutual assured destruction in language worthy of a nuclear abolitionist:

"To look down to an endless future with both of us sitting here with these horrible missiles aimed at each other, and the only thing preventing a holocaust is just so long as no one pulls the trigger, this is unthinkable."

A president so willing to stigmatize nuclear weapons, and to seek alternatives to nuclear deterrence, was completely in character in personally conducting the most remarkable passage in the history of American-Soviet summitry, at a meeting with Mikhail Gorbachev on October 11 and 12, 1986 in Reykjavik, Iceland. Secretary Shultz, Ambassador Paul Nitze, and Don Oberdorfer have all described the Reykjavik meeting in detail in similar terms in their published works. The most startling event of the meeting, one for which the administration was much criticized, was Reagan's proposal to eliminate all ballistic missiles. But this had been foreshadowed in public and private statements by the President; it was not an idea that had sprung out of the intense dialogue between Reagan and Gorbachev.

On July 25, 1986, Reagan sent a letter to Gorbachev in which he proposed the elimination of all ballistic missiles. Both sides would adhere to a modified ABM Treaty for seven and a half years, after which time both sides would be free to deploy SDI. During those seven and a half years, the U.S. and the Soviet Union would negotiate a plan to share benefits of strategic defenses, and for the elimination of all offensive ballistic missiles. President Reagan elaborated on the plan during his address to the U.N. General Assembly on September 22, 1986.

The Reykjavik meeting was roundly criticized for lack of preparation and for its failure to take into account the views of the Joint Chiefs and of U.S. allies, despite the advance warning the President provided. In fact, the Reykjavik meeting stretched the envelope of thinking about arms control. The "Zero Option" for intermediate-range nuclear forces and a nuclear reductions program in START I were realized as treaties, in part, because of the impetus provided by Reagan and Gorbachev at Reykjavik.

2.4. DISARMAMENT – THE ROAD TO CONVERSION

Introductory Remarks

Vlad E. Genin

The "Big Five"... Until now, as many other definitions, covered by "Kremlin Mysteries", only very few people from the top Soviet political echelon knew the real meaning of these puzzling words.

Today, thanks to the memories and thoughts of Ambassador Grinevsky, which he has penned exclusively for this book, many previously unknown chapters in history from the seemingly far-off '70s and '80s have been opened.

One may gain a greater understanding of the "big picture" of the difficult, systematic process of disarmament and the beginning of the demilitarization of the Russian economy.

Oleg A. Grinevsky

From the very beginning of Gorbachev's reforms, conversion and disarmament went together, like twin brothers. These two goals were among the most important priorities of Soviet politics in the area of international security. There was some sort of internal logic in it. The Cold War and the arms race caused immeasurable militarization and increasing military expenses, which were a very heavy burden for the Soviet economy. So these original reasons had to be eliminated.

In May of 1988, Gorbachev described the situation to the innermost circle of his associates as follows:

"16% of the gross national product was spent on militarization every year. Plus 4% for the needs of the Ministry of Internal Affairs (MIA) and the KGB, and you get a total of 20%. The highest military budget in the world. In all other countries it does not exceed 8%. They ravaged the country, kept people starving, destroyed agriculture, but on the other hand we were sitting astride the missiles." [15]

That is why one of the first and the most important goals of Gorbachev's perestroika policy was to create external conditions that would assist in reviving the country's economy, while maintaining a sufficient level of security. In order to do so, the military-political competition within Europe and in the world had to be stopped, and the reduction of the military machine, and the conversion of the defense industry, had to be started.

In his various statements, Gorbachev used different numbers to describe the degree of militarization of the Soviet economy. This slight inconsistency probably reflected the information that was available at that time—in any case, it did not affect the general idea.

The Big Five

The security reforms required the creation of an independent body capable of providing an objective evaluation of external threats and national interests, and of developing a security and disarmament policy. "The Commission of the Politburo of CPSU, observing the negotiations about limitations of strategic arms in Helsinki" became this body.

---

15 Georgiy Shakhnazarov, Price of Freedom (Moscow: Rossika. Zevs, 1993), p. 49.

It was formed in November of 1969, when Soviet leadership had to deal with disarmament seriously for the first time, and existed until the collapse of the Soviet Union. [16]

The activities of this commission were always secretive, and never covered by mass media—which is why it is worth describing in some detail.

Originally, the Commission consisted of six people:

Ustinov, D.F.	Defense Secretary of the Central Committee of CPSU;
Grechko, A.A.	Defense Minister;
Gromyko, A.A.	Minister of Foreign Affairs;
Andropov, U.V.	Chairman of the KGB;
Keldysh, M.S.	Chairman of the Soviet the Academy of Science;
Smirnov, L.V.	Vice Prime Minister, Chairman of the Military-Industrial Commission.

Approximately a year later, M.S. Keldysh was excluded from the Commission, leaving only five members. (Hence the term the "Big Five" appeared in the vocabulary of the bureaucrats.) They prepared reports for the Politburo about the progress of disarmament negotiations and proposals related to the Soviet Union's position.

Of course, the mighty members of the "Five" (three of them soon became members of the Politburo) did not personally develop or write these papers; experts from the Ministry of Foreign Affairs (MFA) and Ministry of Defense wrote all the reports. There was a distribution of

---

16 There was another governmental body in the Soviet Union that dealt with national security issues: the Defense Council, chaired by the General Secretary of the Central Committee of the CPSU. But the Defense Council dealt for the most part with general policy concerning the development of the Soviet Armed Forces.

labor, with specialists from MFA preparing the political aspects of arms limitation and reduction, and Defense Ministry specialists developing the technical details of the Soviet position.

Ustinov and Gromyko supervised this work. They had emphasized a friendly relationship. The two socialized very often; and discussed everything with each other at an early stage. So the experts from their respective ministries had few problems of co-ordination; they followed the example of their ministers, and worked very closely and trustingly with one another.

Of course, sometimes the experts disagreed. But if, let us say, MFA specialists brought these disagreements to Gromyko, they never received his support.

"Defense is the responsibility of the military specialists," he used to say sternly. "So, they know better."

But at the same time, he was always very pleased if, during the expert discussions, his specialists from the MFA proved right about some disputed point. When his subordinates presented him with another "paper", he usually just asked, "Did you confirm it with the military? Does Dmitrii Fedorovich (Ustinov) know?"

Ustinov usually asked his specialists similar questions only about the MFA position. It was sort of a ritual – no dirty tricks. It was unthinkable for Andrei Andreevich (Gromyko) to argue with Dmitrii Fedorovich (Ustinov), or the other way around.

Proposals prepared in such a way by Ministry of Foreign Affairs and Defense Ministry (DM) were sent to the appropriate departments, and then were discussed by the "Big Five." Sometimes there were some corrections, but very insignificant ones, because the joint authority of Ustinov and Gromyko was indisputable. Members of the Commission usually signed what was called a "Note to the Central Committee of the CPSU," and the Politburo approved it without much debate.

Soon the system of preparing the documents by the experts from MFA and DM was enlarged and became official with the formation of the so-called "Small Five," which consisted of specialists from all five Agencies, and which then became part of the Commission. It happened in 1974 immediately after the summit of General Secretary Brezhnev and President Ford in Vladivostok. There was an urgent need to prepare a report about the summit. The Deputy Chief of the General Staff was, by general consent, the leader of the "Small Five." Originally it was General M.M. Kozlov and later Marshal S.F. Akhromeev. [17]

During its long life, the Commission of the Politburo, the "Big Five" as it was called now, had its ups and downs.

After Ustinov was appointed Defense Minister, the new Defense Secretary of the Central Committee (CC) of the CPSU, Y.P. Riabov was not inducted into the "Big Five," so the Commission became the "Big Four" – Ustinov, Andropov, Gromyko and Smirnov – even though it was still called the "Big Five." The administrative staff of the CC was also cut.

It is difficult to say what caused it; the best guess is that Ustinov would not tolerate competition. The "Big Five" met less frequently from then on. All the issues were discussed and decided among Ustinov, Andropov and Gromyko—in fact, we had the "Big Three."

* * *

---

17 Later the position of the leader of the "Small Five" was held by the first deputies of the Chief of the General Staff, namely V.I. Varennikov, V.N. Lobov, and B.A. Omelichev.

Everything changed after Gorbachev came to power. The "Big Five" began a new life.

First of all, he removed his competitor, G.V. Romanov, from the position of Defense Secretary of the Central Committee of the CPSU. The General Secretary liked the new Secretary of the Leningrad Regional Committee of the CPSU, Lev Nikolaevich Zaikov, who for a long time had been the head of the Leninets industrial complex, which repored to the Ministry of Radio Industry, and hence knew the problems of the Defense Industry very well.

Gorbachev offered him the positions of Defense Secretary of the Central Committee (replacing Romanov) and head of the "Big Five". Some time later, the new Head of the International Department of the Central Committee, A.F. Dobrynin, was included into the "Big Five."

By the middle of 1987, the members of the "Big Five" were:

Zaikov, L.N.	Defense Secretary of the CC;
Yazov, D.T.	Minister of Defense;
Shevardnadze, E.A.	Minister of Foreign Affairs;
Chebrikov, V.M.	Chairman of KGB;
Maslukov, U.D.	Chairman of the Military-Industrial Commission;
Dobrynin, A.F.	Head of the International Department of the CC.

In addition, the Secretary of the CC, A.N. Yakovlev, was present at all the Commission meetings, though officially he was not a member, so the "Big Five" became "Seven." And many specialists from the defense industry and research institutions were present at these meetings.

Complicated battles could be observed in its meetings, especially in the hallways. The MFA— to be more exact Shevardnadze—held the most radical position; he urged the clearing of the road for a considerable reduction of weapons. His opponents were the Defense Ministry and its two main representatives, Defense Minister D.T. Yazov and the Chief of the General Staff S.F. Akhromeev. During the meetings of the "Five," they always sat together, although Yazov usually kept silent.

Soon Maslukov started openly supporting the Defense Ministry, while Chebrikov and Dobrynin kept silent neutrality, though it was obvious that most of the time they tacitly quietly supported the military. This partiality was especially noted at the meetings of the "Small Five," where their representatives, B.S. Ivanov and G.M. Kornienko, openly expressed their solidarity with the military position.

Zaikov artistically performed the role of a balancer, trying to develop a unified position. In the process of doing so, it was necessary to get sign-offs from as many as seven departments.[18]

However, there was an alternative way of reaching executive decisions in the Soviet Union. The General Secretary of the CC of the CPSU, later the President of the U.S.S.R., M.S. Gorbachev was above all kinds of "Fives". He could interfere with the process of position development, and force a decision, when the "Five" would "skid" over an issue. And finally, he could simply announce a "political decision," and require the preparation of "concrete results" in time for his next meeting with a foreign leader.

Frequently, Gorbachev would come to an understanding with the leaders of foreign states that they would prepare an agreement prior to the date of a summit. That is exactly what happened with the Intermediate Range Nuclear Forces (INF) Treaty of 1987 and the

---

18 Our American colleagues sometimes complained that it was more difficult for them; they had to obtain thirteen signatures.

Conventional Forces in Europe (CFE) Treaty of 1990. In such cases, the delegations at the negotiations would usually receive instructions to handle any of the remaining issues as quickly as possible.

That is why the leaders of the Soviet governmental agencies tried so diligently to understand what Gorbachev wanted from them. He still possessed the supreme power that he had inherited from his predecessors, the General Secretaries of the Central Committee of the Communist Party of the Soviet Union. The bureaucrats were, therefore, always looking for the opportunity to meet him in order to obtain his support, which alone would enable them to act without fear of reversal.

Shevardnadze and Zaikov were the ablest at aligning themselves with Gorbachev; at the "Five" meetings they acted as a tandem, significantly referring to the opinion of the *"Gensec"* (General Secretary). The way it was staged in 1986 – 1988 is described by Zaikov as follows: "Usually Shevardnadze and I met before the Commission meeting and discussed all the issues with each other, making all the preliminary decisions. Later, during the meeting, he usually kept silent. The ambassador/negotiators, Vorontsov and Karpov, spoke on behalf of the Ministry of Foreign Affairs. We did not have any problems with them.

"We had serious problems with the military. Defense Minister, Sokolov was a nice person, but very stubborn and inflexible. He did not want any compromises that could somehow hurt the military forces. We had to get rid of him. Yazov was appointed Defense Minister. He was much easier to deal with. We could deal with Akhromeev also. He sometimes would make a lot of noise, but continue to search for the right decision." [19]

Thus, the Defense Ministry was forced to make concessions on the disarmament agreements. The tactics used by Zaikov were working, and the meetings of the "Five" went smoothly, with no arguments.

How Did It Work?

One of the first tasks of the renewed "Five" was to develop a new Soviet program for disarmament. This is how it was accomplished.

At the end of 1985, Gorbachev started to invite Soviet Ambassadors from the disarmament negotiations in Geneva, Stockholm, and Vienna, one after another, to visit him in the Kremlin, and asked each of them essentially the same question: "There is only you and me in my office. Nobody can hear us. Tell me the truth – What is happening in your negotiations? Is it possible to come to an agreement and what do we have to do to achieve it? I repeat, I need only the truth."

Each negotiator answered this question from the General Secretary as honestly as he could. Each had his own understanding of how honest he could be with such a person. A few days later, on January 30, 1986, Gorbachev invited all the negotiators [20], this time all together, and said: "And now tell the other members of the Politburo what you told me. We need a concrete, realistic Soviet disarmament program, one without any hype, which can lead us to the suspension of the arms race."

Later, there was another discussion where the concrete steps of disarmament were named and approved, including the following: confidence- and security-building measures in Europe, substantial

---

19 From the personal conversation of the author with L.N. Zaikov in Stockholm on September 1, 1995.

20 They were ambassadors V. P. Karpov, U. A. Kvitsinskii, V. Mikhailov, V. L. Israelyan, and the author.

reduction of the armed forces and arms stationed there, elimination of intermediate-range missiles, reduction of strategic nuclear arms by 50%, cessation of nuclear weapons tests, and banning of chemical weapons. These proposals were to be included in the Statement of the General Secretary that was to be published before the Congress of the CPSU as a part of the International Program of the Communist Party.

Gorbachev defined the task as follows:

"If we can hold the arms race back, imagine what kind of prospect will open for us! Now 40% of our industry is working for defense needs. If we can direct these resources to meet civilian needs, the shelves in our stores will break under the heavy burden of goods. It is high time for making responsible decisions.

"This year is the year of peace. We should prove that we can keep our word and promises. We need to work out all the details of this program, not just for propaganda, but for real situations and real politics. My Statement should be strong. We need to present a wide view of the external political problems and issues that are being discussed at the International Forums."

I wrote then in my diary: "The impression I've drawn from my conversation with Gorbachev is very favorable. Talking to Brezhnev, Chernenko or even Andropov, I felt as if I was dealing with an extraterrestrial. They did not understand you. Here is finally a normal, real man. He gains people's favor with his sincerity. He is friendly and cordial, but you can feel his energy and strength behind it. He likes to talk and to be listened to."

Events unfolded very quickly after that. On January 2, 1986, immediately after the New Year's celebration, the Politburo approved a Note to the Central Committee, presented by Gorbachev.

In the Ministry of Foreign Affairs on Smolenskaya Street and not far from there in the Defense Ministry on Frunze Street, experts were slaving away to polish the General Secretary's Statement. Experts of both Ministries were shuttling back and forth along Arbat Street, trying to sniff out what their "partners" were preparing. Some witty people began calling Arbat Street the "Georgian-Military Road"[21]. On January 6, 1996, the "Small Five" gathered in the office of Army General Varennikov. Both Ministries presented their proposals, and a long and fruitless discussion begun. Everybody left disappointed.

The next day the "Small Five" suggested continuation of the same discussion, but without any ray of hope. Suddenly, at twilight, Varennikov distributed the text of a three-stage program of nuclear weapons elimination within fifteen years—in other words, by the end of 2000.

Representatives of the MFA were against it. They tried to prove that this program would send us back to the epoch of Khruschev's propaganda campaigns about general and complete disarmament. They were convinced that this program was absolutely unrealistic and unacceptable for the West. Since the Soviet Union still had an overwhelming advantage in terms of conventional armed forces, all negotiations about the elimination of nuclear weapons would look like propaganda aimed at fools.

Besides that, this program would cancel those fragile preliminary agreements on the reduction of Strategic Offensive Arms, which had been achieved by Reagan and Gorbachev in Geneva. It basically made the current negotiations over disarmament in Geneva, Stockholm, and

21 A road of the same name exists in the former Soviet republic of Georgia. This is an allusion to the nationality of Shevardnadze, who is Georgian.

Vienna unnecessary. In short, it contravened the tasks given to us by the Politburo.

The Chief of the General Staff walked impetuously into the office in the middle of the discussion.

"We have been working for the whole year," – he started without preamble – "This work was conducted under conditions of the top secrecy. Employees of General Staff who worked in the delegations knew nothing of it. Even the Defense Minister was ignorant of it!"

It was an obvious tall tale. Representatives of the MFA exchanged glances with each other and smiled. Ambassador Kvintsinskii started to laugh demonically and very loudly. But Akhromeev did not even blink, just pursed his thin lips harder for a moment.

"Now everything is ready. Today, General Chervov flew south and presented this program to the General Secretary. He approved it. So the problem is solved."

"We all worked hard to provide security for the Soviet Union. That is why I am speaking here openly and directly. We worked out the issue of reduction of the Intermediate Range Missiles. I have tons of related papers in my office. We cannot accept reduction without taking into consideration the nuclear arsenals of Great Britain and France. To do so would be equivalent to unilateral disarmament. We cannot allow history to repeat itself, when in the '50s we were forced to reduce our Army to 1.2 million people. We still feel the consequences of this reduction, especially in aviation and artillery.

"Understand this: such a reduction blows up, really blows up, our security. If you continue to insist, we will start a fight at the very top. Well, not a fight, but a very serious conflict, a real debate.

"We know that everybody here would do anything to strengthen the Soviet Union's security. But sometimes, some comrades pursue parochial departmental interests. We should not tolerate it. Look, what's happening? We agree to compromise under the terms of certain reservations. And half a year from now, they will suggest writing these reservations off. I warn you, let's work honestly. If we agreed to something – stick to it."

The Marshal left the office as impetuously as he walked in. The negotiators went to the lobby for a smoke break, bitterly laughing at themselves. How artistically Akhromeev twisted everybody around his little finger, in the best traditions of Tsarist palace intrigue! An unbelievable scenario – the Defense Ministry worked for the whole year under conditions of the top secrecy, developing a program of nuclear arms elimination – as if it were a new super-secret missile.

And Mikhail Sergeevich (Gorbachev) agreed with us, and he agreed with the military also! What a man! We did not know at that time that it was his style in general.

What could we do? During that smoke break in the lobby, we developed the following plan of actions. The three-staged program of nuclear weapons elimination, we probably would have to accept – no other options - after Gorbachev approved it. But we needed to make its first stage as realistic as possible. We needed to include in the program all our proposals about the elimination of Soviet and American intermediate range missiles in Europe, reduction of strategic offensive weapons by 50%, cessation of nuclear weapons tests, etc. We also needed to present it so the proposals were not tied up with the whole program, so that they could be conducted independently and without Western approval of the second and the third stage.

The MFA started to promote this plan at the meetings of "Five," though with a lot of difficulties. It was especially difficult to save the newly developed position on the negotiations in Vienna and Stockholm. The military did not want even to hear about it. They believed we no longer needed these new instructions for negotiations, because now we had this "brilliant" program for the total elimination of nuclear weapons.

On January 8 and 9, the "Small Five" was in session early in the morning. The Deputy Minister, Kornienko, was the head of the MFA group now. He firmly supported Akhromeev's three-staged plan for nuclear weapons elimination.

It was also endorsed by representatives of the KGB and the military-industrial complex. This program became the basis for the Statement of the General Secretary. So, it gradually lost all the new and innovative aspects that were earlier suggested to Gorbachev. The elimination of the Intermediate Range Missiles was now tightly connected to the renunciation of the Strategic Defense Initiative and the reduction of strategic weapons.

Gorbachev's Proposals

On January 10, the "Big Five" was gathered in Zaikov's office on the fifth floor of the Central Committee Building on Old Square. They were Shevardnadze (MFA), Chebrikov (KGB) and Maslukov (MIC). The Defense Minister, Sokolov, was absent. We were told that he had left for a Communist Party meeting in some military unit far from Moscow. Akhromeev was there to fill in for him.

It was Akhromeev who presented to the "Big Five" the three-stage plan for nuclear weapon elimination that was developed by the "Small Five." Then, speaking of the negotiations, he admitted that we could not develop solutions for all the problems. The discussion started. Believe it or not, the hottest discussion was about the conference in Stockholm. I would like to offer you the part of the discussion devoted to the Stockholm conference. The following are my notes. They might be of some interest, because they show how the "Big Five" operated; usually nobody took minutes during its meetings.

Zaikov: I see there are some propositions that could make our position in Stockholm more dynamic, and could improve its propagandist aspect. But I do not see whether these proposals could lead us to the agreement. What is the matter?

Akhromeev: The issue is the Notification about the Air Force and Navy maneuvers. This is an issue of vital importance to our security. (Later, for some reason, he spoke of the Air Force only). NATO is conducting a large-scale maneuver in Europe with the participation of several hundred military airplanes. We must know about it. It is a direct threat to our security.

Zaikov: But we know about all their troop movements, including the Air Force activity. What can these notifications give us, if we already know the situation? How can it improve our security?

Akhromeev: The principle of reciprocity should be observed at the negotiations. We compromise – they compromise. There should not be any unilateral concessions. We announced that we are ready to inform them about our military maneuvers from the European part of Russia all the way to the Ural Mountains. And they do not want to inform us about their Navy maneuvers in the Atlantic Ocean.

Grinevsky: The following trade deal could be beneficial for us: the West agrees to confidence-building measures concerning the Air Force activity that bothers Sergey Fedorovich (Akhromeev) so much. We, temporarily, for this stage only, take the question of notification about independent maneuvers of the Navy off the agenda. But we should go beyond that, and suggest postponing this question to the next stage of the negotiations. We do not give up our positions here. Just the solution of the question about the independent Navy maneuvers is postponed.

Zaikov: (to Akhromeev) So what do you think about this suggestion?

Akhromeev: It is difficult to judge when it is just verbal information.

Grinevsky: Here is the text of this proposal. Please have a look.

Shevardnadze: (wheezing from a cold) Why was this issue not worked out?

Grinevsky: We reported this issue to the “Five” twice.

Shevardnadze: Why was this issue not worked out?

Akhromeev: (to General Starodubov) It was never reported to me. Why did nobody report it to me?

Starodubov: We discussed this issue and decided that it would not work. We would have to give up our position without any reason. Why should we make all the concessions?

Zaikov: So why won’t this proposal work?

Akhromeev: I think that it will be better to postpone the question about the Navy maneuvers to the second stage of the

Conference. For now, we should take care of the ground and the air, and leave the ocean to the second stage.

Grinevsky: There is another solution, though not as graceful as the first one. The Soviet Union should control at least some part of the Navy maneuvers.

Zaikov: Well, work out this issue in more detail. A solution probably can be found along these lines.

Later Karpov and Kvitsinskii tried to prove the necessity of eliminating intermediate range missiles first. Israelyan reported the difficulties over the banning of chemical weapons. He was questioned by Chebrikov for a long time.

Mikhailov tried to convince everybody that it was beneficial for us from a political point of view to move the negotiations in Vienna forward. The main problem here was providing undoubtedly false data about the number of our troops in Central Europe. The military, of course, argued, but Zaikov calmly concluded: "We decided to discuss all these difficulties later – behind closed doors." After this, the members of the "Big Five" and Akhromeev secluded themselves in Zaikov's office. What happened there is not known for sure, but because of the known results, we can guess. The three-stage program for the elimination of nuclear weapons by 2000 was adopted. More hype was born. Originally, it seemed that Gorbachev was not going to use it.

But after some arm-twisting, the "stubborn Marshal" agreed to eliminate all Soviet and American intermediate range missiles in Europe, although only as the first stage of implementing the three-stage program implementation. A compromise formula was developed for the Stockholm Conference: "If NATO agrees to notification of any large-scale Air Force maneuvers, the U.S.S.R. agrees to postpone to the second stage of the conference consideration of notification of large-scale Navy maneuvers in the seas adjacent to Europe."

This formula was approved by the Politburo, and later became the basis for all the agreements that were achieved in Stockholm.

On January 10 and 11, the State agencies still argued. On Saturday, January 10, the "Big Five" gathered again. Maslukov (Military-Industrial Commission) tried to undermine our position about verification of chemical weapons, but did not succeed. Intermediate-range missiles were discussed again – resistance from the military was finally broken. On Sunday, the confirmed text of the statement was sent to Pitsunda, where Gorbachev was vacationing. The next day he read and approved it.

Through all this pain, and finally, the famous Gorbachev Statement of January 15, 1986 was born.

* * *

Before my departure to Stockholm, Shevardnadze called me in and asked: "What do you think about the results achieved at the "Five" meetings? Can these results help you as a negotiator in Stockholm?"

"Of course, without Gorbachev's Statements," I responded, "we could never have achieved any change in our position about the Navy. I understand this very well. But honestly speaking, I, as a negotiator, did not gain anything from it. The Statement is public knowledge and the postponement of the issue to the second stage of the negotiations is declared. So what? The Americans listened to it and silently put all our concessions in their pockets. In Stockholm they will tell me: we already have that, what's next? All we will be able to do is to accuse them that we do not have reciprocity.

"On the other hand, if our delegation in Stockholm had been trusted to make this decision, we would never have agreed to postpone the Navy issue without their agreement to cover the Air Force activity with the confidence-building measures (CBM). That would be real diplomatic negotiations."

Shevardnadze laughed: "These are your negotiating skills talking, a merchant of diplomacy. We need a much broader political approach for Mikhail Sergeevich. The Soviet Union needs a new image in the world; we cannot afford to be cheap or narrow-minded. I am worried about a different issue – our relationship with the military. You are in constant contact with them. Tell me, were we able to overcome their resistance? What we are doing right now is just the beginning. We will have to do some serious clearing of all the obstacles that we inherited from our past, in order to start building normal civilized relations with the West."

I replied honestly that our relations with the military were not normal. Those relations were founded on the idea that we need only force them, not convince them. On the expert level, our connections were quite good, but not on higher levels. There used to be an effective channel of communication – with the two First Deputies, Akhromeev and Kornienko, but it did not work any more. Defense Minister Sokolov [22] had completely abandoned the idea of negotiating a solution to our internal political problems; he did not even attend the "Five" meetings any more. Akhromeev ruled the Defense Ministry. The Ministry of

22 The Minister took even more rigid positions than Marshal Akhromeev, and very often he accused the Marshal of agreeing to "unacceptable compromises".

Foreign Affairs had no direct contact with him. What was happening was that experts of the Ministries were having meetings, but at times they could not come to any agreement. Then the highest authorities–Gorbachev and Zaikov—would have to intervene to break the military officials' resistance. The middle level was not working at all. For example, the issue of Navy maneuvers— Akhromeev is an intelligent man with a quick mind, so when at the "Five" meeting everything was explained in detail to him, he agreed. Why couldn't we have such preliminary discussions regularly before the "Five" meeting? Previously, Gromyko had constantly had meetings with Ustinov and Andropov. They discussed all the problems and came to agreement amongst themselves, and then gave instructions to their deputies; based on these instructions, the negotiators prepared our positions…

While I was saying all this, the Minister's face changed from friendly to stone-cold. He interrupted me:

"There will be no return to the previous practice," he said abruptly, and his strong Georgian accent, which he could never get rid of, added a special meaning to his words. "We are not a temporary government. We took power into our own hands, and we will hold it until at least the end of the current millennium."

* * *

Gorbachev's Statement received a unanimous evaluation: propaganda.

Though they noted the new approach to intermediate range missiles and control issues, *Time* magazine wrote: "Gorbachev's plan is a tantalizing mixture of old and new, ambiguity and detail, apparent concessions and repeated demands." [23]

The first reaction of Paul Nitze, who dealt with Soviet issues from the time of the Truman presidency, was very interesting: "I would like to know who in the Soviet Union created this masterpiece?"

Max Kampelman, the main U.S. negotiator in Geneva, said that Washington had serious doubts about the sincerity of Gorbachev's Statement.

But there was one person who accepted Gorbachev's plan to eliminate nuclear weapons right away. It was President Reagan. When Shultz presented Gorbachev's message, the President exclaimed: "Why wait till the end of the century for a world without nuclear weapons?"[24]

The next day he publicly stated at the press conference: "We are very grateful for the offer… It's just about the first time that anyone has ever proposed actually eliminating nuclear weapons."[25]

Journalists left laughing and wondering. Beginning in 1945, Stalin, Baruch, Vyshinskii and Khrushchev had suggested the elimination of nuclear weapons many times. Reagan was known for not paying much attention to little details.

The most interesting fact was that in Washington, everything was seen just the reverse of the way it looked to Moscow. The Joint Chiefs of Staff, the CIA, disarmament specialists, and Sovietologists – all of them were against the elimination of nuclear weapons.

They believed that for the previous 40 years, nuclear weapons had served as a guarantor against global war. Without them, catastrophe

---

23 *Time*, January 27, 1986, p.9.

24 George P. Shultz, Turmoil and Triumph: My Years as Secretary of State (New York: Charles Scribner's Sons, 1993), p.700.

25 *Time*, January 27, 1986, p.9.

would occur; NATO would fall apart, the Soviet Union would exploit its great advantage in conventional arms, and all Europe and Asia would fall into the sphere of Soviet influence.

State Secretary Shultz, as he stated in his memoirs, shared these concerns, and considered a world without nuclear weapons a utopia. But he understood that he could not oppose this idea directly; first, because the President was for it, but also because he believed that Gorbachev's proposals included some measures that could be advantageous for the U.S. That is why Shultz decided to take a Soviet mold, and pour American contents into it.

"Don't worry," he said to one of his main antagonists, Richard Perle, from the Department of Defense. "We can say 'fine' to their three-stage approach, and then front-end load our program in the first stage. Gorbachev's language makes the INF 'zero option' operational; all else is transition to it."

"From that moment," wrote Shultz, "I started to realize that the 'zero option' for the INF talks about intermediate range missiles should be the centerpiece of our next arms control effort.". On January 24, he told Reagan that he would like to set up a special group to work on the U.S.'s broad approach to arms control, and enhance the country's ability to initiate policies and react to those of the Soviets in this new stage. He warned Reagan that most American politicians were against the complete elimination of nuclear weapons. The President was surprised: "If any nation is likely to conduct a first strike, it is the Soviet Union. Why isn't this a problem we want to get rid of?"[26]

---

26 George P. Shultz, Turmoil and Triumph: My Years as Secretary of State (New York: Charles Scribner's Sons, 1993), pp. 701-703.

Nevertheless, Secretary of Defense Casper Weinberger and many other influential persons in Washington were against such an agreement with the Soviet Union, even regarding the "zero option" about intermediate range missiles, which had been suggested by their own President.

Reagan's response to Gorbachev's Statement was developed under such contentious circumstances. Two completely different proposals were prepared. One was developed by the group led by Rosalynn Ridgeway from the State Department, and another by the White House staff.

As a result, on February 23, Gorbachev received a text, written in the President's own handwriting, which discussed in very general terms the necessity of banning nuclear weapons, with main emphasis on the elimination of the intermediate range missiles.

Pause

After Gorbachev's Statement was published there was a long pause. Supporters of a world without nuclear weapons loudly greeted it, but there was no progress at the negotiations. No such progress could occur, because no U.S. leaders, with the exception of Reagan himself, considered the elimination of nuclear weapons a serious possibility, and in the Soviet proposals, realistic arms reduction measures were coupled inextricably with this unrealistic goal.

It was necessary to untie this knot, but the people in Moscow were nervous; they did not understand what was happening. The degree of irritation and resentment was increasing.

At the very beginning of January 1986, Gorbachev counted on a direct dialogue with the Americans. But what happened? He had opened his heart to them, given them his hand, made multiple concessions, and from Washington – nothing; just cold silence. In addition, the U.S. mass media, as usual, claimed noisily that all the proposals were nothing but the usual Soviet propaganda. Being very angry, the U.S. mass media was looking for a way to respond and to hurt at the same time—and the way was found very quickly.

Secretary of State Shultz suggested conducting the next summit in the American capital in June; President Reagan asked that it be held in Geneva. The Soviet response was simple and seemed that it could be effective: we will not agree to this meeting unless the U.S. comes forward with its concessions.

Shultz immediately answered: "This is not a constructive approach", he told Ambassador Dobrynin. "If the Soviet Union is not ready now for this summit, then it cannot be conducted until 1987."

During February and March, there was a tug-of-war between the White House and Kremlin. On March 15, Soviet Prime Minister N.I. Ryzhkov met Shultz at the funeral ceremony of Olaf Palme in Stockholm. He was instructed by Gorbachev to tell Shultz the following: "Honestly speaking, we do not understand what is happening. We were hoping to actively develop cooperation in all areas, first of all in the area of security. There are two prospective topics for our dialogue: cessation of nuclear weapon tests, and eliminating intermediate-range missiles. Unfortunately, nothing is happening. You suggested conducting a summit this summer, but you did not say anything about its content. I am telling you quite honestly – we do not understand what are you trying to achieve."

Shultz answered in a very cold manner: "There is another side to the coin. We also do not understand what is happening."

So misunderstanding was growing. On April 24, 1986 at the Politburo meeting, Gorbachev's anger came down on the MFA and the Defense Ministry: "It is clear now that there is a gap between our political declarations and our positions at negotiations. How did this happen? That is the question. Once a political decision is made, we should act on it – immediately take innovative initiatives—but our positions instead are tied up with old approaches. Where is the splintering of our political decision happening, and why? There is inertia in the MFA and Defense Ministry. If we make a political decision, it should be the rule for everybody. I want the leaders of the Ministries to solve this problem. The one who violates the Politburo decision should be punished. We will not be able to work as a team with such comrades.

"We cannot allow the world to believe that our political decisions are bluffs. Here is a draft of instructions, which are to be approved by us (Gorbachev lifted up a thick pile of papers from the table). When I look at these positions, I see dead ends, which we created with our own hands. We cannot explain it to our partners at negotiations, our friends, or even to our own society. You can see for yourself, we no longer have any valid point to make, but still we resist. Western propaganda profits by it; they say, the Russians bargain and bargain, and at the end give up anyway. So comrades, come to your own conclusions."

Gorbachev ceased talking and looked searchingly at his audience, which had grown quiet all of a sudden. His eyes flashed angrily.

"Any objections? Remarks? Thoughts? Does it mean that everybody agrees? If anybody has any doubt – you should express it. Otherwise, it seems that we all agreed, and afterwards people start whispering in the corners, discussing that this was wrong and that was wrong. These times have passed: we should conduct our business honestly and openly!"

Gradually, though slowly, understanding came: threats will not help. We should replace loud slogans with real business, pay attention to details, and change our positions. Although our souls are nagged by doubts: can we trust the West? What are the goals of the West? Is it possible that the essence of American politics has not changed, and people in Washington are just pretending that they would like to seek agreements with Moscow?

Shevardnadze complained bitterly to his nearest associates: "The situation is critical. We came forward with very serious propositions about the reduction of nuclear as well as conventional arms. But the West did not respond. At the negotiations in Geneva there is nothing but dead ends – about nuclear tests, intermediate-range missiles, and intercontinental missiles. Why? What, don't they trust us? Are they trying to corner us? Instead of meeting us halfway, Washington is playing spy games, deporting our diplomats from New York, sending their warships to Soviet territorial waters. Recently, they struck Libya as a demonstration of their power.

"It is more and more difficult for Mikhail Sergeevich to conduct his strategy. Military officials openly grumble that we are giving up our positions. If this continues, we will have only one option – to close the "iron curtain" again and resume confrontation, as when Andropov was in power. But that will put an end to all our plans for reforming the country."

That is why in 1986, at the beginning of summer, Moscow decided to test the Americans, to see if they were ready to come to an agreement, and what kind of negotiating opportunities we had. The place for this test was chosen to be the Stockholm Conference on European security. We had come closer to an agreement at this Conference then anywhere else, since confidence-building measures are not very tightly connected with the security issues— not like, let's say, the reduction of nuclear weapons. That is why the decision was made to start with Stockholm.

On June 21, Shevardnadze was trying passionately to convince everybody at the "Five" meeting: "Please understand, nobody will believe in our large-scale initiatives about the elimination of nuclear weapons and deep reduction of conventional weapons, if we are not able to solve relatively simple and modest problems at the Stockholm Conference, like difficulties in elaboration of confidence building measures. Now the world cannot wait to see how we are going to conduct our politics in Europe. That is why the Stockholm Conference is attracting so much attention. Success or failure there will be seen as a test of our ability to succeed in the main effort – the revival of détente, and the improvement of the international climate."

Breakthrough

The first important step was not taken until August of 1986, when, after strenuous debates, the Politburo agreed to ground and air inspections within the territory of the Soviet Union.

On August 7, the Ministry of Foreign Affairs reported at the Politburo meeting that there was a chance for a breakthrough in Stockholm. It was quite possible to achieve a dramatic turn in European and international relations, although the problem of on-site inspections was a stumbling block there. Until that day, the Soviet Union refused to permit such inspections. In the eyes of the Soviet Union, these inspections were tantamount to spying. Obviously, inspections would lead to the disclosure of the location and combat readiness of Soviet troops in Europe. But of the same information about American and NATO troops would be revealed, too, and to the same degree.

"Who benefits most from this, from the point of view of security? Openness is obviously a disadvantage for the side that is preparing a surprise attack. Inspections can reveal these plans and frustrate them. The Soviet Union, at the highest level of power stated many times that it will never strike first, neither with nuclear nor with conventional weapons. The best proof of this policy would be our readiness for inspections and we should be interested in them, first of all because the United States and NATO are not ready to commit to a policy of no first use.

"In short, conducting such inspections is in the best security interests of the Soviet Union, which needs stability and peace in Europe, as the most important precondition for implementing our internal reforms and reconstruction. Inspections will lead to greater openness in military activities, and consequently, eliminate the risk of war as a result of a mistake, miscalculation, or misunderstanding of the opposite side's actions. These consequences will allow us to reduce military expenses and decrease our Armed Forces; of course, a reciprocal approach is expected. This way, we can release additional funds for the economical renewal of the country."

Here Marshal Akhromeev exploded: "It is impossible to sit and listen quietly when such things are being said and here of all places – at a meeting of the Politburo! You are trying to convince us that to reveal our combat readiness to our enemies is in the best interest of our Motherland!

This is not just a misunderstanding of elementary principles. This is a conscious plan to harm the country's security! This is betrayal! If we look at it from the political point of view, we cannot call it anything else. How can we tell the Soviet people…"

But Gorbachev interrupted him decisively at that moment: "Stop, stop, Sergei Fedorovich. When you talked about security and combat readiness, we listened to you very attentively. These are your spheres of business. But giving political evaluations, making political decisions, and explaining them to the Soviet people are our prerogatives. I believe that the comrades who presented the Note to the Central Committee of the CPSU defined everything correctly – the conducting of a limited number of inspections will not harm our security."

The Politburo went along with Gorbachev, though without any visible enthusiasm. But this was not the end. Gorbachev sent the Marshal to Stockholm, and instructed him to agree on behalf of the Soviet Union to the conducting of the inspections on the ground and in the air. Let the whole world see that new political thinking has reached even Soviet military officials.

Akhromeev had no choice. With an aching heart, he arrived at Stockholm and spoke at the Conference. His speech caused furor in the world mass media, though journalists could guess the real reason for his visit. The Swedish journal *Dagens Nyheter* wrote, for example, that Moscow sent the Marshal in order to demonstrate the support of Gorbachev's politics by the Soviet Military Forces. The very fact of his arrival in Stockholm was the proof that "there is no disagreement between the Soviet diplomats and the military forces." [27]

---

27 Dagens Nyheter, August 30, 1986.

The final bargaining started at that time at the Stockholm Conference. The bargaining was most difficult and passionate, like that at a Middle Eastern bazaar. Hundreds of technical details had to be discussed and approved, including parameters of notifications and limitations of military activity, methods of conducting inspections, and so on. Another serious problem was limited time. The Conference had to be finished on September19, and not an hour later under any circumstances. That was its most severe mandate.

As of the evening of September 19th, the negotiators were still digging through the details. It was clear to everybody that the agreement would be achieved, but the negotiators just needed more time.

The chairman of the Conference on that lucky day was the resourceful Portuguese man Jose Cuatilero, who suggested that we stop … the clock. Everybody kept silent – it was a sign of agreement. The chairman banged the gavel, and service men turned the clocks off. The clock hands froze at 10:56 p.m.

So time was stopped, but not the work. September 20, 21, and 22 passed in the outside world, but at the Conference it was still September 19. During these days and nights, the agreement was developed in full detail.

Finally, at the last plenary session—it was September 22 outside the Conference—Swedish Ambassador Kurt Lidgard, on behalf of three groups of states,[28] presented the final Document of Stockholm Conference. The chairman asked if there were any remarks, he looked at the audience searchingly. Dead silence was the response. He banged the gavel. Document approved…

28 The Warsaw Pact, Western states, and the non-aligned states.

Two days later, the leader of the Russian delegation visited Gorbachev in his office in the Kremlin.

"Well done!" Gorbachev said, shaking his hand. "You keep your word. The agreement in Stockholm is a breakthrough in the sphere of disarmament, confidence building, and improving the international climate. Let's consider that the first step has been made!"

So the first step was made, the step that initiated a whole series of agreements, which in turn led to the end of the Cold War.

The Insight

The euphoria caused by the signing of the agreement in Stockholm soon vanished. There were practically no changes at the other negotiating forums. The main obstacle at these negotiations was the linking of the specific measures being discussed there with the total banning of nuclear weapons.

The insight came in Reykjavik in the late autumn of 1986. Reagan's agreement on the necessity of eliminating nuclear weapons did not, in itself, change anything—they did not come to any specific agreement there. However, Gorbachev understood that he should untie the knot that he had tied in his Statement on January 15.. He understood that we should start not with the banning of nuclear weapons, but with specific measures leading to it. That was the essence of the summit in the Icelandic capital.

In Washington, on the December 8, 1986, Reagan and Gorbachev signed an agreement stipulating the elimination of 1,846 Soviet and 846 American missiles. This was approximately 4% of the world's missiles.

The real meaning of this agreement went far beyond this: the danger of military conflict in Europe, with the possible use of nuclear weapons, was considerably reduced. The military-strategic atmosphere improved also, especially for the Soviet Union, because it stopped the plan to deploy American Pershings in Europe. This would have created the threat of a sudden strike on Soviet territory, because the Pershing's flight time would be between two and twelve minutes. Besides, the Soviet Union budget savings were about 300 billion rubles.

* * *

On his return from America, Gorbachev called in Shevardnadze and the negotiators dealing with European issues. The General Secretary was definitely in a good mood: he had a twinkle in his eyes, he was smiling very cheerfully, and had barely finished his greetings when he started his solo.

"The signing of the INF Treaty is a breakthrough in our relationships with America, the beginning of understanding reality. Confrontation has definitely lessened. It turned out that disarmament has become the locomotive of our external policy of perestroika. They have started to believe us, and we should not lessen the pressure of our peace initiatives.

"The most serious attention should be paid to Europe. Our interests coincide in a lot of cases, and we should not be afraid of the increasing role of England, France, and even Germany in the world. The key to the change of our relationships is again disarmament. We need to minimize the military threat on the continent."

He was getting more and more excited. "We have more tanks than the rest of the world! And we are counting only the ones that are in service. How many do we have in the armories? Did nobody count, or are they just keeping quiet...? It's the same scenario with infantry fighting vehicles, armored personnel carriers, and artillery. Do we need that much? Do we still plan to put our troops on the shore of the English Channel? I was told that our military still have such plans.

"They say that the United States and NATO have more airplanes. If that's the case, let them eliminate more. And if we have more troops and tanks, we should eliminate the excessive force. But we should negotiate and coordinate this activity. If we need to set an example, well, we are ready to start the process unilaterally.

"We need to work on all these issues very seriously. It has been half a year since I gave the order to find solutions on how to eliminate the imbalance of arms and troops in Europe. But nothing happened; we are still at the same point where we started. Neither the negotiators, nor our military officials did anything. What should we do? Should we use strong organizational measures again?"

Here Gorbachev stopped and looked at the quiet negotiators.

"But elimination of the imbalance is only the first step. We need considerable reduction of troops and arms. Europe is our home, and we are the first ones to be interested in peace and order in this home. That is why we should establish such an order, which would eliminate the very possibility of conducting large-scale military operations or a surprise attack here. How to achieve this... Please discuss all the details at the 'Five' meeting and keep pestering the military."

The conversation was over, instructions received. Discussing the meeting with the General Secretary, employees of the Ministry of

Foreign Affairs came to the conclusion that he was establishing the following hierarchy of priorities for Soviet politics in the area of security:

- Withdrawal of Soviet troops from Afghanistan;
- Elimination of imbalances, and reduction of the Soviet Military Forces;
- Achievement of an agreement on a significant reduction of troops and arms in Europe;
- Achievement of an agreement on reducing the strategic nuclear weapons of the U.S.S.R. and the United States by 50%.

Moreover, Gorbachev decided to start seriously dealing with conventional arms. Besides the European one, there was another, perhaps even more important, aspect of this issue: while the Soviet Union maintained its gigantic advantages in conventional arms, no considerable reduction in nuclear weapons could be expected; that was the essence of deterrence.

The seriousness of Gorbachev's intentions was finally understood in the Defense Ministry. In January 1988, after sharp discussions at the "Five" meetings, its representative agreed that "considering the military-political atmosphere in the world, and taking into account the economic situation," the Soviet Union can undertake the unilateral reduction of its armed forces.

Time was flying by, but no specific actions were taken. The military, at least, submitted to the elimination of intermediate range missiles. But by no means did they want to reduce military forces, or—especially—withdraw troops from Eastern Europe. They used their favorite cunning tactic: the wait-and-see game. Maybe with time the necessity would disappear all by itself; maybe the urge to reform would go away, or the situation would change again, and everything would be as it was before.

* * *

Throughout the spring, summer, and autumn of 1988 Gorbachev was up to his eyeballs in work on the withdrawal of our troops from Afghanistan, and with reform of the political system of the country. He simply did not have the time to deal with European issues and with the planned reduction of the armed forces.

However, in July, immediately after the 19th Conference of the CPSU, he had to give a speech at the meeting of the Defense Ministers of the Warsaw Pact countries. His staff reported to him that the presentation of Chief Commander of the Armed Forces of the Warsaw Pact countries Marshal Kulikov would propose the radically different idea that our forces in Europe should be not reduced, but enlarged.

The Marshal tried to prove that "in spite of the INF Treaty, the danger of military conflict in Europe was not reduced but increased." This proposition was the main theme of his speech, in which he further called for a retaliatory increase in our military force. He suggested devoting more attention to special operation task forces, and also spoke of "the need to increase our fuel reserves and ammunition, creating a bigger reserve of the latter on the territory of Hungary and Bulgaria." To cut a long story short, despite the defense doctrine of the U.S.S.R., it dwelt on preparations for an offensive operation.[29]

---

29 Georgiy Shakhnazarov, Price of Freedom (Moscow: Rossika. Zevs, 1993), p. 335-336.

Then Gorbachev ordered Yazov to change the Marshal's paper completely, and to report what had been done to implement his instructions on the reduction in the size of our forces.

After the 19th Conference of the CPSU, the military officials finally understood that Gorbachev had serious intentions of breaking up the old state mechanism, and that they could not just sit quietly and wait for the steamroller of reform to crush them. That is why an working group dedicated to the task set by Gorbachev was created in the General Staff. It included the heads of the main departments, and also Generals B.A. Omelichev, G.F. Krivosheev and V.V. Korobushin.

Akhromeev reported to Gorbachev that the General Staff was working on the details of the plans for reducing troop strength by three, four, five, six, and seven hundred thousand men. It needed time, because it entailed a lot of research activities, including the conducting of large-scale troop maneuvers under the command of the Defense Minister and the Chief of the General Staff, and also special military games for the General Staff involving all military forces in the different theaters of military operations.

The reduction of forces was being planned so that the existing organizational structure, management systems, infrastructure, and logistics would not be affected at all.[30]

Of course, there was another hidden trick. Besides the wait-and-see game, the military was planning to conduct the reduction so that reducing the personnel number kept the same number of military divisions. Let them be not full strength divisions for the time being—who knows, the situation might change again, and it would be rather easy

30 S. F. Akhromeev and G. M. Kornienko, Through the Eyes of Marshal and Diplomat (Moscow: International Relations, 1992), pp. 211-213.

to fill out the division with new recruits, and everything would be as it was before.

The General Secretary's staff mourned bitterly that the military "displayed an unbelievably artistic ability to report to the political leadership one thing, while thinking and doing something completely different." [31]

But Gorbachev then was too busy to play these games; he especially did not want to deal with the details—he was not a very detail-oriented person. He grumbled that the development of detailed plans was taking too long, and force reduction by 300,000 or 400,000 is far from enough. After all, Khrushchev had been able to reduce the Army by 1.2 million without such problems. However the General Secretary let Akhromeev get away with it for the time being.

Why Do We Need Such A Big Army?

During the summer and autumn of 1988, Shevardnadze raised the issue of troop reductions several times at the "Five" meetings. But every time Yazov and Akhromeev would explain calmly that the necessary work was being done in the General Staff, and upon its completion the political leadership would be informed.

But Shevardnadze was a very difficult person to evade—he kept insisting. But Akhromeev was not born yesterday. Gradually their discussions turned into arguments, which were continued at the "Small Five" meeting.

The discussion can be summarized by the following points:

1. The Nature of the Military Threat for the U.S.S.R.

---

31 Georgiy Shakhnazarov, Price of Freedom (Moscow: Rossika. Zevs, 1993), p. 88-89.

The essence of the Defense Ministry position was that "the threat of the third world war—a nuclear war—is postponed only" because both sides realize that it is senseless, and that it will have catastrophic consequences. "But the danger of a military conflict still exists, because the confrontation of two major powerful military blocs remains."

This was the central topic of the discussion. Representatives of the MFA tried to prove that perestroika in the Soviet Union implied fundamental changes in political approaches to solving the questions of war and peace, in Moscow as well as in Washington. As a result, the threat of nuclear world war was put off, as well as the danger of war in general.

The military disagreed with this point completely. At first sight, their discussion could seem academic. But very realistic, practical positions were behind it. Usually Shevardnadze, as a head of MFA, would structure his arguments this way:

"This new political reality does not require big military forces and military expenses. Just the opposite – their excess is harmful, because our intentions are judged not by our words but by our military capacity. That is why our armed forces should be at the level of 'reasonable sufficiency' – not more but not less. It should be sufficient for our defense capability, and at the same time not so small as to tempt the opposing side. But it should be insufficient to attack the opposing side and overwhelm it. The general idea is not to arouse the fears of the other side."

Shevardnadze's belief in the need for the reduction of Soviet military forces was based on these reasons. However, the military responded in the following way: "The United States still considers the Soviet Union its possible military opponent, and their general military practice does not show any changes. The United States military doctrine has not been changed, their military forces are maintained at a very high level of combat readiness, and they are not being reduced. Their military expenses have not been reduced either. The U.S.S.R. has adopted new defense doctrine, but the United States and NATO rely on the strategy of 'flexible response' and nuclear deterrence, which implies that they can be the first to use nuclear weapons…"

The conclusion, obviously, was completely different: we should not rush the reduction of our forces. If we had to do it because of the political considerations, we might agree to insignificant symbolic gestures.

This kind of discussion continued for a rather long time, until in November Gorbachev intervened, and settled the dispute by decreeing that the military threat was reduced. Then Akhromeev agreed, though with a certain qualification: "the military threat to the Soviet Union is reduced but not eliminated."[32]

2. Militarization's Influence on the Economy

Shevardnadze was passionate in demonstrating that the economic state of the country was extremely poor. [33] And one of the reasons for that was the total militarization of all spheres of life in the Soviet Union. Sixty percent of our industry was working directly or indirectly for the military industrial complex. Seventy nine percent of the budget for research and development work was allocated to military

---

32 *Ogoniok*, No. 50, December 1989, p. 6.

33 The Director of the Institute of the U.S. and Canada, Georgii Arbatov, and its leading expert, Aleksei Vasiliev, helped the MFA greatly in their evaluation of the economic situation. With their help, statistics were compiled that allowed for the first time a direct comparison of the economic potential of the U.S. and the U.S.S.R.

projects. The Gross National Product of the United States and NATO is two and a half times as big as that of the Soviet Union and the Warsaw Pact countries.

The real size of the military industrial complex was camouflaged not only by its secrecy but also by the unfairness of the price policy. Its military products were sold at a price considerably lower than its real cost, while civilian goods were sold at much higher prices than their cost of production.

For example, high prices for agricultural equipment caused the redistribution of funds in favor of the military industrial complex. Thus, millions of rubles nominally allocated in the State budget to agricultural enterprises actually went to the MIC.

In the end, the growth of the MIC branches was stopped because the resources of the national economy were almost exhausted. The real danger that growth threatened was not only to the West, but also to our own country, our own economy.

"As a matter of fact," – Shevardnadze was getting excited – "we drained all the blood from our economy, we ruined and deformed our economy. As a result, we have an inevitable reduction of the population's living standards, and the aggravation of social problems.

"What did we achieve politically, in creating this militarized monster? We scared the whole world, which created a coalition of small and great powers against us. This kind of coalition existed in the world history probably only once – against a Napoleonic invasion. We helped American imperialism and its military industrial complex to extend the Cold War for two decades, and stopped the process of disarmament when it had barely started."

The military usually tried to avoid discussing this subject, and changed the topic conversation to another theme, saying that military forces of the United States and the U.S.S.R. were equivalent to each other, and there was an approximate balance of forces.

At that point the most interesting part of this duel started.

3. Comparison of the Armed Forces of the U.S.S.R. and the United States

When speaking about approximate balance, the military have never used any official statistics. Only very seldom, when they were cornered by their opponents during a discussion, did they refer to the official statistics issued about the military budget of the U.S.S.R., which was only 20 billion rubles, about 2% of the Gross National Product. In 1988, the United States was going to spend $312 billion for their military needs.

According to the Soviet military, in number of troops, NATO and the Warsaw Pact (WP) were approximately equal. Originally, they had said that we also had an approximate balance in the number of tanks. Then they agreed that we had more tanks than NATO, but it was compensated by the fact that NATO had more anti-tank weapons. Later they admitted that WP had 20,000 more tanks than NATO, but the two sides were equal when it came to artillery, while at the same time the West had an advantage in air power—they had 1,400 more planes than we did.

Bottom line – parity: the combat capacity of NATO was approximately equal to the combat capacity of the Warsaw Pact.

Shevardnadze exploded. "Tell me, finally, what is the number of our tanks, artillery, and airplanes, and what is the number of our troops? I know the numbers for the United States and NATO – this data is published. But I do not know how many we have!

"Colonels and Generals from the General Staff come to see me sometimes. They bring for my signature instructions to the Soviet delegation at the negotiations about the reduction of our armed forces in Central Europe. I ask them how many tanks we have;—they just shrug their shoulders, and say that it is a Top State Secret!

"I am a member of the Political Bureau, Minister of Foreign Affairs of the U.S.S.R.! What – am I not eligible to know what any colonel from the General Staff knows? Who is responsible for the defense of our country – the Politburo, or a colonel from the General Staff?"

After this kind of scene, Shevardnadze would complain to the General Secretary, and the latter would call Akhromeev or Yazov on the carpet and severely rebuke them. So, gradually, some official numbers began to appear, one at a time.

When the first numbers on the military budget were produced, it turned out that our annual defense expenditures were not 20 billion, but 77.3 billion rubles.

Then the statistics about the number of the Soviet troops became public: 4.258 million men.

A little later other numbers appeared: the number of our tanks was 64,000, the number of our warplanes – 8,200.

But the discussion was not yet over. The Ministry of Foreign Affairs, with the help of scientific research institutions, analyzed these numbers very thoroughly, and came to the conclusion that these numbers were not true; they were considerably lowered. First of all, the military budget was problematic. If our military forces were approximately equal, how were we able to spend only 77 billion rubles, when the U.S. budget was 312 billion dollars – three times more, at least?

Some NATO sources indicated that the real annual military expenses of the Soviet Union were somewhere between 130 and 160 billion rubles. And according to the calculations of some domestic specialists, these expenses would be about 300 – 350 billion dollars if the calculation of the Soviet's military budget was done using average world prices.

As for the number of troops and arms, to take just one example, our military specialists stated that the number of U.S. troops was 3.3 million. But American specialists insisted that this number is only 2.1 million. Where did this difference come from?

It turned out that our military specialists had been including the National Guard and military reservists in the number of American troops, but when estimating our numbers they did not include military reserves, internal troops, border guards, railway troops, and other types of troops. If they had used the same method for determining the size of the Soviet military forces, the number would be not 4.2 million men but 10.6 million.

* * *

Finally, Shevardnadze lost patience completely and ordered the preparation of a letter addressed to Gorbachev, stating that the military kept deceiving him. And it was a rather big fraud – falsification of numbers concerning the reduction of our troops, about elimination of the military imbalance, and about the development of various types of weapons. This memo, after the Minister edited it himself, looked rather emotional. It was sent to Gorbachev at the end of October.

At that time, Gorbachev's visit to New York and his appearance at the General Assembly of the UN was being discussed very widely, and the memo from Shevardnadze came just in time. Gorbachev was inspired by the idea of his appearance at the UN gathering. For his speech at the UN he needed an original and striking initiative, which could have significant international political potential, and could make his visit to the UN truly epoch-making. What could be more impressive than an announcement about the unilateral reduction of Soviet troops?

On November 3, 1988, the Politburo held another session, where Gorbachev posed the question of the reduction of Soviet troops as the main topic. He did it, as he usually did everything, very generously, on a grand scale. He included his thoughts about troop reduction in the context of the country's political system reorganization. His main idea was that without considerable reduction in our military expenses, we would not be able to solve the problems of perestroika.

"A few days ago, I talked to Ryzhkov (Prime Minister) and Maslukov (Deputy Prime Minister, in charge of the MIC). This conversation, plus a great many letters from our citizens to me, and my recent meeting with Soviet youth, forced me to start thinking seriously about the question, asked during this meeting by a representative of the Young Communist League: Why do we need such a big army?

"The military doctrine we have declared is completely different from our military practice. Not a single country in the world, maybe with the exception of some third world country that we oversupply with weapons while getting nothing in return, spends as much as we do per capita. If we publish the fact that we spend two and a half times more than the United States for our military needs… If we make this fact public, then all our new thinking and all our new foreign policy will go to hell…

"We will never solve all the problems of perestroika if we leave our army as it is.

"The army still swallows the best scientists and designers, the best industrial reserves; it has unlimited supplies…

"I suggest the Defense Council study this issue and report to us at the next session of the Politburo. Does anybody have any doubts?"

Everybody shook their heads.

Ryzhkov: "If we do not do it, we can not even talk about improvements to the living standards of our people. No matter what government rules the country, it will not be able to solve this problem without the reduction of military expenses."

Gorbachev: "If everybody agrees, and we are ready to make major political decisions, including unilateral reduction, and not just what we are obliged to do according to the INF Treaty and Vienna mandate, I believe I should announce it at the General Assembly of the UN."

All members of the Politburo: "Yes, yes!"

Gorbachev: "After the INF Treaty and the decision to withdraw out troops from Afghanistan, it should make a good impression: the whole world will see that what we do is a real peace policy, and not a bluff. The most important reason for all this is our perestroika. Nikolai Ivanovich (Ryzhkov) is right – without the reduction of the army and the military industrial complex, we will not be able to solve all the tasks of perestroika…

"No question about it, we must not give up being militarily strong. But we should be strong enough to provide for our own security, not for scaring the whole world."[34]

So the decision was made. The Defense Ministry was instructed to develop specific proposals on the reduction of the armed forces, and to do so in two weeks.

This time the military acted very efficiently. In the second half of November, the Political Bureau approved the proposals they presented: reduce the Army and Navy by 500,000 men, reduce tanks by 10,000 and airplanes by 1,000 units. In addition, by 1991, withdraw six tank divisions from the German Democratic Republic, Czechoslovakia, and Hungary, and also the special task forces.

It was not the best option – at the "Five" meetings better suggestions had been discussed. During these meetings Shevardnadze had suggested reduction by a million men as a minimum. But as usual, Gorbachev's habit of compromise position, his "golden mean," won.

Stop On The Way To The English Channel

On December 7, 1988, in the morning, Gorbachev walked up to the podium of the General Assembly of the UN and announced the upcoming reduction of the Soviet military forces.

The auditorium exploded with a storm of ovations. Probably, the UN had never seen anything like that before. The mass media compared Gorbachev with Woodrow Wilson, Franklin Roosevelt, and Winston Churchill, the founders of the modern world. The *Washington Post*, for example, wrote that it was one of the most outstanding speeches in the

---

34 A.S. Chernyaev, Six Years with Gorbachev (Moscow: Progress. Kultura, 1993), pp. 255-257.

history of the UN. Mikhail Gorbachev had suggested changing the rules that had been governing this world for the last four decades.

Now the negotiations about the limitation and the reduction of conventional armed forces in Europe lay ahead. That was one of the most difficult negotiations; just the fact that twenty-two states from NATO and WP were participating created a lot of difficulties. When these negotiations started in Vienna, the ratio of the two opposing blocs WP looked roughly like this:

Military personnel:	WP – more than 3 million men, NATO – more than 2 million;
Tanks:	WP – almost 60,000, NATO – 16,500;
Infantry Fighting Vehicles and Armored Personnel Carriers:	
	WP – more than 70,000, NATO – 39,500;
Artillery:	WP – 71,000, NATO – 14,500. [35]

The most important striking power of the Warsaw Pact was the troops in Central Europe. Even its configuration looked like a wedge driven into the middle of Europe. Obviously experiencing nostalgic feelings, the Defense Minister of the U.S.S.R., D.T. Yazov, said during the ceremony of the signing of the CFE Treaty:

"Our forces in Central Europe are the strongest in all of history. All we have to do is say the word, and they will roll, an unstoppable wave, all the way to the English Channel. They could bomb us with nuclear weapons, but it would not matter. The tanks would move ahead. So would the surviving soldiers. Ah, what troops we have!"[36]

---

35 Disarmament and security (Moscow: IMEMO, IZO APN, 1989), p. 281.
36 Oleg Grinevsky, "The Story Behind the Picture," Newsweek, November 22, 1993, p.19.

Now these troops were to go through considerable reorganization and reduction in size, and loose its ability to "arrive at the English Channel." The new Gorbachev approach called for parity in all conventional weapons between NATO and WP, an approximate balance in quality and quantity. During the negotiations the balance was supposed to be developed in detail, systematically dealing with all the levels. In practice, it meant proportionate, not numerically equal reductions; if the Soviet Union had three times as many tanks, it was to reduce their number by three times as many as NATO.

It looks easy only on paper. In fact, hundreds of rather complicated issues had to be coordinated. Issues such as the types of weapons to be reduced, their levels, regional limitations, and verification procedures. Human nature being what it is, each side tried, and will always try, to obtain unilateral advantages. The Soviet Union, for example, suggested the reduction of the strategic air force. But the definition of this reduction looked like a delicate pattern by the best fashion designer -- the suggestion was to cut very neatly and accurately the major part of NATO's air power, while leaving most of the U.S.S.R.'s intact.

On the other hand, the Western military suggested a definition of "tank" such that the majority of their battle crafts would not be reduced. Such examples were evident at every turn.

In some cases the internal position of the Warsaw Pact Organization was better. Most of the weapons were of Soviet manufacture, and that is why most of the internal discussions were about numbers–each country tried to get a higher share of the arms allocated for Socialist countries. In NATO, the negotiations were not only about the numbers, but also about the types of weapons. Some Western countries produced their own tanks, airplanes, and artillery. They tried to save their types of weapons from reduction during the negotiations. Naturally, the Soviet delegation knew about this and used NATO's internal contradiction to their own advantage.

For a little over a year and a half, a very difficult rivalry continued in Vienna. The time frame for such complicated negotiations was rather short, especially if compared to their predecessors. The negotiations over the reduction of armed forces in Central Europe had lasted more than 15 years, and ended without any results.

The Treaty on the Reduction of Conventional Forces in Europe, from the Atlantic Ocean to the Ural Mountains, was signed on November 19, 1990 in Paris, at a summit meeting of the thirty-three European states, the United States, and Canada. During all of human history there had been no battles where such a huge number of tanks, armored personnel carriers, and airplanes were eliminated, as were eliminated during that hour in the Elysee Palace – 50,000 units of various types of weapons.

Now each military bloc, NATO and the WP, could have not more than 20,000 tanks, 30,000 armored personnel carriers, 20,000 pieces of artillery, 6,800 fixed-wing military aircraft, and 2,000 helicopters in their arsenals. But these forces were not allowed to be concentrated in one location. They had to be spread over three geographical zones: central, flank, and rear. Very low quotas were established for European and regional zones. These low quotas made impossible any surprise attack or large-scale military operations on the European continent. Figuratively speaking, a straitjacket was put on Europe.

Obviously, the Treaty could not prevent local conflicts like those that happened in Yugoslavia and on the borders of the former Soviet Union. But preventing such conflicts was not the task of this treaty. The Treaty cleared the air in Europe, ending the confrontation of the two major military blocs. It opened opportunities for the mobilization of forces to suppress national and ethnic conflicts, within the framework of existing European institutions. This is a new and very important role for a treaty under modern conditions.

* * *

Now we had only a few more Treaties to sign: treaties on reducing Strategic Offensive Weapons by 50%, on banning all nuclear tests, and on banning chemical and biological weapons. But these agreements were reached during a different era, when Yeltsin came to power. As a result, the international atmosphere changed dramatically. The road to large-scale conversion of the defense industry was open.

2.5. RUSSIA – U.S.: STRENGTHENING MUTUAL UNDERSTANDING

Introductory Remarks

Vlad E. Genin

After defense conversion's first steps, its further fate depended on the degree of progress in two directions: global disarmament and non-proliferation the most dangerous weapons, and the further development of cooperation and the strengthening of mutual understanding and trust between the two nuclear superpower states.

After the collapse of the Soviet Union, the formation of fifteen Newly Independent States (NIS) on the territory of the former U.S.S.R. had a profound influence on international relationships within the global community. The West now had to deal with a number of new states instead of one country. Nevertheless, Russia got the greatest share of the former U.S.S.R. military legacy: the majority of nuclear arsenals of weapons and stockpiles, and defense plants and R&D centers that had been developed over several decades all over the huge territory of Russia.

During the 1990s the new Russian leadership repeatedly declared its loyalty to the previously chosen political course, aimed at strengthening international cooperation and fulfilling disarmament obligations. They included such major joint projects as the liquidation of nuclear weapons, and the Treaty on the Non-proliferation of Nuclear Weapons (NPT).

These very important steps had a profound effect on relations between United States and Russia, strengthening their mutual understanding and trust.

Mikhail I. Gerasev

The American leadership and the new Russian Federation leadership also faced the problem of the U.S.S.R.'s "nuclear heritage." It was a very important part of a bigger problem – the prevention of the spread of nuclear weapons, and also the prevention of the diffusion of nuclear technologies, including missile technologies.

Under the influence of both countries, the new States—the former Soviet republics—agreed to join the START Treaty, which was signed in 1991. The Soviets' strategic weapons still remained on the territories of these new States. On December 5th, 1994, the United States, Belarus, Kazakhstan, Russia, and Ukraine, exchanged ratification documents, which meant that the Treaty was in force.

By the middle of 1992, all Soviet tactical nuclear weapons were transferred to the territory of Russia. At the same time, the transfer of strategic weapons from Belarus, Kazakhstan, and Ukraine to Russia started. Some of these weapons were intended for dismantlement and elimination. Russian-American cooperation slowly progressed in this area.

For example, the most advanced American equipment for eliminating heavy military aircraft was installed at Russian Long-Range Aviation Bases. According to the international agreement, this equipment was supplied free of charge. According to START I and II, 70 aircraft were to be liquidated on this Aviation Base by the year 2000, but the total number of the aircraft intended for liquidation was 208. The process of liquidation was monitored from space by American satellites, as stipulated in the agreement.

The joint efforts of both countries were also needed to move all of the nuclear arms from the former Soviet Union republics. With U.S. assistance, Russia started to use new Safe Transport Units (super containers), and other state-of-the-art U.S. equipment, which allowed nuclear weapons to be transported safely, preventing catastrophic consequences.

For the first time in the history of Russian (Soviet)–American relations, the possibility existed for destroying nuclear weaponry itself. The preliminary agreement, reached in Helsinki, concerning the development of a mutually acceptable procedure for the elimination of nuclear warheads, was to help eliminate one of the most serious defects of the SALT II Treaty, and to create a very reliable guarantee of the irreversibility of strategic arms limitations.

Having accomplished the transfer of all nuclear weapons to Russia, and the ratification by the former Soviet republics of the NPT, the U.S. leadership was next concerned with the possibility of Russia's losing control over nuclear weapons because of social and political instability. The U.S. was also concerned about the illegal export of nuclear materials from the countries of the Commonwealth of the Independent States (the former U.S.S.R.). These materials were released as a result of the nuclear weapons dismantlement process, and could be used to build nuclear weapons. The Russian leadership had the same concerns as the U.S. government.

In this connection, the United States developed a program called "Cooperative Threat Reduction." Senators Sam Nunn and Richard Lugar initiated this program at the end of 1991. In December 1991, the U.S.

Congress approved the law on reducing the Soviet nuclear threat, which obliged the U.S. President to create an assistance program for the countries of the Commonwealth of Independent States in order to eliminate the weapons of mass destruction that were located on their territories. According to this law, the assistance was to provide safe transportation, storage, and security for these weapons. For the implementation of this program, the U.S. Congress provided 400 million dollars.

The planned elimination of thousands of nuclear warheads caused another complicated problem: the problem of storing them safely and inventorying the huge amount of released weapon materials. At Russia's request, the United States agreed to provide technical and financial assistance to build a large and highly secure storage facility where all of the released weapon materials could be concentrated. American equipment and inventory systems were also used there.

The Clinton administration was a very active participant in projects for mutual control of nuclear weapons elimination. In September 1993, an agreement was signed between the U.S. Department of Energy and the Russian Ministry of Atomic Energy concerning joint development of fissile material protection, control, and accounting measures.

This process received a new impetus during the visit of the U.S. president to Moscow in early 1994. As a result of the summit, both presidents announced that they agreed to prevent the accumulation of excessive fission materials. In March of the same year, a protocol was signed on conducting joint inspections of fissile material production and storage facilities. A month later, an American delegation visited a uranium enrichment facility in the Ural area of Russia, and then a

Russian delegation visited two gaseous diffusion plants in the United States.

A list of facilities where nuclear weapons materials were stored was created during the meeting of the Gore–Chernomyrdin Commission in 1996, including the following: Novosibirsk Chemical Concentrate Plant, the Scientific Research Institute for Energy Technologies (NIKIET) in Beloyarsk, the Sverdlovsk branch of NIKIET, the Radium Institute, the Beloyarsk nuclear power plant, Krasnoyarsk-26, and Sverdlovsk-44. Cooperation between Russian and American nuclear laboratories was developing very quickly.

The April 1996 meeting of G-7 leaders with Russian leaders in Moscow was the first attempt to discuss problems connected exclusively with nuclear materials at such a high level. In the official documents summarizing the results of the meeting, three sets of problems occupied a special place: protection, control, and accounting of nuclear materials; disposition of excess arms materials; and prevention of illegal trafficking in nuclear materials.

The Summit meeting in Moscow received a worldwide response. At the 51st Session of the UN General Assembly, several resolutions were approved. The resolutions called upon all the countries of the world to cooperate effectively in preventing the illegal trafficking of fissionable materials.

Two other very important provisions of the NPT were the following: foreign assistance to the CIS countries for the organization of an effective system of nuclear materials export controls, and assistance with providing employment to Soviet nuclear and missile scientists in order to prevent them from emigrating to countries attempting to develop their own nuclear weapons. The West financed both programs.

In 1992, the West made a decision to gather the post-Communist states into the Forum on the Problems of Cooperation in the Area of Export Controls for State-of-the-Art Technologies." Its proceedings resulted, first of all, in the introduction of restrictions on exports to such countries as Iraq, North Korea, and Lebanon. Since the early 1990s, these particular countries and their regimes have been the subject of very serious concern in the West, especially in the United States.

In spite of some liberalization of export controls on such items to Eastern European and Baltic countries, a prohibition against selling high-tech products and weapons to Russia remained. Russia was particularly dissatisfied by the limitation on the export of some civilian commercial products, such as telecommunication equipment, personal computers, etc. Under such conditions, Russia could not agree to participate in this Forum.

Washington understood that without close cooperation with Russia, which was one of the leading suppliers of weapons to Third World countries, it was impossible to create a new system of export controls. Beginning in fall 1993, the United States started the process of including Russia in such organizations as MTCR (Missile Technology Control Regime) and the New Forum, instead of COCOM.

In November 1993, COCOM made the decision to stop its operations as of March 31, 1994. Simultaneously, work began to form new organizations for controlling the export of weapons and products and technologies that could be used in arms production. Russia was to become one of its founders, but it could not participate until its final stage of activity, a year and a half later. According to Washington, the main obstacle to Russia's participation was its military and technological cooperation with Iran. As Washington put it, the United States would not object to Russian participation in the work on creating the New Forum if Russia stopped supplying weapons to Iran.

Besides the Iran factor, another very important factor affecting the U.S. attitude was that the Russian export control system did not seem reliable. The U.S. was concerned not about the system itself, which in general met international standards of control, but about Russia's ability to control exports in practice, especially to other former Soviet states.

During 1994 and 1995, Russia took several steps to meet U.S. requirements. For example, in September 1994, President Yeltsin announced that Russia would not sign any new weapons contracts with Iran with weapons, yet would fulfill existing ones.

In the middle of 1995, a representative of the U.S. State Department agreed that the fulfillment of the existing Russian contracts did not give new military potential to Iran, and did not affect the military balance in the Middle East. As a result, during the June 1995 session of the Gore-Chernomyrdin Commission, the U.S. Vice President and the Russian Prime Minister reached an agreement to allow Russia to join the New Forum. Two years later, during a session of the U.N., the Russian Prime Minister confirmed that after the completion of the existing contracts with Iran, which were signed in 1989 and 1990, no new ones would be signed.

In 1992, President Yeltsin announced that Russia intended to join the Missile Technology Control Regime. Russia had, in fact, introduced a new system of export controls before becoming a member of this regime. In a Presidential Decree of November 1993, the *List of Equipment, Materials, and Technologies Used to Create Missile Weapons* was introduced. At the same time, the government issued the resolution *On Controlling the Export from the Russian Federation of*

Equipment, Materials, and Technologies Used to Create Missile Weapons. In order to join the export control organization, Russia had to review an agreement with India about supplying cryogenic engines for an Indian space launch vehicle.

In the middle of 1995, the Russian Federation joined the MTCR.

The most significant evidence of the trust developed between the United States and Russia was the fact that some highly sensitive Russian state organizations, research institutions, and missile enterprises opened up for cooperation with American specialists and businessmen.

The State supported the contacts of the defense enterprises with American partners. Moreover, many representatives of highly sensitive research institutes, design bureaus, and defense plants received permission to make business trips to the United States. Previously, defense industry employees could not even visit Warsaw Pact countries, but now they could visit enterprises of the U.S. defense industry. The fact is that from 1992, the relationship between the United States and the Russian Federation changed radically, especially in the very sensitive area of defense industry security.

2.6. AT THE STARTING POINT: SIX "IFS" CONCERNING WESTERN SUPPORT

Introductory Remarks

Vlad E. Genin

Most Russian and Western defense conversion specialists, while referring to the initial phases of the conversion process in Russia, analyze the degree of country's readiness for such a breakthrough and deep reform.

In this context, readiness included several vital and fundamental issues. First among them were the issues of the real recognition of the ideals of both cardinal economic reforms and conversion by the top Soviet leaders, their willingness and readiness to progress toward these ideals, openness in re-evaluating the ideological and economic platform for the new challenges of perestroika, consistency in meeting such challenges, in particular, the conversion plans, as well as preventing potential bureaucratic resistance to truly fundamental reforms, as had happened in the corridors of power many times during unsuccessful campaigns.

Other extremely important issues were readiness of the economic environment for pursuing conversion goals, and the readiness of the whole MIC system. Assuming that all leaders of the country, with no speculations (such as "the West plans to destroy Russia", popular among ultra-nationalists), sincerely believed in the necessity of both disarmament and defense conversion, what was done to create a new economic environment and prepare defense industries for conversion? What was, and was not, in place at the beginning of the Russian defense conversion marathon?

Mikhail I. Gerasev

According to the West, including the American leadership, the following six conditions were necessary for the success of perestroika:

1. Support from the highest echelons of power;
2. Recognition of the necessity for economic reforms;
3. Openness, allowing the re-thinking of ideological and economic theory to justify all the changes;
4. A favorable international political climate;
5. Consistency in development and implementation of the reforms;
6. Ability to overcome the resistance of the bureaucracy.

By 1990, prevailing opinion held that the first four conditions of successful implementation of the reform had been met.

However, the fifth and sixth conditions were very serious problems for Gorbachev. Among the major dangers of perestroika were the following: a weak and incomplete program of economic reforms, which reflected the compromises among the members of the Soviet leadership; the unsuccessful implementation of these programs because of resistance by the bureaucracy; rejection of the reforms by the population because of the loss of privileges and benefits provided under the previous system; and an inability to create a foundation for supporting the reforms. The future of reforms was not clear, and reforms had no legal underpinning.

Western society was very concerned about the general problems of perestroika and economic development. The West promised to support defense industry reforms and conversion programs, provided that the Kremlin implemented all the plans in the economic sphere. Western leaders realized that the presence of effective economic reforms allowed the continuation of large-scale political and social changes in the country. Finally, and not accidentally, the West started to play a waiting game when it came to the question of actual help and investment in defense industry conversion.

Among the economic programs that required the active participation of the West, the following should be emphasized.

First, the expediency of introducing market prices. The Kremlin's actions in this sphere were very palliative until the end of 1991, and prevented the West from providing more active help.

Second, the stability of the ruble. The excess cash created as a result of the huge budget deficit, which was financed with the help of circulating rubles, meant that the cancellation of price controls would cause prices for consumer goods to skyrocket. Selling state property, using Soviet gold reserves to stabilize the ruble, could solve the problem of excess cash, as the West, including Washington, stated it.

Third, free competition and elimination of the monopolies. The distribution of resources must be regulated by the market, not by the planning agencies of the State.

Fourth, legal guarantees for property rights. The parliament approved a law on property. It was considered a compromise. The term "private property" was not mentioned in it. Its failure to allow private property and the direct employment of personnel prevented large private enterprises from developing.

Fifth, rejection of the predatory tax policy and regulations, and the state dictatorship over manufacturers.

According to Western opinion, these measures would help to create a more open society, enhance conversion, and form state institutions not interested in military preparations. And, as a result, the U.S.S.R. could become an equal member of the international community.

The implementation of these conditions required radical reforms, especially in the defense industry, which completely belonged to the State. It consisted mostly of large enterprises, and was highly monopolized. At the end of the 1980s, the production of heavy machinery (the main output of the defense industry) comprised about 80% of the defense industry's total output. The total number of heavy machinery enterprises was about 77% of all enterprises of the defense industry.[37] The implementation of the conversion program was meant to de-monopolize and privatize defense industry enterprises, which during perestroika caused a very negative reaction from the ruling bureaucracy. Thus, the Soviet leadership was either unwilling or unable to meet the conditions suggested by the West.

It was a dead-end situation. The West was not satisfied with the scale, speed, or consistency of the reforms in industry, including the defense industry. The West was not encouraged to participate in the reforms, including investment programs, joint projects, etc. Moreover, the Western attitude toward defense industry reforms became skeptical.

Private organizations, including the Western business world, suggested different options. For example, Western businessmen advised the directors of defense industry enterprises not to expect million-dollar investments. Western investors preferred to study thoroughly the capabilities of the enterprises and send their managers to review their

---

37 *Communist*, No. 9, 1990.

prospects, which were rather problematic at that time, because of national security rules.

U.S. Deputy Secretary of Defense Donald J. Atwood visited Moscow in November 1991. As was stated in the Soviet mass media, during discussions with Soviet government members, Atwood said that he did not notice any progress in conversion. The only activity in this sphere was in the defense industry, which actively searched for Western sponsors. Moreover, Atwood emphasized that very few people in the U.S.S.R. understood the real meaning of defense conversion, and even fewer knew how much it would cost.[38]

Slowly, the interest in joint projects faded. During the same visit, the Americans showed some interest in a few proposed projects, including the creation of nuclear reactors for spacecraft, development of some biological technologies, and cooperation with one of the Soviet aviation institutions in creating land-based devices for the "Siberian Air Corridor" project.

The hopes for foreign sponsorship reflected the general policies underlying Western financial assistance to the Soviet Union. The absence of effective reforms prevented the West from participating in large investment projects in the defense industry. At the same time, the U.S.S.R. received a large line of credit for the purchase of all kinds of goods. Thus, Western exports of goods substituted for investments. Instead of a serious reconstruction of industry to satisfy the needs of the domestic market, the Soviet Union went deeper and deeper into debt, and depended more and more on the import of consumer products.

At the end of 1990, the foreign debt of the U.S.S.R. was more than 55 billion dollars. Fourteen percent of the country's commercial

---

38 *Kommersant*, November 4,1991.

profits went to pay just the interest on that debt. According to Western bank estimates, hard currency reserves of the U.S.S.R. fell from 13-15 billion dollars to 5 billion dollars.[39]

The country went into deep debt within a very few years, which can be explained by the absence of a common system for borrowing and spending credit funds. In 1990, the total sum of credits granted by Western countries was about 6.5 billion dollars. Only one billion dollars were intended for investments, such as the project to construct an automobile plant in Yelabuga City, a project that was frozen for several years.[40] Of the rest, 3 billion dollars, went to import consumer products, and 2.5 billion dollars to pay debts.[41] Data from 1991 also showed that the major part of credit was simply eaten up.

Western credits were just a political gesture of Western support of Gorbachev. As for serious investment, which could help reconstruct the national economy, including the defense industry, it was not even mentioned.

---

39 *Communist*, No.12, 1991.
40 Editor's Note: In 1997, this plant began production of Chevrolet "Blazer" sport utility vehicles.
41 *Communist*, No.12, 1991, p. 65.

PART THREE

The First Steps Toward Conversion

INTRODUCTION

Vlad E. Genin

"The process is underway..." These words by Gorbachev, full of hope and optimism, vividly recall the historical year of 1985, when the Soviet people started to build a new life based on the invigorating ideas of glasnost and a world without wars. It was a time when many new goods appeared in many Russian homes: electronic devices, Western-made furniture, jeans, and Pepsi Cola. A time of a vast variety of consumer goods – modern, affordable, long sought after – instead of tanks and missiles. It was at that time, and in that environment, that conversion was started. What industry in Russia had an opportunity to produce modern high-tech consumer electronics, TVs, VCRs, telephones, car alarms, convertible baby strollers, and sewing equipment for manufacturing designer clothes? The eyes of the whole nation were turned to the defense industry. Hadn't it launched

Sputnik and created unprecedentedly complex missiles, supersonic airplanes, and nuclear submarines? The people of Russia believed in their defense industry potential. That was how conversion began. That was how the process got underway...

Russians had high hopes for the success of defense conversion then. But many experienced plant directors and their technical staffs, while excellent designers and manufacturers, were completely naïve in their business expectations. It seemed to them that since Russia decided to leave the arms race, the West, in exchange for this, should assume full responsibility for converting defense plants to serve the civilian market, including financial responsibility. But this expectation belonged more to the world of hopes and dreams than to the world of business. The international world of economics and business lives by its own rules, and success is based on them, not on emotions.

We all remember the optimistic attitude that sprang up in the United States and other Western countries when the U.S.S.R. started perestroika and conversion of the defense industry complex. The Russian government opened the Iron Curtain a crack, giving the management of defense plants the chance of a lifetime to visit analogous facilities in the West, and study the other parties' technology and production experience. In turn, the West reached out to Russia through the numerous representatives of a whole range of companies, from huge corporations to small businesses. Some businessmen saw Russia as an enormous market for their products; others viewed the country as an infinite source abundant natural resources.

For the very first time, the flagships of Russian high-tech industry, forever geared to the defense complex, were visited by capitalists and entrepreneurs – *"firmatchi"*[1], as the Russians called them. It seemed that the moment was coming when American and Russian plant managers, scientists, engineers, and workers would start working together in close cooperation. At that time, we rejoiced at the achievements of the first international conversion projects, such as the joint project in wireless telecommunication technology between Sun Microsystems from

[1] Editor's Note: Russian jargon for business representatives of foreign firms.

Silicon Valley, California, and "Elvis+"[2] from the electronic capital of Russia -- the city of Zelenograd near Moscow.

[2] Editor's Note: "Elvis+" was a spin-off of Ellas, the Russian major high tech defense enterprise.

3.1. U.S. DEPARTMENT OF DEFENSE SUPPORT FOR RUSSIAN CONVERSION

Introductory Remarks

Vlad E. Genin

From the beginning, the Western countries helped to convert the huge Russian Military Industrial Complex. The optimistic phrase "Don't worry – the West will help us out!" was very popular in the early '90s, when the advanced Western states, along with a number of international organizations, started the first programs of financial and technological assistance to Russia for the purposes of disarmament and defense industry conversion.

President Bill Clinton stated the purpose of American assistance to Russia: to support democracy and market economy reforms, and to decrease the military threat. The logic of such assistance was absolutely plain: to help Russia to convert itself from the "evil empire" to a strong and prosperous country.

It was a time of great expectations for the Russian defense industry; the assistance of the West meant restructuring the production plants, and the development of a new product lines. It was a time when the Gore-Chernomyrdin Commission, led by U.S. Vice-President Al Gore and Russian Prime Minister Viktor Chernomyrdin (and later, his successors) started its historical mission – to launch unprecedented U.S.-Russian scientific and technical collaboration for the first time after decades of confrontation in the Cold War. The positive spirit of this Commission and its participants was the same as that over fifty years ago, during the historical meeting of American and Russian soldiers near the Elba River in Germany in 1945 who battled together against the Nazis. This Commission is a bright example of a wise approach to sensitive issues of mutual collaboration in disarmament and defense conversion.

It was a time, first of all, of U.S. practical support for Russian defense conversion efforts through the Defense Enterprise Fund, the Cooperative Threat Reduction Program and the "Fast Four".

David M. Bernstein

Following the collapse of the Soviet Union, the United States has recognized the enormous stake that it has in the stability of a democratic Russia and that that stability depends in large measure on economic reform and growth. In response the United States has initiated a broad array of programs to assist the economic reform process in material (financial support) and nonmaterial (technical assistance), direct (venture financing) and indirect (institution and infrastructure building) ways. These programs were based on four recognized constraints:

The extent and nature of reform would be largely determined by events and policies in Russia, and the United States could only have a marginal, albeit important, influence and role.

To be acceptable to Congress, programs had to involve substantial participation by American (governmental and/or private) entities, especially in the allocation of resources.

The U.S. government could provide only very limited funds, and therefore its programs had to be designed to achieve high leverage by attracting private capital.

To be effective, the money in these programs would have to go directly to individual enterprises, or even the individual scientist, and not be filtered down through the Russian government.

Some of the programs funded partially or wholly by the U.S. government could be utilized for projects related to defense conversion.[3] A small subset of these programs were initiated by the U.S. Department of Defense, and were designed specifically to encourage the conversion and diversification of the defense research and production complex, particularly that portion involved with weapons of mass destruction (WMD) and their delivery systems. This subset included near-term programs to fund a few model conversion ventures (e.g., the Fast Four) involving U.S. partner companies, the establishment of a fund—the Defense Enterprise Fund (DEF)—to provide a continuing source of government supported financing for similar conversion ventures, the initiation of a few projects to assist in the conversion of factories to the production of housing for retired officers, and an effort to stimulate and facilitate the participation of private capital in additional conversion ventures.

This small but specific focus on conversion was based on the recognition that without diversified productive economic activity for the industrial component, the value of any weapons reduction program would be limited.

---

[3] This chapter deals with programs initiated by the U.S. Department of Defense. Other programs were initiated by other agencies, such as the Department of Energy's Lab-to-Lab, Initiatives for Proliferation Prevention, and the Nuclear Cities Initiative directed toward the nuclear weapons complex, and the International Science and Technology Center sponsored by the State Department and directed to the direct support of scientists. For a summary of U.S. government programs see the annual reports of the Office of the Coordinator of U.S. Assistance to the NIS, *U.S. Government Assistance to and Cooperative Activities with the New Independent States of the Former Soviet Union*.

In 1993, the Clinton administration perceived an urgent need to initiate a cooperative program to assist Russia in converting its defense industries to the production of peaceful commercial goods. This need was based in part on the desire to build a stable market economy, and in part on a hope of encouraging the downsizing of the defense industry. Therefore, defense conversion was one element of the work of the Gore-Chernomyrdin Commission (GCC) that was agreed upon at the Clinton-Yeltsin Vancouver Summit of January 1993. William Perry, who was Deputy Secretary of Defense at that time, was designated to lead this element of the GCC for the United States. In order to implement this mandate, a project was initiated within the Cooperative Threat Reduction (CTR) program, funded by the Nunn-Lugar amendment to the DOD budget, which was already engaged in the cooperative demilitarization of Soviet nuclear weapons.[4]

The first conversion project initiated was the funding of four U.S.-Russian joint ventures, the so-called Fast Four. As the Fast Four projects were being implemented, the DOD also went about establishing the DEF. There was never a basis to expect that the small funds available for the Fast Four contracts (less than 0.01% of the U.S. defense budget) could compensate directly for more than a minuscule amount of the drop in Russian military orders; however, there were strong reasons to believe that if U.S. industry capitalized on the opportunity to utilize some of the technology, trained personnel, and capacity of the Russian defense industry, this could significantly assist the conversion of Russia's military-industrial base, while at the same time being of economic and technical benefit to U.S. industry. However, U.S. industry, especially the

---

[4] The Nunn-Lugar amendment was authorized by Congress in 1991, but the Bush administration did not utilize it for defense conversion.

U.S. defense industry, was not accustomed to looking to Russia for industrial partnerships, and, in fact, had previously been discouraged by the U.S. government (through security and export control regulations) from doing so. Most sources of private capital were similarly unfamiliar with, and averse to, financing ventures in Russia. Therefore, to accomplish the industrial objectives of CTR, the Department of Defense embarked on a program to bring U.S. and Russian industry together for the mutually beneficial utilization of the industrial component of the WMD research and production infrastructure in Russia. At the same time it supported and encouraged programs to train Russian industrialists in Western business practices; to conduct east-west business promotion conferences; and to provide financing, loan guarantees, and political risk insurance.

Since this was an unfamiliar business approach for U.S. industry, with very limited funds available, and a desire to move quickly, the Department of Defense initiated a program to provide financial incentive as well as facilitation for industrial partnerships between U.S. and Russian companies through the Fast Four and the DEF. This chapter deals primarily with these two initiatives.

Objectives Of The CTR Conversion Program

Conversion elements of the CTR program were intended to contribute to the attainment of broad U.S.-Russian security goals, as well as fairly specific objectives[5]. The general overarching objective of all U.S. government programs in Russia is to help create a more stable, constructive, nonconfrontational long-term relationship between the two

---

5 The terms defense conversion and defense diversification were used somewhat interchangeably by the CTR program.

countries. During the Cold War, the United States and the Soviet Union both believed that their primary assurances of security were military preparedness and deterrence. They engaged only secondarily in arms control negotiations, confidence building measures, and other diplomatic initiatives.

In the post-Cold War era, a far broader spectrum of political, economic, and social interactions have become available. These interactions can now probably do far more to reduce the likelihood of military confrontation in the future than maintaining Cold War-levels of military preparedness. Perry has referred to these programs as defense by other means or preventive defense.[6]

Consistent with this, the stability of the relationship between the United States and the Russian Federation depends heavily upon each having a strong, stable civilian economy that is not dependent upon high levels of military spending to maintain economic progress and the well-being of the populations. Attainment of such an economy in Russia depends upon the success of several large economic transitions that are evolving concurrently. The primary transition is from a command economy to a market economy, but a big part of that is the conversion of much of the production and research bases from military output to civilian output. Assisting this conversion within the Russian economy has been the operational objective of the defense conversion element of the CTR program.

This conversion would require investment capital orders of magnitude larger than that available in the CTR program. Even if such capital had been available from the U.S. government, the direct funding

---

[6] Ashton B. Carter and William J. Perry, *Preventive Defense* (Washington D.C.: Brookings Institution Press, 1999).

of projects by the Department of Defense would not have been the appropriate or optimum means of assisting conversion. Private business capital, and its attendant business expertise, is far better suited, and ultimately much of this capital will have to be generated within Russia. However, by starting the process of cooperative conversion projects, the CTR program did have the opportunity to induce the U.S. private sector to move in. The more specific objectives of the defense conversion program were:

- To initiate a few pilot joint ventures that could become self-sustaining, and able to raise the financing necessary after the utilization of the U.S. government funds;
- To stimulate extensive, wide-ranging business discussions and negotiations between U.S. companies and Russian defense enterprises;
- To familiarize other public and private sources of capital with the investment opportunities involving Russian defense enterprises;
- To provide business training for managers in the Russian enterprises;
- To support privatization of the Russian industrial base and, specifically, portions of the military-industrial complex;
- To establish government-to-government mechanisms for facilitating U.S. companies' joint ventures with Russian enterprises; and,
- To contribute to the creation of a legal and commercial infrastructure conducive to foreign investment.

Some critics questioned whether a program, calling it foreign aid; however, it had been proposed and justified solely on the basis of serving U.S. national security and economic interests. Some critics questioned whether a program of this type serves U.S. national security objectives, because it could contribute to both financial support and dual-use technology for the military program in the military-industrial complex.[7] This argument is flawed in several respects. Economic stability in Russia is necessary for political stability and reform. This in turn is necessary for a constructive, non-confrontational U.S.-Russian relationship. Fostering a strong economy, embedded in a democracy, is the best way to constrain the levels of expenditure on military activities. The failure to sustain a civilian-oriented economy would be one of the greatest incentives to go back to a militaristic economy. Furthermore, small spin-off joint stock companies established for U.S.-Russian conversion projects would have a greater incentive to engage in nonmilitary work.

Assisting Russia to more effectively eliminate excess military capacity, and to develop a market economy, will help to make the U.S. and Russia better trade partners. In addition, the reduction of military production and research reduces any military threat both directly and indirectly. The direct reduction follows obviously from the reduced magnitude of military power. If the remaining military power is designed to address legitimate security threats to Russia, this will result in military forces, which are qualitatively as well as quantitatively less threatening to the United States as well, and vice versa. The clearest, and most important examples are weapons of mass destruction (WMD), which relate more to Cold War scenarios than to current security threats. Therefore, the conversion element of the CTR program has focused on WMD.

---

[7] United States General Accounting Office, Report to the Chairman, Committee on National Security, House of Representatives, *Cooperative Threat Reduction: Status of Defense Conversion Efforts in the Former Soviet Union,* 1997.

Another, indirect reduction of the military threat is achieved through increased transparency. The more U.S. and Russian officials and industrialists discuss conversion and production plans and activities, the less chance there is for making unfounded and exaggerated assumptions about potential threats. This openness in turn contributes to the fulfillment of another U.S. objective, which is to be able to reduce its own defense budget. The approximately 50 percent reduction of the U.S. defense budget over the past decade was possible almost completely because of the improved relationship and reduced threats between the United States and the Soviet Union and its successor states, primarily Russia. The dialog that accompanies this transparency provides for resolving misunderstandings as to the intent of specific military research and production programs. Therefore, creating and utilizing a process that stimulated open dialogs about security requirements and military procurement was a very important objective of the program.

Another objective of the program is to inhibit proliferation of equipment, personnel, and technology to other countries that may use such assets in a destabilizing manner. Conversion is one of the factors necessary to achieve this objective. The persistence of a large military-industrial complex (MIC) in the absence of budget funding is one of the main incentives for proliferation of sensitive material and technology as a means to make up the financial deficit in the components of the military-industrial complex. The potential migration of skilled technologists can be curtailed by providing challenging technical work on civilian projects. In addition to curtailing such migration, such work would maintain and augment the technology base on which to rebuild the Russian economy.

The Fast Four[8]

The Fast Four procurement was intended to fund four model projects as quickly as possible as the best means of stimulating the subsequent involvement of U.S. industry and other sources of capital, and of acquainting the Russian defense industrialists with Western business practices. The program was initiated with the consultation of Russian government and industry, and a bilateral Defense Conversion Working Group was established to coordinate the effort.

As pointed out above, the potential direct impact of the Fast Four projects on conversion of the Russian defense industry was bound to be quite small. The Department of Defense also recognized that it was not the optimum organization to administer the financing and operation of commercial ventures; however, it could move more quickly on the first projects by doing so. The program was undertaken with these realizations and the program and peripheral activities were designed to obtain indirect benefits on a significantly larger scale. The activities to stimulate the indirect benefits were conducted both in Russia and the U.S. They included technical assistance at the enterprises; training of enterprise representatives; dissemination of enterprise information to the U.S. business community; facilitating contacts between companies in Russia and the U.S.; and the stimulation of other, much larger, sources of capital (e.g. Overseas Private Investment Corporation - OPIC); and the removal of barriers to U.S.- Russian business ventures. These

---

[8] For a detailed discussion of the Fast Four projects, see David Bernstein and Nicholas Carlson, *The Cooperative Threat Reduction "Fast Four" Defense Conversion Projects in the Russian Federation*, The Department of Defense, January 1997.

interactions with enterprises were for many enterprises, not just for the four.

The simplest indirect effects were those that led to operational improvements in the four enterprises, and facilitated additional business negotiations with the four, or other, U.S. companies. Here again, this had only a fairly small effect on the industry at large. However, it could be quite significant for the conversion of those four enterprises. More indirect still, this growth of conversion activities with multiple foreign partners within a single enterprise served to illustrate ways in which other enterprises could convert, through a series of steps and ventures each of which initially involves but a small fraction of the enterprise's facilities, personnel, and activities. This step-wise conversion can progress in two ways:

(1) Through the growth of small conversion ventures; and,

(2) Through the accelerated initiation of additional conversion ventures facilitated by the contacts, restructuring procedures, infrastructure and business practices that flow from the early conversion ventures.

The next indirect effects were on other Russian enterprises, particularly on a certain 82 of them that increased their efforts to work with U.S. companies. These enterprises were not involved in direct procurements under the CTR program; but they were identified as prospective partners for other sources of funding and for technical assistance in establishing joint ventures with U.S. companies. Many of these enterprises prepared multiple proposals for potential ventures and submitted them, via the Ministry of Defense, to the Department of Defense. They also prepared materials describing their capabilities and interests; made additional contacts with U.S. companies; participated in international meetings designed to bring Russian and American companies together; and started working with U.S. government-funded organizations, such as the International Executive Service Corps (IESC), to find venture partners.

The Defense Enterprise Fund

The Defense Enterprise Fund (DEF) was established in 1994 to take over the DOD-sponsored venture financing role after the Fast Four. It was structured along the lines of the other enterprise funds established for economic development in Eastern Europe and the FSU, except that it was chartered to deal with the specific topical area of defense conversion related to WMD in Belarus, Kazakhstan, Russia, and Ukraine, rather than on a broader set of ventures in a specific geographical area. It was authorized to provide debt and/or equity financing.

The DEF was structured to replace the DOD's venture funding and monitoring with a management oriented toward commercial business. The intent was to capitalize the DEF with approximately $118 million, and for the DEF to raise additional funds through the capital markets. It was ultimately capitalized at approximately $70 million.[9]

Technical Assistance Programs[10]

There were several forms of technical assistance offered to these enterprises in addition to the funding of projects:

---

[9] See Annual Reports of the Defense Enterprise Fund.

[10] Office of the Coordinator of U.S. Assistance to the NIS, *U.S. Government Assistance to and Cooperative Activities with the New Independent States of the Former Soviet Union*, FY 1996 Annual Report, January 1997.

- They were encouraged to apply for the Department of Commerce's SABIT defense-conversion training internships for their personnel.[11] SABIT has trained hundreds of executives and scientists from the NIS, many of these from companies on the list of 82 Russian defense enterprises.
- The IESC worked directly with many enterprises on the list of 82 to assist them in several ways that deal with establishing joint ventures. In some cases they assisted with restructuring and general business development planning. In most cases, they assisted in identifying potential American partners, preparing proposals to them, arranging meetings, and advising on follow-on negotiations.
- The Department of Defense, Department of Commerce, and the OPIC sponsored several bilateral conferences, industry roundtables, and trade delegations to facilitate business development meetings between the managers of the enterprises and those of U.S. companies.
- The U.S. Trade Development Agency (TDA) funded feasibility studies to bring potential business proposals to the point where they could be attractive to public and/or private sources of financing.

Many U.S. companies that bid unsuccessfully for Fast Four projects became aware of the technical capabilities of Russian enterprises and the potential business advantages of working with them, as well as with the U.S. government-sponsored programs to facilitate joint ventures. As a result, many of these U.S. companies continued to explore the possibilities of pursuing their proposed projects either with their own funds or with other sources of finance.

---

[11] Special American Business Internship Training Program for Business Executives and Scientists from the New Independent States of the Former Soviet Union of the U.S. Department of Commerce.

Largely as a result of the diverse types of meetings with U.S. companies and advisers, many of the Russian enterprise directors became aware of the necessity of restructuring their organizations in order to attract a Western partner. It later became clear to them that such restructuring was necessary for their conversion to succeed, either with or without a partner.

The indirect benefits on the U.S. side fall into two main categories, financial and industrial. In the financial area, the main effect was to use U.S. government funds as seed capital to attract far greater sums of more conventional investment capital, as well as political risk insurance. On the industrial side, many U.S. companies that had not seriously considered investment in Russia started to consider the concept, and many of those have gone ahead to make investments. A bilateral commission under the GCC helped remove some of the earlier barriers, and established a mechanism for addressing additional barriers. Other U.S. government-funded operations, such as the American Business Centers and the IESC projects, provided additional practical assistance to U.S. companies starting investments in Russia. There were also other technical assistance programs to help develop the commercial infrastructure and institutions.

Another approach of the CTR program was to combine the results of the indirect effects on the two sides. This was done by a series of conferences, trade delegations, training programs, and publications designed to bring interested parties on the two sides together. The cost of these efforts was much smaller- perhaps 6-8% of the U.S. government investment in the Fast Four - but the resultant leverage has been significant.

There are many sources of both private and public capital that are available for Russian defense conversion ventures, and a few that are specifically designated for such ventures. In addition, there has been extensive investment by companies using their own funds. This money cannot be quantified, because much of it is in contractual investments, which are not tabulated as some equity investments are; however, there are several hundred million dollars of such investments in the aerospace field alone. The Fast Four procurement and the technical assistance programs have provided a backlog of viable projects for consideration by the DEF, other funds, and private industry.

Conclusions

In analyzing any conversion effort in which non-Russian organizations participate, it is necessary to consider them in the context of Soviet/Russian conversion programs as well as in that of the overall economic reform program.

It is still too early to evaluate the success of U.S.-Russian bilateral defense conversion efforts. The Fast Four should be judged as the first step in the process of U.S. government assistance in converting excess defense capacity in Russia to the production of civilian goods. It would have been possible for the four projects to be highly successful in terms of their own business objectives while contributing very little to the broader programmatic objectives. It would also have been possible for the four projects to have been failures in terms of their specific business objectives and still have contributed indirectly, but substantially, to the overall program as well as to the commercial transition of the four Russian enterprises. In reality, the four projects spanned these possibilities.

The experiences of these four projects confirms the hypothesis at the beginning of the program that direct contracts of this type from the Department of Defense are not the best means for the U.S. government to support conversion projects. The effort to start the project as quickly as possible inhibited business relationships between partners and sources of finance from evolving in a logical progression, and they prevented the implementation of the projects to be driven by standard business criteria.

The very first steps were made. They were the most difficult steps because it was impossible to tell with a fair deal of certainty what was waiting down the line. Although, eventually they did lead to some enlightenment. Both Russia and the United States learned their respective lessons, and are now moving ahead.

There were several lessons learned from the DOD's programs thus far:

- Although Russian defense enterprises have gone through an extremely difficult period, they still have substantial human and technological capital, and some have adapted their managerial capabilities to the new challenges. This combination of circumstances makes them more attractive as partners for American companies.
- A successful partnership is far more likely when there is a strong working relationship built up between the partners. While this relationship-building process can grow through the life of the project, it should be fairly well developed before a substantial business partnership is established. Partners should cooperatively develop a complete business plan prior to initiating a major venture. A small contractual project can be undertaken first, and the larger venture's plan can be developed during that contract.

- The prospects of success are greater when the Russian partner has already started a decentralized restructuring that enables sub-units of the enterprise to pursue specific businesses with a high degree of independence.
- U.S. government seed financing, coupled with government-to-government facilitation can be an effective means of initiating joint ventures focused on defense conversion. However, the government's most effective role is in setting general programmatic criteria, establishing and capitalizing financing mechanisms such as enterprise funds, providing technical assistance, and addressing problems at a government-to-government level, but not being involved in direct contractual and business relations.

3.2. COMMAND CONVERSION: POTS INSTEAD OF TANKS

Introductory Remarks

Vlad E. Genin

It is believed that conversion started in 1988, after the U.S.S.R.'s famous statement on arms limitation. This event was preceded by radical economic reforms, which were begun in 1985. One wonders whether the U.S.S.R., under the still-prevailing command economy, had a clear and detailed conversion program.

After the process got underway, rather spontaneously, and after the first two "pilot" years of conversion to production of consumer goods, the U.S.S.R. determined the goals and objectives of conversion, and by 1990, had developed a five-year plan detailing financial issues.

Gradually, it became evident that conversion of the Soviet defense industry presented a most challenging and costly task, comparable in scope only to the Marshall Plan in post-war Europe. It was apparent that the plan for conversion, as a completely new and unprecedented process for reforming Russia, needed a new, thoroughly considered, well-planned, non-command approach.

However, "command conversion" was a child of the Soviet legacy, and was defended as a Russian "specific". This expression is now well known to the international business community. Since perestroika, it has been used by Russians in order to explain the impossibility of transferring pure

Western ways of planning and doing business to their country without adapting them to the specific Russian business environment and the legacy of the old political and command management mentality.

But in the reality, the process of defense conversion in Russia began as a command process.

Alexander P. Kotov

Economic reforms, during the first stage, looked like traditional Soviet "campaigns," but were not real economic reforms for the whole system. In spite of the fact that purposeful reforms started in 1987-88, with the approval of the bill *On State Enterprises*, which proclaimed the autonomy of manufacturers, their freedom was still limited by a system of direct government orders. The specific characteristics and unique status of defense industry enterprises were not completely reflected in the bill. It did not give them market opportunities equal to those of other industries. In reality, a self-financing version of the command system was created. Direct commands were replaced with indirect ones. Compliance with economic regulations, and self-funding norms and standards, were still required.

Enterprises of the defense industry started to operate on a self-supporting basis, with a planned one-year delay. However, by the end of the 1980s, the supporting industries, which were the suppliers of raw materials, components, supplies and spare parts, had eliminated the limitations of the command system and had broken agreements, and the wholesale system had become unusable. All these reasons caused the defense industry to fail to meet its obligations to its customers.

The independence of the supporting industries was narrowed to their right to raise prices and salaries, which immediately affected the financial situation of defense industry enterprises, because these enterprises worked in terms of fixed prices on military products. Uncontrollable salary increases (independent of the expected results of self-financing) were the first push of inflationary processes. The command economy's administrative management was ruined, but the new market system did not yet exist.

The formation of the new main link in the economy -- the *proizvodstvennoe ob'edinenie* (a combination of production enterprises)[12] -- became a notorious nationwide phenomenon. Enterprises located hundreds of kilometers from each other were uniting; the degree of monopolization in some scientific and production spheres was growing.

Diversification directed from above was typical for defense industry operations at that time, and without the creation of any of the necessary economic incentives for organizing civilian production and the regular output of consumer goods. The creation of all kinds of unprofitable subsidiary enterprises was also typical.

The period between 1986 and 1988 was also noted for the beginning of reduced military output, which resulted in the slowing down of economic growth, and the reduction of total output.

The next very important stage affecting the operations of the defense industry in 1989-1990 was the conversion of military to civilian production, and the adjustment of the country's economy to market conditions.

---

12 Editor's Note: Also many *Nauchno-Proizvodstvennoe Ob'edinenie* (combined production and research enterprises) were formed.

The kick-off event was Mikhail Gorbachev's speech at the General Assembly of the United Nations in December 1988, where he proclaimed that the Soviet Union would begin a unilateral and drastic program of reduction of its military forces. This program provided that within two years (1989-1990), the Soviet Union's military forces would be reduced by 12%, the military budget reduced by 12%, and defense industry production reduced by 20%. The scale and depth of the conversion were outlined by a decree of the Presidium of the Supreme Soviet, published on March 21, 1989.

The consequences for the defense industry were these: as a result of the reduction of military expenditures and decreased defense procurement orders, production capacity, funds, materials, and human and financial resources were freed up. All these resources were now available for the output of civilian products.

At that time, more than 400 defense industry enterprises were involved in the conversion process, but only five or six of them totally converted; the others just switched to producing more civilian goods than they had before.

The world's experience shows that the optimal conversion rate is the reduction of military output by 5 – 7% a year. An attempt to convert more rapidly causes the defense industry, and the national economy, to experience certain difficulties, but these problems can be solved with the introduction of certain government rules and regulations.

In addition, the conversion process needed a theoretical and scientific basis, and legal support. Conversion might have succeeded if it had been supported by a unified and coherent plan of action, including scientific research, a legal structure, a financial and technical system, political decisions, a new military doctrine, arms and military technological development programs, and the reduction of the military forces.

From the very beginning of conversion, the logical sequence of its several stages was ignored. In 1988, after the approval of the above-mentioned political decision, the U.S.S.R. reduced orders for arms and military equipment production by more than 20% a year instead of 5-7%. There was no new defense doctrine, no military reform, nor was the concept of conversion developed yet. There was no legal or financial support.

The state program for defense industry conversion and civilian production by the defense industry for the period up to 1995 was not developed until 1990. And even then, it was stillborn, because the State had no funds for its implementation.

The main idea at this stage was to accomplish two things simultaneously: to preserve the production potential of the defense enterprises, while at the same time fostering conversion by allowing civilian industries to use advanced technologies that had been developed earlier for arms production; the use of such technologies, it was hoped, would enable industry to produce high-quality, competitive products.

The scope of the reduction in military production in 1990-1991 is shown in Table 3.2.1.

The decrease in state military orders forced defense industry enterprises to start producing civilian products, including high-tech equipment and general consumer goods. There were serious structural shifts within the volumes and ratios of the military and civilian production. (See Table 3.2.2.)

It is evident that conversion was not only the reason for the structural shifts in the production volume, but also the reason for the

TABLE 3.2.1

The Scope of the Reduction in Military Production in 1990-91

Ministries of the Defense Sector	Number of enterprises undergoing conversion		Reduction in arms and military equipment being produced, by percentage	
	1990	1991	1990 vs. 1989	1991 vs. 1990
Ministry of the Aviation Industry	110	118	11.3	21.9
Ministry of the Defense Industry	108	116	20.3	26.8
Ministry of Machinery	45	45	19.6	30.7
Ministry of the Radio Industry	40	103	10.1	21.4
Ministry of the Ship Production Industry	59	96	1.5	21.5
Ministry of the Electronic Industry	20	48	8.3	21.1
Ministry of Telecommunication Industry	33	55	3.2	14.6
Ministry of Nuclear Energy Production	29	36	46.1	12.7
Total	444	616	21.8 (average)	20.6 (average)

TABLE 3.2.2

Change in Production Volume

Type of production	Change in production volume, by percentage (1991 prices)		
	1990 vs. 1989	1991 vs. 1990	1991 vs. 1989
Military Production	79.5	79.4	63.1
Civilian Production	112.4	113.9	128.0

drop in production. The recession was caused, first, by the need to produce items completely different from those the industry was used to producing. Another cause was that the cost of labor in the defense industry was considerably higher than in civilian industries. That was why the production of civilian goods was unable to compensate for the reduction in defense-oriented output.

The defense industry enterprises had to choose those types of civilian products that most closely matched the technological capabilities of the enterprise, and that would, at the same time, meet the demands of the civilian market.

The State Conversion Program was able to help the enterprises to make the right choice of goods to produce, since the Program offered a list of consumer items that the national economy needed at that time, and the amount of financing that the State was planning to provide for this purpose (about 8 million rubles).

The only defect of the Program was the complete absence of State funds to support it—which is why it was never implemented. The directions outlined in the Program did, at least, prompt the heads of enterprises to concentrate their efforts on the production of civilian technological equipment.

In 1990, there were especially high increases in the rate of equipment production in the following industries (in comparison with 1989):

- for light industry -- 50 %;
- for the food processing industries of the agricultural complex--110 %;
- for the retail industry and restaurant services -- 80 %;
- for the medical industry -- 150 %.

The results of a financial analysis of the conversion effort showed that the defense enterprises worked in an unfavorable economic environment. In 1990, the profits from sales of industrial production dropped by 12%, in comparison with 1989. The profits from military sales went down 20%. However, the profits resulting from sales of civilian technological equipment increased by 4.1%, and from sales of consumer goods by 20.5%.

In 1991, the decrease in profits from military production sales was about 13%, but was not compensated by the increased sales of non-military products. The reason for this was the reduction of total output, along with the simultaneous decrease in profitability, as shown in Table 3.2.3.

TABLE 3.2.3

Product Profitability, %

Description	1989	1990	1991
Military Production	16	16.4	12.1
Technological Civilian Equipment	19.2	17.2	15.2
Consumer Items	16	15	13.4
Defense Industry's Profitability	17	16.2	13.5

The reduction of the defense industry's profitability can be explained by the fact that enterprises could no longer manufacture mass-production items. They had to change the profiles of the production lines, master production of completely new products, and retool and restructure the enterprises. Such retooled and restructured manufacturing is always less profitable than well-established manufacturing of mass-production items.

The low profitability of production in the defense industry in 1991 was caused also by increased costs, mostly salary increases, and the payment of special compensation to employees to cover the increased cost of living. The increase in costs prompted hyperinflation. The fixed prices for defense industry production that were introduced on January 1, 1991 did not reflect all the changes listed above. The defense enterprises had to buy raw materials and components at much higher prices than those originally stipulated in the agreements. This of course drastically affected the cost of the final defense industry product.

The financial crisis in the defense industry was further aggravated by the amount of excess property, materials and goods, which could not be used anymore because of the reduction in state defense procurement orders. By the end of 1990, the estimated cost of this excess property was 3 billion rubles, and by the end of 1991 it was roughly 40% more.

Unfinished military products amounted to 26.7% of total production. The total cost of unfinished production and of excess property and materials was 3.1 billion rubles in 1990, and in 1991 it was 4.5 billion rubles. The property and material needed to be scrapped, because it was impossible to use.

In 1991, conversion expenses were about 1 billion rubles, 170 % more than in 1990, including the state's centralized budget (up by 370%), and the resources of defense enterprises (up by 60%).

In 1990, the expenses for retooling and restructuring defense enterprises were 43% of the total defense conversion expenses, and in 1991 were 41.1%. The rest of the funds were used for the liquidation, conservation, or maintenance of facilities and resources that were not being used, employee compensation payments, severance packages, employee training programs, and other miscellaneous expenses.

In spite of the rather high flow of investments into the production sphere (238.6% in 1990, and 254.6 % in 1991), including the state's centralized sources (296.6 % in 1990 and 329.1% in 1991), the production sphere's portion of the total of conversion expenses had tended downwards from 32.7 % in 1989 to 28.1 % in 1991.

By the end of 1991, the defense industry used 42.5% of capacity to produce military products; 15.2 % of the enterprises stopped their military production; and 60.3% of them were reorganized and retooled for the manufacturing of civilian/commercial products. More that 100,000 people left employment in the defense industry. During this stage, 616 defense enterprises were undergoing conversion.

Moreover, the results were less than modest: 122 new types of products were planned for production, but only 23 types were successfully produced, and only five of them met international standards.

In short, what was called conversion was merely a slight diversification of defense enterprises' production portfolios, with only a couple of dozen defense enterprises among thousands starting real conversion.

The defense industry had very powerful research and development departments, experimental laboratories, and design bureaus. The program proposed that these organizations begin R&D and realization of new products, which had chosen without any common sense. These projects were supposed to be financed after the program was approved.

Defense industry specialists were unanimous in criticizing this program; the concept of "baby carriages instead of missiles, pots instead of tanks, furniture instead of military vessels and ships" was not very popular with either the defense industry employees or the general public. In 1990-1991, the specialists identified the situation in the defense industry as a crisis: its smooth working structure had been dismantled, and it was practically ruined by the extreme reduction in State financing, and by multiple reorganization.

So, the beginning of conversion was conducted with no effective plan, with no consideration of defense enterprises' production capabilities, with no legal support (the law *On Conversion* was still under development), and with virtually no management.

3.3. WESTERN CONTRIBUTIONS AND CONDITIONS

Introductory Remarks

Vlad E. Genin

In the "good old days" of the Soviet command economy, defense plants could not live without protectors. Previously the ministries of the nine defense industries played the role of protectors. After the beginning of reforms the defense plants shifted their expectations to the West—a switch that was encouraged, even mandated, by the top echelons of political power and ministries. Accordingly, Russian defense industry executives, plant directors, and all senior personnel of the defense enterprises were expecting a flood of free Western assistance: shipments of new equipment from America, Germany, Italy, or England. Notwithstanding the fact that the West never promised permanent free assistance, Russians firmly believed in the "Western miracle." Such naïve and inflated hopes were typical of the Russian way of thinking. Historically, the Russian people have always needed to believe in somebody great: in the Tsar, in Lenin, in Stalin, in Khrushchev, in Brezhnev; now it was a new god: the West. Russian propaganda in those years turned the people's faces toward the West, mainly to America...

U.S. support of Russian conversion had really begun. At the start, Russia perceived America as a genius doctor who could quickly cure its industry, which was profoundly affected by the malignant tumor of militarization. (This medical image was probably prompted by the famous Americans who flew all over the world performing their "miraculous," life-saving heart operations.)

But in providing assistance to such a monster of a patient as the Russian defense industry, the West faced too many uncertainties. The West didn't realize the complexity and the sheer size of the Russian militarized industry. Moreover, it was not clear which came first within the system. Was the economy subordinate to the defense industry, or vice versa? This being the case, the probability of a correct diagnosis, and the choice of the proper treatment, was very slim. So it was impossible to prescribe the ideal course of treatment, because the necessary data was missing. The empirical approach seemed to be the only way: cautiously start some practical experiments, study the results, and make corrections as necessary.

The Russian defense industry establishment developed an exaggerated concept of the scale of potential Western assistance. They were sure that the patient, the defense industry, could be miraculously cured with one magic pill called "money". During that early period, Russia seemed to be always saying "give us the money and leave us alone!"

The West did help. But not as much as was expected by the defense establishments and the Russian people. And more importantly, not as much as was necessary for the conversion of the most heavily militarized industrial complex in the world: a huge "defense plant" stretching for 6,000 miles from St. Petersburg to Vladivostok.

Evgeniy M. Kozhokin

Since the early 1990s, some leading Western countries and international organizations have developed programs of financial, scientific, and technical assistance for Russia and other CIS countries to further the demilitarization and conversion of their military-industrial complexes.

These programs were not ordinary assistance to foreign states; they also strengthened the national security of the United States and the other NATO countries by encouraging the destruction of the weapons that were aimed at them, and also by preventing the proliferation of weapons to other countries.

The purpose of U.S. assistance to Russia was announced by U.S. President Clinton in 1993: "to support Russia as a democracy... to support the reduction of the nuclear threat... to support market reforms."

From 1992 to 1995, according to the assistance programs, the United States was supposed to grant the new Commonwealth of Independent States, or CIS, nearly $15 billion, but only $12.7 billion was received by the CIS countries. During this period, Russia received $3 billion in direct assistance and $4.2 billion in credits.

The Nunn-Lugar program[13] was aimed at helping Russia and the CIS countries with demilitarization and defense conversion. This particular program implied that there would be an increase in military contacts between the United States and the CIS countries, with mutual assistance in destroying nuclear, chemical and biological weapons. It also called for assistance in providing for the safe transportation, preservation, protection, and deactivation of weapons of mass

---

[13] Editor's Note: The Cooperative Threat Reduction Program (CTR).

destruction, as well as preventing the proliferation of weapons and their technologies.

By 1995, the U.S. Congress had granted $1.25 billion for the implementation of the Nunn-Lugar program, and the US Department of Defense (DOD) asked for $3.75 billion during the next two years. According to the calculations of the U.S. Congressional Budget Office, by 1994, only 23% of the requested sum had been granted for the Nunn-Lugar program. The larger part of these funds was allocated for disarmament, and only a small part went to the conversion of the defense industry. In official U.S. documents, a significantly higher number is given, but in reality very little was actually received; most of these funds were spent to house and retrain retired officers, as part of the disarmament program.

In 1994, only $20 million of the $36.8 million designated for conversion was received. The U.S. assistance was provided to a very limited number of selected Russian defense companies, four of them in particular—the program's "Fast Four." In research performed by the Russian-American institute Utah-Russia, it is emphasized that most of the U.S. funding that was allocated to the assistance programs went in the end to American corporations, not Russian. This happened because the program was structured to assign to each funded project an American company as leader and treasurer; this strategy may have been unavoidable, but it resulted in a sharp decrease in the amount of money that actually reached the Russian partners.

For example, the funding granted under the Nunn-Lugar program for the development of methods of safe transportation and protection of dismantled nuclear warheads was almost entirely consumed by one American company in New Mexico.

The European Union under the TACIS program also granted assistance to the CIS countries for conversion of their defense enterprises. At the beginning, that assistance was concentrated only on a selected few military plants and complexes. In the 1992 budget for this program, the greatest attention was given to the production and development of agricultural equipment, food industry equipment, medical equipment, and the production of glassware, ceramics, and machinery. Later, the TACIS organization tried to select for assistance those regional enterprises that already had some interesting technologies in aviation, telecommunications, environmental monitoring, electronics, etc. The CIS countries received limited financial assistance from TACIS for defense industry conversion. The Russian Federation received almost 72% of the allocated funds, because of its leading role in the former Soviet military and industrial complex. (See Table 3.3.1.)

TABLE 3.3.1

The TACIS Budget for the Conversion of Military Industry (in millions of dollars)

Fiscal Year	CIS countries (excluding Russia)	Russia
1992	15	10
1993	9.5	8
1994	7.5	5
Total	32	23

In the strategic TACIS document, "Program of the Defense Industry Conversion in the Russian Federation in 1994," the following main purposes of supporting the Russian military industry are listed:

- Maintaining political stability. The military industry has strong influence on the administrative structures of the Russian State, and it is a very serious potential political force.

- Prevention of unemployment, caused by the fast liquidation of jobs in the military industry, especially in the regions where the majority of the population work for the defense industry.
- Maintaining the scientific and technical potential of the Russian economy.

During the implementation of the conversion process, the Western countries that were providing assistance to the CIS countries faced serious difficulties. It was difficult to find viable projects and candidates for assistance in the constantly changing economic situation in Russia. They had to adapt very quickly to the constantly changing reality.

The TACIS assistance was coordinated with Russian state programs for defense conversion. In Russia, the first programs were developed during the beginning of the transition period from a state-controlled economy to a free market economy. Five sectors of industry, selected by TACIS for its first conversion programs budget of 1992, were included in the list of the fourteen programs developed by the Russian government. They were the agriculture and food industry; medical equipment industry; aviation equipment industry; glassware and ceramics industry; and motor industry. For the last three fields, well-known Russian companies had been selected, but for the first two fields partners were not found. All of the projects were located in the regions of Moscow and St. Petersburg. The 1992 budget of the conversion program had funds for a sixth project, which was the creation of a consulting group to help with defense conversion, and to work with local administrations in regions with an especially high concentration of military enterprises.

In 1993, TACIS assistance was expanded to take in other regions (Yekaterinburg and Taganrog). Emphasis was put on technologically advanced projects for the aviation industry; production of helicopters; and the petroleum industry. The budget for 1994 granted assistance to companies that possessed advanced technologies in the aviation industry, telecommunications industry, and environmental monitoring.

In granting assistance, the Western participants of joint projects imposed some conditions on investments for the defense conversion projects:

- privatization of state enterprises is desirable
- funding is limited to selected projects only
- companies receiving funding must operate in the free market
- the companies supported must be highly qualified technically
- the products developed must be highly competitive, marketable or usable by the Western partner
- Western partners should play an important role in the implementation of the projects, and in ensuring the success of the projects
- products must be potentially exportable to a customer who will pay in a hard currency (this condition was later relaxed for those products intended exclusively for the CIS market)

The availability of investments depended on a solid business plan and the availability of a suitable industrial partner, which increased the probability of executing the project within a competitive market.

Representatives of U.S. governmental agencies, research communities, and businesses were indicating their interest in developing and deepening scientific and technical cooperation with Russia. Both countries devoted special attention to solving complex problems of disarmament; in particular, to accelerating the process of converting enterprises and scientific institutions that were part of the Soviet Military-Industrial Complex. The main recommendations to the U.S. government on dealing with the new situation that arose after the disintegration of the U.S.S.R. were made in March 1992 by a group from the National Academy of Sciences of the United States, with some participation from large defense contractors, scientific centers and national laboratories. In the final document, the group recommended the following guidelines for U.S. scientific and technical cooperation with Russia:

- maintaining the scientific and technical potential of Russia at a high level; this was necessary for the reconstruction of the economy and for a "transition to a free market, and open and stable democratic society"; it also furthered the economic interests of the United States, and helped to strengthen its national security.
- reorienting the scientific and technical potential of Russia from military research and development to the commercial sector, civilian industry, and agriculture ;
- carrying out joint research projects with Russian scientists, primarily in fields of direct interest to the American scientific community and American business;
- ensuring American access to scientific and technical innovations of former Soviet scientists;
- ensuring American influence on the Russian leadership in selecting priorities for research and development, scientific and technical education, etc.

Besides the intermediate steps that had already been taken, such as the organization in Moscow of the International Science and

Technology Center, which was set up to attract Russian specialists in the field of nuclear (and other) weapons; the setting up of joint projects with commercial aspects; the signing of treaties concerning scientific and technical cooperation; etc., the U.S. government recommended that the Russian leadership undertake these additional steps:

- opening up those Russian military enterprises and offices that were participating in joint projects to visits from Western partners, and minimizing the restricted areas (i.e., the Russian concept of "higher walls around less territory");
- reducing control over scientists and engineers, so that they could freely and openly communicate with their Western colleagues;
- allowing the installation of electronic telecommunication devices for communication with those foreign military installations that were participating in joint scientific and technical programs;
- guaranteeing access to military laboratories, scientific equipment, and research facilities to those performing non-military work (this is the most important consideration for Western investors);

If Russia observed these conditions, the West would continue working with the scientists and engineers of the Russian defense industry in such fields as the reliable and environmentally safe storage and elimination of stockpiles of nuclear and other weapons of mass destruction; storage and reprocessing of special nuclear materials; ensuring nuclear safety, including studying the biological effects of low levels of ionizing radiation; environmental monitoring and cleanup; civilian power engineering, transportation, telecommunications, etc.

Many foreign observers thought there was a good chance of developing mutually beneficial exchanges between Russian technical institutions and those of the United States, despite the risks of such cooperation with Western countries—especially the United States—and concerns for Russian scientific and technical security. American economists note that the nearly complete absence in Russia of effective legislation for intellectual property protection can result in the use of Russian scientific and technical potential in the interests of foreign companies.

It was also observed that the reduction of state allocations for scientific studies forces Russian scientific and industrial organizations to look for commercial contacts with the West, and to sell them scientific and technical innovations in order to purchase modern equipment for developing their research and technological base. According to some evaluations, more than 60% of the Russian industrial enterprises that urgently needed hard currency had to sell their modern, proprietary technologies and know-how at very low prices on the foreign market.

Another concern was that Russian enterprises and organizations, as a rule, do not have enough experience in scientific and technological marketing, and are unable to estimate the price at which their innovations would be salable in a free market—nor do they know how to protect their intellectual property. There were practically no services in Russia to help them to solve these problems.

Under these conditions, the foreign companies were able to take advantage of inexperienced Russian companies, and to take possession of very valuable scientific and technical achievements, or to obtain key information about them, while investing a minimum in effort and money.

It was generally agreed that this favorable situation for the West is generated by the inability of Russian industry to exploit technological innovations, and by the lack of experience on the part of Russian scientists, especially those in academia, who are used to dealing only with pure science, and not the practical application of their scientific research. So American consultants generally recommended to their businessmen-clients that they purchase (as a rule, with a single low payment) exclusive licenses to the results of chosen scientific research and development projects, at an early stage. In addition, they were particularly interested in purchasing licenses to inventions protected only by a Russian author's certificate, and not by U.S. or other Western patents.

The attention of industrial circles and the scientific community of the United States has been attracted by the achievements of Russian scientists in such fields as high-energy physics, biophysics, genetics, the production of materials in outer space, non-ferrous metallurgy, materials refining technologies, hydrofoil and aircraft construction, titanium alloys, pressure casting, dam construction, the development of semiconductor materials, welding, electrochemical metal processing, super-deep drilling of wells, ophthalmology, architecture and software for 5th generation computers.

The work of Russian specialists in joint ventures with Western partners gives Western partners access to special literature, in which the results of scientific research are published in such a way that they can reconstruct Russian advanced technologies without purchasing licenses and patents. It is no secret that some modern American military developments are based on ideas taken from the analysis of Russian (Soviet) literature (e.g., rocket boosters and space technologies, production of ceramics, and semiconductors).

Several universities in the United States have invited a number of outstanding Russian mathematicians and physicists, who are making considerable contributions to the development of these fields in the

United States, passing on new ideas and approaches to solving scientific problems. Many of these universities invite the best Russian scientists on temporary appointments (for three years, as a rule), or, on occasion, permanent ones.

The expected flow of scientists emigrating from Russia to the United States creates very favorable conditions for strengthening American science. A good example of using Russian "brain potential" in the interests of the United States is the competition for the best article on image recognition that was organized by Hewlett-Packard for the specialists from the CIS countries. The technology of image recognition is considered to be a critical technology, because it is a key element of future "smart" weapon systems, capable of discovering and recognizing targets, including mobile targets. Paramount importance in the competition is given to original theoretical studies (e.g., algorithms, data processing methods, conceptual approaches), which could help in the development of the military industry in the United States at a rather low price. Personal computers and calculators are the prizes given to the competition winners. Obviously, such a competition creates a danger of a free-of-charge transfer of critical technologies to America, as well as another way of finding capable Russian scientists working in this field.

These facts show that on the way to developing scientific and technical contacts and cooperation with the United States, the Russian side can face serious problems, which can be solved only when the economic situation in the Russian Federation is stabilized, and a law is adopted protecting intellectual property.

3.4. THE ERA OF EAST – WEST JOINT VENTURES

Introductory Remarks

Vlad E. Genin

Right after the beginning of perestroika and defense conversion, a phrase was added to the modern Russian vocabulary: *"Mezhdunarodnoe Sovmestnoe Predpriatie"* or *"SP"* (International Joint Venture or JV). The phrase "International JV" sounded like magic. It meant a long-awaited breakthrough into the West, with its new technologies and opportunities of producing in Russia exactly the same commodities, foodstuffs, and equipment that are produced in "well-developed capitalist countries". JV was a symbol of hope for new contacts, relationships, cooperation, and, of course, long-awaited major investments. It was a time of great expectations after the darkness of the cold war. People were expecting immediate domestic production in Russia of previously unknown Western-style cars, VCRs, CD players -- everything that was previously unimaginable in most Russian families.

In the early '90s registration of International JVs was rather active; in fact, it was skyrocketing. However, as further experience showed, the JVs were established without detailed studies of their economic and technical feasibility, or of the very special, unusual, and difficult business conditions in Russia.

In the consumer products area, JVs were supposed to solve several tasks at once, the most important of which was to fill the Russian market with high quality products. Russian consumers have always been very demanding with respect to quality, even during the time of economic hardships, and will not put up with second best. Even the shortage was not a good enough reason for Russians to buy junk. This is a part of the nation's culture, and the greatest mistake of foreign companies was viewing Russia as they did undeveloped countries, and proposing that new joint ventures manufacture products inappropriate for Russia.

Russian industrialists hoped that joint ventures would accelerate many uncompleted major projects, like the new generations of airliners, cars, and industrial equipment. Engineers from Russian high tech plants and research centers started a search for powerful American partnering companies that would help them to complete R&D of the newest types of products and of unique electronic and telecommunication systems, in order to jointly start mass producing them. The Russian Aerospace Agency started mutually beneficial cooperation with NASA on the Mir space station, which was then a masterpiece of the world aerospace industry.

Another task of the joint ventures was to help Russia enter the world market. Yet another was streamlining enterprises themselves, and converting and comprehensively restructuring them.

More than a decade has passed since the Russian defense industry was opened to contacts with foreign firms in the late 80s. This historically short period may be considered an entire epoch in the development of international business cooperation in Russia and, in particular, of

JVs. It comprised both the boom of the first contacts and plans, the period of rather naive expectations and conceptions of each other's capabilities, the time of disappointments, and finally the realistic and balanced relationships, which satisfied mutual interests, opportunities, and needs, and corresponded to the economic, political, and business climate that formed the background of these relationships.

The expectations of Russian and Western counterparts in their approach to JV were more than slightly different. Evaluating differences in those expectations in both countries helps to solve many problems that contributed to the success or failure of many former international JVs. What were the similarities and differences in the primary expectations of Russian defense enterprises and their US partners?

Sergey K. Kolpakov

The answer is obvious. Russian expectations resulted from the extremely difficult situation of the Russian defense industry in the late '80s and early '90s, due to the loss of state orders; the dramatic fall in demand for civilian products, the inability of the state to finance conversion, the non-payment crisis, and galloping inflation. Financial resources were required for Russian industry to survive and to develop properly, and the West was regarded as the main source of financing. Senior managers of defense enterprises believed that the way out of the situation was investment in joint manufacturing (including investments in the form of technology) and access to the world markets. Moreover, the establishment of international joint ventures was considered to be a prerequisite for bringing in foreign investment. Due to the lack of finances, Russian enterprises planned to contribute buildings, manufacturing equipment, technologics, and the results of recent research and technological developments into the charter capital of these JV.

The heads of the defense enterprises wished to establish JVs under their control, which is what caused their sharply negative attitude towards the activities of specialized foreign trade brokerage organizations. According to 1993 polls conducted by the Russian Federation Government Economic Situation Analysis Center, more than 90% of defense enterprise managers did not believe that the brokers knew the status of their products on the world market, or that they were interested in selling them profitably. The way out seemed to lie in the establishment of JVs with Western partners, which would provide access to the world markets for conversion products, technologies, and services. The Institute for Aviation Materials, for example, organized three JVs in the United States alone in order to promote its products there. (To glance forward, all of these ventures ceased to exist before completing any significant transactions.)

What did Western companies expect from joint ventures with Russian defense enterprises?

The first attraction was the vast emerging market nearly inaccessible to them before. Many believed that the market would recover from the crisis phase very soon, and would start developing very fast. Defense establishments announced at Russian-American conferences on conversion that they were opening opportunities for foreign capital to participate not only in wholly converted enterprises, but also in those retaining some military orders.

The second incentive for cooperation was the expectation of being able to access the high technologies accumulated in the Russian defense industry during the long years of its isolated development. Access to these technologies at low prices, as well as to highly-qualified but low-paid personnel, scientists, and engineers was considered by Western industrialists as a way of getting ahead of competition in the market.

The third and last factor to awaken the interest of Western companies involved the declarations made by a number of Western governments of their wish to facilitate conversion in Russia, and their readiness to allocate significant financial resources for this purpose, particularly for support of joint business initiatives. Naturally, the Western companies anticipated receiving a substantial portion of these funds.

When these business contacts began, in the overwhelming majority of cases it was the Russian enterprises that initiated these cooperative projects. Western companies were mostly in a position to choose among proposals. Ministries, government agencies, central and local governments, and numerous intermediary organizations were also very active in the establishment of JVs. At the same time, there was almost no efficient coordination of all these activities. The quality of proposals was poor, and they were not thoroughly examined. The prevailing idea was that investments were relatively easy to attract, and the Western market was ready for conversion products.

Meanwhile, the stream of Western businessmen that rushed into the Russian defense enterprises included not only representatives of firms with good business reputations, but also all kinds of middlemen, and often adventurers who did not seek long-term partnerships, but who tried to collect information and sell it to foreign businessmen. Russian defense enterprise managers, who lacked the necessary information and were inexperienced in testing business partners, could not distinguish the former from the latter. This "disease" infected not just the business managers, but also the authorities supervising the initial contacts. Sound and balanced studies of market opportunities and business conditions in Russia carried out by high-profile Western firms often concluded that partnerships were inadvisable, due to a number of risk factors. On the other hand, the activities of less discriminating firms often resulted in JV registration and eventual disappointments.

Active research conducted by foreign businessmen into opportunities in the Russian defense industry, coincided the leading Western states' pursuit of the demilitarization and defense conversion of the Russian economy, with particular benefits to commercial interests and the financial and technological capabilities of their domestic firms.

This pursuit was primarily motivated by reasons of national security. The United States pursued this policy quite consistently. In October 1992, the U.S. Congress passed a bill dedicated to the demilitarization of the former Soviet Union, which explicitly stated that the Congress finds it necessary in the interests of the United States' national security to support the demilitarization of the large-scale defense-oriented industry of the countries of the former Soviet Union, as well as the conversion of this industry and its equipment for civilian purposes and applications.

Since 1993, the U.S. government has financed a number of special programs and projects to assist Russia in the conversion of its military industry under the auspices of several executive departments and agencies, such as the Department of Defense, Department of Energy, the

U.S. Trade and Development Agency (USTDA), etc. Following the United States, other Western countries and international organizations provided funds for similar purposes. The largest European program to support conversion in Russia was TACIS.

The funds provided were used to arrange meetings between Western businessmen and representatives of the Russian defense industry, assist in the development of proposed projects and business plans, distribute information on potential partners in Russia, finance joint research and design work, and assist in the establishment of JVs.

There were different approaches to developing business contacts. The Russian Privatization and Conversion Center at the Institute of the United States and Canada and Pepperdine University (in the United States), with the financial support of the U.S. Government, analyzed one of the assistance programs for partnership between Russian defense enterprises and American companies. The analysts tried to find out why the program, involving about 140 Russian enterprises, had failed. They arranged meetings with representatives of American and Russian companies, and helped to develop new projects according to world standards.

Immediately after the meetings, all the participants on both sides agreed that they had been useful, and expressed their intention to continue collaborating. In fact, 70% of the participants did continue. But two or three months later, only 25-30% of the participants remained in contact, and in the long term not more than 10-12% continued their relations—and as of today, no joint ventures are known to have been established. The program organizers see the reason for the unraveling of the original plans in the differences between the parties: in the Russian and American parties' widely different motives for seeking partnerships;

in the consequent differences in their ideas about each other's contribution to the partnership; in their business styles; in the professional level and profile of the two sets of negotiators (engineers were prevalent on the Russian side, lawyers on the American); in the treatment of intellectual property (Americans did not yield concerning intellectual property rights); and in business prospects (the Americans were focused on strategic decisions that might not show returns for five or ten years, while the Russians expected immediate profitability).

Western funds were also used for supporting "technical assistance," a program in which numerous groups of consultants were sent to Russia to advise defense enterprises. Most Russian defense enterprise managers saw these consultants as the least useful form of assistance.

First of all, consultants often based their recommendations on Western business practices. They were not always aware of the fact that they were involved in quite an unfamiliar economic and business environment, and that direct application of those practices to Russian conditions may not lead to commercial success, at least in the short term. Furthermore, although these foreign consultants did not represent the investors, actual or potential, that the Russian industry managers eagerly expected, working with them cost the senior managers of enterprises time and sometimes money.

Moreover, some managers had quite specific ideas of the "technical assistance" that they needed, and the inability of consultants to provide that specific type of assistance made the managers skeptical, and sometimes unwilling to collaborate further. For example, the Moscow aviation manufacturing enterprise "MAPO MiG" turned down the TACIS-supported consulting assistance of "Dassault-Aviation" company. Initially, MAPO MiG tried to restructure the assistance program according to its interests. MAPO MiG requested that the assistance not begin with lectures for enterprise managers, as suggested by “Dassault-Aviation”. Instead of lectures, MAPO MiG requested assistance in the certification (according to Western standards) of a number of aircraft parts manufactured by the company for future exports of these parts to the West.

However, this proposal was turned down because it was allegedly impossible to change the fixed procedure of providing assistance. This was the reason why MiG refused the services of Western consultants.

The organizers of foreign training programs for Russian defense industry personnel, particularly the American SABIT program, were faced with similar problems. Certainly, knowledge of business practices in Western countries is generally helpful, but this knowledge neither contributed to the solution of the enterprises’ current problems nor led to the establishment of business partnerships.

The Project “The Fast Four” marked the beginning of progress in the Russian-American partnership. Today, it is evident that the success of future relationships will be determined to a great extent by a thorough analysis of both positive and negative past experiences.

Part of the funds provided within the Nunn-Lugar Program was directly allocated to support the establishment of JVs by American firms and Russian defense enterprises. The total amount of funds earmarked for this purpose was $20 million. Very focused actions to organize four model JVs, the so-called “Fast Four,” were undertaken under the auspices of the Conversion Committee (under the Gore-Chernomyrdin Commission) in order to demonstrate to American business circles and their potential Russian partners the feasibility of successful and profitable business with the converted Russian enterprises. After a competitive selection process, the following business partners received the support of both governments:

- The State Aviation System Research Institute (Russia) and Rockwell International (United States) (JV for the design and production of air traffic control system components, including related software, for upgrading the Russian air traffic control system);
- Istok State Research and Production Enterprise (Russia) and Hearing Aids International (JV for the production of miniature hearing aids);
- Leninets Concern and International American Products (JV for dental chair repair and production of disinfecting solution);
- The Research and Production Machine Building Association and Double Cola Co. (JV for soft drink production).

Two of the four projects have never been implemented. The Research and Production Machine Building Association and Double Cola Co. terminated their relationship, failing to find mutually acceptable approaches to business organization, risk sharing, and utilization of the funds received from the U.S. government. The State Aviation System Research Institute and Rockwell International abandoned the JV idea, and built their relationship on a contract basis. The reason was that the central Russian air traffic control system and its regional branches could not afford the products such a JV would have produced, as had been anticipated, because of the crisis situation with the federal and regional budgets. The relations between the partners have not been terminated, but they have been frozen until better times.

The remaining two JVs were, indeed, organized, but their results have not lived up to initial expectations. The JV set up by Istok State

Research and Production Enterprise and Hearing Aids International has demonstrated the best results of the "Fast Four" projects. The JV launched the production of mini hearing aids that had not previously been available in Russia. However, the distribution and sale of these products turned out to be problematic. In Russia, hearing aids have always been and still are subsidized by the state, as their consumers are supported by the state welfare system. Thus, the success of the JV substantially depended upon state resources. Since all medical equipment and solutions are similarly subsidized by the state, thus presenting the same difficulty even if the JV shifted production to other medical products, the partners are looking to expand sales by penetrating the CIS and international markets.

Joint scientific research projects have been the most successful of the projects and programs funded by the Western countries. Cooperation in this sphere was initiated by the International Science and Technology Center, which was founded by the EU, the United States (the Industrial Partnership program of the U.S. Department of Energy), Japan, the Russian Federation, and some other organizations. Its main task was to provide military scientists and specialists, especially those with experience in the creation of the weapons of mass destruction, with opportunities to transfer to civilian lines of activity. Although these programs had some success in that narrow endeavor, their contribution to JV establishment was insignificant, because most of these projects are not commercial; their aim is not to organize business in a modernized Russia, but to generate new scientific knowledge.

In short, even substantial expenditures by Western countries (it is hard to find the exact scale) neither led to the establishment of many efficient joint ventures, nor succeeded in attracting foreign investment to the converted enterprises. The main reason is that intensive joint venture development was hindered by economic difficulties on the Russian industrial markets.

The JV performance on the civil aviation market exemplifies this problem. In the late '80s and early '90s, the situation seemed favorable for international cooperation in satisfying this market segment.

By then, both Russia and the Western countries had acquired tremendous experience in aircraft design and production, and had well-developed aircraft industries and advanced aeronautical research. This created an objective basis for equal and mutually beneficial cooperation on the newest types of aircraft production, including JV formation.

There were no doubts as to the potential capacity of the Russian market, and more than 2,000 long-range passenger aircraft were already in service in Russia, besides aircraft for local airlines, helicopters, and cargo aviation. Most of the Russian civil aircraft fleet, however, was physically worn out and obsolete. More than half of the long-range passenger aircraft fleet was considered to need replacement by the period 2000 - 2005; the local airline fleet required nearly complete replacement by that time.

It was obvious that the only way for the Russian aircraft industry to maintain its domestic market, not to mention the NIS countries and the international markets, was to produce state-of-the-art aircraft meeting modern world standards of safety, comfort, economics, and environmental "friendliness". The Russian domestic aircraft industry, for both financial and technological reasons, was in need of Western technologies. These factors seemed to be a good basis for technological and investment cooperation in manufacturing new Russian aircraft, first for the domestic market and then for the international markets. This seemed to be a solid basis for joint ventures and projects. The formation of such a JV started in the late '80s and early '90s.

For example, ten JVs were established between 1989 and 1994 in order to improve the performance and international salability of just the Tu-204, and to market the aircraft. These JVs included:

- AVINTCO, for manufacture of aircraft interiors (Russia's Aviastar Joint Stock Company and the British firms Hunting Aircraft Ltd. and Aviation Ventures);
- A JV for the manufacture of air conditioning systems (Nauka Research and Production Association and the Hamilton Standard branch of the American company United Technologies);
- Rubix, for the manufacture of aircraft landing gear (Rubin Research and Production Association and the American company Allied Signal Inc.);
- Aviam, for designing new engines (the Permskie Motory and Aviadvigatel joint stock companies and the Pratt & Whitney branch of United Technologies);
- Russo Berns Aero Products, for aircraft seats and other interior components (Avtomatika Design Bureau and the American company Johnson Berns);
- Bravia, for the manufacture, certification, marketing, maintenance, and servicing of aircraft with Rolls-Royce engines (ANTK Tupolev and Aviastar Joint Stock Company and the British firm Flemings Russia Investment Corp.);
- Sirocco, for marketing the aforementioned aircraft (ANTK Tupolev, Aviaeksport foreign trade association, Aviastar, and the Egyptian Kato Group);

- Eltech, for the marketing and maintenance of aircraft (Aviastar with the Austrian Delta Group).

Joint ventures were also formed for purposes other than Tu-204 production and marketing. For example, the St. Petersburg Klimov Research and Production Association and the Canadian branch of the American firm Pratt & Whitney established a JV in order to manufacture aircraft gas turbine engines on the basis of Canadian and Russian technologies to be used on the new Russian aircraft Il-114 and Be-32.

Regrettably, some of these joint ventures for aircraft development and production have terminated or have frozen their activities; none of them is working successfully and efficiently.

What caused those joint ventures to fail? Is there hope for resurrecting them?

First, there are practically no solvent customers for new-generation aircraft in Russia; in 1996, Russian airlines bought no more than 10 aircraft (in comparison with up to 400 aircraft produced and bought annually by the U.S.S.R. aircraft industry in the mid-'80s).

Second, state support for the final stages of development, certification, and mass production of new-generation civil aircraft proved to be too weak. The most favorable conversion loans promised to the aircraft industry, and the funds envisaged by the Russian presidential Program for Civil Aircraft Development Until the Year 2000, were not provided promptly or in full; in addition, the limited funding that was received by the aircraft industry was used very inefficiently. Production without restructuring led to tremendous overhead costs, inefficient management, financial crises, and unpaid salaries, and resulted in the spending of the available funds for purposes that were very distant from the development and production of new aircraft.

The aircraft industry example is not an extreme one. The situation with the other manufacturers of industrial and technological products was very similar, and so was the fate of JVs in these industries.

Exceptions can be found only among the joint ventures in the export industries. For example, a successful JV was formed by the Khlopin Radium Institute and the consortium of REM Capital, Paine Webber Russian Partners Fund (United States), and Western Bulk Carriers (Norway). This JV specializes in the construction of radiation-processing centers for Russian timber purchased by Western customers. Incidentally, investments in this JV were made not only by its founders, but also later by the Defense Enterprise Support Fund established in the United States within the framework of conversion support to Russia.

The group of relatively successful joint ventures providing industrial and technological products for Russian export industries includes enterprises manufacturing equipment for RAO Gazprom. Among them is the JV Rybinskie Motory - General Electric, which manufactures gas-pumping stations. The success of this JV, and the news that RAO Gazprom needed to replace or upgrade hundreds of gas pumping stations and to construct new stations, encouraged the establishment of new business partnerships (the capacity of this market in the nearest future is estimated as $200 million). Among these partnerships are two JVs with the Lulka Saturn joint stock company, Rolls-Royce and Cooper Camerton (United States).[14]

There were considerably fewer attempts to form ventures in the consumer goods market. While conversion to the manufacturing of other industrial and technological products is a natural path for defense enterprises, conversion to the manufacture of consumer goods is more

---

14 *Kommersant Daily*, Volume 48,1997.

complicated. It often requires a radical change in the general nature of an enterprise, with continued usage of the manufacturing facilities and some of the personnel of the original enterprise. In addition, the technologies for producing modern consumer goods are mostly unknown in Russia, and need to be learned. Thus, Russian enterprises were not so interested in the establishment of such joint ventures. Moreover, the domestic market is saturated with exported goods, often offered on favorable terms, and the remaining limited consumer demand does not favor the domestic production of consumer goods, even with foreign participation. The success of such joint ventures would likely depend on the production of Western-designed goods for sale at lower prices made possible by lower Russian labor costs.

Examples of such joint ventures are the JV for the assembly of Korean Kia cars (at the Yantar shipyard in Kaliningrad), and the JV for razor-blade production (Leninets Concern and Gillette).

Competition on the world commodity and service markets is, of course, extremely tough, and even Western firms themselves experience difficulties in winning market share. Entering the international market with new joint venture products was twice as difficult for Russian enterprises. Accordingly, it was hard to find joint ventures in Russia that sold their products only on the world market.

The organizational and functional problems of the JVs discussed here made contract relations the most acceptable form of cooperation between the Russian defense enterprises and foreign firms. This form of partnership does not require investments, and, because it is less affected by the general economic situation and changes in legislation, involves fewer risks. It also allows the contracting parties to benefit substantially from the international division of labor. Russian enterprises can employ their facilities and personnel, receive the necessary finances, and in a number of cases drastically improve the consumer value of their products, due to the application of foreign technologies. Western firms, in turn, can use relatively cheap Russian defense-industry labor—especially that of researchers, engineers, and technicians, and receive components for their products. One of the main benefits for Western firms is an opportunity to utilize Russian advanced technologies, which allows them to save time on research and design by using results achieved in Russia.

To summarize: the "JV era," which started with a boom in the late '80s - early '90s, for the most part ended by the late '90s without bringing the results expected by the participants and organizers of the process. This outcome seems natural if one recognizes the now-obvious fact that the JV era began ahead of its time. Without macroeconomic stability, a reliable legislative basis, and political consensus in the country, one cannot count on attracting foreign investment and entering the world economic system.

It is unfair to charge the participants and the organizers of the numerous attempts at joint business with shortsightedness. They hoped that JVs utilizing the enormous potential of the Russian defense industry would contribute to the success of the conversion. However, it was not their fault that the JV era was just arising then when Russia faced a difficult choice of paths to economic development. If the chosen way had been more stable, as it was in China, their efforts might have proved more successful. However, Russia chose the way of radical economic reforms, with inevitable painful consequences in the economic, legislative and political spheres. In this situation, a rather small (compared to the scale of the Russian defense industry) "bandage" of foreign assistance for the development of joint ventures could not change the general state of the "patient," even if it had been used optimally.

Nonetheless, the transition period of the Russian economy cannot last forever. The radical economic reform will eventually sooner or later bring macroeconomic stabilization and consequent sustained development. Then, the JV era will come at last.

3.5. GAZPROM: THE BREAKTHROUGH INTO CONVERSION

Introductory Remarks

Vlad E. Genin

Gazprom, the largest natural gas company in the world, and the giant of the Russian gas industry, is constantly referred to as the locomotive of the Russian economy. The breakthrough to the latest technologies and products of the defense industry was vital for Gazprom. For MIC enterprises experiencing a crisis because of the loss of governmental military orders, the transition to meeting the demands of and producing equipment for Gazprom was extremely important. Production of equipment for gas stations meant a chance for surviving, creating new jobs, and keeping intact the accumulated intellectual potential. Thus, attempts to consolidate Gazprom's efforts with the MIC are explained by mutual economic benefit.

Gazprom owns the world's largest reserves of natural gas. Its share of world gas production is approximately 25%. It represents about 8% of Russia's GNP. In 1997, Gazprom entered the Financial Times' listing of the world's top 100 companies in terms of market capitalization. Gazprom's operations range from exploration to processing, transportation, and marketing. It supplies natural gas to virtually every region of Russia, and exports to more than 25 European countries.

Russian-made gas equipment was of rather decent quality, and much cheaper than imported machinery. Experts believe that the most sophisticated Western equipment sometimes can't be used in certain Russian conditions, such as the severe Siberian climate. Besides, service and maintenance of imported equipment are more expensive and present some technical problems. That is why the know-how of the defense enterprises became the lifeblood of the gas giant and the defense industry.

However, Gazprom's participation in defense conversion was just one of a few examples in Russia. The tens of thousands of new jobs that were created by joint Gazprom-defense industry projects were, unfortunately, just a drop in the bucket when considered as a solution to large-scale unemployment, which has been destroying Russian society. The country continues to suffer from its global failures…

Gazprom is a good example of how conversion in Russia might be implemented with the involvement of both domestic investors and the country's own resources. For the MIC, Gazprom was not just one of the first major clients, but an enormous market.

Rem I. Vyakhirev

The Joint Stock Company OAO Gazprom[15] is a natural monopoly, and the sole natural gas equipment consumer in Russia. It is

---

[15] Gazprom's market capitalization: $8.37 billion. The total number of the company's shareholders: 850,000. Gazprom's share (as of June, 1997) in Russia's total gas production: 94%. Share in worldwide gas production: 25%. Natural gas reserves: 33.4 billion cubic meters. Share in worldwide gas sales: 38.7%. Growth of export contracts portfolio: 51%. Company's share in supplying Russia with fuel: over 50%. Share in the federal budget's tax revenues: 25% (this figure reached a peak of 41% in June of 1997).

engaged mainly in natural gas extraction, and sales on the domestic and foreign markets.

Since the 1940s, the country's top political leadership has regarded the development and consolidation of the gas industry as a state priority. The stepped-up development of gas production in the former Soviet Union and, since 1975, in Russia, helped ensure the country's military-strategic parity for some two to three decades during the Cold War.

During the era of centralized planning, Russian companies manufactured equipment in order to meet specific requirements determined by the Soviet State Planning Committee (Gosplan). Neither a buyer's nor seller's market for gas equipment existed, even after the transition to a market economy began.

It was critically important for Gazprom to increase the efficiency of gas-compressor units, equipment diagnostics, communications, environmental monitoring, power supply, automation, and information exchange management. By investing in strategic R&D and the manufacture of new equipment for the gas industry, Gazprom contributed to Russia's economy as a whole.

Besides insufficient funding, defense enterprises faced another problem: the poor prospects and unpredictability of many civilian clients. Gazprom's reliability as a long-term partner for defense enterprises was proven by its plans and the manner of their implementation.

Gazprom has its own system of 25 research organizations employing 5,800 people (1.6% of the company's total staff of over 360,000), 600 of whom hold various scientific degrees. They are supplemented by a total of over 500 research and industrial facilities that are engaged in fulfilling Gazprom's design and R&D orders. Gazprom strove to fulfill its orders by using Russian designers in cooperation with leading foreign companies, thereby improving the equipment and making it attractive to both the domestic and international markets. In order to achieve this goal, Gazprom maximized the use of the defense industry's achievements over the past few decades that were released as a result of conversion. This included the intellectual potential of scientific and engineering personnel, the results of prior R&D, organizational and technological infrastructure, and cooperative ties. The utilization of defense enterprises and organizations has accounted for roughly half of Gazprom's expenditures on new technology development over the past few years. Gazprom regards this allocation of resources as optimal, and intends to continue it in the future.

Though they developed concurrently, the gas industry and defense complex developed in isolation from one another. Like other civilian industries, gas enterprises had no access to military technologies that could be adapted to Gazprom's requirements, and had to rely instead on civilian industrial developments, which were frequently hampered by insufficient funding. Nevertheless, Gazprom gained a certain amount of collaborative experience with the defense sector even in the period when the country was developing according to the laws and rules of a centralized economy.

The gas industry got its first opportunity to obtain access to defense industry technologies in the early 1970s, at the initiative of Academician Kuznetsov, who proposed that NK aircraft engines with expired service lives be used to drive gas-compression units. Due to the use of aircraft engines from 1973 to 1985, the country's gas output reached 52-55 billion cubic meters. The use of 10-12MW naval gas-turbine engines in the gas industry, beginning in 1976, was another breakthrough.

Scientific and technological progress faced formidable problems. Though Russia is fortunate in having a high concentration of gas reserves, 94% of them are located in remote regions of the Far North that have mountainous terrain, difficult geological conditions, an austere climate, undeveloped infrastructure, and fragile ecosystems. All of these considerations mandated that the most progressive methods and technology be used. In the 1990s, therefore, Gazprom began expanding its scope of cooperation with defense enterprises.

Prior cooperation with defense plants and design bureaus made it possible for Gazprom to exploit their scientific and technical potential, but several problems arose. Since Russian military enterprises had lost their main customer, the State, they found themselves in dire financial straits. Gazprom faced the problem of re-training defense industry workers, who were set in a traditional way of thinking, and frequently considered themselves superior to their new colleagues. The company realized that if these problems went unsolved, it might lose potential domestic manufacturers, and be forced to buy from foreign markets. In anticipation of this, some foreign companies started cutting their prices in order to crowd Russian manufacturers out of their own domestic market.

In order to fulfill Gazprom's orders and to master new sophisticated technologies, the defense complex needed to modernize and restructure its production system, and obtain research and test equipment. This required Gazprom to provide large amounts of investments. Gazprom offered low-interest loans, financed R&D, and concluded agreements on establishing joint ventures. Being interested in working with defense enterprises, Gazprom tried to help them retrain personnel in order to preserve their manufacturing, technological, and labor potential—their most important long-term assets.

As the difficulties of the initial period were overcome, Gazprom steadily increased its cooperation with defense plants, research institutes, and design bureaus. Gazprom launched joint scientific and technical activities to develop equipment for its enterprises. Special programs were prepared for sharing know-how. Besides the low-interest financing provided for converting production, Gazprom purchased advanced equipment and leased it to those enterprises.

In deciding how it would interact with certain defense enterprises, Gazprom first took into account the production and technological factors: the more specialized the defense enterprise, the more difficult it would be to switch it over to manufacturing different products. Working with former defense enterprises, Gazprom, as a rule, negotiated direct and long-term contracts.

Defense industry leaders began to associate the possibility of survival with orders from the fuel and energy complex, particularly from major gas and oil companies. Gazprom maintains a fraternal partnership with Russia's leading defense enterprises and organizations. Their powerful scientific and production capabilities have allowed them to produce equipment equal or superior to modern foreign equipment, in both technical and economic terms. Converting defense industry enterprises from the bottom up facilitated the development of dual-use technologies. According to the estimates of defense industry experts, at plants producing technologically sophisticated products alone, Gazprom's orders resulted in the creation of no less than 40,000 jobs for highly skilled defense industry personnel. At enterprises that produced ordinary products, the number was 10-15 times greater.

Gazprom's approach to defense conversion may seem very ambitious, and more appropriate to the State than to a single company, however large.

In 1990 Gazprom began cooperating with the Russian Federal Nuclear Center VNIIEF (Sarov), which was established in 1946 to solve "the uranium problem". VNIIEF created the Soviet atomic bomb in 1949, and four years later, created the thermonuclear bomb. VNIIEF, under its activity diversification program, began assisting Gazprom in designing various types of sensors (for temperature, moisture content, speed, displacement, vibrations, etc.) and factory information-management systems, equipment for certifying systems as explosion-proof, remote-control automation, environmental monitoring, intensifying gas production, etc.

Atommash, which produces equipment for nuclear power plants, began cooperating with the Gazprom subsidiary Astrakhangazprom in 1988. They have mastered sulfur production technology, automatic welding of pipe-to-pipe plate joints, and the manufacture of thick-walled equipment. Significant progress has been made on designing equipment to hydraulically fracture massive rock formations.

The Ministry of Atomic Energy's Scientific Research Institute for Measuring Systems started cooperating with Gazprom in the late 1980s. In 1996, 65% of the orders placed with the Institute were from Gazprom. This dramatic increase in cooperation was due to the compatibility of the Institute 's specialized capabilities with the gas industry's technical requirements. A linear remote-control automation system and other equipment for gas pipelines have been designed, based on experience with military equipment and software; unique high-technology instruments are currently being developed.

Gas blowouts and oil gushers are among the most serious and costly accidents in the gas and oil industry. In the past few decades, 130 blowout/gusher incidents involving gas, gas condensate, and oil have taken place at Russian oil and gas fields. Such an accident can release millions of cubic meters of gas per day, and may take months to contain. One of the most labor-intensive and dangerous accident containment techniques is removing burned equipment from the mouth of the well with military tanks, which shoot virtually blindly at the mouth, destroying usable equipment in the process. For this purpose, in 1992, the Troitsk Institute of Innovative and Thermonuclear Research (TRINITI), which previously worked on many MIC projects, proposed cutting metal up to 40mm thick using a 50kW laser beam, and subsequently designed the MLTK-50 laser system.

Over the past 18 years, the former Ministry of the Gas Industry (subsequently Gazprom) annually imported 300-350 complete sets of well-head equipment, worth up to $35 million. Total annual imports of oil and gas equipment amounted to $5 billion, so developing domestically-produced oil and gas equipment became a priority. As a result of defense conversion, defense enterprises have begun manufacturing these products.

Under the Space-Oil-Gas program, the Voronezh Mechanical Plant (VMZ) started manufacturing oil and gas equipment. Previously, VMZ manufactured rocket engines for Soviet space programs. Its engines were installed in the rockets for Vostok (which sent the first cosmonaut, Yuri Gagarin, into orbit), Soyuz, and Proton. In the early 1990s, on an order from Gazprom, the plant launched R&D activities for a new generation of well-head equipment. In 1994, the gas industry received the first domestically made equipment designed to operate in cold-weather conditions and resist hydrogen sulfide corrosion. Applying advanced dual-use technologies originally developed for aerospace purposes, the plant launched serial production of the new equipment in record time. Gazprom accounts for 45% of the plant's total orders. It helped the plant stabilize its production and create 1500 new jobs in 1997.

Gazprom viewed conversion and system diversification in the space industry as a priority. In early 1996, Gazprom, Energia Space & Rocket Complex, and Gazkom signed an agreement on improving the gas industry's technological level by using new space technologies and conversion developments.

3.6. THE RUSSIAN OIL SECTOR AND CONVERSION

Introductory Remarks

Vlad E. Genin

The Lukoil petroleum company is among the largest companies in Russia, and one whose orders helped implement the first steps of conversion of Russian defense enterprises. Lukoil is the leader in the Russian petroleum business: in extraction, production, and distribution of petroleum products. Lukoil has the largest proven reserves in the world, and is fourth in terms of extraction volume. Its proven reserves are equivalent to 10.7 billion barrels, and all categories of reserves (including probable and potential) equal 17.7 billion barrels.

Cooperation between Lukoil and defense industries has provided mutual economic benefits.

Lukoil became a sort of testing ground for the Russian defense enterprises, where they began to take their first steps down the path toward a free-market economy and away from a command economy.

Vagit U. Alekperov

Cooperation between Russian enterprises in the energy and defense industries has provided mutual economic benefits. This cooperation has made it possible for Russian industry to produce high-quality oil and gas extraction equipment domestically. Russian oil and gas companies are interested in buying domestic-made equipment, for two reasons: First, these products meet world quality standards, yet cost less than imports. Second modern foreign-made equipment is frequently incompatible with existing domestic equipment. Foreign equipment does not always withstand the harsh Russian climate, and can be expensive to maintain and service.

Before 1985, most oil field and drilling equipment was produced in Azerbaijan. Several plants based in Baku had monopolized the manufacture of more than 40 main types of equipment. Lack of competition and other negative aspects of the socialist economy adversely affected the quality of the equipment that was manufactured. As a result, by 1985, technical indicators of the quality Soviet-made oil extraction equipment, such as reliability, specific metal content, automation, etc., were only half as high as those of foreign-made counterparts. Political events in Azerbaijan in 1987, and a general economic decline, caused production of oil extraction equipment to drop significantly.

The Russian oil and gas industry began to experience substantial equipment shortages, so imports of equipment from Comecon countries, Austria, and the United States were increased in order to avoid a crisis. Defense industries made numerous efforts to use government investment grants to start alternative production and expand existing commercial production. Many programs were also initiated at that time to start production of oil extraction equipment under the national defense conversion campaign.

The Comprehensive Program to Develop Oil Extraction Equipment Production for 1991-1995 was one of the largest projects of its kind. It was developed jointly by engineering departments, the Soviet Ministry of Oil and Gas Industry, the Soviet Ministry of Geology, and

Gazprom. This program specifically called for initiating production of 122 types of equipment, which were in high demand, but had not been of satisfactory quality.

However, the program did not live up to expectations. Commercial enterprises had poor production facilities and low labor standards; defense enterprises had excessive production costs. More importantly, the equipment manufactured, in whole or in part, at defense plants did not comply with maintenance requirements or domestic and international standards. This happened because AzInMash and Neftegaz, the main developers of technical guidelines in this field, in order to protect their own proprietary interests, had failed to provide manufacturers with proper information. Manufacturers were left to simply make copies of equipment samples that were frequently outdated. Lack of experience, and sometimes ignorance of major design and production requirements for oil and gas equipment, caused serious problems; many enterprises of the defense sector, even with financial aid from the government, never learned to manufacture oil and gas equipment, and moved on to other civilian manufacturing projects.

The shortages were relieved somewhat by Neftegazmash facilities that had developed production of some types of equipment, including hydraulic engines, circulation system equipment, "Christmas tree" well-head assemblies, and sucker rods. However, their output was insufficient to meet existing demand. Government measures were only marginally effective.

Meanwhile, several defense plants began producing various types of equipment. Perm's Lenin Engineering Plant, Barrikady, and Izhneftemash were among the pioneers. However, their activities were substantially hindered by problems in the market mechanism, which had not developed sufficiently in the aftermath of the centralized procurement system. The decline in production and difficulties experienced by converted defense plants in developing oil extraction equipment caused more troubles on the market.

In the last years of its existence, the Soviet Ministry of Oil and Gas Industry spent $5 billion on foreign-made equipment. For some types of equipment and supplies, the amount imported (including imports from republics of U.S.S.R.), reached or exceeded 45 percent of all new equipment and supplies of those types.

In order to correct this situation, several oil companies, including Lukoil, strove to provide comprehensive support for domestic oil equipment production.

In 1992, as a result of Lukoil's initiative and financial assistance, Izhneftemash began producing cementing units, previously manufactured at the Krasnyi Molot plant in Grozny. OZONig-Lukoil (Lukoil's manufacturing facility) began producing a wide range of industry-specific equipment to mechanize oil-field work, and perform maintenance operations at a higher level. Because of this, it was possible to nearly satisfy the domestic machinery market, and the plant has been working on upgrading its products.

Other companies have engaged in similar activities. Rosneft and Kirovskii Zavod entered into a joint venture to manufacture K-700 tractor-mounted servicing units for underground servicing and repairs, with a carrying capacity of 80-100 tons. These units had not previously been manufactured in Russia.

GlavTyumenneftegaz has also conducted large-scale work to develop production of oil field equipment. Defense plants in Tyumen, Chelyabinsk, and Ekaterinburg mastered the manufacturing of pumping jacks (at Uraltransmash), and elevators and pumps for central gathering points (at the Tyumen shipyard).

The first phase of the conversion campaign has shown that the defense industry was generally incapable of producing world-class oil extraction equipment. This, among other reasons, led to a 30% increase in imports of virtually all oil extraction equipment.

Undoubtedly, conversion has produced some positive results. First and foremost, conversion has determined the winners and losers within the defense industry. As it turns out, there is no correlation between receiving government subsidies for restructuring or conversion and an industry's likelihood of success in converting.

The Special Engineering and Metal Works Joint Stock Company is one of the negative examples. They attempted to develop a mobile complex for deep-penetration hydraulic fracturing. The engineers did not study foreign "know-how", nor did they take the customer's wishes into consideration. They did it their way. As a result, all they accomplished in over six years was to develop a request for proposal. This proves that only those enterprises that created well organized civilian manufacturing and marketing structures under conversion programs were able, though financing was limited, to create competitive equipment and make it salable on the oil extraction equipment market.

PART FOUR

The "Headlong" Command Conversion Marathon

INTRODUCTION

Vlad E. Genin

The year 1992... This year will go down in Russian history as marking the beginning of an economic breakdown of unprecedented scale. "Shock therapy", which freed retail prices overnight—"price liberalization," as it was called in Russia—immediately depressed the population's standard of living.

On the other hand, 1992 also marked the beginning of processes that promised to generate a flourishing economy, increased production, and—very importantly—the manufacture not of military equipment, but of civilian goods.

The conversion of defense enterprises was supposed to lead to the production of not only consumer goods, but equipment for various industries: telecommunications, gas and oil extraction, textiles, shoes, clothing, food processing, furniture, kitchen appliances, bathroom fixtures, western-style cosmetics – in other words, everything necessary for the contemporary way of life.

Hopes were high that the seemingly all-powerful MIC would produce equipment for the civilian industries which traditionally were on the "B-List" (the "A-List" consisted of the defense industry, machine building, power generation, metallurgy, etc.), and never able by themselves to bring about a technological revolution. The MIC was supposed to breathe new life into the "B-List" industries, such as agricultural and food processing, by creating state-of-the-art equipment that met world standards. It was presumed that Russia, which had not only fed itself but exported crops and foods before the 1917 Communist Revolution, would finally stop depending on imports of grain, meat products, and other foodstuffs.

A dramatic decrease in the Ministry of Defense's orders for fighters and bombers seemed to have given the green light to production of such long-overdue passenger and transport planes as the Tu-204 and Be-32. The transcontinental airliner Il-96, aerodynamically one of the most advanced transports in the world, could finally have been equipped with new world-class electronics that met the most rigorous international standards.

A program to revive the shipbuilding industry was being developed, as well as far-reaching reforms in many branches of industry. Finally, the road to mass computerization seemed to have opened up before Russia, which boasts one of the world's most highly educated populations, particularly in the fields of science and technology.

The Russian MIC had the power to bring about phenomenal conversion results. If only a comprehensive approach to conversion had been taken; if only each and every branch of industry connected with the production of now-unnecessary weapons and related materiel had been restructured, the people of Russia would not merely have enjoyed better lives--they would have become rich. A comprehensive approach would have meant deep, radical reforms, which had to embrace all of Russia – the industrial complex stretching from the Baltic Sea to the Pacific Ocean, which not so long ago worked on military orders, but was now turning into a monstrous junkyard. What was needed was a thorough conversion that would have reached down to the essence of this defense plant of a country: a conversion drastic enough to radically change Russia, jump-starting the production of domestic goods and equipment, and generating new technologies.

The time had come when all the intellectual and industrial resources of the country, which had been wasted on preparing for war, should be serving the needs of its people. Everybody in the new Russia already understood that it is just as immoral to promise people a better life while taking absolutely no practical steps to make it happen, as it is to dangle a sword above the whole world.

4.1. THE BEGINNING

Introductory Remarks

Vlad E. Genin

"We meant well, but the results were not what we intended." In the 1990s, this English expression gained a bitter Russian interpretation: "We wanted to do it better, but it turned out to be the usual..." In this context, "the usual" refers to negative results, sorrow, and feebleness. These words, a little bit sad on the one hand, and a little bit humorous on the other, were those of former Russian Prime Minister Viktor Chernomyrdin. Thank to the wealth of the Russian language, these words convey the real feelings of Russians toward "headlong" conversion.

According to the Russian government's plans, the year 1992 was to mark the turning point in the conversion of the MIC and a major step in the overall economic development of the new Russia. MIC conversion, or more accurately, accelerated conversion, was to play a major role in the new economic upswing. These hopes were not groundless. The reputation of MIC was fortified by its past record of impressive military achievements in rocket technology, gigantic nuclear submarines, and supersonic fighter planes. In other words, it seemed to the Russian population that the defense industry could produce anything one wanted. The only question was how to make it happen? How to switch the command-style state enterprises to civilian production without privatizing them? How to create a logical financial mechanism?

> How to go from the first converted production lines to large-scale conversion of the entire MIC, which spanned a territory 6,000 miles wide? There seemed to be no answer—not at the top, in the government and defense ministries, and not at the bottom, on the level of defense plant directors. More precisely, the “top” did not have a thoroughly developed plan of action, and the “bottom”, which was used to living only on orders from the “top”, received one contradictory command after another. But the “bottom” received not only commands, but also unfulfillable promises from the “top” about forthcoming financial, technical, and organizational support. Nevertheless, everybody really wanted “to do it (conversion) better”…

Alexander P. Kotov

The next, intensive, phase of the Russian defense conversion process began in 1992, when the first year of unprecedented reduction in military production for the Defense Industry coincided with the deepening economic crisis.

During this period of defense conversion, the new concept of independent management of the conversion process temporarily prevailed. Enterprises received a certain degree of freedom in choosing new civilian product lines for conversion purposes. Also, their management teams were no longer bound by dozens of regulations, as in command economy times. The Conversion Committee was created under the office of the presidency of the Russian Federation. However, it was never fully formed—it could not withstand the intense struggle over spheres of influence with the Ministry of Industries, and it finally simply disappeared. It was neither harmful nor beneficial, though the mythical idea of "self-financing conversion" is connected with this institution.

The *Law on Conversion*, approved in March 1992, brought about another change. The idea was to slow down uncontrolled conversion and make it a part of the reconstruction of the economy.

After that, the main plans for defense conversion (which had to make up for declining military production) were formulated by the Russian government. The national Program for Defense Industry Conversion for 1992-1995 was developed. It had fourteen different sections dedicated to each of fourteen "sectors" of the defense industry. This program was incorporated into the federal program for reconstructing the entire economy, which was approved in June 1993. This federal program also used the concept of industry sectors such as commercial aviation, commercial shipbuilding, communications and information technologies, and medical equipment.

First, the program formulated the plans for conversion: converted defense enterprises were to manufacture products for selected branches of civilian industries. Second, the program determined which new civilian products would be manufactured, and organized groups of civilian enterprise "clients". These two fundamental provisions were the key factors in the national program for defense industry conversion. It contained fourteen subprograms, which called for the development of world-class equipment, as well as technologies and processes for the development and production of:

1. Commercial aircraft
1. Merchant ships (named "Rebirth of the Russian Fleet");
2. Equipment for fuel and energy industries;
3. Equipment for wood processing industries;

4. Equipment for construction and road building industries;
5. Equipment for agriculture and food processing industries;
6. Equipment for light industries;
7. Equipment for retail trade and the food industry;
8. High-quality durable goods;
9. Development and implementation telecommunications and information technologies;
10. Equipment for environmental protection;
11. New medical equipment and devices;
12. Russian electronics;
13. Equipment and devices for nuclear power industry civilian applications.

Selecting priorities in the conversion process was supposed to help Russia maintain its leading position in the world in areas where Russian achievements in science, research, and development attracted interest from foreign business circles. This selection was also supposed to facilitate the wise use of the little financing that was available for conversion.

The Program allowed each defense enterprise director to decide independently what kind of product to develop. The State was to provide only legal and economic assistance. State financial aid would be provided to the enterprises, which would use the following criteria when selecting conversion production: minimizing expenses, retaining highly qualified personnel, increasing the country's export potential, increasing the use of energy- and resource-saving technologies, employing dual-use technologies, using environmentally friendly technological processes; and stabilizing the market.

However, because these criteria were too general and mutually contradictory, they caused all kinds of difficulties for the defense enterprises. In addition, the program could not protect all the country's interests in the military, technical, scientific, and economic spheres, because the relevant documents were still under development.

Concurrently with the development of the national conversion program, the Russian government decided on the financial support mechanism for defense industry enterprises. Privileged low-interest financing was suggested for the conversion programs. This was reinforced by the government decree *On providing loans to enterprises conducting conversion of military production.*

According to the decree, conversion programs worth less than 5 billion rubles were to be approved by the interdepartmental commission, while programs worth 5 billion rubles and more were to be approved by the Cabinet. The Central Bank was to reach agreement with the Ministry of Finance about providing credit, and the Ministry of Finance, in turn, was to sign specific contracts, and transfer money to commercial banks.

However, this mechanism malfunctioned from the very beginning. For example, in 1992, a privileged credit of 140 billion rubles was needed to finance 1,018 conversion projects, which had been evaluated and approved. This 140 billion rubles credit was needed to develop production of commercial products worth 500 billion rubles. In fact, only 58.9 billion rubles were allocated, which financed only 634 projects, and created about 200 billion rubles' worth of output.

In 1993 the fall in production continued. Although 728 new programs were created, none of them were financed on time, and none of them received the full amount that had been promised. Only 561 enterprises received the new, privileged credit of 254.5 billion rubles.

Moreover, enterprises spent 145 billion rubles of their own working capital to implement the conversion programs. New production facilities for the output of commercial goods were created, but only 543.1 billion rubles (36% of the planned amount) and 213,000 new jobs were created (only 43% of the planned number).

The situation remained the same for the next five years. Financing for the different sectors of the conversion program was always insufficient, and grew progressively worse. In 1996, it stopped completely. (See Table 4.1.1.)

TABLE 4.1.1.

Conversion program statistics, 1992-1996

Indicator		1992	1993	1994	1995	1996
Financing from conversion credits (billions of rubles)	Projected Actual	140.0 58.9	360.0 245.5	1,100.0 475.6	1,100.0 264.3	1,600.0 --
Value of new output produced (billions of rubles)	Projected Actual	500.0 81.9	4,066.0 901.5	17,000.0 2,281.0	7,377.0 1,519.5	16.0 --
New jobs created (thousands)		179.0	213.0	118.0	50.0	--

Conversion took place at the same time as privatization of state enterprises, which was regulated by dozens federal laws, presidential decrees, governmental resolutions, and so forth. The complexity and sheer volume of these laws and regulations, the constant changes to supposedly approved documents, the ambiguity of certain provisions, the unrealistic terms of the method of privatization—all these deficiencies of the legal framework for privatization led to negative results.

Regulatory documents concerning privatization permitted the break-up of companies and consortiums that had existed for years, which resulted in the destruction of defense enterprises' production facilities.

The workers at these enterprises made many of the decisions about privatization. They did not always realize the dangers of the versions of privatization they chose. The governing legislation and constant changes in the rules of the game permitted more than 51% of the shares of the defense enterprises to be controlled by black marketeers who owned large packages of privatization vouchers, as well as by foreign-based and fictitious entities and by domestic financial private institutions, none of which were interested in developing production. In some cases, privatization damaged national security.

Separate privatization for the scientific and production sections took place at the Scientific Research Institute for Avionics. The privatization of the separate structural units of the Arsenal Production Association made this unique enterprise, which produced devices for spacecraft, unmanageable. The uncontrollable sale of shares of the Prommash plant in Saratov and the Kristall Research and Production Association in Dzerzhinskii resulted in the loss of their capacity to produce ammunition cassettes. At the initial stage of privatization, the biggest research and production complexes, like the Sukhoi Design Bureau and the Tupolev Aircraft Design Bureau, lost their production capacities.

The large-scale distribution of shares in the form of vouchers caused the loss of technologies and highly qualified personnel because of the lack of means for investment and restructuring; state property was usually transferred to private corporations free of charge. Forced privatization accelerated the destruction of teams at defense enterprises that had worked well together for many years. Instead of becoming part of a new class of property owners, thousands of highly qualified specialists received no property, but instead witnessed its misappropriation. Workers lost their confidence in the effectiveness of the reforms taking place.

Precise goals and objectives for restructuring the defense industry were never stated. Privatization and the distribution of shares created a poorly coordinated, fragmented structure. State-owned enterprises comprised about 26% of this structure; 30% were joint stock enterprises with state ownership; and 27% were joint stock enterprises that had no restrictions on privatization. About 15% of the enterprises became solely commercial and left the defense industry entirely.

Thus, the command economy approach, the lacks of financing and poor privatization were among the key causes that led to the failure of the defense conversion effort. Although there were positive examples of privatization in the defense industry, they were very rare. The experience of recent years has shown that attempts to force the implementation of defense industry conversion from the top down have failed.

4.2. LEGISLATION, FINANCING, AND INVESTMENTS

Introductory Remarks

Vlad E. Genin

Several decades ago, Western nations demonstrated the advantages and benefits of defense conversion. Yet conversion was possible only because these countries had free market economies and stable legislation; it also required substantial amounts of money. These fundamental issues were well known in Moscow, even before the beginning of conversion, when Russia became an independent state and started its market reforms. Russian leaders were also aware that the country did not have enough money for this huge task.

Unfortunately, it is clear today that the country lost its greatest chance in the 1990s to attract foreign investment for transforming a militarized economy into a civilian one. Such a new economy would already be producing numerous world-class consumer goods.

So many hopes were pinned on conversion at the new birth of the country in 1991. Even today, it is difficult to understand why, at the very beginning of this new pathway for the new Russia, a clear and reliable system to ensure the security of foreign investments was not created. Why did not a single Russian Cabinet dare to form the appropriate legislative system to support the flow of foreign investments?

In fact, the State left its industrial directors, the leaders of its own state defense enterprises, and real patriots of their plants, to the mercy of Fate. The directors, strangled with tight state control, had to try to attract foreign investors by themselves. Not of their own will, but because they had received directives from Moscow.

Russian plant directors attempted, through numerous meetings with 'potential foreign investors', to create a favorable investment climate from the ground up--a process which should have been established from the top down by the State. Government officials doubtless understood that parties with foreign emissaries, often accompanied by drinking and toasting "to Brotherhood" and boat rides along the Volga River, were no substitute for the hard work of legislators and law enforcement agencies to ensure the security of foreign investments. It is difficult to understand what State bureaucrats had in mind when they stimulated these endless exchanges of delegations. Of course, it was definitely beneficial for both parties to get to know each other better. However, such large-scale international networking was only a waste of time, interfering with productive work, aggravating the situations at the plants, and further worsening the living conditions of workers. The leaders of the country understood from the very beginning that the popular "Letters of Intent", signed between 1991 and 1996 after thousands of such meetings, were little more than thank-you notes for the warm receptions. These letters of intent could not serve as foundations for investment projects. Not even being devoted to investments, they had no legal force, and did not replace legislation on the security of foreign investments, the only thing that could protect foreign investors effectively.

High hopes were pinned on some foreign companies, which for the sake of a presence in the new overseas market, could afford to lose money in the short term. Russian plant directors mainly counted on the existence of foreign companies ready to risk their money on Russian enterprises. However, such risk-taking investors were very rare. Some of them succeeded; very few achieved substantial success. But there were many that sustained heavy losses, and left Russia disappointed.

How could the State, which fully intended to reform the country and convert the bulk of its economy (the MIC) by attracting foreign investments, have allowed its own policy to fail in such an ugly way? It is a multi-part question. The two main issues are the following: Was appropriate and enforceable legislature created by the State? And was privatization really allowed to privatize?

Vitaliy Y. Vitebsky

The conversion of the MIC coincided with the time when the Russian economy was in transition from a command/administrative system, totally controlled by the government, to a free market economy. The collapse of the unified and integrated economy of the former Soviet Union caused the termination of cooperation between enterprises and different industries.

Naturally, the success of the conversion process was impossible without proper legislative support. Between 1991 and 1993, the Supreme Soviet (the parliament at that time) approved several laws supporting reforms of the defense industry. These laws regulated conversion, private and state property in enterprises, the process of privatization, export-import activity and investments, product quality and the protection of intellectual property. The Civil Code, which was later passed by the State Duma, included these laws. Despite the fact that they need to be improved, these laws are still in force today.

In 1992, after the beginning of market reforms, the author presented to the Supreme Soviet the bill On Conversion. In March 1992, it was passed and signed by the Russian President. During that period of time, several laws on product standardization and certification, as well as on patents and copyright protection, were approved. These laws are still in effect today; however, they need to be improved to stop the stealing and wasting of Russia's main resource its intellectual property, including advanced technologies.

From the very beginning of the reforms, it was clear that the key element for the production of any new competitive product was financing for the technical renovation of the industry involved. Financing was also needed for reconstruction and modernization of R&D and experimental production facilities. The defense sector needed a separate federal program that would deal with its special conversion and restructuring problems.

High hopes were pinned on foreign investments. In 1992, two key laws were passed to regulate investment activity: On Investment Activity in the Russian Federation and On Foreign Investments in the Russian Federation. The general rules and guarantees given in these laws met international requirements. They created favorable conditions for profitable investing and reinvesting. Joint ventures with foreign companies, which furthered the State's conversion programs, received additional privileges, compared with purely domestic joint ventures.

In 1991, the problem of providing reliable international guarantees in the absence of investment insurance systems urgently needed to be solved. Several steps were made in this direction.

First, in 1992, the agreement on supporting investment cooperation between the governments of the Russian Federation and the United States was signed and ratified. This agreement was intended to help American investors in all aspects of their investments in Russia. More than 250 projects for investing in Russia were reviewed by the two governments in 1993. The total value of these projects was $22 billion dollars.

Second, Russia took steps to join the convention on establishing a special international agency whose mission was to insure investments. The Supreme Soviet ratified this convention in December 1992.

Third, special investment insurance corporations were established in Russia. One of the most famous was the State Investment Corporation. Its main function was to provide guarantees to foreign and domestic investors, to insure their investments. For this purpose foreign banks implemented collateral transactions.

Nevertheless, the expected flow of investments never came to Russia. From the point of view of American specialists who worked for a long time in the sphere of investments and credits, and were also involved in Russian projects, investors were most attracted to those industries for whose products there was guaranteed demand. These industries are oil/gas refining, communications, production of construction materials, and food processing.

There were several dozens defense enterprises in Russia that attracted foreign investors. However, their profitability was below average on the world market. In the mid 1990s the average investment return on the world market was about 15% a year. Moreover, in countries with flourishing economies, return on investments in domestic industry was even higher – 20%-25% a year. If you add the fact that investments in foreign countries, especially a country like Russia, are riskier than investments in one's own economy, it becomes clear why Russia received more promises than real money. In fact, political instability and, as a consequence, high investment risks were among the main reasons for the lack enthusiasm on the part of foreign investors. According to some international evaluations, the investment safety level in Russia ranked 133rd in the world; only countries actually at war ranked lower than Russia. It is true that in March 1996 Russia climbed to100th place in terms of investment safety, and in October to 86th place, but after the crises that started on August 17, 1998, it went back to one of the last places.

That is why it was too early to talk about serious foreign investments even in high-tech MIC industries, although individual companies were implementing several major international projects. However, the number of these companies was very small in comparison to the whole process of converting and restructuring the MIC.

The initially chaotic privatization process in the defense industry was normalized by the presidential decree On Privatization in the Defense Industry in August 1993. All of the Defense Industry enterprises were divided into three groups: 41.7% were state enterprises (including the ones whose privatization was prohibited, and which were to be gradually transformed into state joint stock companies, or stay wholly state-owned enterprises); 31.7% - joint stock companies with state participation (with different stock options or with a "Golden Share" controlled by the State) and 26.6% - private joint stock companies, without state participation. The share of industrial production output of those enterprises was, respectively, 46.1%, 33% and 20.3%. State enterprises remained by far the greatest producers of high-tech products (71.3%).

There was no great difference in the way these enterprises conducted their operations, in spite of the different types of ownership. According to the 1996 survey, joint stock companies without state participation showed the greatest decrease in production, and state-owned enterprises showed the least. Analysis shows that the main problem was not the type of the ownership, but the volume of state orders, which were placed mostly with state enterprises. In spite of irregular payments, these orders allowed state enterprises to survive.

There were so many changes in the defense industry that a new state conversion program for 1995-1997 was developed and approved long before the 1993-1995 State conversion program had ended. The new program was formulated to support very selectively the output of the most important civilian products within very severe budget limitations. To implement this program, 18,6 trillion rubles were needed (in 1995 prices) to be divided as follows: 39% from the federal budget (no returns were expected), 34% from conversion loans (repayment was expected) and 27% from companies' working capital and sales. In spite of the consistent effectiveness of investments in conversion, financing of the program from the Federal budget was nevertheless stopped completely.

That is why the objective of the privatization process was further changed. The new objective was to help enterprises to attract investments for structural reconstruction, and create big competitive integrated structures, primarily financial-industrial groups and holding companies.

At that time, three types of investment competitions (bidding) were recommended: one only for Russian investors, another for both Russian and foreign investors, and a third only for foreign investors. There were some limitations. Enterprises that utilized dual-use technologies and needed equipment modernization would be offered exclusively to Russian private investors. Enterprises that were subject to 100% conversion, and thus completely focused on civilian product output, would be available for bidding by foreign investors.

This investment policy did not sufficiently encourage privatization. Large amounts of shares of privatized enterprises were not sold for several years. The sale of these shares could secure investment for three or four years (about 30 trillion rubles). But in order to attract private investments, quickly profitable projects needed to be developed, based on the exploitation of dual-use technologies.

There were potential sources of financing, such as proceeds from privatization, exports of military hardware, the sale of excess state property and land belonging to the defense industry, the transfer of stocks to a trust, and secondary stock offerings.

At the same time, even taking into consideration the very difficult financial situation in the MIC, shares in some joint stock companies were in great demand among the new generation of domestic investors. Nevertheless, certain measures were introduced in order to prevent their sale to certain parties, regardless of the price they were willing to pay. These means helped to protect enterprises from being destroyed by competitors, and to maintain their capacity for future development. One of these measures called for putting these shares in financial trusts, with the option to transfer funds to the successful joint stock companies—in particular, those that produce export products. In return, the trusts would have the right to sell, pledge, or redeem these shares, and also would have a right to manage any other property, including the right to sell it.

Another source of investment, which has not been actively used yet, is the secondary issue of shares in defense industry joint stock companies, in order to attract additional funds.

To attract more investments, a new bill was drafted that introduced changes and improvements to the existing law on joint stock companies. The bill called for the formation of joint stock companies with 100% of the stock held by the State, and also specified mechanisms for investor participation in the development of these companies.

Due to the constant and rapid decrease in governmental military spending during the 1990s, the MIC, in order to survive, needed deep structural reconstruction. However, during a 5-year period spanning the mid-'90s budget investments in the defense industry were reduced dramatically, by approximately 75%. In this situation the need for investments for reconstruction increased equally dramatically. To implement reconstruction, a new action plan was developed to attract new investments from three main sources: joint ventures, credit lines for projects, and investment portfolios. More than 560 projects and proposals were suggested for the development of the joint ventures and credit lines. Their implementation required more than 8.2 trillion rubles in investments, as well as more than 2 billion dollars.

The results were worse than modest because the hoped-for investment did not become a reality. The long and deep recession in investment activities brought the MIC close to the point at which Russia could lose its status as a technologically developed country.

4.3. CHRONOLOGY OF THE CONVERSION MARATHON

Introductory Remarks

Vlad E. Genin

After a brief preparatory period, the defense conversion marathon started in all corners of Russia. Nearly all defense enterprises participated. The intellectual power of the best designers, engineers, and managers was focused in a new direction: the creation and output of civilian products. Some enterprises were undeniably successful: the Nudelman Design Bureau in Moscow, a leading rocket enterprise, switched part of its capacity to cardiac pacemakers; the Sverdlovsk Avtomatika Research and Production Association, a leading missile guidance systems facility, began producing water meters, incubators for poultry farms, and communications systems for police dispatchers; the Ryazan Instrument Factory, which formerly specialized in weapons guidance systems, began producing avionics for civilian aircraft; the Tikhomirov Scientific Research Institute in Zhukovskiy, Moscow Oblast, a leading MIC plant that designed mobile surface-to-air missile systems and radar equipment for fighter planes, created a unique seismological prospecting device, geological radar for detecting items underground and underwater, and equipment for customs officials; the Nizhniy Novgorod factory Nitel, which formerly produced mobile radar stations, has begun producing VCRs, using technology licensed from the

Japanese company Sharp, state-of-the-art color televisions, and telephones.

However, such examples are rare. The majority of defense plants were unable to achieve respectable production. In short, as a popular saying went in those days, conversion boiled down to the production of shoddy pots instead of tanks, and titanium shovels instead of airplanes.

Imported goods and equipment quickly filled the enormous number of large niches in the Russian market — then the last large, unexplored market in the world. In the unlimited number of newly opened small stores, in each large or small Russian city or town, one could buy practically everything: from Sony TV/VCR combos to nicely packaged Chinese screwdriver sets, from ready-to assemble affordable furniture by Bush Industries to concentrated shampoo by the Quaker company.

Being unable to compete, the majority of MIC enterprises were forced to drop out of the conversion marathon. But worse yet, due to the country’s participation in the global disarmament process and the consequent financial crisis, Russian military production lines were frozen also. As a result, the MIC archipelago started approaching collapse. Thus, Chernomyrdin’s bitter words “We wanted to do it better, but it turned out to be the usual” became prophetical.

Arkadiy I. Yarovskiy

The beginning of the collapse of the defense conversion effort in 1992 coincided with the beginning of the most far-reaching Russian economic reforms. Total output at MIC plants fell 22% because military production dropped sharply. The share of civilian production skyrocketed, due not to the increased output of consumer goods, but to the dramatic decrease in military production.

In 1992 alone, 573 large defense plants (out of 687 that were in the process of conversion) were partially or fully shut down. The majority of them simply waited for better times—they shortened the workweek, and sent some of their employees on indefinite unpaid leave. Several dozen enterprises stopped functioning completely.

Many defense enterprises, regardless of their form of ownership, began to earn income by becoming landlords: renting out available office space, manufacturing and laboratory facilities, cafeterias, conference halls, and sports centers. Their tenants were those new banks, trade organizations, newly born consulting firms, and international joint ventures that were operating successfully, and whose cash flow was frequently in stable hard currency instead of inflating rubles.

In 1992-1993, Russia witnessed the reformation of various types of property ownership. Many state-owned defense enterprises were transformed into joint stock companies with varying degrees of state ownership. Having received permission to engage in commerce, former government officials began reorganizing ministries, agencies, and enterprises into private or joint stock companies, and obtaining their share of ownership in them. But essentially, the only thing that changed was the company sign. As a result, many commercial firms appeared that had gained their freedom from the state monopoly on foreign trade, and were able to avoid paying a number of taxes. This process of privatizing enterprises of the MIC continued without the necessary legal support, and was referred to as "wild privatization" by the public.

After "wild privatization" there came "voucher privatization," which involved the entire population. The government issued each citizen a voucher for a certain fraction of the country's property. Commercial and sometimes criminal organizations, making false promises of large dividends, quickly bought up the vouchers from the people at laughable prices, and used them to purchase, also at ridiculously low prices, the most attractive plants, factories, and institutes, including those in the defense sector. Thus, over 300 large defense enterprises were sold for an average price of $4 million each. This included the giants of Russian industry—Armlet in Sverdlovsk ($3.7 million), Kovrovskii Mechanical Plant, world-famous for weapons production ($2.7 million), and many others. The actual market value of these plants is in the billions of dollars.

Such privatization led to the further dismemberment and destruction of large plants, primarily their management, engineering staff, and workers' teams. At the same time, due to a chaotic absence of control, the process of mass embezzlement of strategic resources—rare materials, steel, precious and non-ferrous metals, as well as unique technologies, equipment, and buildings—began.

In 1993, the decline in production continued. The number of partially and fully shut down enterprises increased to 829. The volume of civilian production in the defense industry fell by 14.1%, and military production fell by 34.3%.

The conversion program adopted in 1994 provided for the creation of civilian production capacity for output worth over $6 billion. But neither the government nor the newly independent enterprises were capable of implementing the program.

In 1995, the conversion program's financial woes reached a critical phase. In 1996, budget allocations for conversion, having decreased every year, disappeared entirely.

Then the State tried to compensate for its lack of money by instituting enormous taxes on enterprises, along with draconian measures to collect them. Nevertheless, in 1996, only 16.9% of enterprises paid all their taxes, while the rest paid only partially or not at all. Defense enterprises learned to get along without money. In some cases they were forgiven for non-payment of taxes, in some they compensated vendors through barter, and in some –they simply stopped paying their employees.

Income from domestic sales or exports (mainly of weapons and other military equipment) was not re-invested in conversion. Not infrequently, the profits from these transactions were deposited in foreign (mainly Western) bank accounts belonging to directors of various ranks (or to various commercial entities to which they had access), or were used to purchase real estate in the United States or Western Europe for the purpose of renting it out or of keeping their families there.

Money ceased to function as a stimulus, since the lack of it no longer threatened bankruptcy; various taboos protected the defense plants from market realities, including bankruptcy. The number of bankruptcies in Russia in the past seven years is less than the number of bankruptcies in US in seven days. The lack of a clear defense policy, of legislative and financial support for defense conversion, and of experience functioning in a market economy aggravated the "headlong" conversion process, and threatened to undermine the entire Russian economy.

In the years of "headlong" conversion, 15 out of 36 leading missile and aviation enterprises stopped developing military products, yet produced virtually no high-tech or competitive civilian goods to take their place. They include the following world-famous enterprises:

- Design bureaus: Salyut (Moscow) Arsenal (St. Petersburg), Vympel (Moscow);
- Aviation Production Associations: Ilyushin, Lavochkin, MiG (Moscow);
- Scientific Research Institutes: Mechanical Engineering NII in Podlipki, NII No.4 (Bolshevo), Keldysh Research Center (Moscow);
- Research and Production Associations: Iskra (Perm), Khrunichev Energia Rocket and Space Complex (Podlipki).

The Kirovsky Zavod in St. Petersburg completely halted production of tanks;[1] most of its equipment is no longer used, and all production units of the factory have been abandoned. R&D and marketing of civilian goods never occurred, and tens of thousands of qualified specialists and workers lost their jobs.

By 1997, the new Russian capitalists—bankers and businessmen, the nascent oligarchy—had gained control over many MIC enterprises, as they had over most of the economy. They were frequently interested solely in personal gain, and not the development of conversion, as they claimed. The criminal world's control over enterprises also increased. According to surveys, roughly 100-150 defense plants were controlled by criminal groups.[2]

All this contributed to the country's course toward political instability and social anarchy. Whole branches of science and industry were lost, and the drying up of cooperation between defense enterprises, which had fostered the development of difficult technologies, became irreversible.

---

[1] TS-VPK Information Agency, http://www.vpk.ru, June 7, 1999.

[2] Leonid Kosals, Rosalina Ryvkina, and Yurii Simagin, *Oboronnye Predpriyatia Rossii v Usloviakh Rynochnogo Eksperimenta* (Moscow: Institut Sotsialno-Ekonomicheskikh Problem Narodonaselenia RAN, 1999).

By 1999-2000, Russia hardly had any facilities left that were actually engaged in the serial production of weapons and military equipment. The country was only able to produce units singly, and at great expense.

Six plants are all that remains of the aircraft industry. Before conversion, the industry produced 545 military planes per year. The current annual production of the remaining plants is only 1-2 planes for the domestic market, and 15 for export.

Production of many types of ammunition, air-to-surface missiles, air-defense systems, and tanks stopped almost entirely. The collapse of conversion and the shutdown of defense enterprises undermined the combat readiness of the Russian Army. The proportion of modern military equipment, particularly conventional equipment, in the armed forces dropped precipitously. By 1997, production volume of the MIC had fallen more than 80%, and the number of employees decreased from 7 million to 2.5 million, of whom only 925,000 continued to work on military goods.[3]

The low point of the economic and financial collapse was the crisis in August 1998, when the government officially admitted bankruptcy. In addition, the number of unsuccessful defense enterprises increased from 700 to 1,200. These enterprises were in bad economic shape, had few orders, and significantly delayed salary payments. Their employees were on the verge of striking.

---

[3] TS-VPK Information Agency, http://www.vpk.ru, November 5, 1999.

In 1998, for the first time in the 70 years of its existence, the defense industry did not deliver a single tank, airplane, or warship to the armed forces—not one armored personnel carrier or artillery piece.[4]

At the beginning of 1999, most MIC enterprises retained only about 40% of their employees. Of those, 9% were considered employees though they did not work, and 25% did not work a full workday. Defense plants, design bureaus, and research institutes operated at about 12-13% of capacity.[5]

According to the Ministry of Defense, in 1999 62% of the 1,600 defense enterprises would have been unable to mobilize in case of war.[6]

In 1999, the following giant enterprises were on the brink of bankruptcy, and faced dubious futures: the Mil - Moscow Helicopter Plant, the Vladivostok Shipyard, Severnaia Verf and Proletarskii Zavod in St. Petersburg, the Zlatoust Mechanical Engineering Factory, Vibropribor in Taganrog, Stankomash in Chelyabinsk, the Cheboksary Electronic Apparatus Factory, Aviastar in Ulianovsk, Poliot in Omsk, etc. Wages at these plants were delayed for up to a year, and employees were paid not for work (there were no orders or income) but for being at the workplace. Hundreds of thousands of defense workers were faithful to their jobs and their coworkers, and waited for better times, when there would be new orders and respectable work. As a result, most enterprises have inflated work forces. In unsuccessful enterprises, the number of "extra" workers is four times greater than the number of useful ones.

---

[4] TS-VPK Information Agency, http://www.vpk.ru, October 26, 1999.

[5] TS-VPK Information Agency, http://www.vpk.ru, October 11, 1998.

[6] Leonid Kosals, Rosalina Ryvkina, and Yurii Simagin, *Oboronnye Predpriyatia Rossii v Usloviakh Rynochnogo Eksperimenta* (Moscow: Institut Sotsialno-Ekonomicheskikh Problem Narodonaselenia RAN, 1999).

In 1999, the situation became even more difficult at MIC enterprises in less fortunate regions, such as Pskov, Tver, Smolensk, Tula, Vladimir, Ivanovo, Saratov, and Orenburg Oblasts; Altai and Primorskii Krais, and the Buryat and Mordovian Autonomous Republics. Though the majority of these enterprises could produce both military and civilian goods, nearly all of them were on the brink of bankruptcy and total economic collapse. This is especially dangerous for those plants in Tula, Vladimir, and Saratov Oblasts and Primorskii Krai that serve as the principal employers in their respective cities.

In early 1999, the structure of the remaining MIC output was as follows:

- Military output for the domestic market—18.2%,
- Military output for export—28.5%
- Civilian output for domestic industry—32.1%
- Consumer goods—9.5%
- Civilian output for export—11.7%

Although the share of civilian output grew, it only reflected reduced military output—in absolute terms, the quantity of goods on the civilian market did not increase.

From 1991 to 2000, MIC enterprises lost a significant part of their technological assets—their unique technology and equipment.

The younger generation of personnel left MIC enterprises shortly after the beginning of the crisis. The average age of the remaining personnel is 55 years and the average of their directors is 69 years.

By the beginning of 2000, the military-industrial complex consisted of 1489 enterprises, including 612 state enterprises and organizations (387 of which cannot be privatized, by governmental decree), 490 joint stock companies with some state ownership of shares, and 387 joint stock companies that are entirely privately owned.[7] Only 10% of joint stock companies are truly successful, having adapted to the market, and 20% are just beginning to recover.

In early 1998, the government's total past-due debt to defense enterprises was 25 billion rubles ($4 billion at the exchange rate at that time). The defense enterprises, in turn, owed the government, the power utilities, and their vendors the equivalent of four years' output. Meanwhile, the budget for the entire country totaled $20 billion.[8]

At present, nearly all defense enterprise directors are negative in their assessment of the results of conversion. During the years of the headlong conversion of the MIC, the majority of conversion proponents turned into its opponents. The program, which received only 10-15% of the necessary financing, collapsed. Without market mechanisms and large-scale investment, the main reserves of conversion—the available intellectual capital and languishing real estate—went unused. At the beginning of the year 2000, the situation in the MIC had not improved.

---

[7] TS-VPK Information Agency, http://www.vpk.ru, July 23, 1999.

[8] A. Shulunov, *Ekonomika i Zhizn,* no. 30, July 1998.

4.4. SYMPTOMS OF PARALYSIS

Introductory Remarks

Vlad E. Genin

Like any unique phenomenon, the headlong conversion of the Russian defense industry has its own distinctive causes. One thing is clear: conversion, as a progressive process, has sustained heavy damage. Analyzing the reasons for the damage, observers—including those in Russia—have differing opinions. Some believe that the failure of conversion initiatives is the result of attempts to reverse the deep militarization of the economy to civilian direction too quickly. In fact, it was virtually impossible in such a short time.

According to others, the MIC simply did not have the adequate technologies or equipment to produce competitive, world-class civilian goods, particularly consumer goods.

A third group believes that conversion, a highly difficult technical and economic process, which required enormous resources, was impossible because not nearly enough money was allocated to support it.

And of course, one may rightly ask, "Who in Russia, apart from the upper echelon of the government, wanted defense conversion and believed in its results?" The plant directors, who prior to reforms had a state-budget mentality, rather than a market-driven mentality? One cannot say that their life was easy during the Soviet period; it was somewhat like life during wartime: under hard leadership, in constant extreme situations with excessive stress. But this was life with guaranteed state orders for weapons and military equipment that they knew how to produce well. Leaving behind this established pattern of work and lifestyle was by no means easy. The transition to producing civilian goods of Western quality, plus the completely unfamiliar, colossal task of marketing and sales, was a surreal nightmare for this past-Soviet generation of defense plant directors. They were the children of the old Soviet industrial system, which, while clumsy worked in its own way.

A new, post-conversion industrial system never solidified. Therefore, many Russian people assess the damage due to conversion by making comparisons to the "good old Soviet times". The present chaotic scenario makes the old system look even better than it did before reforms. Against 1999's reduced (sometimes to zero) economic indicators, the MIC's pre-conversion indicators look spectacular. Such comparisons, like different points of view on the problem of militarized industry, probably have the right to exist. But the country and the people need real goods and equipment produced domestically, but with the quality of imports. And they need them today, not sometime in the future. Therefore, most Russians today would not be satisfied with a comparison of the economic indicators of today and those of the pre-reform period, when MIC workers could buy household electronics only in a very few boutiques selling foreign goods to sailors, foreign tourists, and specialists who went on work-related trips abroad.

Did MIC executives want and believe in conversion? There is probably no clear and direct answer to this question. But this lack of clarity is a factor in their assessment of the collapse of MIC conversion, its past and present, and glimpses of its future.

Alexey N. Shulunov

Since 1992, the socio-economic situation in the country has gotten worse. Russian defense industry, like all industry, has been experiencing a deep crisis. Despite this situation, certain steps to create a market economy in Russia have been undertaken, namely:

- the foundations of financial, insurance, and stock exchange institutions were laid;
- some experience in privatization and stock exchange has been accumulated;
- small businesses are developing;
- price and foreign trade liberalization have been accomplished;
- ruble convertibility is becoming a reality;
- the essentials of a legal system that supports a market economy are being put in place;
- the demilitarization of the economy is under way.

However, economic reform results suggest certain conclusions regarding both the defense and civilian industries. The crisis of the defense industry, unlike all other industries, presents an enormous danger to the country's economy and its defense capability.

The armed forces have increasingly lower percentages of modern armaments and equipment at their disposal. In 1995, the most modern armaments and equipment accounted for 30% of the total, by 2001, it will be 10%, and by 2005 it will be 5-7%. In the armies of the NATO and the United States, the most modern armaments and equipment make up 60-70% of the total.

The unique MIC defense research institutions are disintegrating. These institutions, which were created by the efforts of the whole country, are losing their technological edge in both military and civilian applications. In fact, the first signs that Russia was losing its leading position in advanced technologies and that testing facilities were in poor shape were confirmed by reduced interest in Russian products at international military exhibitions. Experts believe that unless radical measures are adopted, the industry, which is still able to produce modern arms and state-of-the-art military equipment, will be destroyed.

Weak governmental management led to the complete degradation of enterprises, regardless of whether they are technologically integrated or have a single technological focus. Weakness of State control led to the complete disintegration of the enterprises, and their technological cooperation with each other. As a result, products manufactured domestically became non-competitive in terms of price, even on the domestic market, and were absolutely unacceptable on the export market.

The lack of future prospects or a proper understanding of foreign policy, national security criteria, military doctrine, military reform, and arms programs, together with constant changes in government and law enforcement agency personnel, produced great chaos.

Between 1992 and 1999, financing for State defense projects continually decreased. Enterprises involved in fulfilling state defense orders depended completely on state financing. Delays in settling accounts from 1992-1999 led not only to the collapse of enterprises' financial stability but created enormous fines, which are higher than the State's total debt to the enterprises for produced weapons, military equipment, R&D, etc.

The defense industry was left with a large surplus of production facilities. This was due not only to the sharp drop in state orders, but also to the fact that, according to the State requirements, enterprises had to maintain "mobilization " facilities[9] at the same level as in 1986. Enterprises were forced to spend large sums on them, worsening their already bad financial state.

Experts believe that without any emergency measures, we will completely disorganize the industry that once produced weapons and military equipment, unique work teams will disband forever to the detriment of the nation, and we will lose both military and dual-use technology.

The government refused to deal with microeconomics even in the defense sector, believing that the market would sort everything out. The rapid rise in the cost of energy, transportation, and utilities, and the State's harsh tax policy led to difficult consequences for the economic policy as a whole. Constant "changes in course" in Russian industry has had dire consequences for the defense industry. The collapse of the Soviet Union, which meant the collapse of a single economic, monetary, customs, and legal territory, literally knocked out the MIC.

As for the production of civilian goods resulting from conversion, which was supposed to satisfy the demands of all markets by autumn 1992, such large-scale developments, involving structural changes in the entire industry, cannot be implemented without the investment of a lot of money and State coordination. All of the numerous conversion programs failed only because the State wasn't able to finance them.

---

[9] Editor's Note: Facilities for mobilization preparedness.

Enterprises and organizations involved in the development of State defense projects, used money substitutes (e.g., promissory notes) partly to make payments to the State budget, partly to pay for materials, parts, components, equipment, electricity and other municipal services, and partly to pay their debts to the local budgets.

However, when converting money substitutes into money, 40-60% of the total value is lost. As a result, the government is nominally paying its debts, though the situation in the industry is not improving. Thus, the current situation and the future prospects of enterprises fulfilling state orders have become more than critical. Moreover:

- Planned R&D from the Weapons Program and current yearly plans is not being carried out, thereby losing its timeliness and newness;
- The most damaging consequence of not providing funding for many years is the loss of personnel, both young (and highly promising) and older.
- Enterprises that fulfill state defense orders have become virtually bankrupt, with all the attendant consequences.

When one adds the removal of price controls in 1992, which instantly robbed enterprises of their working capital, the resulting inflation, and the State's credit and finance policy, while borders had widely opened to imports of industrial goods, then one understands why even competitive civilian production facilities at defense plants collapsed.

Removal of price controls unleashed inflation, which had not existed since the civil war in Russia (1918-1920), and the industries hardest hits were those that were closely tied to the budget and were not export oriented (first and foremost, the defense industry). The disproportion of prices has reached levels unthinkable in any market economy. One must understand that all economic factors operating in microeconomics are, as a rule, interrelated.

Defense enterprises were forced to pay skyrocketing prices for energy, transportation, and machinery from civilian industries. By 1996, prices for the products of the fuel and power industries had increased by a factor of 16,635; railway transportation--by 10,897; heavy machinery -- by 46,233; MIC military products--by 2,142; and MIC civilian products-- by 1,664. The costs of fuel, power, and transportation reached 50-60% of the cost of the final product. Internal prices for power vary from 40 rubles per kilowatt/hour to 700-800 rubles, and the average price is higher than in South-East Asia by a factor of fifteen, than in China by five, than in Europe by four, and than in the USA and Canada by three-fourths. But many regions of Russia are located much further north, and their increased energy expenditures drive up the cost of the final product proportionally.

As a result, the output produced by MIC manufacturers was unable to compete price-wise on the domestic market, and industry has not adapted to the international market.

The social and economic situation, continued to decline up to the end of 1999, and slight signs of improvement in individual industries were used to create false impressions of a quick recovery, which interferes with strategic goals, since populist tasks are sometimes substituted for effective anti-crisis measures. The reality is much more bleak:

- Degradation of industry and the economy continues; of the manufacturing (including defense), agricultural, and fuel and natural resource industries, the last of the three is dominant, and is focused on exports;

- The budget financing crisis resulting from industrial decline is getting worse;
- Reduced real incomes and demand from the vast majority of the population and increased social stratification have aggravated public problems to the extreme;
- The growth in foreign debt is accompanied by increased contradictions within the groups representing national and supranational interests. The domestic decline in production of goods results in increased strategic dependence on imports of foodstuffs and industrial goods;
- Most industrial facilities and equipment (experts estimate 80-85%) are worn out; modernization and re-fitting is virtually non-existent; high-tech industries, scientific centers, and branches of research are crumbling;
- The government’s tax policy and the developing credit and finance system are markedly anti-industrial in nature. They prevent enterprises from creating (accumulating) working capital to replace what was lost when price controls were dropped in 1992. There is virtually no basis for even simple manufacturing, which has led to the collapse of domestic industry and industrial infrastructure. Not one Western company would choose to take out loan against 100-150% of even the most profitable output;

Since 1992, the MIC’s main endeavor has been fighting for new markets, for both military and commercial products. By 1997, weapon exports had become the main source of money for many military manufacturers.

In other countries that export military products, only 10-20 % of the total volume of military production is exported. However, in Russia, this value is about 60-70%. Aircraft exports are about 58% of the weapon export total volume, and air defense systems are about 25%. At the same time, supplies of military production for the domestic market are at about zero. Export has become the only way for MIC enterprises to survive. Modernization of the manufacturing facilities, and creating state-of-the-art technology and machinery, are usually accomplished with the money received from exports. For example, the contract with India for supplies of Su-30 MKI fighters allowed the Sukhoi Design Bureau to finance the modernization programs for the airplane, its engines, and avionics.

According to experts from the League for Supporting Defense Enterprises, after removing "certain bureaucratic obstacles," it would be quite possible to increase annual earnings as follows:

- Spare parts supplies and post-warranty services - up to $1 billion.
- Scientific/technical cooperation - up to $1 billion.
- Product modernization - up to $500 million.
- Changing financial arrangements - up to $500 million.

What are the reasons for not using the full capacity of the Russian MIC? First, the absence of state support and stimuli for military exports. Second, the insufficient involvement of designers and producers with international military-technical cooperation. In the United States, 1,800 companies are involved in international military-technical cooperation; in Russia, there are only nine. The absence of information about export activity and about the countermeasures of competitors (foreign and domestic), and the substitution of a one-company monopoly for the state monopoly completes the sad picture of weapons exports in Russia.

However, there are untapped opportunities that have not been used for quite a long time:

1. Military-technical cooperation is primarily sales-oriented (it accounts for 95% of all exports). Scientific-technical cooperation is developing slowly, and the potential of all previous R&D and worldwide developmental trends is not being realized. This applies to cooperation with both developing and European countries.

The main limiting factors are the ministerial and agency system of restrictions, lack of understanding of the situation that is unfolding in the scientific sphere, and the lack of structures to promote the development of this type of cooperation.

2. A policy for service and maintenance of military technology sold in the ’70s and ’80s has not been formulated, and therefore has not been implemented.

The MIC industries are disorganized, and if urgent measures are not taken, Russia will be unable to manufacture either military products or high-tech civilian products. Further delay of normalizing the financing of state defense orders will result in the complete paralysis of the operation of MIC enterprises.

4.5. AFTER THE MARATHON: MIC 2000

Introductory Remarks

Vlad E. Genin

Looking at the Russian defense industry after the headlong command conversion marathon is like looking at a mountainside just after an avalanche: monstrous clouds of snow obscure the whole picture, and it is hard to see clearly without oversimplification or emotional exaggerations.

Only one thing is clear -- the mass destruction of the defense industry. Twelve years ago, prior to the first steps of conversion, nobody could have imagined the destruction of the MIC. It was as unimaginable as the collapse of the Soviet Union itself. Even after the beginning of command conversion, and its first failures, it would have been hard to predict the further destruction of the once-flourishing defense industry. However, that is today's reality. The MIC, like a horse that was ridden too hard, now lies on the ground gasping for breath.

To underestimate the MIC's ability to survive is to ignore the spirit of the people who remained inside the MIC: its executives, designers, plant managers, and its ordinary workers. No matter what happened to their industry, either as a result of the state's mismanagement, the casting aside of the defense ministries, or the helplessness of the enterprise's directors, they preserved their sincere dedication to the industry, their great patience, and their strong faith that the day will come at last when they and their production capabilities will be in demand again.

The question is: "Production of what?" Weapons for a new arms race, for supplying terrorists or civilian goods for the people of Russia and other countries?

What is the former defense industry today? How does its military component, still committed to the production of weapons for defense purposes, look? And most importantly, how does its converted civilian component work today?

Arkadiy I. Yarovskiy

The Russian economic crisis has undermined, but not destroyed, the country's military potential. In 1998, Donald Rumsfeld, former US Secretary of Defense, said, "If one were looking down from Mars on the globe and they said, 'what is the nation that has the second most powerful set of military capabilities of various types?' obviously it would be Russia. And to the extent that country's political and economic situation is unfit and turbulent, there is no question that they pose a threat to the world because of the almost inevitability of all kinds of capabilities, knowledge and technicians, as well as capabilities even further dispersed throughout the world." [10]

Of course, implementing arms reduction treaties, drastically reducing defense orders, and shutting down most enterprises has significantly reduced the MIC's capacity, but it still exists and can be reanimated. This is confirmed by the continued production of weapons.

---

[10] "A Clear and Present Missile Danger. An Interview with Donald Rumsfeld," *Intellectual Capital,* http://www.intellectualcapital.com/issues/98/0903/icinterview.asp, September 3, 1998.

In years past, missile development and production was done by dozens of design bureaus and scientific research institutes and hundreds of large factories. They created and serially produced over 500 types of missiles and missile systems. By the 1990s, serial production of missiles and other weapons systems stopped. But 21 organizations continue to develop and modernize approximately 50 missile systems for all branches of the military.

Economic difficulties, and the virtual lack of financing, have forced many enterprises to develop and produce most new super-modern weapon systems in small quantities -- one at a time, using prototype production facilities. These accomplishments are possible thanks to the results of R&D done as long as 20-30 years ago, and will not run out for some time.

These include the *Topol-M*, the newest and most advanced missile system; *Bark* and *Iskander* ballistic missiles; the *Medvedka* and *Bal-E* anti-ship systems; the *Alfa* and *Yakhont* all-purpose missile systems; and the *Ataka, Khrisantema, Malyutka-1, Vikhr, Kornet-E, Kh-65S,* and *Moskit-E* anti-tank, air-based, and sea-based systems.[11]

Special attention is being paid to the development of the following anti-missile systems: the S-400 *Triumf*, S-300PMU *Favorit*, *Antey-2500*, *Buk-M2*, *Buk-M1-2*, *Ural*, S-125 *Pechora*, and *Igla* surface-to-air systems, and the *Tunguska-M* and *Pantsir-S1* artillery rocket systems. A number of systems have been modernized, including the R-27, R-33, Kh-29, Kh-31, Kh-35, S-8, S-13, S-25 air-based missiles, and the TOS-1, *Grad*, *Uragan*, and *Smerch* multiple-launch rocket systems. Despite the severe economic crisis in the country, design bureaus and scientific research institutes, specializing in missiles, continue to work.

---

[11] TS-VPK Information Agency, http://www.vpk.ru, July 6, 1999.

In 1998-1999, a number of systems were produced for delivery to Cyprus, India, and Greece, such as the S-300, *Tunguska-M1*, S-125 *Pechora*, *Osa*, *Tor-M1*, *Tor-M1T*, and *Igla*; Krasnopol and Kitolov guided artillery systems; CLUB-S anti-ship cruise missiles, APR-3ME anti-ship missiles; *Grad*, *Uragan*, and *Smerch* self-propelled MLR systems; and so forth. Although data on specific contracts is not published, the volume of deliveries, as a rule, is no greater than several dozen.[12]

The same is true for the production of fixed- and rotary-wing military aircraft. The Russian aerospace industry includes about 335 enterprises (including 19 large factories and 9 design bureaus)—almost 80% of the former Soviet industry. In the past, they produced 350-500 airplanes and 300 helicopters per year. Today they produce no more than 50 annually, and most of these are for export. In the past five years, the Russian Air Force received 5 Su-30 fighter planes, 8 Ka-50 helicopters, and the Navy received several Su-27K fighters.

A few Russian enterprises that are successfully exporting their goods and occupying a niche in the market include the Sukhoi firm, which unites two design bureaus—Sukhoi in Moscow and Beriev in Taganrog—and three aircraft plants in Novosibirsk, Irkutsk, and Komsomolsk-na-Amure. Increased exports have led the aviation industry to increase production somewhat. These exports are produced mainly under contract with India, Peru, and other countries, and include Su-27, Su-30 MKI, Su-37, Be-200 and Be-103 seaplanes, Mi-17, Mi-26, Mi-28, Mi-35, and Ka-50 ("Black Shark") helicopters, etc.[13]

---

[12] M. Pervov, Ot 'Katiushi' do 'Topolya', *Yadernaia Bezopasnost*, no. 20-21, 1999.

[13] TS-VPK Information Agency, http://www.vpk.ru, March 15, 1999.

Tanks are produced at only two Russian enterprises: Tyazhmash in Omsk, which produces the T-80U and T-80-M1 Bars tanks, and Uralvagonzavod in Nizhniy Tagil, once the largest tank city in the world. During World War II, the plant produced 35,000 T-34 tanks, and in years past, it produced 3,000-4,000 T-72 tanks (and modifications thereof) annually.

For the past two years, the factory has not received any orders from the government, but continues to produce tanks for export. Forty-one T-80U tanks have been produced for Cyprus; 33 for South Korea; three prototypes of the new T-90 tank have been produced for India, which plans to use them to upgrade its tank pool (in 1999 it was expected that India will place the largest tank order in Russian history, on the order of hundreds of millions of dollars); and 16 other tanks have been refurbished for the Russian military. Tank factories, like many other weapons producers, have inventories of unsold finished units. For example, the Nizhniy Tagil plant has 350 tanks on site, according to satellite reconnaissance data.[14]

At the beginning of the '90s, the Russian shipbuilding industry produced a third of the world's military vessels and was the world leader in exports of nuclear submarines armed with ballistic missiles, cruise missiles and torpedoes, which were exported to the navies of 14 countries. Of the 485 nuclear submarines around the world, 249 were built at Russian enterprises. By the beginning of the year 2000, the military shipbuilding centers have received virtually no orders from the state, but they have not stopped working. After several years of finishing works, shipbuilders sent the Navy the *Piotr Velikii* SSBN and the large anti-submarine ship *Admiral Chabanenko*, which were equipped with the

---

[14] *Literaturnaia Gazeta,* no. 40, July 10, 1998.

latest weaponry. And that was all the domestic Navy received. The majority of shipbuilding work goes toward exports. The shipyards are building a few diesel submarines, *Ekranoplans* (wing-in-ground-effect craft), ships with hydrofoils, and destroyers.

Production of firearms has been the least affected. The main producer of firearms is the Federal Center for Firearms-Izhevsk Weapon Plant, where Mikhail Kalashnikov, the inventor of the AK-47, continues to work on new designs. Apart from production of Kalashnikovs, of which there are 70 million worldwide, the factory also perfected the Abakan, the next generation automatic weapon; the Dragunov sniper rifle; the Bizon-2 light machine gun; and other weapons. Izhmash, having finalized contracts worth $8 million, plans to expand its exports to $120 million.[15]

By the beginning of 2000, several MIC enterprises have revived the process of adapting to the market, of restructuring and conversion "from the bottom up." Civilian production from MIC plants is becoming more and more common on the domestic and international markets. Most of it is goods and services for the space and aviation agencies (mainly for the international market) and televisions, automobiles, sewing machines, laser surgery equipment, etc. (for the domestic market).

Russia is quite well represented in the world market for space services. Of the 624 spacecraft in existence, Russia owns 131, including 43 that conduct civilian research tasks and 28 that are used for "dual-use" tasks. In 1998 alone, 12 Russian rockets were launched for civilian commercial programs. One hundred fifty *Dnepr-1* space launch vehicles (converted RS-20 *"Satan"* ICBMs) have found a peaceful profession—they are used to send commercial satellites into orbit. In 1998, the

---

[15] *Zavtra*, no.11 (276), March 16, 1999.

Tubsat-N satellite, created by the Berlin Technical University, was launched from the K-407 *Novomoskovsk* submarine located in the Barents Sea. This unique research project was prepared by the State Rocket Center- Makeyev Design Bureau. In 1999, a series of telecommunications satellites were launched jointly with the U.S. company Globalstar. Russian scientists actively participate in a promising international project to create a thermonuclear power station. According to the general director of the Russian Space Agency, Yuriy Koptev, the total value of work done for international clients for the past five years grew from $48 million to $880 million and will reach $1 billion by the end of 2000.[16]

There are high hopes concerning the creation of two holding companies—Passenger and Transport Airplanes and Russian Helicopters—which will unite designers and production facilities. The Sukhoi military aviation complex has begun producing Su-26 and Su-29 sport aircraft, and a supersonic airplane. Russia's leading aviation firms and institutes—Aviastar, Gidromash, Tupolev Aviation Scientific-Technical Complex, National Institute of Aviation Technology and Central Aerohydrodynamic Institute are part of a Euro-Russian aviation consortium for creating new modern aircraft, including the largest-capacity airliner in the world.

The Nizhniy Novgorod factory NITEL has renewed production of televisions. Izhmash-avto has produced the first batch of all-new Niva VAZ-2131 jeeps. The Sokol aviation plant in Nizhniy Novgorod and the Italian company Aeromacchi are cooperating to produce a Yak-130/AEM training airplane. The main producer of anti-tank, helicopter, and artillery weapons, the Tula Factory, is producing unique civilian

---

[16] TS-VPK Information Agency, http://www.vpk.ru, February 11, 1999.

goods: laser-surgery equipment, sewing machines, and biotechnology goods. The Leningrad Optical-Mechanical Association (LOMO), the only Russian MIC enterprise that has 100% private capital, has kept its leading position in the production of military goods, primarily homing heads. However, though civilian production provides stable income and accounts for 50% of LOMO's output, it is currently unprofitable.[17]

In order to meet State's requirements for mobilization preparedness, the MIC has "mobilization production facilities", which are reserved for use in time of war only. In conditions of financial crisis this is extremely costly. For example, merely maintaining the readiness of a single non-operational tank production line at the Nizhniy Tagil factory costs $8 million annually. MIC enterprise managers believe that the "mobilization" facilities at over 40% of defense enterprises could be used to produce civilian goods instead.

Thus, the MIC weapons manufacturing archipelago has vast opportunities today. How this potential is dealt with will seriously influence Russia's future and international security.

---

[17] TS-VPK Information Agency, http://www.vpk.ru, June 21, 1999.

4.6. CONSEQUENCES OF THE REFORMS

Introductory Remarks

Vlad E. Genin

Today, at the end of the troubled decade of the 1990s, one can see many events and their underlying processes in a different light. Time is not only the best healer; it is the best judge, too.

We may wonder why the economic reforms launched in 1992 resulted in such disorganization of the economic, social, and political life in Russia. Gaidar's government had apparently taken the necessary measures to create a democratic market environment. The one-party system was destroyed, as was the planning system. Controls on production and prices were lifted; competition was introduced, and privatization was launched. However, these measures did not generate any modifications in the mode of operation of the former Soviet enterprises. Although new rules and regulations had been introduced, enterprises, and especially defense enterprises, seem to maintain their former routines and behavior.

It has been suggested that this was due to the preservation of Soviet ways of thinking, and to the resistance of "Red Directors" to the reforms. Although we cannot deny that some directors resisted the reforms, there is clear evidence that most of them supported them, because they provided a freedom not experienced before. Another argument holds that the Soviet system could not be reformed, because it was too rigid and too different from the market. This argument is not without some validity. A system is made up of a large and complex set of rules, behavioral guidelines, and institutions, which provide the system with its own coherence. Changing only a few elements may destabilize the system without generating the expected results. However, it is worth noting that the Soviet system contained the essential elements of the market: employees sold their labor for a salary; goods were exchanged, using money as a means of payment; and prices played an important role in some markets, like the black market. Further, studies of the Soviet economy have clearly demonstrated that the planning system was mainly an instrument of power, and not a mechanism of economic coordination.

Another argument is that the failure of the reforms is due to the fact that they tried to move from one extreme to the other. The elements that characterized the Soviet economy were to be replaced by their mirror image in the market: from state property to private property; controlled prices to free prices; planning system to free enterprise; one-party system to multi-party system; etc. Therefore, they focused on the destruction of the Soviet system, and not the creation of a new coherent system. The question is, what gives coherence to a system?

Sonia Ben Ouagrham

The policy launched in 1992 destroyed some of the elements of the Soviet system that represented obstacles to the emergence of the market. The single-party system and central planning were destroyed. Controls over prices and foreign economic relations were lifted. Privatization was launched, and a banking and financial system was created.

However, the simultaneous implementation of all these measures resulted in the disturbance of the operation of the system without provoking a change in behavior. In fact, the uncertainty that resulted from the destruction of vital elements of the former system encouraged agents to cling to, and even reinforce, customary routines and habits. And the disappearance of the structure that had regulated relations among agents, namely the Party, allowed these behaviors to express themselves with no institutional constraints. This resulted in a fragmented economy characterized by regionalism, inflation, demonetarization, and a concentration of finances and property. Political power was dispersed, and its clientelist feature was reinforced. For enterprises, the manifestation of the new economic and political environment is very similar to that of the former system. We may therefore wonder whether the system has actually changed.

Disturbed Money Flow

One of the consequences of the reforms was that the liberalization of prices and the restructuring of the banking system have resulted in a general indebtedness and the illiquidity of agents.

After the liberalization of prices in January 1992, enterprises found themselves in a situation where prices were increasing quickly, but their financial resources were decreasing sharply. The state had indeed adopted a tight budget policy, and the new commercial banks preferred speculating on the financial markets to investing in the economy.

Such a situation should have handicapped the production system. However, the decrease in production, though significant, was extremely low compared to the inflation level. One of the reasons for this was that enterprises continued supplying each other with goods and services, without paying each other or their employees. This eventually generated a huge enterprise-to-enterprise debt (30 trillion rubles in 1993).[18]

In addition to indebtedness, enterprises were confronted by illiquidity due to various reasons. One of them is that the state tried to control inflation by sequestrating funds that were voted in the budget. Another source of illiquidity was due to the behavior of the newly created commercial banks, which commonly used their clients' money to speculate, thus depriving them of the use of their own funds. Bank loans were also very short-term, and their interest rates were too high for enterprises—especially for defense enterprises. The inability of the state to impose prudential rules on the newly created commercial bank allowed the banking system to develop in an unhealthy manner, which resulted in a series of crises, the latest being the August 1998 crisis.

Demonetization Of The Economy

The general indebtedness and illiquidity of enterprises, and also that of local budgets and individuals, have led to the use of barter as the main means of exchange, as well as to the creation of surrogate money (promissory notes).

As a result, the ruble, which remains the only official unit of account, is neither the only means of exchange nor the only means of savings. Foreign currencies, and especially the U.S. dollar, are usually used for savings: in 1997, 22% of households' income was used to buy foreign currencies.[19]

---

[18] Philip Hanson, "The Future of Russian Economic Reform," *Survival*, Autumn 1994, pp. 28-45.

[19] Sonia Ben Ouagrham, *La Convesrion des Enterprises de Defense en Russie: Une Analyse Regionale,* op.cit.

Although barter and promissory notes have allowed exchanges to take place in spite of the lack of money, they also resulted in the greater segmentation of markets. Because, unlike money, they cannot circulate freely and are not accepted by all agents, they trap their users in a closed network of exchanges.

Fragmentation Of The Domestic Economy

The increase in the price of goods, and also that of energy, transportation, and communications, together with indebtedness and illiquidity, resulted in the splintering of the domestic economy. Exchanges and transactions have withdrawn within regional limits not only because of the high price of goods and services, but also because of the solutions found to solve the illiquidity problem (barter and promissory notes).

Sharp regional differences have also appeared. They express themselves as differences in rate of development (some regions are better off than others), but also in the choice of economic goals. Some regions have indeed adopted a market economy path, others have maintained their Soviet-era organization, and still others have chosen to be rent-seekers.

The fragmentation of the economy and its demonetization has made interregional exchanges very difficult.

Concentration Of Finances And Property

Privatization in Russia had several objectives. It first aimed at making the system change irreversible by creating a class of owners and entrepreneurs who would manage enterprises more efficiently. It also aimed at fostering competition and the demonopolization of the economy. Privatization also aimed at encouraging individuals to participate actively in the process, at attracting foreign investors, and providing the state with income.

However, the method used, and the disturbances created by the reforms, resulted in the opposite situation. The privatization law allowed employees of big enterprises to select the method (among the three proposed) by which their enterprise would be privatized. The majority of them chose the option that allowed them to control 51% of the shares, because outsider involvement was deemed to be a potential threat to their jobs and to the social infrastructure provided by their enterprises. Later, directors became major shareholders, as many of them offered to buy back their employees' shares for cash payments. In a situation where salaries are delayed by several months, this was a very attractive offer. Some of them also forbade, and still forbid, their employees to sell their shares to outsiders, on penalty of being fired.

Privatization also led to increased monopolization of the economy. Some directors, after they bought their enterprises, started implementing an integration strategy that allowed them to control their suppliers and clients. Some use their position as a unique client to impose their will on their suppliers. Others have created banks, bought media, or created important industrial groups. Large Russian banks have also generated important industrial groups.

The upshot is that privatization has allowed the concentration of finances and property among the former Soviet elite – enterprise directors and members of the administration – and financial organizations created during the reforms.

Weakening Of The State

One of the most troublesome results of the reforms and the consequent disorganization is the weakening of the state. While the federal government was subject to internal conflicts, regional actors started fighting for power. As a result, power has dispersed among different actors, and the representatives of the state (governors, mayors) are not necessarily those who hold power in the regions. For instance, some regions are controlled by an important local enterprise, which provides the local budget with the majority of its funding; others are controlled by criminal organizations; and in some cases, power is still being fought over between various actors.

The dearth of public action in the regions, which results both from the struggle for power in Moscow as well as from the absence of financial resources, have allowed local leaders to get increasingly independent. Many make decisions that are not within their competence: issuing new taxes, making decisions that can have an impact on Russia's relationships with foreign countries, etc. Local leaders are all the more independent from the federal government, as they no longer owe their positions to the will of the president: most of them were elected at the universal suffrage.

The independence of the regions also manifests itself in the creation of local interest groups that often integrate federal representatives in the regions: presidential representatives, the police, the army, the tax administration, the courts, etc. They can do this, even though state representatives' salaries are paid by the state, because their lives and working conditions depend on the regional leaders. Like all other employees, state representatives suffer from prolonged salary arrears. In such conditions, the privileges and favors that local leaders can provide become an important part of their income, while the salary itself becomes less and less important.

The result is that the reforms have created an environment that surprisingly resembles the Soviet environment: segmented distribution and money circuits, a monopolized economy, competition for resources, a clientelist system where power is controlled by those who have the ability to distribute privileges and favors, a diminished role for money, etc. This is one of the reasons why most enterprises have resorted to their former routines and behaviors to solve the problems they met. In such conditions, the budgetary policy adopted by the government in 1992 had no impact on enterprises' behavior; they still operated in a world where money and prices play only a marginal role.

However, although the way the new environment manifests itself is very similar to the Soviet environment, the sources, incentives, and constraints of the new environment are very different from those that prevailed in the Soviet period. As a result, the instruments that enterprises use to solve problems do not always operate in the present conditions. This generates a greater uncertainty, which translates into greater rigidities. For defense enterprises the change has been even more radical. While in the Soviet period they evolved in a stable environment where they had an impact on the rules, they now operate in a very volatile and unstable environment.

Conclusion

The obvious conclusion of the developments above is that the reforms focused too much on the framework, and not enough on specific mechanisms. The commercialization of the economy, and the clear separation between economic and political actors, did not receive enough attention from the State. As a consequence, the elements required to support the development of the market (developed transportation and communication systems, market rules and reliable commercial information, a working legal system, authority of the state, etc.) have not been sufficiently developed. A great uncertainty resulted from the conflict between the new explicit rules (introduction of market rules) and the former implicit rules (Soviet behaviors and routines). This allowed the emergence of new institutions that combine some aspects of the Soviet system and some features of the market, yet can be relied on neither as market institutions, nor as Soviet institutions.

In short, the system change has not projected defense enterprises into a new world (the market) but into a parallel world, a mutant system, which is now shaping its own rules and behaviors.

4.7. WEAPONS EXPORTS AND CONVERSION

Introductory Remarks

Vlad E. Genin

The U.S.S.R. formerly armed half of all the world's nations, being one of the world's leaders in the international arms trade. These countries included, at various times, China, Iraq, Iran, Libya, Somalia, Lebanon, Syria, Uganda, Zaire, North Korea, Vietnam, Mongolia, Cuba, and many others.

In previous decades, Russia's latest weapons were highly desirable in many corners of the planet and now, the country's modern missile systems, submarines, combat airplanes, and many types of portable conventional weapons are in high demand in the world.

It is well known that weapon sales yield big profits: not just millions but billions of dollars. For Russia, it would be logical to earmark these moneys for defense industry conversion. The profits from weapons sales together with Western financial assistance could help Russian defense conversion a great deal.

This idea raises a lot of unanswered questions, because all these years the West has been providing assistance for Russia. One of them is: why hasn't the money from weapons export sales helped conversion? If the country really and desperately needs to convert its still militarized economy into civilian one, and at the same time it significantly increases arms exports, if the profits from arms sales are divided among export brokerage organizations, instead of re-investing them into desperately needed

MIC conversion, why would it make sense for the West to provide new, substantial aid?

Mark I. Shteynberg

In all countries of the world, all aspects of arms exports have always been the prerogative of the state and its international and defense policy.

Exporting weapons is a highly profitable business, especially for Russia with its achievements in science, design, and R&D; well-developed military technologies and facilities; special equipment; inexpensive, highly skilled labor; and abundant raw materials. The profitability of this business is based on the fact that, in addition to the weapons (the main component of the export package) there is the second part of the package, which includes: ammunition supplies, spare parts, special equipment, military-technical personnel training, and services (which are particularly profitable). For defense enterprises the "beauty" of the second part of the military sales packages is that customers buy them on a continuing basis. Within the last few years, Russian defense plants dramatically increased their business in that second part of sales packages -- "service and ammunition".

Besides the profitability, there are several other very important aspects of weapons exports. It is true that weapons export orders lead to more jobs. Export orders increase manufacturing volume, serving to promote production efficiency, cost reduction, and profitability. The competition in the arms export race catalyzes scientific projects and R&D. During the last decade, under conditions of the deepest financial crisis, famous Russian design bureaus and research institutes in aviation, space, high technology, and other advanced branches of the defense industry created, designed, and produced innovative models of weapons.

New generations of missiles, ships, combat aircraft, and helicopters were developed in the same period of time, when the federal government could afford to purchase only a very few units per year—or none at all. Most units were produced to fill export orders.

During the Soviet era, weapons were exported to different political regimes. The price of weapons and the payment schedule depended on the political orientation of the buyer. Quantities of weapons were sold to countries such as Libya at relatively high prices, to be paid in hard currency. In some cases, foreign customers paid by barter in the form of consumer goods or foodstuffs.

In the postwar years, after Stalin created the Communist bloc of states, constituting the so-called "socialist camp of fraternal Eastern European countries," the U.S.S.R. needed massive quantities of weapons for their armies. After the establishment of the Warsaw Pact, and the signing of agreements with North Korea, North Vietnam, Cuba, and other allies in Africa, Asia, and later Southern America, the U.S.S.R. took it upon itself to provide weapons for these countries. Evidently the U.S.S.R. saw weapons production as one of its main political priorities, not only for its domestic needs, but also for the "fraternal countries" and other political satellites. In most cases, nations in both classes received weapons for free.

After the collapse of the U.S.S.R. and the Warsaw Pact, the Russian government revoked previously accepted obligations for the shipment of free weapons. The transition toward a free market economy included the commercialization of weapons exports. Russia could no longer afford to make presents in the form several hundred million dollars worth of S-300 missile systems, the newest jet fighters and tanks, and other conventional weapons, as its predecessor did. The new Russia exports weapons for profit.

The main organization that exports weapons from Russia is Rosvoorouzhenie (Russian Armaments). Also, there are others Russian structures and groups, which are involved in the export, such as Promexport (Industrial Export) and Rossiiskie Tekhnologii (Russian Technologies).

By the beginning of the year 2000, Russia is still producing weapons not only for its own use, but also for trade. The market is rather diverse – from repeat customers in the Middle East, Africa, Asia, and South America, and the new armies of the former Soviet republics, to new ones in Southern Europe. Many Russian weapons are re-sold through different channels to many kinds of militarized groups, including terrorist organizations.

China is a very unusual customer. It cannot afford Western products, and that is why it remains one of the major customers of the Russian MIC. The Chinese Army together with the so-called "regular armed police" is approaching four million people. Many nuclear weapons were produced in China using Russian technologies. More than three-quarters of China's military equipment was purchased from the Soviet Union and Russia, or produced in China under Soviet license. China is currently modernizing this equipment, as most of it has aged. However, China has neither sufficient funds to purchase large quantities of modern weaponry, nor indigenous designs and technologies to produce them domestically. Therefore, Chinese military modernization tactics consist of buying small shipments of weapons, and acquiring licenses for their domestic production.

In the Russia, on the threshold of the new millennium, the weapons exports had its own new political lobbyists. There were more than a few politicians and businessmen who argued, "Let us increase weapons exports and re-start frozen defense plants, and hungry Russia will at last be well fed". They strongly believed that only a drastic increase in weapons exports could save the country and radically improve its economy. They claimed it would solve a lot of current problems in the defense industry, the only industry able to rescue Russia. It is a myth—a myth that hid an inability to bring order to Russia, and to complete the market economy reforms. A myth without a grain of common sense. Its authors failed to see that the reason for the collapse of the defense industry was their own mistakes in conversion planning, which resulted from the continuous, destructive struggle for power inside the country in the 1990s. They strongly believed that the source of the MIC's problems was the failure to increase weapons exports. However, here we are entering the sphere of ideology; when stripped bare, this idea turns out to be nothing but political nostalgia for the Soviet empire. It is merely a disguised attempt to get the country back into the same deadlock of weapons escalation and impoverishment of the general economy. Civilian poverty was defended and justified in the Soviet era by slogans about the unity of the Party and its people. That kind of economy required political dictatorship for its maintenance.

It is possible that increasing military orders through weapons exports might feed the Russian population. However, the other side of the coin is that any industry, and particularly any state, that depends strictly on weapons exports becomes "addicted" to them, and stops seeking other means of support. The profits from a nation's weapon sales cannot provide stability for the whole society. In recent years, the many disarmament processes in the world have caused the arms industry to suffer badly. The history of disarmament in the U.S., Russia, and other countries in the early 90s shows that more painful hits were taken by "pure" military enterprises, those that had been engaged exclusively in weapons manufacturing, and now were much less necessary. Only those plants or production units that were able to convert their product lines from military to civilian use were able to survive.

It is not a solution, even a temporary one -- it is a dead end. If adopted as a temporary measure, military orders could at any moment be terminated completely, which would lead to more tragic consequences than even the Russian economic crisis in August 1998, devastating as that was.

The substantial profits received from international weapons sales have not yet played a significant role either in defense conversion programs or in providing for social programs for ordinary people. This money was desperately needed to protect retired veterans of the Russian defense industries, laid-off employees, and their dependants. History will disclose where all this money went, and what influence this diversion of funds had on the willingness of the world financial community to provide further financial assistance to the new Russia.

Undoubtedly, from the beginning of the new century, the Russian MIC plans to dramatically increase its efforts in research, engineering, and production capabilities. The big question is, "for what purpose?" If all efforts are directed toward purely military production, Russia loses its historical chance to make capital improvements in its economy, and to give its own people a better life, which they undoubtedly deserve. If military production dominates, practically all the money for MIC development should come mainly from weapons exports.

But it is hard to believe that exports of weapons or of natural resources will make the Russian economy strong.

Nevertheless, Russia will keep exporting weapons. One hopes that if the revenue from such exports is directed to the conversion of the MIC, and used to immediately and substantially increase civilian production (yet still provide for the necessary weapons production), it will help Russian industries, including the vulnerable defense sector, to "buy time" and overcome the present socio-economic crisis. In this scenario, the majority of the profits resulting from weapons exports would be invested in the conversion of thousands of now-useless military production facilities. Newly converted, profitable civilian production facilities will in turn promote the creation of a regular system to further convert obsolete portions of the Russian MIC.

PART FIVE

The Legacy

INTRODUCTION

Vlad E. Genin

The 1990s have ended, and with them the "headlong command conversion marathon." The long-awaited positive results of conversion never materialized. Instead of the sharp upswing in civilian output that the leaders of the country promised, production at defense enterprises came to a halt. Expensive equipment, much of which had been purchased abroad, became worthless. A certain amount of it was dismantled and sold to private outsiders. Factory floors were half empty.

Highly qualified workers and engineers were no longer needed. Some of them were able to find at least some sort of work; many others became virtually unemployed. For example, at the Kovrovskii Munitions plant, which employed several thousand people ten years ago, we saw completely empty production areas, design bureaus and management offices. Only the director and a maintenance team remain at the factory, in order to prevent fires and utilities supply accidents, clear away snowdrifts, prevent the factory from freezing in winter, and the roof from leaking in summer. This is all that is left of this fully automated factory, once the pride of the Soviet Military Industrial Complex.

In the first few years of conversion this factory began production of high-quality civilian items: equipment for producing decorative textile braids, which were immediately in demand overseas and had been exported to several countries, and executive desk clocks, in which world-class mechanisms were combined with rich artistic paintings, in the style of old Russian Palekh, on the base. But because of the suffocating tax burden, the factory stopped even this production.

The "headlong command conversion marathon" left behind a difficult legacy, and not only for industry.

The environmental situation in the country is a problem, and was so long before the start of conversion. While in some regions with a heavy concentration of defense plants the environment has improved (due to the shutdown of enterprises and the subsequent lack of pollution), the population continues to suffer from poor-quality water and air, and in some regions, elevated radiation levels.

Command conversion resulted in serious social, medical, and demographic consequences for the populace: death rates and illness increased. Birth rates dropped. Crime levels soared.

However, the legacy is not limited to just social, medical, and demographic problems. Apart from conventional weapons, there are deadly nuclear, chemical, and biological weapons. Designs for such weapons, and the technology needed to realize them, remain in the country's heritage, and are ready for immediate use.

As a result of headlong conversion, fundamental science and R&D, which were concentrated in the MIC, lost talented scientists, engineers, and inventors. Many of them left in search of jobs overseas. "Brain drain", the loss of the country's intellcctual capital, began to take place.

5.1. "BRAIN DRAIN": THE LOSS OF INTELLECTUAL CAPITAL

Introductory Remarks

Vlad E. Genin

Bertrand Russell once said, "So far as I can remember, there is not one word in the Gospels in praise of intelligence."[1]

Probably the most deplorable result of headlong conversion is the evaporation of much of Russia's powerful intellectual capital, which, because of the militarization of the economy, was closely tied to the MIC.

According to Dr. Andrei Kokoshin, one of the distinguished world authorities in the military-technological field, "Russia stands out in terms of its human resources, its huge reservoir of intellectual capital. Throughout the history of Russia, there has always been a deep tradition of respect for education, and nowadays the country has a great number of well-educated scientists and engineers. The loss of this human capital, with its high level of scientific and technological knowledge, presents a most serious threat to the national security of the country. It is very important to promote and nurture these potential advantages by way of appropriate economic and social mechanisms, as well as concrete economic benefits."[2]

Russia has always been famous for its thirst for knowledge and its eagerness to put

---

[1] http://fly.to/russell. E.S.O p.14/5.

[2] Boris V.Chugunov, "Tekhnologii VPK – Poslednii Shans Strany," (Interview with Andrei Kokoshin), *Nezavisimaia Gazeta*, vol. 48, March 18, 1999, http://home.mosinfo.ru.

that knowledge to work in practice. It would have been impossible for a country to create a powerful industry that produces the most advanced weapons without a powerful intellectual class. Individual talents and a "culture of knowledge" were intensively nurtured by the State. Jobs in scientific research and design were among the most prestigious in Russian society. Within the last decade, Russians have become some of the best software engineers in the world.

The Russian educational system introduced the treasures of the world's culture, science, and technology to children at an early age, thus forming a foundation for their creative and constructive approach to any tasks. It generated broad-minded specialists, capable of quickly grasping new notions and easily adapting to unfamiliar environments, such as joint international projects.

The state system of free higher education drew a lot of young people to universities. At that time, the notion of private business was nonexistent. That is why the young generation wanted to become specialists – state employees holding the highest university degrees. University students who majored in subjects related to military production were considered to be the elite.

The level of education steadily increased, due to the involvement of universities in almost all centralized research programs run by the State and defense enterprises. Strengthening the ties between the educational process, science, research, and real-world manufacturing practices was one of prime goals of the Ministry of Higher Education. Universities conducted scientific research on a steady, ongoing basis, receiving government orders and secure funding for many years ahead. Practically every university had a large research center, an institution with an intellectual team of professors, researchers, and the brightest students. The fact that the post of university provost—the head of research—was position number three in the school (after rector/president and academic provost), speaks for the importance of science and research in the Russian academic system.

The world-famous Soviet/Russian Academy of Science (RAN) was composed of such distinguished academicians as Sakharov, Landau, Ioffe, Kapitsa, Khariton, Kurchatov, Korolev, Tupolev, Sagdeev, Velikhov, and many other eminent figures. It was not just an association of scientists, but more like a mighty empire comprising subordinate academic scientific institutes and research centers. Many of the Academy's achievements won international fame and authority for their discoverers, and contributed greatly to world science.

Right after the Soviet Union emerged on the political arena as a state, it created the Academy, and gave it the task of creating Soviet military-industrial science. Dozens of so-called "specialized research programs" of the Academy of Science were established. One of the primary tasks of the Academy of Science was national defense-related research.

The second segment of intellectual capital was concentrated in industry. Every branch of Soviet/Russian industry had its own research centers, institutes, and design bureaus. The majority fell under the aegis of the MIC and its nine defense ministries, and worked on military orders. But even the research centers, institutes, and design bureaus of the civilian ministries had military orders in their portfolios.

Thus, most of the highly educated population of the country was involved in research, science, and design projects geared to the defense sector. Those people had received top training, and, consequently, priceless experience. Their degree of involvement in different industries could vary a good deal, from that of the designers of the space station Mir and the latest, state-of-the-art Topol-M ICBM systems, to that of computer programmers and researchers whose work was sought after by leading Western companies, but all of them were part of the "intellectual capital" of Russia.

It is evident that headlong conversion has made many scientists and designers almost unnecessary. This is one of darkest aspects of today's Russian society. The fact is that, as of today, Russia has lost a lot of talented and productive scientists and engineers, those who represented the avant-garde, the best brains of the nation. It was a huge army of intellectuals, who in most cases were poorly paid.

Through the holes in the rusty body of the defense industry, society has been rapidly losing whole groups of intellectual leaders, and consequently whole branches of science and technology. Entire generations of intellectuals have left. Today, some of them are either millionaires (whose wealth is not necessarily based on technological breakthroughs or world class redevelopment of industrial production), or penniless retirees. Many of them occupy modest positions—for example, salespersons in computer or perfume stores. A good few of the former leading specialists are simply poor and unemployed, and, in order to have food for themselves and their children, they grow vegetables and raise chickens at their dachas.[3] The lucky ones became politicians.

Such a life of poverty often drives unscrupulous scientists to become involved in projects related to weapons development in terrorist countries. This was the reason the United States instituted sanctions against several Russian universities in 1999—it had become evident that their activities with sensitive technologies might include secret military and political alliances with terrorist regimes.

In the early '90s, after the defense industry had collapsed, a lot of the "brains" were forced to emigrate to the West. Many talented Russians sought employment in the U.S., Western Europe, and Israel, and a lot of them were lucky enough to find high-ranking, well-paid jobs. Some of them could find employment only in the countries that had previously bought weapons from Russia. It is easy to sympathize with those specialists: they needed money to support themselves and their children. However, the problem lies in the potentially dangerous consequences if their services are provided to terrorist regimes. Who cares, given the devastating consequences, where the missile with the biological warhead came from, whether from the Soviet Union of the 1970s or from terrorists in the 2000s? But if the developer of such a weapon not only changed his address from the former U.S.S.R. to some terrorist country, but also brought to his new home biological weapons technology, it is more than dangerous. It means that all previous painstakingly developed agreements will collapse like a punctured balloon.

---

[3] Editor's Note: A dacha is a small suburban vacation property with 0.12 acre of leased land and a small cabin.

The intellectual capital of Russia has been deprived of the talent of a substantial portion of the young generation, and the country's future pool of specialists has been impoverished. It is hard to comprehend the magnitude of the brain drain from the country that could not or did not care to keep its intellectual capital intact.

It is unclear now whether it is possible to completely restore the former intellectual capital of the country; it may have fallen prey to what is known in the field of soil mechanics as "a process of irreversible failure deformities". To categorize Russia as an undeveloped country does not make sense either for it or for the rest of the civilized world; it may lead to very unpredictable consequences. The question now is what comes first--failure, or recovery.

Alexey N. Shulunov

During the history of Russia, a world-class pool of scientific/technical capital was created. Its best part was concentrated in the MIC. This was a well-developed network of scientific and research institutions and design bureaus.

At the end of 1988, there were 5,111 scientific institutions (including large research departments in universities), and 3,250 research/design institutes (including branch institutes). According to statistical data of that time, over 1,500,000 highly skilled specialists, among them 540,000 Ph.D.s, were involved in scientific research.

In 1990, the MIC conducted 79% of all the R&D work that was done in all Russian industries. However, 53% of all R&D projects were done for defense purposes, while about 41% was done for commercial industries.

By 1991, R&D projects had decreased by 54%. The direction of defense and security-related research was determined by the future demands of the armed forces, taking into consideration the current status, trends, and priorities of global scientific and technical progress, as well as the development of military science.

At that time, the Ministry of Defense (the MIC's main customer) paid very little attention to fundamental and applied research projects; these did not get more than 2.5–3% of the total financing given to R&D projects. This was a paltry share of the financing available for the same category of research projects from the U.S. Department of Defense budget.

During the last years of the U.S.S.R.'s existence, the total amount of financing for R&D projects was 3.6–4.7% of the GDP; nowadays it is 0.3–0.4%. Taking into account that since 1991, the Russian GDP has sharply decreased (to about a fifth or sixth of its earlier level), it is clear that in the late 1990s, the financing of R&D projects had really diminished --by between two and five orders of magnitude, according to expert estimates.

According to Academician Strakhov's data, in 1996 the financing of scientific research per researcher per year was $4,442; in the U.S. the figure was $189,400; in France $177,100; in Germany $158,400; in Great Britain $150,600; and in Japan $148,500. The amounts for these countries are from 33 to 43 times greater than the Russian figure. The expenditures on equipment per Russian researcher per year was estimated at $21,500, which is several dozens times lower than in the countries mentioned.

One result of this shortfall was that Russian scientists, in order to supplement their meager income, had to take second jobs as night guards, stockroom workers, salespersons, etc.

An even more alarming result is "brain drain." From 1991–1999, about 130,000 scientists, academicians, professors, and assistant professors emigrated to Israel, the U.S., European countries, and elsewhere. In 1993 and 1999, the U.S. Immigration Service and State Department adopted special policies that facilitated the immigration of scientists and technicians from the former U.S.S.R. Military-Industrial Complex. As a result, entire scientific fields and production lines have been lost to Russia, and the disintegration has become practically irreversible. The number of employees in scientific research institutes and design enterprises has decreased by 60-70% since 1991, and the disintegration of unique R&D teams has also been taking place.

The results of these losses can be seen in the poor showing of Russian products at international military exhibitions, in the lack of progress in critical technologies, in the poor state of repair of testing grounds, and in the absence of new weapons to be issued to the troops. Even the top priority project, the Topol-M missile complex, has suffered from several years of delays.

Due to the lack and, in some cases, failure of financing R&D work, long-term research work (2 to 5 year projects) can't be performed with short-term (monthly or quarterly) financing, which inevitably causes long delays and interruptions in work. The morale of scientific employees has degraded noticeably, with the most qualified employees leaving first. The country has begun to lose its intellectual capital, scientific potential and, accordingly, a stable foundation for scientific and technical progress.

Arkadiy Yarovskiy

The main symptom of the loss of intellectual capital in Russia is so-called "internal emigration," which is much greater than external emigration. "Internal emigration" means the outflow of highly qualified specialists from science and high-tech industries to trade and administrative structures, which are unrelated to their education and professional expertise, or to the political sphere.

The situation in scientific and academic areas is critical in Russia. Technical progress is in jeopardy. Within the first few years of reform, Russian science lost a third of its staff. Forty percent of today's university faculty members do not have the scientific degrees that are necessary for their positions. The number of annually registered *izobretenii* (Russian equivalents of patents) dropped considerably; 80% of all highly demanded, newly developed technologies and devices do not reach their consumers. Unemployment among highly skilled scientists and engineers in Russia is increasing. The situation is paradoxical – the qualifications of the unemployed are much higher than the qualifications of the employed.

The Russian-speaking population emigrating from the former Soviet republics does not compensate for the brain drain, either in terms of quality or their ability to adapt.

Especially harmful is the flow of young scientists and specialists from scientific academia. These minds form an absolutely irreplaceable part of the most promising intellectual capital of Russia.

According to studies conducted by the Educational Committee of the Council of Europe, the financial damage to Russia caused by the emigration of these specialists is about $50-60 billion annually. It is a very significant financial loss—much higher than the Russian federal budget—but that is less important than the destruction of the most important Russian asset: intellectual capital, formerly concentrated in the defense industry.

Government decrees, presidential statements, the formation of multiple councils and committees, and other such measures undertaken by the government in order to prevent the loss of intellectual capital are ineffective, mostly because of the economic crisis, unemployment, and political instability.

The freezing of progress in science and technology for only one year will cause the country in which they are frozen to fall three years behind other industrially developed countries. If this devastating process is not stopped, Russian research and development labs and design bureaus in the defense industry will not be capable of producing either military or civilian high tech products that will be competitive, regardless of financing or governmental policies. The reason will be simple: the lack of brains. The falling behind of Russia in the area of high technology could become irreversible, and soon Russia could find itself among the undeveloped countries—and stay there, with unpredictable consequences.

Brain drain is not the logical reaction to the processes of disarmament, defense conversion, and economic reforms. Brain drain from the MIC to foreign countries, instead of the use of Russian intellectual capital for building economy of new Russia, is due to the absence of well-developed, state-run social policies. The preservation of intellectual capital can have only one objective – to implement the program of converting and restructuring the military industrial complex. The faster it is implemented, the sooner Russian intellectual capital will work for its own country.

Zhanna Zaionchkovskaya

Intellectual capital has been wasted inside the country on a considerably large scale. As early as the end of 1992, 27% (and in some regions 50%) of the scientific employees of the defense industry had transferred to commercial structures.[4] As long as conversion stagnates, personnel are forced to walk away from their enterprises, research centers, or design bureaus and replenish the army of unemployed or accept any available job, in many cases as low skilled workers.

The average per capita income for employees in the non-state sector is 60% higher than that for state employees. Alternative possibilities of employment, which became available with the development of the private sector, to some extent compensated for the losses associated with the collapse of military production. This alleviated public discontent somewhat, but did not solve the problem. Moreover, business and commerce have had major destructive influences on the scientific and technical potential of the military industrial complex. Highly educated and trained scientific workers who make the transition into commerce no longer apply their technical and professional skills, and tend to lose them as a consequence.

In early 1996, more than one million specialists were employed by the MIC, including 117,000 Ph.D.s. Nearly three out of four of those employed in scientific research and design served the requirements of the defense industry.

Reorienting the accumulated production facilities and intellectual capital from the military to the civilian sector seemed to be the key to success at the beginning of reforms. However, the first steps in this

---

[4] Vestnik RAN, vol. 63, 1993.

direction showed that reorientation was not a merely technical but a complex socio-economic task, since it had to be accomplished on the basis of market relations, from which Russia had departed 80 years earlier.

The situation appeared to be especially difficult for the most specialized employees, whose experience was no longer applicable. Under such conditions of "headlong" conversion as sharp reductions in defense orders and non-payments of wages, these specialists were faced with the need to find their own way out, which meant either emigration or moving to other parts of the domestic economy. For example, in the aerospace and nuclear industries, nearly three-fourths of all specialists expressed a wish to change jobs or to emigrate. This "brain drain" of scientific employees and specialists is continuing and even accelerating.

Not surprisingly, many highly skilled specialists express a desire to work in any country that offers "proper" wages. The great majority (85%) of these workers are motivated by economic interests. About 60% of the employees of the Russian defense industry are even willing to work for the military industry of another country. Taking into account the potential military power represented by such employment, and the existence of "rogue" countries that desire to use their military power for aggressive purposes, it would be extremely undesirable both for Russia and for the developed Western countries for these specialists to assist in building the power of these terrorist or rogue countries.

Currently, highly skilled scientists and professionals tend to emigrate mostly to well developed countries: 66% to Germany, 17% to Israel, and 18% to the U.S. Scientists and professionals are estimated to account for 2-4% of the total emigration flow, which means that from 2,000 to 4,000 specialists leave Russia for other countries every year.

Some of them leave to establish permanent residence abroad; others have temporary jobs as contractors. For example, 20% of the scientific workers in Akademgorodok[5] have already worked abroad, though only 14% of them stayed there for more than a year. Many of those working abroad have the opportunity to maintain their scientific expertise and even to improve it. But the longer the economic instability persists in Russia, the fewer the emigrants who can be expected to return to practice their enhanced skills.

The emigrants who take up permanent residency in other countries are permanently lost to Russian science, and not all of them benefit world science, either. Some emigrant scientists are forced to change their professional specialty, as demand for their old skills may be low, or other obstacles present themselves. The record of successful adaptation by Russian scientists to working conditions in Western countries is uneven, and largely complicated by language barriers and other difficulties in interacting with foreign colleagues and students.

Members of the scientific elite find jobs mainly at universities and at other scientific institutions that combine teaching and research activities. Emigrants with a more ordinary level of expertise usually find work in private industry. It is apparent that future trends in the emigration of Russian scientists will depend more on the internal situation in Russia than on the immigration policy of other countries. Of course, the emigration of specialists is partly compensated by the inflows from the countries of Newly Independent States, where the economic situation is far more difficult than in Russia itself. Still, the average-

---

[5] Editor's Note: The academic town/campus near Novosibirsk where many scientific and research institutions of the Siberian Branch of the Russian Academy of Science are located.

quality immigrant specialists who come to Russia from the NIS cannot be compared to the professionals and the scientific elite emigrating from Russia.

Nevertheless, some optimistic possibilities arise. The process of population aging is also likely to continue. It is expected that by 2015 the portion of the population 60 years old or more will reach 20%. This means that the value of the workforce in Russia will rapidly increase, creating a labor deficit, which would particularly benefit highly skilled labor. Undoubtedly the demand for such labor in the private sector, which has already become a very serious competitor to the State, will rise. It can be expected that the value of intellectual labor, especially in technically complex industries, will not just rise, but soar. The current mindless waste of such labor in unsophisticated commerce will cause enormous losses in the long run.

Of course, there is no doubt that eventually this crisis will come to an end. High-tech specialists and scientists will be needed again, but those who have changed their occupations will be forever lost to high technology. At the same time, it is difficult to count on the new generations, since the present realities force them to work in commercial and brokerage operations rather than acquiring technical expertise and working in high-tech industry. Consequently, the intellectual capital accumulated in the defense industry has been squandered throughout the entire period of reforms. This unfortunate process may deprive the country of future economic growth.

5.2. THE DEFENSE INDUSTRY AND ENVIRONMENT

Introductory Remarks

Vlad E. Genin

After democratic reforms began, Russia honestly faced its acute environmental problems for the first time. Those problems had been accumulating for decades, and had caused the loss of many thousands of lives. Millions of Russians have experienced environment-related health problems, and the life of new generations was at risk. The defense industry was called upon to solve these problems.

The environmental situation on Earth is steadily deteriorating, and much of the environmental contamination is on the territory of the former Soviet Union, including Russia, which constitutes about one-sixth of the land surface of the world.

The results of military and industrial activity in these countries are hazardous not only to themselves, but also to the neighboring states of Central and Western Europe, Asia, and the Pacific Rim. The U.S.S.R.'s disregard for environmental issues gave rise to unprecedented negligence towards human health, flora, and fauna. Even the U.S. cannot escape the environmental pressure generated by Russia (only 60 miles separate Alaska from Russia's Chukotka Peninsula).

Nowadays, politicians all over the world are desperately struggling to prevent the proliferation of Russian WMD, seeing them as a potential source of new military conflicts with catastrophic consequences. But as far as fighting both real and potential environmental "infections" coming out of Russia goes, these same politicians do nothing.

The environmental aspects of the Russian defense industry, and its influence on human health, flora, and fauna, were not monitored at all in Soviet times. Moreover, concerns for environmental safety during construction or renovation of defense enterprises was deemed political sabotage, a threat to national security. The Communist leadership demanded ever-escalating weapons production – more and more defense enterprises to be built in a shorter time. The results of this approach are well known and tragic. The total lack of control over the defense industry (a failure ingeniously disguised as a national security measure) prompted the creation of many forms of environmental chaos in Russia. Water in many regions is not suitable for drinking. Air is polluted to the point when it is hard to breathe. Foul-smelling clouds of chemicals hang over many production plants. Radiation, which has no taste, color or smell, is a problem in many regions.

Ninety years ago, in the beginning of the century, when it was hard to visualize today's dismal environmental situation, Theodore Roosevelt wrote, "The policy [conservation] rests upon the fundamental law that neither man nor nation can prosper unless, in dealing with the present, thought is steadily for the future". [6]

---

[6] Theodore Roosevelt. The Outlook. August 27, 1910 (In Daniel B. Baker. Power Quotes, Detroit: Visible Inc., 1999), p.64.

Victor I. Danilov-Danil'yan

During the past seventy years, defense industry enterprises were, in general, involved mainly in the finishing stages of production. The environmental impact from these operations was rather limited in comparison with the total effects caused by industry as a whole. Thus, an environmental impact can be divided into two parts: defense industry enterprises as the direct source of pollution, and the environmental impact from the suppliers to the defense industry—those that provide raw materials, energy, finished goods, services, etc. The first part can be considered the direct environmental costs of the defense industry, and the second the indirect costs.

To calculate the indirect environmental impact of the defense industry, which is, as noted earlier, higher than the direct impact, it is necessary to calculate all the pollution from the suppliers' production facilities. In the Soviet Union, such information was practically non-existent because of the strict secrecy of the defense sector.

In view of the complex nature of inter-industry links, a share of the total environmental impact from the defense industry (both the direct and the indirect impact) should be regarded as a result of general industrial activity, correlating with the gross domestic product (GDP). The above-mentioned indices would be more reliable if the underlying calculations could be made not only for the defense industry, but for the defense complex (the defense industry and the Armed Forces) as a whole. The available published data vary widely (as indicated in two or three references). The best-substantiated data are those of Shukhgalter[7], who estimated the share of the defense complex in terms of the GDP.

---

[7] M.B. Shukhgalter, *Yadernye Ispytania S.S.S.R.* (Moscow: IzdAT, 1997).

According to his data, that share was 29% in 1991, and 13% in 1996. These indices illustrate the share of defense complex in the environmental impact of all Russian industries.

As a result of the super-militarization of the Soviet economy, in 1991 the share of the defense complex was unprecedentedly high in comparison with the leading industrialized nations. The sharp decrease in this index was the result of the natural reaction of the national economy to the decreased level of super-militarization, and not the result of deliberate policy.

It is not to be assumed that the downsizing of the defense industry, and especially the reduction of expenditures for the Armed Forces, automatically led to a proportional reduction in its share of the environmental impact due to the defense complex.

For an estimation of the direct environmental impact of the defense industry, as distinguished from the indirect impact, an adequate information base is available. The indices of pollution of atmosphere and water sources in some branches of the defense industry[8] are summarized in Table 5.2.1.

In 1994-1999, as a result of the decrease in production, the environmental impact from the defense industry was reduced. The atmospheric release of pollutants was 139,000 metric tons/year, and waste water discharges were 178 million cubic meters/year.

Information on the atmospheric release of pollutants in 1993-1995 is summarized in Table 5.2.2 and Table 5.2.3.

---

8 A.A. Shekhovtsev, et al. *Vliyanie Otraslei Ekonomiki RF na Sostoianii Okruzhaiuschchei Sredi v 1993* (Moscow: Izdatelstvo Tsentr “Meteorologia i Gidrologia”, 1995).

TABLE 5.2.1.

Pollution Produced by Defense Industries

Source of Pollution	Atmospheric emissions (thousands of metric tons/year)	Waste water discharged (millions of cubic meters/year)
Aircraft Industry	56.8	25.5
Ammunition Production	61.8	146.0
Weapons Production	77.0	149.0
Communications Industry	18.6	1.9
Radio Industry	10.1	5.6
Missile and Space Industry	16.6	60.0
Shipbuilding	22.1	20.7
Electronics Industry	11.7	2.9
Total	274.7	411.4

TABLE 5.2.2.

Atmospheric Emissions

Pollutants	1993	1994	1995
Solid pollutants, in thousands of metric tons	43.6	23.6	18.3
Liquid and gaseous pollutants, in thousands of metric tons, including:			
Sulfuric anhydride	68.6	40.6	34.1
Carbon monoxide	87.2	51.7	45.6
Nitric oxide	35.8	24.6	22.9
Light organic compounds	31.5	16.6	14.0
Subtotal, liquid and gaseous pollutants	223.1	133.5	116.6
Total pollution, in thousands of metric tons	266.7	157.1	134.9

TABLE 5.2.3.

Specific Pollutants

Specific pollutants, in metric tons	1993	1994	1995
Lead and lead compounds	15.4	16.7	35.9
Hexavalent chromium	--	11.3	24.9
Arsenic (inorganic compounds)	--	0.1	0.004
Nitric acid	--	226.0	266.0
Sulfuric acid	1,070.0	465.0	597.0
Styrol	--	1,930.0	1,600.0
Phenol	--	23.7	19.6
Butyl acetate	--	639.0	557.0
Ethyl acetate	--	384.0	370.0
Formaldehyde	--	33.4	19.7

Similar data for the same period on the discharge of polluted waste waters are summarized in Table 5.2.4 and Table 5.2.5.

TABLE 5.2.4.

Annual Waste Water Discharge (in millions of cubic meters)

1993	1994	1995
412.0	260.0	178.0

TABLE 5.2.5.

Quantity of Pollutants in Discharged Waste Water

Specific pollutants in metric tons	1993	1994	1995
Chlorides	23,900.0	15,200.00	9,100.0
Fluorine	13.1	9.33	9.64
Zinc	24.0	14.1	6.09
Chromium	25.9	12.4	3.6
Lead	2.92	2.43	0.13
Cadmium	2.73	2.38	0.06
Phenols	0.12	1.27	0.26
Aromatic Hydrocarbons	7.28	0.52	0.22
Formaldehyde	1.09	0.19	0.5
Cyanides	0.23	0.1	0.01

Sudden changes in the indices, and shifts in their direction, are persuasive evidence of instability in the defense industry, which is now breaking up.

The enterprises of the defense industry are located mainly in the large industrial regions of central and northwestern Russia, the Urals, Siberia, and other Russian regions. Frequently, their direct contribution to the total environmental impact is not immediately noticeable. However, in some Russian cities, the environmental situation is directly determined by the defense industry enterprises.

In 1993, in Nizhnii Tagil, the total volume of pollutants discharged into the atmosphere by arms enterprises amounted to 6,900 metric tons; in Irkutsk (aircraft enterprises) – 6,700 metric tons; in Kurgan (arms enterprises) – 6,500 metric tons; in Krasnoyarsk (aerospace enterprises) – 6,500 metric tons; in Roshal (ammunition and special chemical enterprises) – 6,200 metric tons. For the next two years, the volume of pollutants from these largest enterprises was the same, and remained in the range of 6,500 to 7,000 metric tons.

Among defense enterprises polluting water sources, the worst offenders are the defense enterprises of St. Petersburg, which annually discharge more than 80 million cubic meters, including 52.9 million cubic meters (arms enterprises) and 26.3 million cubic meters (aerospace enterprises). In some other regions, discharge volumes of polluted wastewater are: in Kovrov (arms production) - 22.9 million cubic meters; in Kemerovo (ammunition and special chemical production) - 21.7 million cubic meters; in Roshal (ammunition and special chemical production) - 14.7 million cubic meters; in Biisk (ammunition and special chemical production) - 10.6 million cubic meters. Today, these cities are at the top of the danger list in environmental pollution, even though their emissions have been reduced proportionally with those of other industrial enterprises.

But a special place in the military-industrial complex is held by the production of nuclear weapons. This industry is a closely tied with the nuclear power industry. In the past few years, in the nuclear power complex, the civilian component has predominated, but it is impossible to determine the environmental impact of each of them.

The following are the largest enterprises that pollute the environment with radionuclides. Mayak Production Association (PO

Mayak), the Chelyabinsk Oblast weapons-grade plutonium producer, is located about 75 km from the oblast capital. The large cities of Zlatoust, Miass, and Kopeisk are located within 100 km, and the cities of Yekaterinburg, Kamensk-Uralskii, and Pervouralsk are within 120-130 km. In the last twenty years, with a deviation of 15-20%, PO Mayak has annually emitted into the atmosphere the following pollutants: 0.014 curies of artificial alpha-nuclides; 0.338 curies of artificial beta-nuclides; 10,100 curies of inert radioactive gases; and up to 300 curies of various other radioisotopes.

At present, changes in the radiation situation are primarily determined by the wind transfer of the radionuclides from previously polluted territories, and the environmental impact of radioactive waste storage facilities. In this region, the greatest danger is posed by the storage facilities for radioactive waste, and the open natural bodies of water used for this purpose, especially Lake Karachai. Since 1951, 120 million curies of long-lived, medium-activity liquid nuclear wastes have been discharged into this lake. As a result, about 3.5 million cubic meters of industrial solutions containing about 0.9 million curies of beta radiation-emitting nuclides have penetrated into the groundwater.[9] Since 1986, work has been under way to liquidate this lake. Under the lake, a lens of contaminated radioactive groundwater with a volume of 4 million cubic meters, and an area of 10 square kilometers, has formed. It is estimated that the lens may reach the Misheliak River soon after the year 2000.

Within a 100-km radius of PO Mayak, the average annual exposure to gamma radiation is from 10 to 15 microroentgens/hour, the same as the natural gamma background in the Urals region. However, the

---

[9] E.G. Drozhko, et al. *II Symposium po Ekologii*, Obninsk, 1996.

fallout of man-made radionuclides in this zone is much greater than average: strontium-90 is three times the average, and cesium-137 is 8.5 times the average. An unsatisfactory radiation situation exists in the Techa River and its floodplain. For many years, beginning in 1948, liquid radioactive wastes have been discharged into this river. The significant inflow of radionuclides was assisted by several heavy floods, which penetrated radioactive waste storage facilities, and also by the explosion at the Kyshtym storage facility in 1957. During the operational period of this enterprise, 28,000 local inhabitants received a very high radiation dosage (170 rem), and 8,000 inhabitants from 21 settlements were evacuated.

The Krasnoyarsk Mining and Chemical Combined Plant (MCC) is located in Krasnoyarsk Krai (Eastern Siberia) about 80 km from Krasnoyarsk. It houses a radiochemical plant and a plutonium production reactor facility. Solid radioactive wastes are stored in fifteen on-site storage facilities, which are segregated according to the different kinds of wastes involved. Special technologies have been used for the storage of high-level and intermediate-level wastes. They provide a suitable level of safety, provided that strict inspections and regular maintenance operations are carried out. Financial difficulties are preventing strict fulfillment of these conditions. In addition, liquid wastes are being pumped down underground shafts at the Severnyi site, located 12 km from the main production facilities of the MCC.

The waste collects in two underground geological formations: one 370-465 meters below ground, and one at 180-280 meters. Since 1967, 300 cubic meters per day of intermediate-level wastes have been pumped into the first formation; the average level of radioactivity is 0.01 curies/liter.

Since 1972, higher-level wastes (0.1-0.5 curies/liter) have been pumped into this main formation—1,000-2,000 cubic meters at a time, once or twice a year. The second formation has been used since 1968 for naturally occurring, low-level wastes, at a rate of 600 cubic meters per day. Despite the presence of radioactive contamination on MCC territory, its activity so far has not caused conditions that could create danger for the employees or the local inhabitants. But the accumulation of radioactive wastes on MCC territory, the pumping of liquid wastes into the underground formations, and the inadequate radiation monitoring system, create constant anxiety for ecologists.

The Siberian Chemical Combined Plant (SCC) is the largest plutonium producer. It is located 20 km from the oblast capital of Tomsk. The city of Andzhero-Sudzhensk, a major coal production center, is located on the perimeter of the SCC 100-km zone. The city of Kemerovo, the capital of another oblast, is located 150 km from the SCC.

The SCC facility has five reactors designed to produce plutonium. Since 1994, only two reactors are in operation—as required by the programs of conversion and nuclear disarmament, three reactors were shut down, which caused a significant reduction in the atmospheric emission of radionuclides. Different technologies are used for separating, storing, and disposing of radioactive wastes at the SCC facility, including open storage. It is suggested that these storage facilities be eliminated.

In April 1993, there was a serious accident at the SCC facility. In all, over 100 square kilometers were contaminated by short-lived radionuclides. During the investigation of the accident, areas contaminated with 1 to 2 curies/square meter of cesium-137 were found as far as 10 km from the plant. At present, the current radiation situation in the SCC area is no cause for alarm, but there is no guarantee that it will remain this way.

Nuclear weapons tests are particularly harmful to the environment. Reliable information on Soviet nuclear tests and so-called "peaceful nuclear explosions" became public only when a special book by the Russian Ministry of Atomic Energy (Minatom) was published in 1997.

In the U.S.S.R., nuclear weapons tests were carried out from 1949 to 1990. During this time, there were 591 tests for military purposes including:

- 32 surface tests between 1949 to 1962;
- 177 low atmospheric tests between 1951 to 1962;
- one high atmospheric test in 1962;
- four tests in space between 1961 and 1962;
- two above-water tests in 1961 and 1962;
- three underwater tests in 1955, 1957, and 1961;
- 372 underground tests between 1963 and 1990.

In addition, 124 peaceful nuclear explosions were conducted between 1965 and 1988. In many cases, more than one nuclear charge was used, so the number of tests was less than the total number of exploded charges (i.e., a total of 969 explosions, which included 796 for military purposes, and 173 peaceful nuclear explosions).

In general, nuclear weapons tests were carried out at the Semipalatinsk (Kazakhstan) and the Novaia Zemlia test sites. In addition, between 1957 and 1962, ten nuclear weapons tests, including four tests in the ionosphere, one high air test, and four low air tests, were carried out at the Kapustin Yar site in Astrakhan Oblast. In 1954, during general military exercises, one air test was carried out at the Totsk artillery range in Orenburg Oblast near Semipalatinsk Oblast. Also, in 1956, one ground test was carried out in the area of the city of Aralsk (Kazakhstan).

During the first years of the "atomic age", monitoring of events with environmental consequences fell far short of the minimum requirements for reliability and completeness. In particular, in areas near the Semipalatinsk test site, regular monitoring of the radiation level and the health of the population began only in 1957, eight years after the first nuclear test. Even by processing the collected information from that time with up-to-date computers, using the latest models of the spread of radioactive contamination, it is impossible to completely recreate, with any reliability, the situation of 1949-1962. This is especially difficult because of the inaccessibility of much of the necessary information.

The direct impact of the Semipalatinsk nuclear tests was concentrated on a population of several settlements of Altai Krai, which is located near the nuclear test site. As a result of these tests, the population was exposed to a total radiation dose of 42,000 rem.[10] By far the worst test, in terms of its effect on the population, was the first test (August 29, 1949), which exposed the population to 32,000 rem. This dose represents about 76% of the total exposure to radiation, caused by all Semipalatinsk bursts.

By the time the study of the environmental impact from the Semipalatinsk nuclear explosions began in 1990, the level of environmental contamination was reduced to the point that safety measures for the inhabitants were useless. The most significant health effects for inhabitants were recorded in the Uglovskii district, where the

---

[10] A.I. Algasin et al. *Radiation Impact of Nuclear Weapon Tests at the Semipalatinsk. Test on the Population of the Altai Region*, Vienna, 1995, IAEA – SM – 339/829.

level of cancer is 17% higher than normal. The greatest incidence of cancer arises after one receives radiation doses during the ages of 30 to 40, and the risk lasts to the end of the victim's life. As a result, the matter of compensation for damages to the health of the inhabitants, and improved medical services, is a pressing problem in the Altai Krai even today.

During the period of atmospheric nuclear weapons tests at the Novaia Zemlia test site, there was a significant rise of radioactive fallout in the neighboring regions, primarily in the Nenets Autonomous Okrug, Arkhangelsk Oblast, and the Komi Autonomous Republic. Between 1961 and 1962, fallout reached its maximum, reaching 200 to 300 times the levels in 1960. In the settlement of Amderma, daily fallout of beta-nuclides reached about 900 microcuries per square kilometer. In 1988, after a twenty-six year moratorium on land, sea, and atmospheric tests, this level was 0.08 microcuries per square kilometer.

Before the start of nuclear testing, the population of Novaia Zemlia was 400 (Nenets and Russians). After the first tests, they were forced to leave their homes to go to the mainland. Although the most powerful nuclear weapons tests in the atmosphere were carried out at the Novaia Zemlia test site, with the fallout affecting large areas, there are fewer reliable records of the effects on the populations of the specific settlements and adjoining areas than are available for the nuclear explosions at the Semipalatinsk test site.

Nevertheless, the effects of the Novaia Zemlia tests were perceptible not only in the U.S.S.R., but in neighboring northern countries, such as Norway and Finland. The Novaia Zemlia atmospheric tests and the Chernobyl disaster produced similar radioactive contamination in Norway. In 1961, Norway was greatly concerned about the consequences of the nuclear weapons tests. In the northern regions of the country, civil defense stations took radioactivity measurements three times a day. Norwegian military aircraft took similar measurements above the Barents Sea. Special measures to protect the population were carried out, including evacuation.[11]

Arriving at a reliable estimate of the effects of nuclear tests on the health of the populace of specific areas is a very complicated problem. It is estimated that the combined yield of the Soviet nuclear tests is 246 megatons. We don't have the corresponding data for other nuclear-weapons states, but for the U.S., the estimate of 135 megatons is close to the U.S.S.R.'s estimate. It is safe to say that, in general, the U.S.S.R.'s share of responsibility for harmful effects on the world population and the biosphere as a result of nuclear weapons tests is more than 50%.

One more cause of the deterioration of the environmental situation is the destruction of nuclear, chemical, and other weapons. Their destruction is necessary due to three reasons: physical wear and tear, obsolescence, and political considerations—that is, those international agreements, which stipulate the reduction of selected armaments.

Meeting the specific requirements for dismantling weapons can have consequences that are a crucial factor in affecting the environment. To a large degree, this has been the case with the dismantlement of chemical weapons. A general solution to the problem of destroying chemical agents has not been found, because of mustard and lewisite, which contain arsenic. In any case, there are a number of problems in

---

[11] T. Nilsen, N. Bemer, *Istochniki Radioaktivnogo Zagriazneniya v Murmanskoi i Arkhangelskoi Oblastiakh* (Oslo: Bellona, 1994.)

using this technology: financial, organizational, production, and—above all—safety problems. The biggest of these problems is that of where to destroy the weapons: in the field, at the storage sites that were built for them (the "local option"), or at the plants that produced the given chemical agents (the "centralized option")—a solution that often requires that these lethal devices be transported through inhabited areas?

The "local option" has been strongly opposed by the people who live near chemical weapons storage sites. The "centralized option", which calls for the transportation of chemical agents, is not safe because of the poor condition of Russian railways. Although a complete program of chemical weapons destruction so far has not been developed, the "local option" is more likely to be adopted, but the local population would have to be convinced that the transportation of chemical agents would create an extraordinary danger, a much greater danger than that posed by the industrial destruction of chemical agents at the storage sites.

Some reports by the Russian and foreign mass media (the best-known article is by Fiodorov and Mirzoianov[12]) have expressed some doubts about the official data on the stockpiling and deployment of chemical weapons. They also stated that significant quantities of chemical agents were destroyed by unacceptable methods, e.g., dumping in the seas, burial near populated areas, etc. So far, there is no official refutation of this accusation.

According to official data, Russia holds 7,000 metric tons of arsenic-based chemical agents that are intended for destruction. This stockpile is stored near the settlements of Kambarka (Udmurt Autonomous Republic), and Gornyi (Saratov Oblast).

---

[12] L. Fedorov, V. Mirzoyanov, *Moskovskie novosti,* July 20, 1992.

The total amount of arsenic-free chemical agents to be destroyed is 32,000 metric tons. Stockpiles are located in the Udmurt Autonomous Republic, Bryansk Oblast, Vyatka Oblast, Kurgan Oblast, and Penza Oblast. There is no practical use for the end products of the process for neutralizing chemical agents. Destroying them will require vast financial resources, which Russia does not have available. Such financing is being discussed because of the impact on large areas of the Russian economy.

Nuclear disarmament involves not only the removal of nuclear warheads from their delivery vehicles, but also the very complicated process of dismantling the warheads. Unlike chemical weapons, this process is mostly the reverse of the production process, and thus can use similar equipment. This is why choosing the technology and location for dismantlement can be resolved without the consideration of other options, and explains why nuclear disarmament has not elicited as severe a public reaction as the destruction of chemical weapons.

The destruction of conventional weapons creates environmental problems because of the explosives they contain. But solutions that provide for the necessary level of environmental safety are available, and ways to cover the costs are being discussed. As for recovering the explosive materials from ammunition for further use (military or civilian), there are some doubts about both the safety and the economic practicality of trying this.

In analyzing the impact on the environment of the Armed Forces, an important consideration is contamination by petroleum products of both military bases and the surrounding areas. For example, at nine Air Force bases, it had been found that the formation of nine underground petroleum product lenses, with volumes ranging from 2,000 to 30,000 cubic meters, has threatened the contamination of water sources. One must also consider nuclear and chemical weapons and nuclear-powered submarines, which are major sources of radioactive waste. In the former Soviet Union and other nuclear nations, dumping radioactive wastes into northern seas has been a routine practice.

In order to prevent such dumping, it is necessary to construct facilities for the solidification of radioactive wastes at the sites where they are created (the Northern region and the Far East). A joint Russian-American-Norwegian project and a Russian-Japanese project are underway in Murmansk and the Far East, respectively. Their realization will completely halt the dumping of liquid radioactive wastes into the ocean, and make it possible to come to suitable international agreements.

5.3. ENVIRONMENTAL ASPECTS: FUTURE PROSPECTS

Introductory Remarks

Vlad E. Genin

After decades of barbarous abuse, nature will not allow mankind too long a time to correct its mistakes. The environmental situation in Russia is very grim, especially in heavily populated regions. After a lot of defense enterprises stopped production, the environmental pressure in Russia did decrease a little. The correlation is direct and simple: no production--no pollution. For a short moment—by historical standards— it probably has improved the environmental situation in some regions. But what if the huge monster that is the defense industry comes out of hibernation tomorrow, and resumes full-scale production, along with harmful environmental pollution?

After the initial failures, a new stage of defense industry conversion will start sooner or later. This time, environmental issues must not be "just for decoration," as happened before. Environmental consciousness should be as central to the conversion agenda as militarization used to be to the economy. Attention to environmental issues will pay off. The new environmental mentality of the whole society is the key to a new Russian environmental order. In today's Russia, particularly in scientific, governmental, and political circles, there are people who clearly understand the degree of danger of the country's environmental "legacy" – its current environmental problems and their future consequences. Their strong voices contribute to a new mentality toward environmental rehabilitation in Russia. This is no easy task. As Ilya Ehrenburg, the famous Russian sociopolitical writer, said, "It is far more difficult to change the mentality of the people that it is to change a country's political order or even its economy."[13]

Victor I. Danilov-Danil'yan

Russia's environmental situation is extremely varied. On one hand, about 50% of Russia's 17 million square kilometers of territory has never undergone significant economic development, according international standards; it still may be called a wilderness. These wilderness areas are found primarily in Siberia, the Far East, and the Arctic and sub-Arctic regions, including European Russia.

On the other hand, about 15% of Russian territory, where two-thirds of the country's population is located, has sustained significant environmentally damage. Such regions are located in the European part of Russia and the Urals, as well as in areas of Siberia and the Far East where industrial giants and large-scale extraction enterprises are located. This developed territory is the location of the highest population density, major industrial enterprises and infrastructure, and the most advanced agricultural production. However, natural eco-systems have been substantially destroyed by man in this region and cannot cope with the enormous flow of man-made pollutants.

---

13 Ilya Ehrenburg "What I have learned", *Saturday Review*, September 30, 1967. (In Daniel B. Baker. 1992. Power Quotes. Detroit: Visible Ink Press, p. 266.

In the remaining 35% of Russian territory, eco-systems have not been detrimentally affected by industrial activity, but have maintained their viability and their ability to compensate for anthropogenic impact.

Until the 1990s, anthropogenic pressure on the environment in the former U.S.S.R. grew continuously, due to the development of new territories, the increased use of natural resources in industry and agriculture, and increased pollution from all sectors of the economy. Naturally, such pressure would have been much less if economic expansion had taken into account environmental factors and been accompanied by environmental protection measures. In 1995, when production levels were about 50% of 1991 levels, atmospheric emissions of pollutants were reduced by 33%, while the discharge of waste waters was reduced by only 12%. The economic decline was not the only reason pollution was reduced: it is estimated that about 20% of such reductions were caused by the implementation of environmental protection measures.

The discrepancy between drop in production levels and pollution levels indicates the influence on the environment per unit of industrial production. The main reason for the difference is that the drop in production varied from one industry to another. Production declined least in those industries that most affected the environment (the extraction, power, metallurgical, and petroleum refining industries). Also contributing to the discrepancy was increased equipment breakdowns (enterprises do not have the finances to upgrade or repair their equipment) and the reduction of current expenses, with expenditures on environmental protection often being the first to go. But even reduced pollution levels exceed the capacity of the environment, and economic crises may thus be accompanied by environmental crises.

Even if the present economic recession were replaced by economic growth in the near future, that would still not relieve Russia of its environmental problems. Economic growth would itself pose potential threats to the environment through the neglect of environmental protection measures and the expansion into undeveloped regions. These potential environmental dangers are more likely, the stronger the temptation to use extensive growth factors, including not only the environmental resource factors, but also the mass resumption of use of obsolete capital assets. However, such a growth cannot be stable and remain high, because it would not promote the formation of an efficient economic structure.

The internal factors for intensive growth would require, first of all, the mobilization of scientific and technical resources that are mainly concentrated in the defense complex. Even if extensive growth factors play the primary role, and the minimal environmental regulations are followed, growth should still be built upon a very solid scientific and technical base, which is possible only by using the potential of the defense industry. Therefore, economic growth in Russia will not be acceptable from an environmental point of view, unless the defense industry is converted. Providing for the "environmental friendliness" of economic growth is possible only if Russia implements the environmental policy stipulated by the "Sustainable Development Strategy" developed by federal agencies, which takes into account the conversion of the defense industry and environmental regulations.

Despite delays and the insufficiency of positive changes, Russia's environmental protection system, as of 1998, is radically different from that which existed prior to the break-up of the U.S.S.R. A system of territorial environmental protection agencies, including state committees on environmental protection in each constituency of the Russian Federation (in some republics, they are considered ministries) and subordinate district committees, has been fully formed. The territorial agencies have their own inspection, monitoring, advisory, and other relevant divisions, including analytical laboratories and so forth.

What was in its incipient stage in the former U.S.S.R has now become full-scale, regular environmental protection activity in Russia. Major facets of this activity are the following: environmental impact studies; environmental inspections and control; environmental monitoring; economic incentives for environmental protection, based upon the principle of "the polluter pays"; and special energy saving programs at the federal and local levels.

In defining an environmental policy, it is necessary to specify the biota (system of living organisms) that will be affected by environmental regulations. The major tenets of V.G. Gorshkov's theory on biotechnical regulation of the environment[14] are as follows:

1. The modern world's environment is, to a significant degree, a product of the biota's activity, which during the four billion years of its existence has not only adapted to the environment, but has also molded the environment, gradually becoming a regulator of the biosphere (a system that includes both the biota and the environment).

2. The regulatory function of the biota is to keep all the main environmental parameters essential to its existence (e.g., climatic characteristics, chemical make-up of the atmosphere, the oceans, inland bodies of water, etc.), in a rather narrow range, despite various disturbances (i.e., to maintain homeostasis). Like any regulator, the biota

---

[14] V.G. Gorshkov, *Physical and Biological Bases of Life Stability* (Springer-Verlag, 1994).

will maintain this function until the disturbances do not exceed its compensatory ability (assimilation potential).

3. About one hundred years ago, the anthropogenic impact on the environment reached the limit of the biota's natural regulatory capacity (the full economic capacity of the biosphere), and since then has significantly exceeded it. The biota is no longer able to perform its regulatory functions.

4. The development of new technologies (which have an average period of evolution of 10 years) has outstripped the pace of at which the biota evolve (a period of 10,000 years), overstressing and thereby destroying the biosphere.

The spontaneous development of science and technology, unguided economic growth, and uncontrollable population growth, continuously increase the anthropogenic burden on the biosphere.

5. Destroyed natural mechanisms of environmental regulation cannot be replaced with any artificial mechanisms. Any regulation is based upon the flow of information. The capacity of information processed by the biota as it fulfills its regulatory function, exceeds by 12-18 orders of magnitude anything accessible to mankind in the foreseeable future. Meanwhile, a biosphere disaster is quite possible. Even if, theoretically, man could replace the natural regulatory mechanism of the environment, in reality, it would require an infinite amount of time. Also, any assumptions about the possibility of a fully technogenic environment, safely protected from any external influences are purely utopian.

6. Only by reducing the anthropogenic impact on the environment, and by returning to the limits of the biosphere's economic capacity will

save the environment, thereby insuring mankind's survival and development.

7. At the present time, the anthropogenic impact on the environment exceeds allowable limits by a factor of 8-10. Mankind's "anti-biosphere" behavior threatens the collapse of its genome; the decline in the number of species already exceeds the critical level by 2.5 times. Restoration of the biota does not require any special measures; it is enough to stop its destruction.

8. "Sustainable development," which is becoming the main slogan of our era, is naturally defined as development that does not exceed the economic capacity of the biosphere.

The environmental threat is the strongest of all threats to mankind, assuming that the threat of global nuclear war has ended. Mankind must reduce its negative impact on the environment during the 21st century, because time is running out. Such a reduction requires progress in the following three directions: 1) population control and reduction through family planning, 2) rationalization of consumption, 3) reducing the environmental impact of industry.

Whether these tasks are successfully resolved depends on mankind's ability to assume its responsibilities, to act collectively, and to follow a truly human moral code.

Nearly 9 million square kilometers of Russian territory (23% of the world's wilderness areas) are not affected by economic activity. The eco-systems in this area represent an exceptional value for the Earth's biosphere, carrying out major regulatory functions as a part of the planet's biota. Preservation of such wilderness territories is not just a task of national importance; Russia is one of the few countries having enough wilderness to serve as a springboard for global environmental revival.

One of the specific properties of the Russian environmental situation is exemplified by the transfer of pollution across its borders. Compared to other regions, Russia is a net recipient of atmospheric pollution.

For example, the trans-border exchange of sulfur dioxide between European Russia and other countries in Europe is represented by a ratio of 1:10. (This includes Ukraine --1:17, and Germany --1:146.) Nearly half the sulfur dioxide fallout in European Russia is caused by Russian sources, and half is trans-border fallout from other European countries. The situation with the exchange of nitric oxide is similar. In 1994, Russia received 32,000 metric tons of nitric oxide, including nitric oxide produced by Germany, which is not very close to Russia.[15]

Among trans-border environmental effects, the outstanding example in modern times is of course the Chernobyl disaster (1986), which was the most significant environmental catastrophe in mankind's history. That disaster resulted in unprecedented amounts of radioactive fallout in nearly all of Europe, showing that all modern countries have a very strong environmental interdependence.

In 1992, the former Ministry of Ecology of Russia developed a draft of a national scientific and technical program entitled "Defense Conversion and Ecology (Stage 1: 1993-1994)", which became a part of the "State Program for Converting the Defense Industry for 1993-1995." This program was adopted by the Russian federal government, but its fulfillment was complicated by unsatisfactory financing (in 1993, enterprises undergoing conversion received only 67% of the promised financial credits, and in 1994, only 13%).

---

15 *Gosudarstvennii Doklad o Sostoianii Okruzhaiuschei Sredy v RF v 1995g* (Moscow: Ekos-Inform, 1996).

In 1993-1994, the program received only 57% of the promised credit financing. Nevertheless, even with that underfinancing, new industrial facilities were created to producte devices for environmental monitoring and water treatment equipment (Zagorsk Experimental-Mechanical Plant, GNPP Almaz in Saratov, AOOT LOMO in St. Petersburg, NII Giredmet in Moscow; etc.).

As the performance of the program in 1994 deviated widely from the plan, a new State program for the conversion of the defense industry was developed for 1995-1997, requiring that industrial equipment for environmental purposes be developed.

This program is now being carried out. The program supports, as a rule, projects that are in the final stages of development, with completion expected in not more than two years. The program includes: equipment and technologies for water treatment; adsorbent materials; information systems; devices; automated stations and control posts; resource- and energy-saving equipment; special ships for environmental protection, etc.

Ninety research and design organizations were supposed to have been involved in the program's implementation. The greatest success in the environmental sector of conversion has been enjoyed by some programs on shipbuilding for environmental monitoring (the Akvatoria ship complex developed by the defense enterprises of St. Petersburg), and the use of satellites for a global environmental monitoring system.

The "Special Ecological Initiative" program was put forward by the U.S.-Russian Joint Commission on Economic and Technological Cooperation (also known as the Gore-Chernomyrdin Commission) and involves the use of satellite photo archives and other intelligence data in solving environmental problems. For two years, a special working group, consisting of ecologists and representatives from the intelligence services, has started a number of valuable research projects, including the compiling of atlases on the environment of the Arctic Region; geographical information systems for analyzing pollution dynamics on military bases in the U.S. and Russia; investigation of the effects of oil wells on the environment; and of the environmental consequences of earthquakes in Neftegorsk (Sakhalin Island). There is no doubt that conversion projects for environmental purposes need much stronger support from the State.

5.4. MEDICAL AND DEMOGRAPHIC CONSEQUENCES

Introductory Remarks

Vlad E. Genin

Sooner or later, all secrets are unveiled. The Soviet health care system had several hidden aspects. In the empire of the 4th Main Directorate of the Ministry of Health Care, the party and political elite received first-rate treatment, which was inaccessible to the masses. People didn't actually talk about it, but everybody knew about this secret. Talking about this creation of the Communist Party was a strict taboo, as was mentioning the rates of sickness and death due to industrial environmental catastrophes in the country. This was the other, dark half of the Ministry of Health Care. Under the pressure of party leaders, the Soviet Union made it its policy to conceal all terrible truths from society. Gradually, it must have evolved into an unthinking habit. There is no other logical explanation of the actions of the governments of the Ukraine and Belarus after the tragedy of Chernobyl. In the era of glasnost declared by Gorbachev, politicians were telling lies about this major environmental catastrophe, painting it as an unimportant industrial glitch. We all remember that in 1986, five days after the Chernobyl nuclear catastrophe, children in Kiev and Minsk were marching in the May Day parade as the deadly radioactive cloud swept over. As always, political gestures were worth more than human lives.

The defense enterprises, especially those producing chemical and nuclear weapons, will go down in history as the first human institutions that threatened the elimination, or nightmarish mutation, of humankind. Never before had mankind been subjected to such terrible experiments and sufferings. How could all of this not pose a deadly threat to the health of the planet? Would this be bequeathed to our children, grandchildren, and succeeding generations?

There is a small town, Chapaevsk, in Russia. This quite provincial place was selected as a site for the production of deadly chemical weapons, and all the citizens became hostages of the newly built plant. They were born, lived, and died among ammunition filled with mustard gas. Sickness, congenital deformities, and premature death became the norm in Chapaevsk. The health of future generations was in peril.

The tragedy of Chapaevsk did not end when production ended; indeed, it was aggravated. People who had lost their health, were now losing their jobs, and with them their means of existence. Some experienced nervous breakdowns; some died; some plunged into the abyss of drugs and alcohol.

They are the victims of the production of so-called deterrent weapons, which are meant to scare potential enemies from doing them harm. They did not suffer for the sake of a better life for future generations.

Chapaevsk is a typical case of "terminal illness" in a militarized economy ruined by pseudo-conversion. The dry statistical data on Chapaevsk represents a great human tragedy.

Marcus W. Feldman, Elena I. Ivanova, Boris A. Revich

I. Before Conversion: The Military-Industrial Complex

The military-industrial complex in Russia had its origins in the shift from a market economy to a command and central control system that occurred in 1927. The reorganization of industry in 1929 destroyed the last remnants of a private economy or private ownership, as well as any semblance of individual legal protection. These changes made the militarization of industry possible, and this militarization had the effect of suppressing non-military economic development. Thus, the military economy became the driving force behind the state economy, with its own set of rules and procedures that bypassed personal economic well-being.[16]

Between the 1930s and 1980s, the Soviet government focused on the development of military production at the expense of civilian production. Although the Soviet government claimed that it accomplished full employment, this was probably an aberration of the methods of accounting used. American researchers have shown that fewer jobs can be created in military industries than is possible for the same expenditure on civilian industries.[17]

---

16 V.N. Rassadin, "Military-Industrial Complex as System," *Voprosy Prognozirovania: Institute for Economic Forecasting, RAS, Moscow*, no. 1, 1993, pp. 55-56 (in Russian).

17 "Hearings Before the Committee on the Budget, United States Senate." 95th Congress, *National Defense,* vol. 1, no.28, April 1978, pp. 434-438.

In the Soviet system of national accounting, military industries were not disaggregated from national statistics but were included in national statistics on the machine production, chemical production, and nuclear power industries. By the late 1980s, about 60 percent of machinery manufacture was military-related, while from 80 to 90 percent of all national resources went to forming the military-industrial complex. About 75 percent of all scientific research was also devoted to this end. An important feature of this economic change was the high geographic concentration of military production and research facilities. More than 60 "normative" large cities were constructed, each with a high concentration of military production factories and research facilities. In these cities, the pattern of employment was essentially restricted to these military industries.[18] Some 20 other smaller and medium sized closed cities focused mainly on nuclear technology, and these varied in size from some 13,400 people in Ostrovnoi, located in Murmansk Oblast, to 118,600 in Seversk, located in Tomsk Oblast. In order to attract the most skilled employees to these cities, special conditions were created for them and their families. Material and social well-being were better than in comparable non-military cities. For example, health indicators were better than in comparable non-military cities. In fact, comparisons of infant mortality, birth defects, and rate of infant disease between the 20 special cities and, for example, cities devoted to metallurgy, indicate that these health indicators were primarily related to pollution by nitrogen

---

[18] E.E. Kostochkin, *Socio-Economic Characteristics Of Conversion Of Military Industrial Complex In Russia* (Moscow, 1993), p.6 (in Russian).

dioxide and sulfur dioxide emissions from the metallurgical processes, rather than emissions from nuclear plants.[19]

Factories devoted to the production of chemical weapons were located in seven Russian cities: Dzerzhinsk, Volgograd, Berezniki, Novocheboksarsk, Novomoskovsk (Tula Oblast), Chapaevsk, and Kirovo-Chepetsk. More than a million people resided in neighborhoods affected by these enterprises, in which the air became extremely polluted. The first large-scale production of mustard gas was organized in Chapaevsk (Samara Oblast) and in Dzerzhinsk. Altogether, during World War II, 122,000 metric tons of toxic agents were produced in the chemical weapons factories.[20]. The technology used in the production of these toxic agents was the cheapest possible, and there was almost no protection for the factory workers who were exposed to these chemicals, many of whom suffered illnesses resulting directly from their exposure.

The development of Russia's nuclear capability during the post-war arms race also caused environmental deterioration in parts of Russia. This pollution was not connected with nuclear weapons themselves, which were stored safely. Far more dangerous was the radioactive waste material, which was extremely expensive to bury in an appropriate manner. The cost in Russia was more expensive than in the United States, where the cost of deactivating nuclear waste has been estimated at up to $100 billion.[21]

---

[19] L.A. Buldakov, S.N. Demin, E.R.Liubchanski, "Analysis of the Influence of Radioactive and Chemical Environmental Factors on the Health of Newborn Infants in the Region Where Nuclear Industry is Located," *Hygiene and Sanitation*, no. 6, 1991, p. 55 (in Russian).

[20] L.A. Fedorov, *Undeclared Chemical War In Russia. Policy Against Ecology* (Moscow, 1995) (in Russian).

[21] *Technology Review*, August/September 1988, p.42.

The first nuclear accident of major proportions occurred in 1957 in Kyshtym, although it was classified as secret until 1989, when it was made public for the first time. Radioactive pollution as a result of the accident covered some 390 settlements in Sverdlovsk Oblast, in which more than 330,000 people were living. Subsequent studies of the effects of this catastrophe have revealed far-reaching health effects on subsequent generations, including rates of birth defects, cancer, and inherited diseases elevated well above normal for this population.[22] Of course, the notorious catastrophe at Chernobyl is a more familiar example of the terrible consequences of such nuclear accidents.

Accurate assessment of the medical and demographic problems associated with the past operations of the Soviet military industrial complex is impossible. Statistics on mortality and morbidity were, for all intents and purposes, never published. Moreover, in many cities with large defense enterprises, such information was the responsibility of special medical offices belonging to the former Third Directorate of the Ministry of Health Care (also called the Department for Medical and Biological Emergencies), which prevented access to medical statistical data.

II. The Past Decade: Consequences Of Conversion

A. Social Effects

A decade of reform of the military-industrial complex has now passed, and during this time the economy has been converted from a centralized operation, dominated by military and military-related production, to a market system. What are the results of this process?

---

22 The Kystym accident was described in V.Chukanov (ed.) *East-Ural Radioactive Trace* (Ekaterinburg, UrO RAN, 1996) (in Russian).

First, it must be realized that the complexity and scale of the changes in industrial production strategy dominate the process of socio-economic reform that has occurred since 1989 in Russia. Initially, ten governmental organizations were created to finance the process of conversion; altogether some 3,000 conversion projects were initiated.[23] The major elements in the conversion process have been:

(a) an enormous reduction in the output of military-related enterprises, with a concomitant emphasis on developing a market economy;

(b) reorientation of this production capacity, and also the technology base of the military-industrial complex, to a market-based system;

(c) large-scale redistribution of labor to civilian production;

(d) provision of retraining and new employment for personnel formerly engaged in military production, as well as their relocation to new employment sites;

(e) reorganization of the social security system in regions where military factories were previously concentrated.

The first result of this conversion process was "forced" mobility of the personnel involved in the military industries. Before conversion, highly trained workers were attracted to military industries by the relatively high wages, but after perestroika, the emergence of the first private enterprises saw their real and relative salaries drop. Those who stayed in those industries found their wages low, a situation that was

---

23 "Lessons Of Restructuring: Conversion Of Defense And High-Technology Industry In 1992-1994 (Review)." *Voprosy Prognozirovania: Institute for Economic Forecasting, RAS, Moscow*, no. 5, 1995, p. 99, (in Russian).

exacerbated by rapid inflation and non-payment. These, together with the absence of an adequate government policy of social welfare, led even more employees to move to more lucrative occupations. This was particularly true of the youngest and most competent professionals, who fled the military industries. By 1993, this flight had largely ceased, leaving in the military industries mostly people who had failed to find other employment because of their age or their personality.

Young professionals are no longer obliged to work where they are assigned. As a result, there is no source of newly trained personnel for the military industries. In fact, the present employees of these enterprises can be characterized with an inverted age pyramid in which the number of personnel is correlated with age; it is virtually impossible to find professionals under 35 years of age in those organizations.

These effects vary geographically. In some parts of Russia, scientific and educational institutions were completely oriented to the needs of the military-industrial complex. For example, in Tomsk, out of a population of 500,000, about 87,000 were employed by state-financed enterprises. Today these workers have no jobs or support. While in the large cities, such as Moscow or St Petersburg, there are good chances of finding a new job, in cities like Tomsk, or others in the northern and northeastern parts of Russia, it is quite impossible.[24]

Although defense conversion originally appeared to be a focal point for socio-economic reform, the social consequences have not worked out as originally intended. Indeed, there are a number of significant negative consequences: increased unemployment, decreased

---

24 V.N. Rassadin, "Defense orientation of industrial production," *Voprosy Prognozirovania: Institute for Economic Forecasting, RAS, Moscow*, no. 5, 1995, p. 23, (in Russian).

standard of living, curtailment of social welfare (especially in the health field, where access to medical care is no longer guaranteed, and can be extremely difficult), and exacerbation of environmental problems.

The highest rates of increase in unemployment rates occurred in 1994. For the nation as a whole, the unemployment rate doubled in the period from 1990 to 1997, reaching 9% in 1997. Unemployment in the northern and eastern regions, where most cities were focused on military industries, exceeded the national average, reaching 10-12%.[25] In 1997 the volume of industrial production began to increase, new civilian jobs began to be created, and the national unemployment rate fell. Even so, unemployment remains a significant factor in Russian economic life. According to a poll conducted in 1998 by VTsIOM (All-Russian Center for Public Opinion Studies), 66% of respondents viewed unemployment as the most pressing socio-economic problem for Russia.[26]

Per capita incomes dropped by 41.4% between 1991 and 1996. After an initial collapse in 1992, there was a rise until 1994, but in 1994-1996 further reduction occurred, with real wages dropping by 54.5%. The financial crisis of August 1998 affected every Russian family, and resulted in a further drop in the standard of living. The cost of living doubled in a period of several months, reaching 787 rubles (about $31) according to official statistics, although the actual increase was considerably greater. Official estimates placed the average per capita income at 137% of the cost of living, with pensions at only 51% of the cost of living. In 1998, the average monthly wage of workers in heavy

---

[25] B.D. Breev, T.N. Kostenko, A.M. Nanavyan, "Particular Features of Employment Policy During the Transition Period," *Voprosy Prognozirovaniya: Institute for Economic Forecasting, RAS, Moscow,* no. 6, 1998, p. 54 (in Russian).

[26] Breev et al., 1998, p.55.

manufacturing was 946 rubles ($38), while workers in chemical industries received 1174 rubles ($47). In these two industries, employee benefits accounted for 25.4 rubles ($1) and 42.5 rubles ($1.70), respectively.[27]

As a result of the decrease in industrial production, the 1990s have seen environmental pollution undergo a substantial reduction in Russia. In particular, emissions of toxic agents into the atmosphere by industrial sources dropped from 42.5 million metric tons in 1985 to 20.3 million metric tons in 1996.[28] Today the problem of radioactive wastes remains of critical importance. Fifty years of the arms race resulted in the accumulation of huge amounts of radioactive waste materials, and it is extremely difficult to assess the damage to public health caused by these wastes in the regions surrounding their burial sites.

B. Medical and Demographic Consequences of Conversion

The period of 1990-1994 in Russia can be characterized as one of social stress. This stress affected medical and demographic indicators of the population, and the health of the population deteriorated markedly over this period. The most vulnerable sectors of the population, those who were economically marginal and psychologically stressed, suffered most as the situation deteriorated. Rates of occurrence of cardiovascular diseases, alcoholism, and suicide increased markedly. The number of cardiovascular disease cases increased from 10.4% in 1988 to 13.3% in 1995.[29] Every third adult needed some kind of psychological support.[30]

---

[27] *Statistical Yearbook*, 1998 (Moscow: Goskomstat of Russia, 1999), p.263.

[28] *Statistical Yearbook*, 1997 (Moscow: Goskomstat of Russia, 1998), p.282.

[29] *Population of Russia*, 1996 (Moscow: Center of Demography and Human Ecology, 1997), p. 96 (in Russian).

Life expectancy reached the lowest point in the whole postwar period (57.4 years for men and 71 for women),[31] while the greatest increase in mortality occurred in the age group of 30 to 60 years.[32] Economic instability appeared to influence the process of family formation, especially among people of marriageable age. As a result, the total fertility rate declined from 1.89 in 1990 to 1.39 in 1994 for women aged 15-49.[33] The total first marriage rate decreased from 1 in 1990 to 0.77 in 1994, and the total divorce rate reached its highest value for two decades in 1994 (0.64 divorces per male and 0.63 per female).[34]

The period 1995-1998 saw a slight improvement in some of these medical-demographic indicators. Several sociological studies indicate that the population is now going through the first stages of adaptation to the changed economic system. A large part of the population has modified its behavior, and has become able to manage their lives independently of state welfare. On the other hand, there remains a group of socially disadvantaged citizens who are unable or unwilling to improve their economic situation. They remain vulnerable to social and economic disturbance and a negative influence on medical and demographic indicators. However, between 1995 and 1998 there was some improvement in certain health indicators: life expectancy increased, reaching 60.9 years for men and 72.9 for women[35] by 1997.

---

[30] *Population of Russia*, 1997 (Moscow: Center of Demography and Human Ecology, 1998), p. 69 (in Russian).

[31] *Population of Russia*, 1997, p. 87.

[32] *Population of Russia*, 1997, p. 90.

[33] *Population of Russia,* 1997, p. 50.

[34] *Population of Russia*, 1997, pp. 38, 47.

[35] *Population of Russia*, 1998 (Moscow: Center of Demography and Human Ecology, 1999), p.78 (in Russian).

Fertility, however, continued its decline, with the total fertility rate reaching 1.22,[36] the lowest value since World War II.

The medical-demographic situation in cities that formed the core of the military-industrial complex is revealed by official data and our own research. Special attention should be paid to demographic indicators from the former closed cities, namely those oriented towards nuclear industries. At the present time, these formerly elite cities are experiencing pronounced socio-economic depression as their residents find it harder to adapt to the new conditions than those of cities that did not have special status. Psychological stress associated with the rapid drop in living standards, loss of professional prestige, and changed social ideals (earning a good living instead of forging a defensive shield for the motherland) have apparently led to an increase in male mortality from cardiovascular diseases (relative to the average incidence for Russia).

It is difficult to estimate the total number of cities with large metallurgical and machine-tool complexes that were dedicated to the production of tanks, rockets, different types of guns, antiaircraft devices, ships, etc., but it exceeds several hundred. It is reasonable to assume that deterioration of public health can be found in many centers of the Russian defense industry.

Joint studies by Russian researchers and the Harvard School of Public Health showed the influence of air pollution on the population's health. According to these studies, the increased concentration of pollutants in the air led to an increase in prevalence of cardiovascular and respiratory diseases.[37] Panel studies of children with allergic and

---

[36] *Population of Russia*, 1998, p.40.

[37] B. Katsnelson et al., "Daily Variations of Ambient Air Pollution and Acute Mortality of Population in Ekaterinburg and Nizhnii Tagil Cities, Russia;" in

respiratory symptoms confirmed the correlation between the high concentration of such agents as nitrogen dioxide and particulate matter in the air, and an increase in the frequencies of these disorders.[38]

More than ten uranium mines were located in the former Soviet Union. One was in Lermontov, in the Caucasus, near the famous resort of Piatigorsk. In recent years, information about the level of radon in the city's environment and about the population's state of health has been published for the first time. The effect of increased natural radiation on the population was augmented by the influence of the former professional activities of the employees in uranium processing plants. In addition, radioactive building materials were used in Lermontov. The density of the radon stream from the Earth's surface was about fifteen times the average world value. As a result, the population was exposed to an amount of radiation comparable to that of workers at the uranium processing factories. The consequences of high radiation in Lermontov were terrifying. Between 1958 and 1998, mortality rates increased by a factor of three, and the standardized mortality rates from lung cancer in men were considerably higher than average for Stavropol Krai, where the city is located.[39]

Stores of toxic agents in seven military chemical bases constitute an environmental danger to Russia, which signed but did not ratify the

---

"1999 Annual Conference of the ISEE and ISEA: Abstracts," *Epidemiology*, vol. 10, no. 4, July 1999, Suppl., p.45.

[38] L. Privalova, S. Brezgina, B. Katsnelson, S. Kuzmin, S. Voronin, H. Ozkaynak, J. Xue, and J. Spengler, "Ambient Air Pollution, Respiratory Symptoms, and Peak Flow Measurements in Symptomatic and Asymptomatic School Children (Results of A Panel Study in Nizhnii Tagil, Russia;" in "1999, Annual Conference of the ISEE and ISEA: Abstracts," *Epidemiology*, vol. 10, no. 4, July 1999, Suppl., p.53.

[39] S.V. Vereiko, "Radiation And Hygienic Estimation of Working and Living Conditions of the Population of Lermontov" (Moscow, 1998).

convention on the prohibition of the development, production, accumulation, and use of chemical weapons, and their elimination. Medical-demographic data concerning the cities where the military-chemical complexes were located is scanty. Only in recent years has some information on the health of the population of these cities appeared in the media and technical literature. One city where detailed public health studies have been carried out is Chapaevsk, which, like other cities of the military-industrial complex, has experienced high unemployment, rapid reduction in fertility, and increased mortality.

III. Medical and Demographic Indicators in Chapaevsk

Medical-demographic indices in Chapaevsk show substantial deterioration over the past decade. These effects, both long- and short-term, are due mainly to the national socio-economic crisis of the 1990s. Because the economy of Chapaevsk was previously dominated by government-run defense industries, the new socio-economic situation, with its reduced emphasis on the military industry, and increased level of privatization, has had a profound effect on the labor market and population structure.

The population of Chapaevsk decreased by 8,100 during 1990-1997, when, as seen in Table 5.4.1, the rate of natural increase was negative. By the mid-1990s, the birth rate had dropped to its lowest value since World War II.

A major contribution to the drop in the birth rate comes from the aging of the city's population. Chapaevsk has a high proportion of elderly citizens (60 years and older), higher than the average for Russia or for other cities in Samara Oblast. At the same time, of course, the proportion of younger individuals in the population is decreasing. This aging tendency has become the national norm for Russia (life expectancy also increased in the country as a whole until 1989) along with the trend for families to have no more than one child. These characteristics of aging and decreased fertility are typical of the majority of Russian cities.

TABLE 5.4.1.

Population number, natural increase, and net migration in Chapaevsk, 1989-1997.

	1989	1990	1991	1992	1993	1994	1995	1996	1997
Population (1000s)	98.1				94.7	89.2	86.7	83.9	83.6
Number of births	1,011	916	743	686	604	597	617	581	553
Number of deaths	1,194	1,250	1,183	1,278	1,419	1,570	1,582	1,578	1,401
Natural increase	-183	-334	-440	-592	-815	-973	-965	-997	-848
Net migration	-689				358	924	600	384	521

Per 1,000 persons

	1989	1990	1991	1992	1993	1994	1995	1996	1997
Number of births	10.4	9.5	7.8	7.2	6.8	6.7	7.1	6.9	6.6
Number of deaths	12.3	13.0	12.4	13.5	15.6	17.6	18.2	18.8	16.8
Natural increase	-1.9	-3.5	-4.6	-6.3	-8.6	-10.9	-11.1	-11.9	-10.1
Net migration	-7.0				3.8	10.4	6.9	4.6	6.2

Data from Chapaevsk Census Department

In Chapaevsk, the last decade has seen new demographic tendencies. First, there was a sharp reduction in births in the first half of the 1990s compared to the late 1980s--a decrease of almost 50%. On the other hand, mortality rates increased over the same period. By 1994, the number of deaths had increased by 20% compared to 1989. This increase in mortality occurred across all age groups and both sexes (see Table 5.4.2) but was especially high in working-age males. For the age group 40-49, mortality increased by 55% compared to 1990, while the increases were 114% and 66% for the age groups 50-59 and 60-69, respectively. Following a peak in 1995, mortality apparently started to decrease gradually, but there has remained an increasing tendency among the youngest people, men ages 30-39, and women ages 60-69.

TABLE 5.4.2.

Age-specific death rates (number of deaths per 1,000 persons)

Men

Year/age	0-29	30-39	40-49	50-59	60-69	70+
1975	0.22	0.76	0.49	2.88	5.09	15.51
1990	0.19	0.68	1.24	1.92	3.71	15.24
1994	0.25	0.73	1.93	4.11	6.16	17.23
1997	0.29	1.04	1.55	2.74	5.14	14.02

Women

Year/age	0-29	30-39	40-49	50-59	60-69	70+
1975	0.09	0.15	0.41	0.84	1.98	10.09
1990	0.11	0.13	0.35	0.74	1.60	8.81
1994	0.08	0.18	0.51	1.00	2.16	12.78
1997	0.10	0.14	0.42	0.93	2.26	10.43

As can be seen in Table 5.4.1, migration to Chapaevsk from other republics of the former U.S.S.R. has had the effect of ameliorating the decrease in population, which would otherwise have been drastic.

The demographic trends just described interact strongly with changes in the labor market. On the one hand, population aging has reduced the number of employment-age people. On the other hand, the unemployment rate is increasing due to the decrease in the demand for labor. These two effects are typical for areas previously dominated by the defense industries. In Chapaevsk, the number of industrial employees decreased by 14,500 to 27,700 between 1989 and 1997. In particular, employees in defense enterprises decreased by two thirds, from 25,400 to 8,700. Downsizing of the defense industry was partially balanced by the development of new small private businesses, which employed 7800 by 1997. By 1997, there were officially 4,400 unemployed residents of Chapaevsk. These unemployed had a very high level of education (61% had university or college degrees). Most of the unemployed were women (52%) and young people under the age of 29 (31%). However, the relatively low official unemployment rate does not reflect the actual employment situation. For example, in 1997 there was a significant component of "hidden" unemployment, where people were forced to work part-time (3,200) or take long unpaid vacations (8,900). The results were lowered living standards and the disruption of traditional relationships between generations within families. These factors have changed the age structure of the work force: the fraction of the work force of employment age dropped from 88.3% in 1989 to 86.5% in 1997, while the fraction of retirees and teenagers working increased to reach 8.7%.

It is reasonable to assume that these changes in the labor market together with inability of the population to adapt to the changed socio-economic conditions affected the entire demographic spectrum. The most noticeable demographic effects have been the reduction of life expectancy and increased mortality due to specific diseases. The mortality rate in Chapaevsk was higher than average for the whole of Samara as well as other cities. By 1995, life expectancy had dropped to 60.7 for males and 74.1 for females. Cardiovascular diseases were the main cause of death (67% for women, 49% for men). From 1989-1997, mortality rates among employment-age men (especially ages 50-59 and 30-39) increased dramatically. The second most important cause of death was accidents and the third was cancer. A comparison of actual and expected mortality rates (the latter is mortality standardized by age for all of Samara Oblast) shows that the ratio is much higher in Chapaevsk than in Samara (see Table 5.4.3).

TABLE 5.4.3.

Observed and expected mortality rate due to cardiovascular disease in Chapaevsk, 1990-1997

Cause	Gender	Deaths		Ratio (3) : (4)		Standardized rate	
		Actual	Expected*	%	CI, 95%	per 100,000 of pop.	CI, 95%
1.	*2.*	*3.*	*4.*	*5.*	*6.*	*7.*	*8.*
cardio-vascular diseases	Men	2,553	1,532.4	165.4	158.9-172.2	1,182.0	1,135-1,230
	Women	3,349	3,593.6	93.2	90.0-96.2	665.9	643.1-687.7

* *Age-adjusted death rates for Samara Oblast.*

Direct statistical analysis of the influence of labor market changes on the mortality rate has been difficult because of the absence of specific studies. However, an indirect assessment, based on available statistical data, is possible. Thus, the trend towards an increase in deaths caused by cardiovascular diseases is compatible with the trend of increasing unemployment. There is a linear correlation between the dynamics of both indices. Deaths due to cancer are much less frequent than those caused by cardiovascular diseases, most probably because in the case of malignant tumors there were better and earlier diagnostics and better treatment.

Nevertheless, male cancer mortality in Chapaevsk is 1.2 times higher than the average in Samara Oblast, 1.3 times higher than the average in Russia, and 1.4 times higher than in the U.S. In fact, the male cancer mortality rate in Chapaevsk is higher than elsewhere in the whole oblast. These deaths were caused mostly by malignant tumors in the digestive tract, the throat, the lungs, bones, and other tissues. The risk of men dying from these forms of cancer in Chapaevsk is accordingly higher: 1.8, 3.3, 1.8, 3.5, 2.7 times, respectively, than for men in the whole Samara region. Chapaevsk women have a higher risk of dying from breast or cervical cancer. Cancer mortality reduces the average male life expectancy by 2.3 years, and for women by 1.9 years. Lung cancer shortens the average male life expectancy by 0.77 year, stomach cancer by 0.28 year, hemoblastoses by 0.17 year. The average woman's life span is 0.29 years shorter in the case of stomach cancer, 0.27 for breast cancer, 0.15 for lung cancer, and 0.11 for hemoblastoses.

The continuous pollution of the environment with dioxins can be clearly detected upon analysis of breast milk and blood. The presence of dioxins in the breast milk of Chapaevsk women is much higher than other cities in Russia, the United States, Germany, or the Netherlands (Table 5.4.4).

TABLE 5.4.4.

PCDD/PCDF content in human milk, pg/TEQ/g fat

City, country	PCDDs/PCDFs*
Chapaevsk	43.3[40]
15 Russian cities	5-13[41, 42, 43]
Germany	10.0[44]
20 Netherlands cities	23.5[45]
Los Angeles	16.6[46]

**PCDDs/PCDFs — polychlorinated dibenzo-para-dibenzo-dioxins and dibenzofurans.*

Dioxins are considered one of the risk factors for breast cancer, and it is possible that the high degree of contamination of the

40 B. Revich, E. Brodsky and Iu. Sotskov, "Dioxin In Enviromental, Blood, Breast Milk, Cow Milk In Chapaevsk Town," *Dioxin '99: Organohalogen Compounds,* 1999, vol. 44, pp.229 - 232.

41 W.A. Traag and S. Yufit, "The Contamination of Human Milk with PCDD, PCD and PCB in Russia," *Dioxin '97: Organohalogen Compounds,* 1997, vol. 33, pp. 524 - 529.

42 Z.K. Amirova, E.A. Kruglov, E.A. Lozhkina and R.R. Khalilov, "About Level of Dioxins in Breast Milk of Nursing Mothers from Different Cities of Russia," *Bashkirian Chemical Magazine*, vol. 4, no. 4; 1997, pp.70 – 74 (in Russian).

43 A. Schecter, P. Furst, Ch. Furst, W. Groebel, S. Kolesnikov, M. Savchenkov, A. Beim, A. Boldonov, E. Trubitsin and B. Vlasov, "Levels of Dioxins, Dibenzofurans and Other Chlorinated Xenobiotics in Human Milk from the Soviet Union," *Chemosphere*, 1990, vol. 20, no. 7 – 9, pp. 927 - 934.

44 A.K.D. Liem and R.M.C. Theelen, *Dioxins: Chemical Analysis, Exposure and Risk Assessment* (Bilthoven, Netherlands: National Institute of Public Health and Environment, 1997).

45 Ibid.

46 A. Schecter et al., "Levels of Dioxins, Dibenzofurans and Other Chlorinated Xenobiotics in Human Milk from the Soviet Union," *Chemosphere*, 1990, vol. 20, no. 7 – 9, pp. 927 - 934.

environment with these chemicals (even with the decrease in military production) has led to an increase in female mortality caused by breast cancer. This issue can be decided conclusively only after detailed case studies.

5.5. SOCIAL BACKGROUND OF CONVERSION

Introductory Remarks

Vlad E. Genin

A "hungry Russia" is dangerous; that is the warning that various Russian speakers have issued throughout the world—but is Russia really hungry? One cannot avoid the signs of apparent well being: private stores, markets, and shopping centers pop up like mushrooms, and they are filled with customers—this was especially true before the August'98 crisis. The shelves are filled with a vast array of imported goods that were unknown in Soviet times. Between 1991 and 1995, the number of private cars rose steadily, by a factor of 1.4. Traffic jams, unknown in Soviet times, are now commonplace. Russia has one of the highest concentrations of the latest Mercedes S-class and Audi cars. Vacationing abroad in Turkey, Spain, Italy, Germany, the United Arab Emirates, and France is popular among the upper levels of the Russian population. Before the 1998 financial crisis, currency exchange was very active (roughly 19% of people's annual income was spent on this, due to the stability of the foreign currency).

However, not everyone can afford all these things, particularly not the majority of the populace, and not Russia's former industrial and intellectual avant-guard--defense industry specialists. Many of them live in a very different Russia, full of unhappiness, disease, and increased mortality rates. Millions of people aged 55 and up, who could successfully work for many more years, have been forced to take early retirement status, as in the years of the Great Depression in the United States, when there were practically no jobs. Like the Great Depression, the destabilized conditions in Russia have fated pensioners, who have only meager incomes, to a life of deep poverty.

The mysterious, secret "closed cities"—like any other cities, they had real names. However, only their residents and defense industry authorities knew them. The rest of the world knew only the code names, such as Arzamas-16, Chelyabinsk-70, and Penza-19, which did not necessarily give any indications of their real locations. Only the Soviet postal service knew where to send letters by friends and relatives to the residents of these closed cities. This was somewhat similar to the way the postal service operated during WWII, carrying correspondence from America to troops on the front lines in Normandy.

The closed cities were home to secret scientific research, design, and industrial facilities specializing in weaponry, particularly nuclear weapons design, nuclear warheads, weapons-grade plutonium, radioisotopes, communication satellites, and laser technology.

Access to these cities was limited or totally forbidden —not only for foreigners, but also for residents of other regions of Russia or other Soviet republics. The degree of secrecy of a given city's work dictated the degree of openness. Cities with limited access were called "open cities", although they were far from open. Access to cities with highly classified facilities was forbidden to all but a select few. These cities were called "secret nuclear cities". Here they are: Arzamas-16 (Sarov, Nizhnii

Novgorod Oblast), 250 miles east of Moscow; Cheliabinsk-65, (Ozersk, Cheliabinsk Oblast) in the southern Urals; Cheliabinsk-70, (Snezhinsk, Cheliabinsk Oblast); Krasnoiarsk-26, (Zheleznogorsk, Krasnoiarsk Krai) 24 miles from Krasnoiarsk in western Siberia; Krasnoiarsk-45 (Zelenogorsk, Krasnoiarsk Krai); Penza-19, (Zarechnyi, Penza Oblast) in central Russia 200 miles northwest of Saratov; Sverdlovsk-44, (Novouralsk, Sverdlovsk Oblast) in the central Urals, 200 miles southeast of Perm; Sverdlovsk-45 (Lesnoi, Sverdlovsk Oblast); Tomsk-7 (Seversk, Tomsk Oblast) in western Siberia 50 miles from confluence of the Tom and Ob rivers, Zlatoust-36 (Trekhgornoe, Cheliabinsk Oblast) 90 miles east of Cheliabinsk.[47]

Zhanna A. Zaionchkovskaya

Nearly 2 million people lived in several dozen "closed cities", where military scientific facilities and related enterprises were located. Among these cities were 10 completely closed, so-called "nuclear" cities. The majority of the closed cities were located in the Urals and Siberia. The open cities were concentrated mainly in the European part of Russia.

A great deal of theoretical research in areas such as nuclear physics was conducted in open cities such as Obninsk, Dubna, Dimitrovgrad, and Protvino. Aerospace scientific research centers were located in Zhukovskii, Khimki, Votkinsk, Dzerzhinskii, Friazino, Stupino, Koroliov, and other, similar, open cities.[48]

---

[47] Richard F. Staar, *The New Russian Armed Forces. Preparing for War or Peace?* (Stanford: Hoover Institution, Stanford University, 1992), p. 6.

[48] G.Lappo, P.Polyan, "Closed Cities In Slightly Opened Russia," *Problemy rasselenia*, Moscow, 1997.

The closed cities were established to create an optimal setting for scientific activity, and to provide scientists with a standard of living higher than the surrounding regions, higher even than the rest of country. Initially this was a rather effective decision, which allowed Russia, a relatively poor country, to organize and develop world-class interdisciplinary research, and to pass its findings along to production facilities. Graduates of the best Soviet universities aspired to work in these closed cities.

"Headlong" conversion greatly influenced the closed cities. They resorted to "Russian-style" conversion, in which employees were not transferred to civilian production, but simply laid off. These cities still lack a well thought-out system for developing civilian careers, even though it is believed that nearly 80% of former defense professionals could work in civilian fields without retraining. Most of the unemployed in the closed cities lost their jobs because of defense conversion. Moreover, the nationwide average ratio of jobless individuals per job vacancy is 150% less than in closed cities. Between 1994 and 1996, 626,000 people lost their jobs in the defense industry. Only about half of them got new jobs within their respective defense enterprises. There was no corresponding increase in civilian production, which may indicate that conversion has not, in fact, taken place.

In 1992, 26% of the specialists in the closed cities expressed dissatisfaction with the process of conversion, and 54% approved of it. In 1995, however, 62% considered conversion a strategic mistake, and only 12% were still in favor of it. Russian-style conversion has quickly turned its supporters into its opponents, not only in the closed cities, but also in the whole MIC.

At least half of Russian industrial workers, engineers, researchers, and managers worked directly or indirectly for the defense sector. The MIC provided high wages and various types of benefits for a quarter of the population of Russia. The Russian populace was held hostage by militarization; thus, the course of conversion determined not only the fates of those directly involved in national defense, but also the standard of living of the entire population. At present, the most profitable source of income is not manufacturing, which involves the overwhelming majority of specialists, but brokerage and finance, which engages considerably fewer people.

Headlong defense conversion aggravated tensions brought on by the disintegration of the Soviet Union, and the rise of nationalism, ethnic conflicts, civil wars, and terrorism were among the main factors that destabilized the social situation in Russia. The bitter power struggles among the new political elite deepened Russia's economic and social crisis. In addition, demographic factors, the dynamics of the standard of living, and the situation in the labor market were instrumental in forming the social backdrop for the conversion process.

During the course of the last decade, most Russians have suffered from a sense of instability, doubts about the future, anxiety, and even fear. These emotions are the result of the difficulties of undergoing simultaneous political and economic reform; Russia's inexperience in acting under new and rapidly changing conditions; frequent unexpected turns of political, economic, and social events; and a serious distrust in the State, instilled by the totalitarian past.

The disintegration of the Soviet Union not only destroyed a homogeneous, indivisible industry; it also destroyed geographical and technical links between various enterprises. This alone caused a drastic decline in productivity, comparable to the Great Depression in the United States.

The decline set off a chain reaction in the scientific and R&D sectors. First, the formerly integrated scientific research complexes collapsed, thereby reducing the volume of both theoretical and applied research, and eliminating continuity between projects. Second, research institutes rapidly began to lose highly qualified scientific personnel. The inflow of the best university graduates has dropped sharply, while the existing scientific staff is aging. Third, the fate of fundamental research is still largely determined by State financing, which has been declining constantly. State budget allocations for science are currently at the level of the 1940s, which means a four- to five-fold reduction of pre-conversion allocation levels. Such sharp reductions in funding have the greatest effects on enterprises with large staffs. The allocated funds are often so limited that almost 60% have to be used for employee salaries, leaving little for other needs. Even the Russian Academy of Sciences is barely able to purchase any equipment to renovate its basic facilities.

Technological progress in a market economy is closely associated with employee salaries: without appropriate salaries it is almost impossible to create new advanced technologies. However, in Russia's R&D sphere, wages are significantly lower than Western standards. This situation encourages the development of "low technologies," which does not require high-paid workers. Russian theoretical and high-tech research, which previously focused on advanced weapons and military equipment, no longer pays its way.

A survey of defense industry professionals found that 70% consider themselves worse off financially than before, 15% view their situation as unchanged, and the remaining 15% consider themselves better off than before. Defense industry employees are much worse off than other Russian professionals.[49] Many professionals survived by selling their dachas, garages, and other possessions in order to buy food and clothes.

The salaries of defense plant workers (both specialists and those who produce civilian goods at defense enterprises) dropped to two-thirds of the average salary of Russian industry employees. Employees have also suffered from payroll delays, which have become the most widespread problem in the defense industry.

The average desirable salary for highly qualified specialists is five times higher than their actual salaries. The desirable salary is very modest, but covers their basic everyday needs. Indeed, it corresponds to the $400 monthly stipend given to Russian scientists participating in joint projects with the United States. Moreover, this amount is roughly the level of their salaries before reforms and conversion.

The salary changes demonstrate that conversion has not yet produced real positive results. On the contrary, the defense industry appears to be lagging seriously behind. Low wages have forced defense industry specialists to find other jobs or additional sources of income. In the nuclear cities, 40% of the employees “moonlight”, with 18% constantly or frequently involved in outside jobs, and 22% occasionally involved in outside jobs. More men than women have outside jobs—44% of male employees versus 30% of female employees. It seems easier for men to earn additional income than for women. Also, single or divorced men earn additional income more than twice as often as married men. Finding an extra job has been more difficult for older, highly qualified

---

[49] V. Tikhonov, *Closed Cities in Open Society* (Moscow: Institute of Economic Forecasting, 1996).

specialists than for younger, less-qualified workers: the number of employees with advanced degrees that have extra jobs is 27% lower than the number for those without a university education.

For nearly 70% of all employees, their supplemental income matches or exceeds their primary salary. Indeed, these workers' primary jobs become more like secondary jobs, and vice versa. About one-third of those who do not have an extra job would like one. They would prefer to dedicate themselves to their main jobs for modest salaries than to have two or three jobs in order to support their families. Only 20% consider earnings from extra jobs a normal phenomenon of reforms, while 70% believe that this is abnormal.

Nevertheless, recent years have seen the emergence of a certain successful layer of employees who were involved in well-paid projects or private business. Since 1991, they have purchased 8% of all dachas, 33% of all garages and 18% of all cars.

The most destabilizing factor is the recent sharp decline in the standard of living. Real per capita income dropped 40% between 1992 and 1997, while wages declined by one third. Moreover, the wages that are received are frequently delayed. Real pensions declined approximately two-fold, barely covering 80% of minimum living expenses.

The crash of the ruble in August 1998 marked the beginning of yet another sharp decline in the standard of living. In the early 1990s, real per capita income fell by one quarter and actual wages – by one third. Poverty has become rampant: 51.7 million people (35.5% of the population) earn below minimum wage – up from 32.9 million (22.4% of the population) in early 1998[50]

Proper nutrition has also declined: consumption of meat, fish, and dairy products dropped 30-40%, and people are forced to compensate with bread and potatoes.

All these misfortunes combine with increased crime and other antisocial behavior, such as drug abuse, alcoholism, robbery, and prostitution, to create a rather difficult atmosphere in the country. Unemployment is the main factor that intensifies social tension. In the mid 1999, 12.4 % of the workforce was unemployed, according to estimates by the International Labor Organization. However, there is hidden unemployment (this refers to workers for whom there is little or no real work, but who are nevertheless carried on the books as employees) in both the public and private sector.

This situation appears to suit the state, the enterprises, and the employees alike. It deters the threat of social upheaval, thus ensuring stability; the enterprise gain a source of credits and means to pressure the government; and the employees gain the opportunity to earn money in the private sector while retaining their positions in the enterprise. Economists estimate that in 1997, 12 – 14 million more individuals were employed in industry than were really necessary.[51] In order to prevent the threat of further unemployment, the State provided some financial credits to certain enterprises.

Stagnation in the public sector has been accompanied by the rapid development of the private sector, in which 39.9% percent of

---

50 *Russia 1999: Economic conjuncture* (Moscow: Center of Economic Conjuncture, October 1999), p. 19.

51 *Economical Monitoring of Russia*, no 8. INPG, 1997.

population worked in 1997. However, this is only official data. In reality, the percentage of people working in the private sector has been much higher, especially in the cities. This is due to "shadow," or undeclared, employment alongside official jobs in the defense industry.

The declining standard of living, high unemployment rates, low pensions, and delayed wages increased social stratification. Sociologists state that between 1993 and 1996, there was virtually no increase in the potential for organized protests, which maybe explained by the presence of powerful "social shock absorbers", such as commerce, free entrepreneurship, "open doors" to the West and a flexible labor market.[52] However, pessimism and doubts about the future prevail among 70% of public sector employees and 50% of those in the private sector.

Another serious problem is that ethnic Russians employed by the defense industry—scientists and engineers—are emigrating from the non-Russian former Soviet republics. Though they worked and, in many cases, were born there, they are not guaranteed citizenship because of discriminating policies created in some former Soviet republics, now independent states. Among the reasons they have moved are the loss of their rights to pensions, jobs, and property ownership, and acute ethnic conflicts such as the protracted bloodshed in Chechnya. In early 1999, 1,106,300 refugees and forced emigrants from the non-Russian former Soviet republics were registered in Russia. These specialists could in other circumstances assist in converting the Russian MIC, but in an economic depression, emigrants exacerbate unemployment by intensifying the competition in labor markets, a particular problem for those who lost their jobs as a result of headlong defense conversion.

---

52 VTsIOM, Bulletin no. 4. 1996.

Defense conversion's social repercussions go even deeper: the population of Russia has been declining since 1992. Between 1992 and 1999, the population fell by 2 million. Even increased immigration cannot compensate for the natural decrease in population. This demographic crisis is the result of a simultaneous decline in fertility and rise in mortality, particularly among the elderly. This is typical for most Western European countries, where population levels have long been maintained solely by large-scale immigration.

The fertility rate in Russia per 1000 persons was 8.6 in 1997, compared to 13.4 in 1990 and to 23.2 in 1960. In 1997, the Russian population comprised 147.5 million people. In early 1999, the Russian population comprised 146.7 million people.

The degradation in the standards of living has also contributed to the population decline, but not as decisively as social destabilization. In 1997, the average life expectancy for Russians was only 67 years. The 1997 mortality rate in Russia skyrocketed to an unprecedented level—13.8 per 1000 residents. This is nearly twice the rate in the 1960s—7.7 per 1000.

In developed European countries, which have a greater percentage of the elderly, the mortality rate is lower by about one third. Russian reforms have been accompanied by a sharp increase in mortality, due mainly to alcoholism and an increase in murders and other violent deaths. Mortality rates rose particularly high among men, from 11.6 per 1000 in 1990 to 14.9 per 1000 in 1997. The corresponding statistics for women are 10.9 and 12.7. From 1992 through 1997, the population decreased by 4.2 million people or 2.83 %, which is an extremely high rate. If this situation remains constant for a sufficiently long time, the next generation of Russians will be less than one-third the size of the previous one.[53]

The crisis is especially apparent when analyzing the general health of the population. Infant mortality rates in Russia are two and a half times as high as in the United States. The standardized rate of mortality (across similar age groups) in Russia is 1.6 times higher for men and 1.35 times higher for women than in the U.S.

Death rates for women in childbirth are also extremely high—52 cases per 100,000 women, which is 5-10 times higher than in developed countries. Not surprisingly, Russia, in terms of life expectancy, more closely resembles a developing country than a developed one.

Although the roots of this demographic crisis are in the past, the worsening situation demonstrates the lack of social welfare. The coincidence of reforms (including defense conversion) with the transition from a constant rate of reproduction to a natural decline in population is a historical accident with tragic results.

The effects of defense conversion are not limited to the economic and social spheres – they are influencing the political spheres as well. Most defense industry employees are somewhat nostalgic for "the good old days" and their material comforts. They would probably support a retreat from a free-market economy to one that combines state regulation with some market institutions. Employees of the defense industry could make up part of the driving force to restore state interference in the economy. Since reforms began, they have lost more than others, and gained almost nothing. By getting this group on its side,

---

53 *Population of Russia 1998*, (Moscow: Institute of Economic Forecasting, 1999).

the political opposition to reform would gain a highly organized intellectual force.

The situation may get out of control, especially in the closed cities, where employment opportunities and extra jobs are very limited. An example of this has already occurred in the Russian Far East, when workers at the Zvezda submarine shipyard were driven to despair by constant wage arrears. They had been receiving vouchers for bread and canned foods instead of their pay. Outraged, the workers blocked the Trans-Siberian Railroad, a major transportation artery, for several hours. The protesters shouted anti-governmental and anti-presidential slogans. In a similar demonstration of dissatisfaction in July 1997, workers from the Smolensk nuclear power station marched on Moscow, supported by other nuclear industry workers. Because Russians are traditionally patient people, these protests mean far more than demonstrations in democratic Western societies. Such demonstrations are new to Russia, and indicate that the traditional patience of the Russian people may be strained beyond endurance, threatening a resort to mass violence on their part. The vulnerability of the defense sector poses other threats, such as illegal sales of weapons and technology, and difficulty maintaining security at nuclear installations.

Throughout its entire existence, the Russian government balanced social stability and economic necessity, usually giving preference to the former. But all the reserves of the previous economic system have been exhausted, and the economic crisis has made it impossible for the government to give such emphasis to social stability. This has destabilized state structures, led to regional isolation (since the anti-government sentiments of the population were usually targeted at local authorities), and challenged the solidity and effectiveness of the

State. Lack of confidence in the authorities and their chosen course of reforms have steadily grown.

There is progressively less room to maneuver between economic and social interests, and the state is greatly concerned with striking a balance between them. However, the government is consumed by the struggle to control privatization, access to natural resources, and budget allocations; state power structures are being undermined, politically stratified, and corrupted. The authorities are neglecting the interests of the people.

The apparent indifference of all levels of government to the needs of highly qualified defense specialists aggravates a substantial social problem. This indifference will not supply MIC employees with work, food or clothing. These people will not care whose orders– civilian or military – they execute, or who they work for: civilized foreign partners or terrorist regimes; they just need jobs to support their families.

There is a widespread expression: “A hungry Russia is dangerous.” Applying this phrase to the defense sector, one can say that the future of the Russian people depends on the potentially dangerous consequences of such a scornful attitude to the industrial and scientific elite of defense industries.

5.6. ADVANCED RUSSIAN WEAPONS

Introductory Remarks

Vlad E. Genin

In 1999, MIC production increased by 30-40%. Although the sum allocated by the Russian government for weapons purchases has been classified since 1999, the federal budget for this purpose definitely increased. The budget for 2000, according to an announcement by Deputy Prime Minister Klebanov on January 14, 2000, is in the amount of 62 billion rubles.[54]

Today, after several stages of mutual disarmament, Russian weapons and their power is still the subject of much debate.

According to widespread international opinion, the Russian Army was always very well armed. Besides the arms assigned to regular units, large numbers of weapons, intended for mobilization in the case of war, are stored at military reserve bases.

According to the Russian generals, however, the majority of existing Russian weapons are obsolete, and the demand for modern, efficient weapons is not being satisfied. But that opinion is based not only on the generals' military technical expertise and patriotism. It sprang primarily from the Russian political opposition to the country's new course, which was begun by President Gorbachev in 1985 and continued for almost a decade under President Yeltsin. The political opponents of this course strongly

54 Sergei Sokut, Vladimir Sysoev, "Defense Industry was Promised More Money." *Nezavisimaia Gazeta,* http://news.mosinfo.ru/news/2000/nga/01/data/ng012810.html, January 28, 2000, p. 1.

believe that the processes of political and economic reforms in the country, followed by the conversion of the defense industry, are the reasons for the shortage of modern weapons and the obsolescence of the ones in use. In their opinion, this considerably weakened the offensive power of the country, and consequently contributed to the destruction of its defensive capability. Opponents blame the process of conversion not only for the diminishing number of weapons, but also for their out-of-date design. One can get the impression that no modern weapons are being produced by the defense industry today, that the Russian army has nothing left except the legendary Kalashnikov AK-47, obsolete models of tanks, airplanes, and ships, as well as the remaining old formidable nuclear arsenal.

However, it is no secret that the Russian defense industry always worked on future design and developments, even in the most difficult recent years. The State spent its last rubles for these purposes, even leaving elderly people without pensions and below the poverty level. During recent decades, design bureaus created many new models of weapons: missile systems, warships, jet fighters, bombers, artillery, tanks, helicopters, and a wide range of portable arms.

Mark I. Shteynberg

Many conceive of the Russian MIC as morally and physically deficient. However, such conceptions are based either on prejudice or on a lack of information.

Not long ago, the MIC attracted the most talented scientists, engineers, and industrial managers. It enjoyed practically unlimited financial support. Even though circumstances have radically changed today, substantial strengths have been carried over from the 1970s and 1980s, and numerous advanced designs from that time are now being realized.

Above all, this development concerns missiles, including those used for air defense. The combat effectiveness of the newest Russian missile systems created in recent years, particularly the deployed regiment of 10 "Topol-M" intercontinental ballistic missiles with superior accuracy, seems like it is among the best in the world.

The "S-300" anti-aircraft missile system is among the most famous Russian advanced weapons. The latest modification of this complex, known as the S-300 PMU-2 ("Favorit"), for striking targets with 80% - 90% accuracy at distances up to 200 kilometers and heights between 5 and 32 kilometers. "Favorit" looks extremely effective compared to the U.S. "Patriot" system.

Another new anti-aircraft missile system, the S-400 ("Triumf"), completed its testing phase in February 1999. "Triumf" will be able to destroy targets at distances up to 400 kilometers. Finally, a newly developed system, the "Antei-2500," will be capable of defending up to 2500 square kilometers against long-range missiles, and up to 125,000 square kilometers against air raids.

The latest modifications of Russian combat fighter planes, the MiG-29 and Su-27, match the tactical and technical characteristics of America's F-15s and F-16s. But Russia's aviation industry has also developed new technology that surpasses the West. An example of this technology is the bomber Su-33 with an attack radius of more than 1,000 kilometers and a capability of carrying 6.5 tons of high-precision bombs and missiles. Moreover, the newest, fifth-generation, multi-functional fighter-bomber Su-37 (production code 1.44) is expected to arrive to the Russian Armed Forces in 8-10 years.[55] It will be capable of engaging twenty targets simultaneously and compete in performance characteristics with the U.S. F-22 ("Raptor") fighter.

Russian attack helicopters, such as the Ka-50 ("Black Shark"), Ka-52 ("Alligator") and Mi-28N are very serious competitors to the West's newest combat helicopters.

Leading Russian armament systems also include one of the most powerful tanks in the world, the T-90S, the performance characteristics of which exceeds many of its foreign competitors. In March 2000, the newest, more advanced T-95 tank was introduced.

Russian multiple-launch rocket systems also dominate the competition. The famous "Grad" has been replaced by "Smerch" and "Uragan," which, with ranges of 70 and 34 kilometers, respectively, surpass Western systems in both range and weight of ammunition.

The AN-94 ("Abakan"), which is twice as effective in combat as the AK-47 - the legendary Kalashnikov assault rifle-- stands out among the leading examples of Russian machine guns.

Among the novelties in military shipbuilding, there is the world's largest missile cruiser, "Piotr Velikii" (Peter the Great), the missile ship "Bora", and an air-cushion catamaran capable of speeds up to 80 knots. The anti-submarine missile "Shkval" flies under water at a speed several times faster than a torpedo, competing with Western models both in speed and combat effectiveness.

---

[55] Sergey Kolyadin, "The Fighter of the Fifth Generation Will Arrive to the Armed Forces in 8-10 Years." *Nezavisimoe Voennoe Obozrenie,* no. 9, March 17-23, 2000, p.6.

Nuclear weapons remain the most dangerous means of mass destruction. Their storage and elimination are among Russia's most burdensome current problems. The Russian project to ensure the security of military nuclear sites, the greater part of which has been financed under the U.S. Nunn-Lugar program, is still not completed. Many nuclear sites lack anti-ramming barriers, alarm systems with autonomous power supplies, or even a closed-circuit TV surveillance system for the guards, which any Western consumer electronics store has. Meanwhile, weapons-grade plutonium might be a rather attractive objective for terrorists.

According to Russian General Aleksandr Lebed, former Secretary of the Russian National Security Council: "Russia produced 132 nuclear "suitcase" bombs, each with a 10 kiloton yield. Only 48 remain in Russia's inventory; the rest disappeared".[56] Such a "nuclear suitcase" can easily be transported and placed near a dam, an airport, or a nuclear power station. This devastating weapon is remotely operated, and capable of reducing to ruins not only such facilities, but also a medium-sized city. These suitcase-sized nuclear weapons of mass destruction could be planted at "dead drop" sites anywhere in any country and produce a remote-triggered nuclear blast at any desirable moment. (Dead drops are "sites at which one agent could leave an item and another could pick it up".)[57]

Russia still has more chemical weapons than any other nation. Such agents as mustard gas and various mixtures are especially

---

56 "FBI Director Admits Russian May Have Secret Weapons in U.S.," www.stonenews.com/infofolders/Military-all/Military Russia, November 8, 1999.

57 Siobhan Darrow, "Former Soviet spy: Small nuclear devices planted in U.S." www.cnn.com/2000/U.S./01/28/spy.hearing p1, January 28, 2000

dangerous since they have been stored for more than half a century in steel containers. Besides, their service lives expired twenty years ago. Moreover, thousands tons of them, as well as the most dangerous nerve agents (such as VX, sarin, and soman) are still in artillery shells, aerial bombs, and missiles. More than a million of these dangerous munitions are concentrated in five arsenals in central Russia.

Russia developed programs to eliminate these weapons and peacefully destroy their components. However, that requires building expensive special facilities. These facilities have been designed, and technologies have been developed for eliminating chemical weapons. But implementation is stalled by a lack of funds. According to calculations by Russian experts, implementation would require several billion dollars. The West was expected to allocate funds for these purposes, but no adequate funding has been made available so far.

I have described Russian armaments that are superior to those of other countries. Many more systems keep pace with the existing level of world military technology.

Given such achievements, it seems that the Russian Army should be one of the best-armed military forces in the world. Nevertheless, the quality of its arms deteriorated throughout the 1990s, due to the colossal drop in governmental military orders. In some cases, the Russian military forces are not even familiar with many of the aforementioned systems, since the army lacks resources to purchase such arms. In the past decade, the economic crisis and the sharp decline in the military budget and weapons purchases have led to a situation where only a quarter of the Russian military is equipped with modern armaments.

Today, there are many signs that stagnation in the MIC will end and a new cycle in weapons production will begin. The distinctive feature of this cycle is that Russia will produce the latest advanced weapons based on R&D and designs that were done during the deep economic crisis.

But there are no signs that MIC will limit its production of the next generation of weapons to production for the Russian Army alone. There are no signs that MIC will not use its excess manufacturing capacities to produce weapons for foreign armies. As advanced Russian weapons – many of which are equal or superior to their Western counterparts – proliferate around the world, they may become a major threat to international stability in the 21st century if they fall into the hands of international terrorists.

5.7. BIOLOGICAL WEAPONS

Introductory Remarks

Vlad E. Genin

For nearly two decades, the Soviet Union, and then post-Soviet Russia, maintained an offensive biological warfare (BW) program in violation of the 1972 Biological and Toxin Weapons Convention (BWC), which Moscow had signed and ratified. The BWC bans all development, production, and stockpiling of microbial and toxin agents except in types and quantities that can be justified for prophylactic, protective, or other peaceful purposes. Today Russia claims to have eliminated all offensive BW activities, but Western countries remain concerned that research and development with offensive applications may be continuing. The U.S. government, for example, has assessed that some biological production facilities in Russia, "in addition to being engaged in legitimate activity, may be maintaining the capability to produce BW agents." [58]

In addition to these lingering concerns, the legacy of the massive Soviet BW program, together with continued economic displacement in Russia, pose a serious risk of proliferation—the danger that sensitive BW-related materials, production equipment, and know-how will find their way from Russia, Kazakhstan, and other former Soviet republics to outlaw states and

---

[58] U.S. Arms Control and Disarmament Agency, *Threat Control Through Arms Control: Annual Report to Congress 1996* (Washington, D.C.: ACDA, 1997), p. 87.

terrorist organizations seeking a BW capability. A number of countries, including Iraq, Iran, Syria, and Libya, view biological weapons as "the poor man's atomic bomb," and have sought to purchase seed cultures of dangerous pathogens, along with the means to cultivate them in large quantities. Because nearly all of the relevant production equipment is dual-use, with legitimate civilian applications in the manufacture of antibiotics, biological pesticides, vitamins, and fermented products, preventing the spread of this technology is extremely difficult.

Nevertheless, the mass production of disease agents is not the only hurdle to the acquisition of an operational BW capability. Converting deadly or incapacitating microbial pathogens—bacteria, viruses, and rickettsiae—into effective weapons of mass destruction requires drying and milling techniques, additive formulations, and specialized delivery systems that are not widely known, and that require sophisticated scientific know-how to implement—information that former Soviet bioweapons scientists acquired through years of trial and effort, and presumably still retain. According to former senior Soviet BW scientist Ken Alibek, "The most virulent culture in a test tube is useless as an offensive weapon until it has been put through a process that gives it stability and predictability. The manufacturing technique is, in a sense, the real weapon, and it is harder to develop than individual agents."[59]

59 Ken Alibek with Stephen Handelman, "Biohazard: The Chilling True Story of the Largest Covert Biological Weapons Program in the World—Told from the Inside by the Man Who Ran It." (New York: Random House, 1999), p. 97.

What is the current status of the facilities and personnel formerly involved in the Soviet offensive BW program, to what extent do they pose a proliferation risk, and what are the prospects for converting them to peaceful activities?

Jonathan B. Tucker

At least until 1992, the Soviet/Russian offensive biological warfare (BW) program developed a variety of anti-personnel, anti-crop, and anti-livestock agents, some of them genetically engineered for greater military effectiveness, together with sophisticated munitions and delivery systems. The Fifteenth Directorate of the Soviet Ministry of Defense (MOD) operated dedicated military microbiological facilities in Kirov, Leningrad (St. Petersburg), Strizhi, Sverdlovsk (Ekaterinburg), and Zagorsk (Sergiev Posad). In addition, a complex called the Biopreparat All-Union Production Association, made up of ostensibly civilian pharmaceutical facilities, secretly engaged in offensive BW activities.

Biopreparat was founded by the Communist Party Central Committee in 1973, a year after the Soviet Union signed the Biological and Toxin Weapons Convention (BTWC) but before it ratified the treaty in 1975.[60] The rationale for the Biopreparat complex was to establish a clandestine BW program within a civilian entity that would provide an effective cover, although offensive work continued in MOD-controlled facilities as well.[61] More than 60,000 scientists, engineers, and

[60] Even prior to formal ratification, the Vienna Convention on Treaties forbids signatories from taking actions that undermine the basic aims of an agreement.

[61] "Biological Weapons in the Former Soviet Union: An Interview with Dr. Kenneth Alibek," *The Nonproliferation Review*, vol. 6, no. 3 (Spring-Summer

technicians in the Soviet Union worked on BW-related research, development, and production. Biopreparat employed at least 30,000 people, the Fifteenth Directorate of the MOD about 15,000, and the Ministry of Agriculture about 10,000.[62] Additional scientists and technicians did BW-related work under the auspices of the Ministry of Health, the Ministry of Chemical Industry, the KGB, the USSR Academy of Sciences, and possibly other agencies, although the number of personnel involved cannot be reliably estimated. An Inter-Agency Scientific and Technical Council coordinated the flow of information among the various ministries and state scientific organizations involved in the Soviet BW program.[63]

Soviet microbiologists weaponized about a dozen antipersonnel agents, including the microorganisms that cause anthrax, plague, brucellosis, tularemia, smallpox, glanders, and Marburg hemorrhagic fever, and conducted open-air testing of biological munitions on Vozrozhdenie Island in the Aral Sea.[64] A special division of the Ministry of Agriculture was established to research and manufacture anti-livestock and anti-crop weapons under the code-name "Ecology," including variants of foot-and-mouth disease, rinderpest, African swine fever, and psittacosis.[65] The Third Main Directorate of the Ministry of

---

1999), p. 4. Biopreparat was placed under the civilian "cover" of the Main Administration of the Microbiological Industry (Glavmikrobioprom).

[62] Ibid., p. 5.

[63] Ken Alibek with Stephen Handelman, *Biohazard: The Chilling True Story of the Largest Covert Biological Weapons Program in the World—Told From Inside by the Man Who Ran It* (New York: Random House, 1999), p. 158.

[64] Judith Miller, "At Bleak Asian Site, Killer Germs Survive," *New York Times*, June 2, 1999, pp. A1, A10.

[65] Alibek with Handelman, *Biohazard*, pp. 37-38; Steve Goldstein, "U.S. Could Face New Terror Tactic: Agricultural Warfare," *Philadelphia Inquirier*, June 22, 1999, p. 1.

Health also developed biological and toxin agents for assassination and special operations under a program code-named "Flute."[66]

By the mid-1990s, the Biopreparat complex comprised more than 40 facilities, including major research and development centers in Moscow, Leningrad, Obolensk, and Koltsovo (near Novosibirsk). Many of these facilities were dual-purpose and did some legitimate work on pharmaceuticals, biotechnology, and vaccines. For example, the Center for Applied Microbiology in Obolensk devoted 80 to 90 percent of its effort to BW, while the Institute of Immunology in Lybuchany spent about 50 percent of its time on BW and the rest on civilian pharmaceutical research.[67]

After Mikhail Gorbachev came to power in 1985, he approved a five-year plan for the BW program that included the construction of a 630-liter viral reactor to mass-produce smallpox virus at Biopreparat's "Vector" Center for Virology and Biotechnology in Koltsovo.[68] Another top priority of the five-year plan was to alter the genetic structure of known pathogens, such as the bacterial agents that cause plague, anthrax, tularemia, and glanders, to make them resistant to Western antibiotics.[69] In addition, under a project code-named "Bonfire," Soviet military scientists worked to develop regulatory peptides (strings of amino acids)

---

[66] Judith Miller and William J. Broad, "Germ Weapons: In Soviet Past or in the New Russia's Future?" *New York Times*, December 28, 1998, p. A1.

[67] "Biological Weapons in the Former Soviet Union", p. 4.

[68] Alibek with Handelman, *Biohazard*, pp. 117-118. The Soviet BW program was cut back before large-scale production of smallpox virus could take place at Vector.

[69] John Barry, "Planning a Plague?" *Newsweek*, February 1, 1993, pp. 40-41.

that could modify human moods, emotions, heart rhythms, and sleep patterns.[70]

Finally, capabilities were put in place for the large-scale production of BW agents. In peacetime, the MOD facilities at Kirov, Sverdlovsk, and Zagorsk manufactured and stockpiled BW agents such as anthrax bacteria or smallpox virus. The Biopreparat complex also established "mothballed" production lines at plants in Omutninsk, Pokrov, Penza, Kurgan, Berdsk, and Stepnogorsk (Kazakhstan) that would have been mobilized for the manufacture of BW agents in the event of a major crisis or war.[71]

Downsizing Biopreparat

In January 1992, after high-level Soviet defectors to the United Kingdom and the United States had revealed the existence of the top-secret Biopreparat complex to Western intelligence, Russian President Boris Yeltsin admitted that there had been "a lag in implementing" the BTWC by the Soviet Union and then Russia. In April 1992, Yeltsin issued a decree titled *On Ensuring the Implementation of International Pledges in the Sphere of Biological Weapons*, which ordered the halt of all offensive BW activities.

As a result of Yeltsin's decree and the crisis afflicting the Russian economy, the operating and research budgets of many Biopreparat research centers were slashed, and the salaries of thousands of scientists and technicians were delayed from three to six months and

---

[70] Alibek with Handelman, *Biohazard*, pp. 154-155; Miller and Broad, "Germ Weapons."

[71] James Adams, "The Red Death: The Untold Story of Russia's Secret Biological Weapons," *Sunday Times* (London), March 27, 1994, section 4, pp. 1-2.

stagnated at a time of soaring inflation. This financial hardship led to an internal "brain drain" from the leading Biopreparat institutes, including the Center for Applied Microbiology at Obolensk, the "Vector" Center for Virology and Biotechnology in Koltsovo, and the Institute for Ultrapure Biological Preparations in St. Petersburg. Between 1990 and 1996, for example, the Obolensk facility lost 54 percent of its staff, including 28 percent of its Ph.D. scientists.[72]

The downsizing of Biopreparat raised fears in the West that former Soviet BW scientists might be recruited by would-be proliferators and terrorist organizations. Indeed, anecdotal evidence suggests that countries of proliferation concern have made significant recruitment efforts.[73] According to the *New York Times*, Iran has offered former BW scientists in Russia and Kazakhstan jobs paying as much as $5,000 a month—far more than these individuals can make in a year at home.[74]

To prevent further brain drain, the U.S. government launched several initiatives with the Biopreparat institutes to enable former BW scientists to remain at home, support their families, and live in dignity without being tempted to sell their weapons-related knowledge to the highest bidder. Based on a pilot program conducted in 1998 by the U.S. National Academy of Sciences, the Department of Defense is supporting collaborative research projects between former Soviet BW specialists and American microbiologists.[75] These joint projects aim to prevent the

---

[72] Judith Miller and William J. Broad, "Bio-Weapons in Mind, Iranians Lure Needy Ex-Soviet Scientists," *New York Times*, December 8, 1998, pp. A1, A12.

[73] Sergei Pluzhnikov and Aleksei Shvedov, "Terrible Secrets of the 'Ogarkov System'," *Sovershenno Sekretno*, no. 4 (1998), pp. 12-14.

[74] Miller and Broad, "Bio-Weapons in Mind, Iranians Lure Needy Ex-Soviet Scientists."

[75] U.S. Department of Defense, "Expanded Threat Reduction Initiative," March 1999, p. 19.

foreign recruitment of Russian scientists with dangerous knowledge, while increasing U.S. access to formerly secret Biopreparat laboratories.[76]

Additional bilateral support for civilian research by former Soviet BW scientists is provided by the National Aeronautics and Space Administration (NASA), the Defense Advanced Research Projects Agency (DARPA), and the U.S. Department of Energy's Initiatives for Proliferation Prevention (IPP) program. The IPP program funds the development of advanced applied technology close to the market at eighteen former BW facilities, including Vector and Obolensk. The Civilian Research and Development Foundation (CRDF), working under contract to the Departments of State, Defense, and Energy, manages joint research projects and scientific exchange programs involving U.S. and Russian scientists.

In addition to these bilateral initiatives, the Moscow-based International Science and Technology Center (ISTC), an intergovernmental organization sponsored by the United States, the European Union, Japan, and Russia, provides grants to former Soviet weapons scientists so they can work on civilian research projects.[77] A sister-program based in Kiev supports former weapons scientists in Ukraine.

Some security analysts believe that collaborative research projects focusing on highly dangerous pathogens may be counterproductive because they enable former bioweapons scientists to

---

[76] Interview with Andrew Weber, Special Advisor for Threat Reduction Policy, U.S. Department of Defense, February 8, 1999.

[77] Amy E. Smithson, *Toxic Archipelago: Preventing Proliferation from the Former Soviet Chemical and Biological Weapons Complexes* (Washington, D.C.: Henry L. Stimson Center, Report No. 32, December 1999), pp. 22-30.

conduct research that has both civilian and military applications. Such projects, the critics contend, should instead be directed against disease agents that are of public health concern but have no potential BW applications.[78] U.S. government officials respond that Russia will continue to do research on dangerous pathogens in any case, and that it is in the U.S. interest to engage the leading scientific experts at the former Biopreparat institutes and guide their work in peaceful directions.[79]

Conversion of Former BW Production Facilities

Some commercialization of military biotechnologies took place during the Soviet era, when vaccines, antibiotics, and production technologies developed in MOD-controlled microbiological facilities were transferred to Biopreparat for civilian application.[80] Similarly, during the Russian political and economic crisis of the early 1990s, a few Biopreparat facilities pursued commercial joint ventures with European firms in a desperate bid to secure lucrative export markets. Even so, little effort was made to convert existing military facilities to civilian activities, and "conversion" was limited to the attempted commercialization of past research accomplishments and spin-offs from ongoing defense work.[81]

---

[78] Milton Leitenberg, "The Possibilities and Limitations of Biological Weapons Conversion", in Erhard Geissler et al., eds., *Conversion of Former BTW Facilities* (Netherlands: Kluwer Academic Publishers, 1998), pp. 119-133.

[79] Interview with Anne M. Harrington, Senior Coordinator for Nonproliferation/Science Cooperation, U.S. Department of State, February 8, 1999.

[80] Anthony Rimmington, "From Military to Industrial Complex? The Conversion of Biological Weapons Facilities in the Russian Federation," *Contemporary Security Policy*, vol. 17, no. 1 (April 1996), p. 90.

[81] Ibid., p. 91.

After Yeltsin's decree of April 1992, Biopreparat became a joint stock company, and it has since spawned numerous firms and associations that play a key role in Russia's civilian pharmaceutical industry. Nevertheless, former military personnel who were intimately associated with the offensive BW program continue to hold key positions within Biopreparat and the Russian biopharmaceutical industry as a whole, raising doubts about Moscow's commitment to conversion.[82]

The pace of conversion at former BW production facilities has also been limited by a lack of Western investment and assistance. Under the Cooperative Threat Reduction (CTR) program, the U.S. Department of Defense is supporting the dismantlement of fermentor tanks and other equipment designed for the large-scale production of anthrax bacteria at the Biopreparat plant in Stepnogorsk, Kazakhstan. The U.S. Congress has specifically blocked the CTR program from supporting conversion-related activities, however, and private companies in the United States and Europe have so far failed to fill the gap.

A few Biopreparat institutes have managed to negotiate cooperative ventures with Western pharmaceutical firms, but such arrangements remain the exception. In 1997, for example, Searle Pharmaceuticals, a subsidiary of Monsanto Corporation, agreed to invest $6 million in a $32 million joint venture with Biopreparat's All-Russian Center for Molecular Diagnostics and Therapy to build a pharmaceutical production plant at Izvarino, fifteen miles southwest of Moscow.[83] Planning for this facility had begun in 1994 with seed money from the U.S. Agency for International Development. The new plant opened its

---

[82] Anthony Rimmington, "Fragmentation and Proliferation? The Fate of the Soviet Union's Offensive Biological Weapons Programme," *Contemporary Security Policy*, vol. 20, no. 1, April 1999, pp. 86-110.
[83] Ibid., p. 100.

doors on September 15, 1999, and it is currently producing generic antibiotics and drugs to treat cardiovascular and gastrointestinal diseases. As the first pharmaceutical production facility in Russia built to meet stringent Good Manufacturing Practice (GMP) operating standards, the Izvarino plant will be accredited to export medications to Western countries.[84] Nevertheless, this joint venture is not a true example of defense conversion because it was built on a green-field site. Searle considered and rejected the option of renovating an existing Biopreparat facility because of concerns about possible contamination.

Conversion of former BW production facilities will become self-sustaining only if they are able to produce and sell commercial products for domestic or foreign markets. Given the shortage of vaccines and basic medications in Russia, it was widely assumed in the early 1990s that former BW production facilities would be rapidly converted to the manufacture of vaccines and pharmaceuticals. Russian government funding has been lacking, however, and cooperative ventures with Western partners have not materialized. Beyond the problems of chronic political and economic instability in Russia, U.S. and European drug companies have concluded that converting former BW facilities is not worth the trouble and expense.

Although there are pockets of quality among the Biopreparat institutes, years of neglect and lack of funding have taken their toll. Poor construction standards and possible contamination (particularly with persistent spore-forming agents such as anthrax) would raise the expense of renovation above the cost of building an entirely new facility. Moreover, Western pharmaceutical companies have no desire to utilize

---

[84] Telephone interview with Michael Fleming, Searle Pharmaceuticals, Chicago, November 8, 1999.

buildings that may have been involved in BW activities to manufacture products aimed at human consumption.[85] Another obstacle to conversion has been a lack of the managerial expertise needed to adapt former BW facilities to new civilian market conditions. In Kazakhstan, for example, Russian and foreign pharmaceutical companies have carved out a dominant share of the domestic market, limiting the opportunities for Kazakhstani firms.[86]

Given these harsh economic realities, many former Soviet BW production plants have scaled back their conversion plans. Biopreparat has sought to bypass Western regulatory standards by producing pharmaceuticals for markets in developing countries such as Brazil, North Korea, India, Mongolia, and China.[87] Other strategies for the conversion of former BW facilities include the packaging and wholesale distribution of generic drugs produced by Western pharmaceutical firms, or the manufacture of products such as ethanol or biopesticides that do not require a sterile environment or strict quality-control procedures.[88] Following the example of the Searle cooperative venture at Izvarino, Russian managers have also invited Western companies to build new manufacturing plants at green-field sites adjacent to former BW facilities. Such plants could take advantage of the pool of highly trained

---

[85] Anne M. Harrington, "Redirecting Biological Weapons Expertise: Realities and Opportunities in the Former Soviet Union," *Chemical Weapons Convention Bulletin*, no. 29, September 1995, p.4.

[86] Gulbarshyn Bozheyeva, Yerlan Kunakbayev, and Dastan Yeleukenov, "Former Soviet Biological Weapons Facilities in Kazakhstan: Past, Present, and Future," Occasional Paper No. 1, Center for Nonproliferation Studies, Monterey Institute of International Studies, June 1999, p. 24.

[87] Rimmington, "From Military to Industrial Complex," p. 93.

[88] Bozheyeva, Kunakbayev, and Yeleukenov, "Former Soviet Biological Weapons Facilities in Kazakhstan," p. 21.

scientific and technical personnel and the available industrial infrastructure, such as electricity and steam generation.[89]

Perhaps the greatest obstacle to the conversion of former Soviet BW facilities is not economic but political: Moscow's failure to come clean about the full scale and scope of its offensive BW program. Even more troubling, the military microbiological institutes under the control of the Russian Ministry of Defense remain shrouded in secrecy and off-limits to Western scientists, arousing suspicions that they have not entirely abandoned offensively oriented research and development.[90] These corrosive suspicions, fueled by Moscow's lack of transparency, have undermined support for investment in conversion projects by Western governments and corporations. Unless Russia can build international confidence that its BW program is now strictly defensive and in full compliance with the biological weapons treaty, external funding for civilian research, and private investment in conversion activities, will not be politically sustainable over the long run.

---

[89] Rimmington, "From Military to Industrial Complex," p. 93.

[90] Research and development on defensive measures against biological weapons are permitted under the Biological and Toxin Weapons Convention.

PART SIX

Defense Conversion in the World: The Way It Was

INTRODUCTION

Vlad E. Genin

We know, of course, that the problem of converting arms industries to civilian production is neither new, nor peculiar to Russia. The United States, France, Great Britain, China and other countries have partially or totally covered this ground before.

But Russian conversion involves some special and very difficult conditions. On the one hand, these conditions– economic, political and social – reflect the background of reform; the legacy and burden of the past. On the other hand, conversion problems have been aggravated by the conflicting policies and theories of political authorities and government departments in charge of the defense industry, which changed frequently in the 1990s. But the difference between Russian conversion and that in other countries is not limited just to external conditions; there was also a big discrepancy between conversion as planned and conversion as implemented. The interaction of all these factors resulted in a very complex problem, which Russians call "specifics of Russian conversion".

It would be wrong to think that other countries that have previously undergone their respective versions of conversion did not encounter some "specifics" of their own. Each of these countries started its conversion with its own unique background, in its own special conditions, and found its own way to convert its defense industry. However, the many paths to conversion in different countries also had some common aspects. Analyzing the experience of other countries allows us to extract a number of lessons that can be applied to Russian conditions. From the outset of the conversion effort, Russia had the opportunity to analyze the conversion experience and results of other countries, in order to select the most effective ways of implementing conversion in the Russian environment. Russia could have extracted the valuable essence of the American and Chinese experiences, for all three countries are comparable in their geographic and, to a certain degree, industrial conditions. It would have been much easier, and made more sense, than for Russia to go its own way, using trial and error. The effort to restructure the militarized economy might have been a success, and not caused the Russian people the current bitterness and disappointment.

6.1. CONVERSION IN THE UNITED STATES VS. RUSSIA[1]

Introductory Remarks

Vlad E. Genin

From the very beginning of Russian conversion, its authors understood the importance of the American experience. Sooner or later, the process of defense conversion in Russia will enter a new stage, having analyzed all previous mistakes and failures. That is why the thorough study of the earlier American and Russian conversion experience is of vital importance, in providing both the "big picture" and specific details. It is necessary to analyze similarities and differences in order for Russian conversion, which is still in its early stages, to yield concrete results, and break out of the pattern of making the same mistakes over and over again.

David M. Bernstein

Introduction

Comparing conversion in the United States with that in the Soviet Union/Russia (SU/R) is to some extent comparing apples and

[1] For a discussion of conversion in other countries (as well as in Russia and the United States), see the Bonn International Center for Conversion (BICC) *Conversion Survey 1996: Global Disarmament, Demilitarization, and Demobilization* (Oxford University Press, 1996).

oranges.[2] The corporate, economic, and political circumstances in the two countries differed greatly in almost every respect, as did the need for conversion and the options available to companies. A more relevant comparison is that of strategies for adjusting to military procurement reductions, which may include conversion, and the results of implementing those strategies. In addition to conversion, adjustment strategies can include downsizing by reducing employment; disposing of or deactivating assets; and corporate restructuring through mergers, acquisitions, and divestitures. In this section, conversion means the utilization of assets (human, technological, physical, or financial), previously engaged in military activities, for new profit-making civilian activities. The new utilization can be the result of overt actions by companies (active conversion) or of the action of others, such as employees relocating voluntarily (passive conversion).

In the years following the end of the Cold War, both the SU/R and the United States engaged in major reductions in their military forces and procurements. This was largely a new experience for the Soviet Union, whereas the United States had gone through large reductions following World War II, the Korean War, and the Vietnam War. In one of the most dramatic departures from Cold War attitudes, the Soviet Union actually approached the United States for advice on how to convert its military-industrial complex (MIC) to civilian activity.

With the collapse of the Soviet Union, Russia inherited a disproportionately large fraction of the Soviet MIC, and hence the adjustment problem has been greater for Russia than for the other newly independent states (NIS), although it is also a significant issue in several

---

2 SU/R is used herein to denote effects and practices that spanned the end of the Soviet era and the early post-Soviet era in Russia.

of the others. The Russian government continued, and accelerated, the reduction in military procurement as the economy continued to decline. At the same time, Russia also instituted a variety of economic reform programs intended to introduce a market economy. Planners expected that defense conversion would take place within this market (or at least transitional) economy. This potentially helped, in that a market environment could ultimately improve the chances of conversion, but, on the other hand, it exacerbated the near-term problems in that the infrastructure of the command economy, however inefficient, was no longer fully functional, and it had not been replaced by a market-oriented one. The market economy infrastructure is still not yet broadly operational, although much of the basic structure is in place.[3] Many enterprises have chosen, or had little option but, to operate in a non-market economy predicated on inter-enterprise debt, tax delinquency, nonpayment of wages, and de facto bankruptcy.[4]

The assumption that the United States had much knowledge or experience specifically in conversion that was relevant to the Soviet situation was a poor one. The United States has had very little success with conversion, and little of its experience was applicable to the circumstances in the Soviet Union. The rapid increase in civilian production in the United States following World War II was primarily a reconversion of civilian-based assets that had been converted to military production during the war. During WWII civilian producers, such as the automobile manufacturers, turned to making military hardware with the full intent of reconverting in a few years. Following the Cold War,

---

[3] Anders Aslund, *How Russia Became a Market Economy* (The Brookings Institution, Washington, D.C., 1995).

[4] Clifford G. Gaddy and Barry W. Ickes, *"Beyond a Bailout: Time to Face Reality About Russia's Virtual Economy,"* (Brookings Institution, 1998).

companies that had been military producers by choice for decades were faced with adjusting to a loss of demand for their products.

Notwithstanding the lack of utility of the American experience in conversion, the post–Cold War dialog between Russians and Americans has had considerable value. A major benefit was the fact of the dialog itself, and the resulting openness and transparency that it engendered between the government and industrial military establishments on the two sides. An ensuing benefit was the development in the United States of an enhanced understanding of the conversion and general economic reform process in the SU/R, which has informed technical assistance programs and stimulated some public and private investment in Russian industry, even though the level of such investment is still small. Yet another benefit was the exposure of Russians to market economic factors and private ownership, even in the defense industry.

The environment for and processes of conversion in the two countries have far more differences than similarities, and it is of value to understand these differences in order to support the process in Russia, where the need is far more acute.[5] The environment involves not only the size, rate, and nature of the reductions in military procurements, but also the economic system and the state of the economy in which the reductions are embedded. These circumstances, as well as the political system, limit the processes available to deal with the reductions, whether through conversion or otherwise.

---

[5] David Bernstein, William J. Perry, "Defense Conversion in Russia: A Strategic Imperative," *Stanford Journal of International Affairs*, Summer 1993.

The Changes In Military Procurement

It is difficult to measure the decrease in military procurement in the SU/R, because of the inadequacy of budgetary data, the non-market pricing of inputs and the changes resulting from the breakup of the Soviet Union.[6] Estimates of the Soviet military budget differ by about a factor of two, but there is consensus that it was at least a factor of two greater than that of the United States as a percentage of GDP, with estimates ranging up to 25% or more.[7] There is also considerable variation in estimates of the decline in military procurement, but it clearly dropped by approximately a factor of five from the end of 1988 to the end of 1992, with most of the drop in 1991 and 1992. Most of the key points of comparison between the United States and Russia about conversion can be made without quantitatively precise data. It is clear that the reduction in procurement in the SU/R was a demand shock of the order of 5-10% of GDP per year for two years. By contrast, in the United States the military budget dropped by about a factor of two (from about 6 to 3% of GDP) over the decade from the mid-eighties to mid-nineties, or about 0.3% of GDP per year. The difference between the two countries is even greater in terms of jobs. U.S. plants had more modern equipment and cost controls that led to a disproportionately smaller work force than in SU/R. This can be seen from the sheer discrepancy of size of U.S. and Soviet factories engaged in similar production.[8] Therefore the difference

---

[6] For a comprehensive review of the literature on estimates of Soviet defense spending and the reductions in SU/R defense procurements in the early 1990s, see John S. Earle and Ivan Komarov, "Measuring Defense Conversion in Russian Industry," Center for International Security and Arms Control, Stanford, 1996.

[7] Julian Cooper, "Transformation of the Russian Defense Industry."

[8] Clifford G. Gaddy, *The Price of the Past: Russia's Struggle with the Legacy of*

between the jobs lost in the SU/R over that in the United States was even greater than the difference in loss of expenditures. Loss of jobs was the primary concern in the United States from a public policy standpoint. Loss of jobs, economic decline, and the need for domestically produced civilian products were all of importance in the SU/R.

There are other ways in which the reductions had far more impact in Russia. One is that the government was often very delinquent in paying for the weaponry that it did order; this, coupled with the high rate of inflation, exacerbated the situation considerably. In the United States, military procurements, while reduced, were quite predictable, and they were paid for as contracted. In the SU/R, the breakup of the Union and the lack of a clear new military doctrine prevented an orderly, albeit smaller, procurement process. Finally, the availability and price of inputs was extremely uncertain during this period in the SU/R.

The Condition And Structure Of The Countries' Economies

A major cause of the reduction in military expenditure in Russia was the deteriorating state of the economy; in the United States the economy went through normal cycles, but nothing of a magnitude to force drastic reductions in military expenditures. There were also structural ways in which the U.S. economy was far better positioned to deal with reduced military procurements. First, all of the institutions of a market economy were well established. Foremost among these were active capital markets and other financial service institutions to enable a full spectrum of adjustment strategies. There was also a commercial code and markets for consumer and industrial products, as well as competitive

---

a Militarized Economy (Washington, D.C.: The Brookings Institution, 1996).

suppliers of all types of inputs. The Soviet Union had the old command economic system, which had been one of the major causes of the economic collapse in the first place. Following the breakup of the Soviet Union, Russia started to dismantle the command system before it had a replacement for it. The profile of the U.S. economy in terms of the ratio of military to civilian production has been balanced by market forces. In addition to the basic strength of the U.S. economy, and its ability to absorb the small (relative to national industrial capacity) excess capacity of the defense industry, there was also a strong social safety net that was able to support displaced workers fairly effectively. In the Soviet Union a safety net had previously been obviated by the guarantee of full employment, health care, and pensions. In addition, many social services were delivered by the enterprises. The combination of the lack of a safety net and the financial stress on the enterprises created a very difficult situation for the unemployed, underemployed, and retirees. Even many employed workers have not always been paid.

The roles of the defense industries were also qualitatively quite different in the SU/R and the United States. The Soviet defense industry comprised essentially all of the high technology base of the country. Almost all civilian production involving electronics, aviation, and other forms of technology was carried out by the defense industry. Civilian goods comprised about 40% of the output of the military industry.[9] This is in sharp contrast to the United States, where civilian technology, especially in electronics and computers, leads military technology in volume, speed of innovation, and sophistication by a wide margin. Both

---

[9] It is true that some major U.S. corporations (e.g. Boeing, General Electric, IBM) produce both civilian and military products, but the two sides of these companies function as virtually two independent companies.

countries have been attempting to use dual technologies for military as well as civilian applications, but the concept is very different in the two countries. In the United States, the objective is primarily to use advanced civilian technologies and components in military systems; in Russia it is more to use military technologies for civilian applications.[10]

The markets for the products of conversion were also very different in the SU/R and the United States. Conversion works better in the United States when the conversion products are on a comparable scale of technology with the former military production, and existing core competencies are employed.[11] In the United States the basic consumer goods markets are saturated and grow very slowly, but there is a substantial market for new high technology products.[12] In fact, in many cases (e.g., personal computers, fax machines, VCRs, cellular phones) the new products created their own very large market demand. In the SU/R there was a large need for consumer goods, and, until inflation destroyed savings, there was also a pent-up demand. Since the drop in the economy, the market for high technology products has dropped greatly. What markets there are for both consumer goods and technology products has been strongly penetrated by imports, which are often of superior quality and lower price. The market demand for industrial output was further reduced by the breakup of the Soviet Union

---

[10] See Jacques Gansler, "Defense Conversion: Transforming the Arsenal of Democracy," A Twentieth Century Fund Book, 1995, and William J. Perry, “Defense Investment Strategy,” *Foreign Affairs*, Spring 1989, vol. 68, no. 2, pp. 72-92.

[11] Jacques S. Gansler, "Defense Conversion: Transforming the Arsenal of Democracy," A Twentieth Century Fund Book, 1995.

[12] Bonn International Center for Conversion, Conversion Survey, 1996, Chapter 3.

and of Comecon, which reduced trade among the former republics of the Soviet Union and the countries of the Warsaw Treaty Organization.

Structure And Roles Of Companies[13]

In addition to the differences in the external economic environment, the internal aspects of the companies were also very different, with the U.S. companies being far more adaptable to various forms of adjustment. The Russian companies were not fully rounded business units in the market-economic sense. They did not have functions such as marketing, finance, contracts, stockholder relations, and corporate development. To the small extent that any of these functions had been performed at all, they had been performed by the ministries. In addition, the Russian companies did not have an internal structure that allowed for segregation and tracking of direct and indirect costs by business units.[14] Most of the Russian defense companies were still state-owned or just starting the process of corporatization and privatization. Finally, the Russian companies had a far larger role in the lives of their employees and communities. They were the providers of many social services, and they were often the providers and maintainers of community facilities ranging from sports and cultural facilities to infra-structural elements such as roads and local transit systems. The Russian companies, many of which also had nonmilitary activities, also

---

13 "Companies" is used here to refer to Soviet/Russian enterprises regardless of ownership structure.

14 Tatiana Krylova, "Principal Differences in Accounting Systems in Russia and the United States" in David Bernstein, editor, *Defense Industry Restructuring, in Russia: Case Studies and Analysis* (Stanford University, 1994).

experienced a large decline in these activities brought on by the weakened state of the economy.

By contrast, the U.S. companies were complete business units that were already functioning in a competitive market environment. While the defense market was monopolistic, it was still competitive and involved marketing, cost accounting and control, finance, and corporate structural changes when circumstances dictated. The U.S. defense companies were privately owned, and were financially responsible only to their shareholders. They were only responsible contractually to the government. They participated voluntarily in the defense market, in varying degrees over the years. The government did not guarantee their financial viability, nor did they have any obligation to contract with the government or to convert. Many U.S. companies refuse to contract with the government at all. Some defense companies chose to assist displaced personnel in making their professional transitions, but they did not bear any responsibility for their continued employment, nor did they provide any of the basic social needs such as housing. Many of the U.S. companies also had nonmilitary activities, but unlike in the Russian case in general, these were not adversely affected by a sudden reduction in demand, because the overall economy was stable and healthy.

The Roles Of The Governments

In the SU/R the state had an inherent conflict of interest, in that it was both the owner and the customer of the defense (and other) companies. As the customer it was responsible for the decrease in orders, and as the owner it was responsible for the adjustments of the enterprises to this decrease. Its execution of these two functions was not self-consistent. The initial Soviet approach was to stay within the command economic system, and initiate a program intended to convert a substantial portion of the military industry to civilian production. The stated goal was to go from a ratio of military to civilian production of 60/40 to one of 40/60. This was to be accomplished by conversion in production, and by transferring some nonmilitary enterprises under the aegis of the MIC ministries. This change of ratio was achieved but with a sharp decline in both military and civilian production.

In spite of the fact that as customer, the state knew that orders would not be forthcoming for this civilian output, as owner, it failed to take the necessary steps of downsizing and restructuring the enterprises so that they could become competitive. In addition, the state, which also had the role of investor, did not provide the investment capital for conversion. Under these circumstances the state's adjustment strategy was doomed to failure.

In 1992 the Russian government enacted a comprehensive conversion program, but failed to finance it. As a result the burden of conversion fell upon the enterprises, which gained increased autonomy during this period. The program known as *economic conversion* also gained support in this period. This concept called for financing conversion through the profits of increased foreign arms sales. With the possible exception of the combat aircraft sector, this program has also failed. Beginning in 1993 the official programs called for priority to be given to conversion in certain specified industrial sectors, which were similar to those specified in the late Soviet era. These programs, like their predecessors, share the problems of inadequate funding and central control, and have not as yet produced the hoped-for results.[15]

---

[15] Bonn International Center for Conversion, Conversion Survey, 1996, Chapter 3.

In the United States, the government's sole role relative to the defense industry was that of customer. The ownership of the companies was private, and the management was responsible to the shareholders for the survival and profitability of the companies. During the Bush administration, the U.S. government's position was that market forces could and should be the main means to cope with the problems of procurement declines, and the government should not interfere. The Clinton administration assumed a somewhat larger role to ameliorate the dislocations caused by the reductions in defense procurement (and base closures).[16] These programs assisted the displaced workers, the communities whose economies were severely affected by procurement reductions, and some companies requiring assistance in diversification, but the overall expenditures on these programs was very much smaller than the reductions in spending. These programs were not in the form of subsidies to the companies, but were to help plan and implement adjustment programs.

Following the breakup of the Soviet Union, Russia did initiate some major economic reforms, including price liberalization and privatization. It also initiated new conversion programs, but these were underfunded, and still bore the stamp of central planning, although they were somewhat better thought-through than their Soviet predecessors. They did not include downsizing, or the adequate enforcement of hard budget constraints and realistic bankruptcy provisions. The state also resisted privatization of defense plants, and this, among other factors, hampered their ability to attract foreign investors.[17]

---

16 Bonn International Center for Conversion, Conversion Survey, ibid.

17 David Bernstein, *Commercialization of Russian Technology in Cooperation with American Companies*, (Stanford University, 1999).

Alternatives For Adjusting To Procurement Reductions

In both countries, the defense industries predominantly chose other adjustment strategies than conversion. In the United States there are very few cases of large-scale conversion in the defense industry, although there are isolated examples of significant conversion. Ironically, some of the best examples are also examples of cooperative ventures between U.S. and Russian defense companies in the space launch business, and they are therefore cases of successful conversion in both countries. Boeing, Lockheed-Martin, and Pratt & Whitney have all made major investments in the commercial space launch business, based in part upon the use of Russian launch vehicles.[18] Many Russians believe that these examples in this industry can serve as models for both conversion and U.S.-Russian cooperative ventures throughout the defense industry. But the combination of factors that made these examples so successful is not present in other sectors of industry. The primary factor is that the political possibility of cooperation in this previously sensitive sector coincided with a rapidly growing demand for commercial space launches, for which U.S. companies could not successfully compete with the French if they relied solely on U.S. launch vehicles. The Russian systems offered superior technology, cost, performance records, and availability at the same time that there was this rapidly growing market demand. In the absence of these favorable conditions, it is unrealistic for the Russians to expect that this model can be replicated across much of the industrial spectrum.

---

[18] See Matthew Bencke, *The Politics of Space* (Westview Press, 1996) and David Bernstein, editor, *Cooperative Business Ventures between U.S. Companies and Russian Defense Enterprises* (Stanford University, 1997).

Most U.S. defense companies have not looked to conversion as the optimum means of adjustment. U.S. companies' strategies have been dictated by market conditions, and a system in which they do not get government subsidies (although in many cases they are reimbursed for certain costs associated with terminating defense contracts). The absence of subsidies requires that they make their adjustments in advance of the decline in revenues, lest they face large and continuing losses from having costs reductions lag revenue reductions. As a result, most companies in this situation initiated downsizing programs fairly quickly. If they chose to diversify into new products or markets, this required a capital investment, and such decisions were made company by company. If they did choose to invest in some form of diversification, they had access to a fully functional system of capital markets.

There was another approach that dominated the adjustment strategies of U.S. defense companies. Many of the companies, especially the aerospace and electronics defense contractors, engaged in a process of industry consolidation through a series of mergers, acquisitions, and divestitures. Companies making similar products, such as tactical missiles, that saw their markets shrinking but not disappearing bought and sold divisions so that there would ultimately be fewer competitors, and the remaining ones would have large enough production volumes to be profitable. Some companies, such as Rockwell, General Dynamics, and Hughes chose to decrease their defense work through divestiture, and others such as Boeing, Lockheed Martin, and Raytheon chose to increase theirs through acquisitions. Here again, private ownership and the availability of the capital markets was key to these moves. The U.S. government was highly supportive of these consolidations, as long as there were still some competitors left, since these consolidations could lead to more efficient operations, which would be manifested in lower prices to the government. To a major degree, these options are either not available to Russian companies, or they are extremely difficult to implement because of government ownership or regulations, and the lack of capital markets and infrastructure.

The strategy chosen by many, but not all, Russian defense enterprises was neither serious conversion nor downsizing and consolidation. Two conditions, peculiar to Russia, led to their choice of strategy. The first was the privatization process, which, even with State retention of substantial ownership, resulted in the redistribution of enormous assets and power into the hands of factory managers. The second was the weakness of the State, and its failure to enforce hard budget constraints, institute a social safety net, and collect taxes.[19]

Under these circumstances, the accumulation of wealth could be realized far more easily through stripping the assets of the enterprises; capital flight; and the nonpayment of wages, debts, and taxes, than through converting to profit-driven production of civilian goods for a weak economy. Many enterprise managers chose this easier path; others tried conversion, and then took this other path because the economy in which they had to function had these strange new rules of the game.

One could argue that this is simply an example of responding wisely to market forces. It's similar to Willie Sutton's remark when asked why he robs banks: "That's where the money is." This is not, however, a sustainable strategy because the economy is continuing to decline in real terms. It remains to be seen if these managers will seek an opportunity to

---

[19] Michael McFaul, *"State Power, Institutional Change, and the Politics of Privatization in Russia,"* World Politics, January 1995.

acquire their next increment of wealth through the operation of legitimate profit-seeking businesses, or whether the current cycle is unbreakable.

There are several defense enterprises and new companies that have sought to operate market-oriented, profit-seeking businesses. It is difficult to do this when selling to a domestic market where customers, including the State, do not always pay for what they "purchase." Some of the more successful ones derive most of their revenue outside of the country, but this is often a difficult market to penetrate.[20]

While the Russian conversion programs described herein have not been very successful, a major transformation in the industrial profile is occurring. The Russian labor force is redistributing itself from the defense industry to the service sector, as well as from huge state-owned enterprises to small private companies. This passive conversion is occurring through market forces rather than through the overt actions of either the government or the large defense enterprises. This could suggest that this reprofiling could have occurred faster and easier if the state had not initiated any conversion programs at all, but had simply created a better environment for adjustment, such as imposing hard budget constraints earlier, and working to develop market institutions and infrastructure.

Conclusions

Starting in the late 1980s, the defense industries in the United States and the SU/R both faced the need to adjust to reductions in defense procurements. The reductions were much larger and faster, and the economy was much weaker, in the SU/R than in the United States. In

---

20 See Chapter – Toward Cooperative Ventures with Russian Defense Enterprises.

addition, a complete set of market institutions in the United States permitted and, in fact, forced U.S. companies to consider a broad array of adjustment options that would enable them to stay financially viable. In very few cases did U.S. companies utilize conversion as their primary adjustment approach, favoring instead downsizing and corporate restructuring and consolidation. These strategies appeared to involve less financial exposure, and the poor history of conversion was a further disincentive.

In the SU/R these options were not very accessible because of state ownership, and the resultant resistance to downsizing and consolidation; the distortions of economic power from the privatization program; the lack of a well-developed commercial infrastructure; and the weakness of the State. Even when enterprises were privatized, there was still a strong reluctance to utilize these options, and a lack of market institutions to implement them. Thus asset stripping; capital flight; and nonpayment of debts, wages, and taxes often became the adjustment option of choice. Some enterprises attempted conversion, but this was often unsuccessful. It is important to note that even if all Russian enterprises had converted successfully within a couple of years, in the sense of producing products with advantageous features and costs, by then the demand in the Russian economy was far too small to absorb them; the economy had shrunk, and it was over-industrialized to begin with. Thus in concluding that conversion has not been successful, one must remember that only limited success could have been expected.

6.2. U.S., FRANCE, AND GREAT BRITAIN VS. RUSSIA

Introductory Remarks

Vlad E. Genin

With the passage of time, the consequences of failed conversion in Russia have become more obvious. Comparing the experience of conversion in the U.S., France, China, and the countries of Eastern Europe with that in Russia, we clearly see a staggering difference in results: from relative success to tragic failure.

There are very few examples of conversion in the world, and even fewer examples of successful conversion. The most often cited example of successful conversion is that of the U.S. after the Second World War. This was a macro-economic phenomenon, which was realized through a decrease in military activities, and a simultaneous increase in civilian activities, which resulted in the widespread closure of defense facilities.

The difficulties in converting defense enterprises not only in Russia, but also in the U.S. and in Europe in the 1990s, has led many analysts to think that conversion at the micro-economic level—the enterprise level—was impossible, and therefore a macro-economic approach had to be adopted, especially in Russia. But we need to know why conversion succeeded in the 1940s, and why the experience cannot, apparently, be repeated in the 1990s. Is conversion the same phenomenon in both periods? Does conversion have the same characteristics in all countries? In brief, is it a uniform phenomenon, or is it a phenomenon that can differ greatly from one time and place to another? In that case, what causes such differences, and what are the consequences?

Sonia Ben Ouagrham

Conversion In The 1990s

Conversion as an Economic Adjustment Phenomenon: The French and British Examples

Conversion as an economic adjustment phenomenon results from a decrease in the demand for military goods. This implies a micro-economic conversion whose intensity depends on the nature of the events that caused the decrease: it may be mainly an economic event, as in the case of France, or it may result from a political decision, as in the case of Great Britain.

Indeed, until the oil crisis in the late 1970s, the French defense industry exported over 40% of its production, which represented 40% of defense personnel.[21] Exports were mainly to the Gulf countries, and consisted chiefly of aviation equipment.[22] The decrease in oil prices, which affected the financial capacity of the traditional clients of France, was the first cause of the decrease in the foreign demand. That demand further decreased because of the reduction of defense expenditures in Far

---

[21] Jean-Paul Hebert, "Between Disarmament and Sovereignty ? The Issue of the Conversion of Arms Industries/ The French Example," in Brunn A, Baehr L, Karpe H.J (ed), *Conversion – Opportunities for Development and Environment* (Berlin: Springer-Verlag, 1992), p.25.

[22] Ibid.

Eastern countries and South East Asia, and the changes in the geo-strategic context at the end of the 1980s (disarmament agreements, the fall of Berlin Wall, the end of the Cold War).[23]

In the 1990s, the domestic demand for military goods also decreased. This was due to the reduction in French military expenditures that were caused by the changes in the geo-strategic environment, and also the French government's effort to make domestic producers cut their prices. Indeed, the special relationships existing between arms producers and the DGA (General Delegation for Armaments),[24] and the specific mode of coordination of the French weapons market, had caused a constant increase in the cost of weapons, which was not always justified by the cost of high technologies. The French government intended to stop that trend.

However, this did not endanger the existence of arms producers. The French State still intends to maintain an independent defense production capacity. In addition, *conversion* has remained a taboo word among government officials and arms producers. The government has preferred using the term "restructuring," and confirmed its support of defense enterprises by financing controversial military orders. For instance, the "Rafale" fighter plane program has been maintained mainly for the sake of "technological excellence", and in order to protect the jobs created by the program.

---

23 Ibid.

24 The DGA is a department of the French Ministry of defense composed of Armament Engineers. On the basis of the military characteristics determined by the Chief of Staff, the DGA determines the technical characteristics of military equipment, the modalities of their production, negotiates the price with arms producers and supervises the production of the equipment in factories

The adjustments of French defense manufacturers are therefore mainly dictated by the market. As a consequence, the process generated by the decrease in military expenditures is mainly a restructuring process, which resulted in a sharp decrease in personnel. Between 1987 and 1994, 100,000 direct and indirect jobs were suppressed, and 50,000 more were expected to disappear by 2000. Simultaneously, defense enterprises have launched an integration policy with other European weapons producers, which took the form of various types of associations (mergers, alliances, cooperative ventures, etc.) in order to reinforce their position on the international arms market.[25] Some enterprises have started producing civilian goods, but their share of total civilian production remains small. For instance, the DCN (Directorate of Naval Construction – the management of the state shipyards) has started producing oil rigs, and cooperates with civil engineering enterprises to produce bridges. However, the share of civilian production does not represent more than 5% of total production.[26]

French weapon producers have thus responded to the decrease in demand by diversifying their military markets, and only marginally by a shift to civilian goods. Conversion in France is therefore a low-intensity phenomenon, which is highly reversible since an increase in demand on military markets may cause an increase in military production.

British arms producers are in a different situation. Although their conversion is also essentially an economic phenomenon, it is of higher intensity and highly irreversible since it has been generated by a political decision.

---

[25] J.P. Hebert and R. de Penanros, "The Role of the State in the French Defense Industry Conversion," Defense and Peace Economics, 1995, vol.6, pp.207-220.
[26] Ibid.

Indeed, although the geo-strategic changes of the late 1980s had accelerated the decrease in military spending in Great Britain, this was only one aspect of a more general policy aimed at reducing public expenditures. As early as 1985 (before the geo-strategic changes), the Thatcher administration had sharply cut military expenditures, and launched the privatization of weapon producers. The military budget had decreased by 10% in real terms between 1984-85 and 1988-89. In addition, the military-industrial complex, which was mainly composed of state enterprises in 1980 (British Aerospace, Rolls Royce, British Shipbuilders, and Royal Ordnance), now consists of private enterprises.[27] The Thatcher administration also introduced greater competition in the domestic arms market by modifying the mechanism by which military contracts were awarded: priority was not given to British producers any more, and contracts were awarded on the basis of bids and fixed costs.[28]

Like the French producers, British defense enterprises responded to this decrease in demand by restructuring and cutting jobs. Between 1979 and 1991, 160,000 jobs had been eliminated in the defense industry. Some enterprises have tried to diversify their productions by acquiring existing civilian firms. British Aerospace for instance, bought the car producer Rover,[29] which later was resold. But in general, British

---

[27] Paul Dunne, Willet Sue, "National case Studies in Conversion: the United Kingdom" in Brunn A, Baehr L, Karpe H.J (ed), *Conversion – Opportunities for Development and Environment,* (Berlin: Springer-Verlag, 1992), p.210.

[28] Ibid.

[29] Arie Zacks, "Diversification et Reconversion de l'Industrie de D'armement," *Les Dossiers du GRIP*, n165, January 1992, p.32.

defense producers concentrated their efforts on military markets, and developed collaborative projects with foreign arms producers.[30]

Although their responses to demand fluctuations were similar to those of the French defense enterprises, the conversion of British defense enterprises was of higher intensity. The British government's policy of the mid-1980s had indeed broken the special bond existing between defense enterprises and the State, and made military production less profitable for domestic enterprises. Some producers may therefore be led to exit the arms market.

Conversion as a Strategic Orientation: The American Example

Conversion as a strategic orientation stems from a dramatic change in the geo-strategic environment, leading to a modification in military doctrines. This implies a conversion that will take place both at the macro- and micro-economic levels, since the military-industrial complex will have to restructure in order to meet the new defense needs, and defense enterprises will have to adjust individually to the decrease in demand.

The American conversion in the 1990s is a good example of such a strategic orientation. It is indeed directly connected to the end of the Cold War and disarmament agreements, and takes place in a context of changes in military doctrine. This type of conversion generates two different processes. The first leads to a reduction of the burden of defense expenditures on the economy, and to the destruction of surplus facilities that had been created by the arms race. The second involves an economic adjustment to the decrease in demand, and the remodeling of

---

[30] Ibid, p.212.

the military-industrial complex. This results in a much broader and highly irreversible conversion.

The imposition of cuts in the number of some types of weapons called for by disarmament agreements[31] also leads to a reduction of the corresponding production facilities. For instance, the American producer of nuclear warheads at Rocky Flats (Colorado) practically stopped production in 1990. In 1992, President Bush put an end to the production of nuclear W-88 warheads designed for Trident-II missiles, and the site has been converted to the recycling of contaminated metals for the production of containers to store radioactive materials.[32] (The conversion of the site was preferred to closure because the latter was too expensive.) Conversion also aims to allow a slow-paced departure of personnel, so as to avoid the creation of unemployment pockets in neighboring communities. Out of the 10,000 jobs that existed in the facility, 3,000 were eliminated in 1995, mainly through early retirement. And at the end of the century, the number of people employed at Rocky Flats is expected to decrease to 20% of the number in 1994.[33]

---

[31] The treaty on Intermediary Nuclear Forces (INF- 1987) provides for the destruction of all American and ex-Soviet nuclear missiles with a range of 500 to 5500 km. START I (1991) and START II (1993) impose a reduction of nuclear heads from 35 000 for the USSR and 20 000 for the U.S., to about 3000 warheads for each of the countries. They also entail the disappearance of land-based intercontinental strategic missiles located on fixed or mobile sites and armed with multiple warheads (MIRV). The treaty on Conventional Forces in Europe (CFE) did not lead to a destruction of weapons for the U.S., since the American surplus has been transferred to Greece, Spain, Norway and Turkey. Source: Bonn International Center for Conversion, *Conversion Survey 1996* (Oxford University Press, 1996), p.229.

[32] Michael D. Ward, Jordin S. Cohen and Michelle M. Betsill, "The Three Faces of Conversion in the U.S.A.," *Defense and Peace Economics,* 1995, vol.6, pp. 221-235.

[33] Ibid.

In addition to arms destruction and facilities closures, the new geo-strategic situation generated a sharp decrease in military expenditures: from 6.4% of GDP in 1985 to 3.9% in 1995[34]. In 1997, the level of military spending had declined in real terms by one third, compared to the 1989 level, and weapons procurement had been reduced by two thirds compared to 1989[35]. The armed forces have been downsized, and a number of military bases have been closed both in the U.S. and abroad.

In spite of such reductions, the American military-industrial complex is not condemned to disappear. On the contrary, as the only world power left, the U.S. must maintain an appropriate military force, and develop weapons adapted to the new types of conflicts that may emerged.

American defense enterprises adjusted to these phenomena in different ways. They first restructured by laying off a great number of personnel: within one year, between 1990 and 1991, 300,000 job losses had been recorded in the defense industry.[36] Some enterprises responded to the decrease in demand by expanding their activities in international arms markets. Some, like Chrysler and Unisys, abandoned their military activities.[37] Others have tried to convert by obtaining civilian public contracts, while remaining in their field of activity. For instance,

---

34 Ibid.

35 *U.S. Conversion After the Cold War, 1990-1997 – Lessons for Forging a New Conversion Policy,* BICC Brief 9, July 1997, p.5.

36 Gregory Bschack, "Debt Reduction in Exchange For Arms Conversion: The Case for Linking Conversion, Development and Debt Reduction," in Brunn A, Baehr L, Karpe H.J (ed), *Conversion – Opportunities for Development and Environment,* (Berlin: Springer-Verlag, 1992), p.260.

37 Kenneth L. Adelman and Norman R. Augustine, "Defense Conversion: Bulldozing the Management," *Foreign Affairs*, vol.71, no.2, 1992, pp.24-47.

Lockheed-Martin obtained some contracts from the DOE, NASA, the Post Office, and the civil aviation administration.[38] A very few enterprises have converted to a new civilian production.[39] Kaman Aerospace, for example, has started producing guitars, but this new production employs only 100 people, and only 30 of them are former defense employees.[40]

Conversion in the United States thus takes place both at the macro-economic level, through the decrease in the share of military activities in the economy, and at the micro-economic level, through defense enterprises' adjustment to the decrease in demand. It also entails a restructuring of the defense complex, which has to meet new needs under stronger budget constraints.

Whether it results from an economic adjustment or reveals a strategic orientation, the conversion of the defense industry in Europe and in the U.S. receives little financial support from the State. This implies that the burden of conversion lies primarily on the shoulders of defense enterprises themselves, and on those of the communities surrounding them—and the cost of the transition to civilian production is very high for defense enterprises. This is because they are usually highly specialized, and are used to evolving in a market where competition is weak or non-existent. If they are to transition to the civilian sector, they have to develop a new product line, and learn how to sell in a new market. Both elements are time- and money-consuming, and without

---

[38] Michael D. Ward, Jordin S. Cohen and Michelle M. Betsill, "The Three Faces of Conversion in the U.S.A.," op. cit.

[39] Seymour Melman, "Successful Conversion Experiences", in Brunn A, Baehr L, Karpe H.J (ed), *Conversion – Opportunities for Development and Environment,* (Berlin: Springer-Verlag, 1992), pp.338-344.

[40] Kenneth L. Adelman and Norman R. Augustine, op. cit.

appropriate support from the state, conversion is not profitable. This explains why defense enterprises prefer reinforcing their positions on the international arms market, or exiting the military market instead of converting.

The main difference between conversion in France, Great Britain, and the U.S. lies in the fact that for the first two, conversion has primarily economic roots and in the case of the third, conversion is primarily caused by strategic changes. Very logically, French and British defense enterprises have applied "economic responses" to their "economic conversion," while American enterprises have to both apply "economic responses" and comply with the new strategic orientation.[41]

The intensity and reversibility of conversion depends on the importance of the decrease in demand, when conversion is an economic phenomenon, and on the importance of the geo-strategic changes, when conversion stems from geo-strategic modifications. This explains why the British conversion may lead some defense enterprises to exit the arms market, while the French conversion will lead only to a reduction of production for the French market, compensated by an expansion on the international arms market.

The result of conversion (success or failure) must therefore be assessed in the light of the events that caused conversion and by determining whether defense enterprises' responses are adequate.

It should also be analyzed in the light of the attitude of the State towards conversion. The absence of state support may encourage defense enterprises to adopt an exit strategy. This is one common point between

---

[41] The American and European conversion have both economic and strategic aspects. But the primary cause (economic or strategic) of conversion determines the nature of defense enterprises' responses.

the American and the British conversions. In the case of France, the fact that the state aims at maintaining its military independence softens the consequences of a sharp decrease in demand, as the state can support production that have little military significance.

Post-War Conversion: Conversion In The U.S. After The Second World War

Post-war conversion was very different from conversion in the 1990s. First of all, it is a large-scale phenomenon, amounting to the conversion of a whole economy. It is nothing less than a transition from a war economy to a peace economy, with very strong State intervention. Although it takes place primarily at the macro-economic level, it also implies the conversion of enterprises. Indeed, the end of the war entails a sudden decrease in military expenditures to which enterprises have to adapt quickly. However, the categories of enterprises and personnel concerned by conversion are different from those affected by conversion in the 1990s. These characteristics imply that post-war conversion is a very specific phenomenon, which can hardly be compared to conversion in the 1990s.

One of the characteristics of post-war conversion is that it is preceded by demobilization. Personnel in uniform are sharply downsized; the surplus personnel mobilized during war-time to boost weapon production are released; defense enterprises switch to civilian production or are destroyed; controls on prices and production are lifted; and a reconstruction policy is launched.

Since the end of a war is seldom a predictable event, demobilization has often been a sudden and unplanned-for phenomenon, resulting in a deep economic depression. For instance, in the United

States after the First World War, the simultaneous demobilization of 4 million personnel in uniform, and the cancellation of defense orders representing 9 million jobs, resulted in a sudden jump in the unemployment rate from 1.4% in 1919 to 11.7% in 1921.[42] Military and civilian personnel competed on the labor market, inflation increased, and the resulting depression was further aggravated by the crisis of 1929.

Things were different after the Second World War—the memories of the consequences of the Great War and the phantoms of the 1929 crisis had generated a demand for planning post-war conversion both from individuals and enterprises. President Roosevelt gladly responded to these concerns, as he was the father of the New Deal, which marked the failure of President Hoover's policy to curb the crisis. Therefore, demobilization in the 1940s is an exception to the rule: it was a well-planned effort.

Actually, the U.S. government started planning demobilization and post-war activities even before the United States entered the war—as early as November 1940, President Roosevelt asked the National Planning Board to prepare a plan for a smooth transition to civilian activities after the war.[43] Demobilization and the planning of post-war activities became major concerns after the U.S. entered the war: almost each federal administration had created a committee for post-war demobilization.[44]

The states and cities also actively participated to the planning of post-war activities by creating various organizations to help re-train

---

[42] Ballard Jack Stokes, *The Shock of Peace* (Washington, D.C., University Press of America, 1983).

[43] Ibid. p.32.

[44] Ibid, p.35.

defense personnel, develop support programs for enterprises, and create programs to boost economic activity after the war (construction of highways, bridges, playgrounds, etc.).[45]

Industrial and commercial organizations also participated in the planning wave, and their efforts were mainly aimed at coordinating planning efforts and disseminating information on successful examples.[46]

Even though the federal government stopped its post-war activity planning because the war had brought back economic prosperity, the states, cities, and enterprises maintained their efforts. Therefore, demobilization after the Second World War was extremely well planned at all levels. This is one of the main reasons why no depression resulted from the end of the war in the United States, and why the economic boom that started during the war has been maintained in the years that followed.

Many authors have used that argument to assert that post-war conversion has been successful. However, a careful analysis of conversion during that period shows that there were very few examples of micro-economic conversions (transformation of defense enterprises into civilian enterprises). Further, a great part of defense enterprises' personnel during the war did not convert after the war, but instead exited the labor market. Finally, surplus military equipment was generally sold at very low prices or destroyed, but not converted to civilian use.

---

[45] Ibid, p.31.

[46] Description of these programs can be found in: Ballard Jack Stokes, *The Shock of Peace* (Washington, D.C., University Press of America, 1983) and Alexander J. Davidson, "Military Conversion Policies in the U.S.A.: 1940s and 1990s," *Journal of Peace Research,* vol.31, no.1, 1994.

The confusion between a smooth transition from war economy to peace economy for a successful conversion stems from the fact that a great number of the enterprises which had to convert in the post-war period were in fact civilian enterprises that had only temporarily switched to military production in order to meet war needs. After the war, they returned to their former civilian activities, which they had maintained during the war: civilian production represented about 50% of industrial production in war-time.[47] In that case the term *re-conversion* is more appropriate than *conversion* to describe this phenomenon.

A second set of enterprises was composed of firms specializing in military production, which had been created specifically to support the war effort. After the war, these enterprises became surplus facilities, which had no real use in peacetime. Most of them were therefore destroyed.

The third set of enterprises was composed of those defense facilities specializing in the production of weapons that had existed before the war. These enterprises were very few, and after the war they maintained their military profile.

The same argument goes for personnel. Very few of them were specialized defense personnel. Most of them had essentially been hired by the defense complex just for the duration of the war, and only to meet defense needs. Once the war was over, they returned to their former activities.

As no real conversion took place, we may wonder why the transition from a war economy to a peace economy was smooth and no social and economic crisis resulted from the change in priorities. The

---

[47] Ballard Jack Stokes, *The Shock of Peace,* op. cit., p.137.

main reasons lie in the characteristics of the economic situation during that period and in the well-prepared demobilization.

Indeed, the planned demobilization allowed a release of some troops as early as 1944, and this helped avoid a sudden and massive flow of job seekers on the labor market. The G.I. Bill, which was a product of the demobilization planning efforts, also helped to alleviate the pressure on the labor market by allowing some of the veterans to go back to school, or postpone their return to the labor market for various reasons.[48] Further, many veterans found a job after the war, because almost one third of the 10 million employees who held defense jobs during the war were obliged to exit the labor market (women, young people, retired people, and minorities).[49] The decrease of working time to 40 hours a week also created jobs for the returning troops. Therefore, the unemployment rate remained low after the war (3.3% in October 1946) because of a simultaneous exit of a part of the wartime labor force from the labor market (civilians and veterans) and absorption of the labor released by the war.

Demobilization planning efforts also helped clarify the contract cancellation process by determining, among other things, the amount of financial compensation due to defense enterprises.[50] Further, although the federal government did not contribute to the planning of post-war conversion, it had provided defense enterprises with a high level of financing and cash flow during and after the war. Indeed, during the war the profits made by defense contractors amounted in average to $9

---

[48] Ballard Jack Stokes, *The Shock of Peace,* op. cit, p. 137

[49] Ballard Jack Stokes, *The Shock of Peace,* op. cit

[50] *The Army and Economic Mobilization,* Center of Military History, United States Army, Washington D.C., 1985, p.649.

billion a year (after taxes).[51] This provided reserves to finance their future conversion. After the war, the federal government had chosen to cancel defense contracts and compensate defense enterprises quickly and generously so that they could rapidly turn to civilian production.[52] And finally, some civilian goods had originally been developed as military equipment and had therefore been financed from the federal budget: the Jeep is a good example of this.[53]

Further, the decline of defense production has been compensated by the development of other economic sectors, such as agriculture, where seasonal employment rose from 2 to 9 million between February and August 1946; construction; mining; transportation; and the textile industry.[54]

Economic demand also rose after the war, not only because of the shortages endured during the war, but also because both enterprises and households had accumulated large amounts of money: in 1945, they respectively accounted for $80 billion ($22 billion in 1940) and $146 billion ($48 billion in 1940).[55]

In the aftermath, post-war conversion in the U.S. was characterized by the destruction of military activities, which had been compensated by the rise of civilian activities. It generated very few enterprise conversions. This is a typical macro-economic conversion, which succeeded mainly because prosperity and a well-prepared

---

[51] Ballard Jack Stokes, *The Shock of Peace,* op. cit., p.138.

[52] Alexander J. Davidson, "Military Conversion Policies in the U.S.A.: 1940s and 1990s", *op. cit.*

[53] Ballard Jack Stokes, *The Shock of Peace,* op. cit., p.138

[54] Ballard Jack Stokes, *The Shock of Peace,* op. cit

[55] Ballard Jack Stokes, *The Shock of Peace,* op. cit

demobilization allowed a smooth transition from a war economy to a peace economy and the reallocation of resources from military to civilian sectors.

The situation is very different in the 1990s. Defense enterprises are dedicated entities that employ personnel with very specialized skills, and use technologies that do not necessarily have a civilian use because of their specialization or their cost. Conversion in the 1990s also takes place in a context of slow growth and with little help from the federal government.

Conversion In Russia

Conversion in Russia has two important characteristics. The first is that it combines all the aspects of the conversion processes in Europe and the U.S., not only of the 1990s but also of the 1940s. It is simultaneously an economic adjustment phenomenon, caused by the decrease in demand; a strategic re-orientation, caused by the geo-strategic changes and the break-up of the USSR; and a demobilization phenomenon, caused by the end of the Soviet economy and the change to another system. It has to take place both at the micro- and the macro-economic levels. It is a very high intensity phenomenon, which has both reversible and irreversible characteristics. In short, this is a very complex phenomenon that needs to be carefully prepared and planned if it is to succeed.

The second characteristic of the Russian conversion process is that it was launched in a framework that is different from the one in which it is now taking place. This implies that the conception underlying conversion has changed over time. But while the latter was indeed more or less well defined in the Gorbachev era, it has remained very unclear in the Russian context. This resulted in a very disorganized and unguided conversion process.

Evolution of the Notion of Conversion: From Strategic To Economic

Conversion was launched under the Gorbachev administration as the result of a profound change in the Soviet nuclear strategy.

The Soviet nuclear doctrine developed by Marshal Sokolovskii was based on the following principle: should a war break out, nuclear weapons would be used from the very beginning. The USSR would avoid a surprise assault by initiating a massive nuclear strike[56] supported by strong conventional military forces. Such a military doctrine represented a threat to NATO members, and damaged the credibility of the "Flexible Response", which was based on a progressive transition from conventional to tactical nuclear and finally strategic nuclear weapons. NATO responded to such an unfavorable strategic context by designing the "Air-Land Battle" (1982) and "Follow-on-Forces Attack" (1983) concepts. By relying on new technologies, they aimed at attacking the second echelon of Soviet forces in order to deprive the first echelon, the most powerful, of its backup.

The Soviet Union realized how much these NATO concepts threatened its traditional doctrine, which was based on two echelons of massive military formations: any concentration of forces could be forced to commit military action by NATO forces. Further, the offensive approach and the element of surprise, which were the pillars of the Soviet strategy, were challenged by Western technological progress in the fields of reconnaissance and information collection. Aware that a

---

[56] Although the doctrine did not state it explicitly, such an offensive attitude involved a preemptive strike.

nuclear war was improbable, Soviet officers started defining future wars as conventional ones based on smaller, mobile, independent formations, equipped with sophisticated conventional arms able to lead one-echelon combats.[57]

But in order to lead conventional wars, the Soviet Union needed not only modern arms, but also an economic system strong enough to meet war needs and support the survival of the system. Unfortunately, the planned economy had generated a certain amount of dysfunctionality, and the MIC, which still enjoyed priority in the allocation of resources, was unable to meet the requirements of modern technology. Reinforcing the economic system and restructuring industry became vital elements for the survival of the Soviet system. Hence, the new policy of glasnost, perestroika and the accelerated rhythm of disarmament agreements. They mainly aimed at alleviating the burden of the arms race, and allowing time for the USSR to restructure and defeat its enemy.

Thus conversion in the Soviet period was initiated and organized by the State, and had mainly strategic ends.

After the break-up of the USSR, the new Russian government confirmed the Soviet commitments, and continued conversion and the reform policies. However, the disorganization created by the demise of the USSR, the attempt of the Russian government to complete the reforms quickly, and the uncertainty concerning Russia's place on the international scene, did not allow the formation of a new conception of conversion. Actually, the economic reforms became a priority: the government wanted to create a liberal market economy, and this implied getting rid of the vestiges of the Soviet system. In such a situation,

---

[57] Sonia Ben Ouagrham, *Le Desarmement et la conversion de l'industrie militaire en Russie,* op.cit.

conversion was only one element of the industrial restructuring and economic reforms, and consequently it had to be achieved according to the same rules—namely, without financial support from the state.

Thus, conversion in the Russian context lacked two essential elements: from the strategic point of view it did not benefit from a military doctrine to guide it, and from the economic point of view, it did not benefit from an industrial policy. This means that conversion has mainly been conceived as an economic adjustment phenomenon generated by a decrease in domestic and foreign demand. Yet, it is a phenomenon much more complex than that.

A Multiple-Nature Conversion

The second feature of the Russian conversion is that it implies different processes, operating in various time frames. In addition, these processes are complementary, and need to be applied in a predetermined sequence.

First, the Russian conversion implies a post-war conversion process. The Soviet system had indeed the characteristics of wartime mobilized economies: centralized economic management; controls on prices and production; high activity rate; large industrial production basis; priority given to the defense sector; research and technical innovation controlled by the state, shortage of civilian goods, etc.[58] However, the Soviet mobilization is unique in that it was carried out mostly in peacetime, and lasted for more than 60 years.

---

[58] A good description of the American war-time mobilized economy is given in *The Army and Economic Mobilization,* Center of Military history, United States Army, Washington D.C., 1985. For a description of the Soviet mobilized economy, see Jacques Sapir, *L'economie mobilisee,* La Decouverte, Paris (France), 1990.

Indeed, contrary to wartime mobilization, the Soviet mobilization was not a response to an armed conflict. It was used as a development strategy to fill in the perceived gap between the Soviet Union and Western countries in the industrial, economic, social, and political fields. This is tremendously different from ordinary wartime mobilization; it constitutes a long-term economic mobilization. However, wartime economic mobilizations have so far been more efficient than the market in allocating resources for defense needs only because they have been applied in the short-term. When applied in the long term, the behaviors that mobilization generates (hoarding, corruption, bureaucratic competition, quantity production, lower quality goods, etc.) tend to become deeply rooted in the culture and become norms.

Further, all economic mobilizations cause distortions in the economy as resources are channeled towards defense needs. Long-term mobilization, as in the case of the Soviet Union, causes stronger distortions. One of the consequences of the Soviet mobilization was that the defense complex became one of the main employers of the country. The number of employees is difficult to estimate, owing to the secrecy that prevailed at that time, and to the lack of strict demarcation between the military and civilian sectors, as well as to Soviet directors' habit of hoarding personnel in order to meet the plan.

The second consequence of the Soviet mobilization was that it hampered the development of civilian industries. They were either subordinated to the defense sector to the point where they could not develop independently and produce goods adapted to the civilian market, or their development was slowed down due to a lack of resources. As a result, some regions, like the Buriat Autonomous Republic, which possess great natural resources, cannot develop because they lack the required infrastructures to exploit them. In other cities or regions, not only the economy but also the education system is totally dependent on the defense sector. This is typically the case of closed or former closed cities, like Severodvinsk.

The third important consequence of the Soviet mobilization is that it had a strong impact on urban planning. Indeed, according to the Soviet strategic imperatives, the civilian and defense enterprises located east of the Urals were supposed to support a war effort on the western front of the country. The road and railroad systems had therefore been developed to ship goods and people between the eastern and western poles of the country. But there has been little inter-regional and intra-regional development of transportation systems. In the context of a demobilized economy, such a system limits exchanges between regions as well as their development.

In a nutshell, the Soviet mobilization has had several sets of consequences. On the one hand it has had the same results as a war-time mobilization, one of them being the important military equipment and production capacity surplus, and on the other hand, it has had specific effects: distortion of regional economies, and low development of the civilian sector.

Demobilization will therefore have two aspects. First, it implies the destruction of the military surplus, and, second, the creation of a civilian economy (industrial restructuring, public works, etc.). Both processes need to take place simultaneously, since the civilian economy is not sound enough to replace the military economy. This requires strong intervention by the federal government.

The economic system change suggests a conversion process characterized by an economic adjustment of defense enterprises. In the mobilized system, defense enterprises were the core of the national economy. Destroying them would deprive Russia of the greater part of its industrial production capacity. Defense enterprises must therefore adapt to the new economic environment by modernizing their equipment, acquiring new commercial knowledge, a new mode of functioning, etc. This requires that a new economic system has to be created and stabilized. It is a long-term process, which also requires state intervention in order to stabilize the environment.

Finally, the demise of the USSR and the emergence of the Russian Federation in a new geo-strategic environment propose a conversion process aiming at restructuring the military-industrial complex. The latter must indeed meet Russia's new defense needs. This requires from the state a clear definition of its new defense concept.

All these processes have different time frames. Demobilization has to be completed in the short-term in order to allow the civilian economy to take the lead. In contrast, the adaptation of defense enterprises to the new economic environment and the restructuring of the military complex are long-term processes. These processes also have to be realized in a specific order. Defense enterprises cannot adapt to the new system, if the latter has not been created and stabilized, and the market economy cannot be created if the economy is not first demobilized.

Unfortunately, neither in the Soviet context nor in the Russian context, has conversion been conceived as a transition from a war economy to a peace economy. In the Gorbachev era mobilization was, if anything, reinforced, since the defense sector was supposed to lead the reforms. And in the Russian context the economy has only been partially demobilized. "Shock therapy" put an end to the controls on production and prices, and destroyed the management structure of the Soviet system, but defense enterprises remain mobilized. They have to maintain mobilization capacities, and, according to Russian law, no enterprise can refuse to fulfill state orders. Further, the creation of a civilian economy (building and modernization of communication systems, transportation, housing, market infrastructures, regional development policies, etc.) has not received enough attention from the State. In other words, the Russian economy is still structurally mobilized.

Given these facts, the creation of a civilian (market) economy is doomed to fail. The introduction of market rules without the prior creation of the infrastructures required to allow exchanges can only result in a high uncertainty, and encourage enterprises to maintain and even reinforce their former behaviors and routines.

Conclusion

The analysis of conversion in Europe, the U.S., and Russia shows that conversion is a differentiated phenomenon, which may imply various processes that are determined by the prevailing economic, political, and strategic context. In Russia, conversion is a three-stage process, which requires first a demobilization of the economy, then the creation of a civilian (market) economy, and finally, the transformation of defense enterprises into commercial enterprises. However, conversion started before the market was created, and the economic reforms were launched before the proper demobilization of the economy. Defense enterprises have therefore to convert without knowing the features of the economy in which they have to reallocate resources and without being able to make strategic decisions.

6.3. CHINA AND EASTERN EUROPE

Introductory Remarks

Vlad E. Genin

The Chinese conversion experience has special significance for Russia. Both countries started with a similar basis and background for conversion, i.e., a command political system; similar geographic conditions; and most important, production technology and plants built during the Khrushchev era. The new Chinese model of economic development, which started in the 1980s, proved to be not only capable of supporting conversion, but also making it a success.

It is hard to determine which of the Chinese "conversion lessons" are applicable to Russia. Chinese defense conversion did happen in a specific environment comprising both the "new Chinese model" and the old communist dictatorship. Modern Russia, especially its political structure, cannot be compared to China. Russia has long since left the obsolete political system and begun its movement towards democracy and a market economy. That is why, even after extracting a number of valuable elements from the Chinese experience for possible application in Russia, complex analytical tasks still must be solved.

Alexei I. Izyumov

While Russian experience in defense industry conversion has its unique features, many characteristics of this process were shared by other transitional economies. For most of them the transition to the market coincided with the dramatic downsizing of their defense industries. Of approximately 30 transitional economies, the Chinese experience presents particular interest. China is the only country that has a defense industry complex comparable in size to the Russian one. And by many accounts, defense industry conversion in China has been a success. The lessons of defense industry conversion in Eastern Europe may also be educational for Russian policy-makers. The countries of that region are generally ahead of Russia in their market transformation, and patterns of defense conversion there might point to future developments in the Russian military-industrial complex.

In China conversion started in 1978-79, well before the end of the Cold War allowed the goal of conversion even to be formulated in the USSR. Following the death of Mao and the ascent of Deng to the political throne, China declared its now-famous course of the "four modernizations" in agriculture, industry, technology, and the military sphere. Defense industry conversion was an integral part of the overall package.[59] Much like Gorbachev in the 1980s, Chinese reformers hoped that the excess capacities of defense enterprises and research institutes could be used to increase the output and quality of civilian goods. Yet there was a major difference: for the Chinese, conversion from the very start had the equally important goal of modernizing and strengthening the defense industry itself. China did not plan to downsize its defense industry—rather, conversion was meant to *diversify* the defense enterprises. This "dual-track" nature of the Chinese conversion distinguishes it radically from its Soviet/Russian counterpart.

---

[59] Alexei Izyumov, "Formation of a New Economic Mechanism in China." *Problems of Economy*, no. 5, 1998, p. 59-72 (In Russian).

In terms of its absolute size, the Chinese defense-industrial complex is comparable to that of Russia. In the late 1980s it consisted of approximately 3,000 enterprises employing 4-4.5 million workers. By 1996, the number of workers engaged in defense production had gone down to 3-3.2 million, while the number of enterprises stayed about the same.[60] Much as in the USSR, the defense enterprises were, for the most part, isolated from the civilian sector of the economy. In addition to that, no less than a half of the establishments of the Chinese defense-industrial complex were located in the so-called "Third Front" areas--the inland provinces of China, away from the country's borders and main population centers.[61] The geographical distribution of the Chinese defense enterprises was therefore quite similar to that of the former USSR.

Organizationally, the Chinese defense industry falls under dual command: the majority of enterprises report to a civilian body – the State Council. The rest, until recently, operated under the umbrella of the People's Liberation Army, and took orders from its supreme body -- the Military Commission. The overall coordination of all defense industry activities since 1982 was provided by the unified Commission for Science, Technology and National Defense Industry – COSTIND.

From the very start, Chinese conversion proceeded differently from its Soviet/Russian counterpart. Most of these differences reflected the general characteristics of Chinese economic reforms. First of all,

---

60 Conversion Survey (1998), *Global Disarmament, Defense Industry Consolidation and Conversion* (Bonn International Center for Conversion. Oxford University Press), pp. 124, 306; Charles Anderton, "Defense Conversion in China: From Swords to Plowshares?" *Peace Economics, Peace Science, and Public Policy*, vol. 2, no. 2, 1995, p.25.

61 Barry Naughton , "The Third Front: Defense Industrialization in the Chinese Interior." *China Quarterly*, no. 115, 1988,p. 351-386.

Chinese conversion was planned and directed more carefully. Conversion was initially tried in several select enterprises and geographical areas, and only later was spread out to the whole of the defense industry. The approach here followed the guiding principle of Chinese reform in general, formulated by Deng in the form of an old Chinese proverb: "While crossing the river, test every stone carefully".[62]

Second, conversion was coordinated with the broader organizational reform of the defense industry. To free up the initiative of individual enterprises, management of the industry was gradually decentralized and commercialized. The government turned most of the defense ministries into corporations, and allowed enterprises run by the uniformed military to branch out freely into the civilian sector. But in contrast to Russian conversion, Chinese defense enterprises were not allowed to privatize.

Third, the main focus of the Chinese conversion was the domestic market, with the emphasis on low- to medium-tech goods: home appliances, motorcycles, televisions, etc. Unlike their Russian counterparts, Chinese planners and defense industry managers did not have ambitions to conquer the world markets with their newly developed high-tech products. This pragmatic down-to-earth approach, coupled with severe restrictions on imports of foreign consumer goods, proved to be a winning ticket for Chinese defense conversion.

Fourth, conversion in China was greatly facilitated by the relative openness to foreign investments of the diversifying enterprises. Through partnership agreements with foreign companies, and the establishment of affiliates in the coastal Free Economic Zones, many of these enterprises were able early on to tap into foreign technology and

---

[62] Alexei Izyumov, "Chinese Alternative." *Znamia*, March 1988, no. 3, p. 207.

know-how, and capture significant "strategic" segments of the domestic market. Such, for example, was the success story of the Jialing Machine Factory motorcycle venture after it entered into a license agreement with Honda of Japan.[63]

Finally, conversion in China had always enjoyed the strong economic support of the central and regional governments. According to the data collected by the OECD mission to China, from the start of reforms until 1995, government authorities on all levels provided the defense industry with approximately $2.4 billion worth of investment credits, specifically for conversion.[64]

Of course, government assistance also meant the preservation of inefficiencies in the defense sector. According to the same report, the Chinese government has extended additional $3.5 worth of subsidies to unprofitable defense enterprises.[65]

Overall--judging from the information supplied by the Chinese government (presumably erring on the optimistic side) and several studies done by Western observers—the Chinese conversion/diversification experience was a success. Between 1979 and 1997, the share of civilian goods and services in the total output of the Chinese defense industry went up from 8 to 80%, with a comparable

---

63 Charles Anderton, "Defense Conversion in China: From Swords to Plowshares?" *Peace Economics, Peace Science, and Public Policy*, vol. 2, no. 2, 1995, p.26.

64 Conversion Survey (1998), *Global Disarmament, Defense Industry Consolidation and Conversion* (Bonn International Center for Conversion. Oxford University Press), p. 128.

65 *Ibid.* For a detailed review of Chinese conversion see: Jorn Brommelhorster, John Frankenstein (ed.) (1997) *Mixed Motives, Uncertain Outcomes – Defense Conversion in China* (Boulder, CO: Lynne Rienner, 1997).

increase in production volume.[66] In some areas the success of defense industry diversification even prompted the government to apply restrictive measures. Thus in 1998, to control corruption among the military, the Chinese government ordered most of the 15-20,000 commercial enterprises run by the Armed Forces to be separated from the PLA and sold off to the civilian sector.[67]

All of the above-mentioned factors played a role, but the single most important reason behind the success of the Chinese conversion was the phenomenal growth of the Chinese civilian economy in the 1980s and 1990s. Over these two decades, Chinese GDP quadrupled. This created a booming demand for civilian goods in general and conversion goods in particular, and secured the success of the Chinese conversion. The strong economy also gave the Chinese government the necessary resources to assist conversion from above by way of credits, subsidies, and the like. And it is exactly the lack of a booming civilian economy that has made the conversion experience so painful in Russia and in Eastern Europe.

Compared with Russia's economy, the economies of most of the East European countries were much less militarized. At its peak years (1987-88), military production comprised no more than 11% of industrial output in Czechoslovakia, and 3% in Poland and Hungary.[68] By virtue of the much smaller size of these countries, defense enterprises in Eastern Europe were not as isolated from potential civilian markets as

---

[66] Bonn International Center for Conversion, *Conversion Survey 1998: Global Disarmament, Defense Industry Consolidation and Conversion* (Oxford University Press, 1998), p. 227.

[67] *Wall Street Journal*, August 3, 1998.

[68] Judit Kiss, "The Pains of Defense Industry Conversion in East Central Europe." *The New Economy*, vol. 5, no. 2, 1994, pp.10-11.

their Russian counterparts. The proximity of rich Western neighbors presented another potentially positive factor for defense conversion.

Given these conditions, at the start of the market reforms, many managers of East European defense companies hoped that their relatively advanced technology and better trained labor would give them a good chance to succeed in developing and selling new civilian goods. Yet so far, the results of defense conversion in Eastern Europe can hardly be called a success.[69]

With the collapse of the Warsaw Pact and the breakdown of the U.S.S.R., defense spending by East European countries plummeted by 1992 to less than 17% of its peak pre-transition level of 1989. In Russia in the same period, defense spending fell to 23% of its pre-transition level.[70] This coincided with the radical contraction of the foreign export markets for East European military producers. At the same time, the deep decline of the overall economy has denied defense enterprises the hoped-for easy access to domestic civilian markets. These markets were further reduced by the influx of cheap consumer imports resulting from liberalization. However, the hope that Western Europe would open its markets to East European imports was not realized. Western assistance programs to conversion in Eastern Europe proved to be mainly technical in nature, and could in no way compensate for the lack of private investments in conversion.

---

69 For a detailed critical review of conversion in Eastern Europe see: Judit Kiss, *The Defense Industry in East-Central Europe. Restructuring and Conversion* (Oxford: Oxford University Press, 1997).

70 Bonn International Center for Conversion, *Conversion Survey 1998: Global Disarmament, Defense Industry Consolidation and Conversion* (Oxford University Press, 1998), pp. 289, 292.

The reaction of the East European governments to the crisis in their defense sectors basically took one of two paths. Countries more advanced in reform —the Czech Republic, Hungary, and Poland— realizing that they could not finance full-scale conversion out of the state budget, chose the market-led approach to it. Under that approach, the government limits its role to partial employment support and preservation of "core defense capabilities" of the defense sector.[71] In contrast to that, the governments of several other countries, including Slovakia, Bulgaria, Ukraine, and Belarus, tried to direct the conversion efforts "from above". But lack of financial resources and uncertainty about the new defense priorities doomed this government-led approach to failure. Much as in Russia, ever-changing guidelines and unrealistic promises only disoriented individual defense enterprises, and delayed their restructuring.[72]

Approaches to ownership reforms in the defense sector were also different in different countries. In Hungary and the Czech Republic, all but a few "strategic" defense enterprises were privatized. In other countries, most defense establishments were turned into corporations, but only a minority of them was allowed to privatize.[73] Changes in the form of ownership did not produce major changes in behavior and performance of enterprises. As in Russia, both privatized and state-

---

[71] Pawel Wieczorek and Katarzyna Zukrowska, *Conversion in Poland: The Defense Industry and Base Redevelopment* (Bonn: BICC, 1996), p. 33.

[72] Alexei Izyumov, Leonid Kosals and Rosalina Ryvkina, "The Russian Military-Industrial Complex: The Shock of Independence," in *Conversion of the Defense Industry in Russia and Eastern Europe* (Bonn: Bonn International Center for Conversion, 1995), pp. 12-17; *Conversion Survey 1998*, pp. 135-144.

[73] Since its admission into NATO, Poland also moved towards radical privatization. In 1999 the government decided to limit its majority ownership to only 7 of the 34 major defense corporations (RFE/RL Newsline, vol. 3, no. 122, Part II, June 23, 1999).

owned defense enterprises adjusted to their new markets in several stages, ranging from passivity and reliance on government aid, to *ad hoc* survival measures, to sustainable conversion strategies.[74] There were a number of individual success stories in each country, but not enough to ensure the success of the conversion process as a whole.

Now, ten years after the start of conversion, the defense industry of Eastern Europe has been reduced to 10-15% of its pre-reform size—something probably approximating the realistic defense needs of these countries. As for the results of conversion as such, they fell well below expectations. This is particularly true for countries whose governments took upon themselves more conversion obligations than they could fund. In countries that chose a more market-oriented approach to conversion, defense enterprises were generally more successful in diversifying into the civilian markets. Their success was even greater in that these same countries were generally better at reviving their civilian economies. The integration of the Czech Republic, Hungary, and Poland into NATO opened their defense enterprises to Western investment, technology, and managerial expertise. The military production of these enterprises will, in due course, be incorporated into the West European industrial complex, and the rest of their production capacities will be absorbed by the private civilian economy. It is safe to predict that conversion in these countries will be completed before long.

The main lesson of Chinese and East European experience is that defense conversion can only be truly successful in a growing economy. At a recent conference on conversion, a prominent Polish reformer, Jan Bielecki, now Director of the European Bank of Reconstruction and Development, noted, “The only way Eastern European countries will be

---

[74] Wieczorek and Zukrowska (1996), p. 34.

able to meet the combined challenge of economic transition and conversion is if they generate enough income to cover the high cost of conversion".[75] This statement applies to all transition economies, including that of Russia. Thus, all measures that bring closer the sustainable economic recovery in Russia will at the same time be helping conversion.

As for the specific lessons for Russia that follow from Chinese and East European experience, they can be reduced to a few points.

First, the Russian government should define its short and medium-term defense needs as clearly as possible, and based on that, provide defense enterprises with the procurement plans that it can realistically fund. In Russian conditions that includes the speedy repayment of all accumulated arrears for past defense orders.

Secondly, as long as the state in Russia does not have the resources to assist conversion, the government-led approach to it should be abandoned and replaced with the market-led one. This does not necessarily mean accelerated privatization, as privatization *per se* proves not to be a panacea for conversion. But the "core" defense enterprises should be separated from the rest of the defense industry, and the latter part should be allowed to use all of its production capacities as the market dictates.

Thirdly, converting enterprises themselves should discard their excessive ambitions with regard to development of exclusively high-tech products and should aim primarily at the domestic rather than foreign markets. They should also renew their efforts to attract foreign partners, and to seek out foreign investments, licenses and patents.

---

75 Jan Bielecki, *Economic Recovery as a Prerequisite for Conversion,* BICC Bulletin, (Bonn: International Center for Conversion, 1998), pp.1-2.

Finally, to repeat once again, the best recipe for conversion is a general economic recovery in Russia. The defense conversion, however important it may be in its own right, is still just an element of the overall market transition. Ultimately it can be completed successfully only when the transition itself is a success.

6.4. THE CONVERSION OF THE PRESIDIO[76]

Introductory Remarks

Vlad E. Genin

The conversion of the facilities of the former military base in San Francisco, the Presidio, is unique among the world's defense conversion projects. The main challenge of this project was to make the gigantic leap from old defense facilities to a world-class "city within a city" -- a home for higher educational institutions, high-tech companies, charitable foundations, and other such non-military institutions.

This dream became a reality through implementation of a two-part plan: conversion of the site into both a national park and a new modern educational and high-tech center. And not just the function was changed: a new architectural-spatial environment was created for the complex, and historically important buildings were restored, while their architectural heritage was preserved.

The example of the Presidio shows that it is possible to convert former defense

---

[76] The following references were used by the author to prepare this chapter:
Stephen A. Haller, *Post and Park* (San Francisco: Golden Gate National Parks Association, 1997).
Lisa M. Benson, *From Army Post to National Park* (Boston: Northeastern University Press, 1998).
Creating a Park for the 21st Century: From Military Post to National Park. Final General Management, (National Park Service, 1994).
Plan Amendment. Golden Gate National Recreation Area, San Francisco, California.
Final General Management Plan Amendment: Environmental Impact Statement. Golden Gate National Recreation Area, San Francisco, California. (National Park Service, 1994).

facilities not only into complexes with similar functions, but also into complexes with completely different functions. The example of the Presidio might, in many ways, be applicable to Russian enterprises that will be removed from the military or industrial sector, as a result of conversion, and used for new, civilian applications.

James E. Meadows

History

The modern history of the Presidio began with the occupation of the land at the Golden Gate between the Pacific Ocean and what was to be called the San Francisco harbor, by the Spanish in 1776. The Presidio served as the longest continuously operating military post until 1994, when the U.S. 6th Army marched out of its Lombard Gate in a ceremony closing the Post. Between 1776 and 1994, military forces of three countries used the Presidio: Spain (1776 through 1821), Mexico (1821 through 1846), and the United States (1846 through 1994).

As the 20th century dawned, the Presidio's significance as a critical military installation, and as a partner and neighbor of the city of San Francisco, grew. In 1906, the post was a refuge for thousands of civilians fleeing the devastating earthquake and fires in the city. American participation in World Wars I and II cemented the continued development at the Presidio, in part because of its strategic Pacific Rim location. The Presidio was at the forefront in the use of military airpower in the 1920s and 1930s and also pioneered the Army's use of women as nurses. Following World War II, the Presidio nearly was selected as the headquarters for the United Nations. In subsequent decades, the post played an important role in the Korean, Vietnam, and Persian Gulf wars.

In 1989, as a result of a rapidly changing national security environment, Congress determined that the Department of Defense would close its base at the Presidio. In October of 1994, the 6th Army lowered its flag for the last time at the Presidio, ending an era in which that post had participated in every American military endeavor since 1846.

In 1972, Congressman Phillip Burton made a grand gesture in passing national parks legislation, which established the Golden Gate National Recreational Area (GGNRA) in the San Francisco Bay Area, of which the Presidio was to become a part. Congressman Burton inserted into the GGNRA bill a simple sentence that declared that the Presidio, should it ever become surplus to the needs of the United States Department of Defense (DOD), would revert to the National Park System, and become a part of the GGNRA. This one line in federal law had as profound effect on the future of the Presidio as did its discovery by Captain de Anza in 1776.

In 1989 the Presidio was deemed excess to the needs of the U.S. military in the first round of U.S. DOD base/post closures, which was authorized by the Base Realignment and Closure Act (BRAC). During a total of four rounds of base closures between 1988 and 1995, the United States military experienced 97 major base closures, and 387 total base closures, realignments, and relocations. The DOD anticipated that it could sell portions of the Presidio for as much as $500 million. Congressman Burton's provision came as a rude surprise to the DOD.

The Presidio did not go on the DOD sale block, but became part of the National Park System as part of a much larger 77,000-acre coastal preservation area, the GGNRA. The NPS began a planning process in 1990 to convert the Presidio from an Army Post to a sustainable national park in the urban area of San Francisco. The U.S. Army decided that it would retain portions of the buildings at the Presidio for the 6th Army headquarters. Between 1990 and 1994, the NPS put together a plan for the Presidio called the General Management Plan Amendment (GMPA), which formally amended, in order to tailor it to the Presidio, a portion of the General plan created in 1972 for all of the 77,000 acres in the GGNRA in and around San Francisco and the San Francisco Bay. The GMPA showed uses for the historic buildings of the Presidio, and protection for the natural areas. One key element showed a plan to create a scientific and research facility at the Presidio, with the assumption that it would be filled by the University of California at San Francisco. A second portion of the plan acknowledged a continued 6th Army presence, and its attendant capital contributions to the Park. The financial assumptions of the plan called for continuous congressional appropriations of $13-15 million per year in perpetuity to operate the Presidio, subject to the annual appropriations approval process.

Several changes between 1990 and 1995 had a profound affect on the GMPA plan for the Presidio. The research facility plans never materialized. In the third round of base closures, the DOD decided against a continuing Army presence in the Presidio, and disbanded the 6th Army. Congress balked at the idea of a perpetual appropriation for the Presidio that was projected to cost as much as the appropriations for Yellowstone National Park and Yosemite National Park.

Instead, Congress challenged the proponents of the Presidio as a national park to make the park financially self-sufficient. Congress passed the Presidio Trust Act in 1996, which stated that the Presidio would come under the management of a new organization called the Presidio Trust. The Trust would be a federal executive agency with a Board of Directors appointed by the President of the United States. The Trust would be charged with the protection and enhancement of the natural areas, the historic buildings, and the military and cultural legacy of the Presidio. Although some Trust activities would be in partnership with the National Park Service, the Trust would manage 80% of the land area of the Presidio and all of the park's 800 historic and non-historic buildings. The NPS would manage the beachfront areas adjacent to San Francisco Bay on the north side of the Presidio, and the Pacific Ocean and Golden Gate Bridge areas on the West Side of the Presidio. The key element that Congress included in the Presidio Trust Act of 1996 was that the Trust would have to operate the Presidio without any federal appropriations after 15 years (by Fiscal Year 2013) or face the prospect of the Presidio being broken up and sold in part or in whole to private sector buyers.

The Presidio's military legacy and its unique legislative mandate pose many challenges:

- How to preserve the Presidio for future generations.
- How to achieve sufficient annual revenues to offset costs of operations and required capital expenditures.
- How to pay for the environmental damage caused by Army operations.
- How to achieve a true partnership with the National Park Service.
- How to balance a local and national constituency.

Goals And Objectives Of The Conversion

The conversion of the Presidio, a former Army Post, to a national park has created both problems and unique opportunities. The two primary goals of the Presidio Trust are "Preservation of this National Park in the urban area of San Francisco" and "Achieving Financial self-sufficiency by the year 2013". In meeting those twin goals, the Trust has had several requirements laid on it, either by the law that created the Presidio Trust or by goals of the GMPA:

- Under the Trust Act, the Trust must follow the general objectives of the General Management Plan Amendment (GMPA) created by the National Park Service for the Presidio.
- Per the GMPA, the Trust is monitoring the Presidio's jobs-housing balance and housing at the Presidio ultimately will be reserved for people who work there.
- The Trust will provide a full range of housing rent levels to meet the needs of a wide range of employees, taking into account their financial ability to pay for housing in the San Francisco marketplace.
- The Trust will seek market rates for the tenants who lease space at the Presidio.
- The Trust will seek reasonable competition in all contracts, leases and awards.

After 15 years, the Presidio will retain its historic character, but will be enhanced in significant ways. The 800 acres of open space will be increased by as much as 25% to almost 1,000 acres. The historic buildings will be renovated to meet current building codes, seismic requirements, Americans for Disabilities Act (ADA) requirements, and

Historic Preservation guidelines. The Presidio will have a population of as many as 1,300 households and a work force of 4,800 employees.

The Presidio conducts most of the functions of a small community 24 hours a day. As a community, the Presidio provides its own public safety services including police, fire, and emergency medical services. The Presidio has its own utility systems, including water treatment plants, telephone system, and fiber-optic cabling. All maintenance functions, including roads and grounds, landscape maintenance, and control of special events held at the Presidio, are operated by Presidio Trust personnel. In addition, asset management of as many as 1,300 rental-housing units and up to 4,000,000 square feet of non-residential office space will be conducted by Trust personnel, or by contractors hired by the Trust.

Planning – The Concept Plan And Implementation Plan

The Concept Plan for the Presidio of San Francisco is the General Management Plan Amendment (GMPA), published in 1994. The National Park Service produced this plan over a four-year period. The Presidio Trust is bound by law to follow the General Objectives of the GMPA. As a matter of policy, the Trust follows the GMPA as a concept-planning document that lays the foundation for future Presidio planning. The GMPA is a concept plan and many conditions laid out in that plan have changed since 1994. To create implementation plans, and to fill in the gaps created by change, the Trust has commenced a planning process that will focus on the 13 major planning areas of the GMPA, bringing their planning concepts into sharper focus. This planning process will be integrated with the Trust's Financial Management Program (FMP) – a declining schedule of federal appropriations demonstrating how the Trust can achieve financial self-sufficiency. This FMP was required by the Trust Act to be filed with Congress in July of 1998, and received a positive congressional reaction.

To enhance the Presidio as a national park, and to achieve financial self-sufficiency by fiscal year 2013, the Trust will have to raise and expend over $350 million in capital improvements to historic buildings, infrastructure upgrades, historic forest replanting, and natural area expansion.

The implementation plans for the Presidio encompass five major developed areas, which comprise over 400 acres, and planning for the natural areas of the Presidio, which will encompass almost 1,000 acres when completed. These plans have to take into account the historic context of over 500 buildings, which represent five distinct architectural styles, dating from the Civil War era to the 1940s. The natural areas of the Presidio are part forest and part native plant areas. The U.S. Army originally planted the forest 100 years ago. Before that time, the Presidio was an area of coastal sand dunes and scrub oak clusters. The planting of over 200,000 trees not only changed the Presidio's character, but also became a culturally historic part of the Presidio's overall character. Unfortunately, the types of trees selected have a normal life span of 100 years. Consequently, a plan for the orderly replanting of the forest areas has to occur soon to prevent a change in character to the Presidio over the next 30-50 years. Aggressive replanting, combined with methods to enhance the life of existing trees, will assure that no negative change occurs. The overall vegetation planning process for the Presidio is currently under review between the Presidio Trust and the National Park Service. It is called the "Vegetation Management Plan," and will have a public planning component as part of its review process.

Another proposed element is to plan and place into service an integrated, fiber-based communication system for all homes, offices and buildings at the Presidio. The basic fiber-optic loop, connecting all commercial buildings, is already in place. Expansion plans include wiring each home and office building to allow each to become a "smart building" for energy conservation and high-speed access to Internet-related activities. Expansion will also include electronically based program and transmission facilities to allow offices to reach branches or audiences throughout the world. Employees who live and work at the Presidio are part of a jobs-housing balance program that ultimately will reserve all housing at the Presidio for people who work at the Presidio with a sustainability goal of reducing automobile trips.

Financial Resources

The Presidio Trust projects that it must raise $350 million to bring all facilities, infrastructure, and buildings up to current requirements and building codes, including seismic code, Uniform Building Code, handicapped access, and compliance with the Secretary of Interior's Standards for Historic Preservation. In addition, the park must be operated in a way that supports four million visitors a year, and maintains over 800 buildings and at least 800 acres of park open space. The annual operating budget for the Presidio was just under $30 million for 1998. That operational budget is greater than that of Yosemite National Park or Yellowstone National Park, primarily due to the 500 historic buildings and major road infrastructure within the Park that require vigilant care.

In the Presidio Trust Act, Congress mandated that the Presidio become financially self-sufficient by fiscal year 2013. A declining appropriation is anticipated each year, starting at $25 million in 1999, to cover operational costs at the Presidio.

Several sources of income are to be tapped to pay for the $450 million in capital improvements required at the Presidio. First, the Trust has the legal authority to borrow up to $50 million from the United States Treasury to fund improvements. Second, the Trust has the legal authority to have the U.S. Treasury guarantee up to $200 million in loans, to be backed by the faith and credit of the United States. This second source will allow third parties to borrow funds at a lower rate, thus reducing the cost of improvements. Third, the Trust has the legal authority to retain all lease revenues from buildings, concessions, and fees to offset its capital cost requirements and operational costs. Fourth, the Trust will enter into improvement agreements, ground leases, and venture relationships, which will allow third parties to make capital improvements to buildings and facilities in return for reduced rents for a period of time to pay back the costs of the improvements and allow a return on the parties' investments.

The revenue from the leasing of housing at the Presidio is projected to generate almost $21 million of the $37 million needed annually for operations and capital reserves. Currently there are 1116 residential units, and more may be needed as the jobs-housing balance is monitored. The following charts (Table 6.4.1 and 6.4.2) show the major costs involved in operations and sources of revenue.

The one key cost that is most critical to financial self-sustainability is the capital reserve account of almost $12 million needed. The Presidio Trust has no taxing authority, and will have no federal appropriations after fiscal year 2013. The Trust must have reserves in place to pay for building replacement, infrastructure replacement,

TABLE 6.4.1.

2013 Parkwide Operating Costs

	Description	Cost	%
1	Asset Management	$1.2 million	5%
2	Public Safety	$5.1 million	21%
3.	Trust Administration & Overhead	$3.7 million	15%
4.	Facilities	$14.2 million	59%
	TOTAL	$24.2 million	100%

TABLE 6.4.2.

2013 Parkwide Revenue Sources

	Description	Revenue	%
1	Residential	$20.6 million	56%
2	Utilities	$1 million	3%
3.	Non-Residential	$15 million	41%
	TOTAL	$36.6 million	100%

municipal facilities replacement and regeneration of natural areas (trees, native plants and formal landscape/hardscape). Each of these elements has a natural lifespan, and the Trust has calculated how much must be saved each year to pay for replacement at the end of that natural life. (See Table 6.4.3.)

Accomplishments To Date

The primary mission of the Presidio Trust is the preservation and enhancement of the Presidio as a national park in the urban area of San Francisco. Some of the projects that enhance the Presidio as a national park are:

TABLE 6.4.3.

Capital Reserves

Subcategory	Area	Value	Total Value	Life	Annual Funds
Residential Buildings	2,274,340 sf	$75/sf	$170,575,500	75 yrs	$2,274,340
Non-Res (Shell & Core)	1,973,000 sf	80/sf	157,840,000	75	2,104,533
Non-Res TI	1,973,000 sf	20/sf	39,460,000	20	1,973,000
Non Res TI updating	1,973,000 sf	5/sf	9,865,000	7	1,409,286
Roads (infra.)	32 miles	$160,000/mi	5,120,000	60	85,333
WS Lines (infra.)	597,000 lf	59/lf	35,223,000	50	704,460
Utility Plants (infra.)			2,400,000	50	48,000
Wire-Electrical (infra.)	225,000 lf	44/lf	9,900,000	50	198,000
Wire-telecom (infra.)	287,000 lf	36/lf	10,332,000	50	206,640
Telecom Switch			10,000,000	20	500,000
Natural (infra.)	1,000 ac.	$110,000/ac.	110,000,000	100	1,100,000
Landscaping/Hardscape	359 ac.	130,000/ac.	46,670,000	50	933,400
TOTAL			$607,385,500		$11,536,992

- The Presidio is becoming a center for sustainability through partnership efforts of the National Park Service and the Trust. Equally important, the Trust is initiating sustainable practices through water conservation efforts, energy reduction programs, and use of sustainable products, all of which can make the Presidio a model for sustainability.
- The Trust and NPS are working on enhancing the attractiveness of the Presidio to visitors. The Trust is evaluating additional visitor focal points such as proposed affiliations with nationally recognized museums, and additional interpretation of the long history of the Presidio for each visitor. The Presidio story will be told by volunteers and by employees of the Park, as well as through

modern electronic methods, including computer technology and fiber optics to deliver the message.

- New open spaces are being created where there used to be parking lots, fences and aircraft runways. The GMPA calls for an increase in open space from 800 acres to 1,000 acres.
- Historic buildings are being renovated to allow the park visitor to see the five different architectural periods that together make up the Presidio texture.
- A new Vegetation Management Plan is being produced by the NPS and the Trust to manage the Presidio's open space over the next 100 years, including plant and tree replacement as needed.

Preservation of the Presidio requires that the park become financially self-sufficient by the fiscal year 2013. The Trust is on schedule to make its financial forecasts for financial self-sustainability:

- Over 700 homes and apartments have been leased in 18 months. The balance of 416 additional units will be occupied by the end of fiscal year 2000. In total, the current housing at the Presidio will bring in almost $16 million per year in net income.
- Almost 1,700,000 square feet of office space has been leased to date, out of a total inventory of 4,000,000 square feet. These buildings are forecast to produce almost $11 million in net annual revenues to the Trust.
- A preferred alternative has been identified for the single major new construction project at the Presidio's Letterman complex. Once the environmental impacts of this proposed 900,000 square foot project have been studied, the project

may start as soon as late 2000. This project, when completed, will generate over $5 million in ground lease net revenues to the Trust.

The Future Of The Presidio

The Presidio in fiscal year 2013 will look very much like it looks today with the addition of more open space, totally renovated historic buildings, and a rejuvenated natural landscape. All the natural areas of the Presidio today will be natural areas in fiscal year 2013.

The wealth of historic buildings and the urban location make the Presidio of San Francisco uniquely able to achieve financial self-sufficiency. However, many of the individual measures taken at the Presidio, such as sustainable practices, agency cooperation, visitor-experience enhancement, and park stewardship can be used at other locations or by other agencies.

Government funding of the Presidio as a national park was not going to work in the long run. With a perfectly appropriate nudge from the United States Congress, the Presidio will take its place as an enhanced national park that pays its own way, in the urban area of San Francisco.

6.5. DUAL – USE TECHNOLOGY: A KEY TO DEFENSE CONVERSION

Introductory Remarks

Vlad E. Genin

Russia's famous technological potential is without doubt a great achievement of the Soviet epoch, though it cost the Russian people nearly all that they had earned. Even today, Russian technology impresses the world with its novelty and progressiveness. Not all technological innovations were destined to be put into production; this was true of advanced industrial equipment, airplanes, cars, and computers. There was not enough money, private initiative, or technological equipment to complete the R&D phase, much less to build them. But those "lucky" technologies that won the right to existence as products laid the foundation for new Russian weapons and aerospace systems.

Today, Russian "high-techs", the military-technical leaders of the New Russia, must share their production capacity with the civilian sector so that it can mass-produce consumer goods and services. The best military technologies are being introduced into civilian manufacturing. This is the essence of dual-use technology.

Dual-use technology is the child of peace and the forerunner of conversion. It appeared in the United States after WWII, when the time came not only to get rid of unreasonable quantities of weapons, but also to convert military factories to satisfy the quickly growing demand for consumer goods.

For the second decade in a row, Russia is talking about commercializing military technology. One of the main reasons, it is said, for the lack of success is the lack of money. Certainly, it is hard to disagree. Another factor that determines an enterprise's success in commercializing military technology is the executive management's level of preparedness for this difficult process. Whether these statements are true or not, this process was not easy in the United States.

One of the main goals of Russian-international joint ventures was the transfer of technology. This promising process was not successful, however, for a variety of reasons. Among the most important was the inadequate understanding, first of all, by the Russian parties of the nature of international technology transfer, international alliances, and principles of the market economy. The fate of international technological cooperation in Russia depends on the correction of these misunderstandings.

Harry Sello

The History

With the ending of World War II, the United States economy reverted largely to its pre-war status of a peacetime economy. At the same time, however, came a sober realization of the military and financial impact of the Cold War period. For roughly the next forty-five years, until the “soft revolution” (1988-1989), the threat posed by the

Soviet Union convinced planners in the U.S. to maintain a high level of support for the U.S. defense community.

Beginning in about 1950, and all through this Cold War period, high technology in electronics, previously focused on military applications, began to develop and expand into the non-military commercial market. Such previously focused companies included Hewlett-Packard, Varian Associates, RCA, Raytheon, General Electric, Sylvania and others. This period also saw the birth of the transistor and the awarding of the Nobel Prize for 1956 in Physics to Bardeen, Brattain, and Shockley for that discovery. Solid-state electronics was born, and the era of "dual-use technology" came into being. New businesses were formed by Texas Instruments, Motorola, and most notably in Northern California (Silicon Valley), by Fairchild Semiconductor. The latter was an outgrowth of a group gathered by William Shockley — all based on silicon semiconductor technology. This was truly dual-use technology — vital in both military and commercial applications. In California beginning in 1957, upwards of 500 new companies were formed — all based on silicon semiconductor manufacturing technology.

During this period, other new dual-use technologies emphasized by the defense industries in the United States were introduced by many new companies into the civilian markets. Such technologies included computers, telecommunication equipment for business offices, and medical instruments, plus instruments for testing and measurement, including electro-optical sensing and detection. Environmental control was a very prominent dual-use technology. Commercial radio and TV based on semiconductor electronics were early products in both the United States and the Soviet Union.

In this same period, data processing and software were highly developed around large, mainframe IBM 360 computers. The Soviet Union followed this trend. However, in the United States, smaller, minicomputers (1960) emerged for civilian applications such as distributed processing. This was followed, in the early 1980s in the U.S., by the personal computer. While the Soviet Union had developed prodigious strength in software for large computers (for the military), they fell behind in the explosion of mini- and personal computers, which were introduced for the commercial market.

The aircraft industry reacted quickly to the enormous need in the U.S. for civilian aircraft transportation immediately after World War II.

In summary, the start of substantial commercialization of dual-use technology in the U.S. occurred long before the conversion and downsizing of defense plants at the end of the Cold War.

The question can be asked; "Did the advent of dual-use technology in the United States ease the problem of defense conversion?" The answer is, clearly and definitely, yes! By the time the Cold War ended in 1988, new markets had been developed and new companies had been formed which provided a basis for the thousands of new and replacement jobs required by defense conversion and "downsizing." The Department of Defense projected[77] a national budget of $21.6 billion to be spent for defense conversion over the five-year period ending in 1999. Over 60% was earmarked for dual-use and high technology investments.

Due to the intricate structure of defense industries, a wide range of firm sizes is adversely impacted by defense downsizing and conversion. For every job lost at a prime contractor firm, 3 sub-

---

[77] *Defense Conversion,* California Legislative Analyst's Office, January 1995.

contractor jobs and 1.5 service contractor jobs will disappear. Small and medium-sized enterprises (SMEs) represent a large number of these latter two job categories. Because of this, the greatest job loss was found to be in the small and medium-sized enterprises. However, since SMEs are generally able to move more quickly in transition, they can take better advantage of the availability of the civilian aspects of dual-use technology. This certainly does not mean that the larger companies do not have problems related to conversion. They may simply be in a position to bring more resources to bear, and generally have deeper financial pockets. On the other hand, large companies have much built-in inertia to overcome in converting or diversifying. Large companies are in an excellent position, however, to encourage "spin-offs" and assist their small business contractors to form new enterprises in order to quickly introduce new technologies and products into the civilian marketplace.

Following the end of the Cold War, America's high technology employment declined from 4 million jobs in 1990 to less than 3.8 million in 1992 and then rose to 4.6 million projected by 1998.[78] Thus the job loss due to the decreasing defense needs took six years to be restored and surpassed. During this period the high-technology electronics sector became the single largest manufacturing employer in the United States. The leading employment sectors are telecommunications, computers, data processing, electronics, and software. The high technology electronics sector developed during the Cold War, for defense purposes, also gave rise to a myriad of commercial, dual-use products. The most prominent of these were semiconductors.

---

78 U.S. Bureau of Labor Statistics; American Electronics Association Publication, *Cyberstates* 1998.

The Commercialization Of Defense Technology

A program for the successful transition of a defense enterprise to a commercial or civilian-oriented business is essentially the same as formulating a business and implementation plan for an entirely new start-up venture. There are some significant additional complications experienced by defense establishments in addition to those experienced by the usual new commercial start-up companies. Defense establishments are not familiar with commercial markets and do not have effectively trained marketing and sales departments. Such departments have little or no realization of the full importance and impact of competition. The establishments also have little knowledge of identifying market sectors for new products, that is, market development.

There are particular difficulties in the retraining of workers previously skilled in defense products who now must learn the skills of developing and manufacturing new products. To manufacture and sell new products resulting from applying dual-use technology also requires that these products be free of the special regulatory requirements that apply to the parent defense industry. Legal difficulties arising for pure security reasons must not be allowed to choke the commercialization of dual-use technology.

The complications outlined above are common to both the American and the Russian defense organizations. Both suffer from essentially the same problems of commercializing dual-use technology.

The great American advantage, however, for the commercialization of dual-use technology is that country's highly developed, free market economy. Just as in the case of the semiconductor industry, the open market permitted high technology electronic companies to start commercializing their dual-use technology several decades before the actual onset of defense conversion. By 1995, there were already approximately 130,000 high-technology electronic companies in the U.S., employing more than four million people. The striking part of this growth was that the great majority of them were small and medium-sized companies! Very few of the large defense monoliths in the U.S. succeeded in large-scale conversion.

The approach to defense conversion among large companies differed widely and was a difficult process. Grumman Aircraft attempted unsuccessfully to enter autobus manufacturing. General Dynamics elected not to convert, but to focus on military business. McDonnell-Douglas, originally an aircraft manufacturer, entered the new field of wide-body commercial aircraft and suffered initially from a lack of financial resources. Loral Corporation focused initially on electronic upgrades of existing weapons systems, and began expanding into the international market. Lockheed Corporation and Martin-Marietta Corporation leveraged their technologies to diversify more into large closely related commercial markets in an attempt to cope with reduced defense spending by the U.S. government. They suffered business reversals and later merged in order to leverage their strength.

However, U.S. companies, both large and small, still had the advantage of a large U.S. free market economy. Their only problem was how to organize in order to enter and succeed in that market.

The tool for planning and implementing a successful entry into the commercial marketplace is the business plan. A well-organized and carefully laid-out plan does not at all guarantee a successful enterprise, but it is the essential first step. The tendency in Russia has been to assume that a business plan can be prepared for the conversion of an entire defense plant, as one unit, into a commercial business. This has been a mistake. Individual business plans must be written for each product line intended for the marketplace. The plan must then justify the financing needed for the development, manufacturing, marketing, and sales of each of those products.

The most critical need for a new business is the formation of a team of motivated people, who not only have the required technical skills, but who can also manage the new business. The management team of the parent defense plant cannot serve as the top management of the new enterprise. The management of the new business operation must be totally independent of the parent to allow complete freedom of operation for the new venture to establish its own profit and loss record. The lack of this type of managerial independence has been a problem in the downsizing of defense plants in both the U.S. and Russia.

On the other hand, the parent defense enterprise can be extremely helpful by assisting in financial support (in the form of either loans or investment) or by reducing the spin-off company's need for capital. This can be done by providing prototype development facilities, testing, special manufacturing capabilities, and even initial production facilities.[79]

Technology Transfer And Alliances

International strategic alliances, based on technology transfer or alliances built on technology cooperation, represent a powerful approach for U.S. defense companies in penetrating and operating in the global marketplace. For small and medium-sized companies in particular,

---

[79] R.B. Streeter, D.K. Killinger and W.E. Swartz, The Technology Deployment Center, 1995 NATO ASI Proceedings, (The Pinellas County, Florida, U.S. project).

alliances have become almost mandatory in order to cope with the financial and other resource requirements for establishing a "presence" in a foreign marketplace. For large companies, alliances involving technological cooperation have become a valuable part of their survival strategies for diversification, acquisition, and development of new commercial products.

The undeveloped nature of the Russian "open market" makes it difficult, if not impossible, for small and medium-sized U.S. companies to operate in that market. A strategic alliance between a U.S. and Russian company offers a possibility for such operation. However, that approach has not so far been very successful. Careful matching of interests, compatibility of company size, adequate financing, and enlightened management are all required and have been, as yet, nearly impossible to find in Russia.

In the commercial world, many U.S. and European high-technology companies have set up alliances based on technology transfer and cooperation for the purpose of joint development, manufacturing and marketing in Europe.

Since a great deal of the technology in defense companies has been developed under the auspices of defense programs, the transfer and use of such technology or know-how must take into account defense contractual requirements and restrictions on the sharing of technology. It must be kept in mind that not all alliances or cooperative ventures, however, require that technology be transferred. Technological cooperation and joint projects can be set up in which two partners jointly develop new products, and work with each other exclusively in marketing and further developing those products.

The choice of the geographic area in which to operate and market is a matter to be decided between the partners, considering the assets they contribute to the alliance. For example, partnerships between U.S. and Russian companies might select the European, Near East and Pacific Rim as global, operational, and marketing areas — in addition to their own domestic regions. Furthermore, manufacturing sites can be located in one area, and marketing sites in another.

Standards, Quality, And Rules Of Origin

The commercialization of dual-use technology in the global marketplace must take into account the need for and existence of a regulatory environment to meet the quality standards demanded by the commercial marketplace.

- Rules of Origin/Local Content

  The European Community and Russian rules-of-origin regulations require that products marketed in Europe have a significant portion of their manufacturing performed in Europe (local content) in order to qualify as "European origin." Local content requirements can vary from 30% to 100% of the manufactured value of the product. The products on which these requirements are imposed are chiefly those in telecommunications, transportation, microelectronics, data processing, and utilities. The amount of local content required can also vary among the European Community countries, depending upon the circumstances and product. Russia, for example, has local content requirements for telecommunications products to be sold and used domestically.

Such rules can severely impact the capability of a small or medium-sized defense manufacturer to produce for sale in Europe by adding yet another obstacle that must be overcome in establishing European operations.

- Harmonization and Certification

    The EC-92 regulations have brought about the harmonization of product standards and certification across the European Community. This has essentially removed the historical barriers to intra-EC trade that had been caused by differences between the European countries in standards and certification requirements. Certification in one European member-state now qualifies as certification in all.

- ISO-9000

To gain access to the European market, manufacturers must meet International Standards Organization (ISO) requirements. Typically, U.S. high technology products such as aerospace, electronic components, measuring and testing instruments, and telecommunications are either partially or fully in conformity with this system. ISO-9000 standards enable a company to receive a certification on its manufacturing process that provides assurance that there is a quality system in place. Certification must come from an EC organization, which in turn is authorized by an EC member-state government to perform quality-systems audits. ISO-9000 also requires the certification of purchasing, assessment of subcontractors, plus inspection and testing of purchased components. Since ISO-9000 certification for a manufacturing operation located outside of the EC is extremely difficult to receive, a U.S. or Russian firm not manufacturing in the EC will operate under a handicap. They must either manufacture their product in the EC, or if outside of the

EC, seek to have their domestic plants qualify to the ISO-9000 standards. This is taking place rapidly in the U.S., but is lagging seriously behind in Russia. Given two suppliers competing in Europe, a competitive edge goes to the one with ISO-9000 certification. Thus former defense companies seeking to operate in Europe must be willing to open up their proprietary manufacturing lines to a complete ISO-9000 audit.

Local manufacturing has become an effective tool with which to compete successfully in the European marketplace. In the new regulatory EC-92 environment, it has become necessary for a U.S. or Russian firm to establish a "European presence." This means not just selling, but making a deeper commitment such as local R&D, applications and/or manufacturing. Large companies have either already done so, or have the capability to do so. Small companies, on the other hand, usually have to establish cooperative ventures or other types of strategic alliances with European or Russian companies in order to reduce the cost of commitment to the market.

A strategic alliance between a Russian and a U.S. firm, based on dual-use technology, could have advantages for both partners in dealing with the regulatory requirement of the European Common Market.

Conclusion

Defense companies now facing the difficult process of converting to a commercial environment must plan a survival strategy, which includes the need to penetrate and expand into the global commercial marketplace.

To carry out this strategy, they must not only overcome the obstacles enumerated in this chapter but must do so without delay. The intensely competitive commercial atmosphere will not permit them to do otherwise. U.S. defense companies and their "spin-offs," particularly the small and medium-sized enterprises, need assistance in every aspect of starting a new business, especially in financing, planning, training, manufacturing, and marketing. An advantage that such enterprises have is their access to the dual-use technology and products of the cold war period, to possible support from the large defense firms, and above all, to the existence of a highly developed open market.

A potentially advantageous structure for such a new enterprise to consider, in order to aid in the penetration of the global marketplace, is a strategic alliance, or partnership. Such an alliance might be that of a U.S.-Russian business relationship.

Attempts at strategic alliances in the area of dual-use technology between small and medium-sized U.S. enterprises (SMEs) with those of Russia have seldom been successful. As seen from the viewpoint of U.S. companies, there are formidable obstacles. In summary, the major difficulties are:

- Relatively few stand-alone Russian SMEs are available in the field of dual-use technology.
- A U.S. SME will not form an alliance with the typical Russian defense establishment. The latter are too large, have many diffuse interests, and have a very complex centralized management.
- Insufficient knowledge and experience of marketing and market development for the introduction of new products.
- Lack of Russian financial resources to co-invest or contribute to the alliance.
- Shortage of skilled Russian top management or management candidates.

The growth of a market-driven economy in Russia would be greatly enhanced by the conversion of the large defense establishments into smaller business units which could then focus more efficiently on developing the products demanded by an open marketplace. A powerful tool to aid in this sort of market development is the formation of strategic business alliances between U.S. SMEs and their Russian SME counterparts. A well-defined and well-planned alliance with clear business and marketing objectives could then qualify for the financing required to reach those objectives.

PART SEVEN

Toward Restructuring

INTRODUCTION

Vlad E. Genin

From time to time, over the past two years, representatives of various circles in Russia—politicians and economists, industrialists and bankers—have voiced their opinions on the results of the first steps of defense conversion and its future prospects. In many of these statements, they discuss the lessons learned by the failures of the first stages of conversion. The main lesson mentioned is usually that Russia has finally learned that she can count on no one. It is necessary to start many reforms from scratch, relying only on Russia's own strength. In this main lesson learned from the failure of defense conversion plans, very often the West is reproached for providing insufficient support for the conversion process. As was mentioned earlier in this book, Russian defense conversion began with the words "the West will help us!" In the minds of many Russians—both leaders and ordinary people—these words were understood to mean "the West will help us by providing lots of money." Subconsciously, this idea developed even further, turning into "the West will pay for conversion." It is hard to say who cultivated this idea in Russia—the initiators of reform, speaking out of their inexperience at the time, or their opponents, who found it convenient to blame all the country's ills on the West.

Nevertheless, Russia has a number of specialists who provide highly professional and sober assessments of the results of the first stages of conversion. These people, who understand perfectly the extensive processes occurring in Russian society, politics, and the economy, who are well acquainted with the real status and relationships between the various forces in the country, have objectively studied the hard lessons of the past decade, and have determined the true reasons why conversion did not take place. Moreover, they understand and can explain to the public why it could not have taken place in the Russia of the 1990s, given the political setup and legislation of that time.

The West has its own evaluation of the Russian conversion experience, and of the prospects for continuing it. Most likely the best procedure would be for experts from both countries to sit down together, analyze the lessons, and work out viable solutions for the continuance and completion of the Russian defense conversion.

7.1. RUSSIA'S DEFENSE ENTERPRISES: BETWEEN THE STATE AND THE MARKET[1]

Introductory Remarks

Vlad E. Genin

There is no consensus on Russian conversion or the results of the market reforms. According to one group of observers, both were complete failures, and led to economic destruction without yielding any positive results. Another group of observers states that the reforms achieved their goals successfully and did generate a market economy for Russia, albeit one with problems.

The resolution of this disagreement lies in analyzing the trends in changes in industrial capacity and ownership; these are the keys to understanding why the Russian defense enterprises, representing nine branches of the Russian MIC, have been experiencing such great difficulties in trying

[1] This chapter is based on six surveys of directors of defense enterprises, the last of which was conducted in April - May of 1999. These surveys cover a wide range of questions concerning changes in production, changes in the financial position of enterprises, privatization, conversion, change of technological potential, social infrastructure of enterprises, employment and wages, as well as the attitudes of directors of enterprises to economic policy of the government. The resulting data reveal important socioeconomic processes in the MIC enterprises in the 1990s, as well as the institutional, macroeconomic, and political conditions under which these enterprises are attempting to make a transition to a market economy. In this chapter we present the data describing the position of the defense enterprises up to the first quarter of 1999. All analyzed trends continued during the remainder of 1999 and the beginning of 2000, as confirmed by several informal interviews with directors and state officials conducted after the last survey.

to enter the market. Only such an analysis can help us to understand which school of thought is closer to reality.

Time is the best judge. Now, after more than a decade of Russian defense conversion efforts, with their many positive approaches, experiments, trials, errors, accomplishments, and failures, we can begin to see answers to the questions—Did production in the MIC increase at all? Who in today's Russia officially owns the defense enterprises? Who are becoming the real owners of the state and privatized defense enterprises? Who are their directors at present; are they owners or managers? Do the directors want to become owners? Who are the decision-makers in those enterprises?

Answers to these questions would provide deeper insight into the modern trends of conversion as a process for demilitarizing the economy, as well as into the general process of political, economic, and social reforms in Russia during the Yeltsin era. The insights gained from studying the earlier conversion efforts are needed as a basis for trying to understand the new, post-demilitarization conversion efforts and trends that are just now getting under way in the year 2000.

Leonid Ya. Kosals, Rozalina R. Ryvkina, Michael D. Intriligator

The best information available about changes in the output and ownership of defense enterprises is to be found in six surveys of enterprise directors, the last one having been conducted in April-May 1999. These surveys include questions about production, the financial position of enterprises, privatization, and conversion. The trends reported in these surveys continued after the first quarter of 1999, as confirmed by several informal interviews with directors and State officials conducted since the last survey.

What these surveys show is that there was a fall in production at defense enterprises beginning in the mid-1990s. This decline was at first very significant, including a 20 percent drop for 1994, but it diminished as time passed. This loss of production stemmed from a sharp reduction in State funding for defense enterprises, which commenced in 1992. Gradually, however, these defense enterprises began to overcome the shock of this sharp reduction in State funding, and to adapt to the market system by cutting many superfluous departments and unprofitable products, and by laying off many workers. At the same time, these firms had begun to adopt new products and to penetrate new markets. As a result the decline in production stopped at the end of 1996, and a revival of production began in the beginning of 1997, continuing at approximately the same rate until the middle of 1998. By mid-1998, however, this trend had changed again, with production once more beginning to fall. These negative trends bottomed out in August 1998, as a result of the political and economic crisis resulting from the August 17 devaluation and default. While this crisis created many obvious difficulties for the Russian economic and political system, the devaluation did create favorable conditions for Russian producers. The result was an increase in the production of defense enterprises, with a monthly increase of 28 percent in the first quarter of 1999 (and an official estimate of 20 percent). To attain stable economic growth, however, it will be necessary to implement serious institutional reforms in the Russian economic system.

Both survey results and official data show that the mid-1990s marked the beginning of a process of adaptation of defense enterprises to the market system. They conducted their restructuring from the ground up, without any direct guidance from the State. Such spontaneous restructuring was the result of the efforts and entrepreneurship of many directors, who were able to find new possibilities for increased production. However, the legal and economic conditions for full adaptation to the market system were not present. As a result, the restructuring of the defense enterprises and their transition to a market system was not only weak but also dependent on changes in both internal political and foreign economic conditions. These changes, especially the domestic ones, resulted from various technical and institutional factors, the most important of which were the privatization of State property and the creation of new private owners for Russian defense enterprises.

One conclusion that emerges clearly from the surveys is that several important changes in the ownership of Russian defense enterprises have occurred in recent years. First, there was a significant reduction in the shares of the two largest owners, the State and labor. In the mid-1990s they owned 71 percent of the capital in surveyed defense enterprises, but by the late 1990s, their share had decreased to slightly more than half that figure. Second, there was an almost two-fold increase—from 21 to 38 percent—in the shares owned by Russian "outsiders." Third, while the combined shares of directors and labor have decreased, they remain sufficient, at 37 percent, to exert some control over these enterprises. With only rare exceptions, outside owners have not been able to influence the decision-making of defense enterprises. This means that the defense enterprises are no longer under essential State control, as symbolized by the decrease in the share of capital owned by the State, from 100 percent before the reforms began, to 22 percent in 1999. While their directors control these enterprises, they do not have sufficient capital to provide for their development and to become responsible and efficient owners. The nature of the director's control has obviously changed, given the changes in ownership that have occurred over the last three years. Starting in the mid-1990s, shares were transferred from labor to private firms and individuals indirectly controlling the directors. This resulted in changes in the status of the directors, with these shadow owners taking control from the directors. In more than 400 Russian defense enterprises, more than a quarter of the shares were controlled by proprietors in 1999, a level that was 1.5 times higher than that in 1996.

There has been an increasing trend in the number of those who want to become officially acknowledged as proprietors during the period from 1996 to 1999. By 1999 almost half wanted to be real owners, not hired managers. Surprisingly, though, the number of those who want to be officially acknowledged as proprietors decreased in the most recent period, from 61 percent in 1998 to 49 percent in 1999. This refusal to become real proprietors suggests that the directors are in a contradictory position. Two significant and contradictory changes occurred during the period from 1998 to 1999, affecting their motives. First, the importance of motives such as "disorganization in society and in economy" fell to about a fourth of its previous value. Second, the importance of motives such as "excessive taxes, too much responsibility for the fate of the enterprise" rose by almost three-fold. Such motives would make people not want to become an owner. Moreover, as evidenced by our data, the disincentives are stronger than the incentives to ownership. In other words, the perceived costs connected with ownership apparently grew faster than the perceived benefits of such ownership.

We believe that the main reason for the problems affecting the defense enterprises in Russia is the absence of an adequate State economic policy concerning them. In particular, during the whole period of reforms it remained unclear what eventually would be the size of the Russian military-industrial complex. It was also unclear how many and what kind of enterprises would continue to function in this important sector of the economy, what to do with military reserve equipment, how to manage the allocation of State military orders, etc. These are decisions than cannot be decided by the market, as these matters are the prerogative of the State. The State, however, has not performed its proper functions. To implement the reforms that are needed in the military-industrial sector it will be necessary to upgrade the functioning of the State, particularly its political and legal systems.

Two Opposing Viewpoints Concerning Russian Reforms Since 1992

Two opposing views exist concerning the results of the market reforms carried out in Russia since "shock therapy" began under Yegor Gaidar in January 1992. One is that these reforms led to the complete collapse of the economy that Russia inherited from the USSR, with no constructive results. By contrast, the other opinion holds that these reforms achieved their goals, and have led to the development of a market system in Russia, although one with certain peculiarities and defects. These opposing viewpoints are also applicable to the Russian military-industrial complex (MIC), one of the most important sectors of the Russian economy. It is vitally important to decide which of these two opinions regarding the MIC is correct, given that the entry of defense enterprises into the market economy has turned out to be one of the most complex and painful of any of the various sectors of the Russian economy.

The answer lies in a study of two aspects of these changes, namely the growth of output and the changes in property rights.

Is There Economic Growth In The MIC?

There are two main sources of information on these points: the official statistics (as reported by the State Committee of the Defense Industries, the Ministry of the Defense Industries, and the Ministry of the Economy), and surveys taken of the views of the directors of defense enterprises. The information provided by the directors, starting in 1995, exhibits certain important trends, as shown in Table 7.1.1.

TABLE 7.1.1.

Defense Enterprise Directors' Estimates of the Change in Average Monthly Production, 1995-1999 (%)

Estimates of Production Rise/Fall/No change (%)	1995	1996	1997	1998 Early	1998 Middle	1999 Early
Rise	9	15	33	53	26	61
Fall	77	42	34	15	30	11
No Change	14	3	33	32	44	28
Total	100	100	100	100	100	100
Decrease (-)/ Increase (+) in production (%)	-20	-15	+5	+8	-2	+28

Production was on the decline until the middle of 1996. The decline was very sharp at first, amounting to 20 percent in 1994, but it subsequently slowed down. This fall in output was due to severe cutbacks in MIC financing, which began in 1992. Defense enterprises have been able to gradually overcome the shock stemming from sharp reductions in State funding, and they have begun to adapt to the new system. They have cut many superfluous departments and unprofitable products and laid off many workers. They have also begun to adopt new products, create new divisions, and penetrate into new markets.

As these changes occurred, defense enterprises began to sort themselves into those that were comparatively successful, having been able to adapt to the market system and to increase production, and those that were unsuccessful, whose position continued to deteriorate. According to our data, the decline in production stopped at the end of 1996, and production revived by the beginning of 1997. It remained relatively stable until the beginning of 1998. Two factors played a key role here: First, the government and the defense enterprises, using the trading company Rosvoorouzhenie and other firms, increased Russian arms exports. Second, the domestic market for certain civilian products was left to the defense enterprises, which promoted stability. This was not the market for high-tech products, which had already been taken over by foreign companies, but the market for standard equipment and certain consumer goods. The demand for such civilian products has allowed many defense enterprises to stabilize their socioeconomic position. This trend reversed in 1998, however, and declining production once again became the norm. There are two reasons for this downward trend. First, domestic demand for civilian products from defense enterprises fell, a result of the drop in world prices for traditional Russian exports, especially oil. This led to a decline in orders for equipment that the MIC enterprises had been receiving from firms in the fuel-energy industry. Demand for consumer goods produced by the defense enterprises also fell. Second, the country was in a political crisis, as demonstrated by the frequent replacement of prime ministers (first Chernomyrdin, then Kiriyenko, then Primakov); conflict between President Yeltsin and the Duma; and conflicts between the so-called "oligarchs" and the executive branch. This political crisis also led to instability in the region of "military-technical cooperation" (MTC), as seen in the change of management in Rosvoorouzhenie, the establishment of new organizations involved in MTC, and the failure to make urgently-needed decisions on reducing the bureaucracy in this sphere. Simultaneously, many foreign countries cut their own arms programs because of various worldwide financial crises. As a result, there was a reduction in demand for Russian arms exports, and thus in orders for the military products of the defense enterprises.

These negative trends reached their lowest point by the middle of August 1998. The political and economic crisis at that time led to the August 17 decision of the Kiriyenko government to devalue the ruble, to default on foreign debt, and to close bank accounts. These decisions led to a significant outflow of foreign capital, the failure of many banks, and Kiriyenko's resignation. Along with these obviously negative effects on the economic and political system, however, this crisis had one positive result. The devaluation of the ruble created favorable conditions for Russian producers, since imports of foreign goods fell sharply. As a result, many foreign producers left, leaving the home market for Russian firms. The result (see Table 7.1.1.) was an increase in production at Russian defense enterprises. This revival represents only a short-term boost, however, and to attain stable economic growth it will be necessary to implement serious institutional reforms in the Russian economic system, as noted earlier. The cycle of "fall—stabilization—revival—fall," as shown in the production levels of defense enterprises, has been caused by the interaction of the MIC and external factors that are connected with Russia's sociopolitical system and worldwide trends. This cycle can be stabilized only with major institutional reform in the Russian economy.

The other source of production information for MIC enterprises is the official data reported by State ministries. They show the following increases (+) or decreases (-) relative to the previous year:[2] (See Table 7.1.2.)

TABLE 7.1.2.

Production Information for MIC Enterprises

1992	-20%
1993	-20%
1994	-39%
1995	-20%
1996	-27%
1997	-16%
1998	-14%
1999	+20% (first quarter)

From these data it follows that before 1998 there was a continual decline of production that sometimes slowed and sometimes accelerated. This official information, however, also shows that the situation changed after the August 1998 crisis, when defense enterprises were able to use the changed economic conditions to their advantage, increasing their production significantly.

Thus, we can infer from both the survey results and the official data that starting in the mid-1990s, Russian defense enterprises had started to adapt to the market system. They conducted their restructuring

[2] The main difference between the survey data and official statistics is, in our opinion, that the official data does not include information on the 'shadow economy', which is taken into account in the surveys.

from the ground up, without any direct guidance from the State. Such spontaneous restructuring was the result of the efforts and entrepreneurship of many directors, who were able to find new possibilities for increased production. The legal and economic conditions for a full adaptation to the market system were not present, however. As a result, the restructuring of the defense enterprises and their transition to a market system was not only weak, but also dependent on changes in both internal political and foreign economic conditions. Since the most important of these changes were the privatization of State property and the creation of new private owners for Russian defense enterprises, we must closely consider the issue of their ownership.

Who Owns The Defense Enterprises In Russia?

The answer to the ownership question is important for two reasons. First, who manages the capital of an enterprise and who really controls it affects the organization of production and the fate of these enterprises, whether they will survive or go bankrupt. Second, the owners of defense enterprises directly affect the political position of the MIC. In particular, their ownership will partly determine whether they support governmental policy. For example, if there are strong owners of defense enterprises who do not want to allow the State to interfere with their operations, but the government plans to strengthen State regulation, as it now wants to do, many conflicts can be expected between the State and the owners. On the other hand, if the State still possesses the defense enterprises, or if the new owners are only nominal proprietors with no real control, then there will be no serious conflicts between enterprises and government. Discovering who the real owners of an enterprise are is a challenging task for several reasons. First, many categories of owners exist. Second, in Russia at present, real owners usually hide their involvement in these enterprises, keeping it "in the shadows". Third, no official information has been collected on the real ownership of enterprises. These data can be obtained only by means of special studies, including surveys of the directors. Our surveys were designed to collect both direct information on who owns the capital of the enterprise, and indirect information on who controls the enterprise and makes its main economic decisions. It is easier to collect indirect than direct information because management activity is much more evident than information on ownership of property rights. Taking into account this difference, we collected information on the proprietors of defense enterprises since 1995, and we use both sources of information to reveal the composition of ownership and the social problems of management.

There are three peculiarities of the privatization process that determine the shape of ownership of the defense enterprises. First, this process has been going on over a long period. Second, the State's role in the ownership of MIC enterprises is much higher than that in other branches of industry. As of May 1, 1999, "purely private" enterprises, with no State-owned shares, constituted only 26 percent of defense enterprises. The rest either remains completely State-owned (41%) or have been converted into joint stock companies with some State-owned shares (33%).

Third, the process of privatization did not result in effective owners. We presented the defense enterprise directors with a list of 10 possible owners of capital, and asked them to indicate each possible proprietor's percentage of the capital of the enterprise. The results gathered from 1995 to 1999 are shown in Table 7.1.3.

TABLE 7.1.3.

Share Ownership of the Capital of Non-State Defense Enterprises, 1995-1999 (%)

Proprietors	1995	1996	1997	1998	1999
State	24	20	21	15	22
Labor	47	37	38	37	31
Director	5	8	7	7	6
Investment funds	8	6	5	6	2
State enterprises	0	1	2	3	1
Private enterprises	7	13	13	12	18
Foreign proprietors	1	1	1	3	1
Banks	2	2	2	3	1
Individual proprietors	4	10	10	9	16
Others	2	2	1	5	2
Total	100	100	100	100	100

Several points are evident concerning the changing share percentages of the various proprietor types over this period. First, there was a significant reduction in the shares owned by the two largest owners, the State and labor. From 1995 to 1999 their share of the capital of defense enterprises fell from 71 percent to 58 percent. Second, the share of Russian "outsiders," appearing in Table 7.1.3. as investment funds, State enterprises, private enterprises, banks, and individual proprietors, rose almost two-fold, from 21 to 38 percent. The share owned by directors of defense enterprise, according to these direct estimates, was only 5 percent. Third, while the shares of directors and of labor fell, they remained sufficient, at 37 percent, to ensure their control of the property of the defense enterprises. With only rare exceptions, the outside owners do have not a major influence on the decisions made by defense enterprises. While this may be a good thing for protecting sensitive information, it does create problems in attracting capital. Without complete information as to its current situation and with no influence on its decision-making, no potential outside investor would invest in any of these firms.

Thus, the defense enterprises have become non-State ones, as seen in the decrease of the share of the State in their capital, but they do not have access to capital from the responsible and effective owners who would be needed for their development and adjustment to a market economy.

Who Makes The Main Decisions In Defense Enterprises?

There was a special question in our questionnaire devoted to the management of defense enterprises. The answers allowed us to verify the above estimates of the shares of capital held by different proprietors. This question was: "Who among the owners of your enterprise makes the main decisions that define its future?" The answers for non-State enterprises are shown below (see Table 7.1.4.):

TABLE 7.1.4.

The Main Decisions Are Made By (%):

State	13
Labor group	13
Director	38
Investment funds	0
State enterprises	0
Private enterprises	7
Foreign owners	0
Banks	0
Individual Russian proprietors	29
Total	100

Clearly, the main actors in the management of defense enterprises are the directors and labor. Some 51 percent of the directors believe that they and labor made the main decisions concerning their enterprises. By contrast, we have already noted that the directors polled own only 6 percent of the capital, confirming our view that outside owners have relatively little influence on decisions.

A significant role in management decisions, however, is only one aspect of property rights. Another is the issue of who is the real proprietor—who controls the capital of the enterprise, and thus plays a major role in its management.

Who Are The Real Proprietors Of Defense Enterprises?

The answers to two of our survey questions enable us to infer who the directors think have become the real proprietors of Russian defense enterprises and who they think the proprietors should be, in the interest of the country's economy. These questions were 1) "Who do you feel has presently become the real proprietor of the majority of the enterprises in Russia at this time?" and 2) "If you take into account the interests of the development of the Russian economy, who should be the real proprietor of the majority of the enterprises in Russia?"

The answers to these questions were opposite in some cases. These contradictions imply some painful contrasts that exist in reality. The directors criticize the lack of "strong political will" on the part of State. Nearly half of them say that they would like to see the State as the real proprietor of defense enterprises, but only 2 percent say that the State is, in reality, the owner, a result that most directors dislike.

What does this contradiction hide? First of all, directors want to see a strong State, although this desire is not unambiguous. For example, the directors would resist a return to the traditional Soviet-style command role of the State. Since the State's paternalism and detailed control have ceased operating, defense firms have begun to suffer from a different set of government activities, namely the serious defects in its attempted transition to a market economy, which resulted in economic collapse. Defense enterprise directors have suffered from the State's failure to create those economic institutions that are essential to the operation of a market economy: a normal banking system, a system of credit and support for private business, protection from criminals and corrupt officials, and a workable tax system. Moreover, the State failed to create those political, legal, and economic conditions that would be appropriate to a market economy, so the liberalization of the economy led mainly to its criminalization. Taking all this into account, it is easy to understand why the directors hope that the leaders of the present government reinforce the State's role in the economy.

Another divergence is that while 13 percent of directors polled in 1995 thought that the real proprietors of enterprise should be labor; only one percent thought that labor had, in fact, become the owners. The basis of this contradiction is similar to the previous one: while 13 percent of the directors wanted to see Russian business people as the real proprietors of enterprise, as already noted, in practice only 3 percent are the real proprietors (12 percent believe that the real proprietors are criminal gangs). Obviously, there is a great disparity between the wishes of the directors and reality. Since the distribution of property has not yet been completed, one may consider the directors' responses a reflection of the desired "balance of power" in the ongoing process of redistribution of ownership. Significantly, 69 percent of directors polled consider that the real owners of their enterprises are "those who have the money." These replies are also significant in showing that a substantial number of business directors believe that criminal groups have become parasites on industrial enterprises.

It is interesting that 5 percent of the directors believe that directors have become the real proprietors of defense enterprises. This opinion is shared by competent experts on the process of converting directors from managers into real proprietors. When asked about the share of capital in the hands of directors in 1998, they too gave an estimate of less than 10 percent. We think that they underestimated the number of directors who have the potential to become the real owners of enterprises, taking into account the real power of the directors in Russian society. This reflects not so much the real "directorial potential" of these people as it does their disappointment. They feel that they have suffered from the postponement of their sharing in the ownership of the property, having lost in its redistribution.

What does the foregoing imply for the future transformation of property rights at the defense enterprises? To answer this question, it is important to take into account that the majority of MIC enterprise directors believe in strong State governance of the economy on the basis of State ownership. Meanwhile, our analysis of their behavior shows they have already adapted to the market conditions now present in Russia. They deal with commercial banks, have their own small businesses, conduct foreign economic activity, have contracts with Western companies, etc. It would appear that these two aspects of the director's views and behavior—their pro-State economic attitudes and their private business activities—contradict one another. There are no contradictions here, however, since in talking about a "strong State," the directors are not advocating a return to the Soviet State in the form of Gosplan (the USSR State Planning Committee) and Gossnab (the USSR State

Supplying Committee). Far from it. Rather, they want a rational State economic policy, order in the legislative sphere, order in financial payments between State and enterprises, responsibility of the State for its obligations, etc. Besides, they need State support—sometimes less in terms of financial support than of organizational, information, and even moral support. On the basis of the views expressed by the directors, we can conclude that they seek both liberty in their current business operations and those institutions that would promote its realization, including political stability, financial stabilization, and a workable legal system.

What Is The Present Status Of The Directors: Are They Owners Or Hired Managers?

To clarify the role of defense enterprise directors we asked them a series of specific questions on their status. One of them was "What is your role in the enterprise—are you officially acknowledged as the proprietor, are you the actual (though not official) owner, or are you a hired employee?" The answers are presented in Table 7.1.5.

TABLE 7.1.5.

Changes in the Role of the Director (%)

Role of the director	1996	1998	1999
Officially acknowledged as proprietor	7	16	13
Actual owner, though not official	10	11	14
Hired employee	83	73	73

According to these answers, the directors of defense enterprises have "taken power" in that the share of official proprietors in 1999 was twice the percentage in 1996. If we add those who referred to themselves as the "actual, though not official, owner," then more than a quarter of the directors at the beginning of 1999 considered themselves the proprietors or actual owners of their enterprise, a substantial increase over the percentage in 1996. If this is true, it means that a large share of some 400 or more enterprises were owned and run by the directors.[3] This result confirms the suggestion made above that the 5 percent that respondents estimated as the owners of enterprise was a clear underestimate, with the actual share of the director-proprietors being much higher. As for the nearly 75 percent of the respondents who felt themselves to be only hired managers, this group is not homogeneous with respect to their role in management. It includes both those who have formal managerial posts, and those who merely identify with this role, like many of the directors from the Soviet period.

The meaning of "officially acknowledged as proprietor" is not obvious, however. There are two possible interpretations. The first suggests that the director considers himself the proprietor because he is the absolute administrative chief, using both formal and informal instruments of control, as in the Soviet period. The second interpretation is that the director gave such an answer because he indeed is the owner of a controlling interest in the enterprise—that is to say, he is the real owner of the capital of the enterprise.

To determine which is the case for each respondent whose answer was ambiguous, we asked those who are not officially acknowledged as the proprietor the following question: "Why are you not officially acknowledged as the proprietor of the enterprise?" They mentioned the following four major reasons why they are not considered official proprietors. (See Table 7.1.6.)*

---

[3] As of May 1, 1999 there were 1520 defense enterprises in the Russian MIC, excluding the nuclear industry.

TABLE 7.1.6.

Reasons for Not Being Considered as Official Proprietors

It is forbidden to privatize the enterprise	34%
As a result of privatization, the property is dispersed among many different owners	34%
I do not have enough initial capital	25%
The State owns part of the capital	33%

* *The total sum is more than 100%, because respondents could indicate more than one answer.*

Do Directors Desire To Become The Real Proprietors Of The Defense Enterprises?

The status of the directors is more complex than appeared in the answers received. To clarify this situation we asked the directors: "Would you like to be officially acknowledged as the proprietor of the enterprise?" The answers are shown in Table7.1.7.

TABLE 7.1.7.

Attitude of Directors to the Role of a Proprietor (%)

Would you like to be officially acknowledged as the proprietor of the enterprise?	1997	1998	1999
Yes	47	61	49
No	53	39	51

From 1996 to 1999, the percentage of those who want to become officially acknowledged as proprietors increased. More than half in 1999 wanted to be real owners rather than hired managers, which was only a dream for all of them in the Soviet period. Unexpectedly, the share of those who want to be officially acknowledged as a proprietor has decreased lately, and now is almost the same as it was in 1996. To understand why this has occurred, it is necessary to analyze the answers to this question in 1996, 1998, and 1999, as shown in Table 7.1.8.

TABLE 7.1.8.

Change in the Structure of the Motives for Refusing to be an Official Proprietor (%)

Motive for refusing to be an official proprietor	1996	1998	1999
Disorganization in society and in economy	65	75	59
Bad position of the enterprise	12	19	13
My relations with labor will worsen	12	16	11
Excessive taxes, too much responsibility for the fate of the enterprise	7	9	26
Being an owner will not increase my income	7	15	13

Two significant and paradoxical changes in the directors' motives for refusing to be the official owner occurred during 1998-1999. First, the percentage that indicated the reason "disorganization in society and in economy" fell significantly. This change, in itself, shows the role of owner as more attractive in the eyes of the directors. Second, the proportion that indicated "excessive taxes, too much responsibility for the fate of the enterprise" rose by almost three times. This change, by contrast, shows ownership as less attractive. So the factors of repulsion were stronger than those of attraction—the costs connected with this role grew faster than the benefits. Since respondents identified excess taxes as the principal negative factor, their change in attitude was caused by defects in State economic policy. Directors of defense enterprises, then, are in a basically contradictory situation. On the one hand, more than a half of those who are not owners would like to have the official status of proprietors. On the other hand, the objective conditions of their enterprises make them reluctant to take on this role. From our analysis it follows that the responsibility for creating more positive conditions for the directors of defense enterprise to become proprietors lies with the State.

Despite their negative feelings about becoming proprietors themselves, directors sometimes try to act as if they were proprietors, and in doing so find themselves in conflict with the actual new owners of their enterprises. Only 3 percent of the directors polled noted that such conflicts exist, whereas 72 percent answered that relations with the owners are constructive and business-like. The remaining 25 percent said that they have no relations with the owners. This response needs further analysis. It is possible that this last figure indicates that at a fourth of these enterprises the "property factor" does not operate, and thus has no real influence on the behavior of directors. Alternatively, the directors may be the real owners of these enterprises even though they do not admit it. In any case, as is well known from other sources, conflicts between the directors of enterprises and their new owners do occur, and sometimes are acute.

What Are The Reasons For These Trends?

These trends, and the situation concerning the capital of defense enterprises can be explained in many ways. These include the dominance of large enterprises in the MIC, secrecy regulations, political controversies over defense policy, the breakup of economic relationships after the disintegration of the USSR, and others. In our view, however, the main explanation is the absence of an appropriate State economic policy toward this sector. In particular, throughout the entire period of reforms it was unclear what the size of the Russian MIC would eventually be. It was also unclear how many and what kind of enterprises would remain in the complex, what should be done with reserve military equipment, how best to allocate State military orders, etc. None of these decisions could be worked out on the basis of the market, as they are the prerogative of the State, but the State did not perform its own functions with respect to the MIC.

It is true that by the end of 1997 a special program for MIC restructuring was designed under the supervision of the former Minister of the Economy Yakov Urinson and was approved by the government. This program required the following:

1) A reduction in the number of defense enterprises to facilitate concentration of State orders;
2) The transfer of some defense enterprises to the civilian sector;
3) The establishment of a small number of defense enterprises completely controlled by the State, without any participation by private owners;
4) The acceleration of privatization, with a reduction in the number of enterprises whose privatization was forbidden, and the sale of State blocks of shares of other enterprises;
5) The integration of these defense enterprises through the creation of holding companies and transnational corporations and the amalgamation of R&D institutes and production facilities;
6) The separation of military and civilian production;
7) The further conversion of defense firms to civilian production.

Because of the political crisis in 1998, during which Urinson retired, these and other planned measures were not executed. Unfortunately, none of the four governments of 1998 was able to work out a program for the further transformation of the Russian MIC. As of the beginning of the year 2000 there is no reason to hope that any rational program of MIC transformation will be designed or executed. To design and execute such a program, it would be necessary to normalize the functioning of the State, including its political and legal systems.

7.2. THE DECISION-MAKING PROCESS: WHAT AND HOW?

Introductory Remarks

Vlad E. Genin

In judging a defense enterprise's success or failure, we immediately turn to its decision-making process. When talking about headlong conversion and the failure of conversion plans, directors of defense enterprises would refer to external factors and problems, and perhaps not without reason.

But what about the directors' level of professionalism, their marketing and organizational skills, and their ability to make decisions under the new-to-them conditions of a free market economy? Were they always faultless? Almost a hundred years ago, George Moore said, "The wrong way always seems the more reasonable."[4] On what basis do directors make decisions, and how do they choose conversion strategies?

So far, little attention has been paid to the decision-making process that drives the conversion of defense enterprises. How do directors select conversion and restructuring strategies? And why do they change strategies?

To a certain extent, in the environment of defense enterprises, technical characteristics and "genetic inheritance" determine choices, as these factors define

[4] George Moore (1852-1922) Irish Author. *The Concise Columbia*, p.74.

the menu of conversion and restructuring strategies from which an enterprise can choose. In some cases, the menu is very limited, and we can easily explain the choices made by directors. But the task becomes more difficult when the menu is large, and yet the enterprise chooses one of the most constraining strategies. It is even more difficult when directors choose constraining strategies that they know may be harmful to their companies.

So far, the literature has examined some cases of decision-making, mainly those in which clearly opportunistic behavior has been observed. These are the cases in which the directors aim at satisfying their own interests, and divert their enterprises' resources to their own purposes. Choices were made by default.

But these explanations do not allow us to clearly define the modalities of directors' choices. What are their motivations and objectives? How do these two elements translate in terms of choices? Also, how do they affect the outcome of conversion?

Sonia Ben Ouagrham

By enhancing the importance of the environment for conversion in Russia, we may be entitled to believe that conversion is not affected by directors' choices. However, although the regional, historical, and technical characteristics do have a major impact on conversion, directors still have to choose among the options proposed.

Case studies have shown that directors' choices are based on three main elements: survival, profit, and uncertainty. The evolution of the notion of survival and the objectives assigned to it trigger an evolution of the definition given to profit. This will have an impact on the restructuring possibilities for each enterprise.

The third element determining choices is uncertainty. Political and economic changes have created a situation in which market uncertainties have been added to the former Soviet-era uncertainties: production, environment, rules, and situation uncertainties. The type and intensity of the uncertainties encountered by defense enterprises will determine the choices of conversion strategies.

Therefore, by analyzing the conversion of specific enterprises in the light of these three elements, it becomes possible to determine the role played by directors in the success or failure of conversion, and to measure their management and entrepreneurial abilities.

Survival And Profit

In order to understand what lies behind the notion of survival, we need to determine what is a living enterprise and what is a dead enterprise.

In a market environment, the main objective of commercial enterprises is to maximize profits – or at least to make a positive profit – and to minimize losses. Therefore, an enterprise is alive as long as it makes enough profits to increase its activity level, up to the point where it becomes impossible or unprofitable to develop further. Losses are acceptable only in the short term, during a temporary crisis or at the beginning of an enterprise's activities. But in the long term, losses can lead to the death of the enterprise concerned. The accumulation of debts by an enterprise may indeed lead State authorities to declare bankruptcy.

Thus during a crisis, a commercial enterprise will ensure its survival by maintaining a level of activity sufficient to make a minimum profit in order to cover costs. This implies an adjustment strategy, which may translate into a decrease of the range of goods produced as a function of the profits they generate, and/or a stricter management of stocks, a decrease in wage costs, layoffs, or some combination of these.

For Soviet enterprises, life and development in the planning system were not measured in terms of monetary profits. The existence of Soviet enterprises was justified by their producer function, and their survival was directly connected to their negotiating power during the conception of the Plan. Therefore, an enterprise was alive as long as it maintained its production, and an increase in its production as well as in its size generated an increase in its gains in terms of power.

Thus, the survival of defense enterprises was ensured by their ability to implement the Plan. This implied that they possessed sufficient labor and enough material stocks. Consequently, the adjustment of a Soviet enterprise during a crisis did not translate into a decrease in its volume of production and expenses, but an intensification of the behaviors that allowed a maximization of its reserves: exaggerated needs, minimization of production capabilities, and mobilization of all personal connections in order to get the required supplies.

Now, the question is to determine what survival means during the transition period. As the Soviet system has been destroyed, the Soviet notion of survival is not valid any more. On the other hand, the market is not yet established in Russia, which implies that survival is not yet a function of the monetary profits made. Further, we observe that some enterprises have almost stopped producing, but they do not consider themselves dead, while others in the same situation think of themselves as about to die.

As a result, the definition of survival is not only different from that prevailing in the Soviet era or in market economies, but also varies among enterprises. This implies that defense enterprises also have different definitions for profit. It is therefore essential to determine what generated such differences, and what are the consequences in terms of conversion and restructuring.

Survival In The Transition Period

Survival in the transition phase underwent two important periods. During the first period – 1992 to late 1993 – the definition of survival remained very similar to the Soviet definition. The reason behind this was that during that period, many defense directors considered – or hoped – that the changes would be temporary, and that the government would ultimately reverse its policy. Their objective was thus to survive until the situation returned to normal. This meant supporting production and maintaining a sufficient labor force in order to be able to influence decisions.

In a context of increasing inflation, these two objectives implied an increase in salaries, and the consumption of the reserves accumulated during the Soviet era in order to keep producing. During that first period, profit was still measured in terms of power, and the majority of defense enterprises used their connections in the government in order to obtain the required funds to pay salaries and maintain social infrastructures. (Recall that social infrastructures not only represented a major part of an employee's income, but also helped maintain employees on the payroll.) The softening of Shock Therapy in the middle of 1992 confirmed directors in their choices: the fact that the government resorted to extra-budgetary funds to support enterprises, just as in Soviet times (subsidies, low interest-rate loans, tax cuts) proved that it was still possible to take advantage of the clientelist system.

The second period – late 1993 to early 1994 – emerged with the growing instability and the new characteristics of the economic policy. Starting from the end of 1993, the government tried to control its deficit by sequestrating the funds allocated in the budget. The various ministries, and especially the Ministry of Defense and the Ministry of Economics, struggled over the financial issue, as the funds promised by the former were not delivered by the latter. In such conditions, survival could not be efficiently ensured just by using the clientelist system; power had dispersed, and it became increasingly difficult to identify the key actors.

Further, maintaining a high level of production was not "profitable" any more, as the funds received from the State became increasingly irregular and low in value, which implies that they did not compensate for the costs of maintaining production and excess labor any more. Taxes, and especially taxes on salaries, were indeed very high, and this ultimately invalidated the notion of survival based on an oversized labor.

Further, during that period, the financial needs of the State, and the emergence of large financial groups, which concentrated the greatest part of the national wealth, generated new sources of profit, as well as a new elite. Financial speculation ensured higher and more regular revenues than those obtained through lobbying activities, and the federal authorities became more sensitive to the arguments of big financial groups.

In such conditions, the preservation of the former infrastructure and organization became an obstacle to survival. Therefore, enterprises started actively decreasing their production volume, transferring their social infrastructures to local authorities, and laying off personnel.

Profit became financial, but it was not a criterion of profitability yet. And although enterprises had been forced to find new sources of financing, they had not abandoned the idea of a policy reversal, which they did not expect to translate into a return to the command economy, but a preservation into the defense complex. In the aftermath, the restructuring measures applied by defense enterprises only aimed at ensuring their survival under new conditions. But the ultimate goal remained unchanged.

Consequences In Terms Of Restructuring

Although directors were mostly motivated by survival, they did not use the same tactics to reach that goal.

During the first period, they used two main tactics. The first consisted of providing employees with an activity just to keep them busy. The second took the form of an attempt to stabilize the enterprise and its activity.

These two tactics turned the defense enterprises in two opposite directions: the first leads to the preservation of the Soviet organizational system as a whole, as well as to the consumption of the accumulated reserves. The aim of that organizational system was only to produce; the nature of the production had no importance. But this tactic did not provide revenues for the enterprise, as the goods produced were not necessarily sold.

The second tactic leads to a reorganization of the structure, and often to a change in the nature of the goods produced, even while the social infrastructures required to fix the labor were maintained. It could also lead to some investments (new equipment, market research, etc.), and allow the enterprise to make a profit from the sale of its production, or favor a change in mentalities, which is in itself a major achievement.

The second period showed clearer differences in behaviors, and started generating a change in the objectives assigned to survival. Here also, two main tactics have been employed.

The first tactic consisted of getting rid of everything that was considered an unnecessary burden, in order to release funds for speculation. The purchase of government *GKO* bonds, which provided very attractive interests rates in spite of some fluctuations, was one speculation option used by directors. Directors started to actively transfer social infrastructures to local authorities (except in cities where profit could be derived from real estate), or they simply stopped maintaining them. Salaries were sharply decreased or long delayed. Wage arrears are common in Russia, but in this specific case, they were the result of a conscious strategy on the part of management. Resources were therefore diverted from production and enterprises, and restructuring measures were deliberately aimed at decreasing the level of activity as well as the size of enterprises. But they did not result in a reorganization of production for the purpose of producing competitive goods or changing mentalities.

The second tactic used by directors consisted of a restructuring aimed at meeting a real demand, and making a monetary profit. This does not mean that directors did not try to derive some profits from speculation. But unlike the first group of directors, they used at least part of the released funds for production. This tactic also involved unloading, or just minimally maintaining, the social infrastructures. But the wage policy was differentiated: the needed personnel kept on being regularly paid, while the other employees suffered long wage arrears. This ultimately encouraged them to quit.

The evolution of the notions of profit and survival has therefore been divided into two periods, and led to a certain restructuring of defense enterprises, and sometimes even generated changes in behaviors. It also allowed some directors to think about the future of their enterprises, and assign new objectives for their survival. The real chances of conversion success must therefore be assessed as a function of the tactics used during both periods.

The enterprises that used tactics of the first kind previously mentioned in both periods are those, which retain Soviet behaviors. These common practices include the diversion of corporate resources to private use, as when the management uses corporate funds for the construction of private homes or to pay for trips in foreign countries, while employees are unpaid. Enterprises in which such practices are the rule are devastated by them, since their equipment is not renewed, and they lose their competent labor when there are job opportunities in other sectors of the economy. Even if these enterprises start with high technological competence, the destruction of research and work teams due to the loss of personnel will lead to the irreversible loss of knowledge.

The enterprises which used the first tactic during the first period, and the second tactic during the second period, usually selected conversion strategies which allowed them to get acquainted with their environment. The diversification of production is usually the strategy used for that purpose. In that context, enterprises can intensify prior production, exploit their dual-use technologies or start a new production line that has nothing to do with their prior activities, depending on the menu that is proposed by the regional characteristics.

The enterprises, which used the second tactic in both periods, are those that have the greatest chances of succeeding in their conversion efforts, as well as the greatest ability to adapt to a market environment. They have indeed tried to get acquainted with their environment during the first period, and they concentrated their resources on a limited amount of production for which there was real demand during the second period. These enterprises have also created a development strategy, and therefore they are not motivated by pure survival objectives any more[5].

By aggregating these results, defense enterprises can therefore be assigned to three distinct categories. The first is composed of enterprises, which did not assign any new objectives to their survival. Their choices can therefore be likened to reflexes, which in the long term will lead to their death because they are not adapted to the environment. The second category consists of enterprises which did not assign new objectives to their survival, but whose choices are responses to the incentives of their environment. This is a case of "blind" development, which in some situations may lead to successful conversion. Finally, the third category is made up of the enterprises which have explicitly designed a development strategy, and whose decisions are guided not only by the need to survive today, but also by their vision of the future. Russian defense enterprises had therefore to choose between two reactive strategies and one active strategy.

---

[5] Case studies do not show situations when enterprises chose tactic number 2 during the first period and tactic number 1 during the second period. However, if this case actually exists, the shift can probably be explained by a sudden change in the enterprise's environment or its situation.

To summarize, we can say that historical, geographical, technical, and regional factors determine the menu of strategies from which enterprises can choose, but the use and the results of these strategies have to be assessed in the light of each enterprise's objectives. In that context each strategy may lead to different results. Further, when an enterprise reorganizes its production, this does not necessarily indicate a will to convert. It can also be a manifestation of a change in the definition of survival. That is why some enterprises, which possess high technologies and are located in a favorable environment can fail in their conversion efforts, while others that are handicapped by their structure as well as by their environment may succeed. The evolution of the notions of survival and profit has generated restructuring strategies whose apparent similarities hide different objectives. These objectives determine the choice of conversion strategies and direct the enterprises on the path to either success or failure. But the evolution of the notions of profit and survival also depend on the kind of uncertainties that each enterprise has to face individually.

Uncertainty

Uncertainty is obviously a major characteristic of the Russian environment. The economic and political convulsions that Russia has been experiencing since 1992 have led enterprises and a number of foreign observers to consider the past, the present, and the future separately. In such conditions economic decisions are extremely difficult, which of course severely affects the restructuring and conversion of defense enterprises. Both require a long temporal horizon, which does not have its place in the limited time of the present economy.

Defense enterprises are in fact confronted by four types of uncertainties, which stress directors' abilities both to manage present uncertainties, and to make decisions for the future. They simultaneously face a "situation uncertainty" due to the ambiguity of the State, an "environment uncertainty" caused by the system change, a "rules uncertainty" due to the cohabitation of two different economic systems, and an uncertainty related to production.

Production Uncertainty

Today, defense enterprises face three types of uncertainties related to production: one uncertainty at the beginning of the production process, another within the production process, and a third at the end of the production process. These uncertainties existed in the Soviet era, but defense enterprises were then only marginally concerned about them.

The uncertainty at the beginning of the production cycle, i.e., an irregular and difficult supply of materials and services, makes the planning of production extremely difficult. Although this kind of uncertainty existed during the Soviet era, defense enterprises did not suffer very much from it, since they benefited from the priority system. Now, owing to the break-up of the Soviet production links, the splintering of the economy, the cost of transportation, and the increase in prices, defense enterprises, like other enterprises, face great difficulties in obtaining the supplies required to keep their production lines busy.

The uncertainty within the production cycle is also a Soviet legacy, but its sources are different in the Russian context. This uncertainty manifests itself in a lack of competence and personnel to ensure production. In the Soviet time, this type of uncertainty mainly concerned non-priority enterprises, which were served after the needs of the defense sector had been met. Now, with salaries dropping or remaining unpaid, and with defense enterprises often unable to maintain the social infrastructure, they, too, lose competent personnel, and sometimes face serious shortages of them.

The uncertainty at the end of the production cycle also existed in the Soviet context, but it manifested itself only on an irregular basis. As far as defense enterprises are concerned, this kind of uncertainty emerged mainly during doctrinal changes, which could lead to situations where the goods produced were not needed any more, and defense enterprises had to develop new equipment adapted to the new priorities, or exert pressures to change priorities. Today this type of uncertainty is permanent. The destruction of the planning system has succeeded in transferring responsibility for the validation of production to enterprises. Therefore, directors now must organize the distribution and sale of their products, and have to do so in a context of decreased demand, and with almost no information on the evolution and solvency of demand.

In other words, defense enterprises face both modern market uncertainties and old-fashioned Soviet uncertainties.

Situation Uncertainty

The situation uncertainty stems from the inability of the State to clearly decide what enterprises are still needed for defense purposes. The State therefore adopts a very ambiguous attitude towards enterprises: it both deprives them of their former privileges, and keeps them under its control.

Indeed, although the majority of the defense enterprises have been transformed into joint stock companies, the State remains a major shareholder. Sometimes the State acquires "golden shares," which allow it to veto decisions by directors or boards of directors. The State also requires that defense enterprises maintain mobilization capacities, but does not provide them with proper compensation. Finally, military orders are compulsory; defense enterprises, in theory, cannot refuse them. In other words, the State has transferred the costs of its defense policy to enterprises, and places defense enterprises in a very vulnerable situation since they are not protected against an outside intervention (from the State). Owing to the instability of the rules and the specific mode of operation of the Russian government, such intervention can happen any time.

This situation uncertainty thus leads to a shortening of the temporal horizon. It also excludes long-term investments, and eliminates any incentives for directors to assume responsibilities. In short, it helps to maintain some behaviors of the Soviet time. Therefore, the greater this uncertainty, the more defense enterprises will be led to choose survival strategies, and maintain soviet organization and behaviors.

Environment and Rules Uncertainties

The third and the fourth kinds of uncertainties are those related to the environment and to rules.

The environment uncertainty stems from the system change. The destruction of the command economy was not compensated for by the complete creation of a new system. This led to the development of a mutant system, which had aspects of both the Soviet system and an unregulated market. The environment has become extremely noisy: information is not only difficult to obtain, owing to numerous obstacles created voluntarily or involuntarily, but it also changes depending on agents. The splintering of the economy, as well as the dispersion of power, has accentuated this situation. And the adoption of different development paths by the several Russian regions has created further obstacles to the circulation of information, which has therefore become opaque, distorted, and slow.

As a consequence a strong uncertainty about the rules prevails. The introduction of the market has not been accompanied by the creation of the institutions able to generate and implement the rules related to exchanges. And while the framework of the Soviet system has been destroyed, some of the practices that it had generated have been retained. Such an opposition between the explicit rules and the Soviet behavior favors opportunistic behaviors as well as the use of coercive measures.

But if some agents effect the implementation of a contract through the use of violence, they may also use it to implement anything. The weakening of the State and the dispersion of power suggest that there is no set of commonly accepted rules that protect the rights and determine the obligations of agents. In such conditions, the State no longer has a monopoly of force, nor can it arbitrate conflicts. Consequently, the rules vary depending on regions, agents, and the "authority" charged with their implementation.

These four types of uncertainties do not affect all enterprises equally. They vary in intensity depending on the regions and the enterprises, which generates a high heterogeneity within the defense complex.

The situation uncertainty, when it dominates the others by its intensity, is usually the most handicapping, because it blocks the decision-making process. In such situations, defense enterprises tend to choose pure-survival strategies (for example, wide diversification of production) and start producing simple goods, which do not require a high financial and technical investment. The drawback of this strategy lies in the fact that it actually intensifies the production uncertainty. Indeed, as simple goods are usually designed for individuals, demand is usually volatile. If defense enterprises are not flexible enough to follow the evolution of demand, they may end up accumulating unsold goods. In order to solve this dilemma, defense enterprises have developed two responses. If they are too rigid[6] to change, they tend to turn towards the client that they know best – the State – by intensifying military production or by searching for public markets.

If they have the ability to meet and follow the evolution of civilian demand, they try to neutralize the source of uncertainty – the State. For instance, some defense enterprises in Vladivostok have clearly separated their military and civilian production lines, both physically and financially, in order to stop subsidizing military production with the profits derived from civilian production. In addition, they implement military orders only when funding is provided by the State. This kind of response, however, is limited to the enterprises that have enough political clout to pressure the government.

In order to surmount the environment and rules uncertainties, defense enterprises have developed a great number of responses, which we may organize into two big categories. Defense enterprises either try to discover the rules that govern their environment, or they try to create an environment that they can control—in effect, they make their own rules.

---

6 Rigidity is here defined not only by the technical characteristics of the enterprise concerned, but also by its environment and by its "genetic inheritance".

The first response is exemplified by the strategy adopted by some defense enterprises in St Petersburg. They have widely diversified their productions in order to explore numbers of potential markets. As their environment allows them to be flexible, they are able to experiment with various products until one of them actually meets a solvent demand. In order to stabilize the rules, they have created networks of enterprises, each being a supplier of another, where prices evolve only moderately.

The second response is exemplified by the enterprises in Arseniev and Bolshoi Kamen in the Russian Far East. Arseniev and Bolshoi Kamien are monocultural cities, where the economy totally depends on the defense sector. The distance separating these cities from their potential markets, as well as the specific characteristics of local enterprises, do not allow them to convert or produce independently. As a consequence, they decided to become more dependent on the State, and have applied for the status of "closed cities". This allows local enterprises to recreate a command economy, not because they prefer it, but because they know the rules that apply to this kind of environment, and they possess the instruments to pressure the government.

The solutions found to solve one type of uncertainty have an impact on the other uncertainties: they can either diminish or intensify them. The key to understanding the decision-making process is to find out what uncertainty is considered the most dangerous in the light of directors' objectives and motivations. The role of the environment here is that it can have an influence on the intensity of a specific type of uncertainty, which, as a consequence, will direct directors' attention towards them.

Therefore, the choices of conversion and restructuring strategies depend simultaneously on the evolution of the notions of profit and survival, and on the type and intensity of uncertainty encountered by defense enterprises. Enterprises' responses to these issues determine their initial choices and direct them on specific trajectories, which they may find difficult to change.

7.3. CRITERIA OF SUCCESS AND FAILURE

Introductory Remarks

Vlad E. Genin

Many observers have expressed the thought that the success or failure of conversion was a matter of chance, and no real measurement could be realized. Indeed, when observing the conversion process in Russia, we find it difficult to determine whether a given conversion strategy is successful.

Different enterprises have indeed used the same strategies, yet obtained opposite results. Further, the usual belief that some branches of the defense industry, like the space and aviation sector, had better chances of succeeding in their conversion because they possess modern technologies and enjoy a potential demand both on the domestic and international markets, does not seem to have a strong basis in Russia. In fact, the sector factor does not play a major role. Some aviation groups, like MAPO-MiG, play a leading role in Russia, but it is more due to the fact that in the 1990s they have kept a military profile, than to their achievements in conversion.

The conversion process in Russia is much more complex than in Western countries. The general context of economic, political, strategic, and social reforms generated a high degree of uncertainty and instability that need to be taken into account when assessing the results of the conversion process in Russia. Some observers have noted that the success of conversion seems to be related to the geographic location of enterprises: the closer they are to Moscow, the easier the conversion process.[7] Since Moscow is both a political and financial center, it is certainly easier for enterprises located in this area to get the finances and the political support they need for their technical, organizational and economical innovations, as well as access to clientele. As is well known, access to clientele is also based on personal relationships. However, this does not explain the great difficulties met by a certain number of enterprises located near or in Moscow. Obviously, the criteria determining the success or failure of conversion in Russia are not purely geographic, even if the geographic aspect plays a significant role. Owing to the sharp differences in the environment, we cannot evaluate the Russian conversion effort by the same criteria as those used for Western defense firms evolving in stable market economies. What criteria should be used, then, to measure the success or failure of conversion? Are there any success stories in Russia? What factors influence the outcome of conversion?

Sonia Ben Ouagrham

A thorough analysis of conversion in Russia[8] shows that conversion is influenced by four groups of factors, and that success or

---

[7] Interview by Dr. Sonia Ben Ouagrham with Mr. Yeremenko and Mr. Rassadine, Center for Economic and Mathematical Research (TsEMI), Moscow, December 1995.

[8] The author conducted a regional study of the conversion process in Russia between 1995 and 1998. Sixteen cities located in 12 regions of the European part of Russia, Western and Eastern Siberia and the Far East were analyzed. The sector analysis covered about 50 enterprises in the following fields of activity:

failure is not due to chance. The first is the "sector factor". The characteristics of each branch of defense industry may indeed hamper or contribute to conversion. However, the sector factor has much less impact on the success or failure of conversion than the other factors, like the treatment of defense enterprises by the State. The uncertainty that is generated by the State determines the ultimate goal of each defense enterprise (mere survival or true conversion) as well as their choices in terms of conversion and restructuring strategies. Geographic location and the Soviet legacy compose the third set of factors, which determine not only the feasibility of conversion but also the ability of each defense enterprise to convert. The last factor is the regional economic, political, and social environment of defense enterprises. It is the most important factor because the regional characteristics have the power to increase or decrease the effects of all the other factors. It is worth noting that these four groups of factors need to be considered not independently but as a combination, for their cumulative effects can be likened to a chemical reaction, whose result depends as much on the quantity of the various ingredients used as of the order in which they are added.

One interesting feature of conversion in Russia is that defense enterprises have used a limited number of strategies, classified as passive strategies (applied by other organizations or individuals than the enterprise concerned) and active strategies (applied by the enterprises themselves). Each strategy has advantages and disadvantages, but there is no direct correspondence between the conversion and restructuring strategies adopted and the failure or success of conversion. In other

---

naval, ground weapon production, nuclear, aviation and space, electronics, and component production.

words, a given strategy can generate positive results for one enterprise and negative results for another.

However, some strategies are very harmful when used in the long term. For instance, a wide diversification of production and markets usually leads to a dispersion of resources, which may ultimately lead to the death of the concerned enterprise because it seldom has the ability and means to change strategies. In other words, some strategies have a strong lock-in effect.

Some enterprises have used a greater variety of conversion and restructuring strategies while some others tend to use only a limited number of them. Some enterprises also change strategies quite often while others are much less flexible. The degree of flexibility of defense enterprises does not seem to be uniformly related to the lock-in effect corresponding to each strategy—that is, some strategies tend to have a very strong lock-in effect for some enterprises and a much weaker lock-in effect for some others, even if they are used in the long term.

These developments suggest that the positive or negative effect of each strategy is determined by external factors. One of these factors lies in the specific characteristics of each branch of defense industry.

The Sector Factor

The branches that use very specialized equipment and technologies are those, which encounter greater difficulties in conversion. This is the case with the nuclear and naval shipbuilding industries.[9] At first glance, it would seem that naval shipyards could

---

9 Sonia Ben Ouagrham, *Conversion of the Naval Industry in Russia,* Contribution to The Future of Russia as a Maritime Power, conference sponsored and organized by the Department of National Security Affairs, Naval

convert by producing civilian ships: the technologies, the equipment and the facilities are similar. However, naval outputs cannot be easily substituted for one another in terms of workload and profits. Further, the shift from one type of shipbuilding to another is a technical challenge, and one that may require major changes in the layout of production facilities. In addition to technical obstacles, conversion to building civilian vessels may be uneconomic because of a lack of infrastructure (ports, tourist facilities), which does not support an increased demand for civilian ships.[10]

In the nuclear industry, the degree of specialization is even higher than in the naval shipbuilding industry, and the possibilities of a lateral conversion are even lower. The equipment used is extremely costly, and cannot be supported by a commercial enterprise. Scientists are difficult to convert, as they are seldom naturally concerned with economic issues—an attitude that has been reinforced in the USSR, where costs and prices were not major issues, especially in closed cities.

The industries that use dual-use technologies have a greater ability to convert. The aviation and electronic industries, and to a certain extent ground weapon producers as well, can execute a lateral conversion by using their technologies to produce equipment for other sectors. Some ground weapons producers, for instance, have started producing equipment for the oil and gas industry.

Nevertheless, these branch differences have little impact on the success or failure of conversion. Some naval enterprises succeed much better than aviation enterprises. One reason is that geography and the

---

Postgraduate School, Monterey, CA, 16-17 March, 1999.

[10] Sonia Ben Ouagrham, *Conversion of the Naval Industry in Russia,* op. cit.

Soviet legacy of infrastructure and production organization tend to enhance or decrease the impact of the characteristics of each branch.

Geography And The Soviet Legacy

Russia can be divided into three major zones, each with its own degree of advantage for conversion. The first zone is the European part of Russia. It has a very diversified economy and military complex, its communication system is rather well developed, it contains a great number of major power plants, and it includes the two most important financial and political centers in Russia: Moscow and St Petersburg. The central part, from the Urals to Western Siberia, has a much less diversified economy, which is mainly based on heavy industry. The military complex is mainly composed of big production sites, the communication and transportation systems are much less developed, and there are fewer big power plants. The third zone stretches from Eastern Siberia to the Far East, where the economy is mainly based on extraction activities. Though this zone is rich in raw materials, it lacks the processing facilities needed to exploit them. The military complex is less important, but it is much more specialized, and in some cities it is totally composed of enterprises that are either totally dependent on the Soviet organization of production or are simply redundant. The number of big power plants is very low.

This leads to different results: first, defense enterprises will meet the same kind of problems, but in varying levels of intensity. For instance, the heating problem may be a major issue in the second and third zones because of the weather conditions and because of the lack of big power plants. Similarly, defense enterprises located in the last two zones may face greater difficulties obtaining the financing needed for their conversion (except in the regions open to the world, like Vladivostok). Those located in the European part, due to their proximity to the financial and power centers, may experience fewer difficulties in this field. Second, the menu of restructuring and conversion strategies is generally more varied in the European zone, and gets less and less varied in the last two zones. In a nutshell, conversion gets more and more difficult as one goes east.

However, being located in one zone or another does not absolutely determine how extensive the menu of conversion and restructuring strategies will be, or the success or failure of conversion efforts. We can indeed find examples of failed conversion in the European part of Russia, and of successful conversion in Siberia or the Far East. And enterprises located in these last two zones sometimes adopt a wider range of conversion strategies than those located in the European part of Russia. This means that there are other factors that need to be taken into account.

Regional Environment

The traditional analysis developed to assess the dependence of regional economies on the defense sector, and their vulnerability to a decrease in defense expenditures, usually uses several criteria. It measures direct and indirect employment due to the defense sector; and it assesses the solidity of regional economies by analyzing the health of the other economic sectors in the regions concerned, as well as the characteristics of the education system and those of the population. For instance, a region with a diversified economy, presenting dynamic civilian sectors, supported, by well developed higher education establishments and infrastructures, and with a younger population, will have a greater ability to adapt to a decrease in military demand than a region where the only dynamic sector is the defense sector, with few higher education establishments, and an older population.

Although these criteria can prove useful for analyzing the regional aspects of conversion, they present some limits that have been noted in the course of analyses of the vulnerability of European regions. One of them lies in the calculation of direct and indirect employment. The calculation methods used may lead to different results, and therefore they may end up minimizing or exaggerating job dependency.

Another limit lies in the fact that the traditional approach does not take into account the restructuring strategies of defense enterprises: one enterprise may choose to relocate one of its branch in a region heavily dependent on defense expenditures, which will eventually decrease the net effect of the drop in military expenditures for the region as a whole.

The demographic aspect can also be misleading. A younger population may indeed be a promise of dynamism, but it may also be a factor of social unrest if the region concerned is economically depressed.

In Russia's case, the traditional approach may result in an even more biased picture, as it would not take into account the characteristics of the Russian environment. For instance, the clientelist system allows some regions or some enterprises to be less affected by decreases in defense expenditures. Similarly, higher education institutions in defense regions are often dependent on defense enterprises, as they provide them with the specialists they need. In some cases, directors of defense enterprises sit on the boards of local universities, and help define the academic program. In short, the dependence and vulnerability criteria of the traditional approach are not well adapted to Russia. New criteria have to be established, and they will need to take into account the specific environment as well as the "genetic inheritance" of Russian defense enterprises.

The regional analyses have shown that in Russia, five regional factors need to be taken into account when assessing the ability of an enterprise to convert:

i) When Conversion Started

We observe that those defense enterprise conversions launched during the Soviet time tend to have greater difficulty choosing a conversion avenue than those whose conversion was launched after 1992, when defense enterprises quickly decided whether they would convert, remain in the military market or diversify.

One reason for this is that conversion in the Gorbachev era quickly turned into a political battle. Defense enterprises did not agree with the way conversion was dealt with, and they did not immediately address conversion and restructuring issues. Many also expected the government to reverse its policy. Therefore, they mainly aimed at just surviving, and consumed a great part of their resources to that end. When the Soviet Union broke up, they were suddenly projected into a very uncertain environment, with few resources. They consequently needed a few more years to get acquainted with the new context, and they did not actually start converting until 1994.

The enterprises whose conversion started in 1992 had the opportunity to observe the conversion process in other places, and to select the most effective conversion strategies. Many of them were located in closed cities that were opened in 1992, and they continued being subsidized by the State until that date. They did not have to consume their resources to survive, which means that they started their conversion with greater resources. They also immediately understood that if they wanted to survive, they needed to quickly start converting and adjusting to the new economic situation.

The importance of the starting period of conversion lies in the fact that real conversion and restructuring were postponed by several years for the first group of enterprises, but started more quickly for the second group. In a context of resource shortages, timing is a vital issue.

ii) Involvement of Local Authorities

The second factor that influences conversion is the intervention of local administrations in the conversion process. The more local authorities are active in conversion, the easier conversion becomes and vice-versa. This may seem obvious. However, it is worth noting that the involvement of local administrations may lead conversion efforts in opposite directions. Local authorities may indeed encourage the development of a market economy or they may try to preserve the former organizational systems and mentalities.

Nevertheless, case studies show that whatever the direction adopted by local authorities, the action of local authorities mainly helps create a stable economic and political environment, and stabilizes the rules.

iii) Structure of the Defense Complex

The third factor influencing conversion is the local structure of the defense complex. We have already noted that in some regions the military complex is very diversified, and in some others it is more specialized. However, we have to add that diversification or specialization is less important than the ability of a defense enterprise to produce independently. Indeed, some cities like Vladivostok house enterprises representing several branches of the defense industry, but most of them are "doubles" which cannot conduct independent activities. This caused them to be badly hit by the break-up of the Soviet-Union and by the splintering of the Russian economy, and consequently they may have greater difficulties converting. Conversely, the military complex of Kurgan is mainly composed of enterprises representing the ground equipment production sector, but these enterprises can independently design and produce their prior or new products. Therefore, they have suffered less from the disorganization generated by the disappearance of the Soviet system and by the reforms.

iv) Presence of Foreign Investors

The fourth regional factor influencing conversion is the presence of foreign investors. The regional study shows that when foreign investors are permanently present in a region, they foster a quicker evolution of mentalities and a deeper understanding of market rules. This is certainly one of the reasons why the market tends to develop much quicker in the areas opened to the world like the Northeast, around St. Petersburg, and along the Far Eastern Coast, particularly around Vladivostok. And, of course, foreign investors are also a potential source of financing for conversion.

v) Presence of Civilian Sectors

The fifth factor influencing conversion is the characteristics of the local economy and of the local civilian sectors: when local economies are diversified, defense enterprises can find nearby new partners and new customers for their productions. However, not all the civilian sectors have a positive impact on conversion. Civilian sectors can play three different roles as far as conversion is concerned. They may be "locomotives" for conversion, in the sense that as they make enough profit that they can reinvest part of it in the conversion of defense industry.[11] This is mainly the case with the oil and gas industry, which not only determine the new output of defense enterprises, but also finance them and buy their new products. Its role is therefore very similar to that formerly taken by the Soviet industry ministries. The advantage of the cooperation between the oil and gas industry and the defense industry is that it stabilizes the situation of defense enterprises by reducing uncertainty. But the main drawback is that defense enterprises may tend to consider the oil and gas industry as a substitute for the State, remain in their role of "order receivers," and neglect to restructure and adapt to the new economic context. They may become as dependent on their new partners as they were on the State.

Civilian sectors may also play the role of "shock absorbers"—sectors that make enough profits to develop themselves, but not enough to reinvest in conversion. However, their dynamism allows them to absorb part of the personnel no longer needed by defense enterprises, and therefore to minimize the shock of a failed conversion on the economy. For instance, all the maritime industries in Vladivostok are now booming, and have offered permanent or part time jobs to former defense employees. The service sector in St Petersburg plays the same role.

Finally, civilian sectors may play the role of "crisis deepeners". These are typically insolvent sectors, whose linkage to defense enterprises worsens their economic situation. Agriculture is one such sector.

---

[11] Sonia Ben Ouagrham, *Conversion of the Naval Industry in Russia,* op. cit

Impact Of The State On Conversion

The third group of factors that needs to be taken into account in order to assess the result of conversion is the impact of the State. The State exerts two types of influence on the conversion of defense enterprises.

First, the way it works (the clientelist system) does not allow the formulation of a coherent defense restructuring policy. This means that defense enterprises cannot embark on long-term projects, but are obliged to conceive their conversion as a set of short-term measures.

The second effect of the State on conversion is related to the information that the State sends to defense enterprises concerning their place in the Russian defense system. The State has indeed given three kinds of information to enterprises. For some enterprises it has continued to issue a lot of military orders. Other enterprises have suffered a sharp and sudden decrease in military orders, but did not receive any clear information about their future. And a third group of enterprises has experienced a sharp decrease in military orders and subsidies and has received a clear message from the State about their uselessness to the defense system.

The first group of enterprises shows a very low level of conversion, and most of the time Soviet-era mentalities and behaviors have been preserved; the high level of military orders is perceived as a clear message from the State that these enterprises are still needed. There is therefore little incentive to convert or restructure. The third group of enterprises is in the opposite situation. These enterprises have understood that as no support from the State was to be expected, they needed to convert and restructure quickly in order to survive. The second group of enterprises, because of the ambiguity of the message received from the

State, has not been able to make a clear choice between conversion and preservation of military production lines. Therefore, they usually aim only at surviving by means of short-term strategies, and seldom try to convert or restructure.

The influence of the State on conversion therefore lies in the fact that the information it sends to enterprises either block the decision-making process, which hampers conversion, or leads them to make a clear choice between conversion and the preservation of military production lines.

The four groups of factors mentioned above do not completely determine the success or failure of conversion. They create an environment and determine the ability of each defense enterprise to convert in that environment.

Conversion success can be measured in two ways: technical conversion and financial conversion. Owing to the change in the political/economic system, conversion in Russia calls not only for a reallocation of resources from the military to the civilian sector, but also an economically efficient conversion. Therefore, the enterprises which managed to convert just technically by using their technologies, expertise, personnel, and facilities are only half way to the goal; if their new production is not competitive, if it does not meet a solvent demand, then financial conversion has not taken place. In order for it to do so, defense enterprises have to restructure, adapt to the new environment, and adopt a market approach. This means that they must be able to make strategic decisions. This in turn requires that they be independent of the State (demobilization) and that a market environment has been created. We know that these conditions have not met in Russia. As a consequence, the failure of conversion is not necessarily the result of a director's bad choice or refusal to choose. In some regions, the impact of the environment is too strong, and does not allow directors to make decisions. The four groups of factors mentioned above give an indication of the kind of economic policy that the State needs to implement in the regions in order to create the required environment for successful conversion.

Approach Of Successful Enterprises

Having said this, we observe that some enterprises have converted successfully in spite of the obstacles created by their environment, or by using the positive aspects of their environment. Those that have achieved this result have all used the same method, with the same timing.

a) they have first won the ability to make strategic decisions by decreasing their dependence vis-à-vis the State. This was achieved by "physical and moral" privatization. Directors are usually influential enough to be able to get their decisions supported by federal authorities.

b) they have conducted some kind of market research, which allowed them to tailor their new productions to meet existing demand. Their directors met with several potential clients, assessed their needs and the possibility of meeting those needs with the technologies on hand. This is not typically a market approach, since conversion was not generated by market incentives (in fact the directors created their own market). This is due to the fact that most successful enterprises have performed these first two stages in the Soviet era, when the market was still very limited. However, they have been able since then to conduct market research in a more secure and stable environment.

c) they have restructured by getting rid of excess personnel (by means of lay-offs or refusal to pay salary), by getting rid of excess production capacity and most of the social infrastructure burden, by buying new equipment or having their technologies certified, by training their personnel, and by reorganizing their production system (finding new suppliers and clients).

d) they concentrated their activity around a limited number of products, which allowed them to use their resources efficiently.

e) they have sought customers who are solvent, whether foreigners or solvent Russian industries/enterprises.

In other words, these enterprises have demobilized; they have adapted to the market and transformed themselves into commercial enterprises. These are the three stages of the conversion process in Russia, applied at the enterprise level.

Conclusion

The developments above suggest that in order to assess the ability of a defense enterprise to convert, we need to take into account a combination of factors: its technical characteristics; the economic, political, and social environment; and its "genetic inheritance". These elements define the context, the constraints, and the possibilities for each enterprise. Nevertheless, directors' decisions have a great impact on these elements, as they can use their environment or overcome the obstacles they meet, provided they understand that conversion must be achieved at both the technical and the financial level.

7.4. RESTRUCTURING VS. CONVERSION

Introductory Remarks

Vlad E. Genin

Any process starts with terminology, with clear definitions that will lead to identifying correct goals and objectives, and finding the right ways to reach them. Defense conversion is no exception.

More then ten years ago, Russia declared the beginning of the process called Defense Conversion. It was an absolutely clear term, which was used in political and governmental circle and defense industries, as well as in exhibitions like "Defense Conversion - 93" in Nizhnii Novgorod.

Since "headlong" conversion, a new concept has emerged in Russia and generated a new term – "restructuring" instead of "conversion". The defense industry leaders justify the change in terminology by claiming that "restructuring" is a broader notion, dealing with specific Russian realities. The older term, "conversion," has acquired a very negative and somewhat derogatory connotation; in fact, it has become almost a taboo word.

However, there is a much more important reason why the word "conversion" has gradually acquired a very negative meaning for Russians. Conversion in its current form has brought them nothing but endless trouble: unemployment and the squandering of intellectual potential and professional skills that had been polished by years of dedication. Engineers who used to design weapon systems recognized as among the most advanced in the world found themselves in utter poverty. In order to keep their families fed, those engineers often had to work as laborers or vendors at flea markets. Deep troubles of this kind, for society as a whole, but especially for ordinary people, caused illnesses and increased deaths at an early age – and people had to thank "headlong conversion" for all of this. So it is understandable why the word "conversion" became a synonym for trouble.

It seems that at the very beginning, defense industry executives who pioneered Russian conversion had no clear understanding of what kind of process was being launched. The inability to grasp the essence of conversion in the long run prompted "headlong conversion," and started a long string of tragic errors.

The question is, what is the difference between "conversion" and "restructuring"? Could it be that we are dealing with the same notion under different names? It is important to answer this question, because without reaching a consensus on terminology, future international efforts to support Russian conversion in a practical way will be impossible. All the countries that had previously implemented conversion on their own territories always used this term, pointing out its political, economic, and moral meaning, as well as its importance for peace mission in the world.

In the Russian federal law *On Conversion of Defense Industry* dated April 1, 1998, conversion was defined as follows: "Conversion is a state-controlled process of organizational, legal, technical, and technological changes in the defense industry, aimed at partial or total restructuring of production in order to produce civilian goods using facilities, technological potential, and human resources that were earlier targeted for military production".

The Russian website dedicated to the MIC, www.vpk.ru, which is very popular all over the world, includes a section whose name represents a change in this terminology: "Restructuring – Conversion". What is the idea behind this new terminology? How should we understand such a move? What if, under the cover of "restructuring," conversion ideals are being betrayed in favor of a return to full-scale arms production? Is conversion really being pursued by the leaders of Russia, its ministries, and members of the State Duma?

Since 1998, there have been many calls in Russia for strengthening the country's military power and escalating arms exports in order to create new jobs and provide food for the people. Could it be that under the cover of the people's well-being, a new and powerful military-industrial complex is being created?

David M. Bernstein

I use "conversion" to mean change of production from military to civilian goods. "Restructuring" is the change in the structure of the enterprise – the introduction of marketing and finance departments, decentralization, new accounting methods, delegation of management decisions to mid-level managers, etc. These are things that make the enterprise look and function more like a company in a market economy. Restructuring can include conversion because a market-oriented company will plan its products in response to market demand rather than state edicts. You can even include changes in ownership (privatization) under restructuring, but restructuring need not imply privatization. I think conversion is a narrower term than restructuring. I also make a distinction between active and passive conversion. It is active when the enterprise takes active steps to change its production; passive when employees simply leave to work in civilian industry. This latter is conversion via transfer of human capital, and in many ways it has been the most successful type of conversion in Russia.

Arkadiy I. Yarovskiy

The military industrial complex absorbed the best of everything that the USSR and, later, Russia had: the best facilities, technologies, material resources, and intellectual potential. That is why the defense industry is practically synonymous with the Russian national economy, and the conversion of the defense industry practically a synonym for economic reforms. We can also consider the military-technological potential of Russia as practically synonymous with its scientific technological potential.

The English word "conversion" comes from the Latin "conversus", meaning "being changed from one state to another, or transformed". The phrase "conversion of the defense industry" (a process of re-engineering the enterprises to manufacturing civilian goods) appeared in Russian dictionaries only in the 1990s.

During the first years of the reforms, the term "conversion" was used very often in many publications, scientific theses, articles, and state programs. However, after the failure to implement the conversion programs (especially, "the conversion forced from above" which caused a very negative reaction from below, as many workers of the defense industry suffered greatly from it) the terms "restructuring" and "structural reconstruction of defense industry enterprises" appeared in the Russian vocabulary alongside the term "conversion." Sometimes these terms are used as synonyms, sometimes one of them is considered as having a more general meaning. During the last few years, the term "restructuring" (structural reconstruction) has come to be considered more general, especially in government documents. This term implies – besides the reengineering of the defense enterprises to the production of civilian goods – the whole complex of political, economic, social and organizational measures involved in the reforming of the defense industry. Very often these two terms are used jointly.

Sonia Ben Ouagrham

I use "conversion" and "restructuring" to indicate two different phenomena. Conversion consists of transferring resources from military to civilian use. This includes personnel, equipment, facilities, and capital. Restructuring is a process enabling enterprises to adapt to a change in their economic environment. This implies a decrease in personnel, a change in the organization of production, changes in behavior and thinking, and in some cases changes in the structure of the whole enterprise. Generally speaking, conversion concerns defense enterprises, while restructuring is a phenomenon that may concern both civilian and defense enterprises. In Russia, however, conversion and restructuring concern both civilian and defense enterprises. Further, while restructuring does not necessarily imply conversion, conversion cannot take place without prior restructuring.

Owing to the militarized Soviet economy, conversion in Russia applies both to civilian and defense enterprises. Indeed, the Soviet defense complex was composed not just of weapons producers, but also a number of so-called civilian enterprises, which were defense sub-contractors, or otherwise served both the military and civilian sectors. Many civilian enterprises, which did not officially belong to the military complex, also housed military productions within them. For this reason, all these enterprises have been hit by the sharp decrease in defense expenditures. Therefore, they must today reallocate resources and use their personnel, equipment, facilities, and technologies in the civilian sector.

However, their conversion cannot take place without prior restructuring. One of the difficulties of conversion in Russia lies in the fact that it has to take place during the transition from the Soviet planned economy to a market economy. This implies that civilian and defense enterprises have to adopt a form and an organizational system that is in conformity with the market. Soviet enterprises were in general de-specialized enterprises, performing a wide range of activities and productions. They also were social agents, building and maintaining social infrastructures like hospitals, museums, schools, kindergartens, vacation camps, etc. They were organized in "Scientific Production Associations," which gathered a number of similar production enterprises and research institutes, located all over the Soviet Union, that were involved in the development and production of specific products. Finally, they were for the most part huge enterprises, as they were meant to meet the needs of the whole Soviet Union. In a market environment, such a structure does not allow efficient operation. Former Soviet enterprises have to transfer or sell social infrastructures, which are very costly to maintain. They have to decrease the range of their products and activities, and concentrate their resources on profitable ones. They also have to get rid of excess personnel, and reorganize (in some cases create from scratch) their supply and distribution networks. All this implies that they have conducted market research in order to determine what products may be profitable, what portion of their personnel, equipment, and facilities can be used in civilian-sector production, and what type of new equipment and skills they have to acquire for their new activities.

As conversion has to take place within a new economic system, converting enterprises have to restructure before they can actually convert. In that sense, restructuring is the first step of conversion—and a vital step, as it allows for efficient conversion. Restructuring had received very little attention at the beginning of the conversion process, and most defense enterprises started converting without restructuring. In other words, they tried to operate in the market with a Soviet-era structure and organization, which is one of the reasons why conversion has failed. So it is a good sign that the term "restructuring" is more widely used in Russia today. This shows that directors and political leaders are more aware of the need for former Soviet enterprises to adopt a structure allowing them to operate in a market environment.

7.5. THE NEED FOR STRUCTURAL REFORMS

Introductory Remarks

Vlad E. Genin

It seems that the year 1999 was the low point of the MIC crisis, and the year 2000 is poised to become a turning point leading to new developments in the industry. The new leaders of Russia "promise to make the year 2000 the year of the re-arming of the Armed Forces and the restoration of the defense industry." [12]

They consider MIC improvement to be one of their main priorities, hoping that the improved MIC with its production and R&D capacity will become a locomotive for Russian civilian industries.

These initiatives reflect new aspirations; previously, there were too many attempts by different administrations to break through the MIC crisis. Without solving structural problems, which had a long history, it was impossible to overcome the crisis. However, in a deep crisis situation restructuring was improbable. The situation was a "catch-22".

At different times, the MIC, consisting of nine defense industries, was subordinate to many different central governmental entities: *Oboronnii Otdel TsK KP*SS (The Defense Department of the Central Committee of the Communist Party of the Soviet Union); *Komitet po Oboronnym Otrasliam* (The State Committee For

[12] Sergey Sokut, Vladimir Sysoyev "Government Promised Defense Industry Money. However How Much it Does Not Say," *Nezavisimaia Gazeta*, http://www.news.mosinfo.ru/news, January 28, 2000.

Defense Industries); *Oboronii Otdel Ministerstva Ekonomiki* (The Defense Department of the Ministry of Economics); *Komissiya po Voenno-Promyshlennym Voprosam* (The Commission for Military-Industrial Issues), and their other governmental successors in the defense sector.

They kept a firm hand on the "steering wheel" of planning, financing, and controlling weapons production in the USSR and later, Russia. The constant reorganizing of the MIC was strong evidence of the ineffectiveness of each subsequent structure.

Besides the central governmental entities, nine ministers—the "captains" of those industries—had their hands on the steering wheel, and each of them tried very hard to force the wheel to move in the direction he preferred. They tried to persuade the central government to pay the most attention to their particular ministry and their products – arms and military equipment. It was beneficial for the whole ministry: orders, financing, additional social benefits for thousands of engineers and workers, privileges, rewards, and even decorations. As a result, the MIC, a huge system under multiple and contradictory management, was effectively uncontrollable. This uncontrollability manifested itself in the very poor cooperation and coordination of its component parts, as well as overpricing of products.

Russia and its predecessor, the USSR, did not live in a vacuum. The experience and practice of Western countries in the area of weapons production was well known in Russia, especially to defense industries senior executives. One of the main features in Western organizations was the decentralization of defense contractors. This approach worked very effectively in the West. However, the USSR, for fundamental ideological reasons, could not accept this system. It would have meant the collapse of the command economy, as well as the Communist political system itself. Many ministers, being sophisticated and well-informed people, understood the need to decentralize defense production from the economic, technological, and organizational points of view. However, at the same time, each of them understood that suggesting that course of action would cost him his career, his high income and—very importantly—his distinctive privileges.

By the beginning of Russian reforms, the existing organizational structure of MIC was very complicated, illogical, and basically in such disarray that it could not be converted without special preliminary measures. This preliminary stage entailed a global organizational change of the centralized system into a new, decentralized one. Conversion needs an overture, a stage for reforming its environment: the restructuring of the defense industry.

Vitaliy Y. Vitebsky

The unprecedented reduction of the defense industry's output (the volume of which was reduced to one-eleventh), including consumer goods production (the volume of which was reduced to one-fourth) shows not only the catastrophic results of the conversion initiatives, but also that the strategy chosen (sometimes with the help of foreign consultants) to reform the Russian economy, in particular to convert its MIC, was wrong. By the end of 1996, the skyrocketing increase in insolvency caused a deep financial crisis that destroyed a good half of the defense enterprises. The insolvency was caused by numerous uncollectible accounts receivables. Among the main reasons for the insolvency crisis were unpaid-for governmental military orders, lack of essential working capital;, failure in the buying power of industries and ordinary people, non-competitiveness of domestic products for consumers with high income (largely because of the tariff advantages enjoyed by imports), the imperfect tax system (which did not stimulate manufacturers or motivate innovations), and very slow accommodation of industries to the market economy.

One of the main consequences of the crisis was a dramatic reduction in consumer goods production. The reasons for the reduction are very similar to those just given for the solvency crisis; two of them are the most important.

First, the sharp drop in demand among the solvent population. The gigantic stratification of society by incomes prevents the larger part of the population from purchasing durable consumer goods. The projected market demand for such consumer goods is much lower than the industry's production capacities, a fact that must be taken into consideration when making decisions on conversion. There is no need to build new civilian-goods manufacturing facilities, only to make effective use of the existing ones.

At the same time, according to official statistics, 20% of Russian families still do not have washers and dryers, 50% lack vacuum cleaners, 40% have no tape recorders, while only every second family had a TV set. Of all of the durable consumer goods possessed by the population, 40% are obsolete. Although some domestic consumer electronics (color TVs, portable radios) enjoy steady demand due to their affordability, their production was undeservedly reduced or discontinued. So the potential of the market is not exhausted yet.

Second, the majority of the enterprises have practically no working capital. This is the case because interest rates on bank loans are very high, previously available working capital is used to fill governmental orders (which often remain unpaid for years), and enterprises are frequently unable to pay each other. An increase in consumer goods production is impossible today without replenishing enterprises' working capital.

Naturally, any further reforms in the defense industry or a new approach to the implementation of the conversion program will require radical changes, especially now that the implementation of the previous conversion program was ruined by the government.

Among the few positive results of the first conversion programs were the creation and organization of several manufacturing companies producing high quality domestic consumer goods, including high-tech competitive products, which are capable of satisfying the most discriminating buyers – people with high incomes. For these purposes, since 1994, MIC enterprises received conversion loans totaling 475.6 billion rubles, which allowed it to produce civilian goods worth 1 trillion rubles. The new total production capacity made possible the production of goods worth of 2.3 trillion rubles. Production of a wide variety of domestic electric appliances was organized, including power tools, power cultivators, mini tractors, etc. These were good first examples.

Nevertheless, the most important problem remains the lack of financing. From the very beginning of the reforms, it was clear that the key element for the production of any new competitive product was financing the research and development process. However, in 1995, only 18 billion rubles were provided for the purpose of developing 146 new types of competitive consumer goods. This amount is extremely low, and needs to be greatly increased. Such investments must be exclusively dedicated to improving the quality and competitiveness of domestic products, rather than increasing production capacities, as they were previously.

The outrageous skyrocketing of prices for raw materials, parts, energy, and transportation, which exceed world levels, became a national disaster. In some cases, if monopolists set unjustifiably high prices, the government must intervene and take corrective action. The policy of charging such prices for energy in our country, most of which is located in the northern latitudes, makes any kind of production noncompetitive.

Falling production causes overhead expenses to grow as a component of total cost. It makes production inefficient, forcing its further reduction or stopping it completely.

The high level of taxes is also beyond the means of manufacturers. Particularly problematic is the value-added tax (VAT) on purchased materials, parts, and equipment, including imported components, which are extremely important for the production of competitive products. In such a situation, when manufacture of a competitive product is impossible without these parts, payment of VAT makes the final price of a product absolutely noncompetitive. As a consequence, domestic products cannot compete on the market.

Existing customs policies have not protected domestic manufacturers. The absence of properly protective customs duties on the imports of, for example, baby carriages, was one of the reasons why a domestic specialized and automated production line was almost completely liquidated. In 1993, this line produced 135,000 baby carriages. However, in 1995, production dropped to 2,200, while at the same time 95,000 carriages were imported without appropriate customs duties. The same thing happened with mini tractors and power cultivators – again because of poor customs protection. Customs policies are not limited to duties exclusively; import quotas are also used throughout the world to protect domestic industry, but are not used in Russia at all. As a result, there is practically no protection against dumping in the Russian market. It is clear that immediate measures are necessary in order to protect the domestic manufacture of consumer products for which there is high demand.

The absence of State incentives for the export of labor- and technology-intensive civilian products remains a problem of the utmost importance.

In 1996, experts from the Ministry of Economics were trying to project MIC output until 2005. According to their survey, if the industry is not restructured, the total volume of MIC output will be only 36% - 39% of the 1991 total output. If this analysis is correct, the situation can be resolved in one of two ways:

- Either the defense industry will not be able to withstand a few more years of the present stagnation, in which case it will lose most of its human resources, suppliers, and distributors, and its existence will come to the end long before 2005; or
- The number of MIC enterprises and organizations will be reduced by 50%-75%.

The social consequences of either scenario are easy to imagine, especially for the cities whose economies depend on defense plants. Their failure could cause the ruin of whole regions, or even lead to the collapse of the country.

Even if the increase in the production of civilian goods exceeds the best predictions (45%-50% of the 1991 level), there will still be very serious social problems.

The only realistic solution to the problem may be restructuring the MIC. Restructuring must be based on a substantial reduction in military production, and aimed at the encouragement of competitive civilian production. The restructuring should include the following:

First, the identification of the small number (approximately 600) of state defense enterprises in which unique advanced defense technologies and equipment are concentrated. These core enterprises should be separate from those technologically advanced enterprises that have been converted to manufacture civilian products. Only these civilian enterprises, which use dual-use technologies, are better equipped, and have a much better contingent of highly skilled engineers and workers (compared with other industries), can provide significant growth in the output civilian goods, thereby solving two problems simultaneously: meeting the market demands in the high quality domestic product market, and creating new jobs. New, large, integrated structures should be created, such as holding companies, financial–industrial groups, and transnational corporations.

Second, the creation of market infrastructure, including new financial, investment, and insurance organizations.

Third, the protection of the domestic manufacturer through customs policies. This measure could be among the most important factors in protecting and fostering of the production and sales of domestic consumer goods.

Fourth, the provision by the State of incentives for exports, including the introduction of bonuses for exporting expensive high-tech products, could be implemented in many ways, from granting privileged taxation to export bonuses.

Fifth, the protection of intellectual property, including advanced technologies, achievements in software engineering, etc., through more effective state legislation.

Sixth, the creation of mechanisms to stimulate demand for domestic products.

These could include:

- elimination of taxes for three years for enterprises marketing newly developed high-tech products. This will allow them to reduce the products' prices and thus make them more competitive;
- introduction of low- or no-interest state loans to those enterprises which manufacture high-demand products;
- creation of export-oriented exhibitions of civilian products at appropriate expositions, as well as of an inter-industry center for product information exchange and marketing.

Seventh, the development of international cooperation, including such measures as:

- disseminating a wide range of information about investment opportunities in the Russian high-tech sector;
- creating a civilized investment climate;
- forming strategic alliances with leading foreign companies;
- introducing certification of domestic products according to international standards.

Eighth, the establishment of the wholesale system, trading companies, and specialized stores. Since MIC manufacturers have no distribution systems of their own, it would be an effective way to stimulate growth in the production of civilian goods. Financial assistance from the federal and local budgets in providing operating capital could become an effective working solution.

Ninth, the formation of enterprises' own investment funds for civilian production using the proceeds from sales and the leasing of excess production facilities, as well as sales of stocks from privatized enterprises.

Tenth, the reorganization of MIC executive management structures. This would include, for example, combining and enlarging aircraft manufacturing enterprises, concentrating R&D work in new research centers, and the creation national laboratories and research agencies, like NASA in the United States.

These efforts would help in the creation of a new cycle of development of Russian industrial capacity. It would help to overcome the economic and social crisis, and increase employment. One of the main results would be rapid growth in state tax revenues from MIC enterprises, as well as the national population. This would help to make unnecessary many social protection measures, especially in cities dependent on defense plants.

7.6. RESTRUCTURING AND THE FUTURE OF CONVERSION

Introductory Remarks

Vlad E. Genin

Within the last thirteen years, several Russian Cabinets attempted to reform the defense industry, initiating action at least nine times, but no industrial reform policies were ever fully implemented. Attempts to develop a program for converting the Russian defense industry were undertaken by official governmental agencies and by public organizations representing different groups of specialists. Many in the MIC held the following opinion: "Between 1987 and 1990, people looked for optimal management structures, but since 1992 they've just made wild stabs at the problem, each of which has just made the situation worse."[13]

None of the governments could answer the main question: what did the defense industry need in these new circumstances? How many weapons, and of what kind, are necessary for the defense of the country? What numbers of weapons should be produced to export, and what kind of industrial capacity does the MIC need for that activity? How many of the more than 1,700 defense plants should remain under the authority of the military-industrial

[13] Alexey Shulunov, "VPK Crisis: Substitution of Notions. Debates About Imperialism Do Not Solve Key Problems of Defense Industry." *Nezavisimaia Gazeta*, no. 9 (182), http://nvo.ng.ru/concepts, March 17, 2000.

complex? Which of them should be closed, and which transferred to the civilian sector?

And finally, how strong an understanding was there that the future of Russia depended on the successful conversion of its military-industrial complex, and hence on selecting the right way to restructure MIC enterprises?

Arkadiy I. Yarovskiy

Russia's "1998-2000 Program for Restructuring and Conversion of the Defense Industry" envisaged that 600 state-controlled enterprises (out of approximately 1,750) would constitute the core that would continue military production. According to its authors, those enterprises should be major integrated structures: consortiums, holding companies, financial-industrial groups, and new international corporations.

This program laid down the major strategy for reforming defense enterprises, including conversion of military production lines, consolidation of all military production by merger, diversification into various branches of both military and civilian productions, and the complete withdrawal of some of enterprises from the sphere of military production.

It is clear that conversion requires financing. Investments are needed for restructuring enterprises, which will allow the shift to the production of competitive civilian goods. According to the program, $80 billion were expected from the commercial transfer (by lease or sale) of excess production facilities and other property (including land), and elimination of their maintenance costs. The sale of shares in reformed Russian enterprises to Russian and foreign investors was expected to bring $40 billion. Creation of new jobs (about 400,000 in industry and

100,000 in scientific institutes and laboratories) was expected as a result of forming new competitive enterprises to work for the domestic market, producing equipment for power stations, civilian aviation, engines, etc.

The program was to be implemented by the year 2000, and the civilian output of MIC enterprises was to increase by 14%, compared to 1997 levels.

A year before the planned deadline, only 10% of this optimistic program had been completed. Neither domestic nor foreign investors rushed to invest in the defense industry, because they did not trust the management of those enterprises, the local authorities, or even the central government. Hopes of selling the excess facilities or real estate for commercial purposes were not realized. The mechanisms for restructuring and converting the defense industry specified by the official program turned out to be ineffective. The process of reducing the MIC in size is going extremely slowly. During 1998, the number of defense enterprises was reduced by only 221. The number of remaining enterprises is 1,528—a number that the Russian crisis economy will not be able to support. Even the 600 enterprises in the reduced core could be too many.

The problem of finances for conversion and restructuring still has not been solved, and never will be until the State's debts to the defense industry (about $ 2 billion) are paid. This action is necessary, but not sufficient. According to a preliminary evaluation,[14] approximately 1,200 unprofitable enterprises were subject to remodeling (including conversion) after the default of August 17, 1998. The closure, conversion, or restructuring of these enterprises (taking into consideration the number left unemployed as a result) will require about

[14] R.V. Rivkina et al., *Defense Enterprises of Russia*, (Moscow, 1999).

$15 billion, and will take three years to complete. And this does not include the restructuring of the relatively successful enterprises, which will also be expensive.

Because of the absence of noticeable changes in the defense industry, the Russian authorities have come to rely on new organizational measures. In June 1999, the management of the defense industry underwent further changes, in which the deputy prime minister responsible for the MIC now supervised not only the Ministry of Atomic Energy, the Ministry of Science and Technology, and the Space and Aviation agencies, but also some newly organized defense agencies for Conventional Weapons, Ammunition, Shipbuilding, and Management Systems. Apart from these organizations, there are state-managed intermediary companies engaged in exports to and military-industrial cooperation with foreign countries. The new system of managing the MIC reminds one of the Soviet mode of management (though without the State Planning and Supply and Distribution Committees), in which the defense industry was controlled by nine different Ministries. This kind of system offers very little hope for completing conversion and restructuring successfully.

Exports of weapons, as a major important source of income, still play a special role in all governmental programs for many defense enterprises. Russian weapons are 50% cheaper than their American or European counterparts. According to information provided by the ITAR-TASS news agency, the volume of weapons exports was about $2.5 billion in 1998, and reached $3 billion in 1999. While the larger part of the MIC is not yet converted, the export of weapons remains one of the main elements of Russian foreign trade.

The proliferation of modern Russian weapons, especially weapons of mass destruction, is a subject of constant concern for the West, and for good reason. More than once the United States has accused certain Russian institutions and enterprises of having provided Iran with nuclear armaments, as well as of exporting weapons of mass destruction to India, Iraq, Libya, Pakistan, and North Korea. However, the market for weapons of mass destruction is very limited. Attempts to enlarge this market will only complicate the problem of getting Western assistance, and definitely will not solve any of the conversion problems.

Effective planning for conversion is hardly possible without deciding what kind of society will be built in Russia. Obviously, "clan capitalism," which is what existed in Russia in the 1990s, is doomed, as state-controlled groups and criminal elements played the leading role there, not the private entrepreneurs who competed in a free market environment. Those groups and elements created monopolies, controlled the most profitable markets, and kept competitors away. In these circumstances, it was absurd to try to convert and restructure, or to expect to obtain income from privatization. An illustration of this absurdity can be seen in the "sale" of the biggest plants in the defense industry: for instance, the major industrial giant Uralmash was sold for $ 3.73 million; the Kirov Mechanical Plant - for $ 2.7 million; and other 300 large plants went for the same "bargain basement" prices. The cost of similar enterprises in the West would be in the range of billions of dollars.

The key moment for the switch to a market economy and successful conversion of the defense industry was lost. The country failed to create market institutions: the institution of private property, contract law, laws regulating cooperation, trade codes, and banking and financial institutions. Without such institutions, privatization led to a vacuum of power, and a criminalization of the economy. The reforms of the defense industry are just impossible without them. Some Russian economists believe that in modern circumstances, the goal should not be the creation of free competition, but the creation of a mixed economy, with a very powerful state sector. In these circumstances, like in the U.S. and other Western countries, the role of the government is narrowed down to creating market institutions, and guaranteeing that they work.

Alternative programs for conversion and restructuring, as suggested by Russian liberal economists, are based on further progress towards a free market. First of all, the "core" of 600 remaining enterprises in the defense industry, as specified by the program, should be much smaller—not more than 5-10% of the current number. This is a key requirement.

Instead of merging enterprises from the same industry, as suggested by the program, a more expedient and more appropriate strategy for a market economy is merging based upon existing and developing projects. In this case, only the lead enterprise directly receives orders and payments. That lead enterprise manages the developers and the manufacturers as subcontractors, who cooperate based on real demand and available resources. This is how Western high-tech companies, which are focused towards specific market segments, develop. Liberal economists suggest the creation of a special state fund for restructuring. This fund would grant loans using assets such as shares in defense plants and gas, oil, and energy enterprises, as well as tax revenues from the sales of weapons. However, the use of these assets as security for hard currency bonds will be possible only after the liquidation of Russia's foreign debt.

According to independent experts, the main goal of military-industrial reforms would be to transform MIC into an intellectual and manufacturing engine that would revive the country's economy. Twelve percent of the world's scientists are concentrated in Russia, but Russia's share of the world's output of high-tech products is only 0.3%. This sector has accumulated a major reserve of knowledge, technology, and experience in solving extremely complicated problems, including those of global importance, such as creating a system for global environmental monitoring, forecasting and modeling planetary processes, developing renewable energy resources, developing fundamental research in the fields of mathematics and artificial intelligence. Russian scientists and engineers could make great contributions if properly supported.

Russia's future priorities in the area of civilian production should be the development of computer software, civil aviation, launch vehicles for commercial satellites, equipment for gas pipelines and power stations, nuclear power engineering, super-high-frequency electronics, and laser technologies. The creation of "incubators" for start-up high-tech companies similar to those in Silicon Valley (California), would be of the utmost importance for the development of small businesses and entrepreneurship. These are Moscow State University, Bauman Moscow State Technical University, Akademgorodok in Novosibirsk Oblast, and the universities and research centers in St. Petersburg and Ekaterinburg.

There is huge potential for the development of commercial airliners and cargo planes. Within the next 15-20 years, the domestic market alone will demand more than 1,200 new aircraft, in addition to those produced now. Shipbuilding and nuclear power equipment also have great domestic and export potential.

Using the MIC's restructured potential in the joint Russian-American surface-to-air missile systems (similar to the S-300 and S-400) for international security purposes might be quite promising. This would allow savings of significant assets, and prevent an extremely dangerous "brain drain" of nuclear, chemical and biological warfare experts from Russia to terrorist groups and countries. Only the high technologies concentrated within intellectual core of the MIC, once transferred to civilian production, can guarantee the flourishing of the Russian economy. In the near future, Russia could become competitive in 10 to 12 principal technologies, from space and aviation to biotechnologies, with an estimated income of up to $200 billion, if provided with appropriate investments.

This is the issue on which many plans and projects have been wrecked. It is unrealistic to expect the successful completion of any conversion program, or restructuring of enterprises in the Russian defense industry, without substantial Western assistance. Such assistance has several aspects, one of which is dedicated to the nonproliferation of deadly weapons technologies. As Congressman Curt Weldon, Chairman of the U.S. Congress-Russian Duma Study Group, put it:

"In an effort to sustain the work of Russian scientists and prevent proliferation of critical technologies, I have asked Academician Velikhov of the Kurchatov Institute to develop a proposal that would enable Russian scientists and engineers who developed missile technology comparable to that which was transferred to Iran for application in its Shabab-3 to work with the Ballistic Missile Defense Organization in identifying those technologies transferred to Iran and in helping the U.S. counter that technology. In addition, I am supporting other proposals that would ensure continued U.S. support for underemployed Russian scientists and engineers."[15]

A stable Russia is the best option to prevent the threat of brain drain to terrorist regimes. But how to help Russia in the stabilization process? This question is more acute than ever, because the aid already provided for Russian reforms and conversion has seldom reached the intended recipients. It is well known that in 1992, international aid to Russia totaled $20.3 billion, but the major part of it ($17-18 billion) was then laundered through Western banks. The Russian Directorate for Combating Economic Crimes and Corruption stated that in 1998 alone, more than $15 billion of this money finally appeared in the accounts of Western banks or were used for purchasing real estate properties in Western countries. According to the Ministry of Internal Affairs, $50 to 350 billion were taken out of Russia in the 1990s.[16] What strikes most is not just the sum "leaked" but also the enormous uncertainty in the Ministry's estimates.

However, sensible politicians in Russia and the West are fully aware of the fact that without external assistance, Russia will never be able to overcome the crisis. How can the mechanism of assistance be made reliable and effective? The prominent Russian economist and politician, Grigory Yavlinsky, believes that "Russia does not need a fish on the table, but a fishing rod to catch it." According to advocates of Russia's integration into European and world civilization, Western assistance to Russia is needed for two major purposes: supporting

---

[15] Congressman Curt Weldon, "A New Vision for Russia," October 7, 1999, http://www.house.gov/curtweldon/rus-new-vision.htm.

[16] Interview with S. Tesis, Director of the Main Directorate for Combating Economic Crimes and Corruption, Russian Ministry of Internal Affairs, *Izvestia*, May 25, 1999.

institutional reforms, and accumulating funds for privatization and the economic integration of the NIS countries. The destruction of their mutual economic ties was responsible for at least 50% of the economic recession. In the post-war Marshall Plan, the U.S. provided necessary funds in order to support the integration and restoration of Western European countries.

It is impossible to separate the future of the conversion of the Russian defense industry from the future of the country itself. What are the possible scenarios for this future?

For Russia, the most favorable scenario is the formation of a civilized, market-oriented nation, integrated into the European Community. The probability of such a scenario seems to be slight so far, but it would increase in proportion to the nation's success in economic reforms and getting full-scale Western assistance.

Another possible scenario would be the further development of "wild capitalism" hiding behind the slogan of "continuity of the reforms." Such a scenario is quite possible, because the forces implementing it are currently in power.

The scenario that is enthusiastically supported by the Communists and some defense industry executives would be a return to a Soviet society, under the pretense of fighting for "people's interests" and promising them social guarantees. Such a scenario is less likely, as the Communists cannot offer any realistic economic program, but only a myth.

Some fascist groups (like the Russian National Unity) and criminal and military groups, advocate dictatorship, using nationalistic slogans. These forces aren't numerous, and they have neither mass social support nor direct access to the mass media.

There is also the possibility that the country will disintegrate into several small regions, with their own governments and armed forces. Some regions, according to their leaders, have all the necessary resources for independence.

The last four scenarios pose serious threats to the national economy and stability of Russia, as well as to international security. However, sensible forces in Russian society have so far prevented them from being implemented.

Today many Russians understand that there is no alternative to Russia's integration into the community of democratic nations. Here, and here alone, lies the foundation for the full-fledged completion of conversion and restructuring of the military-industrial complex. Without it, it's impossible to reform the economy and achieve prosperity.

PART EIGHT

From a Militarized to a Civilian Economy

INTRODUCTION

Vlad E. Genin

As the year 2000 began, renewed production of weapons for re-arming the Russian Army (the MIC's main priority) became a reality. Also a reality is that many political parties harbor the illusion harbored that arms exports are what is needed to jump-start the Russian economy.

Yet another reality is that restructuring and conversion have begun to produce positive results. The growth of MIC's civilian output reached 15% by the start of the year 2000, which is considerably greater than in other branches of the Russian economy. Although this growth is relative to a period of stagnation, it is nevertheless a positive trend. Dual-use technologies are being used more widely in civilian manufacturing. New civilian products such as Be-200 airplanes for search and rescue operations (Beriev Plant, Taganrog), equipment for poultry farms (Aggregate Plant, Chelyabinsk), cargo ships (Yantar

Shipyard, Kaliningrad), and aircraft engines (Rybinskie Motory, Rybinsk and Salyut, Moscow) have become very popular and have started to bring profitable contracts to their producers. In addition, a new trend has appeared: specialists that left MIC plants during the crisis have begun returning. In the past year, the headcount at Salyut has increased 29%. Unfortunately, such examples are rare, while over 1,500 MIC enterprises are still struggling.

The same trend is apparent in software field. "The country's strongest suit is its homegrown talent. Russians are known for their design and programming prowess. Its hackers are infamous for their ability to break codes. And though Russia's best brains have been draining to Palo Alto[1] and Tel Aviv, now some are staying–or returning–home…Russia's Internet trace is on."[2]

Prior the year 2000, Russia developed three economic growth programs: short-, medium-, and long-term, up to 2010 and

---

[1] Editor's Note: One of America's major high-tech cities, the birthplace of the Silicon Valley and the hometown of the Stanford University. Located near San Francisco, State of California.

[2] Sabrina Tavernise, "Dot-com deals come to the steppes," *Business Week*, April 17, 2000, p. 188.

later. The practical implementation of these programs through conversion and restructuring demands great courage on the part of the individuals working in the MIC. Russian specialists once again analyze past approaches to conversion and recognize strategic mistakes. Many of them understand that the command approach to conversion must be forgotten, since it gave rise to "headlong conversion" and caused significant damage to the defense industry. This approach involved plans that were unrealistic and unfounded. It advocated the "all or nothing" approach, still popular from the Communist era. Nevertheless, there are still opponents of defense industry conversion in Russia. Essentially, they want to return to a militarized economy. But it is hard to imagine other sound alternatives to converting and restructuring the country's industrial-economical legacy. Another question is what this process should be like, given the present socio-economic conditions in Russia.

It is obvious that without help from the West, Russia would be in no condition to implement plans to resolve such a large-scale problem as conversion and restructuring. To ignore this fact would be hypocritical. One simply hopes that a plan will be devised to make this aid decisive and final.

The precursor to a new round of aid from the West must be the creation, finally, of a stable market policy—an economic environment supported by a comprehensive legislative framework. The government must provide full protection from corruption and organized crime rings to MIC factories, especially those that have promising, new, high-tech products. In certain cases, crime rings, some of which are foreign, have tried to establish control over these enterprises through the privatization, subsequent bankruptcy, and liquidation of potential competitors, thereby establishing monopolies.

The time has come at last for the creation and implementation of mechanisms for intensive resolution of today's conversion problems. These mechanisms are necessary for the new round of international cooperative ventures, which would utilize dual-use technologies, create new technologies for the Internet, develop and produce a wide variety of civilian goods, and conduct domestic and international marketing and sales efforts. Certainly, at some enterprises, the conversion process should be started over, from scratch; nothing less will overcome the bad decisions made at the outset, primarily in the areas of marketing and management.

The shameful social problems of the former "closed cities" and other population centers related to “frozen” defense plants must be consigned to the past. Well-educated "brains" (former defense industry managers, professionals and inventors of modern weaponry) deserve to be retrained and given a chance at a better job than selling TV sets in department stores.

The chapters of this part of the book are not "prescriptions" for Russia from the shores of the Potomac or sunny California. They are the visions of people who sincerely wish that Russia will soon prosper and who truly believe in the country.

8.1. TOWARD COOPERATIVE VENTURES WITH RUSSIAN DEFENSE ENTERPRISES

Introductory Remarks

Vlad E. Genin

The experience gained in the course of the past decade by U.S.-Russian cooperative ventures demonstrated many Dos and Don'ts. The two sides of these cooperative ventures had different objectives. The American parties expected to secure entry to huge, new, undeveloped markets in Russia, while the Russian parties frequently saw their overseas partners as a source of capital or a path to major investors. "Although there are many successful Cooperative Ventures in which both partners' goals were met, undertaking a venture with a partner that does not share your goals can set the stage for a problematic or frustrating business relationship."[3]

The lessons demonstrated by the first cooperative ventures indicate that on the path to achieving new international partnerships that will work in Russia, there are still many difficult obstacles to overcome. "Russia features labyrinthine registration rules, arcane accounting, tricky taxes, and other hurdles that call for seasoned counsel." [4]

Nevertheless, the number of advantages offered by the potentially huge Russian

[3] Matthew Edwards, "U.S.-Russian Joint Venture Dos and Don'ts," BISNIS Bulletin, U.S. Department of Commerce, March 2000, p.6.

[4] Ibid.

market, and the new, emerging opportunities to profitably use the engineering and industrial capacities of Russian defense enterprises, will attract more Western companies and private entrepreneurs.

Conducting a deep analysis of the history of the activities of U.S.-Russian cooperative ventures will help not only to create a picture of this previously unknown phenomenon, but will lead to a clear and thorough understanding of the future prospects of cooperative ventures with Russian enterprises, primarily with those belonging to defense industries.

David M. Bernstein

Introduction

During the Cold War, the enterprises of the Soviet military complex had virtually no contact with the West. This isolation went far beyond the controls of defense secrecy, as practiced in many other countries. Although the U.S. Government allowed defense contractors to travel and meet their Eastern counterparts, it put tight limits on the extent of technical communications. As a result, there was little possibility of establishing cooperative business ventures between U.S. companies and Russian defense enterprises. In more recent years such ventures have become politically possible, as the Russian government has greatly relaxed its control over the military research and production complex. Technologists and industrialists on both sides recognized the potential for mutually beneficial cooperation, at least in a general sense. However, the earlier isolation has left a legacy that made it much harder to go quickly beyond this general recognition. That legacy has thus made it much harder to establish cooperative ventures in Russia than in other industrialized countries.

One aspect of this legacy is the lack of information about the structure and capabilities of the elements of the military-industrial complex. Other aspects relate to the isolation of the personnel who were not able to exchange technical information with their counterparts in the West, and had no familiarity with market-oriented business practices. This chapter deals with the approaches that U.S. companies and Russian defense enterprises have taken to establishing cooperative ventures. It is based on a Stanford study of approximately 20 U.S.-Russian cooperative ventures.[5] This sample is fairly small, and some sectors of industry are not included, but many of the models and strategies appear to have broad applicability.

Russian defense enterprises have been in an exigent financial situation, caused by the sharp downturn in their businesses. Different enterprises have taken very different approaches in responding to these problems.[6] Many believed that the economic reform policies initiated by the Gaidar government, in which military procurements were reduced to about one-fifth of their former level, would not endure, and that the state would return to a heavy emphasis on military production. Most such enterprises tried to stand pat, and lobby for state subsidies. Some

---

[5]David Bernstein, ed., *Cooperative Business Ventures Between U.S. Companies and Russian Defense Enterprises,* (Stanford, CA: Center for International Security and Arms Control, 1997).

[6]See K. O'Prey, *A Farewell to Arms?* (New York: The Twentieth Century Fund Press, 1995) and D. Bernstein, ed., *Defense Industry Restructuring in Russia: Case Studies and Analysis* (Stanford, CA: Center for International Security and Arms Control, 1994).

continued to produce military equipment even without orders.[7]

The formation of cooperative ventures with Western companies played an important role in the strategies of many Russian enterprises. As a result of the severe economic conditions, they often tried to find partners and to negotiate agreements quickly. They expected investments to come quickly as a result of what they believed to be the commercial value of their advanced technologies and capabilities in a wide array of fields, and their lack of knowledge of the process and nature of Western-type cooperative venture formation.

By contrast, most American industrial managers viewed the opening of Russia as simply one more opportunity to expand their business, and they examined it in comparison with other, better understood, opportunities; in most cases, opportunities for cooperative ventures in Russia occupied a small percentage of their busy agendas. Few American companies thought there was greater risk of investing in Russia too late, as opposed to too early—although there were exceptions. Companies in the commercial space launch business were one such exception. Soon after the breakup of the Soviet Union, U.S. aerospace companies (e.g., Pratt & Whitney, Lockheed, Boeing) realized that there were large potential economic benefits to utilizing some of the Russian space propulsion technology and systems in the rapidly growing commercial space business. It was important to establish strategic alliances before their competitors did. This would, of course, have been impossible during the Cold War.

Several other U.S. companies had done business in the Soviet Union for a long time, and found re-entry or increased involvement

---

[7] C. Gaddy, *The Price of the Past: Russia's Struggle with the Legacy of a Militarized Economy* (Washington, D.C.: The Brookings Institution, 1996).

relatively comfortable based on their familiarity with the country and its culture. Other exceptions were companies that depend heavily on international revenues, and therefore place emphasis on entering foreign markets as soon as they appear to be approaching viability.

There are, however, large sectors of American industry (e.g., automotive, machine tools, microelectronics, and electrical equipment) that saw neither technological nor market reasons to move quickly toward investment in Russia.

Contemplating A Cooperative Venture

Reasons for Seeking a Cooperative Venture

The large reduction in the state's demand for its output, and the lack of sources of investment capital within Russia was in almost all cases the primary motivation for a Russian enterprise to seek a cooperative venture. Many of them did not analyze how a cooperative venture could be built into a profitable business in a market environment. At least in the earlier years (around 1992–93) they simply assumed that, because of their technical skills, they could succeed as they always had, but with a different source of financing or demand.

The motivations of American companies were far more varied and complex. Some companies were primarily interested in selling their products in the emerging Russian market. Others were primarily interested in utilizing technology and skilled technicians to improve their own products and market position in the West. Some U.S. companies were particularly interested in utilizing Russia's lower labor rates to improve the efficiency of their research and production. Another reason for seeking a cooperative venture with a Russian enterprise was Russia's highly trained labor force, much of it still located at the defense enterprises. Although many skilled technologists and workers have left the industrial sector, they are scattered throughout the economy so that it would be harder to utilize them than to work with an enterprise that still has a strong labor force. Whereas the net benefits of the use of existing factories is open to question, the use of existing highly skilled workers from the enterprises has proven to be sound. In many cases, companies were interested in some combination of these factors. Some sought a combination in a sequential fashion such as the cost-effective utilization of technology while waiting for the market to develop.

Expectations of Cooperative Ventures

The command regime trained enterprise directors to have a view of cooperative ventures that was not at all conducive to understanding such ventures in a market economy. Alliances were made to enhance production, and were frequently only a form of vertical integration. Since the state owned everything, vertical integration was in many ways viewed the same whether it involved one enterprise or more than one. Efficiency, productivity, and profitability were not drivers, only production and secrecy. As a result, the Russian enterprise directors had several unrealistic expectations about cooperative ventures with U.S. companies. They did not see preliminary negotiations as a lengthy fact-finding process, nor as an undertaking that only leads to a cooperative venture in a small percentage of cases. They also did not fully realize that U.S. companies have many investment opportunities, have the resources to pursue only a small fraction of them, and do not have access to state subsidies.

Many Russian directors did not have the background (or

advisers) concerning such fundamental capitalistic issues as intellectual property rights, the different roles of debt and equity financing, the trade-offs between dividends and growth of stockholders' equity, asset evaluation, the time value of money and return on investment, and market-driven product design and pricing. Russian directors generally looked for short-term results, including the provision of up-front working capital. And to them, working capital often meant money to maintain payrolls and social services across the enterprise in addition to capital necessary to pursue the specific business of a cooperative venture. Their capital needs were based on their existing cost structures for the entire enterprise, and not just the requirements of a business plan for a new venture.

In almost all cases, the Russian enterprises wanted to be involved in high-technology projects. Based on data on conversion in the United States, Jacques Gansler has shown that conversion projects have a greater chance of succeeding if they involve a level of technology comparable to that in the company's previous military projects.[8] It may appear reasonable to believe that this conclusion is applicable to the Russian situation, since like ours, their defense enterprises were structured and staffed largely in terms of high technology. There is a difference, however, in market demand as a function of technology level in the United States and Russia, since production of low-technology consumer products had been relatively neglected in Russia in the past. In any event, the Russian approach to selection of projects for cooperative ventures too often tends to be driven more by technology than by market considerations. In Poland, conversion started to be effective when

---

[8]J. Gansler, *Defense Conversion: Transforming the Arsenal of Democracy* (Cambridge, MA: The Twentieth Century Fund Press, 1995).

enterprises shifted away from high-technology products, which they could not produce competitively, and started producing lower-technology products that required less investment, and that could respond competitively to market demands.[9]

There are two general types of cooperative manufacturing ventures—those with a substantial content of Russian technology and those in which products or components are manufactured in Russia to U.S. designs and specifications. The first is typified by the space propulsion sector, where some U.S. aerospace companies have entered into substantial joint ventures in order to utilize Russian launch systems in the global commercial space business. In these ventures, the Russians utilize and advance their own technology, while building a business proprietorship. In the second type, the Russian partner provides a manufacturing service. It does not contribute much technology, nor does it build nearly as much of a proprietorship, but it does gain revenue, valuable manufacturing technology, some modern equipment, market-driven business experience, and a working relationship with a U.S. company.

In the space propulsion sector, the Russians have superior technology, cost, reliability, and performance, for all of which there is a very large, rapidly growing market in both commercial and U.S. government-sponsored projects, and this has led U.S. companies to be very aggressive in forming these ventures. The rapid growth of the space-based telecommunications market coincided with the political availability of extensively tested Russian (and Ukrainian) propulsion

---

[9]Pawel Wieczorek and Katarzyna Zukrowska, *Conversion in Poland: The Defense Industry and Base Redevelopment* (Bonn International Center for Conversion, November 1996).

systems. This sector is probably unique. Many Russians argue that this should be the model for most cooperative ventures, but in other sectors there simply is not the combination of technology, performance, cost, and market demand.

Many Russians believe that they had superior technology in many fields. This is more true if one considers only the seed or fundamental technology, but the integrated set of technologies, including product design and manufacturing technologies, leading to a competitive product, is absent in most fields. It is not the scientific level of the technology that is most important but the potential commercial value of it. Another problem is that research budgets have been severely cut during the last decade, so that technology has not progressed at anywhere near its previous rate. A decade is a very long time at the current pace of global technology when some product cycles are only two or three years.

In most sectors, the Russians have had to function in the second model until their technology and efficiency are sufficiently advanced to be competitive. But in so doing they should strive to build a proprietorship. In addition, the Russians tend to seek large projects. This is partly the result of their desire to save as much of their enterprises as possible, and partly the result of believing that it is relatively easy to plan and organize large projects if only the capital is provided. Along these lines, some enterprises look to cooperative ventures primarily as a source of capital, with far less interest in the other contributions that an American company might make. This approach also ignores the fact that many (although not all) U.S. companies prefer to start with small projects and increase their investments if they are successful.

American companies have a totally different view of the potential utility of cooperative ventures. They were not trying to cope with a crisis, but were seeking to enhance the future earnings of their companies through investment. As a result, they lacked a sense of urgency, and, in many cases, they were very cautious about even considering a cooperative venture. When they did decide to invest, they frequently proceeded slowly and cautiously by investing in increments. As they encountered, or heard about, the various structural barriers inhibiting business in Russia, they wanted to be sure that a cooperative venture could actually function legally and within reasonable cost limits before making substantial investments.

Since they wanted to see an integrated, functioning business, they expected to invest in training, communications, logistics, market research, and the like before plunging into a major production operation. They spent far more time and money than they would have in better established economies on legal and accounting advice to be sure that their businesses were on a sound footing. In some cases they expected to be able to rely on legal/contractual protection more than is practical in Russia. Most U.S. companies have learned that trust, frequent and open communication, and personal relationships are far more reliable assurances of fulfillment of obligations. Once they understood and adopted these criteria, they expected to turn more attention to the actual venture and its operation, and to gain experience in assessing the costs of operation. Only after that did most of them expect to make major investments in facility modifications, new equipment, etc.

During all of these stages, the American companies generally expected to follow up with additional investment if this would improve market access, increase revenues and profits, or yield other outputs of value, such as research data. In only a few cases did they expect to curtail growth; these were cases in which, for example, they had a specific limited research or testing project to be completed. The American companies recognized various barriers to growth, such as slow market development, but they did not expect growth to be inhibited by the limited willingness of the Russian partner to expand operations, which proved to be the situation in some cases.

Russia differs from other emerging markets/economies in ways that require careful attention when the form and terms of the cooperative venture are established. Some of the principal differences, and their impacts on the selection of a legal form of cooperative venture, are:

Financial Condition of Partners

The disparity in the financial condition of the partners has usually dictated that the American partner will provide, or raise, most or all of the capital for the cooperative venture, including virtually all of the working capital, while the Russian partner will make primarily non-monetary contributions.[10] A corollary of the distressed financial condition of most of the Russian partners is that they do not have the financial resources to support their activities when there are unanticipated changes in operations, or unexpected delays that result in lower than anticipated cash flow. On the one hand, the U.S. partner must be prepared to provide contingency funds, and this ability must be anticipated in the initial agreement. On the other hand, the U.S. company

---

[10]A great deal of wealth has been accumulated by some Russians and Russian businesses in the past few years. This wealth includes large ownership stakes in many industrial enterprises, but these parties are generally not investing in the restructuring and growth of these enterprises. The enterprises that are generally pursuing cooperative ventures do not have access to this potential investment capital. The reinvestment of some of this capital into Russian industry is vitally needed.

cannot afford to get into the position of constantly being asked for additional funding, as sometimes happens. A solution to this dilemma that some U.S. companies have adopted is for the U.S. partner to fund some additional contractual work to be done by the Russians. This work need not be directly related to the objectives of the cooperative venture, but because of the integrated approach of the U.S. program personnel, it is generally in the same technical area. If this work does not have urgent schedules, it can be accelerated or decelerated to maintain some base level of support in combination with the cooperative venture's primary activity.

As a consequence of the financial condition of some of the Russian partners, they are not always prepared to capitalize on success in the early phases of a cooperative venture. To an American company, success often calls for expansion, especially if the venture was started modestly, and expansion usually calls for investment. Investment at this stage tends to be financial rather than in-kind investments such as technology, but the Russian partner may not be in a position to provide such investment. This second-stage investment also tends to delay the realization of profits from the activity. All of this can lead to a situation in which both parties are pleased with the progress made, but have very different desires (or capabilities) in terms of future operations.

Another frequent consequence of the Russian partner's financial condition is the utilization of any funds on hand to meet payrolls or other obligations, whether or not that was the originally intended use of those funds. This method of operation is partly a result of the business and staffing habits of the command economy, in which accounting systems, particularly cost accounting systems, were not set up to properly allocate direct and indirect costs throughout the constituent parts of an enterprise.

As a result of these factors (and other management practices), when a cooperative venture is set up with a large enterprise, and the part of the enterprise to be involved in the cooperative venture's activity is not financially and organizationally delimited, serious disputes concerning the assignment of costs (and even of preexisting debt) and application of funds have resulted.

Delimiting the enterprise sub-unit that is involved in a cooperative venture is one of the most important steps, and in many cases one of the most difficult to handle. In some cases the delimiting comes about through the voluntary establishment of a spinoff, the establishment of a joint venture, or the formation of a division or project group with separate management and accounting. In other cases, subgroups split away from the enterprise and form their own joint stock companies. While this is one of the most crucial issues in setting up a cooperative venture from the U.S. company's perspective, it is also one in which the perspectives of the partners are very disparate. It poses difficult negotiation problems, because it is an area where previous experiences and culture are so different and so germane. The incentive structures for the two partners are based on these different perspectives.

From the U.S. company's perspective, the reasons for the delimiting are primarily to have a clear barrier for the utilization and accounting of funds and to set up an autonomous complete business unit that can make and implement business decisions at an operational level. This all seems quite straightforward to an American executive, because it conforms to standard American business practice. In addition, American executives are more familiar with alliances that are formed between viable companies that are seeking opportunities to expand their businesses through investment, and set up such sub-units as the most logical form.

To a Russian enterprise director, decentralization and delegation of authority are major departures from standard practice, and it is very difficult for him[11] to contemplate all of the ramifications and potential outcomes. Decentralization has broader meaning as well, since it relates to issues of ownership and power within the enterprise; Russian general directors generally delegate far less authority than American CEOs do. In addition, the Russian directors frequently fear that if the most viable portions of their enterprises are separated out, the residual portions will not be viable. This fear is often well founded, but sometimes this represents the facts of life in a market economy, and efforts to save the whole can result in saving nothing.

Barriers

Both Russian and American companies have cited various barriers to establishing and operating cooperative ventures. These can be divided into two categories: those that the companies can overcome through their own efforts, regardless of how difficult this may be, and those over which they have very little control. In the former category the most often cited by the American companies are cultural differences, including different ways of thinking about and doing business; the banking system (some earlier barriers, such as currency inconvertibility, have been removed) and the difficulty of completing what should be simple transactions; the lack of reliable and competitive sources of inputs; and the absence of useful and reliable accounting data.

---

[11] I have never met a female general director of a Russian defense enterprise.

The second category comprises those problems that are beyond the control of the companies, and relate primarily to legal deficiencies such as inconsistent and often changing laws on foreign investment; economic and financial crises like that of August 1998; tax rates and customs regulations that are a disincentive to foreign investment; the inability of the state to control crime; the reluctance or slowness of the state to address issues that are key to foreign investment; and U.S. export control policies that are unrealistic in terms of competition and global availability of technology. Some U.S. companies find that these problems can be endured for the time being, but many other companies are citing them as a strong deterrent to investing in Russia.

Planning, Negotiating, And Operating A Cooperative Venture

Deciding Whether to Seek a Cooperative Venture

An American company considering a cooperative venture with a Russian enterprise will view the possible venture as a business opportunity, assess the risks and potential rewards (both of which are often high), compare this opportunity with many other investment opportunities, and make a decision. It has been pointed out that investing in Russia involves a high degree of risk, and that this is one reason that U.S. companies do not invest there. However U.S. companies, especially high technology companies, are quite accustomed to accepting risk in at least a fair fraction of their investments. They are familiar with the risks of competition, and do not expect to win in every competitive venture they undertake. They do, however, want to understand the rules of the competition and to be able to have confidence that they will not be changed capriciously. So the level of risk itself is not an adequate explanation for reluctance to invest. It is necessary to compare the types of risk involved in U.S./Russian cooperative ventures with what U.S. companies are familiar with and willing to accept.

The decision is sometimes to wait, or to start at a very modest level, which is understandably frustrating to the potential Russian partner. Russian enterprises often must find a partner for a cooperative venture to ensure the very survival of the enterprise or a key portion of it, or at least to prevent the enterprise from shrinking further. The Russian enterprise rarely has multiple offers pertaining to one specific business opportunity.

In looking at the partnering decisions of American companies, one can divide the opportunities into two categories—those made at an internal project engineer's level, and those made at a corporate or near-corporate level. The project-level ventures generally involve smaller investments, although they may be substantial in terms of the project's overall budget. They are also usually made on the basis of technology and cost that can improve the project's performance, as opposed to attempts to penetrate new markets, develop new products, or establish new production facilities. Many of the project-level ventures involve the utilization of Russian technology and technologists. Software development and metallurgical process development are two examples, but there are likely others in sectors that we have not studied. As a result, the decision is usually made largely on technological grounds. While advanced technology may be a necessary condition, it is not a sufficient one. In most of these cases, the group performing the technology is a specialty group embedded in a much larger research institute or production enterprise. In this case, the attitude of the parent organization toward the venture is critical. It is extremely helpful if it is supportive of the venture, but if it views the venture primarily as a vehicle for extracting rents for activities not relevant to the venture, this can be destructive. The choice to extract rents is sometimes a result of the Russians' unfamiliarity with the value of equity appreciation. Understanding the attitude of the Russian parent should be a key factor in an American company's decision on whether to invest.

Corporate-level decisions more often involve the strategic business objectives of the American company, and may involve manufacturing and entry into new markets as well. The pursuit of corporate goals will sometimes be executed through project-level investments that would possibly not be initiated if there were no larger, longer-term objectives in mind. A company seeking long-term market penetration, for example, may fund several research projects in Russia. To be sure, there are excellent technical capabilities in the Russian institutes doing this work, and the costs may be significantly lower than at home; however, these would not normally be sufficient reasons for a major U.S. corporation to contract the work out at all, let alone in a foreign country that is undergoing a major economic and political transition. Keeping this work in-house simplifies coordination and project management, contributes to the in-house technical foundation, and reduces the probability of the inadvertent disclosure of proprietary information. However, the company may have an overriding objective of establishing working relations with organizations in Russia and with the Russian government, in order to facilitate future marketing there.

More often, corporate-level goals result in the establishment of major cooperative ventures as opposed to isolated projects. Several U.S. companies in our study depend on foreign markets for a substantial and sometimes growing fraction of their sales. In order to stimulate this growth, they consider it essential to establish manufacturing ventures in the countries in which they seek it; they use in-country manufacturing as a marketing tool. Funding short-term projects and establishing good working relations is a logical precursor to establishing such cooperative manufacturing ventures.

Establishing Goals for the Venture

In the case of project-level investments, the Russian and American goals are frequently quite compatible, even though they may be very different. For example, the American project managers may want certain services, such as R&D, and the Russian manager may want to maintain support for the staff that would provide those services.

In the case of corporate-level investments, however, this may less often be true. The short-term goals may also be different, but compatible; however, the long-term goals are sometimes apt to be incompatible. Sometimes this incompatibility is not apparent, at least at the onset of negotiations. In many such ventures there may be a basic difference in the initial long-term objectives of the two partners that threatens the long-term viability of the partnership (though not necessarily of the business). In these cases the U.S. partner usually provides most of the capital, and seeks an investment that adds to its ongoing business. It views these ventures strategically. By contrast, the Russian partner is seeking financial support to withstand economic collapse, and gladly engages in new ventures that fit its capabilities but that are not a part of its ongoing (or former) business, if indeed it still has an ongoing business. In other words, the Russian partner's view of these ventures may be the same as its view of the project-level ventures.

Because of the substantial risk and complexity involved for an American company in making a major investment in Russia, the company (for corporate-level decisions) wants to understand how the investment can contribute to the fulfillment of long-term corporate goals. These goals are generally couched in terms of increased revenue and profit, new markets, and/or market share. In the strategic ventures the U.S. company frequently starts with a modest investment and a commensurately modest activity as a hedge against failure. It recognizes that this scale of operation would not in itself be worth the effort, and it implicitly expects to expand the operation if it succeeds. The American partner tacitly assumes that if the initial effort is successful, the Russian partner will also be pleased, and also want to expand the operation. But this may not be the case, so it is also important for the American company to hedge against success as well.

If the venture is successful in its early phases, it makes a qualitatively different contribution to the business prospects of the two partners. On the American side, the basic ongoing business benefits, but the greatest profits to the company may come from portions of the value chain that do not include the partnership's activity. For example, the cooperative venture may involve the development of a key technology that improves the efficiency of production or market appeal of an end product, while the cooperative venture per se was not structured to benefit proportionately to the success of the end product.

On the Russian side, the short-term benefits may be primarily the provision of employment and funding to sustain the ongoing development of technology. But the near-term success will not necessarily contribute to other activities of the Russian enterprise since it was not originally part of the value chain of an ongoing business in the enterprise. Sharing in the rights to the technological advances, perhaps in CIS markets, may have some present value, but to benefit from this value it may also require substantial financing, which the Russian partner cannot provide.

As a result of this discrepancy, the two partners could have divergent incentives relative to the subsequent phases of the partnership activity. The American partner may not be concerned about the profits of the cooperative venture per se; in fact, the venture may not even be set up as a profit center. In cases where both partners are interested in the profits of the cooperative venture, their time horizons may well differ. The American partner may want both partners to invest in expanding the cooperative venture to achieve larger future profits, but the Russian may not be in a position to invest further, and prefer instead to maintain and distribute current profits.

The evolution of a cooperative venture between a Russian and a U.S. company can be fundamentally different from one between two Western companies, and it may be in the interest of the American partner to structure the deal initially with a different regard for both the long- and short-term interests of the Russian partner. In a U.S.–U.S. partnership, both partners enter the deal with the expectation that it will contribute to their ongoing businesses. Frequently neither is in desperate economic straits; if one is, it is more likely simply to be acquired.

For the Russian-American case, the divergence of interests following early success poses an interesting challenge in the initial structuring of the deal. American companies generally have broader knowledge of the spectrum of structures and deals possible. In that case it can be in the best interests of the American company to raise the issue in the initial negotiations, rather than considering it to be something that the Russian partner should look out for. This is actually an opportunity for both partners to plan the subsequent phases. It is possible not only to provide incentives for both sides to continue and expand a successful operation, but to do so in ways that will improve the operation from the start. In general, the objective is to provide the Russian partner with an incentive plan in which specific achievements can be considered at least a partial match for future capital investments by the American partner.

There are many possible plans, and the partners should try to find one(s) that suit their circumstances. One example would be to reward the Russian partner for reductions of cost and/or increases in productivity. These must be defined carefully to be sure that the plan is clearly based on elements of cost and productivity that the Russian partner can control, and that do not jeopardize the future prospects of the venture. If such elements can be specified, this plan not only provides the desired incentives and improved operations; it also provides practical experience in sound business practices for the Russian partner.

There are undoubtedly many approaches, and the choice depends on the nature of the business and the business and financial positions of the two partners. Different approaches may depend on whether the venture is contractual, is also an equity deal, or may be phased between the two.

Another approach is to fund other projects that need not be directly related to the principal cooperative venture, but which provide employment and revenue for the Russian enterprise. To be of lasting viability, such projects should be economically sensible in their own right for the U.S. partner.

It is possible to structure ventures that increase the compatibility of the partners' long-term goals in many cases, but to do so, it is important to discuss the long- and short-term goals prior to consummating the partnership, and to structure it in ways that increase their compatibility.

The quest for short-term revenue frequently takes precedence, for the Russian partner, over reinvesting earnings or making other forms of investment to improve or expand operations. Under these conditions it is difficult to build a proprietorship, and to avoid becoming simply a supplier of services. Worse still, if the cost advantages predicated on lower labor rates erode, Russian companies could even lose their advantages as suppliers of services.

Legal Form of the Venture

In general, ventures can be divided into equity ventures, contractual ventures, or a combination of the two. The most common form of equity venture has been the joint venture. Contractual ventures can be contracts for manufacturing, R&D, marketing, services, employment, consulting, and/or licensing. Either form of cooperative venture can, of course, also involve debt. Almost all of the cooperative ventures in our study have the bulk of their operations in Russia, but almost all of them have been structured according to Western legal forms and operated almost completely in conformity with Western business practices. This in itself means that the Russians were on unfamiliar ground in varying degrees, depending on their personal training and their experience with cooperative ventures.

All of the forms are Western constructs, and none of them is in the Soviet tradition. A joint venture, for example, implies equity, which implies a legal entity with divisible, transferable ownership of pooled but separate tangible and intangible assets. And the value of this ownership fluctuates with capital market evaluations. Consequently the concept of accumulation of wealth through the appreciation of equity is also a Western concept. A contract implies liabilities and compensation attached to performance to specifications and schedules.

Americans assume all of this implicitly when we mention a joint venture or a contract, but a Russian manager, who was brought up under the communist system, was not allowed to meet his Western counterparts, or to read Western business literature, doesn't operate with the same set of assumptions. In particular, the potential for accumulation of wealth through the rapid or prolonged appreciation of equity ownership is a very unnatural concept. On the other hand, one must realize that Russian managers are on a very steep learning curve, and both their understandings and positions change fairly rapidly.

The choice of the form of the venture has generally been made by the American partner. The choice may be made on a case-by-case basis, or as a matter of policy. While this choice can be the result of a careful weighing of the alternatives, it is sometimes made for relatively superficial reasons. For example, many cooperative ventures are initiated and negotiated by a mid-level project manager in the U.S. company without major input from the corporate management. In these cases, the project manager usually utilizes the means at his/her disposal. He/she frequently has contracting authority, but not the authority to execute an equity venture. Even though he/she may consider an equity venture to be more desirable, he/she often eschews that option because it takes a great deal of time and effort to push such a proposal up the organizational chain and even more time to negotiate the agreement. In addition to the time and effort it takes to get an equity agreement approved, some project managers believe that their corporate management is less enthusiastic and more conservative about investment in Russia than they are. Forcing the issue could give the manager's project higher visibility and involve more corporate bureaucracy, and this is frequently not what he/she desires. In all cases in our study where an equity venture was selected, the initiative for the project seems to have come from the corporate level in the U.S. company.

In the cases in our sample where U.S. companies made the decisions about the form of venture at a high corporate level, the choices, and the reasons for them, vary considerably. Many of these companies have an extensive history of international business in many countries, and that experience weighed heavily on their decisions. Some of them have fairly firm corporate policies; these tend to be the companies that do the same type of business in all of the countries in which they work. Other companies have varying types of international activities, and tried to adapt more to the specific circumstances in Russia.

If the Russian enterprise has not had much experience in cooperative ventures with American companies, it is frequently desirable to proceed slowly, starting with a small contract, because the attitude and desires of the Russian partner may change as it becomes more familiar with the meaning and implications of a cooperative venture. Russian enterprises entering into joint ventures sometimes try to extract the maximum profits and rents out of the joint venture in order to improve the near-term financial condition of the parent, rather than nurture the joint venture for future long-term appreciation and revenues. This is understandable given the desperate financial circumstances that many enterprises are in, but it is not conducive to building a successful long-term business.

The combination of a joint venture and contractual relationships has often proven to be a good one. The combination can be simultaneous or it can be sequential, with a joint venture being formed after a successful contractual relationship. In that case, it is usually a matter of a growing level of comfort and trust between the partners, leading to an increasing level of cooperative activities. When the two forms are simultaneous it is frequently to accommodate the Russians' need for near-term operating revenue when a joint venture's revenue may be delayed for some time.

It is key that the structure be based on the objectives, and the agreement be tailored to maximize the chances of achieving them, even though the objectives of the two partners may be different, and, in particular, may diverge in the long term. Both partners must have an incentive to continue their participation at every step of the way. With forethought and a complete discussion of objectives, the cooperative venture can be structured to accomplish this. If the form of the venture is dictated excessively by previous company practice and policy, without full regard for the unique circumstances in Russia, it is not apt to meet this criterion.

Identifying Potential Partners and Selecting the Most Appropriate One(s)

The identification of partner for a Russian-American cooperative venture is difficult because of a mutual lack of familiarity with the industrial sectors in each other's countries, insufficient sources of information, and different experiences in the formation of (domestic) cooperative ventures. The lack of information about American companies is caused mainly by the previous isolation of the Russian (especially Soviet-era) managers from the Western world. Once these managers are given exposure to and opportunity to travel to the West, they quickly gain an understanding of the American companies of primary interest to them; however, gaining an understanding of Western business practices, especially those relating to the formation of cooperative ventures, takes considerable time.

Obtaining information about the Russian enterprises is more complex. There are still some security barriers, as there are in the United States, but even if the security barriers are overcome, there is a lack of available information, especially reliable historical financial data. The average Russian knows far less about the profile of Russian industry than the average American knows about American business. In the United States there have always been major sections of the media devoted to business information. There are massive amounts of financial and product information published in the popular media, in resource publications, and in advertising.

Many Russian enterprise managers are disproportionately influenced by their need for capital. This frequently shows a lack of understanding of all that is required to succeed in a competitive market environment. Granting the importance of capital, there are, however, other factors that are very important. Russian enterprises that have emphasized the business synergies of a cooperative venture seem to have been more successful, and as the potential American partner sees these synergies, it is apt to be able and willing to find the financing. Some of the factors that are at least as important as capital are market access and marketing skills; technology for product design and manufacturing; management skills; and the long-term prospects for building a self-sustaining business. The most successful cooperative ventures are those in which the partners have a compatible set of objectives for building the business from the marketing, management, product development, and financial perspectives. In other words, it is important that the Russian enterprises seek a strategic partner rather than just a financial investor.

Since the Russian enterprises have a very short history of operating in a market environment, American companies seeking a partner cannot rely very much on historical performance data to judge the soundness of a Russian enterprise; however, some Russian enterprises have gone further than others in restructuring, in converting to western accounting practices, and in working with western partners. When the enterprise has other cooperative ventures, it is possible to ascertain whether it nurtures these in an effort to make the businesses grow or it attempts to extract revenue and rents from them to the detriment of the cooperative ventures. It is therefore important for an enterprise to seek a variety of ventures, even if some of them are quite small, to demonstrate their constructive approaches. The small ones are quicker to negotiate, and they provide an opportunity to learn and display success in cooperative ventures. They can also lead to larger ventures with the same partner. Some enterprises will only consider large production cooperative ventures, but this can be a losing strategy. It is also useful to be willing to accept lower-technology cooperative ventures; this will show that the enterprise values the business potential of new markets, and it will be quite instructional as well.

The principal restructuring steps needed are decentralization, cost reduction, initiation of Western accounting procedures, and establishing business-oriented departments such as marketing, finance, and corporate development.[12] Privatization is also an important indicator of positive restructuring, but sometimes this is forbidden by the state. This does not necessarily mean that a successful cooperative venture cannot be implemented. In some cases it is possible to have the cooperative venture be a joint venture that is privatized, but has a state-owned enterprise as one of its owners. Contractual cooperative ventures with state-owned enterprises have very often been quite successful, but when major capital investments in equipment are required, the U.S. partner will often retain ownership of it, especially if it can be utilized independent of the cooperative venture.

Some other characteristics of a good potential partner are its practice of reducing costs, including excess labor and social services; good relations with suppliers and government officials; retention of key employees and their availability for working on the cooperative venture; and active programs to train personnel at all levels in essential elements of doing business in a market environment.

Some American companies have made a specific effort to find a partner in the same business, especially for manufacturing cooperative ventures. This has proven to be a mistake in some cases, for various reasons: (1) management capability or restructuring performance may be sacrificed to find a partner in the same business, (2) the Russian partner wants to inject its technology and product design in situations where market considerations dictate staying with well-established U.S. designs, and (3) it may be more costly to use outmoded, energy-inefficient facilities and equipment than to start fresh. In some cases a better partner

---

12 For a more detailed discussion of restructuring, see D. Bernstein, ed., *Defense Industry Restructuring in Russia: Case Studies and Analysis* (Stanford, CA: Center for International Security and Arms Control, 1994).

could be a potential customer, a supplier, or conceivably a bank that could finance the purchase of the product in Russia.

One of the biggest problems many American companies have when trying to decide on an investment in Russia is the inability to make reliable financial projections about the amount of investment required, the costs of operations, and the potential profits or losses. This results from (1) the difficulty of converting Russian accounting data, especially historical data, into Western form, (2) the inability to project costs because of a lack of organizational segregation, cost allocation, and the previous lack of productivity and efficiency criteria in the Soviet system, and (3) the instability of Russian legislation.

Attracting Potential Partners

The prospects of a Russian enterprise attracting a desirable partner are greater when the enterprise has already started a decentralized restructuring program that enables sub-units of the enterprise to pursue specific businesses with a high degree of independence. Many American companies are concerned that all decision-making is done at the highest levels of large Russian enterprises; they are far more favorably impressed if the managers of the sub-units have a substantial degree of authority. When this is combined with solid backing by the parent enterprise's management, it creates a structure more similar to that of most American corporations, and is generally better received by the potential American partner. The further delimiting of a privatized spinoff makes this form even more attractive than a segregated division within a parent enterprise.

U.S. companies also look for well-thought-out proposals. This can include various forms of product design, production, and marketing within the bounds of available resources, and less tangible activities, such as the development of training programs, business plans, and proposals.

Negotiating the Venture

The negotiation of a Russian-American cooperative venture is very different from the negotiation of a U.S.–U.S. cooperative venture. The Russian partner will often have little or no experience in negotiating a Russian-Russian cooperative venture under market conditions, let alone a U.S.-Russian venture. In former alliances between Soviet enterprises, the State made most of the major decisions, and the command system obviated many aspects of a market-oriented alliance, such as the evaluation of assets. The primary difference was that both enterprises had the same owner—the State. In addition, agreements were not formalized in as much detail through contracts in the way that Americans understand contracts, and certainly not through the exchange of stock.

This lack of experience in negotiating with Americans places many requirements on the U.S. partner. In a U.S.–U.S. negotiation, each party assumes that the other understands the rules of the game, and will take whatever steps are necessary to protect its interests. This assumption does not always carry over to U.S.–Russian negotiations. It would be counterproductive for the American company to choose to take advantage of the Russian's inexperience; the agreement would be very apt to come apart later. This puts the American in the strange and difficult position of looking out for the interests of its negotiating partner.

This problem is exacerbated by the fact that many Russians tend to consider negotiations as a zero-sum game, whereas an American will often treat the negotiation as a positive-sum game.[13] He will believe that the outcome must be beneficial to both parties or else it will not be a viable agreement. The situation is further complicated by the psychological difficulty of coping with the decline of the Soviet Union/Russia. The Russian is apt to believe that Americans only want to take advantage of the distressed circumstances in Russia.

A resolution of this problem can be achieved by suggesting that the Russian enterprise have a business adviser who can explain the fundamentals and dynamics of American types of business negotiations, and advise the Russian side on how to protect its interests. The American company can even offer to help pay for such an adviser. In addition to facilitating a faster and mutually beneficial negotiation, this can help build the level of trust that is so important in a cooperative venture.

Other aspects of the negotiation process can be difficult. Several U.S. companies have complained that the Russians will often try to reopen points that have already been agreed.[14] There are other cultural differences that are also troublesome. Since the Russians are accustomed to having more decisions made at higher levels than Americans are, the people who are actually negotiating on the two sides will have different degrees of decision-making authority. This can be an indicator of similar potential problems in the operation of the venture.

---

[13] See Raymond F. Smith, *Negotiating with the Soviets* (Bloomington: Indiana University Press, 1989) and A. Baev, M. Von Bencke, D. Bernstein, J. Lehrer, and E. Naugle, *American Ventures in Russia: Report of a Workshop on March 20-21, 1995, at Stanford University* (Stanford, CA: Center for International Security and Arms Control, 1995).

[14] A. Baev, M. Von Bencke, D. Bernstein, J. Lehrer, and E. Naugle, *American Ventures in Russia: Report of a Workshop on March 20-21, 1995, at Stanford University* (Stanford, CA: Center for International Security and Arms Control, 1995).

The Russians tend to attach greater significance to the personal relationships built up between partners. This being the case, it is in the best interests of the Americans to spend time nurturing these relationships. It is also important to be sensitive to this characteristic when there are changes of personnel.

Some Russian enterprises have not given adequate attention to protecting their intellectual property rights (IPR) beyond the scope of a given venture. They have granted licenses to previous technology that are not sufficiently restrictive (in terms of geography, markets, applications, duration, etc.) as to exclude the option of pursuing other ventures (cooperative or independent) that do not conflict with the cooperative venture being negotiated.

Another way in which some Russian enterprises do not protect themselves is by failure to build a proprietorship in the business. This relates primarily to contractual cooperative ventures. In some cases the enterprise will not secure any residual business rights, such as IPR, if and when the contractual activity ceases. If the U.S. partner pays for the contractual work, it is logically entitled to these rights; however, it may be willing to part with them for applications or markets that go beyond its interests. Another way is to participate in the marketing and planning activities to the greatest extent possible. In some contractual software cooperative ventures, in particular, the Russian partner should attempt to develop business with other customers as long as it avoids conflicting with the interests of its partner.

The American partner will usually take the lead in finding outside sources of financing; however, it is important to have the Russian partner involved and fully informed about the financing proposals. In some ventures the Russian partner has been dissatisfied during the operational phase with the decisions about expenditures of resources. It is better to have these understood and agreed to by both partners before the financing is proposed.[15]

Operating the Venture

After both parties have made all of the decisions leading up to the cooperative venture, the task of operating the venture is still a formidable one. No matter how well the parties have planned and communicated, there are apt to be many unanticipated problems. The first step is to establish a management team with personnel from both partners. This not only brings in a spectrum of talents and backgrounds to deal with management issues, but it also ensures that the Russian parent will be kept informed.

Management teams that include representatives of both partners in roles of responsibility function with a sensitivity to the concerns and traditions of both sides. Operations are smoother if the core management team that makes the day-to-day decisions is on site. Each partner will have personnel above this level in oversight roles; it has proven helpful to have these personnel work together and meet periodically even though they are not on site. There are some ventures in which on-site representation of the American partner is either impractical because of

---

[15] This was a major shortcoming in the implementation by some of the U.S. companies of the so-called Fast Four defense conversion projects funded by the Department of Defense under the Cooperative Threat Reduction program. By law, the USG funds were contracted to the U.S. corporate partners rather than to the cooperative ventures. This in itself could work, but some of the U.S. partners failed to have complete and open discussions of financial issues with their Russian partners. See Bernstein and Carlson, *A Report and Analysis of the "Fast Four" Defense Conversion Projects,* U.S. Department of Defense, 1997.

the small size of the venture[16] or unnecessary because a sufficiently strong understanding and sense of mutual trust have been built up to obviate such presence. Such is the case when there are almost daily communications and frequent reciprocal visits. The management roles of the two partners will often change with time. The role of the Russians frequently increases as they become more familiar with the operations of a market-oriented business. This is in keeping with establishing the venture in Russia, and it is cost effective to reduce the number of American expatriates involved in the venture.

The partners must maintain active communication with each other throughout. This is more difficult in the face of this evolution of management roles and changes in personnel, but it is an identifiable factor in most successful cooperative ventures. Communication of two types is important. The first deals with operational issues. The second is an ongoing process of planning the future course of the venture. This is not only sound business practice; it is also a mechanism for periodically comparing the plans for the venture with the objectives of the partners. An evolving incompatibility of the partners' objectives, which could be a major source of serious future problems in a cooperative venture, can be spotted and addressed early.

A second type of evolution in the operation of successful ventures is the introduction of a spectrum of Western business practices. One of these is the introduction of Western accounting systems and, more importantly, the underlying practice of cost control. In the early stages of many cooperative ventures, especially those engaged in

---

16 Small software development projects, for example, would lose their cost benefits if an American expatriate were stationed on site. See D. Bernstein, *Software Projects in Russia: A Workshop Report* (Stanford, CA: Center for International Security and Arms Control, 1996).

manufacturing, some of the costs of operation may be understated. Existing equipment, while not as modern as desired, may be unrealistically valued as an asset and depreciated accordingly. Some input materials may be taken from supplies on hand, and their costs, which were preferentially set, will not be indicative of current market prices. Intangible assets such as patents are frequently not valued realistically.[17]

Many cooperative ventures do not involve a marketing operation, because the output is utilized by the American partner for incorporation in its products or development projects. In some of these, however, the plan is to go from production of components to production and/or assembly of complete products. In these cases the venture may market at least some of the output in Russia (or more broadly, in the CIS). Then it is important to develop a marketing capability as part of the venture. Some ventures have opted to have Americans do most of the marketing for the simple reason that Americans have more experience in marketing; however, many ventures recognize the importance of having sales and marketing personnel from the country in which the products are sold.

In summary, operation of a cooperative venture in Russia requires attention to four major areas:

(1) General day-to-day operational aspects of a new business in an unsettled environment.

(2) The evolution of the venture into a self-contained business in which

---

[17]See Tatiana Krylova, "Principal Differences in Accounting Systems in Russia and the United States." In David Bernstein, ed., *Defense Industry Restructuring in Russia: Case Studies and Analysis* (Stanford, CA: Center for International Security and Arms Control, 1994).

the Russians take an increasing role in all aspects of management.

(3) The evolution of business plans to ensure that the objectives of the two partners, while different, remain compatible.

(4) Careful attention to personal and cultural issues and differences.

Conclusions

While the level of investment in Russian defense enterprises by U.S. companies has not been large, there have been a variety of significant and successful ventures. These have served to illustrate several models and strategies. In the Stanford study of a subset of these ventures, we have seen some of the important elements of successful strategies. The primary conclusions of this study are:

- The development of a sound personal and business relationship between the partners is of paramount importance. This should cover a deep understanding of each other's goals, problems, and priorities, as well as an understanding of each other's cultures. Building this relationship requires patience.

- The circumstances of the two potential partners are different in several important ways: economic condition, objectives, and ways of doing business. A Russian's near-term criteria are apt to stress survival, as manifested by employment and the maintenance of high-technology research and/or production, whereas an American's focus may be more on the long-term business development.

- Some Russian interests have accumulated a great deal of money and industrial assets; however, they are not investing in the development and restructuring of Russian industry. Such investment could provide the greatest possible boost for both cooperative and domestic ventures.

- It is important for the Russian partner to make structural changes conducive to the formation and operation of a cooperative venture, such as decentralization of authority, governance, and financial management; the adoption of market-oriented business practices such as accounting and cost control; the training of personnel; and a willingness to choose products and services on the basis of market demand rather than just on existing technology.

- The American partner should take the necessary steps (and get the necessary advice) on the handling of the myriad legal and infra-structural issues of doing business in Russia; provide extensive training for the personnel of the Russian partner; and structure the cooperative venture in ways that will maintain compatibility of goals of the two partners.

- Much of the Russian manufacturing technology, equipment, and facilities are outdated. Some, such as highly energy-inefficient facilities, should be abandoned and replaced.

- Some of the enterprises that have been most successful in establishing and operating cooperative ventures are the ones that are willing to produce medium- to low-technology products. This gives them greater opportunities for near-term revenue, experience in market economics, experience and a reputation in cooperative ventures, and opportunities to train personnel in new sets of skills necessary in business.

- U.S. companies are generally more interested in a cooperative venture to produce components, subsystems, or technology to incorporate in their existing products than they are in developing totally new products or investing in existing Russian products.

- There are a few areas, such as space propulsion, in which a cooperative venture can utilize Russian technology that is superior to that of the rest of the world.

- If a cooperative venture is dependent upon sales in Russia, the relevant market as a function of time must be analyzed carefully to determine if and when there will be adequate ability to pay for the products/services; this is true for both state and private customers.

- The legal and commercial infrastructure in Russia is incomplete and inconsistent, and the government has not moved as aggressively as it might to improve it and to make the climate more conducive to foreign investment. The financial and resource sectors have had the political power and desire to prevent this.

- Pandemic crime and corruption, which the state either cannot or will not control, is among the strongest barriers to investment in cooperative ventures.

- Both software and manufacturing ventures can be quite successful. There is probably greater flexibility and ease, less expense, lower-risk, and faster market entry in software, but both can be made to work.

- Strategic alliances based on market considerations and other factors that contribute to the overall business are more likely to succeed than those based solely on financing.

- Successful cooperative ventures can be built either through contracts or by formation of an equity alliance, but the choice should be made after a careful analysis of the specific case, and not just by long-standing corporate policy that may not be as applicable in Russia as in other countries.

- There are many detailed models that can lead to success, and the establishment of a Russian-American cooperative venture can often serve the objectives of both partners.

8.2. THE GAZPROM PHENOMENON: NEW CIVILIAN ORDERS

Introductory Remarks

Vlad E. Genin

In May 2000, MIC factory Rybynskyie Motory, which produces fifth-generation aircraft engines, introduced to President Putin a new line of civilian products: gas-compressor units for Gazprom. Indisputably, the main result of Gazprom's efforts in defense conversion was the breakthrough into the formerly "off-limits" military-industrial complex, achieving positive economic results for both parties. Russia learned that there could be successful collaboration between new major private companies and the old state monsters. It also learned a great deal about the future of the economy and successful development.

Gazprom found that the best contractors for their major projects in the northern regions of Siberia and the Far East could be domestic engineers and manufacturers from defense industries, who are well experienced in the design, installation, and maintenance of equipment for remote regions with severe climates. Their skills are based on the expertise gathered from military installations in such regions. Thus, for defense industries, this is a very large and fruitful market niche. The first experiences and long term plans indicate the vast opportunities for utilizing underused MIC capabilities for civilian applications--not just in the gas industries, but in many others as well.

Rem I. Vyakhirev

Research by the International Institute of Applied Systems Analysis shows that the share of natural gas (relative to other energy sources) in the world's economy will reach its peak by approximately 2030. Experts concluded that the process of replacing energy reserves would be accompanied by improvements and changes in the next 20 years. This conclusion applies in full measure to Gazprom: the history of Russia's gas industry is a continuous process of seeking and implementing the latest Russian and foreign technologies.

The future development of Russia's United Gas Supply System is inseparable from the modernization and remodeling of compressor stations, a basic element of Gazprom's widespread gas-transportation structure. On average, gas is transported a distance of 2,500 km. Thus, the cost of transporting gas is one of the industry's major expenses. By now, a substantial part (10%) of the industry's compressor equipment has exhausted its service life, some of the equipment is obsolete, efficiency is low, and there are large amounts of harmful emissions. The decision was made to replace over 80% of the gas-compressor units (GCUs) now in operation during the next 20 years. According to preliminary estimates, $2.5-3 billion worth of investments will be needed to implement this decision. Naturally, this Gazprom program is of particular interest to the leading manufacturers of gas-compressor equipment in Russia and abroad. However, Gazprom's top priority is the production of domestic modern GCUs, which it plans to do by directing most of its R&D funds to the development of new gas-compressor equipment driven by aircraft and ship engines having an efficiency of 38%.

Gazprom and a number of military aircraft engine-building enterprises are designing 6-25 MW gas-compressor units based on the latest generation of highly efficient aircraft engines. More than 35 types of engines, GCUs, and power stations will be built and put into production, on the basis of new-generation efficient gas-turbine engines.

As the largest consumer of gas-compressor equipment in Russia, Gazprom now finances almost 100% of the R&D for new types of GCUs manufactured at defense enterprises undergoing conversion. The Samara Scientific and Technical Complex NK Engines have accumulated significant experience in this sphere. In order to consolidate their positions on the gas-compressor equipment market, a group of Samara and Kazan defense enterprises set up a financial-industrial group named NK Engines in the mid-1990s. This project is financed through collaboration with the Russian Space Agency and Gazprom.

AO Permskie Motory, AO Aviadvigatel of Perm, and NPO Iskra are jointly pursuing an aggressive technical and marketing plan, and have introduced GCUs with a broad range of capacities based on the PS-90A engine. Gazprom is financing these enterprises, which have developed 2.5, 4, 12, 16, and 25 MW gas-turbine units, and the GCUs and power plants based on them.

One of the largest aircraft equipment manufacturers, the Kazan Engine-Building Production Association (AO KMPO), has launched the mass production of a number of highly economic gas-turbine engines, gas-compressor units, and automatic gas-distribution stations. AO KMPO's relationship with Gazprom has allowed the association to restructure, with relatively few losses in terms of high technology, and to increase the percentage of production dedicated to the gas industry to

50%. AO KMPO specialists feel that cooperating with Gazprom is preferable to participating in Russian federal energy programs.

Participation in Gazprom's projects makes it possible for converted enterprises to preserve their capabilities. For example, the group formed by Liulka-Saturn Design Bureau and the Ufa Aircraft Engine-Building Plant is an important Gazprom contractor and investment recipient. This group is engaged in the development of gas-turbine engines based on Su-27 and Su-37 fighter engines. The group developed the PZhT-21S gas-compressor unit (which Gazprom uses at its compressor stations) jointly with the Italian company Nuovo-Pignone. This cooperation has allowed them to enter the world market.

Gazprom actively promotes and supports cooperation between defense plants that produce GCU engines and foreign companies. In addition to Liulka-Saturn's cooperation with Nuovo-Pignone, AO Kirovskii Zavod has started cooperation with EGT and NPO Iskra is cooperating with MAN-Borzieg, Pratt & Whitney, Dresser-Rand and Thermodyne.

Gazprom has been working with OAO Proletarskii Zavod on developing a mobile 1.5 MW gas-turbine power and heating plants for use at gas-compressor stations, gas and oil fields, and communities located in remote areas such as the Far North. This project is based on a gas turbogenerator used to generate power on naval vessels. Northern Design Bureau, AO Severnaia Verf and NPK Sistema have participated in the joint development and production of containers, auxiliary facilities, and automatic control systems for power stations.

Gazprom will work with defense enterprises on the following four projects:

1. Creation of the Yamal Satellite Communication System to provide communications in remote northern regions, as well as during the construction of the Yamal-Europe gas pipeline and the connection of local computer networks between Gazprom subsidiaries. There are also plans to develop new-generation Yamal-100 communications satellites, and put into operation 120 satellite communications stations. These projects will occupy approximately 15,000 specialists and over 100 rocket and space and defense enterprises.

Gazprom, Energia, and Gazkom have entered into a long-term partnership with the U.S. companies Loral Space & Communications and Space Systems Loral to develop a new generation of telecommunications satellites (based on Yamal-100 satellites) for use in governmental and industrial networks, and for sale on the world market.

2. Creation of a modern information management system for Gazprombank and for directing drilling operations.

3. Creation of a new technical complex for monitoring Gazprom production activities.

4. Development of highly efficient and environmentally safe power plants based on fuel elements, which will allow a five- to ten-fold increase in power supply for underwater equipment and submarines for work on the oceanic shelf. It will be possible during serial production to involve a number of major enterprises from the aerospace, defense, and nuclear industries.

For the construction of the Yamal-Europe pipeline through Baidaratskaia Bay, as well as for future gas and oil developments in the shelf zone, the naval design bureaus Lazurit, Rubin, Vympel, and Korall are developing special-purpose vessels and floating craft, which will be built at naval shipyards in Severodvinsk and Nizhnii Novgorod.

A geological and geophysical survey of Russia's Arctic shelf has revealed vast hydrocarbon reserves. In order to accelerate work to exploit the oil and gas fields of Russia's continental shelf, and to organize the extraction of oil and gas in the Arctic Ocean, a number of defense conversion enterprises have been called upon. Prospecting and exploitation will begin at ten oil fields and three gas fields in the Arctic by 2010.

Unique ocean-based, ice-resistant stationary platforms for the development of the first two explored fields--the Prirazlomnoe oil field and the Shtokmanov gas-condensate field--are now being designed and built. A workforce of 250,000, including workers from defense enterprises, will take part in the development of the oil and gas fields of the Barents, Pechora, and Kara Seas. After this project is completed, social and economic conditions for the population of the entire Northwestern region will be significantly improved. The development of the Shtokmanov gas condensate field alone will lay the foundation for the formation of Russia's northern fuel and energy complex, ensure the supply of gas to the Northwestern regions of Russia's European region, and create at least 100,000 jobs.

Collaboration with converted defense enterprises that have the highest intellectual and industrial capacity allows Gazprom to enhance the performance of its equipment and systems. Gazprom believes that the collaboration of former defense enterprises on the Russian GCU market will significantly increase equipment quality and prevent the formation of a monopoly. Defense conversion involves highly valuable resources, and it demands careful attention. Participation in conversion programs serves as the foundation of Gazprom's innovation policy. The involvement of the defense sector is crucial to achieving strategic state goals in the development of the Arctic shelf's hydrocarbon resources, and the establishment of the oceanic oil and gas extraction industry.

8.3. LUKOIL: TOWARD STABILIZATION

Introductory Remarks

Vlad E. Genin

Among Russian industries there is one – the oil industry – that not only succeeded by itself in the new, market-reform conditions, but also became a primary source of major new civilian orders for the MIC. The flagship of this industry is Lukoil, which, together with defense plants and R&D centers, initiated new large projects that lay the foundation for long-term opportunities for both the development of the oil industry and conversion of the MIC. For defense enterprises, this was also the road toward stabilization.

Vagit U. Alekperov

Despite some overlapping efforts and high costs, Russian manufacturers have begun producing practically every kind of oil and gas equipment previously manufactured in the Soviet Union. Although not yet very significant, there is some competition among domestic manufacturers of some types of equipment.

Lukoil is guided by several main principles in its procedures for procuring equipment and supplies. Among these principles are considerations of quality, cost, technological features, and terms of delivery. The company has developed and implemented a tender-based system of procurement, applying it to both Russian and foreign suppliers.

As a result, imports these days do not exceed 1-2% of total procurements by Lukoil. This allows the company to reinvest its profits, participate in the funding of domestic R & D projects by defense enterprises, and to finance the initial stages of production in order to influence manufacturer pricing.

Today, defense plants are taking their first steps forward in the production of oil extraction equipment. From imitating and copying foreign equipment, they have moved on to the development of innovative equipment designed to meet specific Russian requirements.

One such noteworthy enterprise is Atomkonversmash, which is working jointly with the Krasnodar Compressor Factory, with Lukoil's financial assistance, to develop a nitrogen compressor to be used in well development. This innovative compressor generates nitrogen straight from atmospheric air, bypassing cryoturbation.

Other plants, especially those located in industrial regions such as the Volga Basin and the Urals, have also expanded their range of manufactured goods. Competition, in terms of both pricing and quality, has been on the rise. For example, Ochersk Engineering Plant has practically stopped manufacturing pumping jacks, since it is unable to compete with Uraltransmash's price and quality. After using outdated specs to develop and produce a batch of deep well rod pumps, Tula's engineering plant abandoned its attempts to start lot production.

The creation of a consumer association, open to all oil and gas companies, would help resolve equipment production and quality issues. (Membership should be closed to equipment manufacturers to prevent lobbying.) This association might be a body similar to the American Petroleum Institute. Significant improvement in equipment technology and quality is possible only through the concerted efforts of consumers.

Converting the defense industry to civilian production is a long and difficult process, which requires elaborate preparations and the study of different options. The introduction of protectionist measures (import limits, government R&D subsidies, tax credits, or increased tariffs on equipment imports) is not truly helpful, and is sometimes even harmful. Undoubtedly, the properly managed conversion of defense enterprises to civilian production of oil industry equipment will play a decisive role in stabilizing Russia's economy, and jump-start development of the energy sector.

8.4. THE NEW ERA OF CIVILIAN PRODUCTS: INTERNATIONAL MARKETING CHALLENGES

Introductory Remarks

Vlad E. Genin

In the second half of 1999, after a deep decline, MIC production (including civilian-goods production) began to rise. According to data from the Russian Ministry of Economics, output at Russian defense plants from January to June 1999 was up 24% from the same period in 1998. In the fields of aviation, shipbuilding, and weaponry, output was 30% higher than in the first half of 1998. Compared to 1998 levels, production of washing machines was up 20%; vacuum cleaners, clocks, and telephones—150%; and refrigerators—200%.[18] Of course, the growth in the share of civilian production is a long-awaited, positive trend. It will be followed by new jobs, reduced unemployment, and a domestic market flooded with domestically produced goods. These were the first signs that civilian output in the MIC was improving. Although the production of VCRs, tape recorders, and calculators was not resumed because of stiff competition from foreign manufacturers, production of equipment for the food processing industry and light industry increased by a factor of 1.5 to 2. This new trend shows not only increased production—the sole goal of the Soviet era— but also

[18] *Rossiya-1999 Ekonomicheskaia Koniunktura* (Moscow: Izdatelstvo GoskomStata, 1999), v.3, p. 136b.

high-quality goods, comparable to the foreign goods the Russian people have seen in stores throughout the '90s.

The new trend also marks a new era for exporting a wide variety of Russian civilian products manufactured by the MIC. There is a wide range of civilian products that will create a great deal of interest in Western countries. A very controversial question is how to market them not only on the domestic market, but also on the unforgiving Western markets, avoiding the failures of previous years.

Larisa V. Genin

After The Command Economy: On The Way To Marketing

Since the birth of the Soviet Union, defense enterprises have relied completely upon government orders. Before conversion, Soviet defense enterprises received huge orders from the government to supply unlimited quantities of the latest arms to the armies of the U.S.S.R., Warsaw Pact countries, and various allies under different regimes, thus demonstrating the vast capacity of the country's production facilities.

Because it was fully supported by the government for eight decades, the defense industry was able not only to produce and accumulate the best equipment and technologies, but also to raise several generations of specialists, including world-class scientists, engineers, and workers, and to effectively utilize their brain power for the benefit of the militarized economy.

The advent of *perestroika,* and the beginning of Russia's movement toward a free-market economy, made it obvious that conversion was essential, as the military and aerospace sectors were declining rapidly.

The conversion process was extremely painful for the defense enterprises. It was a problem with many facets, one of which was marketing. Reality dictated that marketing activities, which would be vital to selling civilian products in Russia's new free-market environment, must be established.

However, the initial marketing activities were accompanied by extremely serious problems: the dramatic privatization process, the disintegration of industrial cooperation among thousands of former Soviet enterprises, and competition from thousands of nascent domestic importing companies and leading foreign manufacturers of consumer goods. Surrounded by these problems, enterprises had to fight for state military orders, maintain their remaining production capability, continue the conversion or restructuring process, and improve their products—all at the same time.

The enterprises were still under tight control of the government, which put military production on hold, yet forbade them to restructure and switch to civilian production. The government wanted the enterprises to remain "on call", ready to implement orders as soon as they were issued. Virtually every month, Moscow promised to pay defense plants for government orders, which would allow them to re-start all their frozen military production facilities. Fortunately for world peace and unfortunately for manufacturers, this did not occur until the end of the 1990s. Most defense enterprises were forbidden to leave the MIC “nest”, yet did not receive any significant paying military orders from it. Enterprises were not able to rapidly switch to civilian production and sales. It was against this background that enterprises began their marketing activities.

The initial phase of marketing activities was very difficult, as the enterprises had to make the transition from defense applications to civilian ones while simultaneously making the transition from a command economy to a free market economy. This had never been done in the world, let alone in Russia. There was no way to predict the possible economic, social, and political consequences.

Defense enterprises had never implemented Western-style marketing strategies before conversion, and did not do so afterwards, either. They did not have the appropriate marketing departments in place. Thus, upon entering the free market economy after having lost government guardianship, they were not prepared for the aggressive, world-class promotional methods on the domestic and international markets.

The problem was aggravated by the fact that in Russia, the Western-style marketing environment had not yet developed. If a Western defense enterprise, operating in a well-established marketing environment, switched from military production to civilian production, the only problem it would face would be to hire a qualified marketing staff and establish an appropriate civilian marketing strategy.

For Russia, the situation was much more difficult, a virtual "catch-22": Russia had never had a marketing environment, so there was no need for marketing activities. No need for marketing activities meant that no marketing environment developed. Neither the MIC nor civilian industries employed any Western-trained, experienced marketing professionals.

One of the difficulties in pursuing marketing activities was that Russian defense establishments were not familiar with commercial markets. They had little knowledge of how to create market segments for new products, or of market development. The Russian defense industry had been isolated to a far greater degree than manufacturers of consumer goods, and lacked channels for getting feedback on market conditions.

In the early 1990s, Russian defense enterprises, in order to sell their commercial goods, began their efforts to develop professional marketing activities and formal marketing structures.

However, the vast majority of MIC enterprises had only a limited, outdated understanding of marketing issues. Their promotional methods consisted only of preparing technical literature, proposals, photos, "cold calls", and unsolicited letters. Promotional brochures were poorly worded and poorly printed. The few methods and tools they knew of were used inappropriately and unprofessionally, by Western standards.

One of the most popular marketing strategies in the early 1990s among senior executives at defense enterprises was to conduct face-to-face meetings and negotiations with their new, unfamiliar Western counterparts. Delegations of Russian enterprise directors flocked to the United States, Western Europe, Israel, Southeast Asia, and other well-developed countries. The Russian executives took their first steps in marketing, learning by trial and error. First of all, they were not acquainted with the whole arsenal of existing marketing strategies and techniques, such as trade shows, contests, cooperative advertising, promotions, display equipment, point-of-purchase materials, allowances, product sampling, rebates, premiums, multiple purchase offers, and product placement. In addition, they did not have appropriate public relations departments that would establish and maintain good relations between the enterprise and the public. Of the useful public relations techniques available to them, including news releases, press conferences, TV appearances, and event sponsorships, they used only a very limited number.

Lack of fundamental knowledge and practical experience concerning the free market economy on the part of Russian enterprises caused misunderstandings when they sought business deals and long-term collaboration with Western companies.

The new marketers from Russian defense plants had a completely different mentality and way of expressing themselves than experienced marketers. Until recently, few marketing representatives from Russian defense enterprises were able to sufficiently communicate and negotiate in English with their prospective Western counterparts, in the accepted international way, and thereby reach feasible agreements. All these problems led enterprises to disappointments, causing them to doubt their abilities in marketing and sales.

In the early 1990s, when the country was suffering from its lack of understanding of marketing principles, the first wave of Russian students enrolled in business schools in U.S. and Western European universities. They studied marketing, advertising, consumer behavior, market research, marketing and sales management, international marketing, and international business. Shortly thereafter, Russia received its first professionally trained marketing specialists with Western degrees in business administration and marketing. This small first generation of Russian marketing professionals was able to see the "big picture", knew which marketing strategies and tactics to use, and knew how to create new marketing strategies appropriate for Russian conditions.

Barriers To Successful Marketing And Sales Activities

Between 1990 and 1999, the economic situation in Russia worsened, and the population's buying power fluctuated. After the August 1998 collapse, when the population's buying power dropped catastrophically, international sales seemed to be a great solution. Despite the tremendous efforts made by former defense enterprises during these years, exports did not increase for the majority of civilian products from Russian defense industries. In many cases, they dropped.

From the beginning, Russian defense enterprises faced several major barriers, which prevented them from developing successful marketing and sales activities.

First of all, there was the absence of appropriate marketing channels. The existing marketing channels, where everything depended on middlemen, were mostly ineffective. No reliable marketing channels, including offices and showrooms in foreign countries, were established. All of this created serious obstacles for international sales.

Second, there was a lack of well-trained marketing personnel who could develop creative marketing strategies that would generate significant sales. In addition, no in-depth international market research studies were conducted to clearly identify current consumer needs and demands.

Third, business planning was weak. Prior to perestroika, Russian professionals and government planners had never developed Western-style business plans. The Soviet *tekhniko-ekonomicheskoe obosnovanie* (TEO) was similar to a Western technical feasibility study, but it was based on the principles of a command economy rather than principles of supply and demand. Initially, Russian business plans were based mostly on the biases, assumptions, imaginings, and speculations of their authors.

Fourth, promotional methods were very expensive for defense enterprises, which were in dire financial straits. In most cases, they could not afford world-class advertising, promotional literature, product presentation at trade shows, and participation in conferences. The problem was exacerbated by very high prices—among the most expensive in the world—for parcel shipping and telecommunication services in Russia. In 1999, the cost of telephone/fax communication from Russia to the United States was still over $2 per minute, while in the United States the cost had gradually decreased to 16 cents per minute in recent years. The high cost of marketing presented defense enterprises with a dilemma: to seek investment or not. While it might be possible to borrow funds to create a world class marketing advertising and promotional campaign, numerous failures in international marketing efforts left many defense enterprises wary of increasing their loans while they were just getting started.

Fifth, the geographical factor served as a barrier to successful marketing activities. Enterprises that were struggling financially felt that they were in no condition to pay the cost of transporting goods (via air or sea) from Russia to the West, especially the United States, even though the cost of shipping a 40-foot container of goods (valued between $50,000 to $100,000) from Moscow to San Francisco is only $1,500 higher than shipping it from Moscow to Madrid.

In many cases, the geography factor was less of a physical barrier than a psychological one. For example, a company considering exporting $100,000 in goods to the U.S. for a profit of $20,000 might decline to do so because of the high cost of shipping. That $1,500 decrease in profit was sometimes more important than the loss of huge exporting opportunities in the United States. A popular saying in MIC enterprises was “America is too far away from us”.

Sixth, the Soviet legacy of secrecy and distrust also formed barriers to international marketing. Defense enterprises remained under the tight control of the so-called “First Department”, which was created at each enterprise during KGB-era. This led to conflict between defense plants that could not market their civilian output successfully without granting prospective partners and clients access to their production and design facilities, and the "First Department", which tightly restricted or forbade such access. Thus, an enterprise's secrecy regulations could clash with its new marketing needs.

Availability Of Competitive Export Products

During the ’70s and ’80s, Russia's best manufacturing resources were concentrated in the defense industry, which had first priority in receiving modern equipment and the best domestic and imported supplies. The defense industry had a wealth of the most significant scientific discoveries, engineering innovations, inventions, patents, and intellectual manpower. In the past, defense enterprises developed numerous advanced technologies in order to satisfy Soviet military ambitions. Despite the ongoing crisis, defense enterprises are still able to create a wide range of superior technologies to manufacture commercial products and consumer goods. Defense enterprises that have been privatized and released from governmental controls have a much better chance of succeeding than many civilian enterprises.

The motivation to produce high quality products lies in the general consumer culture in Russia. Russians traditionally are very discriminating European-type consumers, in contrast to some groups of

Western consumers. How else can one explain the fact that after perestroika, when imports to Russia dramatically increased, Russian consumers accepted only the *crème de la crème* of Western consumer goods? For example, demand was high for Sony, Panasonic, and Sharp products, which Russians considered very prestigious, while RCA and Zenith products, which were considered less prestigious, never became "hot". The rationale is simple: it is better to buy one high-quality European dress, than to buy several low- or average-quality dresses. In the early 1990s (after the end of Chinese-Soviet confrontation), Chinese consumer goods appeared on the Russian market for the first time. Though they were reasonably priced, and Russians had low incomes, Russian consumers avoided them because they were perceived as low-quality goods. This Russian cultural characteristic drives the civilian manufacturing industry even today. In many cases Russians strive to manufacture goods they would buy themselves: high-end, quality products.

However, many Western commercial buyers still believe, incorrectly, that Russian industries, including the defense sector, cannot offer quality industrial and consumer goods to international markets. Russian premier goods are not limited to *matrioshki* (nesting dolls) or "Stoli" vodka. There is high demand in the United States for such Russian-made items as aerospace systems, computer monitor components, night vision devices (these are particularly popular), jewelry, crystal, stone carvings from the Urals and Siberia, and many others. To commemorate cooperation with their Russian counterparts, many Silicon Valley "techies" wear Russian Commander watches (*Komandirskie chasy*). In the late 1990s, high-quality Russian consumer goods appeared in major U.S. department stores, including Macy's, Nordstrom, Burlington Factory stores, and Sears.

If Russian goods were marketed in the United States the same way that Chinese goods are, Russia's superior goods would not only replace many Chinese goods on the U.S. market, but also give a new push for new product development and manufacturing. One must also take into account that many products manufactured in (and exported from) China and other Asian countries are based on technologies and semi-finished components created by Russian former defense enterprises.

Russian defense industries have a wealth of so-called intellectual products and advanced technologies that are comparable to the best in the United States and other Western countries. The best example of this is the aerospace industry. The United States decided to make use of Russian achievements rather than spend large amounts of time and money developing their own technologies (e.g., NASA's use of the Mir space station). Much of the R&D for goods and advanced technologies involving new ideas, original solutions, and discoveries is incomplete due to lack of funds. The solution is the development of world-class international marketing.

The Need For A New Era Of Marketing

Russian defense enterprises have entered the second decade of progress toward a free-market economy. The first decade, in which economic uncertainty reigned, was full of marketing and sales attempts, successful and unsuccessful experiments, mistakes, and—most importantly—lessons. It is absolutely clear that Russia needs a new era of marketing for their products.

The new era should bring not only a deep knowledge of the full range of international marketing tools, but also a clear understanding of what is applicable in Russia's unique conditions and business environment.

Because defense enterprises have historically lacked experience with intensive international marketing activities, they should closely and realistically assess their production capabilities, their staff expertise, the potential for applying these to the consumer goods market, and current market trends before creating their marketing strategies. Studies of business plans written between 1991 and 1999 show that Russian defense plants had a tendency to exaggerate their abilities and potential.

In other words, one of the key challenges during the process of defense conversion is the establishment of a vital marketing structure, which should conduct thorough market research and analyses, identify in-demand products and technologies, identify appropriate target markets, select efficient promotional methods, select effective distribution channels, and develop competitive pricing strategies.

Everybody in Russia understands that the funds for costly marketing programs for Russian defense enterprises will not appear overnight. Nevertheless, the origin of many of the problems with defense conversion lies in the difficulty (or occasional impossibility) in marketing and selling the enterprises' products. Without the best strategy for marketing and exporting goods produced by former defense enterprises, and without Western assistance, Russia will continue to experience difficulties in international sales. The most effective solution to this problem is to use Internet marketing.

The revival of the marketing of civilian products provides hope that Russian hard-liners will not call for increased production and exports of weapons in order to "feed hungry Russia". If the numerous problems are resolved and marketing and sales begin, this would decisively influence the resolution of political, military, technological, economical, and social problems.

8.5. CONVERTED ENTERPRISES AND INTERNET MARKETING

Introductory Remarks

Vlad E. Genin

Internet marketing is a new term in the field of marketing. It is only a couple of years old. Nevertheless, Internet marketing has already attained a solid and stable position in the marketing industry. However, the most important fact is that the future belongs to Internet marketing. Moreover, by playing an essential role in the success of e-commerce, it will eventually dominate all of the markets, including international ones.

Internet marketing, and its most important features, easy implementation and availability, can become a very powerful tool for the mass promotion of Russian products, and their deep penetration into Western markets. Its implementation, parallel to defense conversion, can help to avoid the problems of borders; language barriers; and national, cultural, and psychological differences between international counterparts. Even today, Internet marketing could probably bring civilian consumer goods, equipment, intellectual products, and everything prepared for sale during the course of Russian defense industry conversion, to Western markets.

Ward A. Hanson

Connecting The World

Overview

Business evolves by removing barriers. From the industrial revolution to the twenty-first century, communication and transportation improvements pushed the global marketplace forward. New technologies, especially the Internet, continue and accelerate this trend. Companies moving from local markets and noncommercial products to active participation in the global commercial economy need these capabilities.

Defense enterprises converting to the civilian economy will have more success with these tools if they develop a particular type of product or service. An emphasis on intermediate components and business-to-business e-commerce is more promising than an attempt to use the Internet to reach final consumers with complete consumer products. The current capabilities of Internet-based marketing and e-commerce help distant firms with competitive prices and skills to effectively enter supply networks that were formerly expensive or impossible to penetrate. While it may change, current Net capabilities are less suited for developing and pushing final products designed and produced by distant players.

Removing Barriers

At the dawn of the industrial revolution, markets suffered from grossly inefficient transportation, heavy taxation on trade, painfully slow communication, and no models of successful large business organizations. Local production and markets dominated. By the start of the 20th century this had changed radically. Steam power, rapid ship and rail transportation, and telegraph and telephone networks connected distant countries. With this market connection came national, even global, markets. Large markets permit specialization, economies of scale, cheaper and better products. Despite war and ideology, the 20th century continued this trend. Air transportation, advanced ships, trucks, GATT agreements, and global companies further shrank the planet.

But one important feature was still needed. Until the middle of the 1990s, companies needed a physical presence to communicate effectively with distant customers. This involved costly travel and distribution networks to accomplish. While phones and fax machines allow instantaneous communication, they fail to effectively cross language, cultural, and time zone barriers. They are more "order and logistics" mechanisms than "relationship creating and building" mechanisms.

The Internet is the newest planet-shrinking technology. E-mail moves costlessly between individuals, permitting either staggered communication across time zones or near-instant global messaging. Web sites accommodate worldwide visitors. Companies and individuals use new collaborative tools such as electronic bulletin boards, discussion groups, instant messaging, Internet-based videoconferences, telephony, and shared electronic workspaces. This communication is multi-faceted. It can be the routine confirmation of orders, or it can be in-depth and unstructured discussions.

Commerce follows communication. E-commerce has emerged rapidly from Internet usage, even faster than projected by many analysts. Shoppers visit virtual stores with near unlimited "shelf space". Businesses research hard-to-find products without the need for onsite visits and infrequent trade shows. Multiple language web sites partially solve linguistic barriers. Global supply chains incorporate distant and small providers, using the Internet to replace costly and proprietary data networks. Perhaps most importantly, the Internet encourages companies to connect to customers and learn from them directly.

The Internet is a new and powerful ally to Russian firms wishing to convert from a dedicated military market to a global civilian market. It provides crucial missing pieces to the conversion effort. These include rich and deep information, a business support infrastructure, and new lucrative markets previously out-of-reach for Russian products. While no *deus ex machina* magically solving all problems, the Net's rapid rise couldn't happen at a more opportune time.

There is poetic justice in the Internet helping to transform Russian defense enterprises. It was these very same defense firms that stimulated its creation. The original Internet was the result of U.S. military planners concerned about the vulnerability of communication in the case of a nuclear war. Not until the early 1990s, with the demilitarization and commercialization of the Internet, has the Net grown exponentially in connections, users, and content. The key isn't technology, but new ways of connecting, informing, and inspiring people. With new communication technologies came new opportunities.

Marketing Processes

In a previous book,[19] I have discussed how the Internet transforms marketing by digitizing and networking important marketing processes. That is, marketing actions are altered and augmented using

---

19 Ward Hanson, *Principles of Internet Marketing* (Cincinnati, OH: Southwestern Publishing, 1999).

the Internet. For organizations moving from defense production to commercial activities, digitizing and networking marketing processes accelerates the transformation. A careful consideration of marketing processes also reveals why business-to-business markets may be more lucrative in the near term for converting enterprises than business-to-consumer opportunities.

A successful business must find ways of accomplishing the marketing tasks shown in Table 8.5.1.

TABLE 8.5.1.

Essential Marketing Processes for Commercial Enterprises

First-Level Processes					
A. Understand Markets and Customers	B. Involve Customers in the Design of Products and Services	C. Market and Sell Products and Services	D. Involve Customers in the Delivery of Products and Services	E. Provide Customer Service	F. Manage Customer Information
Second-Level Processes					
Understand the Market Environment Understand Customers' Wants and Needs Segment Customers	Develop New Concepts and Plans for Products and Services Design, Build, and Evaluate Prototypes Refine and Customize Products or Services, Then Test Their Effectiveness	Secure Channels of Distribution Establish Pricing Develop Advertising and Promotion Activities Develop and Deploy a Sales Force Process Orders Develop Customers	Offer Broad Delivery Options to Become the "Supplier of Choice" Use Delivery Customization to Attract and Retain Core Customers Identify Customers' Delivery Needs Develop Distribution Capability	Establish "Points of Contact" Excellence Build Cross-Functional "Points of Contact" Cooperation Train Employees to Improve Customers' Expectations for Projects and Services	Build Customer Profiles Establish Service Information Measure Customer Performance and Satisfaction
Source: Table 2-5: Marketing Business Processes That Can Be Digitized. Adapted from Hiebeler et. al., *Best Practices: Building Your Business with Customer-Focused Solutions*					

First level processes are the major marketing functions any organization needs to achieve. Second-level processes further break down these actions into detailed steps. Accomplishing these marketing steps is especially difficult for firms far away from target customers, unfamiliar with new marketplaces, and expanding into new product lines. For each marketing process, the Internet can be used to increase success and lower costs. This is the core connection between Internet marketing and defense conversion.

A. Understanding Markets and Customers

The Internet is rapidly becoming the fastest and cheapest method for high quality understanding of markets and customers. Web sites of current and future competitors can be studied. Products available on the market place can be analyzed. Pricing plans and selling terms can be studied for averages and best practices.

The first step to an active commercial environment is research and understanding of the market environment. This involves mapping the active competitors, understanding the leading products and services, and studying distribution channels. Companies worldwide are using the Internet for this research, dramatically cutting down on the cost of basic market opportunity analysis.

Understanding the needs and wants of customers is one of the biggest challenges facing a new industry entrant. Active industry participants already have a rich history of customer involvement, suggestions, and reactions to earlier products. Online user forums can be a valuable source of information to a distant company seeking to understand a new environment. User forums in a wide range of industries, such as plastics, medicine, construction, chemicals, and computers, regularly post reactions and commentary on available offerings. For a firm trying to break into these industries these commentaries, while unscientific and anecdotal, provide a very valuable context.

A new entrant must conserve resources by attacking the most valuable opportunities first. User forums and industry websites help segment customers and identify the most promising customers and lines of business. Inquiries arising from web site traffic can identify prospects sufficiently interested to initiate contact.

B. Involve Customers in the Design of Products and Services

The market failure of high quality products is often traced back to an inappropriate choice of features. Bad design or shoddy construction isn't to blame; rather it is a lack of communication between designers and customers. Features may be missing, or the design targets the wrong price point. Innovative new online methods help avoid this mistake.

Virtual tradeshows are a resource for distant firms to sample market opinion without the cost of attending actual tradeshows. Shortening the new product development cycle is vital for converting enterprises. Even the most innovative product can look obsolete if it takes too long to construct. Early views of new competitors' features, establishing a connection with lead users, and performing a survey of innovations are important functions of these virtual tradeshows.

Virtual tradeshows are especially valuable for a firm attempting to supply modular components to other businesses engaged in the final product design. Trade shows highlight the broad trends and establish contact between a company and final product assemblers. Trade shows do much worse in predicting and exploring consumer markets. This requires more direct contact with customers.

Business-to-business collaborative design tools are quickly moving from experimental to fundamental. This online collaboration has many faces. It can mean early feedback from important customers, where preliminary versions of products are tried and tested online. Collaboration can be the sharing of sales and inventory levels in order to improve delivery and operations.

The computer supply chain is an example of collaborative supply networks coordinated with the Internet. Dell Computer uses the Internet to create efficiency and understanding with its many suppliers. Through the use of password-protected joint sites, Dell can track many of the details of these independent firms around the world. At the same time, Dell uses the Internet to provide extensive support and personalized information to customers. Cisco follows many of these same paths, being especially successful in lowering the costs of customer technical support.

C. Market and Sell Products and Services

Business-to-business firms find it much easier to use e-commerce and the Internet to market and sell their products than consumer goods companies do. A big reason is the cost of attracting online traffic. A consumer firm must create brand awareness among thousands, even millions, of consumers. This is the most expensive part of many online firms' activities. It is widely commented that many Internet retailers are currently unprofitable. This is inevitable when branding and traffic building expenditures far exceed the normal level of these costs in traditional retail settings.

The situation changes dramatically when business-to-business channels are considered. The much smaller number of potential customers, and their desire to find reliable suppliers, makes it much easier to identify and make contact with good prospects. This is crucial for a struggling new company. A focused, efficiency-driven approach can be effectively implemented with an informative web site, links to industry pages, and registration and documentation with the appropriate search engines. New market intermediaries, which can vouch for credit risk and payment mechanisms, reinforce the e-commerce capabilities online. Online business-to-business intermediaries such as Chemdex in the chemical goods market permit new market entrants to compete much more effectively with established suppliers.

D. Involve Customers in the Delivery of Products and Services

The Internet lets a new industry participant leverage the shipping and logistical capabilities of its lead customers. Joining a supply chain, and performing up to its requirements, provides a valuable endorsement and discipline for a new firm. Previously this required heavy investments in electronic data interchange, limiting the number of suppliers. With flexible Internet connections, and emerging tools such as XML, it is much easier for a new firm with a competitive offering to successfully adopt the tools.

The critical step of identifying customers' delivery needs is much easier when precise shipping data and production needs are available in real time. By enabling suppliers to see the upcoming customer production runs, smart firms can lower total inventory and reduce expensive cross shipments. For firms facing logistical difficulties, as many of the earlier contributors to this book have emphasized is the case with Russian enterprises, this can mean the difference between participation and failure.

On the other hand, improved communications and supply chain control will hurt firms unable to perform and unable to rely on inventory to cover their inefficiencies. Converting enterprises must carefully consider and avoid products where basic specifications change rapidly. This will push many to move earlier in the value chain, toward more basic components. For example, in the computer industry, it would encourage an emphasis on components such as power supplies and controller chips rather than external design molding and other components with rapid obsolescence.

E. Provide Customer Service

Online customer support resources generate substantial cost savings and improved quality when used appropriately. This is especially true for firms facing linguistic, cultural, and time zone differences. Extensive online documentation can reduce the need for expensive telecommunications, lower the worries of customers regarding capabilities, and provide accurate information to a worldwide customer base.

The power of Internet time shifting should not be overlooked, especially its ability to modularize knowledge. A firm anywhere in the world can create a detailed overview of its products, with valuable design and specification information. When necessary these can be password-protected for proprietary reasons, with the passwords given only to trusted partners. Customer support digital environments are not only cheap to share once created, they act as a valuable buffer between the members of an organization that have technical knowledge, and members of the organization with foreign language skills. The best engineers can create the documents in their own words, and then work with translators to ensure it is available in a form usable by foreign customers.

F. Manage Customer Information

The final area where the Internet can help the marketing process is in managing customer information. This is an area where converting enterprises will typically outsource, and partner with market research firms in the important customer markets. For all the reasons outlined above, this will be more effective and cost efficient using the Internet's collaborative tools.

Effective consumer information tracking creates an opportunity to close the loop connecting product design, sales, and profits. Over time a firm develops the ability to evaluate new features, identify the customers that will choose it, and predict the new product's likely success. Effective customer information isn't just bookkeeping, it is a market research asset.

Converting To A Time-Obsessed World Economy

Hunting for market opportunities, just like hunting in the wild, requires anticipating movements and aiming ahead of the target. The faster and more elusive the prey, the more skill required.

In this regard the Internet complicates the task of organizations moving from a command to a commercial setting. There is little debate that the Internet is reducing an already rapid pace of new product introductions. In years past, a technology generation might last three or four years. In some markets, such as personal computers, a generation is now as short as three or four months. Companies accomplish this incredible pace by reorganizing their new product development process, electronically linking with suppliers, and creating a closer connection between themselves and their customers.

This accelerated pace is here to stay, and provides valuable competitive advantage to its lead users. Converting defense firms, especially those seeking commercial opportunities with high margins, must embrace this new reality. This is a stern challenge for any company, requiring painful adjustments and intense efforts. The payoff is equally large. If successful, these new approaches open up a global market.

8.6. GLOBAL E-COMMERCE: CIVILIAN PRODUCTS

Introductory Remarks

Vlad E. Genin

The famous "human factor" has always been a necessary and critical attribute of marketing and sales. In the era of the Internet, computers, programs, and web sites are only tools for marketing, sales, and customer service—domestic and international e-commerce activities. In the early stages of e-commerce (before 2000) the use of these tools was marginally effective. The use of such imperfect tools in the future cannot help merchants attract future clients and motivate them to decide to buy Russian-made high-tech products and consumer goods. This will only take place when the human factor is present in e-commerce, as an organic part of the interactive process.

Russian former defense enterprises should not repeat the bitter experience of unsuccessful marketing (and subsequent failures of sales) in the 1990s, when instead of "human" promotion of products, one saw brochures that looked like inventory lists for liquidation sales at the auctions. However, they were not offering obsolete goods, but frequently world-class products and advanced technologies. It was at this time that many chances to promote many types of Russian civilian goods on the Western market and to begin exporting them were missed—chances to lay a solid foundation for a better fate for the defense industry.

Today one sees that many problems in the MIC are the result of ignoring the human factor in international marketing and sales. Today, in the era of global e-commerce, when influence of the human factor is lost, now is the time to resolve the problems of depersonalized Internet marketing.

Larisa V. Genin

The newest phase of the conversion and restructuring of the Russian MIC is characterized by the challenge in marketing its civilian products, especially internationally. This challenge occurred simultaneously with the birth of Internet marketing and e-commerce. Without doubt, both new marketing challenges in the Russian MIC and the world Internet marketing revolution will develop together. At the beginning of the era of the transition to Internet marketing in all areas of global business activities, there is no other alternative for converted Russian defense enterprises to succeed in marketing and sales, both domestically and internationally.

The United States and many countries of the world, which are moving toward Internet marketing, have a well-developed market economy. The Russian economy in the beginning of the 2000s is still in the period of transition. More than a thousand MIC enterprises still are not in a position to execute effective marketing and sales of their products, particularly exports, which could lead to hard currency revenue streams. They still suffer from the legacy and realities of the post-"headlong conversion" situation in Russia. This is the reason for the gap: while Western high-tech companies rapidly grow their electronic commerce, including international e-commerce, Russian MIC enterprises are still under influence of the undeveloped, old-fashioned marketing, sales, and export system. The situation is aggravated due to rapid, fundamental changes in the international business world, geared toward globalization, that were brought about by the Internet.

The emergence of Internet marketing, as an overwhelmingly effective marketing tool, could nevertheless play a critical role in Russia's breakthrough into the international business world. Therefore, marketing executives at former Russian defense enterprises will have to search for economical ways to create an Internet-based one-to-one relationship with each of their prospects and customers, keeping in mind the following advantages of the Internet:

- The Internet, by its very nature, offers Russian enterprises inexpensive tools, primarily websites, to promote products and services, as well as relatively affordable advertising tools, such as affiliate programs, banner ads, links, banner exchanges, etc.
- Internet marketing will not require Russian defense enterprises' marketing representatives to have superior English oral communication skills. Lack of such skills is still an unfortunate reality in Russia and the Internet could be a good solution to this common problem.
- E-commerce will eliminate borders and geographic barriers, providing greater access to target markets and groups of clients. Converted defense enterprises could bring their products to the right place at the right time.

One of the most distinguishing characteristics of the emerging millennium is the transition from mass communication to more personalized communication.

Many researchers have come to the conclusion that the era of mass communication is over. The era of intensive and effective one-to-one communications is in full swing. If MIC enterprises were to collect more and more information about the prospective consumers of their civilian products, about their profile and expectations, they would be able to deliver to their target audience products with the appropriate characteristics, features, and quality.

By the year 2000, all Internet-enabled countries had accomplished certain first steps in Internet marketing. However, the experience of their accomplishments indicates that certain problems in Internet marketing effectiveness have emerged. Competition in e-commerce has already become extremely high. The process of global Internet marketing and sales of civilian products from MIC plants and research centers will require not only that the scale of Internet marketing be increased, but also that its effectiveness be improved. It is more important than ever to provide customers with not only a highly interactive, but first and foremost, a personalized web environment.

Personalization of e-commerce is among the major current challenges for increasing Internet marketing and sales effectiveness, especially on the international arena. It has become evident that the future of the Russian MIC's success in Internet marketing and e-commerce (domestic and global) in the spheres of new technologies, space systems, equipment, aircraft, software products, and a wide range of consumer goods will significantly depend on the degree of online personalization.

For a long time personalization of the marketing and sales processes was the key element, since people were involved in traditional commerce. The Internet, while it has provided "superhighways" throughout the whole world, has not yet adequately brought personalization to online marketing and e-commerce, either in terms of the use of a comprehensive set of traditional tools for personalization or in terms of the development of new distinctive ones that are applicable to the electronic era.

According to Ward Hanson, one of the leading Internet marketing authorities in the world, personalization can be defined as " a specialized form of product differentiation, in which a solution is tailored for a specific individual."[20] As the Forrester Research states, "As the general content of the Web gets broader, individuals will cease aimless surfing activity and gravitate toward sites that deliver products and services customized to their needs. Sites must plan now to respond to this expectation or risk being left behind as the Web changes to a personal medium."

Like all businesses engaged in e-commerce that want to meet the needs and expectations of its customers in real time, Russia's converting defense enterprises should implement a certain form of personalization. By implementing real-time personalization on their websites, MIC enterprises will be able to change information and products as they learn more about their domestic or foreign customers. Properly integrated personalization in online marketing and sales and service environment will help them to increase revenues in the following ways:

- By presenting civilian products and services to the customers most likely to buy them, sales efforts are more effective.
- Through the tracking of customer behavior, management can understand what appeals to whom.
- By presenting targeted offers and information only to those customers who are likely to find them interesting or useful, vendors increase the

---

20 Ward Hanson, *Principles of Internet Marketing* (Cincinnati, OH: Southwestern Publishing, 1999).

value of their business practices and give customers a reason to return again and again.

One of the important issues is that personalization will help to form lasting and loyal relationships with the MIC's customers by profiling individualized content, information, offerings and services.

Personalization will require from MIC marketing personnel and software developers the creation of a new generation of personalized websites. One of the distinguishing features of the new generation of websites could be individualized marketing and sales approaches, in the form of virtual "personal agents" – highly skilled virtual automated (or semi-automated) navigators that specialize in specific product and service categories, acting in accordance with "one-to-one" principles.

One of the most effective systems of "one-to-one" principles in the world was pioneered in the U.S. by Martha Rogers and Don Peppers.[21] The system provides a clear vision of how technologies that enable tracking and communicating with individual customers, one at a time, will stimulate the creation of totally new businesses, as well as new ways of conducting business. This could serve as the basis for the business operations of MIC enterprises, which need revolutionary, rather than evolutionary, changes while re-engineering and re-tooling their domestic and international marketing.

---

[21] For a more in-depth discussion on one-to-one principles, please refer to: Martha Rogers and Don Peppers, *The One to One Future: Building Relationships One Customer at a Time* (Doubleday, 1997); Martha Rogers and Don Peppers, *Enterprise One-to-One: Tools for Competing in the Interactive Age* (Doubleday, 1999); Martha Rogers, Don Peppers, and Bob Dorf, *The One to One Fieldbook: The Complete Toolkit for Implementing a 1 to 1 Marketing Program* (Doubleday, 1999); Martha Rogers and Don Peppers, *The One to One Manager: Real-World Lessons in Customer Relationship Management* (Doubleday, 1999).

The creation and availability of "one-to-one" virtual personal agents would totally change the way foreign customers perceive many Russian high-tech and other products, which have been waiting to be exported. Personalized services will produce greater buyer motivation than would depersonalized services, as is evident from existing web sites in the U.S., Russia and other countries. As a result, it will lead to a rapid growth in e-commerce sales.

Meanwhile, for the creation of "magnetic" and "sticky" personalized web sites (those that attract and retain customers), new advanced software tools will have to be created. These tools require a foundation of new revolutionary technologies. The so-called "intellectual capital" of the MIC – tens of thousands of scientists and engineers developing advanced software, is still a rich source for such challenging developments. Many well-educated Russian designers have the ability to be good software developers and web masters and to create world-class marketing websites. Leading Russian software professionals have everything in place in order to create world-class Internet marketing tools. Proof of this is that many of them have been hired by Microsoft, Silicon Graphics, and other leading American and Western firms, where they contributed to these companies' success.

For MIC enterprises, one of the alternative approaches to new advanced software tools development might be international strategic alliances. In recent years, new tools for one-to-one marketing systems have begun to emerge. They were introduced by leading personalization software companies such as Net Perceptions, Like Minds and others. Russian defense enterprises possessing unique know-how could succeed by forming strategic alliances with these companies. It would help to further enrich and create new, more powerful generations of highly personalized websites.

Thus, there are two major challenges that Russian defense plants and research centers face today: first, re-tooling their domestic and international marketing through broad implementation of Internet marketing; second, developing new principles and tools for personalization of domestic and international e-commerce processes; and third, creation of a new generation of personalized websites.

The personalized "e-commerce era" will make it significantly easier for defense enterprises to meet their marketing and sales challenges, even for those starting from scratch. Personalization will also help Russian MIC enterprises not only to further expand their domestic markets, but also to reach one of their major target markets—international customers.

8.7. REVITALIZING FORMER "CLOSED CITIES": APPLYING THE U.S. EXPERIENCE

Introductory Remarks

Vlad E. Genin

Historically speaking, ten years is an extremely short time. Ten years ago, there were many who were opposed to the idea of introducing into Russia the widely accepted Western model of doing business. They spoke of the impossibility of instituting it because of "specific and particularly difficult conditions in Russia." Today, we understand that the "specific conditions" rationale of the early 1990s was simply an attempt to hide the opponents' lack of knowledge of these models and, more importantly, lack of understanding of how to introduce them. Fear of the discovery of their own inadequacies prompted all kinds of defensive comments. In practice, however, it took only a few years to begin Western-style business, which has become one of the most important elements of the Russian economy.

Today, the situation is repeating itself in the sphere of developing new models of city management, especially for "closed cities". Many Russians executives criticized as unrealistic the use of the Western model of city management, again because of "specific and particularly difficult conditions in Russia." Obviously, the presence of difficult conditions in Russia is a fact, but they will not last forever. The situation is temporary. Using short-term conditions as the basis for a city development plan is obsolete. It shows a lack of vision for the future of Russian cities in this new era. There is no choice but to base city management principles on further democratization and market reforms.

Western countries, including the United States, created their city management plans in difficult, sometimes crisis, situations, without being able to refer to past experience. In this sense, the American experience would be of great importance for Russian former "closed cities", which will start new type of city management practically from scratch.

To be sure, investment is necessary to revitalize cities. By their very nature, investments are made only in those places that have created logical economic and reliable legal conditions. Many countries, including many in the West, have already gained significant experience in attracting investments for the development and creation of city management. This experience could be utilized by Russia to create a favorable investment climate for the reinstatement and development of city management bodies, particularly in the closed cites.

Randy H. Hamilton

The Background

Throughout the existence of the Soviet Union, especially during the Cold War period, limited and sometimes incomplete information nevertheless filtered through to the West, which, consequently knew of the existence of what are variously known as "secret cities", "closed cities", or "defense cities". These were cities that were fully dedicated to secret nuclear research, space programs, military R&D and full military weapon production. They were comparable to thousands of ordinary cities and towns in the country, with major exceptions. When food supply was low or when living conditions were less than desirable, or other ills beset non-defense cities, the closed cities were the recipients of special favor and special attention that spared them the ills that beset ordinary cities. They flourished, and were considered the best cities in which to live.

They were artificially insulated from the rest of the country and the world. They had the best wage scales, intended to ensure the "secrecy" of the cities. The requirements of secrecy and the tight security controls that were in place have made crime a rarity. And, of course, there was no chance of organized crime invading them.

Similarly, the requirements and nature of the closed cities resulted in a system of civic discipline necessary to military production, the result of which was that, contrasted with other cities, safe neighborhoods and residential areas was the norm. Because the nation's military production depended on full worker participation, these cities provided the best medical facilities, the best doctors, and the best health care for ordinary people. Diagnostic and other aspects of medicine in the "closed cities" far surpassed anything outside metropolitan Moscow, and sometimes surpassed even that standard.

Defense cities, much like Kannapolis, NC (Cannon Cotton Mills) or Pullman, IL (railroad cars) were one-employer or company towns. Soviet defense industries provided all the employment, all the wages, as well as the grocery and consumer goods supply. The normal governance of the cities was subject to the will of the Manager or Director of the city's only employer and major purpose for existence –

the defense industry. While it is true, for example, that the mayor of Rochester, NY, pays attention to suggestions or proposals from the CEO of the Kodak Company, he is ultimately responsible for his actions to the voters of the city, and may or may not comply with the wishes of Kodak.

The local Director or Manager of the defense industry employer ruled the roost, and the Mayor's policies and decisions, of necessity, conformed to the Director's wishes to which the Mayor paid more attention than he did to the will of the city's inhabitants. The Mayor was of lesser importance in all respects than the Director or Manager, to whose tune the Mayor danced.

In the former Soviet system, the various programs and projects for the "closed cities" had directives from defense ministries in Moscow. Expensive projects required approval from the Central Committee of the Communist Party. It was by means of such an administrative "top-down" command system that complete control was exercised, the more especially so as without them there would be no financial support for the projects. With the disbursement of funds from the center came the power. To reiterate a well-known public administration "Golden Rule", "he who has the gold makes the rules".

The process resulting from this system was that a particular Ministry from among those belonging to the several Defense Ministries, in company with the ministry's local representative, the Director or Manager of the enterprise, included in its responsibilities the design, development, and construction of both the defense plant itself and of those portions of the city's governmental apparatus as were necessary to implement the dictates from the center. In a major sense, the Director or Manager was both the operating head of the enterprise and the *de facto* Mayor of the city under whose direction the city's governmental and communal life was conducted – finances necessary for a continuous food and commodity (consumer goods) supply, and the necessities of urban living. Similarly, only with the approval of the Communist Party's hierarchy would there be money for building and maintaining medical centers, schools, colleges, movie theaters, auditoria for community club meeting places, department stores, youth centers, etc. In short, prior to perestroika, the Ministry and the Director or Manager formed a seamless interwoven web, a sole source of financing for the enterprise itself, the development and operational programs of the city and the financing of its everyday life.

With the coming of perestroika, the birth of a new Russia, and the process of global disarmament, orders from ministries for military production declined precipitously, and with them the necessity for the multitude of ministries, many of which simply disappeared. The life-support systems of many secret cites were thereby cut off.

The first-generation governmental structures established to replace the old system were themselves soon abolished. The closed cities lost not only their "commanders" but also their life support systems; financial support, in particular, was withdrawn. Mayors deprived of the support systems formerly coming from the center were "orphans of the storm of progress."

At present, these cities are near total ruin because of the lack of funding and other resources formerly supplied by the center in Moscow. Unemployment, formerly unheard of, has become commonplace. The disintegration of the civic order occasioned by the change gave rise to crime. Alcoholism, drug addiction, and similar anti-social activities flourish, along with prostitution. Children were particularly affected as the social service and civic support systems dried up. With the failure of the health system and the closing of health facilities, the former cream-of-the-crop--highly skilled engineers--began suffering rising death rates as a result of the reappearance of almost forgotten diseases, such as tuberculosis. The skeletal and inexperienced official governments of these cities, lacking their Director's or Manager's link to Moscow, and headed by inexperienced, ineffectual mayors, had neither the ability or tools with which to reconstitute a modern municipal governmental organization. Local taxes were impossible to collect in cities where the unemployment rate was almost 100%. The few residents who were in trade, and who had some means of livelihood, were too few to form a dependable tax base. Tenants have no money to pay rent, let alone pay for utilities and city services. There is no source-sustained income, and no ability to pay for the re-establishment of those services formerly financed from the center.

The Prospects For The Future

It is illogical to expect the crisis noted above to last forever. As troubling as it is, and as intractable as it may seem, its nature and manifestations are well known to the new Russian leaders. Indeed, they may understand it better than anyone else. Hopefully, the substitution of industrial production devoted to civilian rather than military use will emerge as a result of their understanding of the problem and the absolute necessity for doing so. The closed, secret, defense cities have a historic opportunity to re-build modern municipal structures, services and administrative organizations founded on the best municipal practices in the world. They have a chance to replace outmoded, anachronistic, ineffectual civic organizations from top to bottom with the best that modern public administration can offer.

To some extent, there is a parallel between the kinds of municipal organizations characteristic of the United States at the turn of the 20th century[22] and the situation in Russia at the start of the 21st century.

Vast, major and nationwide reforms took place in the United States during the past century. So too can one envision the same happening in Russia. Given the opportunity for change and progress, why would one expect otherwise?

Of primary concern is the necessity to disabuse old mayors and administrators of the notion that more money will solve their problems. In Soviet times, these cities became almost a money mill, utilizing centrally supplied funds for programs and projects, with no thought that the spigot would eventually be turned off and that the flow of funds would halt. While it is true that the administrators of these cities under communist rule claimed to be "servants of the people," the claim was a hollow one, with all hands knowing it not to be true. Given the energy, intellect and abilities of the Russian people, there is no reason to think that Western concepts of public employment cannot be introduced and quickly made administratively effective. Without such concepts, no amount of funding will accomplish much.

Western notions, attitudes, and practices of local government must be introduced with the hope that they will shortly become commonplace in this vast country. Russia's progress towards a free-market economy in a globalized world will be hampered, hindered and

---

22 Lincoln Steffens, The Shame of the Cities (New York: Sagamore Press, Amereon Ltd., 1904, Reprinted in 1957).

delayed unless such systems, attitudes, procedures, administrative structures become commonplace in these cities.

The old top-down, command from the center system simply will not work. A new generation of mayors and managerial talent must be developed, persons no longer dependent on the will and whim of the former local Directors and officials in a far-away Ministry. No longer subservient to a single personage, they will become responsible to and accountable to the residents of the city. This generation needs to be created through both education and international interchange, so that proven Western municipal practices can permeate the municipal world of Russia. Instruments paralleling the growth of modern municipal public administration should become the norm.

With the growth of modern municipal services, it became apparent that new educational processes had to be installed — thus the growth and development of the MPA (Master of Public Administration) degree now offered by more than 200 accredited colleges and universities in the United States—that can provide the kind of education and training so urgently required in Russian cities. The growth of professional education in public administration has been nothing short of phenomenal, including not only pre-entry internships but post-entry, mid-career "continuing education for personal professional development."

For example, the nation of Thailand recognized this imperative 45 years ago. A group was sent to the United States to study municipal management, and after months of study, concluded that a professional city manager should be engaged for the capital city, Bangkok. After a nationwide search, I was chosen and served as municipal advisor/de facto city manager to Bangkok and the Ministry of Interior. Today, there are many professional city managers trained in the United States who are serving the major cities in different countries. My experience tells me that it can be successfully done in Russia, the more particularly so as a result of its closer ties to Western traditions.

The notion of professional management for cities is a century old in the United States. Writing in *California City Magazine* in August, 1899, the Executive Director of the League of California Cities, Mason S. Havern, wrote: "Why should there not be a distinct profession of municipal managers, the same as we now have composed of lawyers, or doctors, or engineers, or accountants and others? ... Municipal Management should be a profession by itself ... Let one city place its affairs in the hands of a competent ... manager and other cities will be demanding one also, for the improvement will be so marked that the citizens of other cities will take note thereof and demand a similar administration."

One hundred years later we find in the United States not only that city managers are widely prevalent, with more than 3,000 cities operating under the Council-manager plan in the U.S., but that professional management is so well entrenched in the nation's largest state, California, that there are city managers in 435 of the state's 471 cities. The success of this approach rests on the perception that there is no political-party way to run a city, or as one scholar has noted "There is no such thing as Democratic or Republican city Fire Department or Police Department or Public Works Department." The concept of neutral competence in the administration of cities in California is enshrined in is Constitution, Article II, Section 6.

a) "All … city offices shall be nonpartisan. b) No political party or partly central committee may endorse, support, or oppose a candidate for nonpartisan office."

When professionally competent city employees work within a system as described above, it is reasonable to expect that in the performance of their duties their imaginations will be freed for hewing to party lines or dictates from above in a "command and control" system. For example, utilizing the distinct resources and opportunities in each city, the search for revenues and investments can be conducted on a professional basis. This would include an inventory of the attractiveness of the city for both Russian and foreign investors – water supply, presence of natural resources and an educated workforce, municipal services that add to the quality of life, installation and organization of municipal agencies specifically and solely dedicated to working with investors – making an inventory of suitable available land, city assistance or reduced taxes to encourage and foster investment with a quid pro quo being the number of new jobs created with the assistance of municipal programs, immediate and direct attention to the issuance of necessary permits for construction or renovation or upgrading of commercial/industrial sites and buildings, etc. In short, "investment" doesn't come naturally. It has to be sought out and accompanied by municipal activities dedicated to that purpose. Obviously, all cities, not just in Russia but also throughout the world, are engaged in activities to attract or retain domestic or foreign investments. Those that are or will be successful are those that have professional personnel organized for and dedicated to fostering investments in their cities.

Municipal efforts in seeking or retaining investments must, of course, be administered in compliance with national laws and regulations, such as laws on the security of investments, the repatriation of profits for foreign investors, protections and/or insurance against internal strife, etc

Given those conditions, the primary objectives for seeking investments, until a well-rounded local economy is in place, should be: creating jobs so that municipal economies are improved, adding to the tax base of the city, capitalizing on natural resources or transportation networks, etc.

Observations And Suggestions Concerning The Future

As the inhabitants of the Russian cities we are discussing well know, we live in an age of science, which inevitably means an age of management. Normal cities engage in activities numbering in the hundreds, not just the dozens that characterized the special-purpose cities, which puts great emphasis on proper management, a term I use as synonymous with co-ordination. And, just as co-ordination was necessary to properly fulfill the purposes and objectives of full service cities as compared to defense or secret cities that relied on one employer, with one purpose and who was responsible for the well-being of all within them.

As the Ministries of Defense industries are no longer the main focus of the closed cities, no single entity is the source of financing of city development, provision of employment, care and feeding of the populace.

The role and functions of former secret-city officials today are, consequently, very different than in previous times. Unfortunately, the lack of infrastructure, local self-government, local financing, local know-how – in short, local management – results in economic hard times, unemployment, lack of investment in infrastructure, lack of investment in productive enterprises and the panoply of ills that accompany the wrenching changes that have come to the closed cities. With the decline of municipal management from the central government, by the central government, and in the main for the central government; it becomes readily apparent that new authority must be provided to replace the old.

Municipal operations must be organized so as to secure maximum results with the minimum expenditure; the elimination of waste, duplication, fraud, and excess effort. The new managers of closed city municipal affairs should abide by the following major principles of modern management.

The first element of management is the utilization of the modern technology. It is an approach that results, for example, in no major project being undertaken unless based on full knowledge. The government landscape throughout the world is littered with the remnants of gross failures of grandiose schemes that promised much but delivered little, if anything.

No dam is to be built until geologists and engineers have explored the foundations. No claim is to be honored until the fiscal officer has certified that the money required for its liquidation is in the city treasury, and that its expenditure has been lawfully authorized. No enterprise is to be undertaken until trained technicians have worked out the details. In this manner, persons capable of utilizing it can apply modern technology to the solution of problems at hand. Increasing numbers of technicians are being employed in the governance of a modern society. The closed cities are fortunate in having a cadre of trained technicians whose skills, attributes, and ways of thinking can be applied to municipal programs, projects, prospects and activities.

The second element of management that will rescue the closed cities from their current plight and condition is closely related to the first. Again, the presence of trained technicians can work to the advantage of the closed cities. I refer to research and administrative planning, activities which have become the lifeblood of modern municipal management. Each city department chief must know his city's statistics, estimate population trends in order to know what facilities or force to ask for, and how to use them once they are in place.

The third element of management involves executive control. Co-ordination means the bringing together and harmonizing of divergent factors, tendencies and agencies. The relentless impact of the necessities of the former closed cities makes this third element perhaps the most challenging of the management tasks.

The fourth element of the new management in the closed cities is the development of modern personnel cadres with defined career paths and recruitment, retention, promotion, and retirement based not on political whim or the dictates of a Moscow-appointed "Director", but on ability and fitness for the tasks at hand. Nepotism and favoritism must be replaced by the various competencies demonstrated by local government employees.

Consideration of local units of the former closed cities government must proceed on a sound, realistic, and modern basis. Two-dozen national governments in Europe adopted a "Convention on Local Self-government" in June1985. The Convention was convened by the United Nations Economic and Social Council in accordance with Resolution #1542 (December 11, 1969). It sets a standard essential for the emergence of the closed cities in the 21st century. We recognize that it will probably be years before the constituent States of the former Soviet Union will put in place the principles of the Convention, but they are reproduced here as criteria for measuring progress.

In some respects, the former closed cities are ahead of the game. To some extent, they write on a clean slate and may be able to reconstitute and reconstruct themselves in ways not possible for other much older and bigger cities with long histories of problems.

The former closed cities should be prepared to attract investments (both domestic and foreign) that promise to reward the investor with justifiable profits. No investor can be expected to put up his capital without assurances of an orderly legal framework in which the investment is to take place, and the further assurance of reasonable profits from well-managed enterprises located in well-managed cities that are responsive to the needs of both their inhabitants and investors. Indeed, the two go hand-in-glove and are not divisible or separable!

Once the necessary national legislation concerning foreign investment is in place, the cadre of well-qualified, well-trained, highly-skilled workers in the former closed cities will be attractive to foreign investors as well as foreign advisors. But, again, it must be repeated that in addition to modern national legislation concerning repatriation of profits, et cetera, the former closed cities cannot expect investments to be made in them for the sake of international amity or some such altruistic goal. The investments must show promise of profitable returns. One need only look at two neighboring cities across the Amur River: Blagoveshchensk in Russia and Heihe in China.

As the *New York Times* mentioned in early 2000, on the Russian side there is unemployment and grimy Soviet-era structures surrounding Lenin Square in the center of what may be called "… the same old dirty village." Across the river is a prosperous, modern city, bursting with new high-rise buildings and other attributes of modern living built with the profits from trade and enterprise that shame the rundown town of Blagoveshchensk.

Technical and professional assistance is available to the former "closed cities" from a variety of institutions. But the prospects for the success of such assistance must be favorable before any of these agencies will agree to assist. It is not just a question of assistance from abroad being able to inform; there must also be the prospect that there will be reform. Failing that, technical assistance to these municipalities will not be forthcoming, or if it is, it will only be pro-forma.

In addition to official agencies such as the U.S. Agency for International Development, a number of private organizations in the United States are quite accustomed to organizing teams of specialists to assist in improving local government administration. A partial list of such organizations in the U.S. source would include the International City/County Managers Association, the National Academy of Public Administration, the American Society of Public Administration, and similar organizations that can provide general assistance. American organizations regularly engaged in provided specific technical and professional assistance include the American Association of State Highway and Transportation Officials, the American Consulting Engineers Council, the American Planning Association, the American Public Health Association, the American Public Power Association, the American Public Works Association, the American Waterworks

Association, Government Finance Officers Association, International Public Works Federation, National Association of Housing Officials, National Association of State Foresters, National Council for Urban Economic Development, National League of Cities, National Recreation and Park Association. These and similar organizations can assist on the "governmental" side.

The International Executive Service Corps, consisting of retired top-level, highly successful business executives willing to assist foreign nations, provinces, and cities, has vast experience in many parts of the world in assisting in the development of investment policies and programs that will attract foreign investments. Consisting as it does of former business executives from the very best American and international business companies, its advice and consultative services have provided the kind of information essential for the former closed cities in their quest for foreign investments.

Local governments serve two very different functions, as most ably documented and related by Professor Banfield of Harvard.[23] One function, he noted, is that of a provider of goods and services that cannot be, or at any rate are not, provided under private auspices. Just as private enterprise provides certain kinds of goods and services to people whom they call "customers", city governments provide other kinds of goods and services to people called "residents" or "taxpayers". The efficiency and value of the goods and services are judged by both taxpayers and customers not only as to make certain that they "get their money's worth", but to determine if they supply goods and services are wanted.

---

[23] Edward C. Banfield, *Unheavenly City Revisited* (Waveland Press, 1990).

When government at any level plans to act, a basic question is whether the proposed activity is an appropriate one for government. Since all government is restricted within limits constitutionally structured by the people, the question may be whether the governmental entity can act as planned. "Home Rule" principles suggest that the answer to this question should be "yes", unless specific legal, constitutional or court decisions say "no".

Basic rules of the game must be established to deal with:

1) The sources of local government powers;

2) Limitations of provincial or state or national power over municipalities;

3) The formation of local governments in accordance with the wishes of the electorate(s);

4) Establishment and alteration of geographic municipal boundaries;

5) Resolution of conflicts between local units of government and state or national governments, based on the principle that "The powers not delegated to the central government, nor to the state or province, are reserved to the cities respectively or to the people";

6) Organization and Operation; definition of officers and employees and their powers; allocation and delegation of powers according to organization of the city; and elections;

7) Rules for the regulation of conduct and of land use;

8) Acquisitions use, and disposition of goods, services and property by the city;

9) Rules concerning contracts, including the prohibition of conflicts of interest, bidding, and other requirements concerning public purchasing;

10) Rules for the taking of private property for public purpose or use, including payment of fair market value for the public taking of private land or property;

11) Rules for the city on acquiring revenues through taxes, fines and forfeitures, licenses and franchises, fees, etc.;

12) Rules giving considerations pertinent to citizen litigation against city governments (the "state" is not supreme, the people are).

What does all this imply for the administrative, organizational, and operational structures of those cities, which were closed cities in the former U.S.S.R.? The suggestions are not meant to be prescriptive but merely descriptive of the kinds of operational realities that should be considered, taking into account the culture, history, political traditions, and local conditions of particular areas. It is not a formula to be imposed on any particular society, but merely an outline within which local conditions will dictate the necessary changes that should be made, so that the ultimate arrangements for the organization and management of the former closed cities will be of the greatest benefit.

8.8. RE-EDUCATING PERSONNEL

Introductory Remarks

Vlad E. Genin

Many observers, who have analyzed the reasons for headlong conversion in Russia, and its poor results, insist that the main reason was the lack of money. They are only partially right. Definitely, funds are a fundamental issue in any project. But such observers underestimate the value of knowledge and expertise in understanding objectives, methods, and business tools for implementing defense conversion. Among the main reasons for headlong conversion was that majority of defense industry executives and their staffs were not equipped with the necessary knowledge, and were not proficient in the latest Western approaches to domestic and international management, to marketing, and to the fundamentals of investments—in short, they were not ready to work in a real business environment. Lack of that knowledge made it impossible for them to succeed at the converting the MIC.

From the beginning of marketing reforms in the 1990s, many Russian universities launched new degree-granting programs with concentrations in Western-type management. It seemed enough to these educational institutions to offer only these programs, which allowed them to bring their schools up to speed, and to make them look modern and well advanced. However, other essential programs, like Western-type marketing, appeared in Russian universities much later. The reasons for this delay were very simple. First of all, Russian society and its leaders didn't fully recognize the urgent need for marketing education. Second, there were not enough highly qualified professors/instructors to convey the spirit of the marketing atmosphere and ways of operating in a market-driven environment.

Thus, all levels of Russian society, from students to formerly well- established industrial and academic executives, had few opportunities to re-educate themselves, and thus lacked the necessary knowledge to move toward a free market economy, including defense conversion. The majority of key personnel, such as enterprise executives and managers, did not receive the necessary re-education. Most of their experience in this new environment had to be acquired by trial and error.

The other key personnel in the advanced technology industries, the Russian engineers and inventors, prevented from bringing their products to the domestic markets because of the economic crisis, tried to explore international opportunities. However, they were not able to promote their valuable products on the international markets either, due to their inexperience in such important fields as marketing and international investments. Very often they seemed to think that the technology-transfer process was simply: "Russian side introduces new technology, Western side invests millions of dollars." Thorough assessments of political and economic risks, of target markets and of competition, were often unknown to them, and as a result often absent from their business proposals. It was only in 1994-95 that specialized consulting companies, staffed with economists, re-educated through short-term Western programs, introduced a new service to Russian enterprises: professional business plans. Even today, enterprises do not commonly prepare professional business plans.

While the field of business administration certainly became popular in the Russian educational establishment, the field of public administration, a very important one for the new Russia, still remains largely overlooked. In a free market economy, business and public administration are equally important. This is especially true for defense enterprises that were located in the former "closed cities", which no longer have governmental support. Democratic reforms in Russia demand a new type of city management and new generation of city managers. However, there are practically no schools in Russia that offer training in this subject that incorporates Western experience in public administration.

Can one state that, as of today, in the beginning of the 2000s, the problem of re-education of Russian executives, managers and engineers for the purposes of defense conversion is solved? Do they still need to obtain training from foreign educational institutions, in addition to their domestic education? Have they the knowledge to manage the next phase of defense conversion? Does their training equip them to be equal partners in future international investment projects? What should the international educational establishment do in order to assist Russia in the preparation of high quality cadres for the real perestroika of its defense industries and cities?

Donald R. Gerth

Future developments of the conversion process of the formerly militarized Russian economy will depend, to a high degree, on people with knowledge, new vision, and experience in Western as well as global practical applications in business administration, public administration, information technologies, and many other areas. Many universities are in the forefront of education and training in these professional fields.

The success of a new generation of Russian specialists will greatly depend on their proficiency in international languages of business communications as well as a deep understanding of the culture and business traditions of other countries, and the ability to apply this understanding in the everyday practice of international contacts. These are key elements of a modern international education.

There are several groups of people who will play a key role in future developments of the conversion process.

The first is the older generation of the director corps, which includes directors of converting Russian enterprises—the individuals who led them within the last several decades, and whose economic training and experience was mostly acquired in Soviet times.

The second group is the generation of directors and senior executives of plants and various companies who started their careers in the new political and economic Russian environment of the 1990s.

This group also includes an administrative class, which only through international education and retraining can be converted into professional public employees responsible to local constituencies, rather than to directives from higher authorities. Those who are interested in a career in the fields of public affairs and public administration will be seeking graduate programs, which meet both their needs and the needs of their country. The types of careers such graduates will embrace are wide and varied.

Some will be generalists who will be employed in central government ministries and in hundreds of local governments, now free to pursue their own destinies under much looser central government control than was formerly the case. Some will be specialists who manage particular areas, such as energy or the environment, public health and sanitation, public works, and similar professional sub-fields of public administration. They must be educated not only as generalists but also in their particular specialties, and also in intergovernmental program administration; they must acquire a thorough understanding of the difference between the roles of the professional administrator and the elected officials who are ultimately responsible to their constituencies, particularly at the provincial and municipal levels. It is in the political realm that public policy is decided upon and adopted. It is in the realm of the professional administrator to put those policies into effect through the issuance of necessary regulations implementing laws establishing policy and monitoring adherence to the law and policy.

What these various careers have in common is that they represent an effort by good and caring people to provide effective services and management in a public organization, which exists to meet some aspect of the common good. People who have chosen public service as a career should be educated and trained as a result of their choice to spend their lives committed to public service.

A third group is the young generation of middle managers, engineers, and marketing specialists who will gradually take executive positions in their enterprises.

A fourth group is composed of emerging graduate students who decide to dedicate themselves to the various fields within business and public administration.

Ten years ago, a democratic and free market economy, in a limited sense, came into being in Russia. Russian people understood many of the approaches and principles of such an economy. Today, based on newly acquired knowledge, they have a different outlook than before perestroika.

Russia has not completed the process of transforming its political and socioeconomic system so as to meet international standards. Business administration and public administration are not conducted, as they would be in a free market economy. In such a transitional environment, people have not been able to get training or experience at world-class levels. This would require masters and doctoral degree programs, accompanied by overseas marketing, management, and executive training programs.

The re-education of directors is very much needed, not only for Russia's sake, but for that of Russia's partners; only thus will the outside world get really equal business partners, with whom it will be possible to do business without making allowances for inexperience. Evidence of such inexperience includes unrealistic investment proposals from former Russian defense enterprises to international companies and financial institutions. Such proposals are often based on the former Soviet "budget" way of thinking more than on principles of a free market economy. The generation of directors and senior executives of the 1990s are not encumbered by the Soviet legacy, so their re-education can be accomplished in a relatively short period of time. "It is never too late to study." (This is a Lenin quote, which was extremely popular in Russia).

Re-educating specialists. With the simultaneous crises in both the entire Russian economy and in the defense industry, substantial numbers of highly skilled employees have left the defense sector and filled new positions in other industries, mostly in fields of trade and commerce. These positions, in most cases, do not match their previous ones, nor draw upon their education and expertise in advanced technologies and high tech production. Numbers of highly skilled defense industry specialists could be re-educated in order to fill positions in modern management, production, or design, to market civilian products related to their particular fields of professional knowledge and experience.

Regardless of whether one undertakes professional degree programs to become a generalist or a specialist, the purpose of a professional degree in public affairs or public administration is to prepare one for a position of leadership in public service. A career of leadership may involve management and/or policy-making at any of several levels of government, in non-profit or in private sector areas where knowledge of government is important. The undergraduate degree in public affairs/administration is useful for entry-level public service positions, while masters and doctoral degrees are directed to those whose positions require more analytical and research skills.

The substance of these degrees is critical. Every graduate program should have both a core program and a "capstone" experience, to provide the general competencies necessary for effective public management, which may be defined as: diagnosing complex problems, collecting and analyzing relevant data, developing alternative courses of action, taking action, evaluating results, and communicating information in a variety of ways. Russia can be at the forefront in providing education for what in other parts of the world is increasingly being called "E-government"—utilizing electronics to provide better, fuller, quicker services and information to the populace.

The most successful curriculum is one designed to enhance public service values, knowledge, and skills to act both ethically and effectively. The following subjects should be covered: 1) the management of public and, as appropriate, third sector organizations, including: human resources, budgeting and financial processes, information technology and computer literacy and application; 2) the application of quantitative and qualitative techniques of analysis in policy formulation, implementation and evaluation, decision-making, and problem solving; and 3) an understanding of the public policy and organizational environment including political and legal institutions and processes, economic and social institutions, processes and organization, management concepts, and behavior.

There are two groups of specialists needed in Russia.

The first comprises those who, upon the success of defense conversion, will be involved in new civilian production, as well in the process of "rebuilding" cities, defense plants, and "secret cities."

The second comprises those who were involved in the production of now discontinued weapons or old-fashioned civilian products, and whose skills have become useless for new production lines, both military and civilian. They need to be fully re-educated.

<u>Educating youth—the future generation of industry and city executives.</u> Today's youth, which has no emotional ties to, or even memory of, the Soviet era, will be the avant-garde of Russia's movement toward reforms and defense conversion. The same is true for the already existing younger generation of government executives, corporate

executives, marketing and management staff, businessmen and entrepreneurs—those who can build a new Russia.

Fields/Specialties in which Russia would need world class and international education. Russia is a world leader in higher education in such subjects as the natural sciences, math, certain fields of engineering, arts, etc. Russia is not yet able to provide higher education of world-class quality in such fields as business administration and public administration. Such education is needed, even critical, for the entire Russian working population. Even those who are not involved in the production or distribution process must be re-educated. Former weapon designers, union leaders, developers of defense enterprises, builders, executives of medical facilities, and the like need this education.

Forms of education. The best arrangement might be full time programs for Russian attendees at international campuses, but very few people can afford costly long-term study abroad. Many of those who need re-education, in particular, executives of enterprises, and other working adults, cannot leave their work and families for a long period.

Distance learning, which is currently expanding significantly in many countries, would not be a solution for Russian advanced and adult students. There is a need for these individuals to reside in countries with advanced economies, even if just for a short period, in order to study and go through internships in different environments.

The solution could be a combination of distance learning, limited campus stays and internships in other countries, and limited visits from international experienced faculty and public policy/administrative professionals, serving as short-term teachers and mentors in Russia. Such a solution would enable Russian students to receive high-quality training in both the ethics and mechanics of modern business.

Types Of Programs That Can Be Provided:

Doctoral degree-granting programs for the following categories of people:

- Those Russians now doing postgraduate research and dissertations; these are for the most part the youngest generation of future executives and scientists.
- Those who have rich professional experience; the older generation of managers, professionals, and scientists.
- Those who dedicated their careers to the field of higher education, but now need new knowledge and international experience.

A combination of distance learning sessions, internships in other countries, and teaching/mentoring in Russia will help to make doctoral programs more effective by applying the accumulated experience of Russian realities, as well as exploiting and disseminating new information, research results, and knowledge among different sectors of Russian society. One of the very important results of this approach is that it will help Russia to prepare its own new generation of internationally qualified professors and instructors in the fields of business administration and public administration.

Master's and executive master's degree-granting programs for all categories of people who would like to get international higher education in various business or public administration fields:

- Managers of the former defense enterprises
- City managers
- Former defense industry professionals
- University graduates who earned degrees in other fields

Short Term Educational Programs for all categories of people mentioned above. Russia needs to intensify the preparation of distance learning educators—professors who will be able to teach distance learning courses, in particular for the suggested international programs.

ESL (English as a Second Language) education and the study of other internationally important languages are keys to understanding international economies and cultures. It will allow Russian executives to work as equals with their counterparts in other countries. These programs could be organized along the same lines as the distance learning programs; they would involve acquiring a certain amount of knowledge through studies in Russia, and further training through distance learning and intensive reinforcement proficiency in English through short-term programs and internships in other countries.

Special programs for children, which would be targeted to helping the youngest generation of future Russian counterparts to understand international cultures. These programs could be organized onsite at major international corporations and organizations. These programs should include both studies in international environments and children staying with families in other countries. Such programs should become permanent fixtures, not a temporary fix.

Internships for many categories of people. Internships can play a most powerful role in the re-education process. Previous internship programs did not show effective results due to the absence of unified programs and absence of educational goals. These looked to other countries more like tourism than hard work and a powerful tool for gathering valuable and needed experience.

There were many reasons for the ineffectiveness of internships. Among these were the hidden agendas or indifference of organizers, and bureaucratic rigid approaches. Leading companies over the world, as well as public jurisdictions, would be interested in participating in such programs. It is absolutely clear that rapid growth of internships with deep involvement in international companies and organizations will speed up the process of re-education.

While the invention and implementation of the “sister cities” programs fifty years ago had governmental internships or “secondings” inherent in the original design, exchange cities, counties, school districts, and special districts did not exploit this aspect of the sister city concept. It fell by the wayside, while other aspects of the program flourished and prospered. A well-rounded educational and training program such as those outlined here would use new approaches to revivify these programs. There is nothing so “international” as the mingling of professionals using the same language and the same techniques in the provision of services needed by the populations of both Russia and other countries.

The international community has helped Russia in the process of re-education. Numerous young Russian people are earning higher degrees from universities in other countries. According to academic reviews at many universities worldwide, Russian students were often among the most outstanding students. In Russia, they are able to successfully apply professional knowledge, international experience, and understanding of socioeconomic principles, to the real needs of their own country obtained within a relatively short period of time.

Now it is hard to find universities around the world that do not have Russian graduates among their alumni. However, it has been a period of hit-or-miss experiments. Until Russia is able to offer its students an international environment with the social values of a free market economy, other nations should assist in doing so.

In helping Russia in its endeavors toward a free society and a market economy, other nations are helping a new country to strengthen its political and economic system. This is what differentiates new and old Russia. Gradually, upon developing a sound educational environment in Russia, as well as an increase in the number of highly qualified Russian educators (institutions and their professors), the need for intensive international assistance in the field of education will disappear.

This special form of international cooperation is a high priority for the economically advanced nations of the world— and the time is now.

PART NINE

The New Century: What's Next?

INTRODUCTION

Vlad E. Genin

Life's turbulent currents always bring new phenomena, including epoch-making ones. Russia has chosen as its new President Vladimir Putin, the second democratically elected president in Russian history. This man has inherited a unique and complicated legacy. Russia of the early 1990s and Russia of the early 2000s are two absolutely different countries. In fact, the first very difficult fundamental steps toward democratic reforms, including human rights, glasnost, a free market economy, disarmament, and defense conversion have already been taken. But there is a mountain of unsolved problems that are so serious, they still threaten socio-economic explosions. Expressing their hopes during the 2000 elections, the Russian people expect their new leader and his government to make practical accomplishments that will help them overcome the crisis not only in the country as a whole, but in their own lives. It is not only the generation of pensioners born before WW II who have nearly lost hope for a better life, but the baby boomers as well. Russian leaders face a very difficult challenge: to convince their own people that the day will come at last when they will live as people in Europe live.

For the rest of my life I will remember the day in 1960 when my schoolteacher, Larisa G. Kreymer, proudly announced to all of us 12-year-old boys and girls that that morning, the Soviet government had declared to the whole world that in 15-20 years, Communism would be complete in the Soviet Union. The government declared that in the "Bright House of Communism" all people would work according to their abilities, and receive according to their needs. There would be enough of all the best, the most delicious food and the most fashionable clothes. Bread would be free of charge. Tens of millions of the most modern apartments would be built. Each family would have its own, rent-free, separate apartment with a bathroom and kitchen. Unfortunately, nothing was said about personal cars. But in our hearts we were certain that since Communism would be complete, there would have to be cars! For everyone!

I remember how eager I was to go home and tell my father what a happy and rich life awaited us in the future! My father, who had been severely wounded defending Leningrad during World War II, who had seen a Gulag when few knew about it, said to me in his quiet, wise voice, "Son, maybe it will happen, but not for 300 years or so." This was a terrible disappointment, and my first-ever lesson about reality.

Today, as before, nobody has the right to give ordinary Russians false hopes that new steps toward deepening market reforms and defense conversion will produce immediate positive results, that it will jump-start the economy overnight. This endangers conversion by making it promise too much, and would only result in making it seem to be the source of all Russia's troubles when it failed to deliver. This would be a great blow to ordinary people.

The defense industry's past has been completely dismal. But today, the industry has promising prospects for conversion, restructuring, and—as a result—a new, decisive stage in its development.

The West always helped Russia. Russia has always truly counted on American support and assistance. Today's Russian schoolchildren need to be told of and reminded about this. About the first Soviet five-year plans, when large new industrial plants were built in Russia with American assistance. For instance, in the 1930s Ford built the gigantic car/truck factory at Nizhniy Novgorod - now the GAZ plant.

They must be told about American convoys of military, technological and humanitarian assistance for the Red Army and the Russian people during WW II. These convoys were bound for Murmansk, a port on the Barents Sea that was under fire from Nazi submarines, ships, and bombers. Some of them did not reach their destination, and were left to lie on the ocean floor; many American lives were lost. Even during the Cold War, when the "iron curtain" was closed between the two countries, thousands and thousands of tons of American wheat were sent, on more than one occasion, to help many survive when the Soviet agricultural sector was not able to feed its own people.[1] And, finally, multifaceted aid from the United States to Russia after the end of the Cold War: financial and technical support for economic reforms, disarmament, and defense conversion; education and training of specialists; humanitarian assistance with food, medicine, and clothing; placement of hundreds of thousands of Russian children and students with American families as part of exchange programs.

We are near the end of our book. One of the distinguishing missions of the year 2000 is to name the new leaders of both America and Russia. They, together with their fellow world leaders, will introduce new policies that will determine the future of international security through a culture of peace, disarmament, and the resulting defense conversion in Russia and other countries—all in the name of human life.

One day in the 22nd century, the chronicle of our 21st century will be written. It will begin with the traditional phrase: "In the beginning of the 21st century…" What

[1] Editor's Note: Before the Great October Revolution in 1917, Russian farmers not only fed the whole population of Russia, but exported surplus wheat, meat, and other agricultural products.

will be written in that history about the beginning of our century and one of its important processes – Russian defense conversion? For us today, this question is still very uncertain; we are asking, "What's next?"

9.1. RUSSIA AND INTERNATIONAL SECURITY IN THE THIRD MILLENIUM

Introductory Remarks

Vlad E. Genin

Russia, one of the world's great nations, is entering the third millennium. The difficult problems with defense conversion that the country is facing are closely tied to issues concerning security guarantees. But not only guarantees for Russian security. The new Russia participates in ensuring international security because, as the UNESCO Constitution states, "since wars begin in the minds of men, it is in the minds of men that the defenses of peace must be constructed."[2] An example of this is the participation of a Russian military contingent, alongside NATO forces, in peacekeeping operations in the Balkans, specifically Bosnia and Kosovo.

Significant political changes in Russia that began in 2000 certainly influenced the creation of the country's new military doctrine, the development of the army, and the Russian defense industry. This new doctrine answers whether it is necessary to produce mountains of weapons, or only the amount necessary to defend the country and to fulfill, as necessary, its new international duty: to work with other civilized countries to defend peace on our planet. The new concept of international duty, instead of the

[2] UNESCO Constitution, 1945. Daniel Baker, Power Quotes. Detroit: Visible Ink Press, 1992. p. 333.

> interpretation that led to Afghanistan, is of key importance. This is how progressive forces in Russia think.

Evgeniy I. Shaposhnikov

In the course of over 70 years, the Soviet Union's domestic and foreign policy was based on secretly developed goals and ideological dogmas, which led to tragic consequences for the Soviet people and state. There are several examples of this from the relatively recent past: Afghanistan, Ethiopia, and Angola. The Soviet Union's policies and actions in these regions, and its participation in armed conflicts, were determined not so much by the interests of the nation as by goals of the party leadership, which in turn were based on an erroneous understanding of international duty.

Russia's attitude to the West in the recent past was based on their conflicting ideologies, and was characterized by a confrontation of systems, blocs, and countries. All this gave rise to the Cold War, the arms race, and mutual distrust not only between countries and leaders, but saddest of all, between the peoples, since government institutions drew them into the fray.

Along with the direct participants in the Cold War, the developing countries were dragged into it, and were forced to take sides. One side had nuclear bombs; the other side had thermonuclear bombs. One side created NATO; the other created the Warsaw Pact.

Beginning in the mid-1980s, mankind began to free itself from the path of the Cold War. Russia's relations with other countries are changing qualitatively: from distrust to partnership, from rivalry to cooperation, from arms race to arms reduction and limitation.

Currently, Russia is striving to develop a security concept based on entirely different principles. This concept must reflect nationwide interests, precisely define goals and intentions, evaluate possible internal and external threats, and designate priorities in the security sphere. The highest priority must be to ensure the security and defense of the vital interests of individuals, society, and the state, and not of doctrinaire ideological goals.

One usually thinks of threats to national security as coming from outside the country, but this traditional understanding of the term is not entirely applicable in Russia today. Examples of this are terrorism and the Chechnya situation. Nevertheless, one cannot discount external factors when providing for Russia's vital interests.

Worldwide changes are, on the whole, providing positive opportunities for the Russian Federation. At the same time, the worldwide political landscape has become more complex and multidimensional, in comparison to the Cold War era. Accordingly, Russia's international security problems have become more complex. Developments in the international situation are becoming more indeterminate, sometimes unpredictable; some previously existing threats have changed form, but haven't disappeared; and since the collapse of the Soviet Union, relations with the "near abroad" have been added to the list of external factors.

The main danger in the economic sphere is that the positive, necessary process of the Russian economy opening to Western capital may reduce economic independence, degrade technological potential, and reinforce Russia's specialization in fuel and raw materials in the world economy.

On one hand, this is related to the deep economic crises in Russia itself, the ineffective system of state defense of the country's economic interests, the negative investment climate, etc.

On the other hand, this danger is increased by a number of external factors: crowding Russia out of a number of foreign markets; limiting its access to cutting-edge technology; uncontrolled flight of capital and strategically important resources out of Russia; and obstacles to Russia's full participation in international mechanisms for financial, economic, and trade regulation.

The basis of mutually beneficial cooperation is the economy. Only joint economic activity will facilitate the appearance of joint capital, which gives rise to joint interest. Only joint interest can serve as a stop sign on the path to confrontation between nations.

In Russia, there is interest in Western technology and investment, and in Western countries there is interest in the Russian economy. Blending these interests serves as a prerequisite for the final disappearance of mutual distrust and the sources of mutual danger.

The Soviet Union, Russia, and the other CIS countries have done much more to further common trust than all the countries of NATO combined, more than the international community expected. In order to increase trust, Russia not only removed all obstacles and barriers, but also in a certain sense is beginning to lose its international authority, its dignity; to seek not only the place it deserves, but also allies with which it can feel more comfortable. Russia has been given the following conditions: no matter what you Russians say, our military bloc is, was, and will always be. Clearly, this is Cold War inertia.

Recent important processes have been difficult and complex, and have received mixed reviews in Russia and abroad. The dissolution of the Warsaw Pact, the re-unification of Germany, the collapse of the Soviet Union, the withdrawal of Soviet troops from Eastern Europe, and other events are viewed by a certain (relatively large) part of Russian society as unilateral concessions to the West. Western politicians, in turn, frequently make statements about winning the Cold War, and in doing so they unwittingly provide support for Russian pro-Communist politicians, who blame the democratic leaders of present-day Russia for all that has happened to the country since 1991. Both views of these events deny the role of Russia's own choice and are a serious threat to both domestic and external security. Such extremist opinions and those who profess them are united in confrontation, the legacy of the Cold War.

At the same time, we must not forget that in the nascent system of international relations, Russia, despite the crisis it is undergoing, remains one of the great powers by virtue of its potential, its influence on the course of world events, and its responsibilities. Russia's ability to influence the world community will increase when the country has made real progress in the areas of social and economic reform. This progress must be facilitated by an effective system for ensuring security, one that quickly responds to threats to the interests of Russia and its citizens.

Finally, one must take into account the unique, global aspects of the present period. The whole world is changing—not just Russia. The end of confrontation that existed between two opposing socio-political systems has created the preconditions for constructive partnership on the regional and global levels. There is clear evidence of tendencies toward forming an international community regulated by international laws. But at the same time, nuclear deterrence and the military approach to resolving political problems still play a significant role. One unique aspect of the contemporary period is also the formation of polycentrism in the world politics. At the same time, there is an aspiration toward unipolarity, which in my opinion is a less stable arrangement.

One of the key factors of the current stage in world development is the collapse of the Soviet Union, which led to the formation of vast regions of instability.

These processes pose a threat to both Russian and international security. An ever-increasing number of countries with differing views and interests are being drawn into these processes.

Depending on its place, role, geostrategic position, and economic status, a given country may fall under one or more global and regional structures. When it does, the country's military force will become non-ideological, more human in its intentions, more controlled and more manageable. Such countries would have one common enemy: extremism, revanchism, adventurism and terrorism.

In the present conditions, strengthening or even expanding one military bloc will not create a new world order; rather, it will create new world disorder, since unipolar systems have always been unstable. Retaining one military bloc will lead to the creation of other blocs. Subsequently, there is a new chance that the world community will slide into the abyss of a cold war, that a bipolar world order will be created, with all the attendant consequences.

Let us imagine the world after the year 2000. Obviously, there will be several "power centers". In the Western Hemisphere, there will be the United States, which will probably have integrated—to some extent—with other countries of the American continent. In the Eastern Hemisphere, the power centers will be the following: Western and Central Europe, with probable integration with the American center; the Asia-Pacific region, dominated by Japan or China; and the Islamic world.

Imagine that this model includes a vast area of land with a population in the millions, great scientific and technical potential, vast reserves of natural resources, and powerful missiles and nuclear weapons. This is Russia and the other CIS states. Naturally, if the Russian Federation is not a power center in its own right at the time, then the other power centers will head toward it with their own interests in mind. This has already happened: the Tatar-Mongol invasion, the Napoleonic invasion, and Fascist aggression. The outcome of these events is well known. When one considers that Russia has nuclear weapons, one can imagine what the results of a similar scenario would be at the threshold of the 21st century. Most likely, Russia would become a black hole of sorts, able to swallow up itself and others.

Another scenario is possible. Suppose that the need for self-preservation prompts Russia toward integration with one of these power centers. Which one? Most likely, either the Eastern or Islamic center. This would give rise to yet another bloc of countries, another military bloc. And that would mean a return to confrontation and the consequences thereof.

There is a third possible scenario. Russia (perhaps with several CIS states) becomes yet another power center—the Eurasian center, able to balance attempts at infringement by other centers. Perhaps this will reflect the interests of most of mankind. Thus, the world community needs a Russia that is sufficiently strong, stable, and democratic, rather than an amorphous enigma with a nuclear cudgel.

This is the essence of multipolarity in the future world order. Ensuring stability, preventing threats, and parrying sources of danger will be implemented through the realization of the concept of bloc-free existence.

This model—multidimensional and free from military blocs; having one worldwide and several regional political bodies, including peacekeeping military structures; united by one ideal: to ensure peace on earth—will meet the interests and aspirations of all people on the planet.

9.2. FROM THE CULTURE OF WAR TO THE CULTURE OF PEACE

Introductory Remarks

Vlad E. Genin

"The more bombers, the less room for doves of peace."[3] These words, anathema to the culture of war, were spoken by former Soviet leader Nikita Khrushchev in 1958, thirteen years after the end of the devastating World War II. However, since WW II, over a period of half a century, the culture of war has triumphed many times.

The leaders of various countries that embroiled themselves in wars of aggression against other countries or their own people have always forgotten that "there never was a good war or a bad peace."[4]

The culture of war has been characteristic of man since the dawn of the human race. The culture of peace was born and developed as man became more civilized. The mission of the disarmament and defense conversion processes is to refute the ideals of the culture of war and to promote the ideals of the culture of peace.

Arkadiy I. Yarovskiy

The culture of a society, understood as the level of that society's development, is expressed in the organization of its people's life and

[3] Nikita S. Khrushchev, speech on Moscow radio, March 14, 1958. Daniel Baker, *Power Quotes* (Detroit: Visible Ink Press, 1992), p. 337.

[4] Benjamin Franklin, letter to Josiah Quincy, September 11, 1773. Daniel Baker, *Power Quotes* (Detroit: Visible Ink Press, 1992), p. 337. p. 320.

work, in their relations and in the material and spiritual wealth they create. In light of this dictionary definition of culture, our time is unfortunately still best characterized as a "culture of war."

The culture of war is evident first and foremost in the hostilities between peoples and states, between nations and faiths, and in the inability to solve conflicts by peaceful means. The sources of hostility lie in distrust, jealousy, and intolerance (some inherent in human nature, some due to material inequality) and the lack of education and upbringing. Hostility is evident in armed conflicts, terrorism, and wars. It is not difficult to view the history of world development as a history of wars. Short periods of peace created an impression that peace, and not war, was the norm for humanity.

Civilized relations between peoples and states, nations and races, and aspirations toward peaceful creation and enlightenment are components of the culture of peace. "A person is free when he is required to obey laws, not people but only laws," wrote Kant.

Attempts to stop or prevent wars and to create a culture of peace—a world order based on legality—have been made throughout all time. One of the first such systems was the Westphalian system, which lasted for about 150 years before being destroyed as a result of the Napoleonic wars. After that, a Viennese system was created that lasted for 100 years, and ended in a world war. The third, the Versailles-Washington system, lasted for only 20 years, ending in an even more destructive war. The last, the Yalta-Potsdam system, has lasted for more than 50 years and so far has avoided a global war. A major contribution towards establishing the norms of the culture of peace has been made by international organizations such as UN, UNESCO, Pugwash, the European Union, and others.

In the latter years of the Cold War, the contesting sides paid great attention to creating the image of the enemy. Unfortunately, it is easier to unify one's side by stirring up hatred than through common sense and a constructive program. The spirit of the Cold War is still present in the mentality of the leaders of both Russia and Western countries. Many politicians have been unable to think differently. Mankind has enjoyed great success in fighting natural disasters, but its abilities in the area of international social cooperation and peaceful conflict resolution are sorely lacking. There is still a discrepancy between the positions of the governments of leading nations, and the opinions of large sectors of the public on such topics as nuclear disarmament, NATO expansion, and the military action “Joint Force”.

With the end of the Cold War, and of the historic East-West opposition, the world has entered a new geopolitical era. For the first time, a fragile hope for the demilitarization of the planet, and for an existence without wars as partners in life on Earth, has emerged. However, even with the end of the Cold War, with East-West confrontation apparently resolved, the danger of nuclear conflict remains, due primarily to the increase in everyone’s dependence on the intellectual capabilities of the ruling elite, who make the decisions. The system of nuclear deterrence does not require mass production of nuclear weaponry. Several nuclear devices are all that is required for any country to prevent a U.S. attack on its territory (despite this, international agreements consider 2,000-2,500 devices to be the minimum). Many politicians and scientists understand this fact. Moreover, political instability and economic crises in nuclear weapons states such as Russia are detrimental to the stability of the world. For that reason, the world is particularly worried about the unsuccessful demilitarization of the Russian MIC through defense conversion.

In regional conflicts in different parts of the world, the dangerous doctrine of their governments' right to coercion, without creating legal and societal control, has triumphed. Instead of persuasion, negotiation, and limited access to weapons, the government often relies on force. As a rule, such a strategy leads to the escalation of violence, more conflict, multitudes of victims, widespread destruction, streams of refugees, and the general spread of hatred in the population. The cost of coercion becomes disproportionate to the declared goals, and the goals themselves remain unattained.

The former U.S.S.R. was among the major contributors to the culture of war. It was the last empire to collapse during the 20th century, and the nostalgia for imperial glory, which always led to bloody conflicts, will long attract modern nationalists and extremists. In their world, there is no room for conversion and observance of international agreements, including nuclear arms limitations.

In its more than 70-year history, the Soviet Union built a military–industrial archipelago, produced mountains of weapons, and armed three-quarters of the world's population with these weapons. Today, the armies of 96 nations are armed with Soviet weaponry. Among them are countries whose governments support terrorism and are unpredictable in their military policies.

Many in Russia and in the West believe that the Soviet era is not yet over. Certain "islands of socialism" (the MIC, the tax system, state ownership of land, etc.) have not disappeared; they are frozen. Nine years of reform, conducted in some cases by criminal methods, have compromised both reformers and the very idea of reform. Western aid for such reforms has also been compromised.

Moreover, huge obstacles to the solution of Russia's key problems (the danger of the collapse of the country, the economic crisis, etc.) require Russia to make a strategic choice: which way will the country go; will it be able to take up the culture of peace that is currently being born?

If modern Russia, the successor of the Soviet Union and its Soviet legacy, makes its firm decision on a culture of peace, it has a historical obligation to ensure a future without wars and international terrorism — an obligation that Russia shares with Western countries. The demilitarization of the Russian economy, and the conversion of the MIC, together with international agreements on arms reduction and other peaceful initiatives, are components of the future culture of peace, which will renounce coercion, militarism, and the abuse of human rights.

This strategy is the basis for developing a strategic partnership with the United States and the new united Europe. Integration into Western economic structures and security systems is the viable alternative.

There exists both a basis and a need to involve Russia in common efforts toward the culture of peace. With huge natural resources and industrial and scientific potential, Russia, together with the leading Western democratic nations, can bring a decisive contribution to the future of the world order without global or local wars, terrorism, genocide, or bloody national conflicts. The best mission for modern Russian weaponry would be to become not only a guarantee of Russia's security, but also to contribute to the security of the international community.

The use by cooperative ventures of the potential of the MIC, particularly its intellectual capital, is especially important. There is a great deal of interest in cooperating with or investing in enterprises involved in space, nuclear power, aviation, and shipbuilding, and other industries in the "closed cities", with their high concentrations of unrivaled specialists and scientists.

However, burdened by its dangerous defense inheritance, Russia is unable to resolve its problems without the help of the West. In his yearly address to Congress at the beginning of 1999, President Clinton proposed increasing financial assistance to Russia by 68% (from $2.5 to $4.2 billion) over the next five years, with the money to be used for dismantling nuclear weapons and strengthening control systems for nuclear and chemical weapons, in order to ensure that they do not "fall into the wrong hands."

Support for transforming the totalitarian regime that was the Soviet Union into a democratic one is a requirement for all those who want to promote openness and cooperation in Russia.

Also necessary are tolerance toward Russia herself, understanding of her internal dynamics, and understanding the mood of her citizens. Often, exaggerated media campaigns against the Russian mafia, fascism, money-laundering, nuclear contraband, etc., serve as the foundation for new images of a new danger, and reestablish fear, mistrust, and confrontation. There are no alternatives to a policy of tolerance and support for a culture of peace.

We know there are historical precedents of such support. Within the memory of our generation, there is the example of the United States helping war-torn Europe to rebuild. The large-scale Marshall Plan, which helped rebuild and develop the economy of seventeen European nations (including West Germany). It is clear what should be adopted from the Marshall Plan while developing a new plan for Russia.

The Twentieth Century began with the most destructive war that had ever been experienced. More than 10 million people became victims of that five-year war. However, all of the horrors of that war paled in comparison with World War II, which began twenty years later, leaving 40 million dead. It is noteworthy that the civilian population has increasingly borne the brunt of conflicts and wars. During World War I, the ratio of military to civilian victims of war was 95% to 5%; during World War II, that relationship was 45% to 55%; and in the Iran-Iraq war, and the national conflicts in Yugoslavia, civilian losses approach 90%, and are sometimes even higher.

The end of World War II was marked by the use of nuclear weapons, and instead of peace, it brought on a new confrontation. After the use of the first atomic bomb, Albert Einstein predicted, "The unleashed power of the atom has changed everything save our modes of thinking and we thus drift toward unparalleled catastrophe."[5] In response to my request to express the vision of applying of Albert Einstein's prediction of "unparalleled catastrophe," to the topic of the culture of peace, American author Ray Bradbury replied, "I see salvation in education and upbringing." Education will be critical to the development of the culture of peace. Psychologists have shown that the tendency toward violence decreases as a person's educational level increases. That is why an education and upbringing in the best humanistic traditions is crucial to the development of civilization. Such qualities as tolerance,

---

[5] Albert Einstein, in a telegram sent to prominent Americans on May 24, 1946, published in the *New York Times*, 25 May 1946; in Robert Andrews, *Cassell Dictionary of Contemporary Quotations* (London: Cassell Wellington House, 1999), p.324.

compassion, and peacefulness are more likely to manifest themselves in an educated person.

The beginning of the 21st century could be the turning point in creating a culture of peace to replace the culture of war that has ruled the minds and souls of people for thousands of years. This movement towards a culture of peace will rely upon the enormous potential of religious and educational institutions.

The play-parable of the Russian storyteller Evgenii Shvartsz talks of the victory of good over an evil, tyrannical dragon. The tyrant is overthrown. However, his death does not cause the flight of evil and hatred from the human soul; it is necessary to kill the dragon within oneself. "We, ourselves," wrote Mahatma Gandhi, "have to be the change that we would like to see in the world."

There is little hope that the question of the organization of human societies can be solved without changing the moral makeup of the individual, without a "conversion" of his conscience. First of all, humanity must save the world from itself.

Humanity has made it into the third millennium only because the lust for power has been restrained by fear of nuclear war, but this restraint is not to be counted on permanently. At the moment, it is hard to say whether we owe our survival more to the instinct of self-preservation or to acquired wisdom. The danger hidden in the separateness of people of different countries, unfortunately, remains a legacy for the next century.

"A global war involving the core states of the world's major civilization is highly improbable but not impossible,"[6] warns Samuel

---

[6] Samuel P. Huntington, *The Clash of Civilizations and the Remarks of World Order* (New York: Simon & Shuster, 1996), p. 312.

Huntington, the famous political scientist and historian, in his book, "The Clash of Civilizations," which Henry Kissinger called "one of the most important books to have emerged since the end of the Cold War of the second part of the 20th century."[7] Huntington's warning is a warning to idealists dreaming about a harmonious world.

Humanity today is capable of overcoming this danger. If it renounces the legacy of the culture of war, it can start down the road of cooperation, peaceful creation, and enlightenment. This is the only road leading to the culture of peace—the culture of the next Millennium.

---

[7] Ibid

9.3. WHAT IS THE FUTURE OF THE DEFENSE COMPLEX IN RUSSIA?

Introductory Remarks

Vlad E. Genin

People always believe in a better future; it is human nature. Russians believe in a better future for the enormous industry still carrying the name MIC. This industry concentrates the brightest minds and the most advanced technologies, the biggest and best industrial capabilities, and can change Russians' lives for the better.

Today, as before, despite the bitterness of the crisis that has affected every aspect of life, Russians still subconsciously respect and are proud of their defense industry, calling it by the pet name "oboronka". But what sort of future for oboronka do the Russians believe in? What do they understand by "a better future" for this enormous industry? An industry that produces more ICBMs with nuclear warheads or one that in a few years will open production of a new generation of super-economical and environmentally friendly automobiles designed by General Motors, Honda, or Toyota? An industry that produces the latest fighters and bombers, while domestic passenger planes, which haven't been replaced in years, become worthless?

Will people continue to love their oboronka if it produces bombsights and military radio locators rather than the latest audio-video components, and those Russians who want home theaters have no domestic models to choose from? It appears that Russians today want a future defense industry that works for them, rather than one for which they have to work, as was the case in previous decades.

The Russian defense industry has numerous unresolved problems. Resolving them is a step toward changing the nature of this industry and leading it out of the crisis, i.e., converting them in the name of the interests of one's fellow citizens. It is the cornerstone of the industry's future. How will the future unfold not only for the notorious "military-industrial potential" of the country, but, most importantly, for the people of the country? This question interests everyone, both in Russia and abroad.

David M. Bernstein

Both the defense industry and R&D complex have gone through exceedingly difficult economic times since the collapse of the Soviet Union. Successful conversion of existing enterprises is rare. Some relatively successful new high technology companies have been formed by former employees of the Military Industrial Complex (MIC), but the number of jobs in these companies is small. Some new companies and older enterprises have entered into worthwhile cooperative ventures with Western companies, but here again the level of activity is low, and in general the Russian partners are dependent on their Western partners for financing and market access, and therefore do not have very favorable arrangements in terms of market rights, sustainability, or levels of profitability. There are exceptions, the primary one being the space propulsion enterprises that have entered into stronger international agreements. There has also been little domestic funding of R&D for about a decade, which is a very long time in the development of technology. All of this has resulted in major reductions in size and technological competitiveness of the MIC. The size reductions were probably inevitable, given the disproportionate size of the defense sector in the Soviet Union, and the disproportionate share of this sector that was in Russia.

This bleak picture was exacerbated by the economic and financial crises of August 1998. It is too early to assess the full effects of these crises, but under these conditions, it is hard to be highly optimistic about the near term prospects for high technology research and production in Russia for either defense or civilian activities. However, there are some positive signs and experiences upon which to build. In order to do this, it is necessary for the Russian government to decide, as Marshal Shaposhnikov has pointed out, which security threats it must prepare for and what industrial and research capability it requires. It must then attempt to support a downsized, but adequately funded, MIC. Enterprises must be able to depend on payment for state orders. The state should also encourage the consolidation of enterprises and bringing R&D and production into the same organizations. This should not be done by the failed process of central planning, but by the issuance of competitive procurements so that enterprises will be motivated to restructure and operate in such a way as to become more efficient if they wish to survive. As enterprises restructure to become financially more viable and operationally more efficient, they will be more successful in diversifying into commercial activities, which is far more likely to succeed than total enterprise conversion. As they diversify, they will probably find it more efficient to separate their military and commercial activities organizationally and operationally.

Under the current circumstances, the idea of supporting the MIC by arms exports is an economic myth. Arms exports contribute to the financial performance of U.S. weapons manufacturers and reduce the costs of defense to the government only because they are an incremental addition to substantial domestic funding for R&D and production, which covers the basic operational costs. In the absence of these domestic procurements, U.S. weapons manufacturers could not survive solely on the basis of exports. If and when the Russian MIC is consolidated and supported domestically, arms exports may become a profitable supplement to their revenue, although there are many other issues involved in this. The export of existing stockpiles can also be economically useful, but maintaining production lines, modernization projects, and maintenance capability solely on the basis of exports will not be economically efficient in general.

There are some bright spots upon which Russia can build. Perhaps the most promising is the natural resources sector. Many Russians have expressed concern about simply becoming a country that exports natural resources. That concern is understandable, but it is important to distinguish between Russia and most other resource-exporting countries. Russia (the Soviet Union) had developed an advanced high technology research and production base. While this base is not in strong shape now, a reasonable portion of it can be revived as a developer of technology for and a supplier of equipment to the natural resource companies. Other countries that rely on the export of natural resources must import this equipment and technology. Rem Vyakhirev and Vagit Alekperov have pointed out the value of this approach in their chapters.

The defense enterprises supplying resource extraction industries can work in conjunction with Western companies to introduce newer technologies, modern manufacturing practices, and management, and they will be able to negotiate far better agreements with the Western companies than other Russian enterprises usually can, for two reasons. First, they will not be totally dependent on the Western partners for financing of the cooperative ventures. Through the Russian natural resource companies, the Russian partners will be able to provide a strong share of the financing, and ventures like this can probably also qualify for financing by enterprise funds and international financial institutions. The second reason is that the Western partners will not be interested in simply getting access to inexpensive labor and Russian technology; they will want access to the Russian markets, which in the case of natural resources have stronger potential growth curves than other segments of the Russian market.

To take advantage of this position it is necessary for the Russian resource and supplier companies to invest the time, money, and effort to be able to negotiate strongly with Western companies, rather than being at their mercy. There is strong competition between the Western companies that supply equipment for resource industries, and this can work to the advantage of the Russian companies. To some extent the Russian space propulsion enterprises took advantage of the competition among Western companies, but they were not in as strong a position as the resource companies and their suppliers, nor did they have the time to develop a strong sense of how to work with Western companies.

There are two other areas in which Russia can utilize the technical achievements of the MIC to strengthen the civilian economy. These are space propulsion and R&D, especially software development.

These do not have the advantages of resource extraction equipment for generating capital, but in many cases they do have the incentive of market access for foreign partners. They also have capabilities that have been and are being sought by Western companies.

Even in the areas where commercial development is somewhat promising, the prospects are limited by the slow development of commercial, market-oriented institutions and infrastructure, the weak economy, and by the pervasiveness of crime and corruption. Until these conditions are substantially improved, many foreign investors will remain quite wary.

9.4. THE NEW WORLD ORDER: DEFENSE CONVERSION IN RUSSIA IS STILL A GLOBAL IMPERATIVE

Introductory Remarks

Vlad E. Genin

We are approaching the end of our book and we have by this time heard enough from our contributors to be aware that attitudes toward the fate of defense conversion in Russia are varied, even contradictory. There are many open opponents to conversion, and there are many steadfast proponents. In the West, the latest attitude toward Russian conversion also takes varying forms. There is disappointment, remembrances of past confrontations, and nostalgia for the era of the arms race. But one of the main, progressive Western attitudes toward the fate of Russian defense conversion, particularly in the U.S., coincides with the attitude of sober-minded Russians. This attitude may be expressed simply: there is no alternative to Russian defense conversion.

John H. Hnatio[8]

It has been almost ten years since the fall of the Soviet Union in 1991. Helping the new independent countries of the former Soviet

[8] Disclaimer: This document represents the personal work and views of the author. It was written for academic expression only and does not represent the policies or positions of the Department of Defense, the Department of State, the Department of Energy, or any other agency of the United States Government.

Union transition to free market democracies has been a foreign policy priority for the United States since that time. The United States has spent and loaned billions of dollars to these countries with mixed results. At the heart of America's foreign policy success or failure in the former Soviet Union lies Mother Russia, with her struggling economy and a superpower arsenal of nuclear, chemical, and biological weapons, materials and facilities.

It is clear that many of the problems engendered by the Cold War have not eased with the fall of the Soviet Union. Economic pressures are such that security controls over Russia's vast arsenal of weapons of mass destruction have deteriorated. The current economic situation in Russia plays into the hands of rogue nations and terrorists in their quest to obtain nuclear and other weapons of mass destruction. It has been said that an ailing Russian economy "puts everything up for sale." In all of this, one thing is clear—who the customer is, and what he intends, will become less and less important if we allow the economic situation in Russia to deteriorate further.

Over the past ten years, many things have happened to change the world geopolitical environment, and with it, the future national and international security landscape. The United States and her European and Asian allies have successfully consolidated the nuclear arsenal of the former Soviet Union in the Russian Federation. Focused aid programs have had only limited and temporary success in the stabilization of the nuclear weapons production complex of the former Soviet Union. More aggressive measures to reduce and eliminate vast existing stockpiles of chemical and biological weapons material, equipment, and facilities, have been much slower. The broader record, on the conversion of other major defense enterprises in Russia, is even less positive.

When we consider Russian defense conversion in its broadest sense, we must understand that the focus of the communist economy of the former Soviet Union was primarily on defense activities. Economists have estimated that between 70-90% of the gross national product of the Soviet Union was dedicated in one way or another to national defense. The best of everything went to defense activities—the most money, the finest materials, and the best minds were focused on this national priority.[9]

Today, the reality of defense conversion in Russia is that little seems to have worked. The managers of large defense enterprises still wait for word from central Moscow on what to do and how to do it, and for the money to pay for it. Unfortunately, the lack of instructions and money from Moscow have left Russia as the most important challenge remaining in the transition of the new independent countries of the former Soviet Union to free market democracies.

Other important things have happened over the past decade on the Russian-American scene. The Aldrich Ames spy scandal proved to be a major bump in the road for U.S.-Russian relations. Ames passed information to the Russians leading to the deaths of U.S. intelligence agents around the world—a rude reminder that the end of the cold war did not translate into the end of espionage and spying. The Ames case also reminds us that trust is fragile. It takes time and a multitude of good deeds to build trust—and only one evil deed to destroy it.

The expansion of NATO has left many Russians skeptical and wary of U.S. foreign policy intentions in Europe. The NATO decision to

---

[9] Bernard Weisberger, *Cold War, Cold Peace: The United States and Russia Since 1945*, (New York: Houghton Mifflin, 1984), pp 43-44; 48-49; 64-82 and 306-318.

attack the Serbs in the war over Kosovo only exacerbated levels of distrust. To many Russians, the NATO air war was seen as an offensive military action designed to test U.S. ability to impose its will on a post-Cold War Europe.[10] To others in the world, the expansion of NATO is perceived as an attempt by the United States to weaken existing international cooperative organizations like the United Nations in favor of a stronger NATO military alliance.[11]

We have seen Iraq develop chemical and biological weapons and defy the international community by interfering with, and then refusing altogether, to allow United Nation's inspections. North Korea, India, and Pakistan have all refused to sign international security agreements intended to prevent the proliferation of nuclear weapons. North Korea is believed by some to already have a nuclear weapons capability. India and Pakistan have conducted nuclear weapons tests as part of their continuing military rivalry.

In the spring of 1999, an Iranian proposal to boost nuclear cooperation with Russia by enlarging a nuclear power plant that they are building with Moscow's help appeared in press reports. The United States has harshly criticized Russia based on fears that Iran may develop nuclear weapons. Moscow, of course, denies the claims.[12] But what really matters to Moscow is that the Iranian nuclear project is a boon to a

---

[10] Alexei Arbatov, "NATO Expansion and Russia," Global Reporting Network, Center for War, Peace, and the News Media, New York University, April 1998, http://www.nyu.edu/globalbeat/nato/arbatov0498.html

12 United States Information Agency, Issue Focus, "U.S. In Kosovo: Arrogant Yankees in Humanitarian Clothes? The View From Latin America and the Caribbean," June 17, 1999, http://www.usia.gov/ [search archives by title and date].

[12] Associated Press (Moscow), "Iran Wants Nuclear Ties With Russia," May 8, 1999, http://www.prop1.org/nucnews/9905nn/990511nn.90.htm [see number 12.]

cash-starved Russian Ministry for Atomic Energy facing severe economic problems.

All of these problems have been exacerbated by the rise of terrorism. The bombings of the World Trade Center in New York and the Murrah Federal Building in Oklahoma City let Americans know that terrorism is no longer something that can only happen in far-away places. In Japan, the Aum Shinrikyo religious cult used deadly gas to attack commuters in Tokyo's subway system. Even more ominous, these attacks show the changing nature of terrorism.[13] For today's brand of terrorist, a simple assassination is no longer enough—now there must be mass casualties.

In April 1999, the Department of State reported that terrorism took a record toll around the world in 1998. In all, 741 people were killed and 5,952 injured. Most of these casualties resulted from the bombings of two U.S. embassies in Africa. In their report, State Department made no change in its listing of the seven countries known to be sponsors of terrorism—Cuba, Iran, Iraq, Libya, North Korea, Sudan, and Syria.[14]

Perhaps Robert Gates, former Director of the Central Intelligence Agency, talking about the post-Cold War world, sums things

---

[13] Judith Miller, William J. Broad, "Clinton Describes Terrorist Threat for 21st Century," *New York Times*, January 28, 1999. Excerpt from article: "President Clinton said Thursday that it is '...highly likely that a terrorist group will launch or threaten a germ or chemical attack on American soil within the next few years.' He made the assertions as the White House disclosed that the Administration planned to ask for $2.8 billion in the next budget year to fight terrorists armed with such unconventional weapons as deadly germs, chemicals and electronic devices."

[14] U.S. Department of State, *Patterns of Global Terrorism-1998*, Office of the Secretary of State, Office of the Coordinator for Counterterrorism, (Department of State Publication 10610), released April 1999.

up best when he says, "...we have come into a world that in many respects is more unstable, more unpredictable, more violent, more turbulent than the world we left behind us. Our hopes for a new world order have been replaced by the reality of a new world disorder."[15]

Disclosures of Chinese espionage and the possible theft of American nuclear secrets have raised serious questions about the national security of the United States. There is growing concern that the possibility of Chinese espionage, amid media reports of years of lax security at U.S. nuclear weapons laboratories, may damage U.S. credibility by raising disturbing questions in the world community regarding America's competence, and its commitment to its own stated nonproliferation objectives.[16]

Few would dispute the idea that the loss of generations of technological investment in America's nuclear weapons design program to the Chinese could be far worse than the Aldrich Ames espionage case. In the Ames case, the U.S. intelligence apparatus was compromised, and many American agents tragically lost their lives. In this new game of "Chinese checkers," however, the stakes are much higher. Instead of costing the lives of a few intelligence agents, the loss of U.S. nuclear

---

[15] Gary Bertsch and Steven Elliott-Gower (eds.), *Proceedings of the Russell Symposium*, Center for International Trade and Security, University of Georgia, October 16, 1995, p. 13.

[16] Several sample citations indicating lax security at Department of Energy nuclear weapons facilities as a serious proliferation problem: a) U.S. Congress (House), Hearing before the Subcommittee on Oversight and Investigations, Committee on Energy and Commerce, Hearing Print: Nuclear Security Coverup, February 3, 1984 (Washington, DC: U.S. Government Printing Office), Serial No. 98-138, passim; b) John Fialka, "U.S. Agency Sets Study to Curb Breaches Of Security at Its Nuclear Weapons Sites," *Wall Street Journal* June 1, 1984; c) Peter Eisler, "Nuclear Arms Stockpiles Vulnerable," *USA Today*, October 22, 1997; and d) Pierre Thomas, "U.S. Nuclear Security Overhaul Promised," CNN Interactive & Associated Press, May 12, 1999.

secrets to China now places whole civilizations at risk.

It was less than five short years ago that Senator Sam Nunn gave the following optimistic assessment of the U.S. national and international security environment, "The world is a safer place today than it has been anytime in the last 50 years. It's safer for America's citizens, and it's safer for our nation. We have less fear of all-out nuclear war."[17] But it appears that things may be quickly changing for the worse.

Ask yourself the simple question—if you were president of Russia, would you reduce your nuclear weapons stockpiles after learning that the Chinese now have the ability to leapfrog forward in the development of their nuclear weapons arsenal? In fact, former Russian President Boris Yeltsin may have already answered this question. During a rare meeting of the Kremlin Security Council in April of 1999, he approved plans to beef up thousands of short-range tactical nuclear weapons that had been unilaterally taken out of service earlier this decade.[18]

For the United States, the future national security implications of the loss of generations of investment in nuclear and other advanced weapons technology to the Chinese should be cause for grave concern. To appreciate the seriousness of the situation, let us consider three things. First, the new strategic geopolitical advantages and military dangers posed by Chinese possession of neutron and multiple-warhead technology. Second, the time saved by the Chinese in the scientific research and development necessary to deploy the new technology. And

---

[17] Gary Bertsch and Steven Elliott-Gower (eds.), *Proceedings of the Russell Symposium*, Center for International Trade and Security, University of Georgia, October 16, 1995, p. 5.

[18] David Hoffman, "Kremlin to Bolster Nuclear Stockpile: Government Fears Short Range Missiles May Be Inadequate," *Washington Post*, April 30, 1999.

third, the huge economic investments in nuclear weapons and missile technology research and development they were able to avoid. China's public proclamations that they now possesses the neutron bomb and threats to use military force to prevent Taiwanese independence may be just the early indicators of a much more belligerent and dangerous China in the decades ahead.[19]

Against this backdrop of significant global change, it may be time for the United States, Japan, Europe, and Russia to reassess the nature and long term importance of their global security relationships. What new types of security arrangements will be critical to the United States, Japan, Europe, Russia, and other democratic nations two or three decades from now, to counterbalance a new super-power giant—China, the most populous nation on earth with a society shaped by thousands of years of Eastern cultural development. How will we collectively engage China from a position of strength if our democratic interests and values are threatened?

This changing geopolitical environment means that the success of democracy and a free market economy in Russia may be more important now than ever before. The United States, Japan, and Europe need a different and stronger kind of partnership with Russia if we are to effectively counter-balance the military and economic growth of China that we are likely to see over the next several decades. Moreover, a stronger partnership with Russia will be essential to any 21st century strategy to stem the tide of proliferation of weapons of mass destruction.

Now let's ask ourselves the important question, why have so

---

19 Bill Gertz, "Chinese aggression toward Taiwan on rise; Albright cites island's vote, 'internal issues'," *Washington Times*, March 3, 2000, and Elaine Kurtenbach, "China Acknowledges Bomb Development," Associated Press, July 15, 1999. Internet available at Electric Library: [search by title and date].

many of our past efforts at defense conversion in Russia been so ineffective? At the core of any success or failure in transitioning Russia to a free market economy is defense conversion. But what does "defense conversion" in Russia really mean? Investing more money in a centralized, non-responsive, command system of obsolete military plant and equipment, or something else?

The defense conversion challenge in Russia is the result of over 70 years under the boot of a central command economy. The focus of the communist economic system was almost exclusively on maintaining a gigantic war machine and a massive production capacity for military materiel.[20] Investments in plant and equipment to meet even minimal Western commercial manufacturing standards were never made. This may be one of the reasons that American industrialists visiting manufacturing facilities across Russia can so often be heard to say, "We'd have to start with a bulldozer and level everything first."

Like the giant dinosaurs of prehistoric ages, Russia's old system of industrial war production faces certain extinction. Without investments in new modern commercial manufacturing capacity, creating a stable free market economy will remain an elusive goal, and the democratization of Russia will remain at risk. In the December 1999 Russian Duma elections, the Communist Party of the Russian Federation remained as the largest party, winning 24% of the vote. Ultra-nationalist Vladimir Zhirinovsky's bloc won 6% of the vote—stark reminders that communism is still waiting in the wings to fill any vacuum left by our failure to do what needs to be done in Russia.[21]

---

[20] Howard S. Katz, *The Warmongers*, (New York: Focus-in Books, Inc., 1979), pp 149-172.

[21] CNN.com, Election Watch-Russia (Parliamentary), December 19, 1999,

In some important ways, Russia's defense conversion challenge is akin to the situation that faced the war-devastated economies of Europe and Asia in the aftermath of World War II. While the collapse of the Soviet Union and the situation in Europe and Asia at the end of World War II have marked differences, important parallels also exist. In shaping a 21st century foreign policy strategy that addresses the critical priority of democratization and the successful transition to a free market in Russia, perhaps there is value in considering some of the lessons we learned from the Marshall Plan.

On June 5, 1947, George C. Marshall gave his famous foreign policy speech at Harvard University outlining the reconstruction strategy for post-World War II Europe and Asia. With all that is happening in Russia today, Marshall's words on that summer afternoon, so long ago, seem prophetic:

"The world situation is very serious. That must be apparent to all intelligent people. I think that one difficulty is that the problem is one of such enormous complexity that the mass of facts presented to the public by the press and radio make it exceedingly difficult for the man in the street to reach a clear appraisement of the situation. Furthermore, the people of this country are distant from the troubled areas of the earth and it is hard for them to comprehend the plight and consequent reactions of the long-suffering peoples…

The feverish preparations for war and the more feverish maintenance of the war effort engulfed all aspects of national economies. Machinery has fallen into disrepair or entirely obsolete. Under the arbitrary and destructive Nazi rule virtually every enterprise was geared into the German war machine. Long standing commercial ties, private

---

http://www.cnn.com/WORLD/election.watch/europe/russia.html.

institutions, banks, insurance companies and shipping companies disappeared through loss of capital, absorption through nationalization, or simple destruction."[22]

It is widely acknowledged that the allies won World War II by turning the overwhelming power of the United States' industrial complex to the task of war production. The United States had a well fed and clothed workforce, the economic resources, the technology, and the determination not only to produce the weapons of war needed by its own forces, but also to supply the allied nations with the weapons they needed to fight. And not only was America's World War II mobilization effort sufficient to produce vast amounts of war materiel, it also had the ability to transport that materiel to all theaters of war—even to the most far-flung corners of the world.

By the end of the war, the United States had a huge, highly efficient industrial war-production capacity. With the end of World War II, however, the need for mass production of war materiel was now gone, and America's economic infrastructure was faced with possible collapse. Demobilization of the armed forces brought millions of servicemen back into the American work force. The United States, unlike Russia today, had vast resources, a past history of commercial production on a grand scale, and the entrepreneurial culture to make defense conversion work.

As the United States began the daunting task of re-converting her mighty industrial capacity back to consumer-goods production the significance of European and Asian markets for American goods became apparent. Europe and Asia were totally devastated by the war and did

---

[22] Library of Congress, "The Marshall Plan and the Future of U.S. European Relations," a foreign policy address presented at Harvard University on June 5, 1947, http://lcweb.loc.gov/exhibits/marshall/m9.html.

not have the economic nor physical means to initiate their own recovery. The United States realized that Europe and Asia, without healthy economies, would never be able to purchase American goods.

In March 1948, legislation establishing a four and a half-year, $17 billion European recovery program was passed by wide margins in both houses of Congress. A key part of the Administration plan to implement the new law was the establishment of an Economic Cooperation Administration (ECA). A single administrator of cabinet-level rank, responsible directly to the president, was made head of the ECA.

A cornerstone of the structure of the Marshall Plan, and key to its success, was the relative autonomy under which the program was allowed to operate. Although President Truman was required to submit quarterly reports to Congress on the status of the program, few other limitations were placed on the ECA. Aside from the initial authorization, appropriation, and screening of reports, Congress played a marginal role in the functioning of the program.[23]

To address the challenge of European and Asian economic recovery, the famous conferences in Bretton Woods brought together nations from all over the world. Out of the Bretton Woods conferences came the organization of the World Bank that allowed European and Asian nations devastated by the war to borrow the long term capital they desperately needed, at terms they could afford, to construct new manufacturing facilities and buy modern equipment needed for

---

23 Morton Berkowitz, P.G. Bock, and Vincent J. Fuccillo, *The Politics of American Foreign Policy: The Social Context of Decisions*, (Englewood Cliffs, NJ: Prentice Hall, Inc., 1977), pp 20-38. Note: See this selection for an excellent overview of the history and implementing structure of the Marshall Plan.

production.[24]

Under the Marshall Plan, the nations of Europe and Asia developed their own recovery strategies, with the United States playing an advisory role. Education of a new generation of European and Asian plant managers was given high priority. Frequent exchanges of industrialists and manufacturing engineers assured that newly constructed manufacturing plants and equipment in Europe and Asia were "state of the art" for their time.

During this period, the United States rapidly converted from the production of war materiel to consumer goods. Of course, one of the most important byproducts of the Marshall Plan was the creation of a huge market for all of the goods and services the United States could supply to Europe, Asia, and the rest of the world as post war re-industrialization progressed. A complex web of economic and political interdependencies among the Marshall Plan nations began to grow as America led the free world into a period of more than 50 years of unprecedented prosperity. The "globalization" of economies and the international security organizations that guided the free world through the Cold War were other important offshoots of the cooperation engendered by the Marshall Plan.[25]

Marshall understood that the devastation of the war was so great that special measures would have to be taken to finance the re-industrialization of Europe and Asia. The World Bank was chartered to become the financial institution to lead the way to re-industrialization. The pre-war business-as-usual approach of raising venture capital based

---

[24] Doug Bandow and Ian Vasques, *Perpetuating Poverty*, (Washington, D.C.: The Cato Institute, 1993), pp. 28-32.

[25] Harlan Cleveland, *NATO: The Transatlantic Bargain*, (New York: Harper and Rowe, 1970), pp 3-12, 182-190.

on the notion of the highest, fastest return on investment gave way to special "patient"—i.e., long term, low interest—lending schemes, that focused initially on rebuilding of the infrastructure and the construction of new plants and equipment.

Resources were accompanied by the education of a new generation of businessmen, industrialists and manufacturing specialists. The focus was on the young with business and technology education, put into actual practice through the construction and operation of "state of the art" manufacturing plants. Learning by doing was an integral part of the process. Building new plants and operating them necessarily meant the introduction and application of modern technology. Investments in commercial production capacity set in motion an evolutionary process of manufacturing improvement. Over time, new generations of Japanese and Germans learned the value of technology to improve the efficiency of production and quality. They also learned the importance of research and development in maintaining a technology lead. The remarkable success of the Germans and Japanese in developing and applying technology across the range of industrial production during the last half of the 20th century serves as a lasting testimonial to the success of the Marshall Plan.

So, how can we apply some of the lessons of the post-World War II re-industrialization of Europe and Asia to the Russian defense conversion challenge?

First, we may want to reconsider the way we have organized ourselves to meet the challenges of defense conversion in Russia. We need better ways to keep the focus of attention on our long-term goals with Russia. We need an overarching strategy that explicitly states these goals, and a more focused leadership structure. The focus of Congress should be on the attainment of these goals, not micro-management. We must avoid gauging the success or failure of our interactions with Russia based on near-term political expediency.

We also need to come to grips with the fact that the challenge of defense conversion in the former Soviet Union is largely a Russian problem. The core of defense production activity was conducted on Russian soil. Much effort centered about maintaining and equipping a huge standing military force. Huge defense enterprises were established to support programs of chemical, biological, and nuclear weapons development and other military production. Across the remote regions of Russia there are ten "closed cities" that were totally dedicated to the national defense. Millions of Russians still live in these cities, trying to survive. Across the country, the best scientific minds remain at hundreds of institutes once exclusively engaged in defense activities unable to leverage their know-how to create a new Russia.

It is a sad fact that most of the industrial production capacity in Russia was never of "state of the art" quality. Much investment went to maintaining military superiority, using the strategy of mass production as a way to offset attrition. The focus was on the large-scale production of "replaceable" conventional weapons platforms such as battle tanks and aircraft. Too often, the focus was on quantity versus quality. Large investments were also made in production of nuclear, chemical, and biological weapons, facilities and equipment—the type of products that can seldom be converted to civilian use.

With a history of amazing scientific and engineering feats like Sputnik, Yuri Gagarin's first venture into space, the MIR Space Station, and their nuclear weapons program, it is easy for us to lose sight of the proper role of technology in Russia's defense conversion challenge.

Like leprechauns in search of the pot of gold at the end of the rainbow, Western companies often come to Russia looking for the elusive technological silver bullet—a technology or process that they can buy on the cheap, patent, and apply for quick profit in their own countries outside of the risky economic environment of Russia. Because the principal focus of Russian scientific and engineering effort was on military activity, more often than not, Western businesses leave Russia disappointed and empty-handed. Unwilling to make the risky investments necessary to let the Russians mature their own technology ideas for commercial application, they leave Russia and never look back.

Too often, Moscow is the focal point for action in Russia. While strong bilateral and multi-lateral government-to-government relationships with the Russian central government are essential, we must also seek out ways to work more closely with regional governments across Russia. De-centralization is key to the types of people-to-people interactions necessary to create a new culture of entrepreneurship in Russia, based on mutual trust, flexibility, and transparency.

Now let us return for a moment to the story about the Western industrialists who visit defense enterprises across Russia only to be overheard saying, "We'd have to start with a bulldozer and level everything first." Ask yourself the question— could it be that they have been right all along? If so, the thrust of our defense conversion strategy in Russia should be focused on the construction of modern, "state of the art" production plants. Just as in post-World War II Europe and Asia, the basic financial need would be the patient capital needed for construction, purchase of modern equipment, and infrastructure development. New opportunities for the Russians to mature their own technology developments for commercial production should be part of the strategy.

We also need to reconsider the methods we are using to finance defense conversion in Russia. The approach of raising venture capital based on the notion of the highest, fastest return on investment, i.e., the best possible business deal, is a cornerstone of modern capitalism. Venture capitalism works well in the environment of a healthy, well-established economy. What is not clear, however, is how well it has worked in the fledgling free market economy of Russia. Some could argue that it has had a detrimental impact by limiting the amounts of foreign investment in Russia available for long term projects like the construction of basic production capacity and infrastructure development. Others argue that the lack of responsible debt repayment structures is leading to capital flight, and allowing the Russians to re-direct loan monies to enhance their military programs.[26] Under the Marshall Plan, fully transparent debt structures that focused on special long-term, low-interest lending schemes for the construction of new plants and equipment were at the heart of a winning strategy.

The European Bank for Reconstruction and Development has been chartered to lead the way in helping the newly independent states make the transition to market economies. Part of their charter is to assist Russia in meeting her huge defense conversion challenge. The Defense Enterprise Fund has a similar mandate. The Overseas Private Investment Corporation strives, through the granting of loan guarantees, to reduce the risk of investment in the volatile economic environment of Russia.

[26] Roger W. Robinson Jr., remarks before the Alaskan World Affairs Council, May 7, 1999, and remarks before the Heritage Foundation panel discussion entitled, "The Meaning of the Russian IMF Bailout," July 23, 1998. Note: Roger W. Robinson Jr., is President and CEO of RWR, Inc., and former Senior Director of International and Economic Affairs, National Security Council.

Working together, we must find more effective ways to make the patient and affordable capital needed by the Russians available to them to construct new, world class manufacturing facilities, buy modern equipment, and invest in improving their infrastructure.

Under the Marshall Plan, the financial resources for new plant and equipment were matched with education. People learned by actually doing. Too often, the case in Russia today is education by consultant. The United States, it seems, has an overabundance of at least two things: lawyers and consultants. As any Russian can tell you, there is no shortage of American consulting expertise in Russia. Not so affectionately referred to as the "Marriott Brigade," thousands of consultants troop in and out of Russia every year. Many of them are paid with taxpayer dollars. They are experts at telling the Russians "how we do it in America." The only problem is that consultants are generally not bankers—they give lots of advice but seldom lend any money.

Consultants by definition are also capitalists. Many are known in the Russian defense conversion game as "cherry pickers." They come to Russia looking for technology to buy on the cheap and take home. Too often, they are not interested in making any long-term difference in the risky economic environment of Russia. Almost always, everyone goes away disappointed after an encounter with a "cherry picker." The "cherry picker" doesn't find the technology he wants and invariably leaves the Russians asking themselves the question, "What kind of help is this?"

We need to seek out new opportunities for Japanese, American, and European industrialists and businessmen to get more involved with teaching the Russians. Creating cooperative ventures where all parties have a vested interest in a good outcome is one way to assure both a good education in the lessons of capitalism and highly receptive students. Linking financial loans to education may be one way to accomplish this important objective. After all, working under a communist command economy has already proven to be very poor preparation for the challenges of a free market. The absence of an entrepreneurial culture under communism means that education coupled with hands-on experience in free market business practice for the Russians is critical to the long-term success of any strategy. Reducing the risk of major investments by providing low cost capital for the construction of new commercial production plants and the purchase of modern equipment under co-ownership and management may be one way to create an environment conducive to both effective teaching and learning.

On May 7, 1999, Federal Reserve Chairman Alan Greenspan gave a speech in Chicago on the astounding vitality of the American economy. He told the audience that an unexpected leap in technology was primarily responsible for the nation's "phenomenal economic performance" and the current extraordinary combination of strong growth, low unemployment, low inflation, high corporate profits and soaring stock prices.[27]

There is no doubt that technology is at least as important to economic development today as it was in 1947, when George Marshall outlined his reconstruction strategy for post-World War II Europe and Asia. It is no secret, however, that the same technology that has important commercial applications can often also be used for military

---

[27] John M. Berry, "Greenspan Credits Technology," *Washington Post*, May 7, 1999. http://www.washingtonpost.com [Search Washington Post archives by title. date, and author].

purposes. Known in government jargon as "dual-use" technology, this has been a major sticking point in U.S.-Russian business development.

For example, two years ago, when former Russian Minister of Atomic Energy Viktor Mikhailov announced that Russia was using American computer technology in its nuclear weapons program, the United States recoiled. It was a disturbing reminder that the same types of advanced technology required for modern commercial production could also be used to produce things like nuclear weapons.[28] Nonetheless, developing a modern commercial production capacity in Russia will require a major infusion of western production technology know-how. Thus, how well we address the thorny issue of dual-use technology may well make the difference between the success of defense conversion in Russia and failure.

Several years ago, former U.S. President Ronald Reagan, in discussions regarding the Strategic Arms Limitations Treaty, coined the famous phrase, "Trust but verify." To make defense conversion in Russia work, the United States and Russia must find a new level of trust. One way to engender trust is through transparency. Transparency means free access, at any time, to plants and facilities to assure technology is being used only for peaceful commercial purposes.

The aftermath of World War II was a unique time in world history. Although the Marshall Plan has been widely heralded as a stroke of foreign policy genius, it would be presumptuous and not very productive to simply dust it off and try and apply it to the current situation in Russia. What we must do instead is seek out the underlying

---

[28] Harold J. Johnson, "Export Controls: Sales of High Performance Computers to Russia's Nuclear Weapons Laboratories," International Relations and Trade Issues, National Security and International Affairs Division, General Accounting Office, (Washington, DC: Government Printing Office, April 15, 1997).

principles of its success, and adjust them to meet today's situation.

Three important principles lie at the heart of the success of the Marshall Plan: the effective application of resources, education, and technology. Applying these principles in the environment of today's Russia means that we must find more effective ways to provide patient capital for new commercial production capacity and infrastructure development. We must seek out better ways to bring Western industrialists and businessmen closer together with their Russian counterparts to educate and learn from one another. And we must do a better job of leveraging technology for peaceful commercial applications.

Since 1991, we have tried many different approaches in Russia. Some things have worked well and others have not. Perhaps the challenge we face today is to identify those things that have worked, and meld them together in the context of the enduring principles of the Marshall Plan to create a uniquely Russian strategy for success. Key to the success of any strategy will be a more focused overarching plan and leadership structure that catalyzes closer cooperation between governments and industry. The more direct engagement of Western industry in Russia must be a cornerstone of the strategy. All sides must have a vested interest in successful outcomes.

One possible way to accomplish these goals might be the creation of a new Multinational Development Corporation or MDC. The MDC would be chartered to develop cooperative ventures that focus on building new commercial industrial capacity and infrastructure development in Russia. The MDC would be given preferential access to patient capital, and work closely with existing international lending institutions such as the World Bank and the European Bank for Reconstruction and Development. New industrial ventures would be co-owned, and link financial lending directly to education and practical learning. Transparency of operations would be a requirement of all MDC business dealings, so as to assure responsible debt structures, and guarantee that dual-use technology is used only for peaceful commercial purposes.

In May 1999, U.S. President Clinton visited us here at National Defense University to speak about the conflict then raging over Kosovo. He discussed the devastation of war and the need to democratize and rebuild the region. Harkening back to the important lessons of history in the aftermath of World War II, he said:

"...Last Saturday was the anniversary of one of the greatest days in American history and in the history of freedom, VE Day. Though America celebrated that day in 1945, we did not pack up and go home. We stayed to provide economic aid, to help to bolster democracy, to keep the peace. And because our strength and resolve was important as Europe rebuilt, we learned to live together, face new challenges together. The resources we devoted to the Marshall Plan, to NATO, other efforts, I think we would all agree, have been an enormous bargain for our long-term prosperity and security here in the United States."[29]

The history of the human race is replete with tragic stories of opportunities lost. Today, we still have an opportunity to do what must be done in Russia. But make no mistake about it; the opportunity with Russia is slipping away. We must all work together and find ways to re-energize our efforts, or risk losing an historic opportunity to stabilize the world and create a new era of global peace and prosperity.

In the summer of 1998, I invited Russian Academician Evgeny

---

[29] William J. Clinton, text of speech, "U.S. Involvement in Kosovo," presented at National Defense University, Washington, D.C. on May 13, 1999.

Velikhov to visit me at National Defense University in Washington, D.C. Dr. Velikhov is Director of Russia's famous Kurchatov Institute,[30] and served as an advisor on national security matters to former Russian President Boris Yeltsin. Dr. Velikhov and I shared our concerns about the slow progress of defense conversion in Russia. During his visit, we discussed the idea of a U.S., Japanese, European, and Russian summit of leading political, economic and industrial leaders to begin a dialogue on the changes now sweeping the world. We agreed that important topics of consideration might include the development of new strategies for defense conversion in Russia and ways to establish new and more effective international arrangements to deal with the new threats posed by weapons of mass destruction. A summit of this type could serve as a platform to re-focus and re-energize our efforts on Russia.

In 1947, George Marshall had the vision and the political courage to pursue a lasting peace with former enemies. For his remarkable leadership, he received the Nobel Peace Prize. At the heart of Marshall's vision for the future was a simple but powerful idea—treat people as people. We can do much to succeed in Russia by making life more bearable for the average Russian citizen, whether he or she lives in Moscow or Siberia. With responsible debt structures, we can stem capital flight from Russia. By directing our investments away from outdated, obsolete Russian defense enterprises with no commercial potential to the construction of new modern manufacturing facilities, we

---

[30] Note: The Kurchatov Institute was originally founded as the I.V. Kurchatov Institute of Atomic Energy during World War II. Today, the Kurchatov Institute is dedicated to a broad range of multidisciplinary research and development in areas including nuclear reactor physics, plasma and electron beam technologies, environmental science, advanced materials, etc. More information regarding the Kurchatov Institute is available on the internet at: http://www.kiae.ru/eng/wel/all/dp1.htm

can create opportunities for the Russian worker to leave the past behind, and move forward into the 21st century.

It will take political courage and persistence by people on all sides to create a new kind of partnership with Russia. To be sure, there will be major bumps along the road. But the stakes are high enough for us to devise a winning strategy and commit ourselves to its success.

EPILOGUE

Vlad E. Genin

Russian defense conversion, its anatomy and chronology of events, its first steps, achievements, and failures, will undoubtedly go down in the history of the new Russia and will become the fundamental determiners of the direction Russia will be taking for the foreseeable future.

The main result of the first stage of defense conversion (1988-2000) is that progressive Russian society saw that demilitarizing the country's economy would allow the acceleration of economic reforms and help Russia to enter the international economic system as an equal partners, reduce dependence on the import of civilian products, and increase the status and the role of the domestic manufacturer.

One of the important positive results is that the experience gained by Russian manufacturers through working with Western countries allowed them to achieve and ensure the production of a good deal of world-class goods, and even surpass the West in the areas of some high-tech and intellectual products. All these years they have worked intensively to master the principles of doing business (previously unknown to them), and achieved great success in a relatively short historical period.

Nevertheless, defense conversion as a whole process—as it was thought up in 1988 —has still not taken place.

Throughout history, after battles in stormy seas, warships have headed home to peaceful harbors. After the end of the Cold War and the unprecedented arms race, defense conversion needed a "peaceful harbor"—a special environment for fostering creation: one that is politically stable and economically healthy. No peaceful harbor existed.

In order to be successful, Russian defense conversion required enormous amounts of money, on the order of hundreds of billions of dollars. Naturally, neither Russia nor the West had that kind of money available. What was possible was the creation of a financial mechanism for Russian defense conversion involving the use of Western seed money, based on appropriate planning and re-investment strategies. What actually happened was that, due to the legacy of the Soviet budget mentality, when Moscow announced the beginning of defense conversion process, most of Russian society believed that money for both economic reforms and conversion would be available too, but from another source – the wealthy West. The expression, "the West will help us," popular in the beginning of the 1990s, which was understood by most Russians to mean "the West will pay for Russian defense conversion," was wide-spread among the population and naturally, never become a reality. This is why many Russian politicians and industrialists on the threshold of the 21st century lost their enthusiasm for conversion, while reactionaries became outright negative, calling for re-conversion and increased arms production and exports.

It is hard to imagine that Russian defense conversion could be implemented during major political battles on the domestic arena, power struggles, frequent and unexpected changes in the Russian Government (particularly Prime Ministers), and the numerous liquidations, resurrections, and reorganizations of ministries and departments in charge of the Military Industrial Complex.

It is also hard to believe that Moscow, which tightly controlled every step and decision of the directors of MIC plants or research institutes, even after announcing democratic and free-market economic reforms, could "baby-sit" each defense enterprise's undergoing conversion.

Thus, in reality, the proper economic environment, mechanisms for financing and eventual self-financing, and organizational plans (matters that are just now being dealt with under the name of "restructuring") were not established to prepare for such a fundamental change in the militarized Russian economy as defense conversion.

The first positive Russian reforms after 1985 roused the world business community. In the late 1980s and early 1990s, it was hard to find a Western industry, company, or entrepreneur who did not want to conduct mutually beneficial business with the new Russia. But the fact is that Russia was unable to take advantage of such a historical opportunity. In the 15 years that have passed since the beginning of Gorbachev's perestroika, Russian legislation has confirmed that to work with this country, particularly on defense conversion projects, is practically impossible, or at least extremely difficult, because of the incomparably greater political risks to investment than are found in most other countries.

The hopes of Russian and foreign corporations and private entrepreneurs for large investment projects in Russia, the creation of international cooperative ventures, the organization of large-scale technical cooperation—everything that should have served as fuel for defense conversion—were not realized. Among the main reasons were the following:

First, because there was insufficient legislation before reforms, and new, civilized, workable laws were not passed while reforms were taking place; as a result, foreign investors have stayed away from Russia, even until the present day.

Second, the attitude of many Russians (based on their Soviet-era legacy) was unable to differentiate between the concepts of financial assistance *for* the country (because it is needy) and investment *in* the country's economy (because it is profitable). Western assistance was viewed in Russia as a permanent "energy supply", not as a "jump-start" measure.

Third, thousands of investment proposals from Russia called for investment in projects where the land and enterprises themselves were not privatized. Even now, hundreds of MIC state enterprises—the majority—remain unprivatized, although they are not part of the core of vital state defense enterprises as determined by Russian specialists. These hundreds of enterprises, which are still owned by the state, find it practically impossible to attract foreign investment.

Besides the lack of guarantees for foreign investment, state policy did not stimulate the domestic manufacture of consumer goods. Moreover, favorable custom duties rates were granted to imported consumer goods, particularly electronics, mainly from Southeast Asia. At the same time, Russian domestic manufacturers were forced to pay astronomical taxes—over 90%. This was one of the main reasons for the birth of the Russian "shadow" economy and of the control of enterprises by racketeers, whose activities led to corruption cases not only in local governments, but also even on the upper levels.

It is extremely uncertain that the trend that appeared in 1999—reorienting the whole of Russia's as-yet unconverted militarized economy in the opposite direction, toward arms production in order to achieve economic success through increasing exports—will lead to a better future for the country and its people. Arms exports development is the prerogative of the Russian government, but it is hard to believe that selling arms to developing countries will make it possible for Russia to feed and clothe the ever-poorer majority of the population, not temporarily, but over the long term; to provide all its people with a stable income adequate to buy homes and to pay mortgages, modern cars, furniture, and annual vacations. As history, including recent Russian experience, demonstrates, living by selling weapons is not the road to stable development. It will not put world-class domestically produced consumer goods on store shelves. Living by selling weapons is a dead-end proposition. This road will most likely lead to a new, more difficult socio-economic turmoil.

In today's Russia, there is an excellent understanding of the obstacles to the conversion process, and to the economic development of the country as a whole. Today, at the advent of a new millennium, a simple question arises: what, exactly, needs to be converted in Russia? One cannot speak of conversion in general or as a whole. One must understand how much needs to be converted.

In the past, the Russian (formerly Soviet) defense industry worked to fulfill a number of goals. First, to support the country's ability to defend itself. Second, to produce enough weapons for the Soviet armed forces located in the remaining 14 republics of the former Soviet Union. Third, to provide weapons to the armed forces of Warsaw Pact countries and Cuba. Fourth, to provide weapons to "friendly allies" in the Middle East, Africa, South Eastern Asia, and South America. Fifth, to participate in the international arms race. Sixth, to export arms to countries paying for them via hard currency or barter.

Naturally, providing the country with the ability to defend itself is the main goal of the defense industry of any country. Obviously, for this goal, and particularly for producing innovative weapons, it is necessary to cultivate the technological potential of a number of core defense enterprises. However, modern Russia is no longer responsible for the ability of the now-independent former Soviet republics, former Warsaw Pact countries, and many former "friendly countries" to defend themselves. Subsequently, the industrial capacities of many of the defense enterprises that filled all previous defense procurement orders are no longer necessary. Therefore, as it applies to the situation in Russia today, "conversion" is defined as the conversion of defense enterprises made redundant by the cancellation of the second, third, fourth, and fifth goals, as well as the substantial revision of the sixth goal – arms exports. In other words, converting the "leftovers" in the Russian arms production order created by the collapse of the Soviet Union, the dissolution of the

Socialist camp, and Russia relieving itself of the responsibility of providing arms to numerous other countries.

The key problem is that there is no real mechanism for implementing the next round of Russian conversion, nor is there a plan. Therefore, the huge sums of money the experts have named should not be provided in one lump sum. What is needed is seed money, plus a mechanism allowing Russia to move toward self-financing conversion activities.

The first tranche of funds should be provided by private domestic companies. One should not ignore the fact that during the last ten years a new generation of Russian domestic capitalists was born and grew up, who would likewise be capable of investing in their country's conversion. The bitter experiences Russian businessmen and ordinary people had when trying to invest money in their own country must be overcome—experiences such as the many recent Russian "pyramid" schemes, and numerous fly-by-night banks, which unfortunately disappeared with the money of working people and pensioners.

The second tranche should be investment by the world community, as Russia simply has not enough money to create and implement the mechanism for a new phase of conversion. The positive results of the Marshall Plan—the revival of Western Europe, as well as vigorous economic growth in Japan and a number of Asian and South American countries—proves the realism of this approach.

Of course, the new stage of international assistance to Russia will make sense only if the new Russian leadership is able to create order in the country, including safeguards against possible corruption.

In the meantime, it is hard to overestimate the potential and the role of foreign private investments in new conversion developments.

Again, the success of this step is up to the Russian government, which must provide guarantees to foreign companies that free-market reforms will not be reversed, and, most importantly, create and universally enforce civilized laws protecting the activities of foreign companies in Russia, and the security of foreign investment. Only the Russian government can free foreign companies from the threat of the State bureaucracy, as well as the criminal circles. The same protection must be provided to domestic investors. To attract these potential investors, it would be wise to create, at last, tax legislation that is mutually beneficial for the State as well as domestic and foreign investors.

The third tranche should be the re-investment of profits earned by converted enterprises, the transition to self-financing for the next stages of conversion, and further business activity.

According to the popular Russian saying, “Moscow wasn’t built in a day”. But it was eventually built, and is becoming more and more beautiful with each passing year—the great capital of the great renascent Russia. People are lining up to use the industrial potential of its former vast defense industry. Conversion, as a process for resurrecting the industrial and intellectual potential of the former Military-Industrial Complex, can cause the Russian people to flourish.

“Do Russians want war?” These are the words from a famous Russian song written by the poet Evgenii Evtushenko in the 1960s. So do ordinary Russians really need war? As the poet asked then, ask today the mothers of the thousands of soldier boys who died pointlessly in Afghanistan and Chechnya. Ask teachers, medics, laborers, farmers or the MIC’s talented and creative technical people. The answer will be No.

Now is the time to accomplish, finally, conversion for the sake of building a better life for the people of Russia, to re-open millions of jobs, to re-start full production of everything that people need—domestically produced foodstuffs (the majority are currently imported), clothes, and medicine. It is the time to improve the terribly polluted environment, which already has claimed the health and lives of millions of people and which still contributes towards the reduction of the Russian population. The time has come at last to provide pensions and decent living conditions for the elderly, who worked honestly for three or even five decades of their lives for the State, and are now forced to look for food in city dumpsters. They still hope. Hope, as the poet said, dies last.

To stop defense conversion halfway, when much of the price has already been paid, would mean to turn back Russia to a militarized economy, to the myths and realities of the Cold War. One of these myths, which has influenced ordinary Russians since Stalin's time, is that of the danger of becoming an enslaved nation. But that myth must be dispelled.

The world does not need a poor, hungry Russia. The modern civilized world, with its human and moral values, aspirations to prosperity, electronically interconnected markets and whole segments of economy, needs an undivided, strong Russia. Not strong by virtue of its tanks; ICBMs; nuclear, chemical, and biological weapons; or intellectual capital capable of committing international cyber attacks—strong because of its civilized laws, morals, high cultural values, and technological achievements to better its own high standard of living.

Many Western companies are ready to invest in the Russian economy, but it is vital to demonstrate to them real results in the movement toward the ideals of world civilization, democracy and free market economy.

That is why today, support for Russia is needed very much. Such support is needed for Russia's efforts to switch the potential of the militarized economy of a gigantic country/defense plant to meet the needs of the ordinary Russian people. The success of the Russian defense conversion effort would change the political climate in the world, making it much warmer. It would give the civilized world confidence in the future of the human race. The West should help Russia in its unique historical endeavor to make defense conversion happen, and make sure that it is irreversible.

CONTRIBUTING AUTHORS

Honorable William J. Perry (B.S., M.S., Stanford University; Ph.D., Penn State) is the *Michael and Barbara Berberian Professor* at Stanford University, with a joint appointment in the School of Engineering and the Institute for International Studies. His previous academic experience includes Professor (half-time) at Stanford from 1988 until 1993, during which time he was the Co-director of the Center for International Security and Arms Control. He also served as a part-time lecturer in the Department of Mathematics at Santa Clara University from 1971 to 1977.

Dr. Perry was the 19th Secretary of Defense for the United States, serving from February 1994 to January 1997. His previous government experience was as Deputy Secretary of Defense (1993-1994) and as Under Secretary of Defense for Research and Engineering (1977-1981). Dr. Perry's business experience includes serving as a laboratory director for General Telephone and Electronics (1954-1964); founding and serving as the president of ESL, Inc. (1964-1977); Executive Vice-President of Hambrecht & Quist, Inc. (1981-1985); and founding and serving as the Chairman of Technology Strategies & Alliances (1985-1993). He serves on the board of United Technologies, The Boeing Company, Cylink and several emerging high-tech companies.

Dr. Perry was born Oct. 11, 1927, in Vandergrift, PA. He attended grade school and high school in Butler, PA. He received his B.S. and M.S. from Stanford University and his Ph.D. from Penn State, all in mathematics. He is a member of the National Academy of Engineering and a fellow of the American Academy of Arts and Sciences. From 1946 until 1947, Dr. Perry was an enlisted man in the Army Corps of Engineers, and served in the Army of Occupation in Japan. He joined the Reserve Officer Training Corps in 1948 and was a second lieutenant in the Army Reserves from 1950 until 1955.

Dr. Perry has received a number of awards, including the Presidential Medal of Freedom (1997), the Department of Defense Distinguished Service Medal (1980 and again in 1981), and Outstanding Civilian Service Medals from the Army (1962 and 1997), the Air Force (1997), the Navy (1997), the Defense Intelligence Agency (1977 and 1997), NASA (1981) and the Coast Guard (1997). He received the American Electronic Association's Medal of Achievement (1980), the Eisenhower Award (1996), the Marshall Award (1997), the Forrestal Medal (1994), and the Henry Stimson Medal (1994). The National Academy of Engineering selected him for the Arthur Bueche Medal in 1996. He has been honored by awards from the enlisted personnel of the Army, Navy, and the Air Force. Dr. Perry has received decorations from the governments of Germany, England, France, Korea, Albania, Poland, Ukraine, Bahrain, Slovenia and Hungary.

Honorable Evgeniy I. Shaposhnikov (Graduate of the Yeisk Higher Air Force College, Kharkov Higher Air Force College, Gagarin Moscow Air Force Academy, the Military Academy of the General Staff of the Soviet Armed Forces) is a Marshal of Aviation.

From 1963 to 1966, he served as a military pilot in Western Ukraine; during his military service, he rose from a combat pilot (more than 4000 flight hours) to Commander in Chief of Air Force, holding numerous military appointments: Commander of the Air Force squadron and later, the Air Force regiment at the Western Group of Soviet Forces in East Germany (1969-75); Commander of Air Force Division in Western Ukraine (1975-79); Deputy Commander of the Carpathian Military District (1979-82); Commander of the Air Force of the Odessa Military District (1984-87); Commander of the Air Force at the Western Group of Soviet Forces in East Germany (1987-88); Deputy Commander of the Air Force of the Soviet Army (1988-90); and Commander of the Air Force of the Soviet Army (in 1990-91).

In 1991, Marshal Shaposhnikov became Minister of Defense of the U.S.S.R. During his tenure as Minister of Defense, the Communist Party relinquished control of the Army. During the 1991 anti-Gorbachev August Coup, he played a key role in disbanding the GKChP.

In 1992-93, he was Commander in Chief of the Armed Forces of the Commonwealth of Independent States. Later in 1993, Marshal Shaposhnikov was Secretary of the Security Council of the Russian Federation. In 1995-97, he was Director General of the "Aeroflot" Airlines. In recent years, Shaposhnikov served as an Assistant to the President of the Russian Federation on space and aviation developments.

He is an Honored Pilot of Russia and has received numerous military decorations from the government. He is an author of several books, published in Russia and France, as well as several dozens of publications on concepts of national security and reforms in the Army and Military Industrial Complex.

Vagit U. Alekperov (M.S., Azerbaijan Oil-Chemical University; Ph.D., I.M. Gubkin Russian State University of Oil and Gas) is president of Lukoil. He worked at Caspian and Siberian oil fields, where he held different positions ranging from Mining Engineer to Director General of Kogalymneftegaz, a major oil production association. In 1990, he became Deputy Minister of the Soviet Ministry of the Oil and Gas Industry. In 1991, Dr. Alekperov founded Lukoil Oil Concern, which combined several Russian oil-extracting and oil-processing companies. Lukoil is a major client of the Russian defense enterprises that started civilian production by manufacturing different types of equipment for the petroleum industry. Dr. Alekperov is the author of 14 publications.

Sonia Ben Ouagrham (M.A., University of Paris; Ph.D. in Economics of Development, ASSS, Paris, France) is a French economist specializing in the conversion of the Russian defense industry. She is currently a Senior Research Associate at the representative office of the Center for Nonproliferation Studies, Monterey Institute of International Studies in Almaty, Kazakhstan. In 1998-99, she was a post-doctoral fellow at the Center for Nonproliferation Studies, where she worked on the evaluation of the American Cooperative Threat Reduction program. In 1997-98, she was a researcher at the Advanced School of Social Sciences, Paris, France where she conducted a study on the regional aspect of conversion in Russia from 1992 to 1999.

David M. Bernstein (B.S., Massachusetts Institute of Technology; Ph.D., Stanford University) is a research associate at Stanford University's Center for International Security and Cooperation. Prior to coming to Stanford, he spent twenty-five years in high-technology companies. For the past ten years, he has done research on the restructuring of Russian defense enterprises, cooperative business ventures between US companies and Russian defense enterprises, and the commercialization of Russian technology. Since 1994, he has also consulted to the Office of the Secretary of Defense on the Cooperative Threat Reduction program. He is currently working on the Department of Energy's Nuclear Cities Initiative.

Victor I. Danilov-Danil'yan (M.S. in mechanics and mathematics, Moscow State University; Ph.D. in Economics, Moscow State University) is Chairman of the Russian Federation State Committee for Environmental Protection. He is a member of the United Nations Environment Programme's Governing Council. Dr. Danilov-Danil'yan worked in different institutes of the Academy of Sciences of the U.S.S.R. and was a professor at Moscow State University. He is a founder and chair of the Department of Ecology at the Academy for the National Economy. He served as the chair of several state commissions on Lake Baikal and the Caspian Sea, and was vice-chair of the commission that coordinated all ministries' environmental protection efforts. Since 1991, he has been Minister of Environmental Protection and Natural Resources of Russia. Dr. Danilov-Danil'yan is a Full Member of the Academy of Natural Sciences, the Academy of Ecology, and the International Academy of Sciences. He is the author of several environmental programs, including one on the economic mechanism for the use of nature and natural resources. Dr. Danilov-Danil'yan is the author of more than 200 articles, books, monographs, and textbooks.

Marcus W. Feldman (Ph.D., Stanford University) is the Burnet C. and Mildred Finley Wohlford Professor in the School of Humanities and Sciences at Stanford University. He is the Director of the Morrison Institute for Population and Resource Studies at Stanford University. He has made important contributions to evolutionary theory and population genetics, including the mathematical analysis of evolution in linked sets of genes and of the means by which cultural evolution, considered alone and in combination with biological evolution, influences human behavior. He has also worked extensively on the demography of the sex ratio in China. He is managing editor of *Theoretical Population Biology* and associate editor of *Genetics* and *Complexity*. Professor Feldman was a Guggenheim Fellow in 1976, and a fellow of the Center for Advanced Studies in the Behavioral Sciences in 1983-1984. He is a member of the American Academy of Arts and Sciences and the California Academy of Sciences, and a member of the board of trustees and science steering committee of the Santa Fe Institute. He is the author of more than 260 publications.

Larisa V. Genin (B.B.A., University of San Francisco; M.B.A., D.B.A., Golden Gate University) is an Adjunct Professor of Marketing at Golden Gate University, St. Mary's College, and the University of Phoenix, teaching High-Tech, Internet Marketing and International Business courses. She is the recipient of several awards and scholarships. Her primary areas of expertise are personalization of e-commerce/online retailing, global Internet marketing of high (dual-use) technologies. Her consulting experience includes business development, strategic marketing, and technical feasibility studies for defense conversion projects. She is a VP of Marketing at IPServe Inc., an Internet based collaborative technology company. In 1994-98, she was Director of Worldwide Marketing and Sales at PSI, Inc. Dr. Genin is a member of the UC Berkeley Faculty Club, the American Marketing Association, the GGU Adjunct Faculty Senate Committee and serves on the advisory board of several high tech companies in Silicon Valley, California.

Mikhail I. Gerasev (M.S. in Nuclear Physics, Moscow Physical Engineering University; Ph.D. in History, Moscow University) is a Deputy Director of the Federal State Company Rossiiskie Tekhnologii. His doctoral dissertation was dedicated to the U.S. decision-making process in the area of strategic arms acquisition In 1997-98, he was General Director of the Center for Economic Analysis. From 1979 to 1997, Dr. Gerasev served in different capacities at the Institute for the USA and Canadian Studies of the Russian Academy of Sciences. He worked at the Institute's Department of Military Policy, was a Deputy Director of the Center for Conversion and Privatization, and was Director of the Center for Strategic and Military Technological Studies. In 1995-97, he was a Deputy Director of the Institute for the USA and Canadian Studies. In 1979, he served as an intern at the Soviet Embassy in Washington, D.C. At the end of the 1980s, he participated in the U.S.-Soviet defense conversion project between Stanford University and the Institute for the USA and Canadian Studies. In 1989 and 1991, he was a visiting scholar at the Center for International Security and Arms Control, Stanford University. Dr. Gerasev is the author of numerous books and articles. His major areas of interest are strategic stability, arms control, and ballistic missile defense.

Donald R. Gerth (B.A., M.A, Ph.D., University of Chicago) is Professor of Government and of Public Policy and President of California State University, Sacramento (since 1984). He was President of the International Association of University Presidents from 1996 to 1999. In 2000, he was appointed by the U.N. Secretary General and the Director-

General of UNESCO to a six-year term on the United Nations University Council, the governing board of the United Nations University headquartered in Tokyo. Dr. Gerth's career in education spans 50 years. Having begun his career within the California State University (CSU) system in 1958, Gerth is one of its senior administrators. He was an Associate Dean of Students of CSU at San Francisco; Professor of Political Science, Dean of Students, Director of International Programs, and Vice-President for Academic Affairs at California State University, Chico; and President and Professor of Political Science at CSU, Dominguez Hills. An active advocate and policy leader in higher education, Gerth served as Chair of the Accrediting Commission for Senior Colleges and Universities of the Western Association of Schools and Colleges (WASC), 1992-1995. He is a member of the Commission on Governmental Relations of the American Council on Education. He is past chair of the Board of the CSU Institute. With UNESCO, he served as a member of the Advisory Committee on Higher Education to the Director-General and as a member of the seven-person Steering Committee for the World Conference on Higher Education (1998).

Ambassador James E. Goodby (M.S., University of Michigan, M.A. in International Affairs, Harvard University, Honorary Doctor of Laws, Stetson University) is a distinguished diplomat and scholar, whose work has focused on U.S. relations with Europe, both East and West. His many posts include principal negotiator and special representative of the president for nuclear security and dismantlement, 1995-96; chief U.S. negotiator for safe and secure dismantlement of nuclear weapons, 1993-94; vice-chairman of the U.S. delegation to the START talks, 1982-83; U.S. representative to the Stockholm Conference on Confidence and Security Building Measures and Disarmament in Europe, 1983-88; and ambassador to Finland, 1980-81. He has served as a member of the State Department's Policy Planning Staff; with the U.S. Mission to the European Community and to NATO; and as deputy assistant secretary of state for European affairs. Winner of the inaugural Heinz Award for work in public policy, Goodby has taught at Stanford, Georgetown, and Carnegie Mellon Universities. He was named Distinguished Fellow by the United States Institute of Peace in 1992, and was Payne Distinguished Lecturer at Stanford University's Institute for International Studies for 1996-97. His publications include *Europe Undivided: The New Logic of Peace in U.S. - Russian Relations* (1998), *The Limited Partnership: Building a Russian - U.S. Security Community* (1993; co edited with B. Morel), *Transforming Nuclear Deterrence* (1997; co edited with Hans Binnendijk), *Regional Conflicts: The Challenge to*

U.S. - Russian Cooperation (1995), as well as numerous articles in edited volumes and journals.

Ambassador Oleg A. Grinevsky (M.A., post-graduate doctoral studies, Moscow Institute for International Affairs; Honorary Doctorate, Southampton University, UK) is an expert in disarmament, European and Middle Eastern problems. Currently, he is the Diplomat-in-Residence at the Monterey Institute of International Studies. In 1997-99, he was a visiting research fellow at Stanford University (Hoover Institution and the Center for International Security and Cooperation). He dedicated 40 years to the diplomatic service at the U.S.S.R./Russian Ministry of Foreign Affairs. During the Cuban Missile Crisis (1961), he worked in the Ministry's Special Group. He was a political adviser to Khrushchev, Brezhnev, Andropov, and Gorbachev. As Chair of the Ministry's Middle East Department, he worked on the peaceful settlement of Arab–Israeli conflicts and the Afghan war. Ambassador Grinevsky was the head of the Soviet Delegations to the CSCE Stockholm Conference, where the first agreement in the perestroika era on Confidence and Security-Building Measures was signed (CSBM, 1986); to the Vienna Conference on Conventional Armed Forces Reductions in Europe (CFE); and to the European Conference on Confidence and Security-Building Measures, which led to the agreement in Vienna on CSBMs in Europe in 1990, and to CFE treaty in Paris (1990). He served as Gorbachev's Ambassador-at-Large. In this capacity, he negotiated with leaders of various countries, including Margaret Thatcher, Franz Vranitzky, Saddam Hussein, and Muammar al-Qadhafi. In 1991-97, he was Russian Ambassador to Sweden. He is an author of seven books published in Russia, Sweden, and Germany.

Randy H. Hamilton (B.A., M.A., University of North Carolina, Chapel Hill; Ph.D. School of International Studies, University of Zurich) is a Visiting Scholar at the Institute of Governmental Studies, University of California, Berkeley. He has been a City Manager of Bangkok, Director of the U.N./IPA Urban Studies program and the Founding Dean of the Graduate School of Public Administration at Golden Gate University (San Francisco). He has been President of the American Society for Public Administration, the California Association of Public Administration Educators, and the Western Governmental Research Association. He is one of 400 Senior Fellows of the National Academy of Public Administration, chartered by the U.S. Congress.

Ward A. Hanson (B.A, University of Wisconsin, Madison; M.A., Ph.D., Stanford University) is on the faculty of the Graduate School of Business and the Center for Electronic Commerce, Stanford University. He has previously been an Assistant Professor at the University of Chicago Graduate School of Business and the Purdue Krannert School of Management. He is a leading innovator in understanding the impact of the Internet on business, especially marketing. His book, *Principles of Internet Marketing*, has been adopted by over 200 universities worldwide for courses in Internet Marketing, Electronic Commerce, and Technology Strategy. He consults for high-technology companies in the United States and internationally, and serves on the advisory board of several Internet companies.

John H. Hnatio (B.S., State University of New York, College at Buffalo; M.L.S., Georgetown University; Ph.D. awarded *honoris causa,* the Urals Branch of the Russian Academy of Sciences) is the Department of Energy Chair and Professor of Strategic Leadership and Decision-Making at the Industrial College of the Armed Forces, National Defense University. In his government career, he has held a variety of national security policy and management positions. From 1994 to 1997, he served as the Department of Energy Founder and Program Director for the Initiatives for Proliferation Prevention Program. The Initiatives for Proliferation Prevention Program brought together the Department of Energy's national laboratories with a consortium of 80 American companies and universities to establish scientific and commercial projects in the Newly Independent States of the former Soviet Union. From 1992 to 1994, John Hnatio was a Department of Energy loaned executive to the staff of Senator Pete V. Domenici (R/NM) where he served as an advisor on the former Soviet Union and preventing the proliferation of weapons of mass destruction. From 1988 to 1992, he served as Director of the Department of Energy's Defense Programs Technology Management Group and oversaw a multi-million dollar portfolio of joint research and development with American industry. In earlier assignments, he was an advisor on domestic and international nuclear safeguards and security matters. He has also served as a consultant to the International Atomic Energy Agency.

David Holloway (Undergraduate degree in Modern Languages and Literature, Cambridge University, Ph.D. in Social and Political Sciences, Cambridge University) is the Raymond A. Spruance Professor in International History. He is the Director of the Institute for International Studies at Stanford University. Holloway was born in Dublin, Ireland

and received his education at Cambridge University. He taught at the Universities of Lancaster (1967-70) and Edinburgh (1970-86) before joining the Political Science department at Stanford University. Since coming to Stanford, he has served as Chair and Co-Chair of the International Relations Program (1989-91), as Co-Director of the Center for International Security and Arms Control (1991-97), and as Associate Dean in the School of Humanities and Sciences (1997-98). In 1996, he was appointed Professor of History, as well as Political Science. His book *Stalin and the Bomb: The Soviet Union and Atomic Energy, 1939-1956* (Yale University Press, 1994) was chosen by the *New York Times Book Review* as one of the 11 best books of 1994 and won the Vucinich and Shulman prizes of the American Association for Advancement of Slavic Studies. He wrote *The Soviet Union and the Arms Race* (1983) and co-authored (with Sidney Drell and Phillip Earley) *The Reagan Strategic Defense Initiative: Technical, Political and Arms Control Assessment* (1984). He has contributed to the *New York Review of Books*, *The Bulletin of the Atomic Scientists*, *Foreign Affairs,* and scholarly journals.

Michael D. Intriligator (S.B., Massachusetts Institute of Technology; M.A., Yale University; Ph.D., Massachusetts Institute of Technology) is Professor of Economics, Political Science, and Policy Studies at the University of California, Los Angeles (UCLA), where he is also Director of the Jacob Marschak Interdisciplinary Colloquium on Mathematics in the Behavioral Sciences. He is also a Senior Fellow at the Milken Institute and the Gorbachev Foundation of North America. He was Director of the UCLA Center for International and Strategic Affairs, the predecessor of the UCLA Center for International Relations, from 1982 to 1992. His publications and other professional activities are in the areas of economic theory, econometrics, health economics, strategy and arms control, and the transition to a market economy in Russia. He is currently Vice-Chair of Economists Allied for Arms Reduction (ECAAR) and was President of the Peace Science Society (International) in 1993. He is a Fellow of the Econometric Society and a member of the Council on Foreign Relations (New York) and the International Institute for Strategic Studies (London).

Elena I. Ivanova (M.A., Ph.D. in Economics, Moscow State University) is a Senior Research Associate at the Center of Demography and Human Ecology, Institute for Economic Forecasting, Russian Academy of Sciences. She was a Research Associate at the Center for Population Studies, Moscow State University (1984-1993). In 1997, Dr. Ivanova was a visiting scholar at the Morrison Institute at Stanford University. She is the author of numerous publications on population studies, as well as a member of Population Association of America (PAA) and European Association for Population Studies (EAPS).

Alexei I. Izyumov (B.S. and M.A., Moscow State University; Ph. D., U.S.S.R. Academy of Sciences) is a Director of the Center for Emerging Market Economies and a Professor of Economics at the School of Economics and Public Affairs, University of Louisville, USA. Dr. Izyumov has been a Senior Research Fellow at one of the leading Russian government think tanks at the Institute of the USA and Canada Studies. He was one of the first Russian scholars to begin research and open public discussion on the problems of converting the Soviet/Russian military-industrial complex. He has served as a United Nations expert on conversion and has published numerous articles and reports on the subject in both the Russian and international academic and general press.

Vitaliy L. Katayev (M.S., Kazan Aviation University) is Director General of the Military Industrial Complex Business Center, which specializes in civilian applications of missile systems (including ICBMs) and other advanced technologies. From 1960 to 1974, he worked in the Soviet aviation industry. He was a distinguished designer and the creator of numerous aviation and missile systems. During his service in the Soviet Defense Industries, he was a curator of the development of strategic ballistic-missile submarines. He was a member of the military policy development group and participated in international negotiations on arms control and disarmament. From 1974 to 1991, Katayev held senior executive positions, including that of Deputy Chairman, at the Department of Defense Industry of the Central Committee of the Communist Party of the U.S.S.R. In 1990-92, he was an advisor to the Office of the President of the U.S.S.R. Katayev has numerous inventions, patents, and publications to his name.

Sergey K. Kolpakov (M.S., Bauman Moscow State Technical University; Ph.D., Moscow Scientific Research Institute of the Ministry of Defense) is a Deputy Director of the Interdisciplinary Analytical Center. Between 1973 and 1991, he worked in the defense industry. He participated in the Soyuz-Apollo joint Russian-American space project. Being a leading expert in defense conversion, he is a member of several international and Russian committees on defense conversion, investment, and cooperation. Dr. Kolpakov is the author and co-author of the first

Russian defense conversion programs, as well as fundamental analytical publications on defense conversion and international cooperation.

Leonid Ya. Kosals (M.A., Novosibirsk State University; Ph.D., Institute of Economy and Industrial Engineering, Soviet Academy of Sciences; Ph.D., Institute for Socio-Economic Problems of the Population, Russian Academy of Sciences) is a Chief Researcher at the Institute for Socio-Economic Problems of the Population, Russian Academy of Sciences. He has been a Senior Researcher in the International Center for Research into Economic Transformation and the Russian Center for Public Opinion Research (Moscow, 1991-1993). In 1992-1993, he was engaged as an expert at the Russian government's Working Center for Economic Reform. He was a researcher at the Institute of Economy and Industrial Engineering, Soviet Academy of Sciences (1980-1990) and Head of Sociological Branch of Economic Department at Novosibirsk State University (Novosibirsk, 1990). Dr. Kosals is the author of 135 publications, including three books, in the fields of the socio-economic factors of innovation, enterprise behavior in economies under transition, and Russia's military-industrial complex.

Alexander P. Kotov (M.S., Ph.D., Moscow Power Engineering University; Ph.D., Institute of Economics of the Russian Academy of Sciences) is the Director of the Scientific Institute of Economics and Industrial Management at the Higher School of Economics State University. He is a past Director of the Central Scientific and Research Institute of Economics and Defense Conversion. He has worked at several research organizations in defense industries and became an expert on economic issues within the Military Industrial Complex during the period of transition toward a free market economy. Since 1990, Dr. Kotov has participated in the creation and development of Russian defense conversion laws and programs, and all Russian defense conversion laws. He is the author of five books and 50 papers.

Evgeniy M. Kozhokin (M.A.; Ph.D. in History, Moscow State University) is the Director of the Russian government's Institute for Strategic Research. In 1980-90, he worked at the Institute of the International Workers' Movement and at the Institute of General History at the Academy of Sciences. During that period, he was a member of the Moscow Tribune Liberal Intelligentsia Club, established by Nobel Laureate Andrei Sakharov. In 1990, Kozhokin was elected to the Supreme Soviet of the Russian Federation, where he headed the

Subcommittee on the Intelligence and International Security. He is the author of 50 papers and books.

James E. Meadows (graduate of the United States Air Force Academy) became the first Executive Director of the Presidio Trust in January 1998. Prior to the Trust, Mr. Meadows was Executive Director of the Lowry Redevelopment Authority in Denver, Colorado, and directed the redevelopment of the former Lowry Air Force Base into a mixed-use; master planned community for the City and County of Denver. Lowry has been nationally recognized as a national model for base closure. From 1991 to 1994, he was Senior Vice-President and head of California and Arizona home-building operations for Castle & Cooke Homes, Inc., a division of Dole Foods. From 1982 to 1991, he managed his own land development, commercial building and home building businesses in Phoenix, San Diego, and Denver. Mr. Meadows is a board member of the National Association of Installation Developers and the Coro Foundation. He has served on a variety of panels for San Francisco area base closures including a ULI Treasure Island Advisory Service Panel, a Mare Island ULI seminar and city panels for Hunter's Point.

Boris A. Revich (M.D., 1st Moscow Medical Institute; Ph.D., Central Institute of Advanced Medical Education, Moscow, Russia) is a Leading Researcher at the Center for Demography & Human Ecology of the Institute of Forecasting of the Russian Academy of Sciences. He is a Professor in the Department of Human Ecology of the Moscow Independent University for Ecological Policy. He was a principal researcher for a number of projects on environmental epidemiology: Database of Experts in Russia (1993-95), Regional Peculiarities in Public Health and Environmental Situations (1990-91), Lead and Children's Health in Russian Cities (1996-2000). He was the head of the Russian component of the international project on PCBs and Infertility (1996-97). In 1999, he was a supervisor for the project "Russian Environmental Health Action Plan". He was a training team leader for the World Bank project environmental epidemiology. At the present time, he is conducting research on the effects of dioxins on male sexual development and their relation to breast cancer. Currently, he is an expert for the United Nations Environment Programme, the World Bank, the Russian Federation State Committee for Environmental Protection, and the Ministry of Health. In 1997, he was a visiting research fellow at the Morrison Institute at Stanford University.

Rozalina R. Ryvkina (M.A., St. Petersburg State University; Ph.D., Tomsk University; Professor, Novosibirsk University) is Head of the Laboratory for Economic Sociology at the Institute for Socio-Economic Problems of the Population, Russian Academy of Sciences, Moscow. She was the head of the Department of Expert Surveys, Russian Center for Public Opinion Research, Moscow (1991-94); Chief Researcher and Head of the Sector of Methodology in Economic and Social Research, Institute of Economy and Industrial Engineering, U.S.S.R. Academy of Sciences (Novosibirsk, 1966-91) and Professor in the Economics Department of Novosibirsk University (Novosibirsk, 1981-88). She helped revive the field of sociology in the Soviet Union in the 1960s, and is an expert in the methodology of social research and economic sociology. She is the author of more than 300 publications, including 10 books in the fields of social factors of the transition period in Russia, managerial behavior, and social issues in labor relations.

Harry Sello (B.S., University of Illinois; M.S., Ph.D., University of Missouri) is President of Harry Sello & Associates. He is recognized internationally for his expertise in the international licensing and transfer of electronic technology. A pioneer in the establishment of Silicon Valley, Dr. Sello worked with Nobel Laureate Dr. William Shockley, at the Shockley Semiconductor Laboratory. This was followed by twenty-two years at the original Fairchild Semiconductor in a variety of senior executive management positions in R&D, manufacturing, and as Operations Manager of the then Fairchild affiliate, SGS Italy. For Fairchild, he was in charge of implementing alliances in Hungary, Italy, Japan, Taiwan, South Africa, and the Netherlands. Since 1968, he has given over twenty technical seminars in Russia (including at MIC enterprises), Eastern Europe, and China. Dr. Sello was an advisor on Militarily Critical Semiconductor Technology for the U.S. Departments of Commerce and Defense. He was an expert witness in sixteen major cases on trade secrets and patents, including at the International Arbitration Court in London. Dr. Sello has been a senior executive in the American Electronics Association. He was a consultant to Olivetti (Italy), LSI Logic U.S., Schlumberger (France), Nippon Steel (Japan), Mentor Graphics (U.S.), and the Flanders Government in Belgium.

Vitaliy V. Shlykov (M.A., Moscow Institute for International Affairs; Ph.D., Institute of the World Economy and International Affairs; Dr. Military Science, Military-Diplomatic Academy) is a military economist. He is a consultant and a member of the Council on Foreign Policy and Defense Policy. From 1958 to 1988, he worked in the area of military intelligence for the General Staff of the Soviet Armed Forces; for 10 years, he was Chief of the Directorate for Assessment of the economy and defense mobilization preparedness of the U.S.S.R. and its potential military enemies. In 1990-92, Shlykov was Deputy Chairman of the State Defense and Security Council, ranking as a Deputy Minister in the Russian government. He is the author of more than 50 books, monographs and papers.

Mark I. Shteynberg (Graduate of the Military-Engineering College, St. Petersburg) is a journalist and military observer of the American-Russian media. From 1945 to 1982, he served in the Soviet Army. He was a Colonel of the Military-Engineering Forces. Shteynberg was also a member of the Union of Journalists of the U.S.S.R. Since 1960, he has published more than 200 articles and reviews in the leading Soviet military newspapers and magazines, such as *Voennaia mysl* (publication of the General Staff of the Soviet Armed Forces), *Voennyi vestnik*, and the central military newspaper *Krasnaya zvezda*. During the 1990s, he published more than 600 military analytical articles and reviews in the U.S. (the Russian-language newspapers *Panorama, Novoe Russkoe Slovo,* and others), Israel (*Globus, Vesti*), as well as in Russia (*Nezavisimoe voennoe obozrenie*) dedicated to different aspects of Russian conventional weapons and WMD.

Alexey N. Shulunov (M.S. in Power Engineering, Ivanovo Textile University; Ph.D. in Engineering, Moscow Technical University) is a Founder and First Vice President of the League for Support of Russian Defense Enterprises and Director of the State Central Institute of Radio-Engineering. Starting his career as an engineer, he rose to the post of director in a defense enterprise. He held the position of Chair of the Department at the Ministry of Radio-Engineering Industry. Dr. Shulunov is a member of Duma commissions and is involved in the creation of legislation, governmental decrees, and regulations on MIC enterprises and defense conversion. He has been awarded the State Prize and is the author of more than 20 scientific publications.

Jonathan B. Tucker (B.S., Yale University; M.A., University of Pennsylvania; Ph.D., Massachusetts Institute of Technology) directs the Chemical and Biological Weapons Nonproliferation Project at the Center for Nonproliferation Studies of the Monterey Institute of International Studies. During the 1999-2000 academic year, he was the Robert Wesson Fellow in Scientific Philosophy and Public Policy at the Hoover Institution, Stanford University. He has also worked for the U.S.

Government in various capacities, including as an arms control fellow at the Department of State (1989-90), an analyst at the congressional Office of Technology Assessment (1990-93), and a foreign affairs specialist in the Chemical and Biological Policy Division of the U.S. Arms Control and Disarmament Agency (1993-95). In February 1995, he was a member of a biological weapons inspection team in Baghdad, Iraq, under the auspices of the United Nations Special Commission (UNSCOM).

Vitaliy Y. Vitebsky (M.S., Ural Technical University; Ph.D., Academy of Defense Industries) is a Deputy Department Chief at the Ministry of Economics of the Russian Federation. He was a Chief Designer at one of the Ural defense plants. During the years of perestroika, he entered politics as a People's Deputy from the Ural Region. Dr. Vitebsky was elected a Deputy Head of the Industry and Energy Committee of the Supreme Soviet of Russia. Since 1993, he has held different senior executive positions within the Russian government of the Russian Federation. Dr. Vitebsky is the author of the Russian law *On Defense Conversion*. He also co-authored the laws on intellectual property protection, and has written 30 books and papers published in Russia and abroad. Dr. Vitebsky has represented Russia at several international conferences and symposiums on defense conversion and cooperation, including the Russian-German Conference on Investments in Russia (Moscow, 1992), European Parliament hearings on conversion in Russia (Belgium, 1993), a conference on Russian and European cooperation (Switzerland, 1993), the NATO Joint Council Meeting (Belgium, 1998), and other hearings in the United States, France, and the United Kingdom.

Rem I. Vyakhirev (M.S., Ph.D., Samara Industrial University) is Chairman of the Board of Gazprom, a Russian natural gas company. He started his carrier in the oil and gas industries as a field manager. Dedicating several decades to this industry, he held a number of executive positions, including Director of the Orenburg Gas Extraction and Tumen Gas Industries production associations. Later, he was promoted to the position of Deputy Minister of the Gas Industry of the U.S.S.R. In 1992, Vyakhirev was one of the founders and Chairman of Gazprom, which within several years became the giant of the Russian gas industry and the largest natural gas company in the world. In 1997, Gazprom entered the *Financial Times*' listing of the world's top 100 companies in terms of market capitalization. Vyakhirev is a recipient of the State Prize, a member of several Russian and International Academies, an honorary professor of Samara University, and has more than 70 inventions and publications to his name.

Arkadiy I. Yarovskiy (M.S., Kiev Polytechnic University; Ph.D., Moscow Power Engineering University) is a Professor–Consultant for 1996-2000 at the Morrison Institute for Population and Resource Studies at Stanford University and a Professor at Frederick Taylor University. Dr. Yarovskiy worked for more than 40 years in Russian defense industries at different rocket enterprises in Novosibirsk and Moscow. For 10 years, he was a chief designer of new military systems. He was among the pioneers of the beginning of defense conversion process in Russia, becoming the director of Delta, a newly privatized former defense enterprise, which was converted to R&D and manufacturing of environmental protection equipment for the gas industry. Dr. Yarovskiy taught in universities in Moscow and Novosibirsk and was the chair of seven doctoral dissertation committees. He is the author of several monographs and books, and has produced more than 60 inventions and papers.

Zhanna A. Zaionchkovskaya (M.A., Moscow State University; Ph.D., U.S.S.R. Academy of Sciences, Siberian Branch) is Head of the Laboratory of Population Migration at the Center of Demography and Human Ecology, Institute for Economic Forecasting, Russian Academy of Sciences. She has held different research positions in the Institute of Economics at the Siberian Branch of the Academy of Sciences and in the Council for Research of Industrial and Labor Resources of the U.S.S.R. State Planning Committee (Gosplan). Dr. Zaionchkovskaya is a specialist in the field of regional and social problems. She is a member of the Executive Body in charge of the Federal Migration Services of Russia and sits on the editorial board of the annual collection of demographic research papers. Zaionchkovskaya was a research fellow at RAND Corporation and at the Morrison Institute for Population and Resource Studies at Stanford University. She is the author of more than 100 books and papers.

EDITORIAL STAFF

Laurel B. Nolen (B.A., Illinois Wesleyan University; M.A. in Russian Translation and Interpretation, Monterey Institute of International Studies) is a Research Associate and the Staff Translator for the NIS Nonproliferation Project at the Center for Nonproliferation Studies of the Monterey Institute for International Studies. Her research at CNS has focused on the civilian nuclear infrastructure and policies of Russia, Belarus, the Baltic States, and Central Asia. She is also a freelance translator specializing in scientific and technical texts, particularly in the nuclear, WMD, and nonproliferation fields. In 1996, Nolen was the primary author of the Russian language module for ACEBO's *Interpreter's Edge* court interpretation instructional materials. From 1996 to 1997, she was the translator for the business magazine *The Russian.* She is a staff translator and editor of this book.

Mark Halpern (B.A., M.A. in English Language and Literature, Columbia University) is a professional editor, literary consultant, and writer. He has published in a wide variety of journals, including *IEEE Spectrum* and *The Atlantic Monthly*, on subjects that include linguistics and English usage. He has also published a book on computer programming (*Binding Time*, Ablex, 1990). In the beginning of his career, he was an officer in the U.S. Army. Later, in the capacity of Lead Technical Writer, he worked with Tandem Computers, IBM, and Lockheed Missiles & Space Company. In the 1990s, he held various executive editorial positions at major Silicon Valley corporations. He was a Lead Writer/Editor for the Sedona Project at Oracle Corporation, a Senior Developmental Editor at Tesseract Technology and a Senior Developmental Editor at Siebel Systems, Inc. (ex-Scopus). Mark Halpern taught the Advanced Editorial Workshop course at the University of California, Berkeley Extension. He was twice Chairman of the Special Interest Group in Writing and Editing for the Silicon Valley Chapter of the STC. He edited the landmark paper on cryptography titled "Privacy and Authentication," by Whitfield Diffie and Martin E. Hellman, which won the Donald E. Fink Award in 1980 as "best expository paper to appear in a IEEE publication." He is a staff editor of this book.

Rita V. Archibald (M.A., Tver State University; M.B.A., Frederick Taylor University) is a bilingual specialist in international business and human resource management, English as a Second Language instructor, translator, and editor. As a Senior Instructor, she taught ESL during 6 years at the Tver Polytechnic University. Since 1985, she has participated in numerous international projects, such as the Canadian-Russian educational project "Team Canada" (under auspices of the U.S.-Russia global disarmament agreement), aimed at helping demobilized Russian officers to obtain new skills applicable to civilian sectors of the economy. With VEGA, she participated in the development of several business plans for defense plant conversion. She was the coordinator and interpreter for multiple U.S.-Russia exchange projects between business and educational institutions, including Christian Missionaries and Global Volunteers. She is a staff translator and editor of this book.

Olga Uraltseva (M.A. in Journalism, Moscow State University) is a distinguished journalist, who has worked in the central Russian media for more than twenty-five years. She was one of the founders of the Russian independent newspaper *Megapolis Ekspress*, one the first independent newspapers, with a circulation of 3 million, where she was an editor, Department Chair and Deputy Chief Editor. For the last two years, she has been a foreign correspondent for *Megapolis Ekspress* in Los Angeles. She is also a contributing writer for several Russian-American newspapers, as well as Netsperanto, the first multi-ethnic website. She is the author of more than one thousand articles and radio reports in both the Russian and U.S. media and a member of the International Union of Journalists.

Galina Zheltova (M.A., Central Asian State University; Ph.D., Moscow Historical-Archival Institute) is a Professor of History and Historiography. She is a past Chair of the History Department at Tashkent Pedagogical University and a pioneer in the scientific field of historiography in Central Asia. Dr. Zheltova was a member of the Committee on Historiography at the Institute of History of the Russian Academy of Sciences. She was the chair of more than twenty doctoral dissertation committees and is the author of more than 100 publications.

Ekaterina Drozdova (B.A., Stanford University; M.A., Stanford University; Ph.D. candidate, New York University) is a Researcher at CISAC and a member of the Consortium for Research on Information Security and Policy (CRISP) at Stanford University. Specializing in international security and human rights in the information age, she conducted study of national laws in fifty countries to determine the extent of international consensus against cyber crime. She participated in the organization of the Stanford Conference on International Cooperation to Combat Cyber Crime and Terrorism.

Inna Sayfer (B.A. in Quantitative Economics and in International Relations, Stanford University; Ph.D. candidate in Political Science, Stanford University) specializes in Russian policy and integration into the international trading system. Her paper "The Process of Creating Market-Based Financial Systems in Eastern Europe" was nominated as an outstanding economics honors thesis at Stanford (1994). She was a teaching assistant at the Center of International Security and Cooperation (CISAC) at Stanford University (courses: "International Security in a Changing World" and "Introduction to International Relations"). She has been awarded numerous research grants, including from the Center for Russian and Eastern European Studies at Stanford University.

APPENDIX 1

Exchange Rates - Russian Rubles to U.S. Dollars (approximate values)

Year	Exchange Rate in Rubles/per USD
1992	125
1993	From 572* to 1,231**
1994	2,020
1995	4,077
1996	4,077
1997	5,560
1998***	From 5.96* to 17.8**
1999	From 20.6* to 24.2**
2000 (June)	28.27

* Exchange rate in the beginning of the year

** Exchange rate at the end of the year

*** In 1998, there was a denomination of the ruble – 1 new ruble became equivalent to 1,000 old rubles.

INDEX